CALIFORNIA SCHOOL LAW

CALIFORNIA SCHOOL LAW

Fourth Edition

DEAN T. ADAMS AND
MARGARET A. DALTON

Earlier editions authored by Frank Kemerer and Peter Sansom

STANFORD UNIVERSITY PRESS
Stanford, California

Stanford University Press
Stanford, California

The first edition of this book, by Frank Kemerer, Peter Sansom, and Jennifer Kemerer, was published in 2005. Kemerer and Sansom then revised and updated the second and third editions, published in 2009 and 2013, respectively. For the present, fourth edition, authorship has been transferred to Dean T. Adams and Margaret A. Dalton, who have significantly updated and revised the text.

© 2005, 2009, 2013, 2026 by the Board of Trustees of the Leland Stanford Junior University. All rights reserved.

No part of this book may be reproduced or transmitted in any form or by any means, electronic or mechanical, including photocopying and recording, or in any information storage or retrieval system, without the prior written permission of Stanford University Press.

Library of Congress Cataloging-in-Publication Data

Names: Adams, Dean T., author. | Dalton, Margaret A., author.
Title: California school law / Dean T. Adams and Margaret A. Dalton.
Description: Fourth edition. | Stanford, California : Stanford University Press, 2026. | "Earlier editions authored by Frank Kemerer and Peter Sansom." | Includes index.
Identifiers: LCCN 2025009084 (print) | LCCN 2025009085 (ebook) | ISBN 9781503644373 (ebook) | ISBN 9781503640450 (cloth) | ISBN 9781503644366 (paperback)
Subjects: LCSH: Educational law and legislation—California.
Classification: LCC KFC648 (ebook) | LCC KFC648 .K45 2026 (print) | DDC 344.794/07 23/eng/20250—dc05
LC record available at https://lccn.loc.gov/2025009084

Cover design: Jan Šabach
Typeset by Newgen in 10/13.5 Minion

The authorized representative in the EU for product safety and compliance is: Mare Nostrum Group B.V. | Mauritskade 21D | 1091 GC Amsterdam | The Netherlands | Email address: gpsr@mare-nostrum.co.uk | KVK chamber of commerce number: 96249943

CONTENTS

	Tables and Figures	*xv*
	Abbreviations	*xvi*
	Preface	*xix*
Chapter 1	**Law and the California Schooling System**	1
	What Constitutes School Law?	1
	Constitutional Law	2
	Statutory Law	6
	Administrative Law	9
	Contract Law	12
	Judicial Law	13
	The California Schooling Structure	15
	Parent Rights and Responsibilities	22
	Choosing a Private School	22
	Homeschooling	24
	Rights Within Public Schools	25
	Expanding Parent Choice	26
	California Charter Schools	30
	Starting a Charter School	31
	Operating a Charter School	33
	Constitutionality of Charter Schools	38
	California Private Schools	39
	Voucher Programs	41
	Summary	44

Chapter 2	**Attendance, Safety, Instruction, and Assessment**	**46**
	Attendance	47
	The Compulsory Attendance Law	47
	Attendance Records	53
	Exemptions from Attendance	53
	Absences and Truancy	55
	Safety	57
	Maintaining a Safe and Healthy Learning Environment	57
	Curriculum and Instruction	70
	Curriculum Content Standards	70
	Curriculum Censorship	76
	Classroom Instruction	78
	Class Size Reduction	78
	Educating Targeted Groups	79
	Teacher Preparation and Evaluation	81
	Copyright Law	84
	The Internet	88
	Controlling Access to Inappropriate Material	89
	Privacy and the Internet	92
	Distance Learning and New Internet Privacy Rights Laws	93
	Artificial Intelligence	98
	Assessment and Accountability	102
	The Influence of the No Child Left Behind Act	102
	Summary	106
Chapter 3	**Equity, Adequacy, and School Finance**	**107**
	Does Money Matter?	108
	The Quest for Equity	110
	Foundation Funding	110
	Litigation	112
	State Court: *Serrano v. Priest I* (1971)	112
	Federal Court: *San Antonio Independent School District v. Rodriguez* (1973)	115
	State Court: *Serrano v. Priest II* (1976)	116
	Proposition 13	119

	Changes to the California School Finance System	123
	Revenue Limit Funding	125
	Categorical Aid	126
	Local Control Funding Formula	128
	Local Control and Accountability Plans	131
	Federal Funds	132
	Student Fees	132
	Other Sources of School Revenue	134
	Facilities Funding	135
	Funding Charter Schools	136
	The Block Grant System, LCFF, and LCAP	136
	The Special Case of Nonclassroom-Based Charters	138
	Facilities	139
	The Movement Toward Adequacy	140
	Summary	145
Chapter 4	**Unions and Collective Bargaining**	**148**
	The Three Stages of Collective Bargaining	149
	Unionization Stage	149
	Contract Negotiation Stage	151
	Contract Administration Stage	152
	Collective Bargaining Under the Educational Employment Relations Act	153
	The Role of the Public Employment Relations Board	154
	Covered Employees and Schools	155
	Deciding on the Appropriate Bargaining Unit and Choosing a Representative	156
	Scope of Bargaining	157
	Contract Negotiation	163
	Contract Administration	170
	The Grievance and Arbitration System	170
	The Role of the Arbitrator	171
	Unfair Labor Disputes	174
	Organizational Security Arrangements	175
	Future Challenges	180
	Summary	186

Chapter 5	**Employment**	**188**
	Classifications and Categories of Public School Employees	189
	Property Rights in Employment	191
	Certificated Employees	192
	Credentials	192
	Classifications	194
	Substitute	194
	Temporary	195
	Probationary	200
	Permanent	202
	Evaluation and Reassignment	204
	Discipline of Probationary and Permanent Employees	206
	Non-Reelection and Dismissal of Probationary Teachers	208
	Dismissal of Permanent Teachers	210
	Immoral or Unprofessional Conduct	211
	Unsatisfactory Performance	214
	Evident Unfitness for Service	215
	Persistent Violation of or Refusal to Obey School Laws	216
	The Dismissal Hearing Process	217
	Layoff	219
	Classified Employees	223
	Categories	223
	Evaluation and Discipline	225
	Dismissal and Layoff	226
	Merit System School Districts	228
	Administrators	229
	The Personnel File	230
	Public School Employee Leave Rights	231
	Federal and State Antidiscrimination Laws	235
	Title VII	235
	Americans with Disabilities Act and Section 504	237
	Fair Employment and Housing Act	240
	Summary	242

Chapter 6	**Rights of Expression**	**244**
	Educator Expression Rights	244
	Speaking Out on Matters of Public Concern	244
	Mt. Healthy Test	247
	Complaints About Working Conditions	251
	Expression Through School Channels	254
	Use of Electronic Communication Devices	259
	Educator Association Rights	260
	Whistleblowing	261
	Student Expression Rights	263
	Face-to-Face Communication	264
	Expression Targeting Protected Identities	269
	Expression Through Electronic Communication Devices	271
	School Regulation of Off-Campus Speech	272
	Expression Through School Channels	274
	Student Dress, Grooming, and Uniforms	279
	Right of Association	281
	Expression Rights in the Classroom	284
	Teacher Academic Freedom	284
	Student Classroom Expression	288
	Summary	290
Chapter 7	**The School and Religion**	**292**
	Federal and California Constitutional Law	292
	No Government Establishment of Religion	292
	Protection for Free Exercise of Religion	295
	Manifestations of Religion on Campus	296
	The Pledge of Allegiance	297
	School Prayer	298
	School-Sponsored or Endorsed Public Prayer	299
	Private Prayer and Religious Exercise	301
	Religion in the Classroom	304
	Teaching about Religion	305
	Student Religious Papers and Presentations	309
	Holiday Observances and Religious Music	310
	Graduation Prayer and Religious Speeches	311

	Access of Religious Groups to Campus	313
	Student Religious Groups and the Equal Access Act	313
	Community Use Policies	318
	Religiously Based Exemptions	321
	Transgender Students, Public Schools, and Religion	323
	Aid to Religious Private Schools	324
	Direct Aid Programs	325
	Indirect Aid Programs Through Vouchers and Tax Credits	326
	Summary	328
Chapter 8	**Students with Disabilities**	**330**
	Special Education Law	330
	A Brief History	330
	Sources of Special Education Law	334
	The Language of Special Education	335
	Free Appropriate Public Education (FAPE)	337
	Procedural Component	337
	Substantive Component	338
	FAPE and the Least Restrictive Environment (LRE)	341
	Child Find, Referral, Assessment, and Eligibility	343
	Child Find and Referral for Initial Assessment	343
	Initial Assessment	345
	Eligibility	348
	Independent Educational Evaluation (IEE) and Reevaluation	350
	The IEP Process	351
	IEP Team Meetings	351
	IEP Contents	353
	Special Education and Related Services	355
	Extended School Year (ESY)	357
	Behavior-Related Assessments and Plans	357
	Mental Health Services	359
	Placement	359
	Transition Plans, the Age of Majority, Exiting Special Education, and Revocation of Consent	360
	Transition Planning and Age of Majority	360
	Exiting Special Education	361

	Private School Students and IDEA	362
	Due Process Hearings	363
	Stay-Put During Hearing	365
	Due Process Rights	366
	Due Process Remedies	367
	Compensatory Education	368
	Reimbursement for Educational Expenses	368
	Attorneys' Fees	369
	Section 504 and the Americans with Disabilities Act (ADA)	371
	Section 504 of the Rehabilitation Act of 1973	371
	Americans with Disabilities Act (ADA)	374
	Summary	375
Chapter 9	**Student Discipline**	**378**
	The Importance of Student Discipline Rules	378
	California's Legal Framework for Student Discipline	380
	Who Can Discipline	381
	Due Process of Law	381
	Types of Discipline	384
	Discipline Short of Suspension	384
	Suspension	384
	Expulsion	391
	Mandatory Recommendation for Expulsion	391
	Mandatory Recommendation for Expulsion Unless Inappropriate	394
	Discretionary Expulsion	394
	Discipline for an Act Not on School Grounds	396
	Involuntary Transfer	398
	Dismissal from a Charter School	399
	The Expulsion Process	400
	Recommendation for Expulsion	400
	The Expulsion Hearing	401
	Final Determination by the Governing Board	405
	Postexpulsion Educational Programming	408
	Readmission Following Expulsion	409
	Appeal of an Expulsion Order	409

	Discipline and Special Education	412
	Different Types of Disciplinary Removals	413
	Short-Term Removals	413
	Long-Term Removals	413
	Interim Alternative Educational Settings and a *Honig* Injunction	415
	Students Not Yet Identified as Special Education Students	416
	Summary	417

Chapter 10 — Public Access, Privacy, and Student Search and Seizure — 419

	Public Access	419
	Open Meetings Under the Brown Act	420
	Key Provisions	421
	Defining Open Meetings	424
	Exceptions to Open Meetings	426
	Enforcement	429
	The Public Records Act	429
	Personal Privacy	436
	Employee Lifestyle	437
	Student Lifestyle	439
	Student Records and Surveys	441
	Student Records	441
	Student Surveys	446
	Student Search and Seizure	447
	Student Searches	447
	Standards	447
	Individual Searches	452
	Group Searches	457
	Student Seizures	461
	Summary	462

Chapter 11 — Race and Gender Discrimination — 464

	Racial Discrimination	465
	Racial Discrimination Under Federal Law	465
	Racial Discrimination Under California Law	468
	Historical Perspective	468

	Remedying Racial Isolation Regardless of Cause	470
	Limits on Busing	473
	Limits on Affirmative Action and Racial Balancing	474
	Finding Other Means of Fostering Diversity	478
	Gender Discrimination	480
	Constitutional Dimensions	481
	Title IX and Its Regulations	484
	California's Sex Equity in Education Act	487
	Racial and Gender Harassment	489
	Racial Harassment Under Title VI	489
	Sexual Harassment and Abuse Under Title IX	492
	Sexual Harassment and Abuse Under the California Education Code	494
	California Unruh Civil Rights Act	495
	Summary	497
Chapter 12	**Legal Liability**	**499**
	Liability Under California Law	499
	California Tort Claims Act	500
	Injury to Students on Campus	503
	Liability when School Employees Act Outside the Scope of Their Employment	508
	Injury to Student Athletes and Cheerleaders	511
	Is There Liability When Students Don't Learn?	516
	Injury to Students off Campus	517
	Injury to Nonstudents	520
	Dangerous Condition of School Property	523
	Waivers of Liability	525
	Counselors and the Duty to Warn	526
	A Word about Insurance	528
	Fair Employment and Housing Act	530
	Liability Under Federal Law	531
	Liability of Schools Under 42 U.S.C. Section 1983	531
	Liability of School Employees Under 42 U.S.C. Section 1983	534
	Summary	538

Appendix A: Glossary of Legal Terminology   *541*
Appendix B: Finding and Reading Statutes and
   Judicial Decisions   *549*
Appendix C: References   *554*
List of Cases   *557*
Index   *576*

TABLES AND FIGURES

Tables

Table 1.1	Key Federal Statutes Affecting California Public Schools	7
Table 2.1	Selected California Penal Code Provisions for Maintaining Order at School	62
Table 2.2	Copyright Law Guidelines	86
Table 3.1	Major Components of California's School Finance System until 2013-2014	124
Table 3.2	Tests for Determining a Minimum Base Funding for Schools under Proposition 98	125
Table 4.1	Stages of Collective Bargaining	150
Table 4.2	Key Mandatory, Consultative, and Nonnegotiable Topics under EERA	158
Table 9.1	Disciplinary Acts and Consequences	385
Table 11.1	Major Developments in California Desegregation Law	479
Table 12.1	Key Provisions of the California Tort Claims Act as Set Forth in the Government Code	502

Figures

Figure 1.1	Relationship of Law to Establishment and Operation of California Public Schools	3
Figure 1.2	California State Structure for School Governance	16
Figure 4.1	Teacher Contract Negotiation in California Public Schools	164
Figure 4.2	Resolving an Impasse over Negotiating Mandatory Topics of Bargaining under the EERA	166

ABBREVIATIONS

AB	Assembly Bill
ADA	Americans with Disabilities Act of 1990; also average daily attendance
ADEA	Age Discrimination in Employment Act of 1967
API	Academic Performance Index
AUP	Acceptable Use Policy
AYP	Adequate Yearly Progress
CAHSEE	California High School Exit Examination
CAPA	California Alternate Performance Assessment
CBEST	California Basic Education Skills Test
CCTC	California Commission on Teacher Credentialing
CDE	California Department of Education
CELDT	California English Language Development Test
CFRA	California Family Rights Act
CFT	California Federation of Teachers
CIF	California Interscholastic Federation
CIPA	Children's Internet Protection Act
CPC	Commission on Professional Competence
CSEA	California School Employees Association
CST	California Standards Test
CTA	California Teachers Association
DFEH	Department of Fair Employment and Housing
EAA	Equal Access Act
ECD	electronic communication device

EEOC	Equal Employment Opportunity Commission
EERA	Educational Employment Relations Act
EAHCA	Education for All Handicapped Children Act of 1975
EIA	Economic Impact Aid
EMO	educational management organization
ERA	Equal Rights Amendment
ERAF	Educational Revenue Augmentation Fund
ESEA	Elementary and Secondary Education Act
ESY	extended school year
FAPE	free appropriate public education
FEHA	Fair Employment and Housing Act
FERPA	Family Educational Rights and Privacy Act of 1974
FMLA	Family and Medical Leave Act
GATE	gifted and talented education
IDEA	Individuals with Disabilities Education Act
IEE	independent educational evaluation
IEP	Individualized Education Program
LEA	local education agency
LCI	licensed children's institution
LRE	least restrictive environment
NAEP	National Assessment of Educational Progress
NCIPA	Neighborhood Children's Internet Protection Act
NCLB	No Child Left Behind Act
NEA	National Education Association
NLRA	National Labor Relations Act
NPA	nonpublic agency
NPS	nonpublic school
OAH	Office of Administrative Hearings
OCR	Office of Civil Rights
OSEP	Office of Special Education Programs
OSERS	Office of Special Education and Rehabilitation Services
PAR	Peer Assistance and Review program
PERB	Public Employment Relations Board
PPRA	Protection of Pupil Rights Amendment
PRA	Public Records Act
PTA	Parent-Teacher Association
PTSA	Parent, Teacher, and Student Association
QEIA	Quality Education Investment Act
RSP	resource specialist program

RTI	response to intervention
SAIT	school assistance and intervention team
SARC	School Accountability Report Card
SAT	Scholastic Aptitude Test
SBE	State Board of Education
SELPA	Special Education Local Plan Area
SLD	Specific Learning Disability
SPI	superintendent of public instruction
STAR	Standardized Testing and Reporting program
UCP	Uniform Compliant Procedure
USDOE	United States Department of Education

PREFACE

As noted in the previous editions of this book, the law affecting the day-to-day operation of schools is seldom static. As with the earlier editions and subsequent updates, the authors' goal is to make understandable to legal and nonlegal audiences the maze of legislative laws (statutes), administrative rules (regulations), judicial decisions, and policies that constitute "education law." This is particularly true for a large state like California, where education law emanates from a variety of both federal and state sources and encompasses a host of topics.

This fourth edition of *California School Law* provides a comprehensive and current description of the law that affects the operation of the state's traditional public schools, charter schools, and private schools. It is intended for a wide audience including governing board members, school administrators, teachers, education professors and their students, policy makers, education law attorneys, parents, and members of the general public. To serve such a broad constituency, we have somewhat simplified the legal analysis of cases and provided numerous illustrative figures and tables. While cases are referenced generally in the text, their legal citations are included in an index at the end of the book.

In the book's twelve chapters, readers will find a detailed account of the many ways in which the law structures the delivery of public education services in California. Chapter 1 begins with an overview of the legal framework governing California schooling. This chapter may be especially helpful for readers who may want to gain an understanding of what education law is, the sources from which it emanates, and the components that make up the state's schooling system. The chapter includes the rights of parents and the status of charter schools, which are publicly funded, and private schools, which typically are not.

Subsequent chapters discuss the law in detail as it affects attendance and the instructional program; the financing of California traditional public and charter schools; the collective bargaining process; employment; teacher and student free speech, including use of electronic communication devices; religion; the delivery of services to children with disabilities; student discipline; open meetings and records; privacy and student search and seizure; race and gender discrimination and harassment; and legal liability. Within each of these areas, myriad legal matters are examined. Readers who are interested in particular topics are advised to consult both the table of contents and the topical index.

In addition to a comprehensive discussion of how law affects the operation of California schooling, readers will find appendices providing a glossary of legal terms relating to education law, a discussion of how to find and read statutes and judicial decisions, and sources for additional information. The index of cases provides page references for those seeking to locate a particular judicial ruling.

California School Law is designed to provide information regarding the subject matter covered and does not take the place of expert advice and assistance from a lawyer. It is published with the understanding that neither the authors nor the publishers are rendering legal services. If specific legal advice or assistance is required, the services of a competent professional should be sought. For this fourth edition, we especially want to thank the following University of San Diego law students who provided important contributions throughout this edition: Elise Johnson, Jeffrey Mihalik, and Joshua Sarsfield, whose research and writing were exceptionally helpful in the preparation of this book. We also want to thank Sasha Nunez, Publication Services Library Coordinator, whose research, analytical and technical skills were vital to the successful completion of the book. The benefits of understanding the law and following its dictates are immeasurable. We hope this book will assist readers in that endeavor.

Dean T. Adams
Margaret A. Dalton

CALIFORNIA SCHOOL LAW

1 LAW AND THE CALIFORNIA SCHOOLING SYSTEM

The extensiveness of the California schooling system adds to its complexity. California elementary and secondary schools enroll over 5.8 million students. Traditional public schools enroll about 90 percent of them, with another 709,630 enrolled in charter schools. Some 500,000 students attend private schools enrolling twenty-five or more students. It is estimated that well over 100,000 students attend very small private schools or are homeschooled. The California public school system encompasses 1,015 school districts of various types. There are some 9,997 public schools and 1,283 students. The law that governs this vast system emanates from several sources and has become extensive over time. Because the provisions of the Education Code have been enacted in piecemeal fashion over the years, they are difficult to find and often overlap. As early as 1922, a California court recognized the complexity of the Education Code: "At the outset it may be observed that any attempt to apply literally all the various provisions of the school law would lead to hopeless confusion." (*Horton v. Whipple*, p. 190, 1922)

The interplay among the various sources of school law adds to the complexity. The purpose of this introductory chapter is to identify the sources of California school law, the major players, and the structure of the system. Also covered are the rights and responsibilities of parents, the role of private schools, and the efforts to expand schooling options through charter schools and voucher proposals.

WHAT CONSTITUTES SCHOOL LAW?

School law is essentially a combination of constitutional, statutory, administrative, contract, and judicial law. This section (including the flowchart in Figure 1.1) covers each type of law and describes how the types relate to one another.

Constitutional Law

Constitutional law is the highest form of law because it sets forth basic principles of governance. Constitutional law has two sources: federal law and state law. The federal law, the U.S. Constitution, is an important source of school law for two reasons. First, it reserves to states the responsibility to establish and operate a schooling system. Article I, Section 8 of the U.S. Constitution lists the powers given to Congress; Article I, Section 10 lists powers prohibited to the states. Because education is on neither list, it becomes a state responsibility under the Tenth Amendment to the U.S. Constitution, which provides that all powers not specifically delegated to Congress or prohibited to the states are the prerogative of the states.

The federal Constitution is also an important source of individual rights. The Bill of Rights lists such fundamental rights as freedom of speech, the free exercise of religion, and the right to be free from unreasonable searches and seizures. It was a condition of state ratification of the Constitution in 1789 that the Bill of Rights be added to protect these fundamental rights from hostile action by Congress. Justice Robert Jackson explained the purpose of the Bill of Rights in a 1943 ruling that prevented the state from compelling all students to salute the flag. He wrote, "The very purpose of a Bill of Rights was to withdraw certain subjects from the vicissitudes of political controversy, to place them beyond the reach of majorities and officials and to establish them as legal principles to be applied by the courts" (*West Virginia State Board of Education v. Barnette*, 1943).

The due process clause of the Fourteenth Amendment extends nearly all the original Bill of Rights protections to persons in the state setting, and many of them now apply to public school employees and students. The due process clause reads, "Nor shall any State deprive any person of life, liberty, or property, without due process of law." Not only has the U.S. Supreme Court construed the word *liberty* in this clause to protect persons from state governmental intrusion on their constitutional rights; the Court also has ruled that these rights cannot be taken away without "due process of law." Thus, both educator contract termination and the disciplinary removal of students from public school must be done in compliance with the due process clause. These events are covered in later chapters.

The Fourteenth Amendment also provides that no state shall "deny to any person within its jurisdiction the equal protection of the laws." Beginning in 1954 with the famous *Brown v. Board of Education* desegregation case, the equal protection clause has figured prominently in efforts to integrate schools and, for a time, to ensure equalized funding as well. When the U.S. Supreme Court backed away

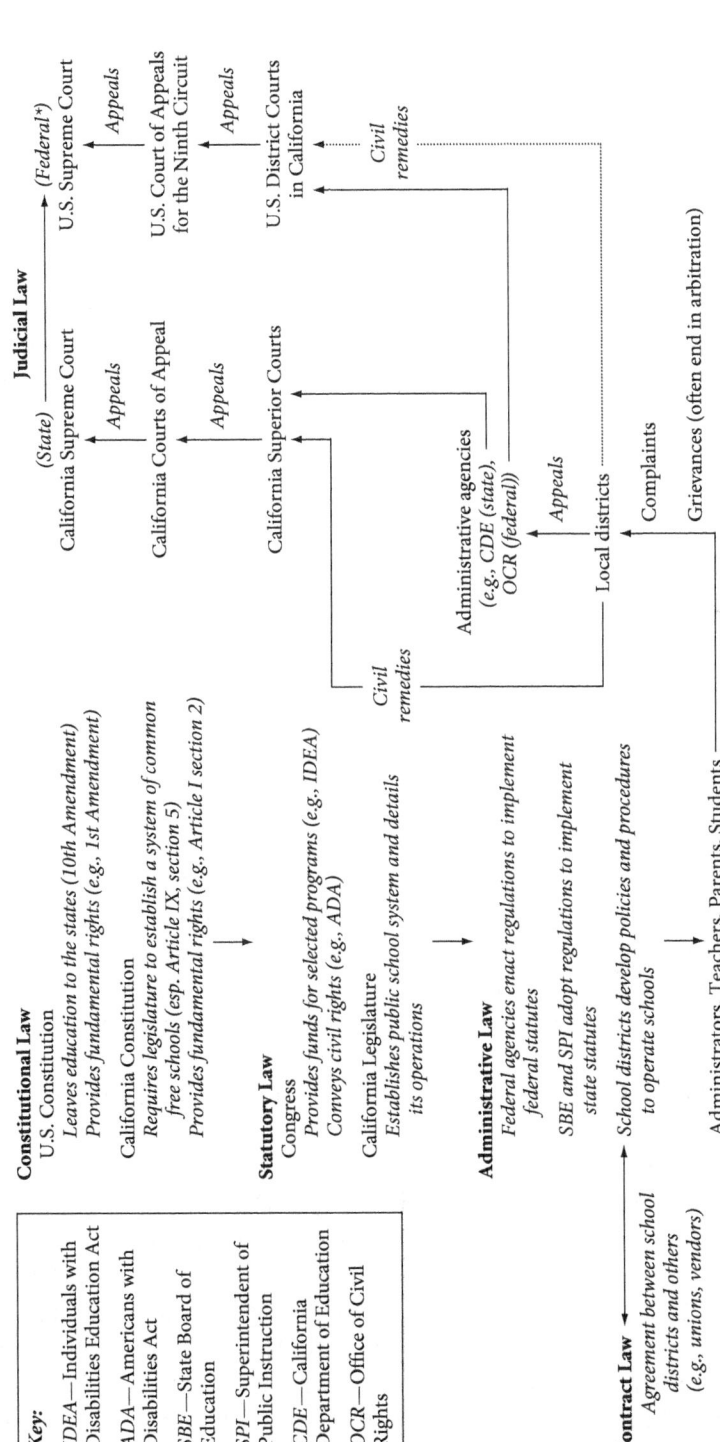

Figure 1.1 Relationship of Law to Establishment and Operation of California Public Schools

[Some matters such as disputes of U.S. constitutional rights can be taken directly from school districts to federal district court. Hence the dotted line.]

from becoming involved in equalization of school finance, state courts bridged the gap. Both of these matters are discussed in detail in subsequent chapters.

Although public school districts and charter schools are included within the ambit of the Fourteenth Amendment, private schools are not. This is because the amendment is phrased in terms of "states." It requires some semblance of state action for the amendment to apply. Because private schools are not part of the state, they do not have to observe the constitutional rights of their constituents. The relationship between a private school and parents, teachers, and students is essentially contractual, just as is true of a private corporation and its employees. At the same time, private schools are subject to other types of law that limit their autonomy.

As a general rule, federal law prevails when there is a conflict between state and federal law. This is the thrust of Article VI, Section 2 of the U.S. Constitution, which states:

> This Constitution, and the Laws of the United States which shall be made in Pursuance thereof; and all Treaties made, or which shall be made, under the Authority of the United States, shall be the supreme Law of the Land; and the Judges in every State shall be bound thereby, any Thing in the Constitution or Laws of any State to the Contrary notwithstanding.

This provision is known as the federal supremacy clause. Precisely when a state law may survive a supremacy clause challenge is a very complicated legal question and thus is not covered in this book. The supremacy clause figured prominently in the 1995 federal district court decision striking down the portion of Proposition 187 that had excluded undocumented persons from California public schools (*League of United Latin American Citizens v. Wilson*, 1995). The U.S. Supreme Court had ruled in 1982 that the exclusion of undocumented immigrant children from tuition-free public schooling violates the equal protection clause of the Fourteenth Amendment (*Plyler v. Doe*). Based on the federal supremacy clause, the federal judge in *League of United Latin American Citizens v. Wilson* declared such exclusion by California's Proposition 187 unconstitutional. Later, most of the other provisions of the proposition were supplanted by federal law.

Although the Tenth Amendment leaves education to the states, it does not specify that the state must create a schooling system. In fact, the amendment merely reads, "The powers not delegated to the United States by the Constitution, nor prohibited by it to the States, are reserved to the States respectively, or to the people." Picking up where the federal constitution leaves off, Article IX, Section 1 of the State of California's Constitution states: "A general diffusion of knowledge and intelligence being essential to the preservation of the rights and liberties of the people, the Legislature shall encourage by all suitable means the promotion of intellectual, scientific, moral, and agricultural improvement." Article IX, Section 5 specifies, "The Legislature shall provide for a system of common schools by which a free school shall be kept up and supported in each district." Article XVI, Section 8 (a) specifies, "From all state revenues there shall first be set apart the moneys to be applied by the State for support of the public school system and public institutions of higher education." Taken together, these provisions not only require the California Legislature to provide for a public school system but also make a student's entitlement to education a fundamental right. This determination was essential to the California Supreme Court's ruling in *Serrano v. Priest* (1976) that expenditures across districts must be equalized, a matter addressed in some detail in Chapter 3.

The California Constitution also is an important source of individual rights. For example, California courts have held that the entitlement to free speech for students is greater under the California Constitution than under the First Amendment to the U.S. Constitution. Article I, Section 2, subdivision (a) of the California Constitution reads: "Every person may freely speak, write and publish his or her sentiments on all subjects, being responsible for the abuse of this right. A law may not restrain or abridge liberty of speech or press." In 1979, the California Supreme Court ruled that this provision protects the right of high school students to circulate a petition in a private shopping center (*Robins v. PruneYard Shopping Center*), a decision it affirmed in 2007 when it struck down a shopping mall ban on all forms of speech urging customers to boycott a store (*Fashion Valley Mall, LLC v. National Labor Relations Board*, 2007). In the eyes of the court, the shopping center is the equivalent of a public forum where people exchange views. The U.S. Supreme Court had ruled earlier that the free speech clause of the First Amendment to the U.S. Constitution does not apply within the confines of a private shopping center (*Hudgens v. National Labor Relations Board*, 1976).

While federal law is supreme over state law when there is a conflict between them, the U.S. Supreme Court has recognized that state constitutions and laws can be *more* protective of civil liberties than the U.S. Constitution but not less so. Just as the California Constitution is more protective of free speech than its federal counterpart, it is also more protective of privacy. For example, in cases involving teacher lifestyle choices, a portion of Article I of the California Constitution has surfaced, providing that among the inalienable rights Californians enjoy is the right of "obtaining safety, happiness, and privacy."

Statutory Law

A "statute" is a law made by a legislative body. Both the statutes enacted by Congress and those passed by the state legislature have significant influence over the operation of California schools. Congress has enacted numerous laws affecting education. A synopsis of some of the most important is provided in Table 1.1.

Because Congress does not have direct authority over education, most—but not all—of its enacted statutes are pursuant to its spending authority. The first provision of Article I, Section 8 of the U.S. Constitution is that Congress has the authority to collect taxes and provide for "the general welfare of the United States." Congress uses this power to provide conditional monetary grants to states, trading federal dollars for state compliance with Congress's political agenda. For example, a school district could lose federal funding if it condoned the release of personally identifiable information about students or their families without complying with the provisions of the federal Family Educational Rights and Privacy Act.

Some federal statutes affect both public and private educational institutions regardless of whether they receive federal funding. These statutes are enacted pursuant to Congress's authority to enact laws affecting interstate commerce under another provision of Article I, Section 8. Recently, Congress has been less inclined to enact laws under the interstate commerce clause, in part because doing so limits the autonomy of states and in part because the U.S. Supreme Court has been more protective of the concept of federalism—the division of power between the central government and states. Nevertheless, as noted in Table 1.1, some very important federal statutes that are based on Congress's power under the interstate commerce clause remain and have significant influence over the operation of both public and private schools. Included among them are Title VII of the 1964 Civil Rights Act, which, with few exceptions, prohibits discrimination based on race, color, religion, sex, or national origin in both public and private employment, and the Americans with Disabilities Act, which does the same for persons with disabilities.

Another important federal statute included in the table is a civil rights law known as 42 U.S.C. § 1983. Enacted after the Civil War, this law was designed to enforce the provisions of the Fourteenth Amendment by enabling persons to file lawsuits in federal court involving alleged violations of federal rights. The law was Congress's effort to provide meaningful relief to victims of discrimination because state courts had not proven up to the task. Known generally as "Section 1983," the statute provides:

TABLE 1.1
Key Federal Statutes Affecting California Public Schools

42 U.S.C. § 1981	Accords all persons the right to make and enforce contracts free of racial discrimination and retaliation for filing complaints based on racial discrimination in both the public and private sectors. Based on Congress's power to enforce the terms of the Thirteenth Amendment to the U.S. Constitution outlawing slavery and its trappings, this law also applies to discrimination occurring during the contract term. Thus, a private school student subjected to racial discrimination after enrolling would have a cause of action. Penalties include injunctive relief and monetary damages.
42 U.S.C. § 1983	Allows suits for injunctive relief and compensatory damages against persons acting as public officials or employees under state law who deprive others of constitutional and federal statutory rights. The U.S. Supreme Court has interpreted the word *persons* in this statute to encompass state political subdivisions such as cities, towns, school districts, and individuals. However, for reasons explained in Chapter 12, California school districts are not subject to suit under this statute, nor are private schools and their employees.
Title VI of the 1964 Civil Rights Act	Prohibits intentional discrimination in the context of race, color, or national origin in federally assisted programs. Loss of federal funding, injunctive relief, and monetary damages are available. This law was instrumental in desegregating public schools in the South during the 1960s and 1970s.
Title VII of the 1964 Civil Rights Act	Prohibits direct discrimination and retaliation for filing complaints based on race, color, religion, sex, and national origin in all aspects of public and private employment. In addition to equitable relief such as back pay and reinstatement, this law allows monetary damages for intentional discrimination. Title VII does not apply to organizations with fewer than fifteen employees for each working day in each of twenty or more calendar weeks in the current or preceding year. It also does not apply to religious organizations with respect to the employment of individuals of a particular religion to perform work, for example, in a Catholic school.
Age Discrimination in Employment Act of 1967 (ADEA)	Prohibits discrimination against individuals aged forty and over in both public and private employment unless as a bona fide occupational qualification reasonably necessary to carry out job responsibilities (for example, airline pilots). Thus, with few exceptions, there is no longer a permissible mandatory retirement age. Also prohibits retaliation for filing age-related complaints. Penalties are similar to those for Title VII.
Individuals with Disabilities Education Act (IDEA)	Requires public schools to identify children with certain specific disabilities and provide them with a free, appropriate public education. IDEA affords parents extensive due process rights. Penalties include loss of federal funding, compensatory relief, and attorneys' fees. This law is procedurally complex and has spawned a vast network of federal and state regulations that school administrators must follow. This is discussed in detail in Chapter 8.
Section 504 of the Rehabilitation Act of 1973	Prevents discrimination against persons with disabilities in programs receiving federal financial assistance. Regulations issued by the Office for Civil Rights require a free appropriate public education and services for children who have a mental or physical handicap that substantially limits one or more major life activities. Penalties are the same as under Title VI of the 1964 Civil Rights Act.
Americans with Disabilities Act of 1990 (ADA)	Accords persons with disabilities meaningful access to the programs and facilities of most businesses in the country. The ADA also prohibits discrimination against persons with disabilities in public and private employment and requires employers to make reasonable accommodation for disabled persons to enable them to perform their jobs. Penalties are similar to those for Title VII for public entities. The statute provides an exemption for religious organizations or entities controlled by religious organizations. Thus, a religious school would be exempt from the ADA, at least in most cases.

(Continued)

Title IX of the 1972 Education Amendments	Prevents discrimination against persons on the basis of sex and gender in educational programs receiving federal financial assistance. Also prohibits retaliation for filing sex discrimination complaints. Penalties against educational organizations can encompass both money damages and the loss of federal funding. Title IX has taken on renewed importance in recent years in the context of employee-on-student sexual harassment and student-on-student sexual harassment.
Family Educational Rights and Privacy Act of 1974 (FERPA)	Prohibits disbursement of personally identifiable information contained in records, files, documents, and other materials containing information about any student and prevents disclosure of such information except to parents or with parental permission. Exceptions include a legitimate educational interest (for example, sending records to a substitute teacher). The statute also gives parents the right to request that directory information about them and their child (such as names, phone numbers, and addresses) not be revealed through class rosters, athletic programs, and the like. A violation of FERPA can result in loss of federal funding.

> Every person who, under color of any statute, ordinance, regulation, custom, or usage, of any State or Territory ... subjects, or causes to be subjected, any citizen of the United States or other person within the jurisdiction thereof to the deprivation of any rights, privileges, or immunities secured by the Constitution and laws, shall be liable to the party injured in an action at law, suit in equity, or other proper proceeding for redress [in federal court].

Discussed at some length in Chapter 12, Section 1983 is the primary means by which claims involving deprivation of constitutional rights, such as free speech and free exercise of religion by municipalities and public employees, are taken directly to federal court. While school personnel in California public schools can be sued individually under this statute, school districts in the state are not subject to suit because they are viewed as part of the state, and the state itself is immune under the provisions of the Eleventh Amendment. The same is true of most, if not all, charter schools.

The California Legislature has enacted a vast number of statutes involving education in response to the California Constitution's educational mandate that it do so. Because the legislature is in session every year, new statutes are constantly being added and old statutes revised or repealed. State statutory law reaches deeply into the operations of public schools and, in some cases, private schools as well.

Most of the statutes affecting education are grouped together in the California Education Code. The code establishes the structure of the system and details its operation. Provisions of the Education Code are a major focus in ensuing chapters and can be found in their entirety on the California Department of Education (CDE) website. Other important state laws also affect education. A case in point is the section of the California Government Code setting forth the Educational Employment Relations Act (EERA)—also known as the Rodda Act after its sponsor.

EERA provisions spell out how collective bargaining is to be conducted in public schools. It will be explored in some detail in Chapter 4.

Administrative Law

When legislatures enact statutes, they cannot possibly write them specifically enough to give them full operational value. This is where administrative law comes in. Administrative law is the body of law developed by administrative agencies under the authority of the legislature to carry out their statutory responsibilities. Congress has given federal agencies like the U.S. Department of Education the authority to develop administrative regulations implementing various federal statutes. For example, the department's Office for Civil Rights has developed regulations for determining how Title IX of the 1972 Education Amendments is to apply to curricular and extracurricular activities so as to ensure gender equity. Likewise, the department's Office of Special Education and Rehabilitation Services (OSERS) has developed extensive regulations to implement the terms of the Individuals with Disabilities Education Act.

The California Legislature has given the California State Board of Education (SBE) broad authority to adopt whatever rules and regulations it deems necessary for the operation of elementary and secondary schools (Cal. Educ. Code § 33031), subject only to demonstrating their need to the Office of Administrative Law. As a practical matter, however, most of the SBE's rulemaking is in response to specific legislative directives. For example, Education Code Section 47605 (j) requires the SBE to adopt criteria for the review and approval of charter school petitions presented to it. Like all state board rules, the set of regulations the board has developed for this purpose is included in Title 5 of the California Code of Regulations and can be found on the California Department of Education website or directly on the California Code of Regulation's website at https://oal.ca.gov/publications/ccr/. The state Superintendent of Public Instruction (SPI) also has limited authority to adopt administrative regulations, which can be found as well in Title 5 of the California Code of Regulations. The administrative rules and regulations from the state board and SPI detail the operation of many facets of California schools, including special education, pupil accounting, student records, and the formation or reorganization of school districts.

While the complexity of modern government gives the legislature little alternative but to enfranchise administrative agencies with broad authority, accusations sometimes arise that the legislature has delegated too much of its authority to administrative entities. Historically, as one California court of appeal noted, "Reasonable grants of power to administrative agencies will not offend the nondelegation doctrine so long as adequate safeguards exist to protect against abuse of that power" (*Wilson v. State Board of Education*, 1999, p. 760). So long as administrative agencies stay within the scope of the authority the legislature has given them, their regulations will be upheld. That is no longer the case.

As Chief Justice Roberts said in the opinion in *Loper Bright Enterprises v. Raimondo* (2024), "[W]e have sometimes required courts to defer to 'permissible' agency interpretations of the statutes those agencies administer—even when a reviewing court reads the statute differently" (p. 2254). That requirement was established in *Chevron U.S.A. v. Natural Resources Defense Council, Inc.* (1984) and generally occurred when a statute was ambiguous, which is not unusual, as statutes are meant to set the law generally, whereas regulations set the specifics. That approach had a number of strong detractors over the next forty years, culminating with the U.S. Supreme Court taking up the question again. The *Loper Bright* decision was not unexpected: Chevron was overruled and agency power seriously diminished, a major shift toward creating more powerful courts without the historical and expert opinion of the agency professionals.

For school personnel, the best illustration of administrative law can be found in school board policies. California Education Code Section 35010 requires school boards to develop and enforce rules for governing their district. The rules they adopt must not be in conflict with other law, including the rules prescribed by the SBE. In larger districts, board policies are accompanied by a set of district administrative procedures that detail the implementation of board policies at the school and program levels. Taken together, board policies and administrative procedures are best known as "the law of the district." It is important for all school personnel to know and follow them because failure to do so can be grounds for contract termination and employee and district liability. It is important for school district officials to regularly review district board policies to verify that the policies and regulations are current and do not conflict with state or federal law.

When disputes arise over the application of statutes and their accompanying administrative regulations, administrative agencies often play a role in resolving them. In effect, they exercise quasi-judicial authority. At the federal level, for example, the Family Educational Rights and Privacy Act (FERPA) is enforced by the U.S. Department of Education through its Family Policy Compliance Office and its Office of Administrative Law judges. Until 2002, a student or the student's parents could file a lawsuit in federal court claiming a violation of FERPA and seeking money damages and attorneys' fees. But the U.S. Supreme Court cut off this manner of enforcing the privacy law by holding that the statute's enforcement mechanism is exclusively through the U.S. Department of Education (*Gonzaga University v. Doe*, 2002). The department's toughest sanction is the termination of federal funding. Judges cannot award monetary damages to victims. So, to some extent, FERPA is no longer taken as seriously as perhaps it should be.

As with federal law, California administrative law also governs the resolution of certain types of disputes. A process known as the Uniform Complaint Procedure (UCP) has been established within the CDE to channel and resolve complaints involving alleged violations by local agencies in administering federal or state laws or regulations governing specific educational programs or committing unlawful discrimination against students. The UCP specifies the procedures and timelines for processing complaints within the school district and provides a right of appeal to the CDE. Its provisions can be found in Title 5 of the California Code of Regulations, Section 4600 et seq.. For example, if a parent claims that the football coach improperly cut a student from the team because of racial discrimination, the parent could utilize the UCP complaint process. School districts are now required to use their uniform complaint process to help identify and resolve deficiencies relating to instructional materials, condition of facilities, teacher assignments, and instructional services provided for students (Educ. Code § 35186).

This provision was added in 2004 as part of the settlement of the *Williams v. State of California* school finance lawsuit, described in Chapter 3 in the section "The Movement Toward Adequacy." Complaints are first channeled to the principal or other appropriate school official, who then has up to thirty working days to resolve them and forty-five days to report back to the complainant. If not satisfied, the complainant can appeal to the governing board and, if the complaint involves dangerous conditions of school facilities, to the SPI. The statute requires notices in all classrooms that sufficient textbooks and teaching materials are to be provided and that facilities are to be clean, safe, and well maintained, and informing complainants of where complaint forms are available in case of a shortage. The notice also must inform parents that there should be no teacher vacancies or misassignments. A "misassignment" means the placement of a teacher in a position for which the teacher does not have the appropriate credentials under state law. If such is not the case, the UCP provides a means of seeking redress.

Not all disputes involving federal or state law are resolved through the UCP. As explained in Chapter 8 in the section "Due Process Hearings," a different process must be followed for disputes over the identification and placement of children with disabilities under IDEA. Matters involving gender discrimination under Title IX go directly to the Office of Civil Rights in the U.S. Department of Education, whereas employment discrimination disputes are routed to the California Department of Fair Employment and Housing. The law is filled with such complexities, often requiring a specialist to sort them out.

Administrative bodies have a role in resolving disputes to avoid flooding courts with matters that can best be resolved by knowledgeable experts who are close to the scene. Often complainants are required to "exhaust administrative remedies" before they seek judicial relief. However, not all disputes involving federal and state law are subject to the exhaustion requirement. Some matters can be taken directly to state court. For example, a parent may be able to go directly to state court to try to obtain an order overturning a principal's decision to exclude the parent's child from graduation ceremonies. Additionally, disputes involving the violation of federal constitutional rights generally can be taken directly to federal court without pursuing state or federal administrative remedies. For example, a parent's allegation that the elimination of his or her son from a team was racially motivated can be taken directly to federal court. The dotted line in Figure 1.1, going from local districts to the federal court system, shows how matters involving federal claims can bypass the state administrative and judicial process altogether. The solid line linking school districts and California courts illustrates a similar bypass for civil remedies.

Contract Law

Most school employees are aware of the importance of contract law simply because they have an individual or collective contract that spells out the terms and conditions of employment. Contract law is also very involved in the daily operation of schools through purchasing, property acquisition, and lease arrangements. Campus-level administrators sometimes have concerns about whether they have the authority to enter into contracts with vendors such as the purveyor of team uniforms. While the governing board can delegate its power to contract to the superintendent and persons the superintendent designates, Education Code Section 17604 requires that the governing board must approve all contracts binding the district. If this is not done, then the contract is invalid. If an official given the power of contract in accordance with this section engages in unlawful behavior, the official is personally liable to the district for any money paid out.

In the private school sector, contract law is an important determinant of the relationship between the school and its parents, students, and teachers. This is so because constitutional rights generally do not exist within the private sector, relatively few provisions of federal and California law pertain to private schools, and the CDE has little influence over private school operations. To determine the relationship between the private school and its constituents, one must consider the agreements between the school and its constituents, as well as the school's policies that are incorporated by reference in the contract. In some private schools, teachers do not have employment contracts but rather serve at the pleasure of the governing board; in others, students can be asked to leave at the school's discretion. The rights of teachers and students are determined by the school's policies. If the policies are not to a person's liking, he or she is free to go elsewhere.

The collective bargaining agreement is another form of contract law. The contracts negotiated between employee unions and school districts impose rules governing school operations that should not be ignored. Included in most collective bargaining contracts is a grievance process that specifies how complaints arising under the administration of the contract are to be channeled and resolved. Because of their importance to the operation of California public schools, Chapter 4 focuses specifically on unions and collective bargaining.

Judicial Law

The last source of school law involves the rulings handed down by courts. Much of school law, particularly student and teacher rights, is controlled by judicial law. Because there are two judicial systems—one federal and one state—we discuss each separately.

California has a three-tiered judicial system. At the bottom are the superior courts, which have jurisdiction over civil matters and criminal matters such as misdemeanors, felonies, and traffic offenses. Located in each of California's fifty-eight counties, the superior courts are the state's basic trial courts. Because important matters involving schools begin here, we include them in Figure 1.1. A single judge staffs each court. The superior court system has an appellate division for certain types of cases. Three judges staff each of these courts, unless a party requests the full panel after a ruling. Decisions from the appellate division may be published in volumes known as court reporters, depending on their importance in establishing a new rule of law, resolving conflict in the law, dealing with an important public interest, or making a significant contribution to the legal literature.

Decisions of the superior courts are appealable to the California courts of appeal, of which six are scattered around the state. These courts hear cases in panels of three judges. The role of the appellate courts is to determine whether the law was applied correctly in cases decided by superior court judges. The decisions of the courts of appeal may be reported in the official court reporters, depending on their importance and at the court's discretion. The highest state court is the California Supreme Court. Composed of seven justices who sit as a panel, this appellate court is the court of last resort for matters of state law. The justices have the authority to choose most of the cases they hear, and their decisions are published in the official court "reporters." Because of the precedents established by California courts of appeal and the California Supreme Court in many education matters, they are often cited in school board policies and various publications on California school law. California judges are elected either directly or, for appellate judges, through a retention election following appointment by the governor.

In addition to these three courts of record, there are specialized courts for certain types of cases. For example, with exceptions for violent acts such as murder or rape, persons under the age of eighteen who violate state or federal laws or municipal ordinances other than those pertaining to curfew violations are within the jurisdiction of California's county juvenile courts, typically called *delinquency court*. Persistent student truancy matters are directed to these courts.

Federal courts hear cases involving the federal constitution and federal statutes. They also have the authority to hear disputes involving citizens from different states on matters of state law where the amount in controversy is greater than $75,000. This so-called diversity of citizenship jurisdiction rarely involves education matters. In addition, federal courts occasionally hear state claims when they are combined with federal claims. Article III of the U.S. Constitution specifies that there is to be one supreme court and such lower federal courts as Congress wishes to establish. In response, Congress has established the federal district courts and the federal courts of appeals, which, together with the U.S. Supreme Court, constitute a three-tiered federal judicial system. At the bottom are the U.S. district courts, four of which are located in California, with each having jurisdiction over a portion of the state's fifty-eight counties. The federal district courts are trial courts, each staffed by a single judge. Decisions reached by one federal district court are not binding on another federal district court, although judges will consider each other's decisions carefully in the interest of uniformity of law. The same is true of state court judges. The only time a decision of one court becomes a binding precedent on another court is when the former is in the same circuit and higher in the judicial hierarchy. Decisions from the federal district courts in California are appealed to the U.S. Court of Appeals for the Ninth Circuit, whose jurisdiction extends over nine western states, including Alaska and Hawaii. Usually hearing cases in panels of three, the Ninth Circuit decisions are binding on the federal district courts within the geographic jurisdiction of the Ninth Circuit (which includes all of California).

The decisions of the Ninth Circuit Court of Appeals can be appealed to the U.S. Supreme Court in Washington, D.C. However, the chances of the Supreme Court accepting a case on appeal are very slim. From some 10,000 cases filed annually for review, the high court has chosen to hear fewer than 100 in recent years. When the Court does accept a case, all nine justices hear it together. The Court's decision will bind the entire country. As with other courts where more than one judge hears a case, the justices often disagree, and there will be several concurring and dissenting opinions. A concurring opinion means that the justice writing it concurs with the majority's decision but for different reasons.

All federal judges are appointed by the president, with the advice and consent of the U.S. Senate. This explains why the confirmation process is often so heated, as presidents typically seek to appoint judges who share their political philosophy. However, there are never any guarantees that a federal judge may not change his or her judicial philosophy over time.

In sum, these are the five primary sources of California school law, and, as noted in Figure 1.1, there is a pattern to their interaction. Constitutional law is preeminent over all other types of law. A statute that conflicts with either the state or the federal constitution may be ruled unconstitutional and thus null and void. Both federal and California statutes and their related administrative law regulations play important roles in establishing the structure and governance of California schools. Contract law, often in the form of collective bargaining agreements, shapes the relationship between the school and its employees and, in the private sector, with parents and students as well. Contract law also governs the relationship between the school and various entities such as contractors and vendors. Unless subject to a contractually negotiated grievance process, disputes between the school and its constituents are usually first processed administratively at the school level or before an administrative agency before being appealed to the judiciary. Some matters, such as a request for an injunction against a school policy or practice, can be taken directly to court without first exhausting administrative law remedies. Generally, matters involving state law are routed to state courts, and matters involving federal law are routed to federal courts. Cases start at the trial court level and can be appealed to higher courts, with the California Supreme Court (state law) and U.S. Supreme Court (federal law) having the last word.

THE CALIFORNIA SCHOOLING STRUCTURE

As noted at the beginning of the chapter, the California Constitution directs the legislature to establish public education. In essence, the legislature controls the state's public schooling system. In a characterization that has been repeated many times, the California appellate courts have termed the authority of the legislature over education as "exclusive, plenary, absolute, entire, and comprehensive, subject only to constitutional constraints" (*California Teachers Association v. Hayes*, 1992, p. 706). (See Figure 1.2.)

The governor is a key player in setting the legislative agenda and making compromises necessary to the success of the governor's proposals. The governor can veto legislative enactments, but the legislature can overrule that action with a two-thirds vote. Equally significant, the governor controls the education budget and can use the line-item veto power to reduce or eliminate the funding appropriated by the legislature for education programs. The two-party system ensures that conflict will occur in the legislative arena, stimulated by intensive lobbying from

16 | LAW AND THE CALIFORNIA SCHOOLING SYSTEM

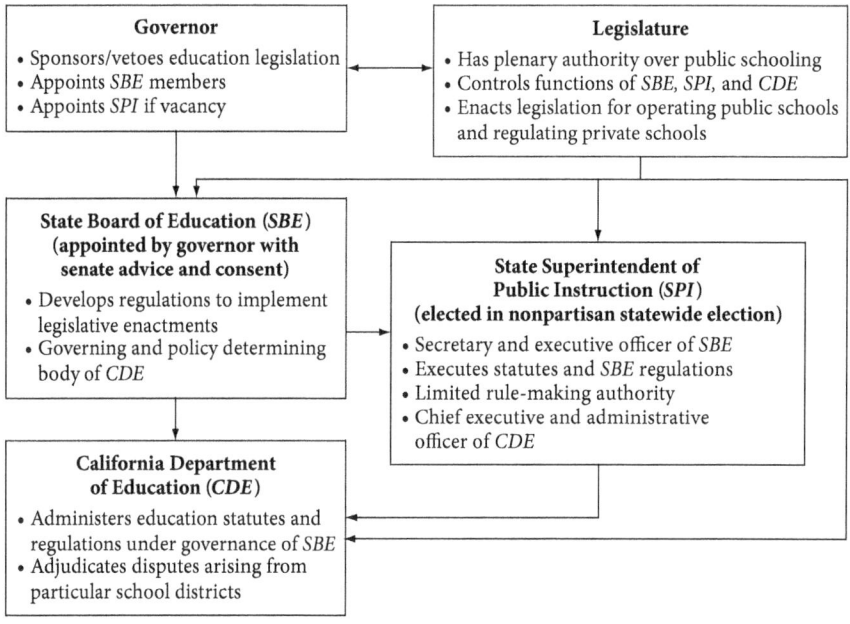

Figure 1.2   California State Structure for School Governance

powerful interest groups. Still, reality dictates that a person who wants to change the California schooling system is best advised to lobby the legislature and gain the governor's support.

The California Constitution itself ensures that politics is an integral part of educational policymaking in the way that it structures the state's educational system. Article 9, Section 7 of the California Constitution requires the legislature to provide for the appointment or election of the State Board of Education (SBE). In response, the legislature has established a ten-member board appointed by the governor for four-year terms with the advice and consent of two-thirds of the State Senate (Educ. Code § 33000 et seq.). A student is similarly appointed to the board for a one-year term. Assisted by a small office staff and meeting at least six times per year, the SBE oversees the policies drafted and implemented by the California Department of Education (CDE) and is the liaison between the federal government and the state. The board elects its own officers and establishes its committees. As noted earlier, one of the most important functions of the SBE is to adopt administrative regulations detailing how state statutes are to be implemented at the school district level. Among the multifaceted responsibilities placed on the SBE by the legislature are the following: engaging in statewide study and planning for schooling, developing teacher evaluation guidelines, adopting instructional materials for K–8 grades, granting waivers of various Education Code provisions for both traditional public and charter schools, approving proposals for the unification of school districts, and approving and overseeing statewide curriculum content and performance standards, student assessment, and the public school accountability program.

Article IX, Section 2 of the California Constitution provides for the selection of a state superintendent of public instruction (SPI), who is the *ex officio* director of education, in a nonpartisan election, meaning that the candidates are not identified by political party on the ballot. The state superintendent takes office after the first day of January following the gubernatorial election and can serve no more than two terms. If there is a vacancy in the office, the constitution provides that the governor appoints the SPI. The legislature has designated the superintendent as the secretary and executive officer of the SBE and responsible for executing its policies (Educ. Code § 33100 et seq.). Although the legislature cannot alter the constitutional status of the SPI, it can change the superintendent's powers and duties. The legislature has given the SPI numerous responsibilities, just a few of which include superintending the schools of the state; developing regulations pertaining to arrangements with the federal government; administering state funding and budgeting; working with the state board to develop and implement the state's curriculum standards, instructional materials adoption, school district reorganization, assessment, and school accountability programs; and compiling a directory of information on private schools.

The CDE and its various subunits administer the education laws under the oversight of the state board and at the direction of the SPI, who is the CDE's chief executive and administrative officer (Educ. Code § 33300 et seq.). The legislature has placed a wide range of duties on the CDE, including such functions as disseminating information, developing budgeting guidelines and holding training workshops, gathering and reporting test results and other outcome data, coordinating the identification and development of effective programs and practices, supervising physical education and interscholastic athletics, and evaluating the effectiveness of programs for learning English. With regard to secondary school interscholastic athletics, the department works in collaboration with the California Interscholastic Federation (CIF), a voluntary organization composed of school and school-related personnel. CIF responsibilities are set forth in Education Code Section 33353 et seq.. The CDE is also charged with assisting the California Commission on Teacher Credentialing, an agency created by the legislature to establish professional standards, assessments, and examinations for entry and advancement in the education profession. Chapter 2 covers the commission and its responsibilities in more depth. Though pared down significantly in recent years, the CDE still has some 2,700 employees to carry out its responsibilities and those of the state SPI.

Given that the CDE is subject to the authority of both an elected state superintendent and an appointed board, it is not difficult to imagine that tensions would surface. Indeed, turf battles have spanned more than seventy years, reaching a high point in 1993 when the state board filed a lawsuit against the state superintendent for not carrying out its directives (*State Board of Education v. Honig*, 1993). Prior to the lawsuit, the California attorney general was called on on several occasions to clarify the responsibilities of each. In 1943, for example, the attorney general advised that the state board is similar to a board of directors and the state superintendent to its executive head. The former makes policy, and the latter executes it through the education department. The problem with this view is that, unlike the chief executive officer of a company, the state superintendent is not selected by the state board and may not feel any particular allegiance to it. Indeed, that was the situation in the 1993 lawsuit—the state board had directed the state superintendent to do certain things, but the superintendent refused, saying he had no obligation to do so.

The judges in *State Board of Education v. Honig* (1993) first rejected the state superintendent's argument that, because the SPI is a constitutionally recognized official, the legislature is without authority to define the superintendent's duties. The legislature can increase or diminish the powers of the SPI as it wishes. Likewise, the authority given by the legislature to the SBE in Education Code Section 33031 to adopt rules and regulations governing its own appointees and employees is sufficient to require the state superintendent to comply with the board's directives. Regarding the dispute, the court ruled that the state board could direct the state superintendent to nominate a deputy SPI and three associate SPIs for board approval, per Article 9, Section 2.1 of the California Constitution. The state superintendent had refused to nominate them. The state board can also seek additional staff and direct the state superintendent to include them in the CDE budget. However, although the state board can review the performance of key personnel, it is without authority to exercise detailed budget oversight of the CDE. Such an activity, said the court, would overstep the board's role as a policymaking entity and involve it in micromanagement. Finally, the court ruled that the state board could hire outside legal counsel to represent it in its lawsuit against the state superintendent and have the state superintendent pay the costs out of state department funds.

The state educational governance structure is replicated in California's fifty-eight counties. Each one has a county office of education, a county superintendent, and a county board of education. The county superintendent is elected in all but five counties. In three of these—San Diego, Santa Clara, and Sacramento—the County Board of Education appoints the county superintendent. In Los Angeles

County, the county superintendent is appointed by the County Board of Supervisors, and in San Francisco County the San Francisco Unified School District superintendent is the county superintendent and operates under the auspices of the County Board of Supervisors. The county school board comprises five to seven members elected from trustee areas within the county.

The California Education Code includes extensive definitions of the responsibilities of county boards (Educ. Code § 1000 et seq.). The county board approves budgets submitted by the county superintendent, adopts rules for the administration of the office of the county superintendent, and implements legislative directives. The county school board also serves as an appeal board for adjudicating student expulsion appeals, interdistrict attendance appeals, and charter schools whose applications are rejected by school districts. The county superintendent operates county schools where they exist (e.g., court and community schools).

Provisions of the Education Code relating to students who may be involuntarily enrolled in a county community school (often called court schools) were amended in 2014 to (1) exclude homeless children, (2) add conditions to referrals made on the recommendation of a school attendance review board, and (3) limit types of juvenile offender referrals. Referrals are not to be made initially unless it is determined that the county community school has sufficient space; can meet the needs of the student; and the parent, responsible adult/guardian has not objected to the referral because of factors such as safety, geographic distance, lack of transportation, and concern about meeting the student's needs. The student has the right to return to the student's previous school or another appropriate school within the district at the end of the semester following the semester when the acts leading to referral occurred. The right to return continues until the end of the student's eighteenth birthday, except for students with special needs. In that instance, the right to return ends when the student turns twenty-two. The statute then addresses conditions for county community school enrollment of students on probation with or without the supervision of a probation officer and consistent with the order of a juvenile court. All these changes are quite detailed and should be reviewed directly. See Education Code §§ 1981 and 1983.

The county school board likewise serves as an intermediary between the local school districts within each county and the state (Educ. Code § 1200 et seq.). Among the superintendents' duties are operating programs for children with disabilities, parenting teens, and childcare for students who are also parents. In Kern County, the county superintendent even operates a county library and zoo. County superintendents provide myriad services to school districts, including fiscal oversight, curriculum support and training, and media services. They are now also responsible for monitoring the sufficiency of textbooks and instructional material in low-performing schools that are not under review through state or federal intervention programs.

School district boards of trustees are responsible for governing school districts. They generally are composed of five members, who are elected to serve staggered four-year terms so that half are elected in each odd-numbered year (Educ. Code § 35000 et seq.). A unified school district (one that operates both elementary and secondary schools) may have a governing board of seven members elected either at large or by trustee areas as designated in the proposal for unification. An increasing number of school districts are now switching to trustee elections in which voters in a portion of the district elect a candidate of their choice under the 2001 California Voting Rights Act (Election Code § 14025 et seq.). That law prohibits state political subdivisions, including school districts, from running at-large elections that thwart the ability of minority groups to elect candidates of their choice.

For many years, the legislature has promoted the unification of small districts in contiguous areas to promote efficiency and uniformity. In 1935, there were 3,500 school districts in the state. Today, there are about a third as many, with 345 unified school districts, 517 elementary, 76 high school, 10 high school with a junior high program, 58 county districts, 22 SBE charters, and a few additional schools operated by the California Youth Authority and by the state. These figures are subject to change because consolidation continues. The governing board of an elementary school district other than a union or joint union elementary district consists of three members elected at large. In districts with high schools, boards also must include at least one nonvoting student member if the students submit a petition requesting student representation. Education Code Section 35160 gives school boards broad authority to operate schools as they see fit—so long as their actions are not inconsistent with or preempted by law and are not in conflict with the purposes of school districts. This general grant of authority reflects an amendment to Article 9, Section 14 of the California Constitution added in 1972 and is often cited in school board policies, administrative regulations, and judicial decisions. In addition, Education Code Section 33050 allows school district and county boards of education to request the State Board of Education to grant waivers from some provisions of the Education Code and the board's implementing regulations after a public hearing. The statute includes a significant list of exceptions to the waiver option.

In recent years, legislatures in several other states have enacted measures enabling city mayors in specific cities to appoint some or all of their city school district governing board members or otherwise influence district governance. Such an effort was tried in California in 2006 when the legislature enacted the Romero Act to establish a Council of Mayors and a Mayor's Partnership in Los Angeles that together transferred powers normally possessed by the Los Angeles Unified School District school board to Mayor Antonio Villaraigosa. These included appointing and removing the district superintendent and taking control over three clusters of low-performing schools. The Romero Act was declared unconstitutional by a California court of appeal because it violated Article IX, Section 16 and Section 6 of the California Constitution (*Mendoza v. State of California*, 2007). Section 16 grants charter cities the right to determine whether their boards of education are to be elected or appointed, and the Los Angeles City Charter provides for an elected board. There are currently 120 charter cities out of a total of 482 cities in California. Section 6 provides that no public school or any other part of the public school system is to be transferred to an authority not included in the public school system. The system encompasses the state superintendent of public instruction and state board of education, county superintendents and boards of education, and local school districts with governing boards. Mayors are not included. Thus, the constitution would have to be changed to empower mayors. This may be true even for charter cities if voters were to give the mayor authority to appoint the entire school board.

The law sets the maximum ratios of administrative employees to each 100 teachers as nine in elementary schools, eight in unified school districts, and seven in high school districts (Educ. Code § 41402). School superintendents constitute the chief executive officer of school districts (Educ. Code § 35035). Among the superintendent's duties set forth in Section 35035 are preparing and submitting budgets, assigning school district credentialed employees, and entering into contracts on behalf of the district. Other duties are specified elsewhere throughout the Education Code, usually in connection with programs or particular school district responsibilities. The qualifications for superintendents are set forth in Education Code Section 35028 et seq.. Superintendents must hold a valid administrator certificate and a valid teaching certificate, unless the person is employed as a deputy, associate, or assistant superintendent in a purely clerical capacity. However, a local governing board may waive any credential requirement for the chief administrative officer of the school district under its jurisdiction. Any individual serving as the chief administrative officer of a school district who does not hold a credential may be required by the local governing board to pursue a program of in-service training conducted pursuant to guidelines approved by the commission.

Public school principals, who basically serve at the pleasure of the school district, must hold an administrative credential and one or more teacher or services credentials (Educ. Code § 44860). However, a substitute principal with only a teacher's credential may be employed in an emergency for not more than five months in a school year, as long as the credential matches the grade level at the school to which the substitute principal is appointed (Educ. Code § 44861). The powers and duties of principals are not detailed in the Education Code. Thus, what they do is determined largely by school boards and central office administrators. Included among the powers and duties listed in the Education Code are making annual reports to the school superintendent if directed to do so and suspending students from school. These are simply two responsibilities that in practice are almost endless. Likely, as a result of that, the legislature has established a grant program to provide administrator training in leadership activities (Educ. Code § 44681 et seq.).

Principals also may work with school site councils and advisory committees. For example, Education Code Section 52176 requires each school with twenty or more limited English proficient students to have an advisory committee of parents and staff to assist the principal with planning and reviewing bilingual education.

PARENT RIGHTS AND RESPONSIBILITIES

Despite the significant involvement of the state in schooling, education is a shared responsibility with parents. In fact, before there were public schools, parents either sent their children to private schools or educated them at home. With the advent of public schooling and compulsory attendance laws in the late nineteenth and early twentieth centuries, the role of parents in educating their children themselves declined. Parents were still responsible, of course, for child rearing and training during the first few years of life. But beyond that, education increasingly became a government responsibility. What rights do parents retain over the education of their children? With growing interest in school choice, this is an increasingly important question.

Choosing a Private School

The leading U.S. Supreme Court decision on parent rights is *Pierce v. Society of Sisters* (1925). That case involved an Oregon statute requiring every child between the ages of eight and sixteen to attend a public school. Failure to do so was a misdemeanor offense. A Catholic school and a nondenominational military school challenged the law, arguing that they would be forced to shut down if the law were strictly enforced. The U.S. Supreme Court unanimously declared the law to be an unconstitutional infringement on both the rights of parents and the rights of private schools.

As to parent rights, the Court noted that Oregon's compulsory public school attendance law "unreasonably interferes with the liberty of parents and guardians to direct the upbringing and education of children under their control." In a key passage, Justice James McReynolds observed that

> The fundamental theory of liberty upon which all governments in this Union repose excludes any general power of the state to standardize its children by forcing them to accept instruction from public school teachers only. The child is not the mere creature of the state; those who nurture him and direct his destiny have the right, coupled with the high duty, to recognize and prepare him for additional obligations. (p. 535)

Thus, parents have a constitutional right to enroll their children in private schools, and the state cannot require all children to attend public schools.

The Court reaffirmed its position on parent rights in a 2000 ruling. The case involved a Washington State statute giving state judges the authority to override a parent's objection to child visitation rights by grandparents. While a majority of justices reaffirmed the *Pierce* decision, four members of the Court went further to observe that the interest of parents in the care, custody, and control of their children "is perhaps the oldest of the fundamental liberty interests recognized by this Court" (*Troxel v. Granville*, 2000, p. 65).

It is clear from these decisions that parents have a right to select private schools for their children in lieu of public schooling. But, beyond the choice of a private school, the constitutional dimensions of parent educational rights appear quite limited. In a 2005 decision, the U.S. Court of Appeals for the Ninth Circuit rejected a parental claim that having elementary-age children respond to survey questions dealing with sex and sexual activity violated the parents' rights to control their children's upbringing (*Fields v. Palmdale School District*, 2005). The survey was administered by a mental health counselor with the approval of the school. Parents were given an opt-out, but several who did not exercise it became incensed when they discovered the nature of the questions, some of which related to sex. In 1925, the appeals court observed that parent rights under *Pierce v. Society of Sisters* are limited to choosing the school their child attends. The judges observed, "Parents have a right to inform their children when and as they wish on the subject of sex; they have no constitutional right, however, to prevent a public school from providing students with whatever information it wishes to provide, sexual or otherwise, when and as the school determines that it is appropriate to do so"

(p. 1206). However, the court did not rule on the application of state law to the claim. By statute in California, parents have a right to exempt their children from sex education and HIV/AIDS prevention education, as well as assessments pertaining to them, although the exemption is typically presented as a passive "opt-out" rather than an active "opt-in" (Educ. Code § 51938).

While the Old Order Amish were able to convince the U.S. Supreme Court that they should be able to withdraw their children from public school after eighth grade and educate them at home based on their separatist religious heritage, no other group successfully has done so (*Wisconsin v. Yoder*, 1972). Even in that case, the justices observed that the *Pierce* ruling provides "no support to the contention that parents may replace state educational requirements with their own idiosyncratic views of what knowledge a child needs to be a productive and happy member of society" (p. 239). However, the stated difference in the *Yoder* decision was the central role of the Amish faith in family life and the education of the children within the Amish community for hundreds of years. Chapter 7 considers the extent to which the free exercise of religion clause may enhance parent rights to control their children's education.

Homeschooling

Stated disillusionment with public schooling, coupled with the explosive growth of online learning, has resulted in the soaring popularity of homeschooling. However, federal courts have yet to extend the *Pierce v. Society of Sisters* (ruling to encompass it. Thus, the right to homeschooling is a matter determined by state law. While California requires children between the ages of six and eighteen to attend school full-time during the typical academic year, there is an exemption for attendance at a full-time private school and for instruction by a tutor (Educ. Code §§ 48222 and 48224). The latter provides that children may be instructed for at least three hours a day for 175 days a year by a tutor in the subjects taught in the public schools. The instruction must be between 8 a.m. and 4 p.m. and in English. The statute provides that, unlike teachers in private schools, the tutor must hold a state credential for the grade taught.

For a number of years, parents who taught their children at home were considered tutors by the California Department of Education and consequently had to meet the credential requirement. Many, however, believed that the California Legislature had in fact viewed homeschooling as a form of private schooling and that parents did not need to have a credential. This position was confirmed in 2008 by a California court of appeal. Though the legislature has never been explicit, the judges concluded after examining various statutes that homeschooling is a form of private schooling and not the equivalent of tutoring. In so ruling, the state court construed the liberty right of parents to control their children's upbringing to be sufficiently strong to require a compelling governmental purpose to restrict homeschooling. A finding by a dependency court (sometimes called juvenile court) that parents are not fit parents can fulfill that requirement. The court concluded by observing that California has no laws overseeing homeschooling and that once a parent files an affidavit that he or she is teaching his or her children at home, the matter is at an end. The judges advised that in the interest of quality education, more clarity in this area of the law could be helpful (*Jonathan L. v. Superior Court*, 2008).

Parents who want to educate their children themselves have found a new venue in the form of charter schools that combine supervised homeschooling with various online and on-site programs. Independent study programs are also available in many traditional public schools and can consist of non-classroom-based instruction as well. State law imposes conditions on independent offerings in both settings, including a restriction on offering courses required for high school graduation in this manner (Educ. Code § 51745). In addition, traditional public schools often offer alternative programs that provide credentialed teachers to assist parents who homeschool their children.

Rights Within Public Schools

Several sections of the California Education Code give parents rights within public schools, recognizing that they are partners with public schools in their children's education. Generally, the term *parent* means the natural parent or adopted parent, or one who stands in a parental relationship with a child, such as a legal guardian or foster parent. One section of the Education Code details parent access to student records and the right to challenge information contained therein (Educ. Code § 49070 et seq.). Another gives parents the right to inspect instructional materials and assessments, teacher manuals, films, tapes, and computer software and to observe instruction and other school activities that involve the parent's child (Educ. Code § 49091.10 et seq.). Chapter 10 details the privacy rights involving both students and parents.

The Parental Involvement Act added by the legislature in 1998 conveyed additional rights to parents, including the right to observe their child's classrooms, to meet with their child's teachers and principal, to request a particular school for their child and to receive a response from the district, to refuse to permit psychological testing involving their child, to have a safe school environment, and to be eligible for membership on a school site committee (Educ. Code § 51100 et seq.). The statute also reinforces other federal and state law provisions giving parents access to, and the right to challenge, their child's records. The statute requires school districts to develop a policy, in consultation with parents, outlining parental responsibilities and suggesting how parents and guardians can support the learning environment for their children. Suggestions may include checking student attendance, ensuring that homework is completed, monitoring television viewing, volunteering at school, and helping extend their children's learning activities at home.

The right of parents to access the school campus to visit with school personnel and to observe their children's classes is not unrestricted. Parents, guardians, and nonstudents over the age of sixteen who willfully interfere with classes or school activities are subject to criminal penalties (Educ. Code § 44810). A companion section provides that any parent, guardian, or other person who materially disrupts class work or extracurricular activities or who creates substantial disorder is guilty of a misdemeanor (Educ. Code § 44811). Penalties include fines and imprisonment. Parents also can be liable up to $10,000 for willful misconduct of their child resulting in injury or death to public or private school students, school personnel, or volunteers, as well as for damages caused by their child to property belonging to the school or school personnel (Educ. Code § 48904). This same section permits schools to withhold the grades, transcripts, and diploma of students who willfully damage school property or fail to return loaned property until the damages have been paid. If the minor and the parent or guardian are unable to pay the damages or return the property, the school must provide a voluntary work program to secure the release of academic records and diploma.

Expanding Parent Choice

The school choice movement has not escaped the attention of California legislators. While parents have always had the right to choose private and public schools for their children through choice of residence, the options within traditional public schools were often limited by geography. Starting in 1994, governing boards have been required to adopt an intradistrict open enrollment policy (Educ. Code § 35160.5 (b)). Intradistrict open enrollment means that parents or guardians may select any school in the district for their children. The policy must include a random, unbiased selection criterion for chosen schools that are oversubscribed. Athletic and academic performance may not be considered, though the latter may be used for placement in gifted and talented programs. Specialized schools such as a mathematics academy can continue with existing selection criteria. Districts are allowed to give special consideration to students who seek transfers even to overcrowded schools within the district because of unsafe and dangerous conditions to those students at their assigned school. Districts also may give priority to siblings of students already in attendance at a chosen school or whose parent(s) or guardian(s) work there. However, transferring students cannot displace students currently residing in the chosen school's attendance zone.

One provision of this statute stands out. It provides that school districts retain the authority to maintain appropriate racial and ethnic balances among their schools, either at their discretion or pursuant to a court-ordered or voluntary desegregation plan. At the same time, Proposition 209, added in 1996 to the California Constitution, prohibits discrimination against, or preferential treatment to, any individual or group on the basis of race, sex, color, ethnicity, or national origin in public employment, public education, or public contracting. A central concern with school choice dating back to the desegregation era of the 1960s is that it could result in racial and ethnic isolation. As discussed in some detail in Chapter 11, the concern is real, and the measures to prevent it are limited.

Congress gave parents increased choice opportunities within school districts when it enacted the No Child Left Behind (NCLB) Act in 2001 in the form of a reauthorization of the Elementary and Secondary Education Act that provides federal funding for the education of disadvantaged students. Under NCLB, parents whose children are in low-performing public schools receiving Title I funds could transfer their children to higher-performing traditional and charter schools in the district. Chapter 2 covers this issue further.

Building on NCLB, the California Legislature enacted the Parent Empowerment Act in 2010, known as the "Parent Trigger" law (Educ. Code §§ 53300–53302). The law applies to no more than seventy-five Title I traditional public and charter schools that have an academic performance index of less than 800 under the California school assessment system. The 800 score is the statewide performance target. Thus, these schools need not be among the lowest performing, as with NCLB. However, after one school year, they must remain subject to corrective action and continue to fail to make adequate yearly progress. The "trigger" provision provides that if at least one-half of the parents or legal guardians of students attending the school, or in combination with at least one-half of those whose children in elementary or middle schools will move on to the school, request the school district to implement one of four interventions including restructuring or closure, the district must do so unless it can show why the option cannot be implemented and instead describes what other options it will implement in the subsequent school year.

Parents can also seek to have their children attend other school districts pursuant to transfer agreements between two or more districts. The agreements spell out the conditions for transferring, subject to conditions set forth in Education Code Section 46600 et seq., including associated rights of appeal. At the request of the parent or guardian, priority for attendance is to be given if a student is determined by either the resident district or the district of proposed enrollment to have been a victim of bullying by personnel in the resident district.

The state also has an interdistrict school choice program whereby school districts may accept transfers from other districts (Educ. Code § 48300 et seq.). Sections 48300–48317 of the Education Code relating to the interdistrict school transfer program were revised in 2017 to spell out the program's components in more detail. Chief among them was a requirement that on or before July 1, 2018, a school district opting to become a district of choice must register with both the Superintendent of Public Instruction and the county board of education where the district is located. Starting the next school year, a school district of choice was not to enroll students until the district had completed this registration. Also, a district of choice must give first priority for enrollment of siblings of children already attending schools or programs within the district, second priority for attendance to students eligible for free or reduced-price meals, and third priority for attendance of children of military personnel (Educ. Code Section 48306). These legislative provisions were due to sunset on July 1, 2023, but the legislature extended the statute so that it becomes inoperative on July 1, 2028, and will be repealed on January 1, 2029, unless the legislature again extends the provision.

If governing boards accept transfers, they must ensure that no resident student is displaced and that transferring students are admitted through a random, unbiased process. Preference may be given to siblings of children presently enrolled. While no consideration may be given to academic or athletic performance, existing entrance requirements for specialized programs or schools may be applied. Either the district of residence or the chosen district may refuse to permit a transfer if it would negatively impact a court-ordered or voluntary desegregation plan or the racial and ethnic balance of the district. The validity of this condition is questionable for reasons discussed in Chapter 11 on racial segregation.

The district of residence may not block or discourage out-transfers. However, a district of residence with fewer than 50,000 students may limit the number of students transferring out to 3 percent of its enrollment. Education Code Section 48307 also provides that the district of residence may limit the maximum number of students transferring out "if a county superintendent of schools determines that a school district of residence would not meet the standards and criteria for fiscal stability" as specified elsewhere in the provision.

According to the state attorney general, school districts may not charge an interdistrict transfer processing fee (Opinion No. 04-501, September 14, 2004). Further, districts are encouraged to hold informational meetings to inform parents of the options available, and parents are to be notified within ninety days after the chosen district has received the application if the transfer has been approved. The chosen district may not deny a transfer if the additional cost would exceed the amount of additional state aid received for the student, but it may refuse to accept a student transfer if a new program would be required to serve the student. It also may revoke the transfer if the student is recommended for expulsion. Once admitted, high school transfers may be automatically renewed, even if the district later cancels its transfer program, but that is not a requirement in the statute. If parents so request, the chosen district may provide transportation assistance within the boundaries of the district in the same manner as for resident students.

Finally, the legislature expanded parental choice when it enacted the Open Enrollment Act (Educ. Code §§ 48350–48361) in 2009, providing parents of children enrolled in low-achieving non-charter public schools with the opportunity to attend higher-performing schools in the district of residence or another district (termed the "school district of enrollment"). The act is limited to parents whose children attend schools listed on the superintendent of public instruction's list of 1,000 low-performing schools. The school district of residence is required to notify parents in the low-achieving schools that they have these options. The district of enrollment may deny admission because of a lack of space and lack of funds. However, both the sending and receiving districts can limit or refuse transfers if doing so would negatively affect a court-ordered or voluntary desegregation plan or upset the racial and ethnic balance of the district consistent with federal and state law. If the school is oversubscribed, students are to be selected randomly for available spaces, although priority is to be given to those with siblings already enrolled in the school and students coming from program improvement schools. Relatively few families take advantage of these interdistrict transfer programs because children do not wish to leave their neighborhoods and because of transportation burdens. It is also important to note that the California Interscholastic Federation requires a one-year moratorium on playing the same contact sport if a student transfers from a private or public school to another school without a change of parent residence.

CALIFORNIA CHARTER SCHOOLS

Charter schools have grown in the state since the Charter Schools Act was passed in 1992. A charter school is essentially a newly created public school that is relatively free of state regulation. Students are there by choice. The purpose of charter schools is to give parents increased options for their children's education and to generate new approaches to schooling. Because they are public schools, charter schools must recognize the constitutional rights of their students and teachers under the terms of the federal and state constitutions—just like traditional public schools. Thus, for example, teachers and students are entitled to constitutional rights of expression, the right to associate, and the right to due process. And like traditional public schools, charter schools must be neutral toward religion. They are subject to the federal statutes listed in Table 1.1 and must follow California statutes, such as the open meetings law, generally applicable to governmental entities. They also are bound by local building, health, and zoning laws. However, they are exempt from most other state laws applying to traditional public schools.

A lengthy section of the Charter Schools Act spells out the details for charter schools' approval, operation, and accountability (Educ. Code § 47600 et seq.). State Board of Education regulations augment these provisions. As an aid to understanding these requirements, the CDE maintains a charter school website that provides answers to commonly asked questions (www.cde.ca.gov/sp/cs/). Charter schools must be either converted from traditional public schools or newly created. Private schools cannot convert to charter school status. Previously, the law limited the number of charter schools to 250 in 1998–1999, with up to 100 charter schools authorized in each successive year. Subsequently, as of the 2022–2023 school year, California has more than 1,300 charter schools across the state and seven all-charter school districts. Furthermore, 11.7 percent of all public school students in California attend charter schools.

The petition to convert an existing public school to a charter school requires the signatures of at least 50 percent of the permanent teachers at the school. The petition to start a new charter school must be signed either by at least one-half of the parents or guardians of students expected to attend or by at least one-half of the teachers interested in teaching in the school.

In 2002, the California Legislature amended the Charter Schools Act to require charter schools to operate within the same geographic boundaries as the authorizing school district, subject to the exceptions noted below (Educ. Code § 47605). The charter school may encompass any grade levels and operate as a single school or at multiple sites within the district, so long as they are within the same geographical boundaries. Further, for a charter to operate at multiple sites, it must either identify the additional locations within the initial petition or later amend the charter to include the additional sites. If amendments to the charter are made, they are then subject to the material revision requirements to determine whether the additional sites satisfy the criteria described in Education Code § 47605.

It bears noting that the Charter Schools Act includes a few limited exceptions to the geographical boundary requirement for multiple sites, including an exception for a resource center, meeting space, or other satellite facility located in an adjacent county, provided certain conditions are met. The Act also includes exceptions in instances when the charter school has been authorized by the county board of education as a county charter school (Educ. Code § 47605.6) or by the State Board of Education as a state charter school (Educ. Code § 47605.8).

The Third District Court of Appeal directly confronted the question of where charter schools may be authorized to operate in *Anderson Union High School District v. Shasta Secondary Home School* (2016), 4 Cal.App.5th 262. In that case, the court noted that, absent one of the previously mentioned exceptions, charter schools may not locate a non-classroom-based independent study resource center outside the geographic boundaries of the authorizing school district. The court also held that a resource center that provides educational support to students and is located outside of the school district's geographical boundaries does not meet one of the exceptions under Education Code Section 47605 and is therefore impermissible under the Charter Schools Act.

As noted earlier, the State Board of Education may also approve a statewide charter. To be approved as a statewide charter, the State Board of Education must find that the entity will provide instructional services of statewide benefit. In other words, the statewide charter option is targeted to entities that would serve a statewide populace. It is not to be used for a charter organization that can accomplish the same statewide benefit by operating each of its schools under individual charters approved by various school districts or county boards (*California School Boards Association v. State Board of Education*, 2010).

Charter schools that serve a large geographic region within the state are often the equivalent of a newly created school district. In federal and state statutory parlance, they are called "local education agencies," or LEAs. The same is true of start-up charter schools that operate independently of their authorizers. We will see the significance of the LEA classification in later chapters.

Starting a Charter School

Components of the petition to start a charter school are described in detail in Education Code Section 47605. Among them are a description of the governance system; the educational program, its goals, and measurable outcomes; methods to measure student progress, employee qualifications, admission requirements, and facilities; start-up costs and a three-year cash flow projection; the manner in which annual financial audits will be conducted; student suspension and expulsion procedures; a dispute resolution process; and procedures to be followed if the school closes. Also to be included are the rights of school district employees who leave employment in the district to work in the charter school and any rights of return, as well as the manner in which staff members will be covered by the State Teachers' Retirement System, the Public Employees' Retirement System, or Social Security. Commonly labeled "Petitioners," those who wish to start a charter school must affirm that their school will be nonsectarian; shall not charge tuition; and shall not discriminate against students on the basis of disability, gender, gender identity, gender expression, nationality, race or ethnicity, religion, sexual orientation, immigration status, or any other characteristic contained in the definition of hate crimes described in Penal Code Section 422.55.

Public schools converting to charter school status must give preference to students living within the previous attendance area. Petitioners also must affirm that the charter school will admit all comers but, if oversubscribed, will admit students by public random drawing. Preference is to be extended to students already attending the charter school and those residing within the school district. Other preferences, such as for siblings of enrolled students, must be approved by the chartering authority, often labeled the "authorizer." If a full-time student is expelled or drops out, the charter school must inform the superintendent of the student's last district and provide a grade transcript and health information.

The charter petition also must specify "the means by which the school will achieve a racial and ethnic balance among its pupils that is reflective of the general population residing within the territorial jurisdiction of the school district to which the charter petition is submitted" (Educ. Code § 47605 (b)(5)(G)). Achieving this requirement may present a challenge to charter school operations in light of the state constitution's prohibition against affirmative action. It is important to note that the racial balance provision requires charter schools to reflect the racial balance of the *general population* within the school district, not the school district population. Because many persons do not have children or do not send them to public schools, the racial makeup of the community may be quite different from the racial makeup of the district's student body.

Without efforts to ensure integration, however, charter schools may become more racially isolated than traditional public schools. This matter is discussed in some depth in Chapter 11. District governing boards are to give preference to charter school petitions focused on low-achieving students. Another provision permits charter schools located in the attendance area of an elementary school with upward of 50 percent of the student population eligible for free or reduced-price lunch to give preference in admissions to students enrolled in the school or living in the attendance area (Educ. Code § 47605.3). The law, however, does not specify that preference must be restricted to those who are actually receiving free or reduced-price lunches.

Once completed, the charter petition is presented to the authorizing school district's governing board for a public hearing, followed by board action to approve or reject the petition. If the charter school is to serve students enrolled in schools operated by a county, such as schools for adjudicated youth, or to provide instructional services that are not provided by the county office of education—and that, in the county board's judgment, cannot be provided as effectively if the charter school were to operate in a single district—then the petition is presented to the county board of education. Education Code Section 47605.6 details the requirements for approval.

Petitions for charter schools to be operated statewide may be presented directly to the State Board of Education pursuant to Education Code Section 47605.8. A petition may only be denied if the chartering entity can establish, in writing, that the petition is incomplete, the educational program is unsound, the petitioners are unqualified, there are not enough signatures on the petition, or the petitioners have not agreed to comply with statutory conditions for operating a charter school.

If the charter petition is rejected by the district governing board, the petitioners may revise and resubmit the proposal or appeal to the county board of education. If the county board rejects it, petitioners may submit the petition to the State Board of Education. However, petitions for countywide charter schools rejected by county boards may not be appealed.

Operating a Charter School

Under current law, charters may be granted for up to five years and may be renewed for additional five-year periods (Cal. Educ. Code § 47607(a)). Additionally, following the COVID-19 pandemic, Education Code section 47607.4 extended the renewal dates for all charter schools whose term was set to expire on or between January 1, 2022, and June 30, 2025, by two years under certain circumstances. In addition, any charter school whose term expires on or between January 1, 2024, and June 30, 2027, was to be extended by one year. The schools may operate as, or be operated by, a nonprofit benefit corporation; if so, the school district granting the charter is entitled to one representative on the board of directors of the nonprofit public benefit corporation. This means that nonprofit educational management organizations may receive charters and must adhere to California laws applying to nonprofit corporations. Although California charter school recipients must be nonprofit, they may contract with for-profit education management companies to operate the school. In either case, the charter school remains a public school.

Charter schools are monitored by their authorizing entity (or "authorizer"), which must conduct annual site visits and perform specific oversight activities. County school boards also have the authority to investigate charter schools operating within the county if there is a reason to do so, including auditing expenditures and internal controls of a charter school and reporting findings to the charter school and the school's authorizer.

Charter schools must submit annual financial audits to the chartering entity, State Board of Education, state controller, and county superintendent of schools unless encompassed in the authorizer's audit. Except for the charters it grants directly, the SBE may delegate its supervisory responsibility by agreement to any local agency in the county, to the school district that originally denied the charter petition, or to any other third party. To underwrite its monitoring cost, the chartering entity may charge up to 1 percent of the revenue of the charter school—an amount defined as general-purpose and categorical block grant funding—unless the charter school obtains rent-free facilities from the entity, in which case the sponsor may charge up to 3 percent. In addition, some charter schools contract with their school district authorizer to provide services such as printing, payroll, and maintenance. In many instances, the school district works to help charter schools flourish, viewing them as partners rather than rivals.

The authorizing entity may inspect the charter school at any time and may revoke the charter if it finds substantial evidence of a material breach of a charter term, failure to meet any of the student achievement outcomes specified in the charter, financial mismanagement, or a violation of the law. The authorizer is required to consider increases in student academic achievement for all groups of students served by the charter school as the most important determinant in a revocation decision. Before revocation, the authorizer must give the charter school a reasonable opportunity to correct the deficiencies unless student health and safety are at risk. Details of the process for revocation are spelled out in Education Code Section 47607.

To bolster credibility, some charter schools are seeking accreditation by the Western Association of Schools and Colleges, one of six regional accrediting bodies recognized by the U.S. Department of Education. While accreditation does not insulate a school from having its charter revoked, it does indicate that the school is conforming to generally accepted operating standards. A charter can be renewed by its authorizer or grantor for five-year periods if the school continues to meet the conditions set forth for granting the initial charter and if the school meets specified academic proficiency standards. Data concerning charter school progress may be accessed through the California School Dashboard, which is available at https://www.caschooldashboard.org/. The standards are discussed in the "Assessment and Accountability" section in Chapter 2. Renewals and revisions of charters are to include any new requirements enacted into law after the charter was originally granted or last renewed.

While generally exempt from state law applying to school districts pursuant to the Charter Schools Act (Educ. Code § 47600 et seq.), charter schools are not completely autonomous. Charter schools must observe the minimum age for school attendance and must meet the same statewide student testing requirements as traditional public schools. Teachers of core subjects must hold a state credential. There are restrictions on independent study and non-classroom-based instruction. These are intended to preclude excessive funding for schools with no facilities or traditional classroom teaching (e.g., virtual schools offering online instruction).

Those who start charter schools must establish their qualifications for doing so, and charter schools must prepare financial and attendance statements and undergo auditing and periodic inspections. Charter schools must comply with the California Building Code as adopted and enforced by the local building enforcement agency unless the school already complies with the Field Act regarding building construction and repair or unless the facility is owned or controlled by the federal government or other entity not subject to the building code (Educ. Code §§ 47610–47610.5). Collective bargaining is permitted if teachers wish it. For this purpose, the charter must specify whether the charter school or the school district is the employer. If the teachers in a charter school choose to unionize, the union may bargain over teacher discipline and dismissal procedures because state employment law, much of which is not bargainable, does not apply to charter school teachers.

Some of these accountability measures are part of the original charter petitioning process, and others were added when the Charter Schools Act was amended in later years. In 2002, the legislature severely limited the ability of charters to operate satellite campuses outside the geographic boundaries of the chartering entity after financial abuses surfaced at the satellite schools. The burden of overseeing a wide network of campuses springing from a single charter proved too great for school district authorizers. The closing of a network of sixty charter schools operated by the California Charter Academy in 2004 demonstrated the point. As seen in

Anderson Union High School District v. Shasta Secondary Home School (discussed earlier), with very limited exceptions, a charter school must operate within the geographic boundaries of the district granting the charter. Restrictions like these reflect a tendency found in several states for the legislature to impose more regulatory controls over time as charter schools become more numerous.

Additional regulation from both the legislature and state education agencies remains a central concern of school choice proponents. New accountability measures are often added when stories arise regarding misuse of funds, excess profits going to charter school management companies at taxpayer expense, and efforts to teach unorthodox curricula. This additional cost of doing business results in fewer charter schools started by entrepreneurs and more by nonprofit organizations that can attract grant money and realize the efficiencies of operating a network of schools. Some charter school proponents contend that rising costs will drive entrepreneurs out of the charter field altogether, leaving vast networks of carbon-copy schools little different from traditional public schools. In response, charter support and advocacy entities, like the California Charter Schools Association and the Charter Schools Development Center, have been established to advance the cause for charter schools and ward off restrictive legislation.

Start-up and facility costs are also major concerns, but the federal Public Charter School Grant Program administered by CDE, together with the Charter School Facility Grant Program (Educ. Code § 47614.5) and the Charter School Revolving Loan Fund for charter schools (Educ. Code § 41365), have ameliorated those costs to some extent. Facilities funding is discussed in more detail in Chapter 3. To assist with facility needs, Proposition 39, which passed in 2000, requires school districts to make facilities available to accommodate a charter school's in-district enrollment if the school enrolls eighty or more students (Educ. Code § 47614). The facilities must be comparable to other district schools, including furnishings and equipment. They remain the school district's property, which may charge the charter school the portion of cost for the facility that the district would otherwise have to pay.

While facilities offered by a district to an in-district charter school do not need to match exactly those of comparable district schools, the district must make a good faith attempt to identify and quantify the facilities available to the comparison group of similar schools with regard to teaching stations, specialized classroom space, and nonteaching space. This is clear from a 2011 ruling involving a challenge by the Bullis Charter School to facilities offered by the Los Altos School District. Operating out of portable buildings on a portion of a junior high school in the district, the elementary charter school alleged that the district had violated the comparable facilities requirement in various ways. The court agreed, noting that the State Board of Education has set forth regulations detailing how charter facility determinations are to be made (Admin. Code Title 5, § 11969.1 et seq.). Here the district had not complied with the directives (*Bullis Charter School v. Los Altos School District*, 2011).

Further, under a 2012 California appellate court ruling, school districts may use their own student-to-classroom norming ratios to determine the number of classrooms to be offered charter schools. In that case, the Los Angeles Unified School District counted classrooms actually provided to students in the district attending comparison schools. Classrooms used for other purposes, not yet constructed, or at closed school sites were not included. Thus, classroom allocations for charter schools were based on a much larger student-to-classroom ratio than is characteristic of many charter school classrooms (*California Charter Schools Association v. Los Angeles Unified School District*, 2012).

The school district also must make reasonable efforts to provide the charter school with facilities near where the charter school wishes to locate. Litigation between Ridgecrest Charter School and the Sierra Sands Unified School District focused on the meaning of these requirements. Ridgecrest sought a contiguous facility to accommodate its 223 elementary and middle school students. Desiring to minimize displacing its students, the district offered Ridgecrest the use of 9.5 classrooms at five different school sites separated by sixty-five miles. Ridgecrest rejected the offer. The California court of appeal noted that a district must give the same degree of consideration to the needs of charter school students that it does to students in district-run schools, starting with the assumption that all charter school students will be assigned to a single site. Because the contiguous requirement had not been addressed, the school district had abused its discretion (*Ridgecrest Charter Sch. v. Sierra Sands Unified Sch. Dist.*, 2005).

Sequoia Union High School District lost a court battle in 2003 over whether it, rather than the Redwood City Elementary School District, had to provide facilities under this provision for the Aurora Charter High School. The Redwood City Elementary School District, which lies within Sequoia's borders, had granted the Aurora charter. Because Aurora served the minimum number of students who otherwise would be attending the Sequoia district, the appellate court ruled that the latter was responsible for providing facilities (*Sequoia Union High School District v. Aurora Charter High School*, 2003). The court noted that if a charter school served students in several districts, it could request facilities from all of them if it met the requisite minimum enrollment requirement in each.

In 2004, a California court of appeal ruled that a charter school's facilities request must be based on a showing of enrollment projections supported by relevant documents. The court supported the Centinela Valley Union High School's refusal to grant a facilities request when the charter school would not provide names, date of birth, and other information regarding its students (*Environmental Charter High School v. Centinela Valley Union High School District*, 2004).

Constitutionality of Charter Schools

The Charter Schools Act survived a major court challenge in 1999 when a California court of appeal upheld its constitutionality. Noting that charter school legislation was designed to cut through the tangle of rules pervading the California public school system, the appellate court held that the legislature had not unconstitutionally delegated its constitutional duty set forth in Article IX, Section 5 of the California Constitution to provide for a system of free common schools. The court noted, "From how charter schools come into being, to who attends and who can teach, to how they are governed and structured, to funding, accountability and evaluation—the legislature has plotted all aspects of their existence" (*Wilson v. State Board of Education*, 1999). Charter schools, the court noted, are very much part of the California common school system. Their teachers have the same credentials as other public school teachers, the curriculum must meet state standards, and students are assessed in the same manner as other public school students.

Similarly, the court rejected the contention that charter schools are not school districts and thus violate Article IX, Section 14, which gives the legislature the power to provide for the incorporation and organization of school districts of every kind and class. The court pointed out that the legislature had specifically classified charter schools as school districts in Education Code Section 47612(c) for purposes of funding and compliance with the constitution. The court ruled that the charter legislation also conforms to Article IX, Section 6, which states that no part of the public school system shall be directly or indirectly transferred to any authority other than public authorities. Nor does the charter school program violate Article IX, Section 8 of the constitution, which states that no public money may be spent to support any sectarian or denominational school or any school not under the exclusive control of public school officials. The destiny of charter schools, the court noted, is controlled by public entities. Charter schools must be operated on a nonsectarian basis and cannot be controlled by religious organizations. Therefore, there is no violation either of this article or of Article XVI, Section 5 prohibiting public entities from spending public money to help support or sustain schools controlled by religious organizations. The appellate court's decision gave a major boost to the further development of charter schools in California. At the same time, charter schools are public schools and subject to a great deal of public law, as we note in subsequent chapters.

CALIFORNIA PRIVATE SCHOOLS

While private schools have a right to exist by virtue of the *Pierce* decision discussed earlier, the justices recognized that the state has the right to regulate them, even in the absence of any public funding. In a key passage that many private school and voucher advocates often overlook, the Court noted:

> No question is raised concerning the power of the state reasonably to regulate all schools, to inspect, supervise and examine them, their teachers and pupils; to require that all children of proper age attend some school, that teachers shall be of good moral character and patriotic disposition, that certain studies plainly essential to good citizenship must be taught, and that nothing be taught which is manifestly inimical to the public welfare (*Pierce v. Society of Sisters*, 1925, p. 534).

How much regulation is reasonable? When Hawaii imposed very restrictive regulations on its private foreign language schools in the 1920s to promote Americanism, the U.S. Supreme Court declared them unenforceable (*Farrington v. Tokushige*, 1927). Among the requirements were paying an annual per-student fee for an operating permit; restrictions on when the schools could operate; teacher permits and pledges; and specifications on entrance requirements, subjects, courses, and textbooks.

Conversely, if a state legislature were to permit private schools to operate with no regulation, it could be argued that the legislature has unconstitutionally delegated its central responsibility for schooling to unaccountable private entities. Although the unconstitutional delegation claim has lost much of its persuasive effect in federal courts, it remains viable in state court. Many commentators and private school organizations believe increased regulation of private schools is an inevitable by-product of publicly funded voucher programs.

In accordance with *Pierce*, California provides an exemption from public schooling for children who attend private full-time day schools (Educ. Code § 48222). Teaching in these schools must be in English except when bilingual education is necessary or when students proficient in English are taught in a foreign language. Classes must be taught by capable teachers and cover the several branches of study required in public schools. Pupil attendance must be taken. Though California does not require private schools to be state accredited, they must file an affidavit annually with the state Superintendent of Public Instruction (SPI) providing information on such matters as the school's operators, size of the teaching staff and enrollment, courses of study offered, names and qualifications of the teachers, and fingerprint and criminal record information (Educ. Code § 33190). The filing of the affidavit is not meant to confer any state approval, recognition, or endorsement of private schools, and it is not to be construed as a license or authorization. Recently, the affidavit requirement has been extended to heritage schools, which enroll children who are at least four years and nine months to eighteen years old and who also attend a public or private school full-time (Educ. Code § 33195 et seq.). Heritage schools offer education and/or tutoring in a foreign language and focus on the culture, traditions, and history of a country other than the United States.

Most private schools are accredited through the Western Association of Schools and Colleges or by the associations to which they belong, such as the California Association of Independent Schools. An umbrella group of private schools, known as the California Association of Private School Organizations, maintains contact on behalf of its members with the California Department of Education (CDE) and state legislators.

Other provisions of the Education Code pertain to the operation of private schools. Among the more significant are those requiring private schools to comply with earthquake construction measures (Educ. Code § 17320 et seq.); earthquake emergency procedures (Educ. Code § 35295 et seq.); school safety measures such as fire drills, access gates, the wearing of eye-protective devices, having first-aid kits, avoiding toxic art supplies, and preventing hazing (Educ. Code § 32000 et seq.); school bus regulations (Educ. Code § 39830 et seq.); and employee sex offense notification requirements (Educ. Code § 44020). Private schools also must comply with local health and zoning requirements. Most of these provisions have exemptions for very small private schools and, by implication, homeschools.

While the regulations may appear extensive at first glance, it is important to note what is not regulated, such as student admissions, teacher credentialing, textbooks, the instructional program, and reporting and finances. California private schools may participate in the state's student assessment system but are not required to. In essence, California private schools are relatively autonomous organizations. Intuitively, the general "hands-off" approach exists because a majority of California private schools are religiously affiliated. For reasons discussed in the next section and Chapter 7, the California Constitution erects a substantial barrier between church and state. In this regard, it is more stringent than the federal constitution.

As a matter of federal law, private schools do not have to observe the constitutional rights of their constituents because the schools are not government entities. For this reason, they and their employees are exempt from lawsuits under 42 U.S.C. Section 1983 (see Table 1.1). While private schools can select students based on gender and religion, they cannot discriminate on the basis of race. The U.S. Supreme Court ruled as much in 1976 (*Runyon v. McCrary*). The Court cited 42 U.S.C. Section 1981, a federal statute enacted after the Civil War to implement the Thirteenth Amendment's ban on slavery (see Table 1.1). That amendment and implementing statute apply to both public and private schools. The private schools in *Runyon* had argued that the statute would undercut the right of some parents to choose to have their children educated in racially segregated schools. But the justices pointed out that the state has the authority under *Pierce* to regulate the parents' choice of schooling for their children and that the schools could still teach whatever values they wanted, though presumably under the *Pierce* decision, the state could prevent the teaching of racial hatred. Later, the Court ruled that tax exemptions can be denied to private educational institutions that practice racial discrimination, even if those practices are religiously motivated (*Runyon v. McCrary*).

Private schools are subject to several important federal statutes. Included among them are Title VII of the 1964 Civil Rights Act and the Americans with Disabilities Act (see Table 1.1), though there are exemptions for very small schools, for those controlled by religious organizations, and for persons involved in ministerial roles. The U.S. Supreme Court has ruled that who falls into the latter is left to the discretion of the religious school (*Hosanna-Tabor Evangelical Lutheran Church v. Equal Employment Opportunity Commission*, 2012). Unless private schools receive federal funding—and most do not—they are not subject to certain federal statutes such as the Individuals with Disabilities Education Act, Section 504 of the 1973 Rehabilitation Act, and Title IX of the 1972 Education Amendments. Interestingly, California law requires private secondary schools to observe the free speech rights of their students in the same manner that public schools do (Educ. Code § 48950). In subsequent chapters, we provide additional information related to this and other statutes affecting private schools.

VOUCHER PROGRAMS

When the U.S. Supreme Court ruled in *Pierce v. Society of Sisters* that parents have a constitutional right to choose private schools for their children's education, it said nothing about any responsibility on the part of the state to finance the choice. Many parents view the *Pierce* decision as inequitable because only families of means can afford to exercise the right. Private schools are beyond the reach of most low-income families. Lacking the means to pay private school tuition or move to another district, these families have had little alternative in the past but to send their children to the assigned public school. In some urban areas, this often meant a dilapidated school with less experienced teachers and fewer high-achieving students to serve as positive role models. With the advent of magnet schools, intra- and interdistrict transfer programs, and charter schools in California, more parents have been able to exercise control over where their children attend school. But their choices are all within the public sector. Private schools remain beyond the reach of many families, a reality frequently mentioned by parents who seek a faith-based education for their children. Both federal and state constitutional laws require public schools to be secular. By contrast, more than three-quarters of private schools in the nation are religiously affiliated.

Enter vouchers. At its purest and grandest, a publicly funded voucher system gives parents the means to send their children to the public and private schools of their choice. A voucher system represents a fundamental change in education financing because the money goes to parents, not schools. In effect, education becomes a market system whereby schools compete for students. Proponents believe that selection of schools should be an integral part of individual choice in a free society. Some low-income families favor vouchers because they open the door to private schools. Middle- and upper-income families who send their children to private schools find vouchers attractive because they resent paying taxes for public schools they generally do not access. Many private school operators see vouchers as a means of shoring up their financial base and expanding enrollment.

Opponents of vouchers believe a voucher system will, among other things, undermine the common learning experience provided by the nation's public schools by removing scarce resources from public education. They fear that many parents will not choose wisely, or at all, and that accompanying regulations will undermine the autonomy of private schools.

So far, experience with voucher programs has been limited. The first significant voucher program involved the Alum Rock school district on the east side of San Jose in the early 1960s. Launched by the Office of Economic Opportunity as an experiment in assisting low-income families, the program created a firestorm of opposition from many quarters and eventually was limited to giving parents a choice of thematic public schools in the Alum Rock district. Within a few years, the program disappeared.

Growing concern about the quality of some public schools in the 1980s generated renewed interest in vouchers and resulted in the development of private school voucher programs for low-income families in Milwaukee and Cleveland in the early 1990s. Florida enacted a private school voucher program in 1999 for parents with children in failing public schools and later expanded it to include the parents of children with disabilities. The portion pertaining to low-performing schools was declared unconstitutional by the Florida Supreme Court in 2006.

Congress approved a voucher program for the District of Columbia in 2004. Research findings on these programs remain mixed. While parent and student satisfaction levels are generally higher than in traditional public schools, student achievement remains about the same when all the variables, including the influence of the act of choosing, are controlled.

Vouchers attracted interest in California too, but proponents quickly realized that the state afforded an inhospitable constitutional climate. Article IX, Section 8 of the state constitution is very explicit: "No public money shall ever be appropriated for the support of any sectarian or denominational school, or any school not under the exclusive control of the officers of the public schools. . . ." Article XVI, Section 5 further provides:

> Neither the Legislature, nor any county, city and county, township, school district, or other municipal corporation, shall ever make an appropriation, or pay from any public fund whatever, or grant anything to or in aid of any religious sect, church, creed, or sectarian purpose, or help to support or sustain any school, college, university, hospital, or other institution controlled by any religious creed, church, or sectarian denomination whatever. . . .

Faced with these constitutional barriers, California voucher proponents nevertheless launched two initiatives to amend the state constitution to permit vouchers. Neither was successful. Proposition 174, known as the Parental Choice in Education initiative, was rejected by more than a two-to-one margin in 1993. The National Average School Funding Guarantee and Parental Right to Choose Quality Education Amendment, Proposition 38 failed by an even larger margin in 2000.

Proposition 174 would have provided an educational scholarship of $2,600 for every resident school-age child in California. Scholarships could have been redeemed at any scholarship-redeeming school, which included public, private, and religious schools that met minimal requirements. The initiative strictly limited the regulation of scholarship-redeeming schools.

Proposition 38 would have given parents $4,000 to send their children to private schools. It, too, would have severely restricted the ability of the legislature and other governmental entities to regulate private schools.

A flat voucher of the type proposed in these initiatives is generally too small to be of much benefit to low-income families. Unlike the voucher programs targeted to low-income families in Milwaukee, Cleveland, and the District of Columbia, both initiatives were criticized for diverting taxpayer money to the wealthy. Fiscal concerns were also apparent because families already in private schools presumably would apply for the scholarships. Opponents saw the shift of money to private education as draining funds from public schools and shortchanging the education of children left behind. Restrictions on the state's ability to hold choice schools accountable raised fears about misuse of the money. Opponents capitalized on all of these design features to soundly defeat the voucher initiatives.

In the past several years, renewed interest has been shown in vouchers and other forms of indirect aid to private schools in the wake of U.S. Supreme Court decisions that clarified the law regarding their constitutionality to some extent. Because these decisions involve the interpretation of both federal and state constitutional provisions involving government support for religion, we include them in our discussion of religious issues in Chapter 7.

SUMMARY

This chapter has presented the basic sources of school law and discussed how they interrelate. School law is not a cohesive category of law. Rather, it is a multilayered mixture of constitutional, statutory, administrative, contract, and judicial law. Given the size and complexity of the California school system, it is easy to get lost in the details.

The federal constitution leaves the creation of an educational system to the states. California constitutional law places the major responsibility for establishing and operating the schooling system on the legislature. While the legislature has enacted a host of laws describing how schools are to operate and has placed considerable oversight responsibility in state agencies, it has left the day-to-day operation of schools to county and district boards of education. Still, given that schooling is one of its most important functions and consumes more than 40 percent of the state budget, the legislature is never far away. With that said, the legislature does not operate in a vacuum. Rather, it is significantly influenced by the governor, powerful interest groups, and the electorate. And it cannot act contrary to either federal law or state constitutional law.

While the state and its political subdivisions have a major role in the education of children within its borders, so too do parents. Both the federal and California governments have increasingly recognized the role of parents in the education of their children. An example of the former is Congress's enactment of the Every Student Succeeds Act in 2015, which gave states the flexibility to develop accountability systems that best measure student success in their respective states rather than the universal accountability system that existed under the previous No Child Left Behind Act. An example of the latter is the California Legislature's Parental Empowerment Act of 1998, which specifies parents' rights within the public schools. Increasingly, parents have been given a choice of public schools they wish their children to attend through intra- and interdistrict choice programs and the development of charter schools. Indeed, charter schools have become an integral part of the California schooling system. Many pending disputes in California related to several matters, including subjects that may be taught to students and parents' desire to opt out of certain instruction, will likely continue to shape parents' rights.

For many students, the California private schooling system and homeschooling have provided a viable alternative to public schools, especially for those seeking a faith-based education. While parents have long had a constitutional right to choose private schools, most lack the means. The newest systemic reform is publicly funded vouchers that enfranchise parents with the right to select private schools. While California voters have decisively defeated two voucher initiatives, their design features played a large role in their demise, and other voucher efforts are likely to arise in the future.

With our overview of the legal framework for California schooling and of the major players involved in their operation completed, we now turn to an examination of how law affects school attendance, teacher preparation, and the instructional program.

2 ATTENDANCE, SAFETY, INSTRUCTION, AND ASSESSMENT

Before instruction can begin, students have to be in school or under the supervision of a teacher. Accordingly, this chapter begins by examining California's school attendance law and describing the consequences for those who violate it. The focus then shifts to the instructional program. Increasingly, emphasis has been placed on specifying what students are to learn as they move from grade to grade, how their learning is to be assessed, and how schools are to be held accountable. Because teacher quality is an important influence on student learning, teacher preparation and credentialing have also received attention. An important stimulus to reform in these areas comes from Congress. When Congress reauthorized the Elementary and Secondary Education Act (ESEA) by passing the No Child Left Behind Act (NCLB) in 2001, it mandated high standards for teacher quality and student achievement as a condition of receiving federal funding under the act. ESEA is the principal federal program affecting elementary and secondary education. Title I of the Act provides funding for the education of disadvantaged children, and 60 percent of California public schools receive such funding. Prior to the enactment of NCLB, California had made significant strides in developing curriculum content standards, student assessment, and school accountability. NCLB stimulated further reform.

A number of other legal issues arise in the context of curriculum and instruction. A prerequisite to effective learning is an orderly environment, and state law conveys some important tools for school administrators to use to ensure it. While the authority of policymakers over what occurs in the classroom is extensive, it is not unlimited. The growing role of computers and the internet in the instructional program poses a unique set of legal concerns. Copyright law imposes some important restrictions on the use of classroom instructional material. The education of English learners has undergone major change in California due to the passage of Proposition 227 in 1998. These and other concerns are addressed in this chapter.

A word to readers: What broadly can be termed "curriculum law" is in a state of flux as reformers and policymakers seek to improve the performance of the public schooling system. For example, technical education and digital learning are expanding significantly. Because many topics in this chapter are controlled by state law, we frequently cite the statutes for ease of reference, even though this may interfere a bit with the flow of the discussion. It is also important to note that many of these statutes are very detailed and frequently amended. Thus, they should be consulted directly when the need arises. This can be done easily through the California Department of Education website at www.cde.ca.gov (click "Laws and Regulations").

ATTENDANCE

The Compulsory Attendance Law

Education Code Sections 48200 and 48204 provide that, unless otherwise exempt, students between the ages of six and eighteen are to be admitted to public schools of the district on a full-time basis under the following conditions:

- Either the parent or legal guardian lives in the district. To make this determination, the district can request the parent or legal guardian to show name and address through such documents as property tax payment receipts; rental property contract, lease, or payment receipts; utility bills; pay stubs; voter registration; and the like. Not all are required. In the alternative, a parent or legal guardian may execute a declaration of residency. Excluded from this requirement are homeless and other students who must be admitted under federal and state law (Education Code § 48204.1).
- The student is placed in a licensed children's institution or foster home in the district.
- The student is admitted pursuant to an interdistrict transfer agreement under Education Code Section 46600.
- The student lives in the district and is emancipated from the control of parent or guardian. This means that the student is or has been married, is on active duty in the armed forces, or has been declared emancipated by a court.

- The student lives in the home of a caregiving adult in the district who is over the age of eighteen and who has filed a caregiving affidavit to this effect as specified in Family Code Section 6550, unless the school district determines to the contrary. The affidavit asks only for the name and address of the caregiver to authorize enrollment in school and to authorize school-related medical care. For any other medical care, additional items must be completed on the affidavit by a relative. If these items are not completed, then additional medical care can be authorized only by the minor's parent or guardian.
- The student resides in a state hospital located in the district.

In addition, districts may admit a student if one or both of the parents or guardians are physically employed within the boundaries of the district for a minimum of ten hours within the school week (Educ. Code § 48204 (b)(1)). Students who satisfy the residency requirement pursuant to parent employment need not reapply so long as at least one of the students' parents remains employed within the school district's boundaries (Educ. Code § 48204(b)(8)). If a district refuses to admit these students, it must not do so on the basis of race, ethnicity, sex, parental income, scholastic achievement, or any arbitrary consideration. Education Code Section 48204 (b) provides that either the sending or the receiving district may deny admission to a student whose parent or guardian works within the district's boundaries if the admission would negatively impact a court-ordered or voluntary desegregation plan. The receiving district may also deny admission if the cost of education would exceed the amount of state aid received for educating the student. The statute encourages districts that reject these transfers to communicate with parents and to record the reasons accurately in governing board minutes. The statute does not authorize out-of-district transfers beyond specified limits unless approved by the sending district. Once a student whose parent or guardian works within the district's boundaries is admitted, the student does not have to reapply each year and may continue through the twelfth grade, subject to the conditions just described:

> What if a child lives in a home that is only partly within a district's geographic boundaries, and the bulk of property taxes paid by the home's owners goes to a second district? Can the first district refuse to admit the student? A California court of appeal ruled in the negative in 2004, holding that Education Code Section 48200's requirement that students attend school in the district "in which the residence of either the parent or guardian is located" must be interpreted to include a residence that is only partly within a school district's boundaries. The fact that the

bulk of property taxes may flow to another district is unfortunate—but a matter for the legislature, not the courts. Additionally, the fact that the county office of education construed the law otherwise was irrelevant because the judiciary has the final say (*Katz v. Los Gatos-Saratoga Joint Union High School District*).

A school may believe it needs to investigate whether a student meets the residency requirements. Prior to initiating an investigation, "the school district must have an investigatory policy adopted at a public meeting of the governing board" (Educ. Code § 48204.2 (a)). Among other things, the investigatory policy is to identify the circumstances for conducting an investigation, describe the methods used, prohibit surreptitious photographing or video recording of students being investigated, and provide an appeal process (Educ. Code § 48204.2 (b)). "Surreptitious photographing or videorecording" means the covert collection of photographic or videographic images of persons or places subject to an investigation and does not include the collection of images when the technology is used in open and public view (Educ. Code § 48204.2 (b)).

Governing boards, with the approval of the county superintendent of schools, may admit students in adjoining states to its schools pursuant to an agreement with the district of residence or the parent or guardian reimbursing the chosen district for the cost of education (Educ. Code § 48050). The attendance of these students cannot be included in computing the average daily attendance for purposes of state funding. Students who live in Mexico and regularly return there within twenty-four hours may be admitted to district classes and schools with the approval of the governing board if they are otherwise eligible to attend school (Educ. Code § 48051). However, because they are not permanent residents, their parents or guardians must reimburse the district for education costs (Educ. Code § 48052).

Foster children present a special challenge to California public and private schools. In the school year 2019–2020, there were over 45,000 foster children enrolled in public schools in the state, most of whom experienced multiple placements in foster homes and licensed children's institutions (LCIs), which results in frequent transfers among schools. Education Code Sections 48850–48859 stipulate that foster children are entitled to the same educational opportunities as other children and detail the notification requirements regarding educational options for children placed in LCIs. Agencies placing children in these institutions must notify the local county office of education, school district, and any charter schools participating as members of a special education local plan area. Limits are placed on the authority of the placement school.

Section 48853.5 requires every school district and county board of education to have an education liaison for foster children and details that person's responsibilities to ensure proper educational placement of foster children and assist with the transfer of their credits, records, and grades. Either the liaison or another person designated by the district superintendent must notify the foster child's attorney and appropriate county child welfare agency representative of pending expulsion proceedings and, if a special needs child, of a pending manifestation determination. If there is a change in a foster child's residential placement, the school of origin must permit the child to remain enrolled through the duration of the jurisdiction of the court or, if the jurisdiction of the court ends prior to the end of the academic year, through the remainder of the school year, if in either case it will best serve the needs of the child.

Foster students in high school can remain in the school of origin through graduation. These determinations are based on deliberations of the school district's foster care liaison, the person who holds education rights for the child, and the child. If no change is made, the school district of origin may provide the student with transportation but is not required to do so unless the student has special needs and transportation is a necessary related service. If it is determined that a foster child should be enrolled in a school other than the school of origin, the new school must admit the child immediately without regard to past due fees, fines, or textbooks at the previous school and without regard to the absence of records such as proof of immunization and proof of residency or inability to comply with a dress code. The educational liaison at the new school must contact the previous school within two business days to obtain all required records, and the educational liaison at the former school has two business days to supply them.

Other important Education Code provisions relating to foster children include Section 49069.3 (access of foster care agencies to student records), Section 49076 (access of persons without written parental consent or judicial order to student records), Section 49069.5 (timely transfer of records for foster children and no academic penalties for school absences related to placement changes), Section 48645.5 (awarding credit for coursework completed satisfactorily at another public school, private nonsectarian school, or juvenile court school), and Section 42920 and following sections (establishment of foster youth educational services programs).

Many of the rights of foster youth are now extended to students who are unhoused, including the right to remain in their school of origin (Educ. Code 48852.7 (a)), to receive partial credits for courses if they switch schools during the year, and to meet only state graduation requirements if they transfer high schools after their second year (Educ. Code §§ 51225.1–51225.2). Districts are also required to notify the district-appointed liaison before expelling these students. There are some exceptions, and these provisions are complicated. Districts are wise to develop clear policies for schools to follow.

Education Code Section 48215, enacted following approval of Proposition 187 in 1994 excluding undocumented immigrants from various public services including public schooling, was not removed from the Education Code until 2014 when Governor Jerry Brown signed a bill deleting it but it had not been operative for many years. The provision conflicted with a 1982 U.S. Supreme Court ruling (*Plyler v. Doe*) to the contrary and was declared null and void in 1995 (*League of United Latin American Citizens v. Wilson*).

Section 48216 gives governing boards the authority to deny admission to students who have not been immunized, but provisions of the state Health and Safety Code provide an exemption for medical reasons (Health and Safety Code 120325, 120335, 120370). The school must require documentary proof of the required vaccinations or approval for an exemption (Code § 120375). A group of parents filed a motion in federal court for a preliminary injunction to halt enforcement of immunization changes, but the suit was rejected (*Whitlow v. California*, 2016).

If there is good cause to believe a student has been exposed to one of the listed diseases requiring immunization, and there is no documented proof of immunization, the student may be temporarily excluded from school until the local health officer is satisfied that the student is not at risk of developing or transmitting the disease. Additionally, parents must provide evidence of an oral health assessment unless they are "excused from this requirement if they indicate that the assessment could not be completed due to financial burden, lack of access to a dental professional, or they do not consent" (Educ. Code § 49452.8). The requirements do not apply to home-based private schooling or an independent study program that does not encompass classroom-based instruction.

Children whose parents choose to enroll them in kindergarten must be admitted at the beginning of the school year or anytime thereafter if the child will be five years old on or before October 1 of the 2013–2014 school year and September 1 of the 2014–2015 school year and thereafter (Educ. Code § 48000). Children whose fifth birthday is after this date may be admitted on a case-by-case basis. To receive funding for students enrolling in the first year of a two-year transitional kindergarten program, a school district or charter school is to ensure that, for the 2013–2014 school year, a child is to be admitted if the child's fifth birthday is between October 2 and December 2, and for the 2014–2015 school year and thereafter the fifth birthday is between September 2 and December 2. Transitional kindergarten is the first year of a two-year kindergarten program that uses a modified kindergarten curriculum that is age- and developmentally appropriate.

To be admitted to the first grade, students must be six years old on or before the same dates as noted in the preceding paragraph for kindergarten (Educ. Code § 48010). A child who has completed a year of kindergarten in a private or public school must be admitted to first grade unless the parent or guardian and the school district believe the child should remain in kindergarten for another year. A child who is in kindergarten and judged ready for first grade may be admitted to that grade at the discretion of the administration and with the consent of the parent or guardian if the child is at least five years of age (Educ. Code § 48011). The attorney general has opined that a student who has completed a year of kindergarten in a private school is not automatically entitled to be admitted to first grade in a public school when the student does not meet the minimum age requirements. The decision is left to the school administration if the child is at least five years of age (66 Ops. Atty. Gen. 135, 1983).

Like most states, California equates quality learning with time spent in school. The minimum and maximum lengths of the school day for various grade levels are set forth in Education Code Section 46111 and following sections. While these provisions are quite detailed and contain numerous exceptions and conditions, the general thrust is to limit kindergarten to a minimum of 180 minutes and a maximum of 240 minutes per day, exclusive of recesses (265 minutes per day in a multitrack year-round school). The minimum school day for the first through third grades is 230 minutes except in opportunity schools, classes, or programs. For grades four through eight, the minimum school day is 240 minutes, not counting the lunch period and recess. For junior and senior high schools, the minimum school day is 240 minutes. The minimum is 180 minutes per day for eleventh and twelfth graders also taking courses on a part-time basis for academic credit at a junior college, the California State University, or the University of California. With some exceptions, seniors must take at least five courses each semester.

As we will note later, California limits the amount of time students can spend learning on the internet, though the law in this area is changing. Minutes of instruction per grade level for charter schools also are specified (Educ. Code § 47612.5 (a)(1)). These are, at a minimum, 36,000 minutes per year in kindergarten, 50,400 minutes in grades one through three, 54,000 minutes in grades four through eight, and 64,800 minutes in grades nine through twelve. These cannot be waived by either the State Board of Education or the state superintendent of public instruction; only the Legislature can make a change.

Areas of study for grades one through six are set forth in Education Code Section 51210 and include a minimum of 200 minutes of physical education every ten school days. The parent of an elementary student challenged a district's decision to schedule no more than 120 minutes. The school district, backed by the California Department of Education, argued that the minute allotment was discretionary in that Section 51002 recognizes that a common curriculum may need to be modified because of local economic, geographic, physical, political, and social diversity. The California court of appeal, in an unpublished decision, rejected the assertion, noting that Section 51210 uses the term "shall" and is discretionary only in allowing a district to exceed the minimum (*Doe v. Albany Unified School District* 2010).

Attendance Records

Parents and guardians enrolling a child in kindergarten or first grade must present evidence that the child has reached the minimum age (Educ. Code § 48002). When students transfer to a new school, administrators can request records from the former public or private school. Such records cannot be withheld from the requesting school because the student or parent has not paid fees. According to the attorney general, the withholding provision in Education Code Section 48904.3 applies to the student and the student's parents, not to a school to which a student is transferring (64 Ops. Atty. Gen. 867, 1981). This is so because another section of the code requires both public and private schools to forward student records to the new school on request (Educ. Code § 49068). The county board of education may require the reporting of various types of attendance severance at both public and private schools. Such reporting is required for children with disabilities (Educ. Code § 48203).

The California Administrative Code classifies student enrollment and academic achievement records as permanent records, which must be kept indefinitely. Other information, such as the names of persons other than educators given access to a student's records, health information, participation in special education programs, progress slips, and results of standardized tests administered within the preceding three years, are disposable in accordance with California law (5 C.C.R. §§ 432, 16023). Additional information on student records is found in Chapter 10.

Exemptions from Attendance

Students who are exempt from having to attend public school include those who are attending a full-time private school and those who are being homeschooled by credentialed tutors or by parents (Educ. Code §§ 48222, 48224). Students who hold a permit for working in the entertainment industry are permitted a maximum of five absences per school year of up to five consecutive days each (Educ. Code § 48225.5). They are to receive instruction from a qualified studio teacher. Students participating with a not-for-profit performing arts organization in a performance for a public school audience must be excused for up to five days per school year if the parent submits a written request. In either case, students must complete reasonably equivalent assignments and tests missed during the absence for full credit. Students who hold permits to work are exempt from the compulsory school attendance law but must attend part-time classes. A student who is fifteen or older may take a leave of absence for up to one semester for supervised travel, study, training, or work not available in school if the district has a policy to this effect (Educ. Code § 48232). The child's parent or guardian must sign an agreement indicating the purpose and length of the leave, as well as the need for meeting periodically with a school official during the leave. The leave may be extended for an additional semester. The statute limits leaves of absence to no more than 1 percent of student enrollment in the district.

School districts, county boards of education, and charter schools may permit independent study for various reasons, such as providing access to content not included in the curriculum and continuing education to students traveling (Educ. Code § 51745 et seq.). Beginning July 1, 2021, with the exception of pupils participating in independent study programs due to an emergency, as described in Sections 41422 and 46392, not more than 10 percent of the pupils participating in an opportunity school or program, or a continuation high school, calculated as specified by the department, shall be eligible for apportionment credit for independent study pursuant to this article. To include these students in average daily attendance for funding purposes, the district, county, or charter school must require the students to sign a detailed independent study agreement. It is not sufficient to have a general policy governing independent study (*Modesto City Schools v. Education Audits Appeal Panel*, 2004).

The statute delineates the required components of the agreement in some detail (Educ. Code § 51747). Included among them are how completed work is to be submitted and evaluated, the resources to be made available to the student, and the duration of the agreement. State funding is not available for independent study if funds or anything of value is provided to these students that is not provided to students attending regular classes. Nor is funding available if funds or anything of value is provided for independent study, including home study, that could not legally be provided to a student in regular attendance or to the parent (Educ. Code § 51747.3). According to a 1995 attorney general opinion, the purpose of this provision is to prevent charter schools from offering "sign-up bonuses" to parents for home study so that the schools could obtain state funding. It does not prevent a charter school or other local education agency from spending funds for special education aids and materials that make independent study meaningful (78 Ops. Atty. Gen. 253, 1995).

Absences and Truancy

The law permits students to be excused from school for justifiable reasons such as illness, doctor's appointments, family emergencies, and attendance at religious retreats (Educ. Code § 48205). The attorney general has advised that a school district cannot require prior written parental consent before releasing a student to obtain confidential medical services under this section. The district also cannot notify the parents when a student leaves school for this purpose. The attorney general noted that although parental permission is required under this statute for justifiable reasons, such as appearance in court, attendance at a funeral, and observance of a holiday, such is not the case for absences for medical, dental, optometric, or chiropractic services (87 Ops. Atty. Gen. 168, 2004). Students who have excused absences must be allowed to complete missed assignments and tests for full credit; they cannot be penalized for missed assignments and tests on the day of an excused absence. Religious retreats are limited to one school day per semester. The latter limitation may invite dispute from devout parents, who may argue that it intrudes on their free exercise of religion. Another provision of the code gives school districts the option of releasing students for up to four days per month to attend religious exercises or receive religious and moral instruction off campus. Such absences are not to be included in computing the average daily attendance.

Truancy provisions in the education code are elaborate (Educ. Code § 48260 and following provisions). A student is considered truant and must be reported to the attendance supervisor or school superintendent if he or she is absent from school without a valid excuse for three full days in one school year or is tardy or absent for more than any thirty-minute period during the school day without a valid excuse on three occasions in one school year or a combination thereof. Parents and guardians of truant students are to be notified and reminded of their responsibility to see that the student attends the regular or alternative school program. Failure to do so can result in criminal penalties against the parent following an investigation and referral to a county-based school attendance review board, which, among other things, has the authority to direct parents and students to participate in community services to address the truancy problem. Penalties include a fine of up to $100 for the first conviction, $250 for the second conviction, and

$500 for the third or subsequent convictions or, in lieu of these fines, placement in a parent education and counseling program. Failure to pay the fine or attend the program will result in a contempt citation. The municipal court judge also may order that a parent immediately enroll the student in school with proof to the court. Failure to do so is punishable as civil contempt with a fine of up to $1,000 but not imprisonment. Fines collected under these provisions are to be credited to the school district to support activities of the student attendance review board and the parent education and counseling program.

Truant students also suffer penalties for nonattendance. School attendance supervisors or designees, police officers, school administrators, and probation officers have the authority to take custody of a truant student during school hours. Custody is not considered punishment but rather a step toward remediation by returning the student to school or to the student's parent or guardian. At the same time, police officers who have probable cause to suspect that a youth is truant may have grounds to conduct a search of the student and the student's belongings (*In re Humberto O.*, 2000). A first-time truant may be asked to make up the missed classes and, together with the parent or legal guardian, be requested to meet with the school counselor or other appropriate school official to discuss the causes of missed attendance and develop a remediation plan. A second truancy in the same school year may result in a written warning by a peace officer and the student's assignment to an after-school or weekend program. The school may make a record of the truancy. A third offense within the same school year results in the student's classification as a habitual truant, provided school officials have made a conscientious effort to hold at least one conference with the parent or guardian. Habitual truants may be referred to the school attendance review board or a truancy mediation program. School attendance review boards may be established at the county and district level. They include a diversified membership reflective of the school community and are empowered to improve coordination among agencies dealing with student attendance and behavioral problems, as well as to develop alternative ways of dealing with truant students in the juvenile court system.

A fourth truancy in the same year may place the student in the jurisdiction of the juvenile court, which could adjudge the student a ward of the court. If this occurs, the student will be required to do one or more of the following: perform court-approved community service, pay a fine, attend a court-approved truancy prevention program, or have driving privileges suspended or revoked. The court may also require the parent or guardian to bring the student to school. Districts are to submit data to the county superintendent of schools on the number and types of referrals to school attendance boards and juvenile courts.

There is no easy method of dealing with truant students. Students usually are truant because they do not see a benefit from attending school or because of problems or needs in the home. The legislature has enacted legislation encouraging school districts and county boards of education to adopt pupil attendance policies that incorporate active student, parent, and community involvement. At the same time, it discourages the use of suspensions for these students (Educ. Code § 48900 (w) (1)). The legislature has directed the state superintendent of public instruction to disseminate information on effective attendance strategies to school districts. Perhaps most useful is the development of alternative education programs and charter schools for at-risk students. Under Education Code Section 48432.5, for irregular attendance, a high school student can be assigned to attend an alternative school, which may offer a more flexible instructional approach and smaller class size. The officials involved in the final decision to make an involuntary transfer of a pupil to a continuation school shall not be a member of the staff of the school in which the pupil is enrolled at the time the decision is made (Educ. Code § 48432.5 (f)).

SAFETY

Maintaining a Safe and Healthy Learning Environment

Students learn best when classes are safe and orderly and they have access to a healthy learning environment. Article I, Section 28 of the California Constitution provides that "All students and staff of public primary, elementary, junior high and senior high schools have the inalienable right to attend campuses which are safe, secure, and peaceful." The legislature has responded by passing several laws that give administrators at public, and in some cases private, schools the authority to maintain a safe learning environment. We describe some of those many laws below.

Safe Place to Learn Act. To address the increasing concern over student harassment and bullying, Education Code Section 234, known as the Safe Place to Learn Act, prohibits discrimination, harassment, intimidation, and bullying at public schools and school activities. Among the characteristics that fall into this category are disability, gender, gender identity, gender expression, nationality, race or ethnicity, religion, sexual orientation, or association with a person or group that has one or more of these actual or perceived characteristics. Local education agencies are required to have a policy prohibiting harassment and bullying and a process for receiving and investigating complaints related to them. We will detail other provisions of the Education Code that set forth grounds for disciplining students in Chapter 9. Here we discuss laws that restrict outsiders from interfering with campus activities.

Civic Center Act. It is important to note at the outset that, while a traditional public or charter school is a public place and thus must observe the constitutional rights of individuals, it also serves a special purpose. Thus, unlike a public park or street corner, individual rights are generally more circumscribed in this setting. This is particularly true for outsiders. At the same time, the Civic Center Act allows governing boards to open school facilities for use by community organizations for literary, scientific, recreational, educational, and similar purposes (Educ. Code § 38130 et seq.). The act requires governing boards to permit nonprofit organizations such as the Girl Scouts, Boy Scouts, veterans' organizations, farmers' organizations, school-community advisory councils, senior citizens' organizations, parent–teacher associations, and the like formed for recreational, educational, political, economic, artistic, or moral activities of the public school district to use its facilities so long as doing so does not interfere with schooling or other permissible uses. Additionally, recreational youth sports leagues that charge participants a nominal fee (an average fee of no more than $60 per month) may also access school facilities. The school district may charge a fee for allowing outside organizations to use its facilities. While the district is liable for injuries arising from its negligence in maintaining the facilities, the outside group is liable for injuries arising from its negligence in using them.

Comprehensive School Safety Plan. The legislature has implemented a multitude of programs and efforts to ensure the safety and security of school facilities. For example, effective March 1, 2000, each school, including charter schools, community schools, and court schools, must develop and implement a comprehensive school safety plan (CSSP) designed to ensure a safe and secure learning environment for all students by, among other things, addressing campus risks and preparing for emergencies (Educ. Code §§ 32280–32289.5). Each school must review and update its CSSP by March 1 each year and submit the CSSP to its governing board for approval thereafter.

The CSSP must be developed, revised, and updated by the school site council (SSC) or another group comprised of the school principal or their designee, at least one teacher who is recognized by the certificated employee organization, a parent whose child attends the school, a classified employee who is recognized by the classified employee organization, and other desired members. The SSC must consult with law enforcement, the fire department, and other first responders when writing and developing the CSSP.

The CCSP must include strategies to ensure compliance with existing school safety laws. For instance, the CSSP must address, among other things, (1) child abuse reporting procedures; (2) disaster procedures (including adaptations for students with special needs); (3) earthquake procedures with building disaster plans and protective measures in the event of an earthquake and staff training related to the same. The CSSP may include provisions related to the release of pesticides and/or toxic substances from properties located within a quarter mile of the school.

In addition, the CSSP may include "tactical responses to criminal incidents" that may result in death or serious bodily injury at school sites. The tactical responses to criminal incidents should include safeguards to protect students and staff, secure the affected area of the school, and apprehend the criminal perpetrator(s). Portions of the CSSP that include tactical responses to criminal incidents are exempt from public disclosure, including requests for information under the California Public Records Act. In addition, the school district's board may meet in closed session with law enforcement officials to approve the tactical responses portion of the plan but must publicly disclose the final vote on such portion of the plan.

Further, schools are encouraged to include clear guidelines related to the roles and responsibilities of certain staff who provide service pursuant to the plan. Specifically, the CSSP guidelines should identify how the following staff members, if needed, will provide service under the plan: mental health professionals, community intervention professionals, school counselors, school resource officers, and police officers when they are on the school campus.

The California Department of Education has issued CSSP recommended components; methods to improve CSSPs; and practical considerations at the school site, district, and county office of education levels. CDE's guidance may be accessed at: https://www.cde.ca.gov/ls/ss/vp/cssp.asp.

Transportation. Following a series of tragic events involving students on school buses, the Legislature imposed safety plan requirements on superintendents of county schools, superintendents of school districts, leaders of charter schools, and the owners or operators of private schools providing transportation to or from school or school activities (Educ. Code §§ 39831.3, 39860). Specifically, in compliance with certain safety procedures and mandates, the plans must ensure, among other things, that students are not left unattended on buses. In addition, the requirements mandate the Department of Motor Vehicles revoke the school bus driver certificates for those drivers who fail to comply with such procedures. Each school's safety plan must also designate an adult chaperone other than the driver to accompany students on "school student activity buses," operated by a common carrier under a contract with the school district. Finally, the Department of Motor Vehicles requires that each school bus, school student activity bus without one or more adult chaperones, youth bus, and child care motor vehicle for more than eight persons (including the driver) is to be equipped with a child safety alert system at the interior of the bus to ensure that the driver confirms no students are not left unattended at any time (Vehicle Code § 28160).

School Visitors. The legislature has also adopted efforts specifically targeting outside threats. For instance. after declaring that a disproportionate share of crimes committed on school grounds are committed by outsiders who have no lawful business there, the legislature added provisions to the California Penal Code in 1982 requiring outsiders to register with the principal or principal's designee during school hours (Penal Code § 627 et seq.). Outside individuals cannot simply enter campus to interact with staff members and students at will. School hours are defined to mean an hour before school begins and an hour after school ends. Registration is to include the visitor's name, address, and occupation; proof of age and identity; the purpose for being on campus; and any other information that may be relevant. Failure to register is a misdemeanor offense. The statute also provides that if it appears reasonable to a school official that an outsider may disrupt school activities, the official can direct the person to leave. Failure to comply also is a misdemeanor, as is the reentry of a person onto school grounds within seven days of being asked to leave.

A California appellate court defined the scope of this important statute in a 2000 decision involving the Golden West Middle School in Fairfield (*In re Joseph F.*). The case involved a juvenile offender who challenged his conviction for violating this law and for committing battery on a police resource officer assigned to the school. The police officer testified that the assistant school principal asked him to detain the youth for questioning after the youth was unresponsive to the assistant principal's questions. In attempting to do so, the officer met with resistance and had to use force to subdue the youth. The youth was placed on probation and restricted from associating with gangs. He argued that he did not have to register because the school day had ended and the officer had no reason to stop him for questioning. In a two-to-one decision, the court of appeal rejected his arguments. While the statute's registration requirement is restricted to school hours, the majority noted that nothing prevents a school official from inquiring why an outsider is on campus at any time. Contrary to the youth's assertion, it was not necessary for the officer to specify any particular law that was being broken. In a key passage, the court observed that unlike the rules applicable to public places in general, school officials, including police who assist in maintaining general order on school campuses, need not articulate a specific crime which appears to be violated in order to detain an outsider for the limited purpose of determining the fundamental factors justifying an outsider's presence on a school campus, such as who he is, why he is on campus, and whether he has registered. (p. 986).

The court upheld the conviction of the youth for battery and resisting arrest.

Outsiders' Use of Campuses for Speech-Related Purposes. The question of whether the school campus is a public forum that must accommodate outside groups intending to communicate with students surfaced in a 2003 California appellate court ruling (*Reeves v. Rocklin Unified School District,*). The case involved an antiabortion organization that sought to register with the school principal for the purpose of handing out leaflets and engaging in communication with students at Rocklin High School. When the request was denied, the group filed a lawsuit, arguing that its First Amendment rights had been violated.

The court of appeal rejected the claim. It noted that the U.S. Supreme Court declared in a 1983 ruling that, in order to serve its dedicated purpose, some public property may not be open to communication by outsiders (*Perry Education Association v. Perry Local Educators' Association*). A high school campus is such a place. If the high school were considered a public forum, not only the antiabortion group but other organizations as well would have to be granted the same right, because the government cannot discriminate on the basis of speech content in a public forum. The educational functioning of the high school and the safety of the students would be jeopardized as a result.

The antiabortion organization argued that Penal Code Section 627 prohibits school districts from impinging on protected rights of expression. But because the high school is a closed forum to outsiders, this provision is inapplicable. In any case, the court noted that the group could still communicate with students by doing so at a public intersection near the school.

It is important to note that this case involves the speech rights of outsiders, not students or teachers. The expression rights of students and teachers are discussed in Chapter 6. In a juvenile court proceeding, a student tried to argue that, because *Reeves v. Rocklin Unified School District* held that schools are not public property open to communication by outsiders, Penal Code Section 594.1, which makes it an offense to possess etching cream or aerosol paint on public property, does not apply to schools. The California court of appeal rejected the contention, noting that schools may be considered public property for certain purposes but not others. Here, the legislative goal of eliminating graffiti from public schools is furthered by viewing them as public places (*In re Miguel H.*, 2010)).

Individuals Who Willfully Disrupt School Operations. It also bears noting that the Penal Code authorizes school officials to prohibit certain individuals from entering or remaining on a school campus. For instance, Penal Code Section 626.4 establishes certain procedures that permit school officials to prohibit those who willfully disrupt the orderly operation of the school or facility from entering that school or facility. Under these procedures, school officials may direct those individuals through a "stay away letter" to remain away from schools or facilities for up to fourteen calendar days, and the individual may retain only very limited appeal rights. Individuals who willfully and knowingly enter or remain on the campus or facility are guilty of a misdemeanor and subject to arrest.

Safety-Related Penal Code Sections. A number of other Penal Code provisions may be accessed by school officials and law enforcement to maintain a safe schooling environment. A few of the more relevant provisions, including Section 626.4, are set forth in Table 2.1.

TABLE 2.1
Selected California Penal Code Provisions for Maintaining Order at School

Section 626.2	Penalizes unauthorized entry on public or private school grounds by a student or employee after written notification of suspension or dismissal for disrupting school operation.
Section 626.4	Permits the campus's "chief administrative officer" or designee to withdraw consent to visit the campus or facility of any person who has "willfully disrupted the orderly operation of the campus or facility" for up to 14 days. Anyone failing to leave the school premises after consent to remain there has been withdrawn because of concern about disruption of school operation is guilty of a misdemeanor.
Section 626.7	Permits chief administrative officer or designee of a public or private school or facility to request that an outsider who enters a nonpublic business area is to leave the campus if disruption appears likely. Failure of the person to leave, or return without following the posted requirements, is a misdemeanor offense. An exception is a parent or guardian who needs to reenter the campus to retrieve a student for disciplinary reasons, medical attention, or family emergency.
Section 626.8	Applies to outsiders who enter public or private school premises or adjacent public area without written permission of the school principal or designee and disrupt school activities or threaten the safety of students arriving, attending, or leaving the school. It is a misdemeanor offense if the person (1) remains after being asked to leave, (2) reenters within seven days of being asked to leave, or (3) has otherwise established a continued pattern of unauthorized entry.
Section 626.9	Known as the Gun-Free School Zone Act of 1995, Penal Code Section 626.9 prohibits possession or discharge of a firearm in an area in or on the grounds of a public or private school without written permission of the superintendent or designee. Individuals holding a valid license may carry a concealed firearm, but not ammunition, in an area that is within 1,000 feet of, but not on, the grounds of a public or private school. Among the exceptions are firearms carried by active or retired law enforcement and unloaded firearms and ammunition if kept in a motor vehicle and a locked container or in the locked trunk of the vehicle. (Penal Code §§ 626.9 and 30310).

Safety-Related Education Code Sections. Provisions of the Education Code also give school officials authority to maintain order. Some of these statutes have their roots in the student activist period of the 1960s and early 1970s, when civil rights and Vietnam antiwar demonstrations were common across the educational landscape. One statute provides that minors over the age of sixteen or adults who enter school grounds and willfully disrupt classes or interfere with the administration of the school are guilty of a misdemeanor (Educ. Code § 44810). A companion statute provides that a parent, guardian, or other person whose conduct "in a place where a school employee is required to be" materially disrupts classwork or extracurricular activities is guilty of a misdemeanor (Educ. Code § 44811).

An exemption is permitted for lawful union activity such as picketing and distribution of handbills. These statutes state that repeated offenses will result in increased penalties, including both a fine not exceeding $1,000 and imprisonment.

Education Code Section 32210 provides that anyone who willfully disrupts a public school or a public school meeting is guilty of a misdemeanor punishable by a fine of up to $500. Education Code Section 32211 directly relates to the classroom and mirrors many of the Penal Code provisions previously discussed. It provides that nonstudents who are requested to leave because the principal or designee is concerned about disruption of classes or other school activities must do so promptly and not return for seven days. Included as nonstudents are parents, guardians, and off-duty school employees other than a union representative engaged in representational activities. Failure to comply will result in a misdemeanor charge. The individual accused of disrupting the school may file an appeal later with the school superintendent and, if the appeal is unsuccessful, with the school board.

The attorney general has stated that under this section, school administrators may require members of the news media to register on campus and comply with whatever conditions the school has for interviewing students and observing events or teaching. If their presence would interfere with school activities, they may be requested to leave (79 Op. Atty. Gen. 58, 1996). This statute also requires that a notice setting forth school hours be posted at every entrance to the school and grounds. School hours are described as either the period one hour before classes begin and one hour after classes end or the time period defined by the governing board.

Workplace-Violence Restraining Orders. Of course, in emergencies or when appropriate under the circumstances, school staff may rely on local law enforcement for assistance. In more extreme cases where a parent or other individual has harassed, made a credible threat of violence, or engaged in violent conduct against a staff member, board member, or volunteer, school officials may pursue workplace-violence restraining orders (WVRO) pursuant to Section 527.8 of the California Code of Civil Procedure.

If issued by the court, the WVRO often directs the offending party to, among many other things, avoid contact with the protected person(s) and stay a certain distance from the protected person(s), their workplace, home, school, children's school, vehicle, and other locations. The WVRO typically imposes those limitations for a period of three years. In addition, the WVRO prohibits the defendant from owning, possessing, purchasing, or receiving guns, firearms, or ammunition.

When appropriate, the WVRO may also extend its protections to family or household members. When a WVRO restrains a parent or guardian of a student or students attending the school, school officials are well advised to consider ways to minimize the impact on the student(s), such as arranging acceptable pick-up/drop-off locations and procedures and incorporating the same into their request for a WVRO.

Workplace-Violence Prevention Plan. In 2023, the legislature approved, and the Governor signed, legislation requiring school districts to include certain safety measures within their injury prevention protocols. Specifically, Senate Bill (SB) No. 553 requires school districts and other employers to establish, implement, and maintain an effective workplace-violence prevention plan. SB 553 further requires school districts to log violent incidents and provide training to employees related to the plan.

SB 553 also expands the scope of who may pursue workplace-violence restraining orders. Specifically, SB 553 permits the collective bargaining representative to pursue and obtain a workplace-violence restraining order for certain employees. Prior to pursuing a workplace-violence restraining order, the collective bargaining representative must provide the named employee or employees the opportunity to decline to participate, and the representative must honor the employee's or employees' preference.

Background Checks. In addition to protecting staff and students from external threats, the law imposes safeguards to ensure that staff and other individuals who may come in contact with students on school campuses and/or during school-related activities complete specific background checks. For instance, school district employees must ensure that all employees complete an extensive background check by submitting their fingerprints to the Department of Justice (Educ. Code § 45125). Likewise, contractors working in the school environment, such as non-public-agency (NPA) staff members, must also complete a criminal background check, and on a case-by-case basis, school districts may require an entity with whom it has a contract to submit the employees' fingerprints to the Department of Justice (Educ. Code § 45123.1).

The law also protects students by prohibiting school districts from hiring individuals who have been convicted of certain crimes. For example, individuals who have been convicted of a sex offense or certain controlled substance crime may not be employed in public schools (Educ. Code § 45123). However, if an individual's conviction is reversed and the person is acquitted of the offense in a new trial or the charges against him or her are dismissed, Section 45123 does not prohibit the individual's employment thereafter. Finally, a school district may employ a person convicted of a controlled substance offense if the governing board of the school district determines, from the evidence presented, that the person has been rehabilitated for at least five years (Educ. Code § 45123(d)).

Sports. It also bears noting that the Legislature implemented efforts designed to create a safe and inclusive school environment through the elimination of certain offensive terms in the sports context. For instance, the Education Code prohibits public schools from using the term "Redskins" as a school or athletic team name, mascot, or nickname. The initiative became effective on January 1, 2017, and allows for an exception for uniforms or other materials bearing that name that were purchased before the enactment date if: (1) the school selects a new school or athletic team name, mascot, or nickname; (2) the school refrains from purchasing or selling uniforms to students or employees that bear the "Redskins" name unless necessary to replace damaged uniforms up to 20 percent of the total number of uniforms used by a team or band at the school during the 2016–2017 school year and purchased prior to January 1, 2019; (3) the school refrains from purchasing or acquiring for distribution to students or employees any yearbook, newspaper, program, or similar material that includes the name in its logo or cover title; and (4) the school does not purchase or construct a marquee, sign, or fixture that includes the "Redskins" name, and for facilities that already bear the name, the name shall be removed during maintenance. (Educ. Code §§ 221.2–221.3).

Healthy Foods and Activities. Part of maintaining a safe and healthy school environment is to ensure that students receive nutritional foods and beverages while at school. In recent years, the legislature has enacted laws requiring that full meals must be served during breakfast and lunch at elementary schools, that food served during breaks meet specific standards, and that consumption of nutritious fruits and vegetables be promoted outside the lunch period (Educ. Code § 49430 et seq., § 49565).

In an effort to combat childhood obesity in schools, legislators passed the Distinguished After School Health (DASH) Recognition Program in 2014. The DASH Program requires the California Department of Education (CDE) to implement a process for identifying high-quality after-school programs in coordination with other legislation that has also been enacted to promote student health and safety. These accompanying laws include the 21st Century High School After School Safety and Enrichment for Teens (ASSETs) program, the After School Education and Safety program (ASES), and similar initiatives that focus on healthy eating and physical activity. The former can be found in Education Code Sections 8420–8428 and provides grants through the CDE that partner traditional public and charter schools with communities to provide academic support and constructive alternatives for high school students and that support college and career readiness. The latter can be found in Education Code Sections 8482–8484.6 and provides grants through the CDE for educational and literacy support and enrichment encompassing technical education and physical fitness, among others, to kindergarten through ninth-grade students.

Under DASH, schools have the option of demonstrating how their program meets the criteria set forth in the statute. The CDE's website includes a list of recognized schools meeting the criteria. Details of the DASH program are set forth in Education Code Sections 8490–8490.7.

The Free or Reduced Price Meals Program also strives to improve overall school nutrition, recognizing that school lunch is a critical aspect of student health and well-being and that nutrition is a necessary component of brain development and learning. For many low-income, refugee, and immigrant students, food insecurity is a daily problem. However, research demonstrates that receiving free or reduced-price school lunches reduces not only food insecurity but also obesity rates and poor health.

In the interest of improving access to free or reduced-price meals by children from refugee and immigrant households, Education Code Section 49557 has been amended to require that school district governing boards and county superintendents of schools make applications available online, subject to specified requirements, including a link to the website on which translated applications are posted by the U.S. Department of Agriculture with instructions on how to submit it. The instructions must be clear for families who are homeless or migrants. These changes will allow families to access the application readily and without any language barriers.

Additionally, as of 2017, Education Code Section 49557.5 requires public schools, school districts, county offices of education, and charter schools serving free or reduced-price meals during the school day under the federal National School Lunch Program or the federal School Breakfast Program to ensure that students whose parent or guardian has unpaid meal fees is not shamed, treated differently, or served a meal that differs from those served to other students. Nor shall disciplinary action implemented against a student result in denial or delay of a nutritionally adequate meal.

Physical Education. In addition, legislative concern about obesity, coupled with litigation throughout California, has heightened California Department of Education's duty to assure through categorical program monitoring that each school is providing not less than 200 minutes of physical education each ten schooldays to students in grades one through six and not less than 400 minutes in the same time frame to students in grades seven through twelve, except for exempt students (Educ. Code § 33352). As noted earlier, there is no discretion in offering fewer than these minutes of physical education.

AEDs. The Legislature has also implemented safety measures related to automatic external defibrillators (AEDs). Specifically, the Health and Safety Code requires that both public and private school principals notify school employees where an automatic external defibrillator (AED) is located in the school and ensure that staff members receive information on how to use it. The principal also is to designate the trained employees who shall be available during instruction and school-sponsored activities to respond to an emergency that may necessitate the use of the AED. The Education Code insulates the school employee and the school or district from civil damages resulting from any act or omission in rendering emergency care or treatment, except in instances of gross negligence or willful or wanton misconduct resulting in personal injury or wrongful death (Educ. Code § 49417). The Education Code notes that, to access the liability protections described in Section 49417, the school district must comply with all requirements described in Health and Safety Code Section 1794.196.

Health and Safety Code Section 1797.196 requires principals to ensure that when an AED is placed in a public or private K–12 school, administrators and staff receive information describing sudden cardiac arrest and the school's emergency response plan. The principal must also ensure the following: (1) All administrators and staff understand the proper use of the AED; (2) instructions on how to use an AED are posted in fourteen-point type next to every AED; and (3) at least annually, school employees are notified as to the location of all AEDs on the campus.

Smoking. In response to statewide concerns regarding student smoking and drug use, legislative changes have also been made to anti-smoking laws. For instance, Education Code Section 48901 prohibits smoking or the use of a tobacco product on public school grounds, while attending school-sponsored activities, or while under the supervision of school employees. To target vaping, Section 48901 also incorporates the use of an electronic smoking device that creates an aerosol or vapor and any oral smoking device for the purpose of circumventing the prohibition of smoking. In addition, any school district, charter school, and county office of education that receives a grant from the State Department of Education for anti-tobacco education programs must address the consequences of tobacco use, reasons why adolescents use tobacco, peer norms and social influences that promote tobacco use, and skills for resisting social pressure promoting tobacco use (Health and Safety Code § 104420).

Further, California Health and Safety Code Section 104495 prohibits persons in playgrounds and youth sports events areas from using any tobacco product within 250 feet of the location. Failure to comply will result in a $250 fine for each violation.

Performance-Enhancing Drugs. The California High School Coaching Education and Training Program, which is set forth in Education Code Section 35179.1 and following sections, provides information about the harmful effects of the use of steroids and performance-enhancing dietary supplements. Education Code Sections 49030–49034 specify which performance-enhancing substances are prohibited, restrict schools from accepting sponsorship from manufacturers of dietary supplements, and require that the California Interscholastic Federation's constitution and bylaws be amended to require participating athletes to sign a pledge not to use dietary supplements or anabolic steroids without a prescription. Parents must also sign a notification form regarding these restrictions.

Child Abuse and Neglect. Finally, public and private school teachers, teacher aides, administrators, board members, and classified staff at public schools are among a long list of persons who have a mandatory obligation to report suspected child abuse or neglect under the terms of the Child Abuse and Neglect Reporting Act (CANRA) (Penal Code § 11164 et seq.). The report must be made to law enforcement, a county welfare department, or a county probation department if authorized to receive it. The report is to be made as soon as the reporter knows or suspects abuse or neglect. An initial telephone call is to be followed up by sending, faxing, or electronically transmitting a written report within thirty-six hours.

Failure to report may result in county jail confinement for six months, a fine of up to $1,000, or both. Parents may also file an action for negligence. However, if a mandated reporter fails to make the report and the employee moves to another district where the employee abuses a student, the parents of the victim of that abuse cannot seek damages against the former employing district and employees under this law, though there may be other ways to do so (*P.S. v. San Bernardino City Unified School District*, 2009). In the recent past, county district attorneys' offices have taken a more aggressive approach in investigating and prosecuting mandated reporters who fail or refuse to comply with the mandated reporter requirements.

We expect this trend to continue in the future, and all mandated reporters are well advised to adhere closely to all reporting requirements.

The law requires employers to provide training in the duties of child abuse and neglect reporting within the first six weeks of each school year and within six weeks of an individual's employment. (Educ. Code § 44691.) Employees who have a mandatory duty to report must be provided with, among other things, a statement regarding their reporting obligation, confidentiality rights, and potential criminal liability for failing to report.

As part of its ongoing efforts to eliminate child abuse and neglect, the Legislature added Section 33133.5 to the Education Code, requiring the Superintendent of Public Instruction to develop a poster notifying children of the appropriate telephone number to report abuse or neglect and to post downloadable version of the poster on the California Department of Education's website. Among specific elements, the poster must include information advising victims and others to dial "911" in emergencies and to be produced in five languages. School districts, charter schools, and private schools are encouraged to display appropriate versions of the poster in areas where students congregate.

Suicide. In closing, the Legislature has implemented specific efforts to prevent student suicides. For instance, Education Code Section 215 requires all school districts, county offices of education, state special schools, and charter schools to adopt a policy on student suicide prevention in collaboration with school and community stakeholders, school-employed mental health professionals, and suicide prevention experts. These efforts were first implemented in 2017–2018 for schools serving students in grades seven through twelve and were later adapted in 2020–2021 to be more age appropriate for students in kindergarten through sixth grade.

The Legislature adopted these provisions as part of a broad effort to address student suicide at every stage, including prevention, intervention, and postvention. The legislative goal is to raise awareness while also equipping teachers and other school staff with the training necessary to prevent student suicide. The policy is also intended to specifically address the needs of high-risk groups, including, but not limited to, the following: youth bereaved by suicide, youth with disabilities or mental illness, youth experiencing homelessness, and the LGBTQ community.

The legislation requires local educational agencies to provide training for teachers on the following topics: suicide awareness and prevention, how to identify appropriate mental health services, and when and how to refer youth to mental health services. Further, the legislation requires that employees act only within the scope of their credentials, and it does not authorize or encourage school employees to diagnose or treat mental illness that they are not specifically licensed to treat.

CURRICULUM AND INSTRUCTION

Curriculum Content Standards

Like legislatures in other states, the California Legislature has responded to criticism of public schools by specifying an elaborate set of academic content standards in each of the core curriculum areas of reading, writing, mathematics, history and social science, science, visual and performing arts, physical education, and foreign languages (Educ. Code § 60605 et seq.). The standards were developed by a broad-based commission appointed and approved by the State Board of Education (SBE) and are intended to serve as a model for the development of school district standards (Educ. Code § 60618).

Because the state student and school assessment program is tied to the standards, school districts have little alternative but to adopt them in some form. The standards are designed to specify the content that students need to acquire as they progress through public schools. These standards reflect the judgment of educators and others about the knowledge students should possess and the skills they need to succeed as adults. Accompanying the content standards are performance standards established for measuring student academic achievement at various grade levels. The state assessment system is elaborate and provides feedback not only on student achievement but also on how well schools are doing.

The content standards are specific to grade levels. The English-Language Arts content standards provide an illustration. They specify the content students need to master by the end of each grade level or cluster of grades. The standards are separated into the four domains of reading, writing, written and oral English language conventions, and listening and speaking. These, in turn, are further broken down into specific categories with performance objectives set for each.

For example, the reading domain for kindergartners includes three categories, one of which is literary response and analysis. Under this category are specific information and skills students are to acquire. Included are distinguishing fantasy from realistic text, identifying types of everyday print materials, and identifying characters, settings, and important events.

While the four domains and subcategories remain the same for successive grade levels, the specific information and skills students are to acquire become increasingly complex. Thus, for eleventh and twelfth graders, the literary response and analysis category includes a long list of specific information and skills students are to master, such as analyzing the way in which authors through the centuries have used archetypes drawn from myth and tradition in literature, film, political speeches, and religious writings.

California is one of forty-eight states that have worked with the Council of Chief State School Officers and the National Governors Association Center for Best Practices to develop a common content core in English language arts and mathematics. The purpose is to align states regarding the curriculum content in these subjects so that there is a clear and consistent K–12 progression regarding what students are to master regardless of where they live. The SBE adopted the common core state standards in August 2010. Education Code Section 60208 requires the state superintendent of public instruction (SPI), in collaboration with others, to develop professional development activities for teachers and administrators to be used as the common core academic standards are implemented. For further information, go to www.cde.ca.gov/ci/cc/.

Similarly, in 2013, the SBE adopted the Next Generation Science Standards for Public Schools for kindergarten through grade twelve (NGSS). The NGSS focus on physical science; life science; earth and space science, and engineering, technology, and applications of science. The NGSS includes three dimensions: science and engineering practices, disciplinary core ideas, and crosscutting concepts.

In recent years, increasing emphasis has been placed on integrating career technical education with traditional academic courses, given the rapid advance of technology in all aspects of daily life. Section 52372.5 and following sections of the Education Code address in some detail the value of high school career technical education (now often labeled "multiple pathways" or "linked learning") in broadening the scope of education and providing students with a full range of postgraduation choices from postsecondary options to career entry.

In 2010, the legislature expanded existing law relating to career technical education to encompass promoting work-based learning (Education Code § 51760 et seq.). School districts and community colleges that receive funding to provide career technical education may include a work-based learning component in these programs.

Work-based learning means an educational approach that combines rigorous college preparatory education with demanding career technical education. Work-based learning offers opportunities to learn through real-world experiences like job shadowing, mentoring, intensive internships, real or virtual apprenticeships, and school-based enterprises. It may be delivered by California Partnership Academies, regional occupational programs, and programs developed in association with community colleges.

The legislature also has broadened the mission of California Partnership Academies to encompass students who are not at risk of dropping out of school and to encourage the establishment of academies addressing the needs of developing technology (Educ. Code § 54690). The academies were started to provide combined academic and occupational training for high school students at risk of dropping out of school. Occupational education and skill development encompass California's fifteen different industry sectors, including computer technology, alternative energy, environmental design and construction, and space. Up to one-half of partnership academy enrollment now may be those who do not meet the criteria of at-risk students.

Among the conditions for receiving state funding, a district must establish the partnership academy as a school-within-a-school and assure instruction in at least three academic subjects per school term that prepares students for a regular high school diploma and, where possible and appropriate, to meet the subject requirements for admission to California State University (CSU) and the University of California (UC). The legislature also has broadened the definition of supplementary instructional materials that are to be selected for use in public schools to encompass relevant technology that further engages interactive learning.

School districts and county offices of education that offer career technical education courses must include the completion of such a course as an option for satisfying the high school graduation requirement of one course in visual or performing arts or foreign language (Education Code § 51225.3). The district or county office must include a list of its career education courses that satisfy specific subject-matter requirements for admission to CSU or UC.

The Legislature also implemented support for bilingual education. Following the November 2016 election, a majority of voters successfully endorsed the California Education for a Global Economy Initiative, repealing Proposition 227, which had replaced bilingual education with English immersion. Under the new measure, parents may choose a language acquisition plan that best suits their child's needs. Additionally, as of the bill's enactment in 2017, school districts and county officers of education are required to provide English learners with a structured English immersion program to ensure they have access to the academic content necessary to become proficient in English. School districts and county offices also are encouraged to provide opportunities for native English speakers to become proficient in one or more other languages to the extent possible. Finally, the Legislature repealed the right of parents to sue for enforcement and receive damages and attorneys' fees under the prior English immersion program.

In a related manner, Section 313.2 of the Education Code requires the Department of Education to obtain and disseminate information regarding the number of students in each traditional public and charter school who are, or are at risk of, becoming long-term English learners. That section has also been amended to require the Department of Education to obtain and disseminate information concerning the ways English development programs will meet student needs and age-appropriate academic standards.

In addition to curriculum standards and detailed curriculum frameworks for teachers to use in developing standards-based lesson plans, the legislature has established requirements for selecting and disposing of instructional material (Educ. Code § 60000 et seq.). Among other things, the legislature, with certain exceptions, requires the SBE to adopt for each elementary grade level and subject-matter area at least five separate basic instructional materials that are aligned with the curriculum content standards; requires school governing boards to involve teachers and community members in the adoption of instructional materials; requires instructional materials to portray cultural and racial diversity; specifies that instructional materials are to address certain topics in certain ways (e.g., the necessity for environmental protection and the harmful effects of tobacco, alcohol, narcotics, and dangerous drugs); and requires religious neutrality.

Discrimination against lesbian, gay, bisexual, and transgender persons in the selection and disposal of textbooks also is prohibited. In addition, the Legislature has implemented efforts to ensure the accurate portrayal of certain groups in the curriculum. Specifically, schools must ensure that social science instruction includes a study of the role and contributions of people of (1) all genders, (2) Native Americans, (3) African Americans, (4) Latino Americans, (5) Asian Americans, (6) Pacific Islanders, (7) European Americans, (8) LGBTQ+ Americans, (9) persons with disabilities, (10) and members of other ethnic, cultural, religious, and socioeconomic status groups, with particular emphasis on portraying the role of these groups in contemporary society (Educ. Code §§ 51204.5, 60040).

The Legislature also implemented certain efforts to ensure accurate Native American studies curricula. For example, in 2017, the Legislature revised Education Code Section 51226.9 and directed the Instructional Quality Commission and the State Board of Education to develop and approve a model curriculum in Native American studies. The model curriculum was developed with the assistance of Native American tribes in California and serves as a guide for school districts and charter schools to adapt related courses to reflect student demographics in their communities.

Following the adoption of the model curriculum, each school district and charter school maintaining any grades from ninth through twelfth that does not offer a standards-based Native American studies curriculum is encouraged to offer such a course of study as a social sciences or English language arts elective. The course is to be made available in at least one year of a student's enrollment. An outline of the course must be submitted as an A-G course for admission to the University of California and California State University.

When a particular group is misrepresented in social science course materials, litigation is a common remedy. For example, the California Parents for the Equalization of Educational Materials (CAPEEM), a group that seeks to promote an accurate portrayal of the Hindu religion, filed a lawsuit against several members of the State Board of Education (SBE) and the California Department of Education (CDE) asserting that the history-social science sixth-grade standards and framework were patently anti-Hindu. Among other claims, CAPEEM alleged the standards did not describe Hinduism as virtuous and did not mention Hinduism's divine origins and central figures. The SBE moved to dismiss the claim.

The federal district court determined that the standards did not: (1) intrude on the liberty rights of parents to control their children's upbringing under the Fourteenth Amendment due process clause, (2) violate the right of parents to freely exercise their religious beliefs under the free exercise clause of the First Amendment, or (3) discriminate against Hinduism in violation of the Fourteenth Amendment equal protection clause. However, the court denied the SBE's motion to dismiss CAPEEM's claim that the standards and framework violated the First Amendment establishment clause. The court cited as an illustration the comments of a sixth-grade student who alleged that, when her class was divided into castes, she felt discriminated against on the basis of her religion, because she said other students and the teacher considered Hinduism as cruel, primitive, and unjust. The judge noted that the student formed this impression from the framework's statement to teachers to make clear that the caste system was both a social/cultural structure as well as a religious belief. Based on this assertion, the judge denied the SBE's motion to dismiss the establishment clause claim (*California Parents for the Equalization of Educational Materials v. Torlakson*, 2017).

On appeal, the court affirmed the district court's dismissal of all but one of the plaintiff's claims and its summary judgment in favor of the defendants on the remaining claim. The court held that, absent evidence of unlawful intentional discrimination, the parents could not raise an equal protection challenge to the curriculum. Further, the court denied the parents' free exercise claim as the curriculum content did not penalize, interfere with, or otherwise burden the exercise of their religion. Finally, the court found that the parents failed to produce a valid due process claim. The court ultimately denied the parents' claims related to the curriculum, hours of instruction, and extracurricular activities (*Cal. Parents for the Equalization of Educ. Materials v. Torlakson*, 2020).

Instructional materials are to be free of charge to public school students. Private schools may order instructional materials adopted by the SBE at cost.

Critics argue that the detailed nature of the content standards, in combination with state-approved curriculum materials, diminishes the autonomy of the school district and the classroom teacher, as well as dampens classroom spontaneity. The English-Language Arts content standards alone encompass nearly 100 pages.

While charter schools are relatively free to develop their own instructional program, they cannot, as a practical matter, stray far from the state standards because their students must participate in the state assessments. To ensure the students are successful on those assessments, charter schools must address the content standards in their curricula.

Critics also express concern that the backgrounds and characteristics of some students (e.g., students with disabilities, certain English language learners, or those from impoverished backgrounds) stand in the way of their mastering the standards, and they do poorly on state assessments as a result. This places a special responsibility on educators to ensure these students have an equal educational opportunity to learn. There are serious consequences for schools and educators who fail to do so.

Along with curriculum standards and requirements, the Legislature placed restrictions on schools assigning students to "course period[s] without educational content." These restrictions originated in response to a lawsuit focused on high school students assigned to content-absent courses because of a lack of funds or teachers. Sections 51228.1 and 51228.2 have been added to the Education Code, specifying that personnel in school districts with any ninth through twelfth grades are prohibited from assigning students to a course period without educational content for more than one week in a semester.

The term "course period without educational content" includes:

1. sending a student home or releasing the student from campus before the conclusion of the school day;
2. assigning a student to a service, instructional work experience, or an otherwise named course in which the student is to assist a certificated employee but not complete curricular assignments during that period and where the ratio of certificated employees to students assigned to the course for curricular purposes is less than one to one; and
3. assigning the student to no course during the relevant course period.

The restriction does not affect other curricular programs such as community college dual enrollment, evening high school, independent study, work-study courses, or work experience education. It also does not apply to students enrolled in alternative schools, community day schools, continuation schools, and opportunity schools. Notwithstanding the strict prohibitions, such assignments may be made if the parent or adult student provides written consent and the school official believes the student will benefit from such an assignment.

A similar restriction applies to efforts to assign a high school student to a course the student has already completed and received a grade sufficient to satisfy admission requirements to a California public postsecondary institution and the school's graduation requirements. However, the student may repeat the course if the parent or adult student and the school official believe that the student will benefit from repeating the course. Alternatively, the student may repeat the course if the curriculum has changed and they would benefit from taking the course again. And as above, this provision does not apply to dual enrollment programs, evening high schools, alternative schools, and so on.

Curriculum Censorship

The U.S. Supreme Court has been reluctant to intrude on state and school governing board authority in developing curricula and selecting classroom instructional materials. Its general orientation to the issue was well expressed in a 1968 decision: "By and large, public education in our Nation is committed to the control of state and local authorities" (*Epperson v. Arkansas*, 1968). However, the authority of state and local school officials to control the classroom curriculum is not unlimited.

In a seminal 1969 decision, the Court observed that "state-operated schools may not be enclaves of totalitarianism" (*Tinker v. Des Moines Independent Community School District*, 393 U.S. 503). The problem is one of balance. As one California appellate court has observed, "[T]here exists an inherent tension between two essential functions of a school board, exposing young minds to the clash of ideas in the free marketplace and the need to provide our youth with a solid foundation of basic, moral values" (*McCarthy v. Fletcher*, 1989)).

The difficulty is determining when the exercise of curricular authority crosses the line of constitutionality. In the *McCarthy* case, the school board in the Wasco Union High School District school board removed two books, *Grendel* by John Gardner and *One Hundred Years of Solitude* by Gabriel Garcia Marquez, for use as supplemental reading in a senior English class. School administrators believed the books were antireligious and contained too much profanity, vulgarity, and sordid imagery to be appropriate. The school board approved a revised book list that did not include the two books. A teacher, student, parent, and taxpayer argued that the board's action constituted unconstitutional censorship. The appellate judges noted that school officials must have legitimate educational reasons for their curricular decisions. They cannot substitute "rigid and exclusive indoctrination" for the right to make educational choices. The case was sent back to the trial court to determine the motives of the school board members in approving the altered reading list.

A particularly sensitive Arizona case came before the U.S. Court of Appeals for the Ninth Circuit in 1998 (*Monteiro v. Tempe Union High School District*, 1998). The geographic jurisdiction of the Ninth Circuit encompasses Arizona and a number of other western states in addition to California. In that case, Black parents objected to their children reading *The Adventures of Huckleberry Finn* by Mark Twain and *A Rose for Emily*, a short story by William Faulkner, in a ninth-grade English class. The parents argued that the required readings were racially offensive and asked the school board to remove them. They alleged that, following the assigned reading, their children were subjected to racial harassment.

The Ninth Circuit ruled that a student's First Amendment rights are infringed when approved instructional material is subsequently removed due to the threat of lawsuits. Furthermore, the removal of books that some parents find objectionable would establish a dangerous precedent. The court noted that whites might seek the removal of books by Toni Morrison, Maya Angelou, and other Black authors; Jews might file lawsuits over the writings of William Shakespeare; and females might seek damages for assignments of works by Tennessee Williams. The court pointed out the value of reading materials with which one disagrees.

At the same time, the judges were sensitive to the parents' allegations about a racially hostile environment. They held that under Title VI of the 1964 Civil Rights Act, school authorities have a responsibility to take action to stop racial harassment as soon as they learn it is occurring. Title VI prohibits discrimination on the basis of race in any federally assisted program. Failure to do so can result in liability, a matter discussed in more detail in Chapter 11. One judge in the case wrote a short concurring opinion in which he noted that a school board's requiring students to read books with overt messages of racial hatred may well violate Title VI.

Further, school districts, county offices of education, and charter schools are prohibited from refusing to approve or prohibiting the use of any textbook, instructional material, or other curriculum or any book or other resource in a school library because it includes a study of the role and contributions of any of the above-noted individuals or groups. Likewise, school districts, county offices of education, and charter schools may not prohibit the continued use of an appropriately adopted textbook, instructional material, or curriculum on the basis that it contains inclusive and diverse perspectives (Educ. Code § 51501). The California Department of Education issued guidance to assist with managing conversations about race and gender and how to review instructional materials to ensure they represent diverse perspectives and are culturally relevant, which may be accessed at: https://www.cde.ca.gov/ci/cr/cf/ab1078guidance.asp (Educ. Code § 60040.5).

Commercial content in curricula has also become the focus of litigation. Specifically, a California appellate court ruled in 1994 that school districts can contract with a commercial entity (in this case, Channel One) to provide a current events video program for classroom viewing, provided there is an opt-out for students who object to viewing the program because of its advertisements. The court could find no justifiable educational purpose to require students, who are compelled to attend school and thus are a captive audience, to view advertisements (*Dawson v. East Side Union High School*, 1994). Under prevailing constitutional law, commercial speech is not entitled to the same degree of constitutional protection as noncommercial speech. Additionally, as noted earlier in the chapter, outsiders do not have unfettered permission to enter public school campuses for expressive purposes.

It bears noting that parents' ability to opt their students out of certain LGBTQ+ materials became a significant source of litigation near the time of publication of this book. Shortly prior to publication, the United States Supreme Court held that a school district's refusal to permit parents to opt their young students out of "LGBTQ+-inclusive" story books violated the parents' right to free exercise of their religion (Mahmoud et al. v. Taylor et al., 2025). Readers are encouraged to review Mahmoud and its progeny when analyzing this issue.

Classroom Instruction

Class size reduction. In past decades, attention has been directed to reducing class size as a way to improve student learning. Teachers, teacher organizations, and parents regularly strongly advocate for reduced class sizes. If classes are smaller, teachers typically may provide greater attention to each student.

California embraced class size reduction in 1996 by enacting a voluntary program that encouraged school districts and charter schools to reduce class size in kindergarten through grade three from thirty to twenty students (Educ. Code § 52120 et seq.). Similarly, the state enacted programs to reduce class size for ninth through twelfth graders (Educ. Code § 52080 et seq.).

However, these policies came to an end in 2015 when the state legislature repealed both Section 52120 and Section 52080 and replaced them with California's new school funding and accountability system, the Local Control Funding Formula (LCFF). As discussed briefly below and in detail in Chapter 3, under the LCFF, schools receive funding from grade-span-specific base grants on the basis of average daily attendance, which reflects adjustments for grades K–3 class sizes and grades 9–12 classes.

The legislature also maintained funding penalties on districts and charter schools that exceed designated maximum class sizes (Educ. Code §§ 41376 and 41378).

But reducing class size has not been accomplished without complications. Policymakers and administrators have been concerned about finding sufficient highly qualified teachers, sufficient space to accommodate additional classes, and adequate funding to implement the reforms.

Smaller class sizes are least likely in districts serving high concentrations of low-income minority students, because of limited resources, and teacher qualifications have declined in these schools as more experienced teachers transfer to other schools. Recent budgetary problems at state and school levels have prompted some pullback from class size reduction efforts. Other strategies to improve classroom instruction have focused on tailoring programs to special categories of students and improving teacher quality.

However, implementation of the LCFF sought to target these and other disparities. In particular, the LCFF provides additional funding in the form of supplemental and concentration grants for certain groups of students based on their demographic information. Namely, the LCFF targets funding for students who (1) are English learners, (2) meet income or other categorical eligibility requirements for free or reduced-price meals under the National School Lunch Program, or (3) are foster youth. These students are often labeled the "unduplicated count," meaning each student is counted only once for purposes of supplemental and concentration grant funding under the LCFF. We provide additional information regarding the LCFF and the Local Control Accountability Plan (LCAP) in Chapter 3 concerning equity, adequacy, and school finance.

Educating targeted groups. Several student groups have been identified as needing special instructional attention. Clearly, children with disabilities are the most prominent. In Chapter 8, we describe how their instructional needs are met. Other groups with tailored programs include English learners, gifted and talented students, and those who are educationally disadvantaged.

In June 1998, California voters approved Proposition 227, which largely replaced bilingual education with English immersion. At the time, legislation incorporating the terms of Prop. 227 began by noting that "all children in California public schools shall be taught English by being taught in English" (Educ. Code § 305).

In 2016, California voters approved Proposition 58, effectively repealing the English-only requirement described in Proposition 227 and increasing school district authority to implement various programs to assist students in learning English. Proposition 58 was intended to ensure all students in California's public schools master the English language, receive high-quality instruction, and access innovative and research-based language programs that prepare them for the future.

Courts have acknowledged that schools must assist students in overcoming language barriers that limit their ability to learn. For instance, in a 1974 U.S. Supreme Court case involving the San Francisco Unified School District (*Lau v. Nichols*, 1974), the Court ruled that regulations accompanying Title VI of the 1964 Civil Rights Act required school districts to eliminate language barriers that deny students an equal opportunity to learn. Because English is the primary language of instruction and a graduation requirement, the school board was required to take affirmative steps to rectify language deficiencies. Simply placing Chinese students who spoke no English in all-English classes would not suffice.

Both state and federal law require school districts to administer tests of English language proficiency for students in kindergarten through twelfth grades. First administered in 2001, the California English Language Development Test (CELDT) tracked students' progress toward full English proficiency, a determination also encompassing teacher evaluation, parental views, and basic skills testing. Parents were not permitted to opt out of the CELDT, because English-language assessment is both a federal and a state requirement. Parents were informed of their children's scores on the CELDT; results at the school, district, county, and state level were also published online.

In 2018, California replaced the CELDT with the English Language Proficiency Assessment for California (ELPAC). The ELPAC must be administered to all students whose primary language is other than English. The ELPAC is aligned to the 2012 California English Language Development Standards and includes two separate assessments: (1) an initial evaluation to identify English learners, and (2) an annual summative evaluation designed to measure the student's progress and English language proficiency. California publishes the initial and summative ELPAC results at https://caaspp-elpac.ets.org/elpac/.

Additionally, school site and district advisory committees afford parents a role in their children's education, including their children's language acquisition. (Educ. Code § 62002.5). For instance, each school district serving at least fifty or more English learners must establish a District English Learner Advisory Committee (DELAC) (unless the DELAC responsibilities are delegated to an existing district-wide subcommittee). The DELAC must advise the school district's governing board concerning the following items (Educ. Code § 52063):

1. Development of a district master plan for English learner programs and services, including consideration of any school site master plans.
2. A district-wide needs assessment conducted on a school-by-school basis.
3. Implementation of district programs, goals, objectives, and services for English learners.

4. Development of a plan to ensure compliance with any applicable teacher and/or staff requirements.
5. Review and comment on the school district reclassification procedures.
6. Review and comment on the written notifications required to be sent to parents and guardians.
7. Review and comment on the annual update of the Local Control and Accountability Plan (LCAP).

Teacher preparation and evaluation. While the content standards somewhat diminish teacher autonomy and local control, they do not end it. School districts, principals, and teachers still must design instructional strategies to bring about mastery of the subject matter. Research has consistently shown that teacher quality and experience play a significant role in student achievement. This is especially true in high-poverty schools. Unfortunately, these schools have trouble attracting and retaining high-quality teachers. Federal and California law are seeking to address the problem.

These efforts included Congress's enactment of the No Child Left Behind (NCLB) Act in 2001, which was as much concerned about the quality of teaching as it was about student performance. Accordingly, the law required that all public school teachers, including those in charter schools, must be highly qualified to teach the core academic subjects of English, reading or language arts, math, science, foreign languages, civics and government, economics, arts, history, and geography. This requirement did not apply to private school teachers.

Effective at the start of the 2017–2018 school year, the Every Student Succeeds Act (ESSA) replaced the NCLB. The ESSA eliminated the need for waivers from requirements such as ensuring adequate yearly progress in all students' proficiency on math and reading tests to not lose federal funding. The annual progress requirement has been eliminated, and consequences for schools that do not satisfy certain performance standards have escalated.

ESSA continues to require students to be tested in reading and math from third to eighth grade and at least once in high school. States are required to intervene to assist low-performing schools, including those with underperforming subgroups. School evaluations must include at least one other measure beyond student test scores, such as graduation rates or English proficiency for nonnative speakers. California's changes in student assessment and financial accountability are described below and in Chapter 3.

California has sought to address teacher quality by developing a comprehensive system of credentialing over the years and updating that system as schools and student needs dictate. It is beyond the scope of this book to provide a detailed description of the credentialing system, which is set forth in Education Code Section 44200 and following sections and in the regulations developed by the California Commission on Teacher Credentialing (CCTC). Generally speaking, the CCTC requires individuals who wish to obtain a multisubject teaching credential to complete a baccalaureate degree in professional education in addition to meeting the basic skills requirement through one of four assessments, such as the California Basic Education Skills Test (CBEST), and to complete both a teacher preparation program and a performance assessment approved by CCTC (Educ. Code § 44225 (a)(1)).

Elementary teachers also must pass the Reading Instruction Competency Assessment. The preparation program must be linked to state curriculum content and student performance standards, and its teacher assessment component must be linked to the research-based competencies set forth in the California Standards for the Teaching Profession. These encompass six areas: engaging and supporting all students in learning, creating and maintaining effective environments for student learning, understanding and organizing subject matter for student learning, planning instruction and designing learning experiences for all students, assessing students for learning, and developing as a professional educator. Among the specified course requirements is a foundational computer technology course that includes general and specialized skills in the use of computers in educational settings. Other requirements for obtaining a credential include studying alternative ways of developing English-language skills, completing a subject-matter program aligned with the state content and performance standards, demonstrating knowledge of the U.S. Constitution, and showing competency in the use of computers (Educ. Code § 44259 et seq.).

General education teaching credentials in California fall into two categories: multiple subject and single subject. Generally speaking, a multiple-subject teaching credential is necessary for teaching in the elementary school self-contained classroom. A single-subject credential is required to teach the subject in middle schools and high schools. Candidates for both must demonstrate competency in their subject area either by taking a subject-matter test or by completing an approved program at a college or university. For elementary teacher candidates, the test covers the multiple subjects taught at this level, such as language studies, mathematics, and science. Teacher candidates who meet basic credentialing requirements and are recommended for a credential by their teacher preparation institution are given a preliminary certificate valid for up to five years. During this time, they complete additional requirements, including a school-based induction program, to receive a professional clear credential. The professional clear credential is valid for life so long as the holder functions effectively on the job and submits a renewal application and fee every five years.

There is a similar program for credentialing administrators in traditional public schools. Administrators in charter and private schools are not required to hold a state credential. Like teacher credentialing, the requirements for an administrator credential are ever-changing. For current information about the California credentialing system, review the above-described Administrator Assignment Manual and/or visit www.ctc.ca.gov.

As noted earlier, all teacher and administrative credential candidates are required to take the CBEST, which assesses basic reading, writing, and mathematics skills, unless exempted. Among those exempt are candidates receiving scores on the Graduate Record Exam, Scholastic Aptitude Test, or the ACT Plus Writing test at a level determined by the state superintendent of public instruction. Also exempt are persons who have a teaching credential from another state and have passed a basic skills test in that state.

Because nonwhite candidates have received disproportionately failing scores on CBEST, several organizations challenged its validity under Title VI and Title VII of the 1964 Civil Rights Act. As noted earlier, Title VI prohibits discrimination on the basis of race in federally assisted programs. Title VII prohibits discrimination on the basis of race, color, religion, sex, and national origin in both public and private employment. In a divided decision, the judges of the U.S. Court of Appeals for the Ninth Circuit ruled in 2000 that the test is a valid measure of minimum competency for both teaching and nonteaching positions and that the passing rates were appropriately established (*Association of Mexican-American Educators v. State of California*, 2000).

The legislature has directed the state Superintendent of Public Instruction and the CCTC to develop a system of teacher support and assessment to help beginning teachers become effective and weed out those who are not (Educ. Code § 44279.1). For some time, California has required school districts to have a uniform system of evaluation and assessment of performance for all certificated employees. Districts are required to evaluate performance as reasonably related to student achievement on grade-level assessments and, if applicable, the state-adopted content standards; instructional techniques and strategies; adherence to curricular objectives; and the establishment of a suitable learning environment (Educ. Code § 44662). Details on employment are discussed in Chapter 5.

As part of the California Education Information System, the legislature has directed the California Department of Education, in association with the Commission on Teacher Credentialing, to oversee the development of an individualized tracking system for teachers to be called the California Longitudinal Teacher Integrated Data Education System (CALTIDES) (Educ. Code § 10600 et seq.). Teacher data tracking provides a central repository of information for enhancing understanding of the teacher workforce and the effectiveness of teacher preparation programs.

CALTIDES was intended to become a comprehensive system that integrated existing databases, enabling the retention of longitudinal educator data in order to facilitate assignment monitoring and to conduct high-quality program evaluations. (Educ. § 10601.6). However, CALTIDES has been defunded and the program is no longer administered by the California Department of Education.

Copyright Law

Article I, Section 8 of the U.S. Constitution provides Congress with the authority to "promote the progress of science and useful arts, by securing for limited times to authors and inventors the exclusive right to their respective writings and discoveries." While copyright law is designed to protect authors' rights over their works, these protections are not unlimited. Thus, the Copyright Act enacted by Congress in 1976 specifies that copyright protection does not encompass "any idea, procedure, process, system, method of operation, concept, principle, or discovery regardless of the form in which it is described, explained, illustrated, or embodied" in a published work (17 U.S.C. § 102 (b)).

The most important limitations to author rights are embodied in the doctrine of "fair use" and are codified in Section 107 of the Copyright Act. The principle of fair use attempts to balance the author's and the public's interests in the dissemination of information and is rooted in consideration of four factors: (1) the purpose and character of the use, including whether it is for nonprofit educational purposes; (2) the nature of the copyrighted work; (3) the amount and substantiality of the portion used in relation to the whole work; and (4) the effect of the use on the potential market for or value of the work.

These factors accord educators in nonprofit educational environments some latitude in reproducing portions of works for classroom use but do not clarify the extent to which school personnel may fairly use copyrighted works. Because the law left the scope of fair use in the educational setting somewhat ambiguous, a committee of educators, authors, and publishers has established a set of guidelines for the use of copyrighted materials in nonprofit schools. These are set forth in Table 2.2.

Additionally, the U.S. Copyright Office published a specific guide titled Reproduction of Copyrighted Works for Educators and Librarians, which can be found at https://www.copyright.gov/circs/circ21.pdf. These guidelines are extensive and should be considered prior to use of copyrighted materials.

If teachers wish to use copyrighted materials over a period of years, their best approach is to request permission from the publisher. A publisher's permission preempts the standard copyright limitations, and many publishers are quite accommodating when the material will be used for educational purposes. Others may charge a fee, and in some cases, teachers may find it less expensive simply to purchase the printed work. However, if teachers wish to make photocopies for course use without permission, they should have a good faith belief that the copying qualifies for permissible uses.

Many school personnel assume that materials posted on the internet are freely available for reproduction and use. This assumption may be rooted in the absence of a copyright notice on many materials readily found on the internet. The federal Copyright Act of 1976 specifically includes the internet, and nearly everything on the internet is or can be copyrighted. Thus, the safest approach is to assume that, unless specifically indicated otherwise, any material or design on the internet is copyrighted.

The law relating to web page links is unsettled, but teachers may post a link to another site if they are not publishing the material. However, teachers should not provide a link to a site that violates copyright law, such as a site that allows free downloads of copyrighted software or music. A website's "Terms of Use" will also detail requirements for linking. Sites that require a username and password do not permit linking to circumvent that requirement. A teacher may not bring the material onto the class site.

Other concerns related to internet materials include downloading material to a teacher's computer. Downloading is an electronic copy, and printing the downloaded item makes another copy. A copyright owner may prohibit both. Additionally, it is important to note that the website holder might not be the copyright holder.

Copyright violations may also occur when using microcomputer software. The Copyright Act of 1976 includes computer software in its protections and defines a computer program as "a set of statements or instructions to be used directly or indirectly in a computer in order to bring about a certain result" (17 U.S.C. § 101). The media containing the software and its accompanying manual are protected by copyright laws. Educators may make backup copies of purchased software but may not make additional copies unless pursuant to a lease or purchase agreement. Software must be licensed for networking to be included on a school or district computer network.

TABLE 2.2

Copyright Law Guidelines (See Appendix C for updating sources)

Type of copyrighted material	School personnel may	School personnel may not
Books, newspapers, magazines (specific items)	Make multiple copies for classroom use of the following: • 250 words or less from poems printed on two pages or less • 2,500 words or less of an article, short story, or essay • 1,000 words or 10%, whichever is less, of a play, novel, or letter (Note: No matter how short the work, educators may copy up to 500 words without risking copyright infringement.) • Two pages or 10%, whichever is less, of illustrated books such as picture or comic books	Copy consumables such as workbooks and standardized tests Copy items for use term to term Copy more than one poem, article, or essay by the same author, nor more than two excerpts from a collection
Music, Lyrics, Music Video	Make emergency copies for performance with the understanding that the emergency copy soon will be replaced with a purchased copy Make multiple copies less than a performance unit so long as the copy does not exceed 10% of the entire work, but no more than 30 seconds of music or lyrics from an individual musical work. Simplify or edit printed music so long as the changes do not alter the fundamental character of the work when editing. Make single copies for exercises or exams	Make copies in order to substitute for the purchase of a complete work Copy consumables Copy for performance (unless an emergency) Add or alter lyrics
Multimedia (Microsoft PowerPoint)	Play multimedia presentations that support direct instruction that include • 10% or 3 minutes, whichever is less, of a video, film, or television recording • 10% or 1,000 words, whichever is less, of a novel, play, story, or long poem • Poems of 250 words or less in their entirety • Up to 10% but not more than 30 seconds of a musical work • 10% or fifteen images, whichever is less, from a collective work but no more than five illustrations from a single artist or photographer • Up to 10% or 2,500 fields or cells, whichever is less, of a copyrighted numerical data set	Use the same multimedia presentation for more than two years
Software	• Distribution over the educational institution's network • Make backup copies of purchased software	Make copies (other than backup) unless pursuant to lease or purchase Network software unless it is licensed for networking (be aware of license limitations)

The increasing use of programs such as Microsoft PowerPoint and Hypermedia in school settings raises concerns when presentations incorporate materials from copyrighted sources. Generally, educational institutions may digitize images and multimedia works for one semester while permission is being sought from the copyright holder. Teachers and students may also incorporate portions of other copyrighted multimedia materials along with their own material, such as notes or commentary. The copyright guidelines for multimedia presentations are quite detailed and are included in Table 2.2.

Video and audio recordings that directly relate to instruction may be used in the classroom even if these recordings are labeled "for home use only." These recordings may not be used for the purpose of entertainment or reward (e.g., during noninstructional periods or as a reward for performance on a difficult test).

Off-air recording of television programs is permitted so long as the recording is used within ten days of taping and is destroyed within forty-five days. Teachers may not routinely copy a program for use in the classroom or copy in anticipation of need. In addition, teachers may not alter or combine off-air recorded copies or make backup copies of their recordings.

Teachers may publish copied materials on their web pages, even for course use, because websites are not considered traditional, face-to-face teaching. Cable-only channels such as HBO, The History Channel, and The Disney Channel have developed their own off-air recording policies. Educators must comply with these policies when recording from cable-only networks.

Teachers in traditional face-to-face teaching environments enjoy broader fair use exemptions than do teachers who present their lessons via distance-learning arrangements. The 2002 Technology, Education, and Copyright Harmonization (TEACH) Act allows the display and performance of nearly all types of work for distance learning. TEACH amended Section 110(2) of the Copyright Act to allow nondramatic and dramatic works, including videos, films, plays, operas, and musicals, to be shown as clips in "reasonable and limited portions" in distance-learning teaching arrangements. A display comparable to what would be shown in a live classroom setting is also allowed. Works that are not allowed are those marked "primarily for performance or display as part of mediated instructional activities transmitted via digital network" and works that were not lawfully acquired under the U.S. Copyright Act, if the educational institution "knew or had reason to believe" they were not lawfully made and acquired. Schools may record or maintain copies of the distance-learning transmission, even if it includes copyrighted content. The act permits the digitalization of some analog works, but only if the work is not already available in digital form.

To benefit from TEACH, educators must supervise the transmission, the transmission must be an integral part of a class session, and the materials must be directly related to teaching the content of the transmission. Simply stated, instructors must be in charge of the use, and the materials must serve educational pursuits. Teachers may not upload chapters of a book in lieu of purchase by the student. However, occasional handouts with short works may be permitted.

TEACH also prohibits converting materials from analog into digital formats unless the amount converted is appropriate in conjunction with the Copyright Act's Section 110(2) and a digital version of the work is not available or secured behind technological protection. This means teachers must take two steps: (1) Ensure the material being converted is within the scope of allowed materials, and (2) Check for digital versions available or any access protections.

Because lawsuits charging copyright infringement against schools have increased in recent years, administrators are well advised to develop clear policies regarding the use of copyrighted work and to monitor their compliance. In addition, administrators may wish to take the extra step of marking equipment capable of copying with reminders of copyright limits and liabilities. Web-based learning presents unique challenges. Administrators need to be particularly vigilant in seeing that TEACH and/or fair use guidelines are followed when copyrighted material is incorporated into web-based courses. This includes seeing if a license to include copyrighted material on the website is necessary and requiring enrolled students to have a PIN or password. The use of streaming formats will help prevent student copying, and student access should be limited to the duration of the course. Teachers should include a notice that the material on the website is provided under fair use and may be used only for personal, noncommercial educational purposes. Both administrators and teachers need to be particularly vigilant in keeping up to date with legal developments in this area of copyright law.

The Internet

From the educational perspective, the internet is a vast electronic library that is increasingly being used to secure information and enrich learning.

As a vast communication and information-conveying system, the internet has become the focus of litigation. In response to this and prodded by the federal government, school districts have developed internet user agreements generally called Acceptable Use Policies (AUPs). These policies spell out the conditions for the use of the internet and other technology by school personnel and students. They typically specify the purposes for which school technology and equipment can be used, set forth applicable rules, inform users about the extent of privacy, and spell out such matters as copyright and privacy requirements. As a condition of employment, teachers must adhere to the AUP terms. Because students are not employees, they and their parents generally sign the policy, indicating that they have read, understand, and agree to abide by it. Failure to do so can result in disciplinary action. However, school personnel and student use of their own computers and other electronic communication devices (ECDs) at school and especially away from school on their own time generally is beyond the scope of AUPs, given free speech protection. We discuss this complicated area of the law in Chapter 6.

Email warrants separate mention. For schools, e-mail is an electronic form of the school mailbox system. And just like the mailbox system, the school can control and monitor the contents of its email system. In the Perry decision discussed earlier, the U.S. Supreme Court ruled that school mailboxes are not automatically open forums for any type of communication among school personnel, their unions, and other persons. Because the mailbox system is a channel of communication owned and operated by the school, the school can control how it is used. For example, the school could limit the mailbox system to business only. Or it could open the system for certain types of communication but not others. This is called a "limited open forum." Once open to a particular category of communication, the school cannot discriminate within that category. For example, if the school permits its mailbox system to be used for school business and community announcements, it cannot prohibit certain types of community announcements.

Frequently, school districts will specify that the district reserves the right to monitor email usage as well as any and all files on computers or servers connected to the district's network and that no employee or student should have any expectation of privacy as to his or her usage. When students and parents sign a responsibility contract incorporating this provision, they agree to the condition. The same is true of employees who must abide by the district's AUP. Obtaining consent in this way dissolves any reasonable expectation of privacy; thus, the school can monitor email or internet use without violating the Electronic Communications Privacy Act, a federal law criminalizing the interception of email communications unless at least one party to the communication gives consent to the interception.

Controlling access to inappropriate material. Obscenity is not entitled to any constitutional protection under the First Amendment. This was the teaching of the U.S. Supreme Court in *Miller v. California* in 1973. In that case, the majority set forth a three-part test for determining when a material is obscene: whether the average person, applying contemporary community standards, would find that the work, taken as a whole, appeals to the prurient interest; whether the work depicts or describes, in a patently offensive way, sexual conduct specifically defined by the applicable law; and whether the work, taken as a whole, lacks serious literary, artistic, political, or scientific value. Pornography that is determined to be obscene under these standards is not constitutionally protected under either the federal or California Constitution. The California Penal Code has provisions providing criminal penalties for distributing or possessing obscene materials.

In 1990, the Supreme Court ruled that, while adults have a right to possess and view in their own homes pornography that is not legally obscene, a state can criminalize the possession and viewing of pornography involving children (*Osborne v. Ohio*, 1990). This is so because, unlike adult pornography, child pornography is always obscene (*New York v. Ferber*, 1992). Adult possession of obscene materials, including child pornography, is not protected by the speech or privacy provisions of the California Constitution either (*People v. Luera*, 2001). The California Penal Code has provisions imposing criminal penalties for distributing or possessing obscene materials.

The federal Children's Internet Protection Act (CIPA), which took effect in April 2001, requires public libraries as well as schools using federal E-rate or Elementary and Secondary Education Act funds for internet use or connections to have filtering devices in place to block out visual depictions deemed harmful to children. Failure to do so can result in loss of federal money (20 U.S.C. §§ 7131, 9134 (f)). Inappropriate material includes visual depictions that appeal to a prurient interest in nudity, sex, or excretion; that depict actual or simulated sexual acts or lewd exhibition of genitalia; and that lack serious artistic, literary, political, or scientific value to minors. CIPA provisions apply to students seventeen years of age and younger. For adult library patrons who wish access to pornography that is not obscene, CIPA permits libraries to disable the filters. In 2003, the U.S. Supreme Court upheld the statute (*American Library Association v. United States*, 2003).

Although CIPA provisions pertain to pictures, images, graphic image files, and other visual depictions, they do not apply to internet text. However, along with CIPA, Congress added a measure called the Neighborhood Children's Internet Protection Act (NCIPA) to require libraries and school districts to develop an internet safety policy as a condition for receiving federal assistance (47 U.S.C. § 254 (h)(5)). The policy must address access by minors to inappropriate matter on the internet and the Web; the security and safety of minors when using electronic mail, chat rooms, and other forms of electronic communication; hacking or other illegal activities; unauthorized disclosure, use, and dissemination of personal identification information regarding minors; and measures designed to restrict minors' access to material deemed harmful to them. What is deemed "harmful" is to be determined by the school or library.

While the application of CIPA to school computers gives the governing board considerable control over what material can be accessed on the internet through school computers, the control is not unlimited. As a vast electronic library, the use of the internet in public schools is likely to fall within the parameters of the U.S. Supreme Court's 1982 decision that school boards may not remove books from the school library merely because they disagree with their contents (*Board of Education of Island Trees v. Pico*, 1982), although the law is in flux with the current U.S. Supreme Court and should be checked before applying this ruling. In that case, three members of the Court held that students have a "right to receive ideas" as a necessary correlate to the right to express them. Two other justices did not endorse such a right but nevertheless appeared to agree that the First Amendment limits the board's discretion in removing library books (but the Court said nothing about refusing to purchase library books). In response to this decision, school districts usually employ some type of deliberative process for handling complaints about library books so that there are legitimate pedagogical purposes for their removal. These might include inappropriateness for the age level of the students, obsolescence, and redundancy. How much authority California districts have to remove books from the school library remains uncertain. While Education Code Section 18111 gives governing boards the authority to exclude books, publications, or papers of a sectarian, partisan, or denominational character, doing so may well constitute unconstitutional viewpoint censorship and discrimination against religion.

In the context of internet access in public schools, when does filtering or blocking go beyond the school district's legitimate right to control the content of the curriculum to constitute impermissible or inappropriate censorship? This is a difficult question with no easy answer. Such restrictive screening could be considered an intrusion on protected free speech because it prevents access to various forms of commercial and intellectual discourse. Likewise, a school district that prevents internet access on the district's high school library computers to material with the words *gay*, *lesbian*, and *homosexual* because the governing board opposes a gay lifestyle could run afoul of the thrust of the *Pico* decision. Because there may be print materials in the library containing such terms, the inconsistency inherent in such a policy is readily apparent. Matters like these are of less concern in the classroom because the U.S. Supreme Court has recognized that school board control in this setting is extensive (*Hazelwood School District v. Kuhlmeier*, 1988). As noted later in this chapter and in Chapter 6, both teacher and student rights in this setting are quite limited.

The best safeguard against losing in court is to employ a blocking or filtering system that is narrowly tailored to achieve its goal of eliminating access to inappropriate material without at the same time eliminating material that is entirely appropriate for library and classroom use. This is easier said than done because no screening system is foolproof. Some districts acknowledge up front that their screening system is imperfect and warn parents in their AUPs that students might encounter inappropriate material when using the school's computers. The assumption is that parents will accept some responsibility for educating their children about inappropriate internet use. CIPA also now requires schools to include an internet educational component designed to educate students about appropriate online behavior, including interacting with other individuals on social networking websites and in chat rooms, as well as cyberbullying awareness and response. Lessening district concern about liability is the federal Telecommunications Act of 1996, which provides that interactive computer service providers are not considered content providers but rather information conduits.

Privacy and the internet. As discussed in greater detail in Chapter 10, the federal Family Educational Rights and Privacy Act (FERPA) prevents disclosure of personally identifiable information about students and their families contained in school records without prior parent permission (the student's permission if the student is over eighteen years of age). California Education Code Section 49061 and following sections track this law. Educational records are those that are directly related to the student and are maintained by the school. The term is defined more broadly than just information in the student's cumulative folder. As defined in FERPA, education records include "records, files, documents, and other materials which contain information directly related to the student" maintained by the school or its personnel (20 U.S.C. § 1232g (a)(4)(A)). FERPA also requires that parents be notified of the posting of directory information by the school (names, addresses, and so on) and be given an opportunity to opt out prior to posting (Id. at (a)(5)(A)-(B)).

Privacy becomes an issue when personally identifiable information (e.g., a student's academic record or photograph) or school directory information (such as names and statistics about the district's football players) is included on the school's website. This is particularly a cause for concern when students create their own websites at school to upload to the internet. In these instances, parents should be informed and given the opportunity to decline to have personally identifiable information posted. If students and faculty members grant their permission, their original works may be published on school websites.

Distance learning and new internet privacy rights laws. Provisions have been added to the California Business and Professions Code protecting minors from commercial marketing by internet providers (Bus. & Prof. Code §§ 22580–22582). Federal law (the Children's Online Privacy Protection Act (COPPA)) already requires operators of 12 commercial internet sites or online services to provide notice of what personal information is collected and used, and gives parents the option of refusing to permit collection of additional data for children under age thirteen. Entitled the Privacy Rights for California Minors in the Digital World, the new California law expands this protection to minors under age eighteen by prohibiting operators of websites, online services, online applications, or mobile applications from marketing or advertising certain products or services to them. The restrictions apply as well to advertisers. The long list of restrictions includes alcoholic beverages, firearms, aerosol paint containers capable of defacing property, tobacco, drug paraphernalia, electronic cigarettes, and obscene matter. Disclosure of personal information about minors to third parties is prohibited. Operators also must permit minors who are registered users to remove or request to be removed content or information posted by them. This does not apply to information posted by third parties.

Another law added to the California Business and Professions Code is the Student Online Personal Information Protection Act (§§ 22584–22585). Effective January 1, 2016, this detailed law prohibits operators of websites, online services, online applications, or mobile applications used primarily for K–12 school purposes from using student information to target advertising to students, parents, or guardians; using covered information to amass student profiles; or selling student information. Disclosure of covered information is also prohibited unless in furtherance of a K–12 purpose germane to the site, service, or application under certain conditions set forth in the statute. Operators are to establish security measures and are required to delete student information if requested by the school or district. Operators are allowed to disclose information if required by federal or state law or if for legitimate research purposes. The law also allows the use of deidentified or aggregated student information for certain purposes, such as improving its educational products or to demonstrate the effectiveness of the product. Given both its importance and complexity, the statute should be viewed in its entirety.

As of 2023, this also extends to operators providing proctoring services in an educational setting (Student Test Taker Privacy Protection Act, Bus. & Prof. Code § 22588).

Newly enacted legislation, effective in 2025, renames this section the K–12 Pupil Online Personal Information Protection Act, reorders some subsections, and adds new language to California Business and Professions Code Sections 22584 and 22586. This language requires operators to delete a pupil's covered information under the operator's control and not subject to the California Consumer Privacy Act, provided that the pupil's parent, guardian, or education rights holder (or pupils themselves if 18 or older) requests the deletion and the pupil is no longer enrolled at the school or district for at least 60 days (2024 Cal. Stat. Ch. 935). The operator must also be provided with documentation that the student is no longer enrolled at the school or district.

A provision has been added to the Education Code requiring school districts, county offices of education, and charter schools to inform parents of programs they propose to use to monitor their students' social media activities and to collect and store the data and postings (Educ. Code § 49073.6). Many schools seek to gather this information to help prevent bullying, sexting, school violence, and student suicide. An opportunity for public comment must be provided at a regularly scheduled board meeting before such a program is adopted. Presumably to deter litigation over information collected about them from social media and to make corrections or deletions. To protect student privacy over the long term, all such information must be destroyed within one year after the student turns eighteen or is no longer enrolled. This legislation applies as well to third parties hired by the governing board to undertake this task.

Another provision added to the Education Code protects student privacy rights when schools enter into a contract with third parties to provide services including those that are cloud-based for digital storage, management, and retrieval of student records (Educ. Code § 49073.1). The law does not apply to existing contracts in effect before January 1, 2015, when the new law went into effect until their expiration, amendment, or renewal.

The establishment of the California Cradle-to-Career Data System became effective September 27, 2024 (Educ. Code § 10860). The data system will be "a source for actionable data and research on education," among other categories and "provide for expanded access to tools and services that support the navigation of the education-to-employment pipeline . . . including insight regarding early learning and care to grade 12, inclusive" ((a)–(b)(1)). The state expects the system to address disparities in opportunities and outcomes and support student guidance, among other goals (2)(A)–(B).

As digital learning becomes increasingly incorporated in school instructional programs, more federal and state laws protecting parent, student, and teacher privacy are likely to be enacted.

The Education Code defines distance learning as "instruction in which the pupil and instructor are in different locations and interact through the use of computer and communications technology" (Educ. Code § 51865(a)). Distance learning is generally delivered in two forms. First, synchronous instruction involves live two-way communication between the student and the teacher. Second, asynchronous instruction involves learning that occurs outside the teacher's presence and typically involves the student accessing resources and completing assignments issued by the teacher.

Although its use increased exponentially during the COVID-19 pandemic, distance learning was implemented several years before the pandemic. Specifically, starting in the 2014-2015 school year, school districts and county offices of education were permitted to include synchronous online instruction in computing average daily attendance for students in grades nine through twelve (former Educ. Code § 46300.8). The Education Code permitted instruction by distance learning through a certificated teacher who was required to confirm student attendance through visual recognition and ensure the student attended for the entire class. The Education Code also prohibited school districts and county offices of education from denying enrollment to students because they did not have access to computer hardware or software. The teacher-student ratio for synchronous online classes remains the same as for all other educational programs unless negotiated otherwise in a collective bargaining agreement.

Education Code Section 51865 authorizes the use of distance learning for the following four educational goals:

1. Equity in education, which requires that every pupil in California's public schools, and every adult in the state, have equal access to educational opportunities, regardless of where he or she lives or how small a school the pupil attends.

2. Quality in education, which would be enhanced through the creative application of telecommunications, as pupils are given the opportunity to interact with pupils from other cultures and geographical locations, and with outstanding educators from other educational institutions.

3. Diversity among educational institutions, which has been recognized in California through the support of various types of public educational institutions as well as of independent and private colleges and universities. Distance learning technology permits greater diversity in the means of instruction and in the delivery of educational and training services to an adult population that is more and more likely to seek education outside of

the traditional baccalaureate program designed for four consecutive years on a full-time basis shortly after graduating from high school.

4. Efficiency and accountability, which receive increasing emphasis as state budget resources become increasingly restricted. Distance learning technologies can be effective only through the cooperative efforts of individuals from different institutions, a collaboration that has the potential to reduce costs and increase efficiency. A technology-integrated educational delivery system would allow for the electronic transmittal of files and reports, thus providing the information needed for accountability more rapidly and at a lower cost, and for video teleconferencing for state and local education and other government agencies, thereby diminishing travel requirements.

Distance learning has many advantages. For example, distance learning may be used to offer instruction to students in certain rural areas who lack the means to access specialized classes. It also enables students in different settings to explore a common topic together. Distance learning may be used to interactively teach students (synchronous instruction) or can be made available to students when it is convenient for them to learn (asynchronous instruction). Online courses also enrich the education for students attending schools with limited educational offerings (e.g., no AP classes or qualified teachers for hard-to-staff subjects).

Distance learning also has its disadvantages. For instance, among many other reported disadvantages, student participation in lessons drops significantly and it can be difficult, if not impossible, for teachers to adequately monitor students through distance learning. Likewise, students often struggle to effectively manage their time which may result in diminished academic performance and increased anxiety. Distance learning and, in particular, asynchronous instruction, can impede immediate feedback resulting in misunderstandings and learning loss. Also, the costs associated with site-based instructors and technicians can be excessive. There are also some disadvantages, chiefly cost, the cost of having site-based instructors and technicians. Distance learning can also require extensive parent participation to ensure its success, but many parents may be unable to provide the needed level of assistance given work and other commitments.

During the onset of the COVID-19 pandemic in March 2020, and throughout the 2020–2021 school year, most school districts offered instruction to students through various forms of distance learning. Research revealed that the implementation of distance learning varied across the state as many districts struggled to obtain and introduce technology and other means necessary to deliver instruction to students. Research also revealed that students struggled to access significant portions of the curriculum, especially those who are English learners, students with special needs, students of color, and low-income students. Finally, teachers report significant academic, social, emotional, and behavioral concerns in students who learned primarily through distance learning during the pandemic.

The state's approach to addressing student education and related needs has resulted in litigation. For example, in the case of *Cayla J. v. California*, several students attending school in Los Angeles Unified School District and Oakland Unified School District, two of the state's largest school districts, sued the state contending that the state failed to provide adequate oversight, support and guidance during the pandemic resulting in significant gaps between the resources available to low-income student and students of color as compared to their wealthier peers. Ultimately, the matter settled with the state agreeing to dedicate $2 billion in evidence-based supports to remedy the learning loss suffered by those students most adversely affected educationally by the pandemic and the state's response.

As part of an effort to remedy some of the impacts of distance learning during the COVID-19 pandemic, the legislature made funding available to school districts through the Expanded Learning Opportunities Program (ELOP). Expanded learning offers before school, after school, summer, and intersession programs that are designed to assist kindergarten through sixth-grade students with developing academically, socially, emotionally, and physically through engaging learning experiences (Educ. Code § 46120). The legislature also intended the program to offer pupil-centered, results driven educational opportunities that include community partners and complement, but not replicate, learning activities during the regular school day. School districts are expected to focus their ELOP programs on schools located in its lowest income communities while maximizing the number of schools with ELOP programs throughout the school district's attendance area.

To access funding associated with ELOP, school districts must develop a plan that complies with all requirements described in Education Code Section 46120. The plan must be adopted by the school district's board of education in a public meeting and available through its website.

Distance learning also presents unique challenges related to materials. On the one hand, web-based curricula are easily updated and eliminate hard-copy texts. However, there are concerns about protecting students from commercialism that often accompanies web-based learning. Commercial vendors often mine the data to develop targeted advertising aimed at students. Education Code Section 35182.5(c)(3) prohibits school districts from entering into contracts for electronic services or products that require dissemination of advertising to students unless the district (1) at a public hearing, finds that the electronic product or service is essential for education; (2) determines that the district cannot otherwise afford the product or service; (3) provides written notice to parents that advertising will be used in the classroom or learning center; and (4) offers parents the opportunity to request in writing that their child not be exposed to advertising.

Virtual schools create new opportunities for homebound students and for homeschooling parents who lack the time or qualifications to provide a quality education for their children. An increasing number of charter schools in California offer some or all of their programs online. In addition, some schools have continued to offer virtual schools following the COVID-19 pandemic to meet the needs of students who succeed through distance learning or require that form of instruction for various reasons.

The movement toward more online instruction was apparent prior to the COVID-19 pandemic. Although distance learning presented several benefits for students and some certainly benefit significantly from that form of instruction, distance learning for most students and subgroups of students does not appear ideal. As described in the next chapter, charter schools classified as "non-classroom-based" are entitled to state funding, although the funding may be less than for their classroom-based counterparts.

Artificial intelligence. Artificial intelligence, commonly known as AI, likely represents the most significant technological trend in education at the time of publication. Simply put, AI comprises computer systems that are capable of learning, reasoning, and/or acting in a manner that would ordinarily require human intelligence, or speeds beyond what is possible through human intelligence.

It is expected that public schools will integrate AI into many aspects of their daily activities and services to students. For instance, the use of AI-driven resources may be used to evaluate student progress, address student needs, increase student engagement, and assist with data-driven decisions. Similarly, AI may be used to provide tutoring for students requiring assistance in specific areas, voice typing for students with disabilities, and translation support for students who require it. Further, as AI becomes increasingly integrated into the workforce, students must possess certain skills and understanding related to AI to be effective in the workforce.

It is critical that teachers receive sufficient professional development to assist them in effectively integrating AI into the classroom in a manner that safely enhances student learning. This professional development should include, among many other things, information related to the ethical use of AI, including privacy, appropriate sharing, plagiarism, and cyberbullying.

CDE recommends that schools integrate the "5 Big Ideas of AI" into curriculum to meet students' developmental needs. The "5 Big Ideas of AI" include the following:

- **Perception**: Understanding how AI systems perceive the world is fundamental. This includes image and speech recognition, natural language understanding, and sensory data processing. Integrating this idea into education enables students to comprehend how AI systems interact with the environment.
- **Representation**: AI relies on data and information representation. Teaching students how data is structured and organized empowers them to work with AI models and make informed decisions about data usage and manipulation.
- **Reasoning**: AI systems use reasoning to make decisions and solve problems. Integrating this idea helps students develop critical thinking skills, algorithmic reasoning, and the ability to assess the logic behind AI decisions.
- **Learning**: Machine learning is at the core of AI. Teaching students about machine learning algorithms, training models, and the concept of learning from data prepares them to understand the AI systems that surround them.
- **Societal Impact**: Recognizing the societal impact of AI, including ethical considerations and bias, is essential. This idea encourages students to engage in discussions about AI's role in society and its ethical implications. (See https://www.cde.ca.gov/pd/ca/cs/aiincalifornia.asp#:~:text=By%20 utilizing%20AI%20for%20planning,and%20make%20 data%2Dinformed%20decisions.)

Like many technological advancements, the law lags significantly behind the development of AI. Nonetheless, certain executive and legislative efforts have been implemented to address AI.

For instance, on September 6, 2023, Governor Newsom signed Executive Order N-12-13 designed to prepare California for the progress of AI. The Executive Order was designed to ensure the development of ethical, transparent, and trustworthy AI in California. The Executive Order directed various state agencies to develop risk-analysis reports to identify potential threats to California's infrastructure related to AI.

The Executive Order also required state agencies to (1) develop procurement procedures designed to improve the efficiency, effectiveness, accessibility, and equity of government operations; (2) identify the most significant benefits of AI to the state; (3) develop guidelines to analyze the impact AI tools may have on vulnerable communities; (4) provide training to state employees on the use of AI to achieve equitable outcomes; (5) establish partnerships with the University of California, Berkeley, and Stanford University to consider and evaluate the impacts of AI and identify efforts the state should take to advance its leadership in the industry; (6) engage legislative partners and stake holders in the development of policy recommendations, and (7) periodically evaluate the impacts of AI on an ongoing basis.

On November 21, 2023, Governor Newsom's office released the first report required under the Executive Order. The report includes a preliminary analysis of risks and high-risk use cases along with the economic and transformative benefits of AI; examines how the state could prioritize the use of AI; identifies potential uses of AI to improve accessibility of government services, including groups with certain barriers, such as language barriers, and those who may be disproportionately not accessing available services; and describes potential AI risks.

Similarly, on October 30, 2023, President Biden issued an Executive Order on Safe, Secure, and Trustworthy Artificial Intelligence. The Executive Order is intended to "seize the process and manage the risks of artificial intelligence" by directing a variety of different actions. Namely, the Executive Order includes safety and security standards designed to test AI mechanisms and share the results of that testing with the government; develop standards to ensure AI systems are safe, secure, and trustworthy; protect against the use of AI to develop dangerous biological materials; protect against fraud; and develop proper military and intelligence community use of AI.

The Executive Order acknowledges that AI may be used to improve product, service, and education, but notes that it may do so at the risk of Americans' safety. The Executive Order aims to address these concerns and protect consumers, patients, and students by requiring the development of a safety program to receive reports of, and remedy, unsafe practices. In addition, the Executive Order seeks to shape AI's potential to transform education by creating resources to support educators in implementing AI-enabled educational tools such as personalized tutoring in schools.

The Executive Order also addresses Americans' privacy and acknowledges the heightened risk AI poses to privacy given that AI makes it easier to extract, identify, and exploit personal data, particularly by companies that use data to train AI systems. The Executive Order seeks to accelerate privacy-preserving techniques, strengthen privacy research and technology, evaluate agency use of commercially available information, and strengthen privacy guidance for federal agencies, and develop guidelines for federal agencies to evaluate privacy-preserving techniques.

The Executive Order aims to advance equity and civil rights and acknowledges that irresponsible use of AI may result in discrimination, bias, and other injustices. The Executive Order provides guidelines for landlords, federal benefits programs, and federal contractors designed to prevent AI algorithms from exacerbating discrimination. The Executive Order also coordinates training, technical assistance, and coordination between the Department of Justice and federal civil rights offices concerning the best practices for investigating and prosecuting civil rights violations related to AI. Finally, the Executive Order seeks to develop best practices in the use of AI for sentencing, parole, probation, pretrial release, detention, risk assessments, surveillance, crime forecasting, predictive policing, and forensic analysis.

The Executive Order also targets a multitude of other areas and seeks to develop resources, guidelines, and other measures to protect Americans. The other areas include workers' rights, innovation and competition, American leadership abroad, and responsible and effective government use of AI.

Administrative agencies have created many resources for educators related to the use of AI in schools. For example, the U.S. Department of Education's Office of Technology has issued a policy report titled "Artificial Intelligence and the Future of Teaching and Learning: Insights and Recommendations" that addresses the need for sharing knowledge, engaging educators, and refining technology plans and policy for AI in education (see https://tech.ed.gov/ai/.)

Likewise, the California Department of Education has issued guidance related to learning with and about AI. The guidance describes several resources, explains, among many other things, the safe use of AI, pros and cons of AI, and social impacts of AI. (See https://www.cde.ca.gov/pd/ca/cs/aiincalifornia.asp#:~:text=By%20utilizing%20AI%20for%20planning,and%20make%20data%2Dinformed%20decisions.)

It is anticipated that many pieces of legislation related to AI will be proposed and enacted in the coming months and years. Readers are well advised to closely review legislative advancements when addressing AI issues as many changes are expected following publication of this resource.

As demonstrated through the separation between students and teachers during the COVID-19 pandemic, technology cannot replace personal relationships. Educators and those responsible for ensuring student success should ensure that AI is used to augment, and not replace, the value and importance of personal connections and relationships with students. Educators should also be particularly sensitive to ensuring the use of AI does not perpetuate inaccurate or biased information or expose students to hate, racist, or bigoted information. If implemented effectively, it appears that AI could be used to allow the educator to reduce their focus on certain tasks and dedicate additional time to supporting students in targeted areas and building relationships with them.

ASSESSMENT AND ACCOUNTABILITY

Along with the specification of curriculum content standards has come unprecedented emphasis on performance for students, their teachers, and their schools. The roots of so-called high-stakes testing go back to 1983, when the U.S. Department of Education issued a report on the relatively poor performance of American public school students. Entitled *A Nation at Risk,* the report called for renewed emphasis on academic rigor and assessment. Over the intervening years, many reforms have been instituted, yet student performance is little improved, if at all. Administered by the U.S. Department of Education, the National Assessment of Educational Progress (NAEP) is the nation's only representative and continuing assessment of what students know and can do in various subject-matter areas. It is known as "the nation's report card," though its findings have been viewed with some skepticism because states have different participation rates. In recent years, for example, only about 35 percent of the nation's fourth and eighth graders performed at or above the proficient level on the NAEP reading and math tests. For California, the percentage is lower. Along with tightened state curricular requirements has come more frequent and rigorous state assessment to determine how well students, their teachers, and their schools are doing. California students do better on state tests than on NAEP, largely because these tests relate to the curriculum taught in the state's public schools. In 2011, for example, 64 percent of fourth graders and 57 percent of eighth graders scored proficient or higher in English language arts on the California Standards Test. However, the scores varied significantly by student subgroup.

The Influence of the No Child Left Behind Act

Concerned that the federal government's expenditures under Title I to improve the education of disadvantaged students have increased dramatically over the years with relatively little improvement in student achievement, Congress reauthorized the Elementary and Secondary Education Act in the form of the No Child Left Behind (NCLB) Act in 2001. NCLB required states to assess annually every public school student's progress in reading and math in grades three through eight, and once during grades ten through twelve. Tests in science were required not less than one time in grades three through five, grades six through nine, and grades ten through twelve. The tests had to be aligned with the state's curriculum standards, and each school had to make adequate yearly progress as determined by the state on the state's assessments toward having all students achieve 100 percent proficiency by 2013–2014. Achievement data had to be broken down by race, ethnicity, gender, English-language proficiency, migrant status, disability status, and low-income status. In addition, states were required to participate every two years in the NAEP math and reading assessments for fourth- and eighth-grade students. This requirement was designed to compare results in one state with those of another state, as well as to demonstrate the degree of rigor of a state's assessment program. Penalties were required under NCLB for persistently low-performing schools on the state's assessment tests, though the penalties applied only to schools receiving Title I money. The force behind NCLB was the loss of some or all federal funding for education. Starting in 2012, states could apply for waivers from major portions of the act.

In part because of the lack of success as measured by student performance, in 2015 the NCLB Act was replaced by the much less controlling Every Student Succeeds Act (ESSA). The revision eliminates the need, among other provisions, for waivers from requirements such as assuring adequate yearly progress toward all students becoming proficient on math and reading tests or face loss of federal funding. The annual yearly progress requirement has been eliminated along with escalating consequences for schools that do not measure up. ESSA still requires that students be tested in reading and math from third to eighth grade and at least once in high school. States are to intervene to assist low-performing schools including those with underperforming subgroups. School evaluation is to include at least one other measure beyond student test scores such as graduation rates or English proficiency for nonnative speakers.

California has had mixed success in meeting the requirements of the ESSA. For example, in 2019, the U.S. Department of Education (DOE) had placed the state on high-risk status, finding that California satisfied one of the measures but not others. As late as 2022 in a letter to the California Department of Education, the U.S. DOE made clear that California's remaining issues had not been resolved. California has developed a seven-year plan to improve performance. More detailed information on this complex area of accountability can be found at the CDE California Accountability Model and School Dashboard at https://www.cde.ca.gov/ta/ac/.

The state's earlier assessment and accountability standards, as evidenced in the Standardized Testing and Reporting (STAR) System and the California High

School Exit Examination (CAHSEE), were replaced by the movement to implement common core curriculum content standards. Governor Jerry Brown signed Senate Bill 484 in October 2013, which embraced the development of academically rigorous content standards in all major subject areas and sets forth a new assessment system. The purpose is to model and promote high-quality teaching and learning activities across the curriculum so that students can acquire the knowledge, skills, and processes needed for success in the information-based global economy of the 21st century (Educ. Code § 60602.5). The student assessment system is designed to hold schools and districts accountable for the achievement of all students in meeting the standards.

Identified as the Measurement of Academic Performance and Progress (MAPP) in SB 484, the new system has been renamed the California Assessment of Student Performance and Progress (CAASPP). It replaces most of STAR (Educ. Code § 60640). The new system is based on the work of a multistate organization called the Smarter Balanced Assessment Consortium that developed assessments aligned with the common core state curriculum standards. In 2017, the California High School Exit Exam (CAHSEE) ended, given its lack of linkage to the common core. In the next year, the legislature replaced the Academic Performance Index (API) with a "single multiple measures public school accountability system" (Educ. Code § 52052 (a)). All references to API were deleted in the Education Code.

The current assessment system reports student academic performance in relation to state academically rigorous content and performance standards and in terms of college and career readiness skills. When appropriate, the performance reports include a measure of growth describing the student's status in relation to past performance. From the funds available for that purpose, each local educational agency shall administer assessments to each of its pupils as identified in CAASPP. These assessments shall include the use of accessibility resources, as may be determined by CDE. (Educ. Code §60640(f)(1).

Students with special needs unable to participate in the testing shall be given an alternate assessment (Educ. Code § 60640 (k)).

CAASPP encompasses a summative assessment in English language arts and mathematics for grades three through eight and grade eleven that measures content standards adopted by the State Board of Education (SBE); grade-level science assessments in grades five, eight, and ten until a successor assessment is implemented; the California Alternate Performance Assessment (CAPA) in English language arts and mathematics in grades two to eleven and in science in grades five, eight, and ten until a successor instrument is implemented; a voluntary early assessment program for grade eleven students in English language arts and mathematics; and a primary language assessment program aligned to English language arts standards for students enrolled in dual language immersion programs. By March 1, 2016, the Superintendent of Public Instruction (SPI) was to submit to the State Board of Education (SBE) recommendations for expanding CAASPP to include additional assessments in such subjects as history and social science, technology, and visual and performing arts.

CAASPP assessment in English language arts and mathematics was field-tested in the 2013–2014 school year. There was no assessment in these areas pursuant to the old California Standards Text because the common core curriculum together with CAASPP transforms databases and disrupts trend analysis. Adding to the transition was the adoption of the Local Control Funding Formula.

The adoption of the new assessment system affected the calculation of school and district scores. In addition, Senate Bill 484 addressed a number of matters relating to student assessment and school accountability. Several of the more significant include:

- Based on recommendations from the Superintendent of Public Instruction, the State Board of Education must set performance standards on the CAASPP summative tests. Once adopted, these performance standards are to be reviewed by the state board every five years (Educ. Code § 60648).

- The CDE must determine how school districts are progressing toward implementation of a technology-enabled assessment system and the extent to which assessments aligned to the common core standards in English language arts and mathematics can be fully implemented (Educ. Code § 60648.5).

- A paper and pencil version of any computer-based CAASPP assessment is to be made available for students who are unable to access the computer-based version of the assessment for a maximum of three years after a new operational test is first administered (Educ. Code § 60640 (e)).

- With approval of the SBE, the CDE is required to develop a three-year plan of obtaining independent technical advice and consultation regarding ways of improving CAASPP. Areas to examine include studies focused on validity, alignment, testing fairness and reliability, reporting procedures, and special student populations such as English learners and students with special needs (Educ. Code §60649).

For the latest information about CAASPP, go to www.caaspp.org.

SUMMARY

This chapter began with a detailed examination of California school attendance law. But there is more to quality education than getting students to attend school. The learning environment must be safe and engaging. It must reach each child where they are and provide each of them the tools to develop the skills necessary for successful adult life. There are numerous provisions in California law to make it so. Equally important, the curriculum must be challenging, teachers must be of high quality, and instruction must be effective. California has embarked on an ambitious route toward school improvement; the curriculum content standards, and the accompanying student assessment system (CAASPP), support the need for data to measure success.

NCLB was important because it placed great pressure on states to make sure that all students become proficient in mastering state standards. The ESSA built on that system and the efforts continue today. The danger is that the resources and teaching skills may not be available to improve performance, especially for all students. California has taken steps to bridge the gap by specifically targeting many of its reforms to disadvantaged students and others needing special instructional attention. In particular, the state's class size reduction program and enhanced teacher preparation measures are designed with these students in mind. How well federal and state-mandated reform of traditional public schools will succeed remains to be seen.

3 EQUITY, ADEQUACY, AND SCHOOL FINANCE

Throughout the 1960s and early 1970s, California's spending on public education was among the highest in the nation, with average per-pupil expenditures that were 10 percent higher than schools in other states. Throughout the 1980s, California's school spending declined to the national average. By the mid-1990s, it fell well below the national average, with per-pupil expenditures as much as 17 percent below those of the rest of the nation, according to the National Center for Education Statistics. In the past several years, the state has ranked near the middle among states in per-pupil expenditure. The state drops to the bottom ten when adjusted for personnel costs, which are higher in California than elsewhere.

What has caused this dramatic change in fortune for California's schoolchildren? As this chapter indicates, the answer is multifaceted. Throughout the 1970s, California courts wrestled with the issue of equitable school funding in the landmark *Serrano v. Priest* school equity case. The *Serrano* rulings prompted the legislature to overhaul the distribution of California's school resources. A significant setback to funding schools occurred in 1978 when California voters limited their property tax burdens by approving Proposition 13. The approval resulted in a centralized system of school finance that slowed the growth of per-pupil expenditures at the very time the California school system was both expanding and undergoing significant demographic changes. This combination spawned new litigation and stimulated reform efforts.

Understanding the problems of the state's school finance system is made more difficult by its sheer complexity. As one state appellate court noted in 1992, California's system of funding schools is "Byzantine in its intricacy and complexity" (*California Teachers Association v. Hayes*, 1992). Such complexity merits more than a chapter's discussion, and in fact, a book-length treatment of the subject may prove insufficient to fully address the many forces that have shaped California's approach to funding public education, how the system works in day-to-day school budgeting, and its effect on schoolchildren. Instead, this chapter examines the role of money in schooling and seeks to explain how California's school finance litigation has shaped how both the state's and the nation's schools are funded. We describe the litigation and how it changed the way schools are funded. We also look at competing approaches to funding public education that frame the legal arguments. In addition, we examine how both traditional public and charter schools are currently funded in California. At the outset, it is important to note that changes in the current system may soon result from litigation and legislative reform.

DOES MONEY MATTER?

The relationship between school spending and student achievement has been the source of heated debate since 1966, when the federally commissioned study Equality of Educational Opportunity—commonly known as the Coleman Report, after its principal investigator, Professor James S. Coleman—asserted that schools have little influence on student performance that can be separated from family background. Since then, researchers have worked to identify educational production functions that measure the effect of a wide variety of student, parent, community, and school influences on students' academic achievement. School spending is a key ingredient in such analyses as well as one of the most hotly disputed. Clearly, money is important—it buys school buildings and textbooks and pays the salaries of trained teachers, counselors, and administrators—but how much money is necessary to educate students effectively? The research is divided on this point because school spending does not demonstrate a clear or consistent relationship with student achievement. Many high-spending districts have disappointing student outcomes, while many low-spending districts are able to produce high levels of student achievement.

Class size reduction is an interesting case in point. It makes intuitive sense that teachers can better affect the learning of smaller student groups, but the research on smaller classes and achievement increases is disappointing. California presents an interesting example. In 1997, the California legislature approved funding to reduce the size of K–3 classrooms to twenty students. Evaluation of the program during its early stages by a consortium of research institutions found that math scores increased slightly, and reading scores were unchanged despite an expenditure approaching $2 billion a year. What does not appear to be studied is the impact on social-emotional growth, especially for students with challenges in this area.

While class size reduction has had a weak effect on California's student achievement, it has proved a strong force in the state's labor market for teachers. Reductions in the number of students per teacher create an increased demand for teachers as more teachers are needed to teach the same number of students. In California, this increase in demand was not met with a corresponding increase in the supply of credentialed teachers.

Many teachers working with hard-to-serve student populations in predominately low-income schools moved when class size reduction created new teaching positions in what they viewed as more desirable districts. Administrators in many predominately low-income schools were unable to find credentialed teachers to fill vacancies and were forced to hire uncertified teachers with little or no classroom experience.

> The lack of convincing research on the relationship of funding to student achievement was one of the reasons the U.S. Supreme Court gave for ruling that interdistrict funding disparities are not unconstitutional, even when there is disparate impact among a group of families who were both poor and Mexican-American (*San Antonio Independent School District v. Rodriguez*, 1973).

Common sense suggests that funding does indeed matter. Justice Thurgood Marshall, dissenting in *Rodriguez*, noted ironically that if financial variations do not affect educational quality, "It is difficult to understand why a number of our country's wealthiest school districts, which have no legal obligation to argue in support of the constitutionality of the Texas legislation [which reduced interdistrict funding disparities but did not eliminate them], have nevertheless zealously pursued its cause before this Court" (p. 85).

The central policy concern is not that money doesn't matter, for clearly schools with modern and well-equipped facilities, a strong and comprehensive curriculum, and high-quality teachers are preferable to schools with poor facilities, a sparse curriculum, and unqualified teachers. Instead, the central policy issue is how best to distribute school resources to maximize learning opportunities for all students . For a time, the preferred means to achieve this goal centered on ending the often glaring per-pupil spending disparities among school districts. More recently, attention has shifted to ensure that every child is provided the necessary resources to reach a certain level of proficiency on state-mandated achievement tests and overcome learning loss associated with the COVID-19 pandemic. These are very different goals, and, as we will see, California policymakers have wrestled with both.

THE QUEST FOR EQUITY

Foundation Funding

The local property tax has long been the primary funding source for local governments in the United States. In most states, the property tax is levied by local governments, and each taxing jurisdiction sets its tax rate through the budgetary decision-making processes, voter initiative, or both. The generally decentralized and local character of property taxes allows for local communities to have a strong voice in how the tax is levied and how much support is provided to public schools.

In many states, property taxes satisfy the principles of horizontal and vertical equity because landowners in similarly situated residences can expect to pay about the same in taxes, and homeowners residing in more expensive homes can usually expect to pay more. As discussed later in this chapter, Proposition 13 has largely eroded horizontal equity in California's property tax structure by restricting the reassessment of a property's market value until it is sold or changes ownership.

One advantage of using property taxes to fund public schools is that they are a generally stable source of revenue. Unlike the sales and income tax, which are highly sensitive to economic trends, property values—and subsequently, property taxes—are less affected by short-term economic fluctuations and remain relatively constant through economic downturns. Thus, funding public education through property taxes ensures a stable funding base for schools during difficult economic times.

Property taxes are ad valorem taxes, which means they are calculated as a percentage of property value. Different types of property may be taxed at different rates depending on how the properties are used. Residential, business, and agricultural properties generally are taxed differently. To determine the amount of tax, a property's assessed value is multiplied by the locally determined levy rate. For example, a homeowner living in a home with an assessed value of $150,000 in a community that levies a property tax of $1.50 per $100 of assessed value would pay property taxes in the amount of $2,250.

Historically, California was a wealthy state, and it was well able to fund its public schools by relying on the local property tax, augmented by a system of state-funded flat grants for all students. This was true until the 1940s, when the state experienced rapid population growth. The emergence of communities with sizable amounts of industrial and residential property meant that they were able to raise far larger amounts of revenue through the local property tax, and at relatively low tax rates, than more sparsely settled regions of the state could raise with higher tax rates. This resulted in growing disparities across the state in the amount of revenue communities could raise for local public services, including schooling. Pressed with the need to develop a more efficient method of funding its rapidly expanding public education system, California adopted the foundation plan approach to school finance in 1947.

Foundation programs have been a popular method of funding public education. Organized around the principle that students throughout a state should receive some minimum level of educational services, foundation plans strive to offset local district wealth and equalize the distribution of educational resources by ensuring that each student has access to a basic education, which is paid for by a threshold level of education spending. Each school district is responsible for a share of this funding through its property tax effort at some predetermined uniform tax rate; for districts with revenues that fall short, the state makes up the difference.

Because state resources are distributed in inverse proportion to a local district's ability to raise revenue, poorer districts with low assessed property values receive more state support while wealthier districts receive less.

In the years before the *Serrano* decisions discussed below, California operated two foundation programs: one for equalization aid and a second for supplemental aid. Although state equalization contributions diminished as a district's per-pupil wealth increased, the California Constitution had provided each district with a basic aid floor of $120 per student regardless of wealth since 1952 (Article IX, § 6). The basic aid provision, a holdover from the state's early flat-grant program, ensured that even the wealthiest districts received some state aid. For supplemental aid, however, the foundation level was set just above the median assessed property value per pupil, and most supplemental aid went only to low-wealth districts.

Foundation plans equalize spending up to the established minimum foundation level, but local districts generally enjoy latitude in generating additional school funding beyond that minimum. In principle, this ensures that local communities with differing preferences for schooling are able to obtain their desired level of educational services through local tax efforts. In practice, however, differences in the fiscal capacity of local districts frequently translate into wide variances in the amount of revenue available for schools. Noting that the differences in the amount of resources available to wealthy and poor school districts implied differences in the quality of education provided, school finance reform efforts began to address concerns about the equity of school finance systems that relied primarily on local property tax bases for school funding. The concern over inequity in the distribution of school resources was well aligned with the changing legal interpretations of the equal protection clause in the Fourteenth Amendment to the U.S. Constitution and, later, state constitutions as well.

By the 1960s, it was apparent that the equal protection clause had taken on new meaning in the eyes of the U.S. Supreme Court. Worded simply, the clause specifies that no state shall "deny to any person within its jurisdiction the equal protection of the laws." In 1954, the U.S. Supreme Court relied on the clause to find segregated schools unconstitutional in the landmark case *Brown v. Board of Education*, 347 U.S. 483. The Court held that "separate educational facilities are inherently unequal" and that the inequity created by segregated schools deprived Black children of the equal protection of the laws. Although the Court stopped short of defining education as a fundamental right under the Constitution, its language straightforwardly addressed the importance of education to American society:

> Today, education is perhaps the most important function of state and local governments. Compulsory school attendance laws and the great expenditures for education both demonstrate our recognition of the importance of education to our democratic society. It is required in the performance of our most basic public responsibilities, even service in the armed forces. It is the foundation of good citizenship. (p. 493)

The importance that the high court gave to education in *Brown* and the aggressive stance it took in the 1960s to compensate the victims of racial segregation by requiring school integration caught the attention of school finance reformers. If the equal protection clause could be used to halt unequal treatment based on race in schooling, could it also be used to halt unequal treatment based on wealth? This thinking led to litigation in both state and federal courts on applying the equal protection clause to interdistrict disparities in school finance. What does not appear to be studied is the impact on social-emotional growth, especially for students with challenges in this area.

Litigation

State court:* Serrano v. Priest I *(1971). On behalf of a class of public school students in all but the richest school district in California, John Serrano filed a lawsuit in state court against the state treasurer Ivy Priest and others who administered the California school finance system, contending that it denied them the equal protection of the laws under the federal and California constitutions. It would become a seminal ruling in school finance. The question for the California Supreme Court was whether the trial court judge correctly dismissed the case.

The justices began by noting that over 90 percent of public school funding in the state was derived from local district property taxes and aid from the state foundation program known as the State School Fund. The local property tax was by far the major source of these funds, contributing over half of all educational revenue. The amount of money a local district could raise depended on the assessed valuation of real property within its borders and on its tax rate. Tax bases varied significantly across California school districts. While the state had placed a cap on the property tax rate, nearly all districts had voted to override the statutory limit. The central problem was that, even with a high tax rate, school districts with low assessed valuations could not match the spending levels of property-rich school districts.

The court noted that the state's foundation program did little to ameliorate funding differences. While the equalization component of the foundation program varied inversely with the district's property wealth, substantial disparities remained. In the Los Angeles County school district of Baldwin Park, the school district of plaintiff John Serrano, per-pupil spending for the 1968–1969 school year was $577. For the same school year, the nearby Beverly Hills school district spent $1,231 per pupil. The source of this variance in spending was not the willingness of Beverly Hills residents to tax themselves at a higher rate. Instead, the difference emerged because Beverly Hills had much greater property wealth than did Baldwin Park. For the 1968–1969 school year, Beverly Hills had $50,885 in per-pupil assessed property value, and residents paid school taxes of $2.38 per $100 of assessed property value. In marked contrast, Baldwin Park had a per-pupil assessed property value of $3,706. Its residents paid $5.48 per $100 of assessed valuation, yet they were able to spend less than half as much on their children's education. Similar differences existed across the state.

In overturning the trial judge's ruling by a six-to-one margin, the California high court chiefly relied on the Fourteenth Amendment equal protection clause. The majority indicated in a footnote that the court previously had construed several provisions of the California Constitution to be the substantial equivalent of the equal protection clause. These included Article I, Section 11 (now Article IV, § 16), which provided that "all laws of a general nature shall have a uniform operation," and Article I, Section 21 (now Article I, § 7 (b)), which provided that no citizen or class of citizens shall be granted privileges or immunities "which, upon the same terms, shall not be granted to all citizens." The court's footnoted observation would become central to its second *Serrano* ruling in 1976 (discussed later in this chapter).

The justices began by noting that, although the U.S. Supreme Court had not directly ruled that wealth, like race, was a "suspect" classification under the equal protection clause, it appeared to be poised to do so. This distinction is important because a suspect classification requires the state to establish a compelling justification for the unequal treatment, a very high criterion. The California Supreme Court rejected the claim of state defendants that wealth could not be a suspect classification like race, because wealth is related to school districts, not individuals. The court was equally unimpressed by the state's assertion that levels of educational expenditure do not affect the quality of education. Nor was it necessary for the plaintiffs to prove that the state had intentionally discriminated against residents in property-poor districts. The court pointed out that it had held eight years before that racial segregation in schools was unconstitutional regardless of cause (*Jackson v. Pasadena City School District*, 31 Cal. Rptr. 606 (Cal. 1963)) and that it should be the same with wealth discrimination.

The justices also accepted Serrano's argument that education is a fundamental constitutional right even though it is not mentioned in the U.S. Constitution. The court pointed to the U.S. Supreme Court's observation in *Brown v. Board of Education* that "education is perhaps the most important function of state and local governments" and noted its own observation in the *Jackson* decision that education must be made available to all on an equal basis. While citing U.S. Supreme Court decisions to support this assertion, the justices also referenced the California Constitution in discussing why education is so fundamental that its funding must be equalized.

Having concluded that wealth is a suspect classification and education a fundamental right, the justices rejected the state's argument that deference to local control satisfied the compelling interest criterion. Under the present system, the court noted, "Such fiscal free will is a cruel illusion for the poor districts" because, although they express their willingness to tax themselves high for quality education, they are precluded from matching the spending levels of the rich districts (p. 620). The justices also rejected the contention of the state defendants that, if spending for education had to be equalized, so would spending for other social services. Education, they wrote, is unique among public services.

The case was sent back to the trial court for further proceedings, meaning that the trial judge was in a position to order the state to develop a system of school financing that would satisfy a compelling interest test. Meanwhile, *San Antonio Independent School District v. Rodriguez*, another case on the same issue (discussed later in this chapter), would soon reach the U.S. Supreme Court. The question among school finance reformers was whether the California Supreme Court had accurately prophesied how the justices on the nation's highest court would rule. It had not.

Federal court: **San Antonio Independent School District v. Rodriguez *(1973)*.** As noted earlier, the California Supreme Court based its *Serrano I* decision primarily on the Fourteenth Amendment's equal protection clause. *San Antonio Independent School District v. Rodriguez,* mentioned earlier, is an important case from Texas. It reached the U.S. Supreme Court in the early 1970s, giving the Court the opportunity to rule definitively on the subject.

In the late 1940s, Texas established the Minimum Foundation School Program (MFSP) to help ameliorate glaring inequities among school districts in per-pupil expenditures. The program involved local and state contributions to a special fund to help pay for teacher salaries, operating expenses, and transportation costs in property-poor school districts. Eighty percent of the funding came from the state, with the remaining amount coming from local school districts on an ability-to-pay basis. Each district was required to levy a property tax to support its contribution, and any excess could be retained to support local schools.

MFSP helped reduce the inequities but did not eliminate them. For example, in 1967–1968, Edgewood Independent School District, serving a predominately Mexican American population in the inner city of San Antonio, retained $26 per pupil in local funding above its MFSP contribution at a property tax rate of $1.05 per $100 of assessed evaluation. MFSP added $222 per pupil, with an additional $108 coming from federal funds. Altogether, Edgewood had $356 per pupil to spend. By contrast, Alamo Heights Independent School District, located in an affluent area of San Antonio, retained $333 per pupil for its schools beyond its MFSP contribution at a property tax rate of 85 cents per $100 of assessed evaluation. MFSP added $225 per pupil. An additional $36 from federal funds gave the district a total of $594 per pupil, nearly twice that of the per-pupil expenditure in Edgewood. Differences like these existed elsewhere in Texas and in states across the nation.

As in *Serrano,* the property-poor districts argued that education is a constitutionally protected fundamental right and that a public finance system that discriminated against poor districts violated the equal protection clause of the Fourteenth Amendment to the U.S. Constitution. They also argued that poverty, like race, is a "suspect" classification under the Fourteenth Amendment, requiring the state to establish a compelling state reason to justify inequality in school finance. Texas agreed it could not justify its finance program if poverty were to be declared a suspect classification. For its part, the state sought to argue that education is not a fundamental right protected by the U.S. Constitution and that poverty is not a suspect classification. This being the case, all the state had to do to prevail under the equal protection clause was to show that its program served a rational purpose.

The state was confident that the fact that MFSP did ameliorate the differences, though imperfectly, would satisfy this lower criterion.

By a narrow 5–4 margin, the Court agreed with the state. The majority noted that education is not specifically identified as a constitutional right in the U.S. Constitution and chose not to infer it from explicit constitutional protections like freedom of speech.

With regard to the suspect classification argument, the majority noted that, unlike racial minorities, the "poor" are not easily definable. Indeed, the Court noted that there was no evidence that the poorest families were necessarily clustered in the poorest school districts. Thus, all the state had to do to prevail concerning the equal protection challenge was to establish that its plan was rational. And while imperfect, the MFSP did reduce the disparities significantly.

The decision came as a great blow to those who had hoped that the Court would do for the poor what it had done for racial minorities. And for school finance reformers in California, the decision came as a serious setback because the California Supreme Court had based its ruling in *Serrano* primarily on the Fourteenth Amendment equal protection clause.

The U.S. Supreme Court majority did offer some hope, conceding that inequities in school finance were apparent. Wrote Justice Lewis F. Powell: "We hardly need add that this Court's action today is not to be viewed as placing its judicial imprimatur on the status quo. The need is apparent for reform in tax systems which may well have relied too long and too heavily on the local property tax." He added, "And certainly innovative thinking as to public education, its methods, and its funding is necessary to assure both a higher level of quality and greater uniformity of treatment" (p. 58). However, any reform in school finance would have to come from state legislators and state judges. With the door to the federal courthouse closed, attention shifted back to these entities in California.

State court: **Serrano v. Priest II** *(1976).* Meanwhile, the California Legislature swung into action following the California Supreme Court's *Serrano I* decision and passed Senate Bill 90 and Assembly Bill 1276 in 1972. These bills attempted to comply with the *Serrano* decision by increasing both the foundation level of state aid and the computational tax rate used to assess the districts' share of funding.

Under these bills, all districts continued to receive basic aid of $125 per average daily attendance (ADA)—$120 of which was constitutionally mandated. What had changed was a substantial increase in the foundation level, the minimum amount the state guaranteed to all districts from state or local funds. For elementary students, the foundation level rose from $355 to $765, and for high school students, from $488 to $950.

Increases in the maximum computational tax rate meant that local districts' share of the foundation plan funding also increased. The rate rose from $1 to $2.23 per $100 of assessed valuation at the elementary level and from $0.80 to $1.64 at the high school level. If districts were unable to reach the foundation levels at these rates, then the state made up the difference. Of course, many districts could do so at much lower tax rates. The bills provided some property tax relief by increasing the homeowner exemption for residential property and the property tax exemption for business inventories.

The most lasting and significant effect of this legislation was the introduction of the revenue limit system. Under this system, a district's initial or base revenue limit in 1973–1974 was determined by its total per-pupil funding from both property tax revenues and noncategorical state aid for the 1972–1973 school year. A district could not levy taxes at a higher rate that would increase its 1972–1973 base revenues beyond a permitted yearly inflation rate unless the voters decided otherwise.

Wide variances in districts' assessed property values resulted in large differences among districts' initial 1973–1974 base revenue limits, with the wealthiest districts generating three to four times as much in per-pupil funding as the poorest districts, often at very low tax rates. To equalize these differences over time, districts having a tax rate that produced revenues in excess of foundation levels received inflation adjustments from the state, which decreased in magnitude as those revenues rose above foundation levels.

Districts having base revenues that, when added to the full inflation allowance, did not reach the foundation level were permitted growth rates of up to 16 percent of the preceding year's revenue limit. The goal of this approach, known as the "squeeze formula," was that per-pupil spending of high- and low-wealth districts would converge over time—the spending of low-wealth districts would be leveled up, and the spending of high-wealth districts would be leveled down.

While the central intent of the legislation was equalized per-pupil spending, it allowed districts to increase their revenue limit spending by increasing the local tax rate if a majority of voters approved an override. The rationale was that, because education is a local enterprise, the residents of a particular district ought to have the discretion to decide how much they wish to spend on their school systems. Many districts adversely affected by the constraints of the revenue limit and squeeze systems were able to pass such initiatives and thus weaken the effect of the law. Viewing the revised finance system as still inequitable, the plaintiffs filed suit again. Citing *Serrano I*, the trial court struck down the revised finance system, and the plaintiffs appealed the decision to the California Supreme Court.

By a 4–3 vote, the California Supreme Court ruled that the unconstitutional features in *Serrano I* remained despite the legislative reforms. The basic aid allotment required by the California Constitution had an anti-equalizing effect because all districts, rich or poor, received the same amount per pupil. Property-rich districts could reach their foundation levels with a tax rate below the computational level. The new revenue limit system perpetuated inequities that already existed in the 1972–1973 school year by making that the base year. As a result, the system would require up to twenty years to achieve convergence between property-rich and property-poor districts. Even if convergence were to occur, there would still be inequity because the property-rich districts could achieve the foundation level at less than the computational property tax rate. And the entire revenue limit system was compromised by permitting property tax rate overrides so that districts could secure additional property tax revenues.

As to the nature of the constitutional wrong, the majority noted that they based their *Serrano I* decision on the federal and state constitutions. They also noted that the state constitution now contained its own equal protection clause with the passage in 1974 of Proposition 7, adding Article I, Section 7: "A person may not be deprived of life, liberty, or property without due process of law or denied equal protection of the laws." Holding that education is a fundamental right and interdistrict funding disparities a form of wealth discrimination under the California Constitution, the majority of the justices ruled against the state once again.

As to how the system could be rectified, the majority identified several options that the legislature had the authority to pursue. Among them were full state funding through a statewide property tax, consolidation of school districts into geographic areas with equalized property valuations, shifting of commercial and industrial property taxation from local to state control, instituting a school voucher system, and school district power equalizing. As articulated by school finance experts, district power equalizing reduces the effect of local property taxes on school finance by having the state assume a much greater role in assuring some basic level of funding. In addition, district power equalizing permits unequal spending in a way that works to end the correlation between spending and district wealth. Given finite state resources and the large role of local property taxes in school funding, this usually means that excess revenues raised at a state-mandated minimum tax rate in wealthy districts are distributed by the state to poorer districts.

Aside from a shift in the control of school finance away from local districts to the state, district power equalizing generated resentment among residents in property-wealthy districts who saw their tax dollars diverted away from their schools. But for a time, what was dubbed "the Robin Hood system" intrigued state policymakers around the country. Whatever system the state used, the justices affirmed the trial court's decision that the California school finance system was unconstitutional and had to be remedied within six years.

Following the *Serrano II* ruling, the matter of school finance reform was back in the hands of the California legislators. They responded by enacting a bill that increased revenue limits and embraced a form of district power equalizing intended to increase the financial capacity of property-poor districts. The bill was short lived as a result of propositions.

Specifically, on June 6, 1978, California voters approved Proposition 13, which the antitax activist Howard Jarvis spearheaded in a revolt against perceived high property taxes. A year later, voters approved Proposition 4, known as the Gann Limit, after its sponsor, Paul Gann. Proposition 4 amended the state constitution to limit spending growth among state and local governments, including school districts, to the rates of inflation and population growth.

Proposition 13

Because in most states the property tax is a largely decentralized form of taxation, local tax jurisdictions must employ assessors to determine the fair market value of properties even if those properties will not change hands. This results in what many taxpayers refer to as "paper wealth." When property values increase, the property owner is subject to higher taxes even though he or she has not experienced a parallel increase in well-being. The taxpayer still lives in the same home, but when the assessment establishes a higher value for the home, that homeowner is subject to higher property taxes even when the tax rate remains unchanged.

During the early 1970s, housing values began to increase rapidly in many communities, resulting in increased property taxes. At times, counties reassessed properties every six months and raised the homeowner's property tax. When soaring assessments were not met with lowered tax rates, homeowners became restless. In 1972, a proposition known as the Watson Initiative that would have reduced property taxes and effectively converted them into a state property tax was defeated at the polls. But by the end of the decade, homeowners reversed direction and supported Proposition 13.

Proposition 13 limited property taxes to 1 percent of assessed value (Calif. Const. Article XIIIA, § 1). It also required a two-thirds vote of the legislature to increase state taxes and prohibited the imposition of a statewide property tax. It prohibited increases to property taxes except for a specified percentage each year (discussed later) and required a two-thirds majority vote for cities, counties, and special districts to impose any special taxes. It eliminated voter overrides on state-set local property tax rates, a significant blow to property-rich school districts.

Theoretically, Proposition 13 established a system that taxed everyone at the same low rate and centralized authority over school funding at the state rather than the local level. It resulted in a substantial benefit to home and business owners who saw their property tax bills drop by more than 50 percent because of the combination of rolled-back assessments and the reduction in tax rates. This reduction in property tax revenues required that California use other funding sources, such as sales and income taxes, to fund its public schools. Many critics argue that this shift in revenue sources, coupled with the centralization of school funding at the state level, has resulted in a system of school finance that is more sensitive to California's economic fluctuations and less responsive to the needs of individual school districts.

Under Proposition 13, the assessed value was established at the 1975–1976 assessed value of the property, and inflationary increases of this value were limited to no more than 2 percent a year. Property is reassessed at market value only when it is sold. Homeowners may challenge assessments and frequently seek reductions when property values drop. Because the assessed and market values may differ substantially, many property owners pay real property taxes that are less than 1 percent of the assessed value. In addition, Proposition 13's requirement that reassessment occur only when the property is sold or changes hands results in large differences in the taxes paid for similarly situated properties. Under this framework, a taxpayer's property tax burden depends on when the home was purchased, and new homeowners pay considerably more than tenured residents for the same schools, fire and police protection, trash collection, and other public services.

Ironically dubbed the "welcome stranger" law because a newcomer to the community will contribute much more in taxes for local government than settled neighbors, Proposition 13's constitutionality was challenged in 1990 by Stephanie Nordlinger, who found that the tax bill for the Baldwin Hills home she purchased in 1988 was more than five times that of her neighbors living in similar homes. Nordlinger argued that the burden imposed on new homeowners deterred people from moving to California and violated the constitutional right to travel. She further argued that the law was a violation of the equal protection clause of the Fourteenth Amendment because it treated taxpayers differently without legitimate justification.

California state courts rejected Ms. Nordlinger's arguments, and the case made its way to the U.S. Supreme Court in 1992. In an 8–1 decision, the Court also rejected Nordlinger's claims. The Court noted there was no infringement on her right to travel because she already resided in California prior to purchasing her home. On the equal protection clause claim, the Court held that a state needed only a "plausible policy reason" to impose differing property taxes contingent on purchase dates. The justices held that Proposition 13 met this standard. The Court reasoned that California had a legitimate interest in preserving local neighborhoods by discouraging the rapid turnover of homes and businesses. Furthermore, the Court found that the state may distinguish between a new owner and one who has vested rights in retaining his or her property (*Nordlinger v. Hahn*, 1992).

Following the enactment of Proposition 13, the California Legislature returned to the drawing boards on school finance. After a one-year state block grant stopgap measure, it enacted Assembly Bill 8 (AB 8) in 1979. Under AB 8, high-wealth districts received very low inflation increases each year to their revenue limits, and low-wealth districts received high inflation increases, a continuation of the convergence or "squeeze" approach of the previous foundation program.

AB 8 restricted the revenue limit concept to general operating funds, excluding categorical funding for such purposes as educating children with special needs, providing transportation, and deferred maintenance, which vary from district to district. Because the legislature could no longer recapture excess property taxes from high-wealth districts and had no immediate source of state revenue to raise funding levels in low-wealth districts, per-pupil funding levels expanded much less rapidly.

But the *Serrano* litigation had not ended. Plaintiffs returned to court following the implementation of AB 8 to argue that it, too, was inequitable. The trial court disagreed, and the decision was upheld by the Court of Appeal for the Second District, whose judges were so impressed by the superior court judge's carefully reasoned opinion that they incorporated it as their own (*Serrano v. Priest*, 226 Cal. Rptr. 584 (Cal. App. 2 Dist. 1986) [*Serrano III*]), cause dismissed (Oct. 27, 1989).

A good deal of controversy surrounded the standard for determining equity. The superior court judge looked back to the trial judge's decision in 1974 following the California Supreme Court's decision in *Serrano I*. In that decision, the trial judge determined that, other than categorical funding, wealth-related disparities between districts had to be reduced to insignificant differences, meaning considerably less than $100 per pupil, within six years. While the California Supreme Court affirmed that decision in *Serrano II* in 1976, it had not specifically discussed the extent of permissible interdistrict disparities.

Referring to the earlier judge's ruling, the superior court judge, whose decision was embraced by the California Court of Appeal for the Second District in *Serrano*

III, concluded that the term "insignificant differences," as applied to base revenue funding across districts, did not mean that the $100 figure had to be rigidly applied. Rather, it was to serve as a guide, and the revised system imposed by AB 8 and subsequent legislation achieved the desired equity.

The judge also noted that the plaintiffs first had to establish that their fundamental right to education under the state constitution was substantially impaired before the court would scrutinize the constitutionality of funding legislation. This threshold requirement is necessary to avoid having judges second-guess every legislative funding enactment that may treat persons and districts differently. For example, it may be more costly to educate a secondary student than an elementary student. Such a funding difference would not by itself warrant judicial review.

Serrano v. Priest finally came to an end. While equity appeared to have been achieved, it came at the expense of local control of school funding. In addition, the shift to state-centered funding resulted in a system of school finance that was less responsive to the needs of individual districts and that failed to keep pace with the need for additional school funding.

As a result of *Serrano*, the passage of Propositions 13 and 4, and a rapidly growing schooling population, California's per-pupil spending grew more slowly relative to other states. By the 1990s, the state's average per-pupil expenditures were well below the national average. Some attribute the slowdown to the reticence of California's political leaders to introduce new taxes. While this explanation may have some merit, it is undermined by state public spending patterns over the past decade.

While school funding has lagged, other public services have not, leading some to conclude that the lack of resources for public education is the result of deliberate decision-making on the part of policymakers and voters. These critics point to demographic changes as the source of California's school-funding problems, asserting that white voters are reluctant to invest in schooling for the state's increasingly nonwhite and low-income school population. In 2011–2012, 71 percent of California public school students were students of color, over half came from low-income families, and one-quarter were English learners. Others contend that legislators no longer believe that increasing school funding will lead to improved student outcomes.

Whatever the reason, the shape of equity in the wake of *Serrano* was not what reformers had expected. Rather, the failure of California school funding to keep pace with other states fostered a growing perception that California's public schools were rapidly becoming equally mediocre.

CHANGES TO THE CALIFORNIA SCHOOL FINANCE SYSTEM

Following *Serrano* decisions, the state revised its practices and procedures to fund public education through a variety of state, local, and federal sources. The major components are listed in Table 3.1 and described in this section. At that time, state funds generally accounted for about 60 percent of California's school revenues and were derived largely from state sales and income taxes. Local sources, such as designated property taxes for schooling, which the state collected and allocated to school districts, and developer fees, constituted about 30 percent. Remaining revenues came from federal funding for categorical aid programs, receipts from the state lottery, and other miscellaneous sources.

The amount of funding derived from each source varies from year to year depending on the decisions and compromises made by the legislature and governor in developing the state's budget. This process begins in January, when the governor releases a proposed budget, and generally concludes sometime in July or August, when the finalized budget is formally adopted. While the California Legislature has substantial influence over how California's schools are financed, its authority is not exclusive. California's K–14 education system has been guaranteed a minimum level of funding by the state's voters.

Proposition 98, approved in November 1988, amended the state constitution to establish a funding floor for the state's public schools and community colleges (Article XVI, § 8). It also focused on educational outcomes by requiring the establishment of the School Accountability Report Card (SARC) discussed in Chapter 2.

The Proposition 98 funding floor was initially set at 40 percent of California's general-fund tax revenues, but during the recession of the early 1990s, this minimum was reduced to about 34 percent. To keep public education funding largely intact, the legislature and then Governor Pete Wilson enacted the Educational Revenue Augmentation Fund (ERAF) in 1992. ERAF made up for the lost general-fund revenues by shifting some of the property tax revenues of counties and cities to public schools. In the decades since, other actions have occurred in response to the state's budget problems.

Proposition 98 provides that state revenues for school districts and community colleges in high-revenue years are to be the larger of the first two formulas in Table 3.2. Formula three is applicable in low-revenue years.

The first formula was used when economic times were good, general-fund revenues high, and where the portion of the budget for schools was 39 percent. This formula was first introduced in 1988–1989.

TABLE 3.1
Major Components of California's School Finance System until 2013-2014

Revenue Limit Funding
- Set percentage of state general-fund tax revenues for public schools and community colleges (Prop. 98)
- State and local property tax funds (latter controlled by Prop. 13)

Categorical Aid
- State sources
- Federal sources

Other Sources
- State lottery revenue
- Parcel taxes
- Private contributions
- Interest income
- Leases and rentals

Facilities Funding
- State and local bonding process
- Developer fees
- Mello-Roos Community Facilities District Act (1982)
- Leroy Greene School Facilities Act (1998)

The second formula was available only in fiscal years when the growth in per capita income is less or equal to the percentage of growth in per capita general-fund revenues plus .005 percent. This formula was used most often because it is not as heavily dependent on economic factors as the other two.

The third formula was used when general-fund revenues did not grow as rapidly as per capita income. And, as noted in Table 3.2, the proposition gave the legislature the further option of suspending the proposition's base funding provisions for one year by passing urgency legislation, which happened for the first time in 2004.

Shortly after Proposition 98 was passed, several groups, including the California Teachers Association, argued that the proposition had shifted authority away from the state and had given school districts the exclusive right to decide how to spend their allocated funding. The argument was rejected (*California Teachers Association v. Hayes*, 1992). The California court of appeal ruled that the proposition did not alter the legislature's plenary authority over school funding.

TABLE 3.2
Tests for Determining a Minimum Base Funding for Schools under Proposition 98

High-Revenue Years	
Formula One	The same share of state general-fund taxes received in the base year of 1986–1987, adjusted for the shift of property taxes to schools under ERAF.
Formula Two	The same amount of state and property tax funding received in the previous year with adjustments for increases in enrollment and inflation.
Low-Revenue Years	
Formula Three	Same criteria as Formula Two but inflation defined as the growth of taxes per capita plus .005 percent. Any reduction compared to the previous year must be no worse than cuts in state spending per capita for other budgeted services.

State has the option of suspending Proposition 98's base funding provisions for one year by passing urgency legislation requiring two-thirds approval of both houses and signature of the governor pursuant to Article IV, Section 8 of the California Constitution.

General-purpose funds made up about two-thirds of California's school revenues. The legislature provided these funds to school districts on an unrestricted basis. Consisting of a combination of local contributions through the applied property tax and the state's contribution toward the district's predefined revenue limit, general-purpose funds are primarily devoted to teacher salaries, utilities, and general operation expenses. The remaining one-third of school revenues came from state and federal categorical funds, which were earmarked for specific educational purposes, such as programs for low-income students, students with limited English proficiency, and children with special educational needs.

Revenue Limit Funding

Until the 2013–2014 school year, districts continued to receive the bulk of their general-purpose funds through revenue limit foundation funding (see Table 3.1). A district's revenue limit was calculated through a complex formula that adjusted a base revenue limit amount according to a variety of factors, including increases for inflation or cost-of-living adjustments (COLAs) and decreases for deficits, as well as adjustments for summer school programs and policies that extended the school day and year.

The amount of funding a district received under the revenue limit system was calculated by multiplying the per-pupil amount of its revenue limit by its average daily attendance, or ADA. Additional funding was provided for "necessary small schools" located in geographically isolated areas with low attendance levels. To protect against revenue losses caused by declining enrollments, districts were permitted to use either the current or the previous year's ADA when calculating their revenue limit funding.

The legislature combined state funds with local property tax revenues to meet the revenue limit requirements. Because districts were generally prohibited from receiving money in excess of their revenue limit, the exact mix of state and local funds was of little concern. Each year, however, between sixty and eighty districts had property tax revenues that either met or exceeded their revenue limits. These districts were not subject to a state recapture plan and were designated as "basic aid" districts until the 2003–2004 school year because they kept their property tax receipts and received the basic aid guaranteed by the California Constitution—a flat grant of $120 per pupil. In 2003, however, legislators agreed to eliminate state basic aid to these districts, reasoning that all districts receive the constitutionally guaranteed minimum in the form of categorical aid. The districts were still permitted to retain their excess property tax revenues, which were designated as "excess tax" districts.

By largely eliminating the connection between local wealth and school spending, the revenue limit system moved California's public schools closer to a position of equality relative to general-purpose funding. Differing revenue limit growth rates forced a convergence to a median level for all districts. In the late 1970s, some high-wealth districts had revenue limit funds that were more than 30 percent above the revenue limit median, and some low-wealth districts had per-pupil revenue limit spending that was less than 85 percent of the median. By the 1990s, however, the upper level on spending had been reduced to about 7 percent, and the lower level had been increased to about 99 percent of median revenue limit funding. However, while per-student revenue limit funding moved toward equalization across school districts, there was some variance by type of school district (e.g., elementary, secondary, unified).

Categorical Aid

During revenue limit funding, about one-third of California's school funds were committed to specific purposes that aligned with the State's priorities, commonly labelled "categorical aid" (see Table 3.1). Funding for categorical programs was drawn from both federal and state sources and was generally accompanied by regulations ensuring that the money was used for the educational purpose or special student population for which it is designated.

In California, the largest share of categorical funding was dispensed for special education. Because federal and state categorical aid falls short, districts must contribute some of their general funds to make up the difference—a practice known as "encroachment." As its name indicates, this practice results in less expenditure in other areas and can generate resentment from those who view funding for regular students as siphoned off to make up the shortfall in special education.

Encroachment is a continuing source of controversy and generates assertions that the federal government has, in effect, imposed an unfunded federal mandate on the states. Although the federal government is required to pay 40 percent of special education funding to states, it presently provides far less.

The needs of low-income students and English learners were another important focus of categorical aid in California. Economic Impact Aid (EIA) was the primary state program supporting low-income and limited-English-speaking students. EIA funding is determined on a per-pupil basis, and districts receive funding based on the number of low-income and English learners they serve. Federal funding for these students was divided into two programs: Title I provides funding for low-income students, and Title III funds programs for students with limited proficiency in English.

In addition, California's public schools received varying amounts of funding for some fifty other categorical aid programs (this number may vary depending on how "programs" are defined). These included federally funded programs for preschool students, child development and nutrition, and vocational programs, as well as state-funded programs for school improvement, desegregation, and a variety of compensatory educational programs. Like special education, programs for class size reduction, early childhood development, and adult education received state and federal funding. The number of programs and the amount of funding per program varied from year to year, reflecting legislative preferences.

In 2004, the legislature consolidated over twenty categorical programs, accounting for 18 percent of annual categorical funding, into six block grants. These included pupil retention, school safety, teacher credentialing, professional development, targeted instructional improvement, and school and library improvement. School district and county office of education officials welcomed the provision, which gave them the discretion to transfer up to 15 percent of four of the block grants (pupil retention and teacher credentialing are excluded) to cover costs in other block grants or categorical programs not to exceed 120 percent of the total amount allocated for those programs. Before this can be done, the district or county board of education must discuss the matter at a public meeting.

In 2009, the legislature eliminated spending restrictions through 2014–2015 in some forty categorical programs, representing about 30 percent of categorical funding. What was labeled as "flex spending" gave school districts and schools discretion in deciding how the funding should be spent. Doing so helped alleviate funding cutbacks as a result of the recession.

Through the revenue limit years and continuing to present, the issue of "unfunded mandates" by the state has proved contentious. The antitax Proposition 4 corollary to Proposition 13, approved by voters in 1979, added Article XIII B to the California Constitution. Section 6 of this article requires the state to reimburse local governments whenever the legislature or state agency mandates a new program or higher level of service. The term *program* in this provision has been construed to encompass public education (*Long Beach Unified Sch. Dist. v. State of Cal.*, 1990).

Because of the state's budget shortfalls, the legislature provided only nominal funding to cover mandated cost reimbursements, deferring remaining payments to the future. In one year, for example, the legislature provided $1,000 for each of thirty-eight mandates, with a total cost estimate of over $160 million. A California court of appeal ruled that this "credit card" approach is unconstitutional. However, the judges also ruled that the judiciary is without authority to compel the legislature to provide the funding. Rather, the remedy is set forth in Government Code Section 17555 and following sections. These sections state that if the legislature provides only nominal funding or no funding for mandated programs, school districts either are relieved from having to fulfill those mandates under certain circumstances or must seek judicial relief from having to do so (*California School Boards Association v. State of California*, 2011).

Local Control Funding Formula

In the 2013–2014 school year, the state began implanting a major overhaul to the school finance system. Labeled the Local Control Funding Formula, or LCFF, the state attempted to simplify the school funding throughout the state and target the student groups that require additional resources. With the exception of the differences described in the later section "The Block Grant System, LCFF, and LCAP," the LCFF requirements apply to both school districts and charter schools. For simplicity, *school districts* in this LCFF section and the following Local Control Accountability Plan sections applies to both school districts and charter schools.

Prior to the implementation of LCFF, the revenue limit system was highly criticized for, among other things, its complexity and use of more than fifty categorical programs to allocate funds for specific purposes, with each categorical program including its own specific restrictions and allocation formulas. The revenue limit system was also considered inequitable because it failed to adequately target student needs, inefficient because it required school districts to focus on compliance rather than coordination of activities for students, and antiquated since it relied on outdated factors.

During the Great Recession, from 2007 to 2009, the state suspended many categorical programs. As the state exited the Great Recession, it began to consider significant revisions to school funding, including categorical programs. The state replaced the revenue limit system with the LCFF, which has been heralded as more effectively targeting student populations with the greatest need, simplifying school funding, and treating school districts similarly through state funding.

Under LCFF, school districts continue to receive funding on the basis of average daily attendance, or ADA, which includes a base amount of funding determined by grade spans. However, nearly 20 percent of the funding available to school districts under LCFF is based on the proportion of the student population that include English learners, low-income families (students who qualify for free or reduced-priced meals under federal law), and foster youth. Students falling into one or more of these categories are often referred to as "unduplicated pupils," meaning that they are counted only once for LCFF purposes.

The LCFF comprises four components: (1) base grant, (2) supplemental grant, (3) concentration grant, and (4) add-ons. The first three components constitute approximately 98 percent of each school district's LCFF apportionment. The LCFF apportionment constitutes approximately 80 percent of school district funding.

The base grant includes a uniform level of funding per student based on grade spans. The base grant also includes additional funding for the span of kindergarten through third grade, so long as each school site maintains an average class enrollment of not more than twenty-four students in grades kindergarten through third grade (Educ. Code § 42238.02) or another collectively bargained ratio. Additional funding is also available through the base grant to address costs associated with career technical education, or CTE. The base grant also includes funding for "Necessary Small Schools," or schools serving 2,500 or fewer students who would be required to travel long distances to attend school or face other obstacles that would make busing an unusual hardship.

The supplemental grant includes additional funding for each school district's unduplicated count. This grant specifically includes an additional 20 percent of the school district's base grant for each student who is an English learner, low income, or foster youth. The supplemental grant is calculated based on a three-year rolling average.

The concentration grant recognizes that schools serving student populations with high unduplicated counts face the greatest educational challenges and includes funding above the supplemental grant for unduplicated pupils. Specifically, it provides an additional 65 percent of the adjusted base rate for each English learner, low-income student, and foster youth when unduplicated pupils account for more than 55 percent of the school district's enrollment. Both the supplemental and concentration grants significantly increase funding allocated to the school district through the LCFF.

Finally, the add-ons include monies associated with the Targeted Instructional Improvement Block Grant, transportation, and other specified items. The add-ons are the smallest of the four components, totaling just over 2 percent of the total LCFF allocation in the 2022–2023 school year.

The state imposes certain requirements to ensure school districts satisfy mandates related to the supplemental and concentration grants. Namely, school districts must ensure "proportionality" between the funding received and services to unduplicated pupils. In addition, school districts must ensure that any unspent supplemental and concentration grant funding must be tracked and used to improve services for unduplicated pupils in future years. Finally, school districts must use a certain portion of the concentration grant to increase staff who provide direct services to unduplicated pupils. We discuss these requirements and monitoring in greater detail in the following section.

The LCFF requires the state to apply a cost-of-living adjustment, or COLA, to the LCFF allocation. The COLA is based on a federal price index tied to changes in the cost of goods and services. However, if required Proposition 98 funding is inadequate to account for the increased COLA, the COLA increase is reduced to align with available funding.

Like the revenue limit system, the LCFF relies heavily on local property tax revenue. Specifically, the state identifies an LCFF target for each school district and then credits that school district with its local property tax revenue. In most instances, the local property tax falls short of the LCFF target. In those instances, the state makes up the difference. The LCFF allocation for these school districts is typically heavily dependent on the district's ADA.

However, in certain instances, the local property tax exceeds the LCFF target. In those cases, the school district, commonly referred to as a "basic aid district," may use its excess property tax revenue on the district's educational priorities. Basic aid districts are typically unaffected by changes in ADA in the same manner as their non-basic aide districts. It also bears noting that school districts can transition in and out of basic aid status from year to year depending on the LCFF allocation associated with that year.

Local Control and Accountability Plans

In an effort to ensure transparency and accountability related to the use of LCFF funds, the state requires all school districts to develop Local Control Accountability Plans, or LCAPs. LCAPs are three-year plans that must be reviewed and updated annually. Each school district must develop its LCAP in accordance with stakeholder involvement and specific requirements.

In developing the LCAP, each school district must develop a proposed plan, solicit written comments concerning the plan from the public, present the plan to parent advisory committees for comment, and solicit recommendations and comments through a public hearing. In addition, the school district must consult with bargaining units, employees, students, and parents. Following that process, the school district must adopt its LCAP at a public hearing.

Each school district must integrate goals in the following eight priority areas in the LCAP:

1. Basic Conditions of Learning
2. Implementation of State Standards
3. Parent Engagement
4. Student Achievement
5. Student Engagement
6. School Climate
7. Course Access
8. Other Student Outcomes

Along with each of those areas, each school district must set performance targets for all students and student subgroups for the coming school year and the following two school years.

The LCAP must also identify the actions the school district plans to implement to achieve each of its goals and include information demonstrating that the district will increase or improve services to its unduplicated pupils in proportion to their supplemental and concentration grant funding. Each of the actions must be aligned to the school district's budget.

Once the LCAP has been developed and approved, the school district must submit it to the County Office of Education for review and approval. Through that review, the county office of education must ensure that (1) the LCAP complies with the required template, (2) the school district's expenditures are sufficient to implement the strategies described in the LCAP, and (3) the expenditures comply with all supplemental and concentration grant requirements. The county office of education may suggest amendments to the LCAP, which must be considered by the school district at a public hearing. However, the school district is not required to accept those recommendations.

Federal Funds

As noted earlier, approximately 80 percent of school district funding comes through the LCFF apportionment. School districts also receive a variety of federal funds. For example, the federal government provides funding pursuant to Title I for school districts with large populations of low-income students. Additionally, school districts receive funding pursuant to the Individuals with Disabilities Education Act (IDEA), although the funding provided pursuant to the IDEA falls far short of the monies required to provide services required under the IDEA and routinely requires school districts to dedicate substantial general funds to meet the IDEA requirements. Finally, the federal government allocates funds to school districts under the Child Nutrition Act to provide certain nutrition programs and impact aid to school districts with children residing in areas with military bases, reservations, and other areas.

Following the COVID-19 pandemic, the federal government implemented unprecedented funding to assist schools and students. For instance, the federal government implemented three relief packages through the Elementary and Secondary School Emergency Relief (ESSER). ESSER funds were generally available to assist with any activity aligned with federal programs, such as services for students with disabilities and low-income students. ESSER funds could also be used for activities related to COVID-19, such as addressing learning loss resulting from the pandemic and improving school facilities.

Each ESSER funding package, divided into ESSER I, ESSER II, and ESSER III, includes different dates by which the funds must be committed. ESSER I funds must have been committed by September 30, 2022; ESSER II funds must have been committed by September 30, 2023; and ESSER III funds must have been committed by September 30, 2024.

Student Fees

To help with budget shortfalls, some districts have charged student fees for cheerleading outfits, instruments and uniforms for band participation, and the like to help support these programs. However, charging such fees is impermissible unless specifically authorized by law. Under California Education Code Section 49011(a)(1), schools are required to provide students with "all supplies, materials, and equipment needed to participate in educational activities" at no charge. This policy aligns with the California Constitutional requirement that schools provide students with a free public education. Therefore, school supplies such as books, paper, or other necessary supplies must be provided to students at no charge (Educ. Code § 38118). Additionally, required reading materials, transportation to and from school (Educ. Code § 39807.5(b)), and student ID cards may not be charged as student fees.

In contrast, the law permits certain fees. For instance, school districts may charge fees associated with certain food items (Educ. Code § 38082), exam fees such as those required to take the SAT (Educ. Code § 52240–52244, 52920–52922), and fees associated with parking on campus (Educ. Code § 35160). With that said, it is permissible for schools to distribute a list of school supplies to parents and request donations for classroom supplies on a voluntary basis. For many reasons, including the fact that student fees have been a topic of significant litigation, school districts are well advised to make clear that such donations are entirely voluntary.

Courts have also analyzed fees in the context of extracurricular and other activities. For instance, the California Supreme Court ruled in 1984 that all educational programs including extracurricular and athletic activities fall within the right to a free public education under Article IX, Section 5, of the state constitution. Thus, once offered, an extracurricular or athletic activity must be provided at no charge (*Hartzell v. Connell*, 1984).

The constitutional provision specifies that "the Legislature shall provide for a system of common schools by which a free school shall be kept up and supported in each district." The high court later ruled that bus transportation is not included within the right to a free public education because it is not an educational activity (*Arcadia Unified School District v. State Department of Education*, 1992). Accordingly, Education Code Section 39807.5 states that a school district governing board may require parents and guardians to pay a portion of the cost of transportation to and from school. However, other provisions of the Education Code provide state reimbursement for school bus transportation.

While fees may be involved in field trips and excursions, Education Code Section 35330(b)(1) provides that no student is to be prevented from participating because of a lack of funds. Similarly, Section 35183 provides that if a school district has a uniform dress code, resources must be provided for economically disadvantaged students. Driver training is educational, and therefore, student fees cannot be charged (*California Association for Safety*, 1994). Education Code Section 49010 and following were added in 2012, specifying fees that are not to be charged and requiring the State Board of Education every three years, beginning in 2014–2015, to provide guidance to school officials on the matter. The new provisions also specify how disputes over fees are to be resolved through the Uniform Complaint Procedure discussed in Chapter 1.

Other Sources of School Revenue

There are several other sources of school revenue, as outlined in Table 3.1. In 1984, California voters approved a constitutional amendment enabling the creation of a state lottery, with 34 percent of revenues tagged for public education. Although the lottery provides less than 2 percent of K–12 funding, the money is valuable to districts because it may be spent at the district's discretion on any school expense except school construction or the purchase of property.

Despite the centralization of California's system of school finance, districts still retain some local avenues for school funding, though only about 6 percent of school funding comes from these sources, with great variance among districts. Districts are able to generate local revenues through leases and rentals of school property and earned interest on general-fund balances. In addition, with two-thirds voter approval, districts are permitted to levy parcel taxes on parcels of real estate to raise revenue for specific school purposes. The tax may be variable or a flat per-parcel rate, but it may not be levied *ad valorem*. That is, the tax is levied on the parcel itself and not on the value of the parcel. The voter approval requirement makes the parcel tax a somewhat cumbersome funding mechanism for many California districts, and parcel tax revenues are enjoyed only by districts in which voters are willing to approve the tax. Only a handful of districts conduct parcel elections annually, with about a 50 percent pass rate.

The slowing pace of increases in California's per-pupil spending has caused many local districts to rely on voluntary private contributions to support school programs. In the wake of Proposition 13, an increasing number of California districts have established nonprofit educational foundations to raise private revenues for local school districts. More than 500 of these foundations currently operate in California. Districts located in affluent areas are more likely to raise substantial funding this way. At the school level, however, the primary source of private revenues continues to be parent groups, such as the Parent-Teacher Association (PTA) and booster clubs. In most school districts, private donations contribute less than $100 per pupil, though there can be wide disparities among schools in the same district.

Facilities Funding

Rapidly increasing enrollments coupled with aging school buildings have placed considerable pressure on California's public school districts to build new school facilities and renovate existing ones. In 2001, the California Legislative Analyst's Office estimated that one-third of California's school-aged children attended school in an overcrowded or outdated facility.

California's system for funding new schools and school renovations is independent of its basic school finance system and relies heavily on the state and local bonding process. Prior to the passage of Proposition 13 in 1978, local school districts held the primary responsibility for financing school facilities through general obligation bonds. Districts that experienced rapidly increasing enrollments and had reached the limits of their bonding capacity were eligible for state school construction aid. With the passage of Proposition 13, property taxes were restricted to 1 percent of assessed valuation, and local districts were no longer able to use general obligation bonds supported by a local ad valorem tax as a funding source for school construction.

At the state level, voters have passed bonding measures in recent years that have generated billions of dollars for school land acquisition and facility construction or repair. For instance, Proposition 47 raised $11.4 billion in 2002, and Proposition 55 generated $10 billion in 2004. As discussed later in the chapter, the settlement of a class action lawsuit brought by poor districts generated additional funds.

From 1978 to 1986, the state held a primary role in school facilities funding. In 1986, California voters passed Proposition 46, which restored local district authority to issue general obligation bonds with two-thirds voter approval. Bond issues for school renovations and repair required a simple majority of voter approval.

From 1987 to 1999, revenue raised through local general obligation bonds paid more than 30 percent of California's school building and renovation costs. Despite the passage of Proposition 46, the state still retained considerable control over school construction because state school construction bonds could be passed by a simple majority vote instead of the two-thirds vote required by local districts.

In November 2000, however, California voters approved Proposition 39, which reduced the voter approval threshold needed to pass local school facility bonds from two-thirds to 55 percent. The reduction in required voter approval makes it substantially easier for school districts to generate funds for school construction.

In addition to Proposition 46, the year 1986 also saw the approval of Assembly Bill 2926, which permitted local districts to levy developer fees on new commercial, industrial, and residential construction projects. Districts are permitted to impose the fees when they can demonstrate that the new construction will create a need for additional school facilities (Educ. Code § 17620 et seq.). The law initially permitted fees of up to $1.50 per square foot for residential construction projects and up to 25 cents per square foot for commercial and industrial projects (Govt. Code § 65995). Increases in inflation were permitted in 2000 and every two years thereafter, as determined by the State Allocation Board. Developer fees provide substantial revenue in rapidly growing communities but are not important sources of revenue in stagnant communities.

School districts may also raise capital revenues through the creation of Mello-Roos districts with two-thirds voter approval. Introduced in 1982, the Mello-Roos Community Facilities District Act enables local districts to create special financing districts to raise money for community construction needs such as schools, libraries, and roads (Govt. Code § 53311 et seq.). In recent years, Mello-Roos has given way to the formation of school facility improvement districts for the conduct of a bond election pursuant to Education Code Section 15300 and following sections.

The Leroy Greene School Facilities Act of 1998 also assists schools with funding for facilities. Under the terms of the Act, eligible school districts may apply to the State Allocation Board for school construction funds (Educ. Code § 17070 et seq.). The Act requires schools to meet state-developed criteria for inadequate school facilities according to a point system. The application process is competitive and complex, and schools that qualify must match state funding with local revenues.

Voter approval in November 2006 of Proposition 1D channeled $7.3 billion of the $10 billion measure into K–12 facility modernization, new construction, relief grants for overcrowded schools, career technical education facilities, charter school facilities, environmentally friendly projects, and joint-use projects such as gyms and libraries. In each case, local contributions are necessary for the release of funds. It is estimated that some 1,800 schools (20 percent of all schools) are eligible for overcrowding grants.

California's spending on school facilities has increased steadily since the mid-1980s. Still, differences in local communities' ability to pass general obligation bonds, as well as differences in the amount of state aid received, have resulted in wide disparities in the amount of facilities funding available to California school districts.

FUNDING CHARTER SCHOOLS

The Block Grant System, LCFF, and LCAP

Prior to 1999, California's charter schools were largely funded based on the revenue limit system used by traditional school districts. Thereafter, the system of charter school funding was restructured to develop a simpler method of providing charters with operational funds equivalent to those received by traditional school districts serving similar student populations.

The revised system of charter school funding was composed of two block grants (Educ. Code § 47633 et seq.). The first, a general-purpose entitlement, replaced revenue limit funding. The charter school general-purpose entitlement was computed annually by the Superintendent of Public Instruction and funded through a combination of state aid and local funds; it was distributed to charter schools on the basis of average daily attendance across a set of four grade ranges: kindergarten through third, fourth through sixth, seventh and eighth, and ninth through twelfth. Charter schools receive per-pupil funding equivalent to the statewide average revenue limit funding of traditional public school districts serving similar student populations. Like the revenue limit funds received by a traditional district, a charter school's general-purpose entitlement is unrestricted and may be used for any school purpose. Charters are restricted, however, from receiving necessary small-school revenue limit funding available to traditional schools (Educ. Code § 47633). Although this is currently the law governing charter school funding in California, it bears noting that, without legislative action or other changes in the law, section 47633 will remain operative until July 1, 2033, and will be repealed as of January 1, 2034.

The second, a categorical aid block grant, replaced some of the categorical aid available to traditional schools. In place of applying separately for certain categorical aid programs, charter schools received a categorical aid block grant that included funding for general categorical programs and for educationally disadvantaged students. For 2007–2008, the SPI set a base funding level of $500 per ADA that was to be adjusted each year thereafter for inflation. Charter schools enjoyed greater flexibility than traditional schools in the use of state categorical aid funds and were not bound by programmatic restrictions. Like the general entitlement funds, a charter school could use these block grant funds for any school purpose (See former Educ. Code § 47634.1(h)).

As noted earlier, with the implementation of the LCFF and LCAP, charter schools receive most of their apportionment based on a per-student formula. Like school districts, nearly 20 percent of all charter school funding is based on the proportion of students who are considered unduplicated pupils.

However, unlike school districts, charter schools are funded based on their current year's average daily attendance. Charter schools also receive kindergarten through third-grade apportionment but are exempt from the class size requirement. Similarly, charter schools are not required to submit their LCAP to the county office of education for review.

At the time of publication, charter schools were not qualified to receive certain add-on funds. For instance, they are ineligible to receive reimbursement for certain transportation costs.

A charter school may elect to receive funds either directly or through the local authorizing agency that granted its charter or was designated as the oversight agency by the state board of education (Educ. Code § 47651). Charters that choose the direct funding option have their funds deposited in the school's appropriate account in the county treasury. The same is true for charters that have been granted by the State Board of Education (SBE) but for which the board has not delegated oversight responsibilities.

For charters that are funded through their local authorizing agent, the funds are deposited in the account of the authorizing local education agency and then dispensed to the charter. The method of allocating funds affects neither the amount of funds provided to charters nor the oversight responsibilities of the local authorizing agent. Charter school authorizers are permitted to charge an administrative fee of up to 1 percent of a charter school's revenues for oversight responsibilities or up to 3 percent of revenues if they provide the school with substantially rent-free facilities (Educ. Code § 47613).

The method by which a charter school chooses to have its funds allocated may affect its ability to apply for state and federal categorical aid. Those schools that have their funds allocated directly may apply for categorical aid individually, just like a school district. If the funding flows through the local education agency that granted the charter or has been designated by the SBE as the oversight entity, then the charter school may receive considerable administrative support in the application process and in managing the program from that agency. In addition to state and federal funding sources, many charter schools rely on private donations to offset start-up costs, provide instructional materials, and substitute for categorical aid programs for which the charter was ineligible or failed to apply.

The Special Case of Nonclassroom-Based Charters

The Education Code defines a charter school's program as "classroom-based instruction" when the following four criteria are met: (1) The charter school's students are engaged in educational activities and are supervised by a teacher who holds a valid teaching certificate, (2) at least 80 percent of instructional time is offered at the school site, (3) the charter school site is used principally for classroom instruction, and (4) the charter school requires its students to be in attendance at the school site for at least 80 percent of the minimum instructional time required by law for the appropriate grade level (Educ. Code § 47612.5(e)(1)). In recent years, about 20 percent of California's charter schools did not meet these criteria and were classified as "nonclassroom-based instructional programs." These charters offered programs for independent study, home study, and work study, as well as distance and computer-based instructional programs.

The California Legislature has instituted a reduced funding schedule for nonclassroom-based charter schools. Nonclassroom-based charters may receive an amount not more than 70 percent of the per-ADA funding provided to classroom-based programs (Educ. Code § 47634.2).

The State Board of Education may determine that less or more funding is appropriate based on the amount the charter school spends on certificated employee salaries and benefits, school site expenses, teacher-student ratio, and other factors the board considers appropriate to school funding. One caveat is that a nonclassroom-based charter school may only receive state funding for instruction of students who reside in the county where the school is chartered or in an adjacent county (89 Ops. Atty. Gen. 166, 2006). This is because the State Board of Education requires nonclassroom-based instruction in any school to comply with independent study requirements. State funding is available only for independent study programs when the students are residents of the county in which the school is located or an adjacent county (Educ. Code § 51747.3(b)).

Facilities

Obtaining adequate school facilities has been a central obstacle for many charter schools and for start-up charters in particular. While conversion charters often occupy the same facilities they use as traditional public schools, start-up charters must contend with locating appropriate facilities, as well as rental costs and maintenance and utility expenses. Responding to the difficulties inherent in starting a new school, California has implemented various legislative changes designed to assist charters with capital expenses.

As part of Proposition 39, voters in 2000 approved a measure requiring traditional school districts to provide charter schools serving eighty or more in-district students with facilities sufficient to serve those students (Educ. Code § 47614). As noted in Chapter 1, the facilities must be "reasonably equivalent" to those of other schools operating within the district. These facilities must be "contiguous, furnished and equipped" and remain the property of the host school district. Districts are required to provide facilities even if unused facilities are not available and must make reasonable efforts to accommodate the charter school with facilities in the area of its desired location.

Charter school facilities must be provided even if districts will incur costs in providing them. Districts are permitted to charge charter schools a pro rata share of school facilities costs, which the school district pays for with unrestricted general-fund revenues. Because districts use nongeneral funds for most capital expenditures, general-fund expenses are likely to include only costs for maintenance and upkeep. Districts are not required to use their unrestricted general-fund revenues for charter school capital expenses and instead may use state or local bonds to fund the facilities.

Proposition 47, approved by voters in November 2002, provided up to $100 million for the construction of new charter schools and presented the first opportunity for charter schools to apply directly for state facilities bond funds. These funds were rapidly depleted when more than twenty charters applied for funding in the spring of 2003. In March 2004, however, voters approved Proposition 55, which included provisions granting charter schools an additional $300 million in state bond funds for facilities.

In 2003–2004, California implemented Senate Bill 740 and established the Charter School Facility Grant Program, which is designed to assist charter schools with the costs of renting and leasing facilities (Educ. Code § 47614.5). Subject to conditions set forth in the statute, eligible charters may receive up to $750 per pupil as reimbursement for up to 75 percent of the annual cost of leasing or renting a school facility. The California Department of Education is charged with informing charter schools about the program and determining eligibility requirements. Charter schools are eligible for the program (1) if they are located in the attendance zone of a public elementary school in which at least 70 percent of students are eligible for free or reduced-price meals, and the charter gives preference in admissions to students who either attend the public elementary school or reside in its attendance area, or (2) if they enroll 70 percent or more students eligible for free or reduced-price meals. The availability of funds depends on the state's budget for each fiscal year, and funds are not appropriated until the subsequent year's fiscal budget has been approved.

THE MOVEMENT TOWARD ADEQUACY

The fiscal complexities and political difficulties inherent in equalizing school resources across districts, coupled with an increased emphasis on state-mandated educational standards, led to a subtle but significant shift in school finance reform efforts in the 1990s across the nation. This shift was marked by a movement away from concern over equitable school funding to discussion of adequate funding and school quality. Instead of pressing equal protection clause arguments alone to shape more equitable distributions of school resources, school finance reform advocates now focused on the education clauses of state constitutions, arguing that the clauses obligate states to provide a minimum level of education for all students. These efforts were better aligned with the growing curriculum standards movement than were the arguments for increased equity. An important stimulus to the adequacy argument was the enactment of the federal No Child Left Behind Act in 2001. That act, which is discussed in Chapter 2 and has now been replaced by the Every Student Succeeds Act, required that all students must achieve proficiency levels or higher on state-mandated assessments by 2014.

The focus on the adequacy of school resources has placed school quality at the center of the debate over how best to distribute school revenues. Although a school's quality is not necessarily a function of its revenues, some students require more resources than others do to attain minimum levels of achievement, which is recognized by the LCFF and serves as a central tenant to the funding methodology. It is anticipated that the LCFF will assist in closing the achievement gap between the students and their peers.

Urban schools serving large populations of low-income students of color, in particular, are challenged to provide an adequate education for their students, many of whom arrive at schoolhouse doors with significant educational deficiencies resulting from a lack of family financial resources, limited-English-proficient households, or a host of other concerns that have an impact on their learning. These students have greater educational needs and frequently require additional resources to bring their achievement in line with state-required minimum standards.

While California's poor record of academic achievement may be linked in some way to school finance, it is likely that the state's changing demographics also have influenced educational outcomes. California's immigrant population has grown rapidly, and students from low-income families and from households with limited English proficiency on average earn lower scores on standardized measures of academic achievement. California's students are more likely to come from minority and recent immigrant households than students in many other states.

Irrespective of student outcomes, many critics of California's reduced expenditures for public schooling fault Proposition 13's restrictions on property tax revenues and point to the increased susceptibility to economic conditions of state-based systems, such as California's, that rely heavily on sales and income taxes. These critics argue that the economic downturns beginning in the early 1990s were particularly hard on California and that later recessions, coupled with other unique factors, are at the center of California's school finance difficulties.

Critics point to the influence of Proposition 98's minimum funding for education. They argue that since Prop. 98 was implemented in 1988, funding for California's schools has declined relative to other states while spending on other government services has remained high. They suggest that the California Legislature has focused somewhat narrowly on meeting the minimum school-funding requirements without giving much thought to the actual costs of educating California's current public school population. This focus on meeting school districts' past funding levels has effectively transformed Prop. 98 from a funding floor to a funding ceiling.

Adding strength to the argument are statistics showing that the current California funding system have historically remained inequitable despite over decades of pursuing equity. A class action lawsuit that was filed in May 2000 against the state by civil rights organizations clearly demonstrates the point by focusing on the deteriorating facilities, absence of textbooks and materials, and inadequately prepared teachers in schools serving students who are disproportionately nonwhite and poor. These conditions are not just apparent across districts. They also show up among schools within particular districts.

Similarly, the plaintiffs in *Williams v. State of California* detailed substandard conditions in forty-six schools across the state attended by the named plaintiffs. Relying on its numerous expert witnesses, the plaintiffs provided statistical information documenting disparities. For example, they presented a table showing that at schools with upward of 90 percent students of color, a quarter of the teaching staff was noncredentialed. This compared with about 4 percent for schools with less than 10 percent students of color. The same inverse relationship was evident in schools serving children from poor families.

The plaintiffs further argued that these conditions not only violated the California Constitution but also constituted racial discrimination under Title VI of the 1964 Civil Rights Act and violated Education Code Section 51004. The latter states that it is the policy of California to provide every student, without regard to race, creed, color, national origin, sex, or economic status, an educational opportunity sufficient to enable the student to secure a job.

Plaintiffs' expert witnesses maintained that the state must ensure that the quality of facilities, textbooks, and teachers is sufficient to enable students in all schools to reach levels of proficiency. This means a funding system that recognizes that some schools will need disproportionately greater state-guaranteed funding than others as a result of student needs. Under an educational adequacy funding system, districts that already meet the adequacy standard would be free to spend more, assuming they have the discretion to do so and that voters agree.

The problem with the educational adequacy funding system, however, is that it is hard to define. If set too low, then adequacy begins to look like the discredited minimum foundation programs that triggered the first round of school finance litigation. The difficulty of identifying the standards necessary to determine educational adequacy was the central thrust of the reply brief filed by the state defendants in the *Williams* litigation. The state argued that the plaintiffs had not specified the minimum standards for teachers, textbooks, and facilities under the California Constitution and that the state had fallen short.

Commentators generally agree that once school facilities are made safe and accommodating, simply spending more money in low-performing schools by itself is no guarantee of improved student outcomes. As noted at the start of this chapter, the key concern is *how* the money is spent. It is also important to make sure that the money finds its way through the district and school bureaucracy to reach targeted students. But first, the factors that directly improve student achievement must be identified and the extent of their influence determined. Funding would be directed to those factors that are most positively correlated with student outcomes. This requires significant social science research, and concurrence among experts is likely to be elusive, particularly when the needs of schools and students often vary.

For instance, consider teacher quality. Is it measured by the possession of a state teaching credential or a subject-matter degree? From a state university or a virtual university? By years of experience, participation in professional development training, the accumulation of continuing education credits, positive evaluations from administrators, or high student scores on state assessments? Is research methodology sufficiently sophisticated to separate one from the other and to control for other factors that positively influence student learning, such as the family, student ability and motivation, and student peer groups? If high-quality teaching is an art, then can it be taught?

Additionally, some factors that are positively correlated with student performance may only be minimally affected by how schools are funded. For example, spending more money on the education of low-income students in racially isolated schools does not address the positive impact on learning and socialization of student bodies that are integrated by both race and class. Nor does it influence parenting skills.

Research on teaching and learning is inexact, and politics plays a major role in determining standards and assessment. Given that education is a fundamental right under the California Constitution and measured against constitutional provisions requiring a general diffusion of knowledge and equal protection of the laws, how a school finance system built on the concept of educational adequacy will fare in court is open to question. Late in the summer of 2004, the parties in the *Williams* litigation agreed to settle the case rather than engage in a long and expensive court battle. The settlement affected more than one million students across the state in schools that rank in the bottom 30 percent on state tests. Most of the money was to be spent on instructional materials and facilities improvement. In the end, it appeared the focus was more on addressing educational inequity and less on adequacy.

Despite the new money resulting from the *Williams* settlement, the California Teachers Association and other educator organizations criticized the governor's failure to restore $2 billion taken from Proposition 98 when it was suspended by the legislature to deal with a budget shortfall in 2005 on the promise that the funding would be restored. These organizations joined the State Superintendent of Public Instruction (SPI) in a lawsuit to force the governor to pay back the money plus the increase in school funding that would have accrued to public education if Prop 98 had remained in effect—a total of over $3 billion. The lawsuit was dropped when the governor agreed to restore the money by adding $2 billion to Prop. 98 base funding for 2006 and an additional $3 billion in "settle-up" funds through 2013. The funding was committed to low-performing schools ranking in the bottom two categories (or deciles) of the state's Academic Performance Index (API) categories and was administered in accord with the Quality Education Investment Act (QEIA) (Educ. Code § 52055.700 et seq.).

The state's top political leaders have acknowledged the need for fundamental school finance reform. In 2005, Governor Schwarzenegger established the Governor's Advisory Committee on Education Excellence. Together with legislative leaders, the Advisory Committee requested a comprehensive study of school finance and governance. The study, titled *Getting Down to Facts*, was released in the spring of 2007. Composed of twenty-two reports by an array of researchers from thirty-two institutions across the country and orchestrated by the Institute for Research on Educational Policy and Practice (now the Center for Education Policy Analysis) at Stanford University, "Getting Down to Facts" provided a critical look into the school finance and governance systems of California's public education system.

While few support California's historically byzantine system of school finance, developing a consensus as to when and how it should be reformulated has been and will continue to be no easy task. Once again, we may see the judiciary enter the fray as it has in the past.

For instance, in 2016 and following the implementation of the LCFF, a California court of appeal rejected two related lawsuits challenging the state's current school finance system as a violation of the state constitution. In arguing for an adequate school finance system to assure a quality education for all schoolchildren, the appellants cited Section 1 of Article IX of the California Constitution requiring the legislature to "encourage by all suitable means the promotion of intellectual, scientific, moral, and agricultural improvement" in the interest of a general diffusion of knowledge and intelligence, and Section 5 requiring the legislature to establish a system of free common schools. The majority in this two-to-one decision ruled that neither provision sets forth a right to a public school education of a particular quality. Nor do the provisions require the legislature to provide a particular level of funding. While agreeing with the appellants that a quality education is an important societal goal, the constitutional sections cited do not give the courts the authority to "dictate to the Legislature, a coequal branch of government, how to best exercise its constitutional powers to encourage education and provide for and support a system of common schools throughout the state."

In August 2016, the California Supreme Court, by a 4–3 vote, denied the appellants' petition for appeal. While the majority gave no reason for the rejection, Justice Goodwin Liu noted in a lengthy dissent: "It is regrettable that this court, having recognized education as a fundamental right in a landmark decision 45 years ago (Serrano v. Priest (1971) [citation omitted] should now decline to address the substantive meaning of that right. The schoolchildren of California deserve to know whether their fundamental right to education is a paper promise or a real guarantee. I would grant the petition for review" (*Campaign for Quality Education et al. v. State of California/Robles-Wong v. State of California*, 2016).

SUMMARY

The lack of a strong positive correlation between money and student outcomes is one reason the U.S. Supreme Court has refused to mandate reform. The California Supreme Court has expressed no such inhibitions. In 1971, the California high court ruled in *Serrano v. Priest* that the great disparities in per-pupil funding in districts across the state caused by excessive reliance on the local property tax were unconstitutional. Simply put, property-rich districts could spend more at lower tax rates than property-poor districts, and this amounted to a violation of the equal protection clause of the Fourteenth Amendment. That decision was undermined somewhat by the U.S. Supreme Court in its 1973 *San Antonio Independent School District v. Rodriguez* decision. But the California Supreme Court ruled the same way in a 1976 installment of the *Serrano* case, this time based on provisions in the California Constitution.

Thereafter, state policymakers sought to revise the system to curtail funding disparities so that per-pupil expenditure among students varied only insignificantly across school districts. The idea was to institute what was then known as district power equalizing: Excess revenues from the property taxes in rich districts would be siphoned off to raise spending levels in poor districts at a state-determined tax rate. This noble venture, however, was sidetracked by the passage of several propositions, the most famous being Proposition 13, that limited the yield obtainable from local property taxes.

The *Serrano* decisions in combination with Proposition 13 resulted in a significant shift of school financing control to the state. And faced with limited resources, the state responded with various measures to secure equity in per-pupil spending. Pursuant to Proposition 98, enacted in 1988, public schools generally are guaranteed a basic percentage of the state's general tax revenues. School districts receive the bulk of their general-purpose funds through the LCFF apportionment. While restrictions on issuing local school facility bonds have eased in recent years, voters in many districts are reluctant to pass them. The lack of sufficient funding to maintain school buildings has resulted in rapidly deteriorating facilities in many districts, especially those serving low-income students of color.

Charter schools also have budget challenges, especially start-up charters that require facilities to operate and nonclassroom-based charters that receive less state funding than their classroom-based counterparts. Facilities costs have eased somewhat because the state now requires traditional school districts to provide charter schools with facilities if they serve a certain number of in-district students. Charter schools have also been able to access private funding more readily than traditional public schools have.

A class action lawsuit filed in 2002 threatened to bring state courts once again into the school finance fray. This time, the argument was that the state had shirked its responsibility of providing sufficient resources for all students to receive an adequate education. Rather than seeking equalization, reformers sought to tie funding to the needs of students. From this perspective, the state should guarantee disproportionately greater funds for schools serving students facing greater educational challenges, so that the students can succeed on state-mandated proficiency tests. In 2004, the parties reached a settlement that channeled millions of dollars to secure textbooks and other instructional material for these students and upgrade the facilities they attend.

In 2010, a new school finance lawsuit was filed, claiming that the current school finance system does not enable all students to meet state curriculum standards. At the same time, legislators and the governor began considering a weighted student formula funding system where the amount spent per student would vary depending on the educational needs of the student. This system would combine many categorical funding programs with general revenue funding and would give school officials greater discretion in deciding how money should be spent. But the greater question remains: How should limited resources be spent in the best way for all students to achieve academic success?

Beginning in 2013–2014, the state implemented the LCFF and LCAP. This school finance system purports to target the students with the greatest level of need and to require school districts to provide services to assist those students. Although the COVID-19 pandemic set education back throughout California and the country, some research suggests LCFF has had positive impacts on closing the achievement gap between underserved groups of students, including unduplicated pupils, and their peers. Additional time will reveal the ultimate effectiveness of the LCFF, but controversy is sure to continue to follow school-funding decisions and mechanisms.

4 UNIONS AND COLLECTIVE BARGAINING

Unionization has become a way of life in American public education. Today, most states either have such statutes or permit bargaining without them. Only a few prohibit collective bargaining outright. Over 70 percent of teachers in American public schools are represented by unions. Like other states, California began with so-called meet-and-confer legislation that required management to confer with unions but did not permit the negotiation of a binding contract. California's meet-and-confer legislation gave way in 1975 to the Educational Employment Relations Act (EERA), also known as the Rhodda Act. With the legal framework in place, unionization progressed rapidly.

Today, nearly all of California's approximately 940 school districts are unionized. Of these, the California Teachers Association (CTA), an affiliate of the National Education Association (NEA), represents teachers, counselors, and other certificated employees in the majority of districts; its major competitor is the California Federation of Teachers (CFT), an AFL-CIO affiliate. The California School Employees Association (CSEA) is the largest classified school employees' union in the country, representing nearly 250,000 public employees in California. CSEA is affiliated with the AFL-CIO. However, unions have not made as much headway in representing employees in charter schools. Unions are not a presence in California private schools. Further, certain members of educational management in public schools are ineligible for unionization under EERA.

EERA, like other public sector collective bargaining laws, is modeled on the federal National Labor Relations Act (NLRA). The NLRA provides full bargaining rights to many employees in the private sector as well. Briefly stated, full bargaining rights consist of

- the right of employees to organize collectively if they so choose;
- the right of employees to be represented by a single agent;
- bilateral (management–labor) determination of wages, hours, and other terms and conditions of employment;
- the right to a binding collective bargaining agreement (commonly labeled the "contract") between the employer and the union; and
- the right to strike or to negotiate binding arbitration of both grievance disputes (those arising under the contract) and interests disputes (those arising from the negotiation of a new contract).

By virtue of the EERA, teacher unions in California have become major players in public education. They sponsor legislation, influence school board elections and state politics, negotiate collective agreements, and represent employees on the job. The collective bargaining contract they negotiate is a source of requirements that rivals school board policy in governing day-to-day school administration.

The three stages of collective bargaining described below provide a sense of how the process works. Then we examine in detail how the EERA shapes collective bargaining in California and the implications for union members and school administrators. We conclude by exploring the challenges that school restructuring and reform pose for traditional teacher union bargaining.

THE THREE STAGES OF COLLECTIVE BARGAINING

Once a collective bargaining law conveys bargaining rights to employees, the collective bargaining process generally follows three stages, depicted in Table 4.1.

Unionization Stage

During the unionization stage, unions compete to gain the representational rights of employees within the bargaining unit. The Public Employment Relations Board, commonly known as PERB, determines the bargaining unit based on a community of interest among employees (e.g., all teachers and certificated employees, other than administrators, within a school district).

Depending on how much support a union has among employees in the bargaining unit, the employer may either recognize the union as the exclusive bargaining agent or ask PERB to schedule an election. Evidence is usually required that at least 30 percent of the bargaining unit supports a union before an election can be scheduled. This is termed a "showing of interest." Once a union is chosen by a majority of employees in the bargaining unit, that union becomes the exclusive bargaining agent for all employees in the unit, even those who voted for a different union or no union.

This concept of "exclusivity" is central to collective bargaining. It gives the union significant power at the bargaining table as the single spokesperson for all employees in the bargaining unit. Conversely, the individual employee loses the right to negotiate individually with the employer. With few exceptions, relations with the employer related to the mandatory subjects of bargaining must go through the union unless the union decides otherwise. In this sense, collective bargaining is about group rights, not individual rights, though the provisions of the contract serve to protect individual rights. It is the union that negotiates the collective bargaining contract, and it is the union that sees that it is enforced. In return for exclusivity, the union has a legally enforceable fiduciary responsibility to represent all employees fairly, whether or not they are union members.

The unionization stage is very political, as unions compete among themselves to represent employees in the bargaining unit and as the employer seeks to avoid having any union chosen by a majority of the employees. Once the majority of employees choose a union to represent them, the focus shifts to the bargaining table.

TABLE 4.1
Stages of Collective Bargaining

	Unionization stage	Contract negotiation stage	Contract administration stage

Character	1. Drive to organize unions
	2. Competition among unions
	3. Elections for certification and decertification
		1. Bilateral (employer/employee)
		2. Often Adversary ("we-they" mentality)
		  a. Least common denominator
		  b. Use of sanctions
			1. Parties meet and confer
			2. Grievance processing
			3. Adjudication by arbitrators

Results	1. One union selected as exclusive representative
	2. Contract negotiation begins
		1. Written agreements or tentative agreements with language specificity
		2. Differentiation of role relationships
		3. Contract expansion over time
			1. Rationalization of organizational processes
			  a. Define role relationships
			  b. Legitimize exercise of authority
			  c. Channel and resolve conflict
			2. Highlight contract inadequacies, pointing way for new rounds of negotiation

Contract Negotiation Stage

Because there is only one union representing all employees in the bargaining unit at the bargaining table and only one employer, negotiations are bilateral. As an interest group, the union often employs the familiar tactic of asking for more than it expects to get. Management, in contrast, is generally insistent on maximizing productivity from its employees within its limited budget resources. Thus, the parties often begin from the least common denominator and work toward an agreement. This is particularly true when the bargaining relationship is new and relationships between management and labor have yet to form.

In general, collective bargaining statutes identify the subjects of bargaining. Mandatory subjects of bargaining refer to those matters that the parties must bargain about if one side wishes to do so. Typically, economic matters such as wages and hours of employment fall into this category.

Permissive subjects of bargaining are those that the parties may negotiate if both parties agree to do so. Prohibited subjects of bargaining are those that cannot be bargained even if both parties wish to do so. When there is disagreement about whether a particular subject is bargainable, PERB and perhaps the judiciary will be called on to decide the matter.

As the parties work through the negotiation process, they will reach "tentative agreements" subject by subject. Eventually, the parties will reach tentative agreements on all subjects and sign a collective bargaining agreement. The tentative agreement is then subject to ratification by the union's membership and the school district's board of education. If one or both do not approve the tentative agreement, the parties will return to the bargaining table for further negotiations in an effort to resolve the concern(s) that prevented ratification. With the exception of salary and health and welfare benefits, which are typically negotiated each year, the parties typically implement the collective bargaining agreement for up to three years but may agree to a shorter term.

The contract will have certain characteristics. First, most terms will be very explicit. The specificity of contract language ensures that little ambiguity exists that could trigger interpretation disputes later on. The union's role will be defined as it relates to involvement in school district operations. The same is true for delineating management's role.

As time goes on, there is a tendency for collective bargaining contracts to expand. This is so for several reasons. First, despite efforts to be as explicit as possible, areas of ambiguity are certain to remain, in part because the parties chose to compromise on some issues to reach agreement. During the next successor negotiations, the parties will seek to clarify the ambiguity. Second, the negotiation teams will anticipate as many conflict situations as possible and include contingency mechanisms for their resolution. Third, new legislation may provide topics for negotiation (e.g., benefits resulting from the enactment of the federal Family Medical Leave Act and the grade span adjustment described in Chapter 3).

In addition to economic benefits, the union is equally concerned about working conditions and will strive to negotiate matters that fall within the permissive area of bargaining. This is particularly true of unions representing professional employees. The union might contend, for example, that the development and implementation of a new middle school curriculum will affect the preparation time of teachers, a mandatory subject of bargaining. To avoid having to build more preparation time into the contract, school district negotiators may decide to provide teachers with a greater say in curriculum development. In these ways, the scope of bargaining expands, and contracts can become lengthy.

Contract Administration Stage

In contrast to the political character of the unionization and contract negotiation stages, the contract administration stage tends to be more impersonal and bureaucratic. Similar to a government constitution, the agreement regulates the diverse activities of individuals with conflicting interests within the same organizational setting. It rationalizes organizational functioning through a set of mutually acceptable work rules that define the respective roles of the employer, the employees, and the union. It legitimizes the exercise of management authority. It fosters communication between the union and management through periodic deliberative sessions regarding the administration of the contract. And equally important, the grievance provisions, including arbitration by a neutral party, are a channel through which disputes may be resolved. Inevitably, of course, contract ambiguities and inadequacies will surface during the years the contract is in force. These, coupled with changing conditions, often become the focus of the next round of negotiations.

The presence of collective bargaining is no assurance that employees will not be too weak to check absolute, arbitrary administrative power. Or conversely, there is no guarantee that management can preserve sufficient authority to direct the organization and prevent worker demands from becoming an impregnable wall against needed innovative change. At best, collective bargaining represents a workable balance between management prerogative and membership rights that is not externally imposed but decided by the parties themselves.

Having sketched out the collective bargaining process, we turn now to examine how collective bargaining in California operates under the terms of the EERA and what the implications are for both administrators and teachers.

COLLECTIVE BARGAINING UNDER THE EDUCATIONAL EMPLOYMENT RELATIONS ACT

Before the enactment of the Educational Employment Relations Act (EERA) in 1975, unions had been around for many years in California. In fact, CTA and CFT date back to 1863 and 1919, respectively. CSEA was started in 1927. However, the absence of a collective bargaining law kept them from having much leverage with school districts.

Until 1961, school districts could unilaterally determine working conditions. That year, the California Legislature became one of the first states to move toward public sector collective bargaining by enacting the Brown Act, which gave public employees, including public school staff, the right to join or not join employee organizations and recognized the right of these organizations to meet with employers to discuss working conditions. However, the school board retained the prerogative to make the final decisions, and there was no process for adjudicating disputes over the application of the Brown Act.

In 1965, the California Legislature passed the Winton Act for public school employees, thus separating them from California public employees in general. The latter were accorded collective bargaining rights with the enactment of the Meyers-Milias-Brown Act in 1968.

The Winton Act continued the meet-and-confer provisions of the Brown Act for school employees but added measures establishing dispute resolution mechanisms such as fact finding and mediation. While the Winton Act provided teacher unions greater influence, it did not accord them full bargaining rights. That came with the enactment of the EERA ten years later. Because unions are active, unionization moved quickly after the legislature passed the EERA.

The EERA does not impose collective bargaining on school districts. It leaves the decision to form and join a union to employees and the process of negotiating a contract to both the union and the school district. However, the EERA does provide the legal framework for collective bargaining. This lengthy and detailed statute can be found in California Government Code Sections 3540–3549. The EERA's purpose is to promote the improvement of personnel management and employer–employee relations within the public school system of the State of California by providing a uniform basis for recognizing the right of public school employees to join organizations of their own choosing, to be represented by the organizations in their professional and employment relationships with public school employees, to select one employee organization as the exclusive representative of the employees in an appropriate unit, and to afford certificated employees a voice in the formulation of educational policy. (Gov't Code § 3540)

The EERA sets forth a number of unfair or prohibited labor practices for both public school employers and employee organizations. For instance, it is unlawful for both employers and unions to (1) penalize employees engaging in protected activities under the EERA, (2) refuse to meet and negotiate in good faith, or (3) refuse to participate in efforts to resolve differences when negotiations break down.

The EERA also requires good-faith negotiations over mandatory subjects of bargaining before employers can impose a change unilaterally. In addition, employers are prohibited from denying unions their rights under the EERA and from seeking to dominate or interfere with unions by such actions as contributing financial support or preferring one union to another.

Government Code Section 3540 notes that the EERA is not to supersede the provisions of the California Education Code and the rules and regulations of public school employers relating to tenure or a merit or civil service system, and courts have recognized this limitation. For example, the California Supreme Court has ruled that a teacher union cannot negotiate due process rights for the nonextension of probationary teacher contracts as the non-reelection of probationary teachers is controlled by the Education Code (*Board of Education of the Round Valley Unified School District v. Round Valley Teachers Association*, 1996; see also Educ. Code § 44929.21).

The Role of the Public Employment Relations Board

The EERA is administered by an independent state agency known as the Public Employment Relations Board (PERB), which comprises five members appointed by the governor with the advice and consent of the State Senate. The governor also appoints the chairperson. The PERB selects an executive director, who in turn appoints a staff and general legal counsel.

The PERB's principal functions include (1) deciding appropriate bargaining units; (2) conducting representation elections and certifying the results; (3) determining the matters within the scope of negotiations and of meeting and conferring; (4) investigating unfair labor practice claims; (5) establishing lists of mediators, arbitrators, and fact finders; and (6) undertaking any other actions necessary to implement the EERA. To this end, PERB has developed a set of administrative regulations that can be found in Title 8 of the California Code of Regulations, beginning with Section 31001. The regulations are also included on the PERB website, at www.perb.ca.gov.

As a quasi-judicial administrative entity, PERB has established a body of labor law through the thousands of decisions it and its administrative law judges have issued over the years. PERB decisions may be accessed at www.perb.ca.gov/decisions/. PERB enforces its orders and decisions by court action, where judges accord its judgments substantial deference. In 1988, the California Supreme Court observed that "PERB's interpretation will generally be followed unless it is clearly erroneous" (*Banning Teachers Association v. Public Employment Relations Board*, 1988).

Covered Employees and Schools

The EERA governs public school employers and public school employees. The term "public school employer" includes the governing board of a school district, a school district itself, a county board of education, a county superintendent of schools, a charter school that has declared itself as such (and not the district that granted the charter to be the public employer), and a joint powers agency where two or more educational entities operate collectively (Gov't Code § 3540.1 (k)).

The EERA defines "public school employee" as any person employed by any public school employer except persons elected by popular vote (e.g., school board members), persons appointed by the governor, management employees, and confidential employees. The EERA also recognizes supervisory employees and imposes special limitations on their access to representation.

Management employees are those who have significant responsibilities for formulating and administering district policies who have been designated by the public school employer subject to review by the PERB.

Confidential employees are those who develop or present management positions with respect to employer–employee relations or whose duties normally require them to access confidential information that is used to contribute significantly to management positions (Gov't Code § 3540.1).

Management and confidential employees are permitted to represent themselves individually in employment matters with the school district or through an organization of similar employees. However, the organization cannot meet and negotiate with the governing board. The statute specifically prohibits the organization from negotiating any benefit or compensation for these employees. As we noted in

Chapter 1, school principals, as members of management, essentially serve at the discretion of the school district (Gov't Code § 3543.4).

Supervisory employees include employees who have the authority to hire, transfer, suspend, lay off, recall, promote, discharge, assign, reward, or discipline employees. Supervisory employees also include those employees who have the responsibility to assign and direct work, to adjust employee grievances or effectively recommend adjustments to those grievances, and to exercise independent judgment regarding the matters reserved for supervisory employees. Supervisory employees are permitted to engage in bargaining, providing the bargaining unit includes all supervisory employees employed by the district and does not include employees they supervise (Gov't Code § 3545). In some districts, principals use the supervision designation to form a union.

Deciding on the Appropriate Bargaining Unit and Choosing a Representative

Commonly labeled the "exclusive representative," the EERA permits one organization to represent all employees within the bargaining unit on matters specified in the statute. If there is a conflict over which positions should be included in the bargaining unit, PERB makes the determination based on "the community interest between and among the employees and their established practices" (Gov't Code § 3545(a)).

A negotiating unit that includes classroom teachers is not considered an appropriate unit unless it includes all classroom teachers employed by the school district. Likewise, and as noted above, a negotiating unit of supervisory employees is not deemed appropriate unless it includes all supervisory employees employed by the district. However, supervisory employees cannot be included in the same unit with persons that they supervise, nor can classified and certificated employees be included in the same unit, because their interests are different.

If an employee organization can satisfy a public school employer that it represents the majority of all employees in an appropriate bargaining unit, the employer must recognize the organization as the exclusive bargaining agent unless the employer doubts the appropriateness of the unit. The employee organization must post its request for recognition on employee bulletin boards in all the district's facilities and submit proof of its majority support claim to the PERB for verification.

Verification of union support is established through a review of dues deduction authorizations, notarized membership lists, or signed petitions. The employer does not have to recognize the union as the exclusive representative if another employee organization contests the bargaining unit or submits—within fifteen days of the first organization's posting—a competing claim that is supported by at least 30 percent of the members of the unit. In the latter scenario, the PERB schedules an election.

No election can be held if a collective bargaining agreement is already in existence unless the request for recognition by another union is filed in accordance with timelines set forth in the EERA. No election can be scheduled if the employer has recognized another employee organization as the exclusive bargaining agent within the past year.

If by January 1 of any school year, no employee organization has established majority support in the bargaining unit, a majority of employees may submit a petition to the public school employer asking for an election to be conducted by the PERB. An employee need not be a member of an employee organization to sign the petition. Any employee organization that establishes support from at least 30 percent of members of the bargaining unit may appear on the ballot.

As the overseeing agency, the PERB has the authority to investigate and resolve matters submitted to it by petition involving the appropriateness of a proposed bargaining unit and recognition or withdrawal of recognition of a bargaining agent. If PERB finds that a question of representation exists, it will order an election by secret ballot and certify the results. Timelines and procedures are specified in the statute. Ballots must include "no representation" as one of the options. Each voter is entitled to choose only one option. If no choice on the ballot receives a majority, then a runoff election is conducted between the two highest contenders. Once an employee organization is selected as the exclusive representative, it has a duty to "fairly represent each and every employee in the appropriate unit" (Gov't Code § 3544.9).

Scope of Bargaining

While the Winton Act permitted education unions to meet and confer over a wide range of items, it did not require management to negotiate and reach an agreement over any of them. The EERA increases the power of unions by specifying that certain matters are mandatory subjects of bargaining and according representatives of certificated employees the right to consult on certain matters. All other matters are left to the discretion of the public school employer. Within certain limits, the parties are free to expand the scope of consultation and negotiation should they so desire. An item that is not a mandatory subject of bargaining can trigger a duty to bargain if it impacts a matter that is within the scope of bargaining. Table 4.2 provides an overview of the categories discussed in this section.

As indicated in the table, mandatory topics of bargaining encompass matters relating to wages, hours, and other terms and conditions of employment. Government Code Section 3543.2 identifies specific topics that fall within "terms and

TABLE 4.2

Key Mandatory, Consultative, and Nonnegotiable Topics under EERA

Mandatory bargaining	Mandatory consulting	Management prerogative
Wages Hours Terms and Conditions of Employment • Health and welfare benefits • Leave, transfer and reassignment policies • Safety conditions • Class size • Evaluation procedures • Organizational security agreements • Grievance procedures • Layoff of probationary certificated employees • Alternative compensation or benefits if adversely affected by pension limitations Other topics (per PERB decision) if: • Logically and reasonably related to wages, hours, and an enumerated term and condition of employment • Conflict likely to occur if not negotiated • Will not significantly undercut management prerogative	Representatives of certificated employees have the right to consult on the following: • Definition of educational objectives • Determination of course and curriculum content • Selection of textbooks Note: The parties may agree to consult on other matters.	All matters not specifically enumerated are reserved to the public school employer and may not be a subject of meeting and negotiating unless the employer and union agree otherwise and the matter is not preempted by the Education Code. EERA does not limit the right of the public school employer to consult with any employees or employee organization on any matter outside the scope of representation.

*If the parties are unable to reach agreement, provisions of the Education Code control.

Note: Matters that are not themselves mandatory topics may trigger a duty to bargain if they impact an item that is within the scope of bargaining.

conditions of employment," including health and welfare benefits; leave, transfer, and reassignment policies; safety conditions; class size; evaluation procedures; organizational security arrangements (to be discussed later in this chapter); grievance processing procedures; layoff of probationary certificated employees (limited to districts with an enrollment of 400,000 or more); and alternative compensation or benefits for employees adversely affected by pension limitations.

In an important decision, the California Supreme Court has ruled that the mandatory subjects of bargaining may range beyond those specifically listed in the EERA but may not supersede provisions of the Education Code. The case involved unfair labor charges filed with the PERB against two school districts for their refusal to bargain in good faith on selected topics. The first district, San Mateo City School District, refused to bargain over instructional duty and preparation time and the effects of unilaterally changing the length of the instructional day. The second district, Healdsburg Union School District, refused to negotiate a list of items presented to it by the California School Employees Association.

When the unions filed unfair labor practice charges against the districts, the matter came before PERB. The school districts argued that because the matters were not specifically listed in the statute as topics of negotiation, they did not have to be bargained. PERB disagreed with the school districts' position, ruling that a subject is negotiable even if not specifically enumerated in the statute. PERB developed the following three-part test to determine which topics are mandatory for bargaining:

1. The subject is logically and reasonably related to hours, wages, or an enumerated term and condition of employment;

2. The subject is of such concern to both management and employees that conflict is likely to occur, and the mediatory influence of collective negotiations is the appropriate means of resolving the conflict;

3. The employer's obligation to negotiate would not significantly abridge its freedom to exercise those managerial prerogatives (including matters of fundamental policy) essential to achieving the district's mission.

Using an earlier version of this test, PERB ruled that all contested items in the San Mateo case and some items in the Healdsburg case were negotiable. The California Supreme Court endorsed the use of the test, noting that the legislature had not exclusively identified all negotiable items in the statute. Rather, by using phrases such as "matters relating to," it left such a determination to PERB's expertise. The Supreme Court noted that, while explicit provisions of the Education Code may not be bargained, such as layoffs of classified employees, language pertaining to those provisions may be added to a collective bargaining agreement. Doing so, wrote the court, "would not supersede the relevant part of the Education Code, but would strengthen it" (*San Mateo City School District v. Public Employment Relations Board*, 1983).

It also bears noting that the EERA places an affirmative duty on school employers to notify the exclusive representative of its intent to make any changes to matters within the scope of bargaining. In addition, school employers must provide the exclusive representative with a reasonable amount of time to negotiate regarding the proposed changes (Gov't Code § 3543.2(a)(2)). Depending on the changes, the school employer may be required to negotiate only the impacts and effects of the decision or both the decision and its impacts and effects.

On request of either party, the EERA also includes within the scope of bargaining causes and procedures for disciplinary action other than dismissal for certificated employees, including suspension of pay for up to fifteen days, procedures for the layoff of certificated employees for lack of funds, payment of additional compensation based on criteria other than years of training and experience, and a salary schedule based on criteria other than uniform allowance for years of training and experience. If no mutual agreement is reached, then the provisions of the Education Code control. These are, respectively, Sections 44944 (disciplinary action), 44955 (layoff), and 45028 (uniform salary schedule).

The provision dealing with additional compensation based on criteria other than years of experience puts a union in the difficult position of negotiating provisions that may benefit some bargaining unit members but not others. The matter was an issue in a 2002 California court of appeal ruling involving a onetime retroactive payment of 3 percent of base salary to teachers who returned to work or who had retired at the end of the previous year, but not to eight teachers who had resigned or left. Although the payments complied with the terms of a mediated settlement package reached with the teachers' union, the agreement was negotiated with difficulty and involved the work of a mediator. The union subsequently sued the school district, contending that the payment was not additional compensation but rather a uniform salary payment under Education Code Section 45028 that should have been given to all teachers. The section provides that, except for those holding administrator or supervisor credentials, each person employed in a certificated position is to be classified on a salary schedule based on uniform allowance for years of training and years of experience unless the union and employer agree otherwise.

The questions for the court in this case were whether the one-time payment to all teachers except those who resigned or left after the school year could be characterized as a salary payment or as additional compensation. If additional compensation, was it based on criteria other than years of training and experience? The court answered yes to both. As a one-time payment, the 3 percent emolument was additional compensation. And the criterion on which it was based was whether or not the teachers had returned to work for the 1998–1999 school year or had retired at the end of the previous year. The teachers in question had resigned or left, so they did not meet the criterion. Thus, the one-time payment provision in the contract was justified as an incentive payment and did not violate the uniform pay provisions of Education Code Section 45028 (*California Teachers Association v. Governing Board of the Hilmar Unified School District*, 2002).

A few years later, the Education Code provision on uniform salary schedule blocked the Stockton Unified School District and its teacher union in their effort to catch up with the salary levels of neighboring school districts by accelerating teacher pay through compression of steps on the salary schedule. While this benefited teachers on the lower levels of the schedule, it worked the reverse on teachers who were on the eliminated steps. These teachers were shifted to lower steps and thus had to work longer to attain higher salaries. They filed suit, arguing that the compressed salary schedule violated the uniformity requirement. Both the trial court and the appellate court agreed, noting the absence of new criteria in the collective bargaining agreement, such as teaching in an economically depressed area or teaching special needs students to justify the differential treatment. The compressed salary schedule could remain in place, but the district was required to adjust the affected teacher salaries so that the uniformity requirement was met (*Adair v. Stockton Unified School District*, 2008).

As noted earlier, the Winton Act's meet-and-confer approach was carried over to the EERA in the form of mandatory topics for consultation between the union and the public school employer. Consultation means that the parties may discuss the topics but are not required to bargain over them unless both parties agree to do so. As noted in Table 4.2, Government Code Section 3543.2 (a) specifies that the exclusive representative of certificated employees "has the right to consult on the definition of educational objectives, the determination of the content of courses and curriculum, and the selection of textbooks to the extent such matters are within the discretion of the public school employer under law." Several of these matters, such as curriculum content, are significantly influenced by the Education Code and implementing regulations, thus leaving less discretion to the employer. While the substance of these matters is not bargainable, PERB has concluded that the procedures by which consultation takes place are subject to negotiation.

Beyond bargainable and consultative topics are those reserved to the public school employer. Government Code Section 3543.2 (a) states, "All matters not specifically enumerated are reserved to the public school employer and may not be a subject of meeting and negotiating." At the same time, in a 1983 decision, the PERB noted that in enacting the EERA, the legislature did not intend to deny employees without an exclusive representative the opportunity to speak to their employers individually or through a nonexclusive representative about matters affecting employment, a right that they had under the predecessor Winton Act. Thus, in this situation, the employer has an obligation to provide reasonable notice and a time to meet and discuss fringe benefits and other matters of fundamental concern to the employment relationship before making a final decision (*Service Employees Industrial Union v. Los Angeles Unified School District*, 7 PERC P 14069 (1983)).

Even when there is an exclusive representative, the statute provides that "nothing herein may be construed to limit the right of the public school employer to consult with any employees or employee organization on any matter outside the scope of representation" (Gov't Code § 3543.2 (a)). School districts and individual schools have any number of advisory committees and channels of communication for receiving information and commentary about matters other than those governed by the EERA.

As noted above, the EERA permits the union and employer to extend the scope of bargaining and consultation should they wish to do so. However, PERB has concluded that when a school district agrees to bargain over a permissive topic of bargaining, the topic then does not become a mandatory topic. In other words, a district may withdraw the topic from bargaining during negotiations (*Poway Federation of Teachers v. Poway Unified School District*, 12 PERC P 19102 (1988)).

As noted earlier, charter schools now fall within the ambit of the EERA. As amended in 1999, Education Code Section 47611.5 specifies that the school's charter must indicate whether it is to be the exclusive public school employer for purposes of collective bargaining if the school's employees opt to unionize. If the charter school is not so designated, then the school district where the charter school is located becomes the employer for this purpose.

At the same time, Section 47611.5 provides that the approval or denial of a charter petition by a charter authorizer is not controlled by collective bargaining agreements, nor is it subject to review or regulation by the PERB. To date, unions have made relatively limited progress in organizing charter school employees, although in some districts, the conversion of a traditional public school to a charter school has continued employee union representation.

Following the 1999 amendment to the charter school law, conflict arose in a few districts over the employer designation issue. For example, controversy arose in the Ravenswood City School District over the termination of several teacher contracts by the Edison Brentwood Academy, a charter school operating in the district.

In that case, the teachers' union brought an unfair labor practice charge against Ravenswood, contending that the teachers were terminated for engaging in union activities and citing language in the collective bargaining contract that the district was the employer. The district claimed that the charter school was the employer and should face the charges. In compliance with the statute, Edison Brentwood Academy's principal had sent out a letter confirming that it, and not the district, was the employer.

The teachers' union argued that this declaration did not change the fact that the district had authority over personnel matters at the school. The PERB administrative law judge observed that while the collective bargaining agreement between the teachers' union and the Ravenswood district did have provisions setting terms and conditions for the employment of charter schoolteachers, the charter stipulated that these provisions did not apply if they were in conflict with the design and operation of the school. Thus, the charter school had unilateral discretion in making personnel decisions about its teachers. This being so, the charter school was the employer and was the proper entity to face the unfair labor charge (*Ravenswood Teacher Association v. Ravenswood City School District*, 26 PERC P 33118 (2002)).

Complicating the matter in the Ravenswood case was the fact that the charter school was operated by Edison Schools, now known as EdisonLearning. While the management agreement between the charter school and Edison recognized that the company and the Ravenswood School District would be involved in teacher selection and evaluation, that teachers remained public employees, and that the district would provide due process protections in the event of contract teacher termination, the administrative law judge ruled that the charter between the district and the charter school took precedence. Conflict of this type is not unusual when multiple agreements are involved—here, a collective bargaining contract between the union and the school district with some provisions applying to the charter school, a charter document between the district and the charter school, and a management agreement between the charter school and the private educational management organization.

The 1999 amendment to the charter school law states that if the charter or the charter school does not specify that the school will comply with statutes and regulations governing tenure or a merit or civil service system, then the discipline and dismissal of teachers at that charter school become mandatory topics of bargaining. This depends on who the employer is, the terms of the charter, and whether the teachers at the school have opted to unionize. At the same time, the statute directs the PERB to take into account the Charter Schools Act when deciding cases coming before it involving these institutions, suggesting that the innovative character of charter schools should be safeguarded whenever possible.

Contract Negotiation

Negotiations involving public schools significantly implicate the public. Thus, the EERA requires all initial proposals of the parties to be "sunshined," or presented, at a public meeting and notes that the initial proposals are public records. Negotiating cannot begin until the public has had a reasonable time to become familiar with the proposals and express its views at a governing board meeting. Though negotiation sessions are not open to the public, new subjects arising in the course of negotiation must be made public within twenty-four hours, and the public must be informed of any votes cast on the subject by the governing board within the same time period.

Prior to approval of the written agreement, the provisions and implementation costs are to be presented at a public meeting. In addition, commonly labeled the "AB 1200," the school district's superintendent and chief business officer must certify that the district will meet its financial obligations during the term of the agreement and such representations are subject to review and confirmation by the county office of education.

The public disclosure requirements are based, in part, on the assumption that if the negotiating stance of the governing board and costs associated with its position are not supported by the public, board members will feel the pressure and conform to public wishes. However, as a powerful interest group, the union can sometimes have significant influence on school board elections, especially when voter turnout is low.

If school board members realize that union members constitute a significant portion of their support, they may be particularly attentive to union interests. And while school board members are always concerned about public opinion, unions are adept at influencing it. As portrayed in Figure 4.1, the union's presence thus can be felt on *both* sides of the bargaining table. This is less true of charter schools whose governing board is the employer, because the members of charter school governing boards are not elected but gain their status through the granting of the charter. However, if the school district remains the employer of charter school employees and charter school employees agree to unionize, the union can exert any political influence it has on the governing board. Figure 4.3 illustrates these lines of union influence.

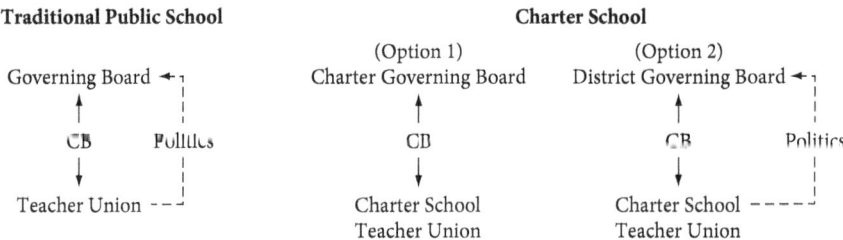

Figure 4.1 Teacher Contract Negotiation in California Public Schools

In many districts with a long history of amicable relations between the union and the governing board, collective bargaining is not extremely adversarial, and agreement may be reached quickly. In other situations, however, strained relations in combination with limited resources often lead to conflict at the bargaining table over key issues such as salary and benefits.

During the negotiation process, the parties may reach an impasse, meaning that they have been unable to reach agreement on a contested item of bargaining. The EERA defines *impasse* to mean that the "differences in positions are so substantial or prolonged that future meetings would be futile." One or both parties may declare impasse by filing an impasse declaration with PERB. If PERB agrees that an impasse exists, several things can happen, as outlined in Figure 4.2. Note that a district's locking out or discharging teachers is not among them. Nor can a union resort to a strike except in rare circumstances, as described later in the chapter. The reason is that public schooling is a constitutional right under the California Constitution, and its continuation takes precedence over the interests of the governing board and the union.

The impasse procedures include several steps as noted in Figure 4.4. First, the PERB must appoint a mediator to assist the parties in reaching agreement. Alternatively, the parties may develop their own mediation procedures.

Some years ago, the PERB declared that the South Bay Union School District committed an unfair labor practice by declaring an impasse over negotiating a provision restricting the union's right to file grievances in its own name. The contract was eventually signed without the provision. The district insisted that the matter was a mandatory topic of bargaining because it related to negotiating a grievance system. The union argued that, because it has a statutory right to file grievances, the district could not force it to bargain over the matter to the point of impasse.

The district appealed PERB's ruling without success. Noting its obligation to give great deference to the judgment of the PERB, the California court of appeal cited several PERB decisions holding that a union has a statutory right to file a grievance in its own name. Thus, the district's declaration of an impasse over this nonmandatory bargaining topic constituted bad-faith bargaining (*South Bay Union School District v. Public Employment Relations Board*, 1991). The EERA was amended in 2000 to permit employees to file grievances in their own name without the union's involvement as long as the resolution is reached prior to arbitration and is not inconsistent with the terms of the collective bargaining agreement. However, the public school employer may not agree to a resolution of the grievance until the union has received a copy and has had a chance to file a response (Gov't Code § 3543 (b)).

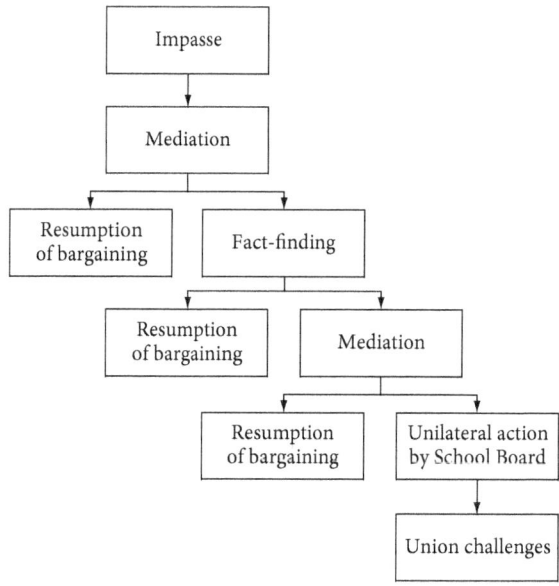

Figure 4.2 Resolving an Impasse over Negotiating Mandatory Topics of Bargaining under the EERA

Government Code Section 3548 provides that a mediator may meet with the parties or their representatives either jointly or separately and take whatever steps necessary to assist the parties in resolving the impasse. Like negotiation sessions, meetings held by the mediator with either or both parties are not open to the public. If the mediator is unsuccessful within fifteen days of the appointment, then either party may request that their differences be submitted to a three-person fact-finding panel, although parties may, and often do, waive this timeline and others associated with the impasse process.

If the matter proceeds to a fact-finding panel, each party selects a person to serve on the panel, with the chairperson selected either by PERB or by mutual agreement of the parties. Unless the parties agree, the chairperson cannot be the same person who served as mediator.

Unless waived by the parties, the fact-finding panel meets with the parties within the time frames specified in the statute, holds hearings, and conducts investigations. These activities take place in private. The panel has the power to compel persons to attend, give testimony, and produce evidence. Unlike traditional adversarial hearings, such as Commission on Professional Competence hearings related to teacher dismissals, the panel member selected by each party typically confers with the party who selected them and may assist with the presentation of their positions during the fact-finding process.

Following a set of criteria described in the statute, the panel sets forth its findings and settlement recommendations. These recommendations are advisory only and are submitted to the parties before being released to the public. The mediator previously appointed may resume mediation based on the findings of fact and recommendations for settlement. Throughout this period, the parties must continue to seek a resolution of their differences, and when impasse is broken, they must resume bargaining in good faith.

The EERA permits the school district to take unilateral action to implement the last offer the union has rejected (Gov't Code § 3549). When can this occur? A California court of appeal ruled in 1983 that a school district may impose unilateral changes in employment conditions within the scope of bargaining only after the impasse procedures have been completed. The court agreed with the PERB that allowing the employer to do so prior to this time would generate conflict, undercut effective employee representation, and diminish the bilateral duty to negotiate (*Moreno Valley Unified School District v. Public Employment Relations Board*, 1983).

Even after fact-finding, however, if one party makes concessions, the duty to bargain resumes. Thus, the employer cannot simply impose the last best offer rejected without returning to the bargaining table if the union makes concessions. Further, when a unilateral change is implemented, it must be reasonably consistent with the last offer (*Public Employment Relations Board v. Modesto City Schools District*, 1982).

Of course, even after post-impasse actions have been exhausted and the employer unilaterally implements changes in the terms and conditions of employment, the matter is not likely to end. Union challenges are likely on a variety of fronts, including going out on strike. The EERA does not expressly approve a post-impasse right to strike, but neither does it prohibit that right.

In 1979, the California Supreme Court analyzed the right to strike in a matter involving the San Diego Unified School District. In that case, each party filed unfair labor charges against the other. The school district obtained a judicial restraining order suspending the strike. The parties then agreed to resume negotiations. A few days later, the trial judge filed contempt charges against the union and its president for violating the restraining order. Both were subsequently found guilty. The union and its president were fined and the latter sentenced to jail for a short time.

They appealed, arguing that while Section 3549 does state that a provision of the Labor Code permitting strikes is inapplicable to public school employees, the

EERA does not itself prohibit strikes. The Supreme Court did not rule directly on their argument because it found the district improperly pursued the injunction without following the steps the EERA provides when the parties fail to reach agreement, including seeking PERB's assistance in pursuing the restraining order. While the court noted that the impasse procedures discussed earlier "almost certainly were included in EERA for the purpose of heading off strikes," it did not preclude strikes after exhaustion of the impasse procedures (*San Diego Teachers Association v. Superior Court*, 1979). The court invalidated the contempt order and penalties against the union and its president.

Taking its cue from the California Supreme Court's *San Diego* decision and a 1985 decision by the same court refusing to apply an automatic ban against strikes that do not pose an imminent danger to public health and safety (*County Sanitation District No. 2 v. Los Angeles County Employees Association, Local 600*, 1985), PERB subsequently developed a two-part test to determine whether a post-impasse strike constitutes an unfair labor practice. Specifically, in a case involving Compton Unified School District, PERB held that a post-impasse strike must cause a total breakdown of basic education and be used to leverage gains at the bargaining table by holding education hostage to constitute an unfair practice (*Compton Unified School District v. Compton Education Association*, 11 PERC P 18067 (1987)).

In *Compton*, teacher work stoppages coincided with failure to reach agreement on a contract and continued intermittently, lasting sixteen days. The school district was unable to replace most of the striking teachers. Over the four months when periodical work stoppages occurred, attendance was down 40 percent and reached 70 percent during the height of the work stoppages.

Several other disruptions occurred. For example, strikers and others disrupted a school board closed meeting, resulting in police action. The district asserted that strikers encouraged students to join the picket lines around the district's schools or sent them home when they arrived for school. Several fires of suspicious origin occurred in the district's schools.

Viewing education as a fundamental right, the majority of members of the PERB found that a considerable number of the district's students received little or no meaningful education during this period. Based on the facts and its lengthy analysis of the importance of education, PERB held that the strike constituted an unfair labor practice and sought a court order against it.

In contrast, the PERB upheld a strike when analyzing an unfair labor practice claim filed by the Vallejo Unified School District against its teacher union over a two-day walkout occurring after impasse procedures had concluded. Though only 100 teachers out of a normal day attendance of approximately 800 arrived for work, the district was able to replace all of them with substitutes. While student attendance decreased by half during the strike, there was no evidence that attendance suffered beyond the week of the strike. Nor was there evidence that the strike caused a breakdown in negotiations, because neither side sought to continue negotiations during the time when the strike occurred (*Vallejo City Unified School District v. Vallejo Education Association*, 17 PERC P 24166 (1993)).

It is important to note that the PERB has not supported a union's right to strike either before or during an impasse to achieve economic goals, because such a strike undermines the mandatory procedures set forth in the EERA to end the impasse. For example, the Irvine Teachers Association resorted to several tactics to advance its cause in contract negotiations with the Irvine Unified School District in the mid-1980s. Included among the tactics were a work-to-rule job action and a one-day strike. The work-to-rule job action meant that the teachers refused to perform any discretionary duties beyond those specified in their contracts. The strike occurred on the first day of the beginning of the spring semester. Three-quarters of the 750 members of the bargaining unit participated in the work stoppage. The work stoppage was conducted peacefully, with striking teachers spending most of the day engaged in informational picketing at their respective school sites.

The PERB administrative law judge concluded that the work-to-rule job action was a lawful bargaining tactic, but the strike was not. The strike was unlawful because it was motivated solely by the teacher union's desire to advance its economic demands at the bargaining table. In effect, the strike amounted to a refusal to negotiate contrary to the mandatory procedures set forth in EERA (*Irvine Unified School District v. Irvine Teachers Association, CTA/NEA*, 1987).

A few years later, the PERB ruled that the post-impasse intermittent strike was impermissible under EERA. In a matter involving the Fremont Unified School District, PERB considered whether a series of short work stoppages by teachers in the Fremont Unified School District in 1990 following an unsuccessful effort to reach agreement violated the EERA. Each of the strikes coincided with an impasse in negotiations and lasted no more than two days.

The district filed an unfair labor practice charge against the union. The PERB noted that the intermittent strike was an unfair pressure tactic because it enabled employees to retain the benefits of working and striking at the same time. It also precluded the district from hiring long-term substitutes. Because the intermittent strike disrupted the delivery of education services and violated the duty to bargain in good faith, post-impasse intermittent strike was both unprotected and unlawful

(*Fremont Unified School District v. Fremont Unified District Teachers Association*, 14 PERC P 21107 (1990)).

The past several years have seen a significant increase in the number of teacher strikes in California and across the United States. For instance, in 2019, teachers' unions implemented strikes in the New Haven Unified School District, Forestville Unified School District, and Sacramento City Unified School District. Also in 2019, teachers in the Los Angeles Unified School District implemented work stoppage until the school district agreed to a six percent wage increase. Likewise, the Oakland Unified School District's teachers engaged in a seven-day strike that same year, achieving an eleven percent on-schedule salary increase over four years and a three percent off-schedule payment.

Strikes continued in both the Los Angeles Unified School District and Oakland Unified School District. Specifically, in the Los Angeles Unified School District, employees engaged in a three-day strike related to wages and staffing in 2023. Likewise, in 2023, Oakland Unified School District teachers engaged in a strike before reaching a tentative agreement on issues including pay, class size, work hours, and other issues.

Given its increasing use in the recent past, it is likely that unions will continue to resort to strikes to obtain economic and other benefits. As strikes become more common, it is likely that the PERB will be required to intervene in additional unfair practice allegations and resolve disputes between school districts and unions.

Contract Administration

Once a collective bargaining agreement, commonly labeled a contract, has been signed and is in force for up to three years, its provisions must be implemented in day-to-day school and district management and operations. At times, a labor-management or joint contract administration committee is established to assist the parties in handling matters that arise in applying contract provisions, such as disagreements related to contract terms, access to district premises, use of association leave for association business, reviewing reports, and developing a collaborative approach to achieving alignment of standards, curriculum, staff development, and student assessment.

Occasionally, disputes arise that cannot be resolved informally. To resolve those disputes, contracts typically include a grievance and arbitration clause.

The grievance and arbitration system. A grievance system is a standard provision of a collective bargaining agreement. It consists of a number of steps by which an individual employee can, with or without union support, seek a remedy for a violation of the contract. The first step normally involves bringing the matter to the attention of the employee's immediate supervisor. If no satisfactory adjustment is forthcoming, the employee and/or union may appeal to a higher level, and so on, through the grievance steps. If no agreement can be reached, the matter usually is referred to arbitration.

EERA provides that a public school employer and exclusive representative may include in the agreement final and binding arbitration for disputes involving the interpretation, application, or violation of the agreement (Gov't Code § 3548.5). Even if the agreement does not include such an arbitration clause, both parties mutually may agree to submit a dispute to final arbitration in compliance with rules established by the PERB. Compliance with an agreement to arbitrate is enforceable by court order. Once an arbitrator has made an award, the award is final and binding on the parties. Subject to certain exceptions, it is also enforceable by court order. An arbitrator's award may be challenged in court only on limited grounds (Code of Civil Proc. § 1281 et seq.).

Alternatively, the parties may agree to advisory arbitration in place of binding arbitration. Although the arbitration hearing procedures are typically identical to binding arbitration, the arbitrator issues only an advisory decision to the school district's board of education. The board of education typically has the discretion to accept, modify, or reject the arbitrator's decision. In school districts implementing advisory arbitration, the board of education's decision is typically final and not subject to review, unless the board of education's decision is unlawful.

The role of the arbitrator. The arbitrator's role is particularly significant to the ongoing relationship between the employer and the union. Often, under pressure to reach agreement, negotiators will leave certain clauses relatively ambiguous simply to avoid further conflict. Naturally, the parties will interpret these clauses differently, each to their own advantage.

Eventually, the conflicting views will coalesce around a specific grievance. The resolution of the question will be up to the arbitrator, who has been given the power by the parties to convene a hearing, review evidence related to the dispute, and render a decision.

In some cases, all provisions in the contract are subject to the arbitration clause; and in others, the arbitrator has the authority to determine whether a grievance is arbitrable. Judges are reluctant to disturb the arbitrator's broad powers to decide both procedural and substantive issues arising under a contract, except for very limited circumstances, such as the arbitrator's unwillingness to admit and consider relevant evidence. Thus, the arbitrator plays an important adjudicatory role in the continuing relationship between the parties and, in the process, provides a way of settling disputes without expensive and time-consuming litigation.

Despite the authority of the arbitrator and the reluctance of judges to interfere, there are limits to the arbitrators' authority, and violations of that authority have led to litigation. For example, in 1996, the California Supreme Court was faced with a school district's refusal to arbitrate a dispute with its teacher union over the nonextension of a probationary teacher's contract. The union negotiated a clause into the collective bargaining agreement extending due process rights to probationary teachers in such situations.

During the term of the contract, the school district notified a teacher of contract nonextension without complying with the clause. The Education Code provides that probationary teachers have no due process rights (absent unlawful conduct by the school district) other than notice of non-reelection by March 15 during the second consecutive year of their probationary contract (Educ. Code § 44929.21). In effect, probationary teachers may be non-reelected without a showing of cause, without a statement of reasons, and without a hearing or right to appeal (although school districts are well advised to ensure that legitimate, nondiscriminatory reasons support any non-reelection). A California lower court ordered the district to submit the dispute over the contract nonextension to binding arbitration in compliance with the collective bargaining contract. The arbitrator later found the district violated the agreement and ordered it to comply with the due process procedures it had agreed to. The school district challenged the decision.

Although the California Supreme Court recognized that arbitrator awards are accorded great judicial deference, exceptional circumstances may justify judicial involvement. Here, the arbitrator's decision conflicted with a provision of the Education Code governing nonextension of probationary teacher contracts and, hence, violated a provision of EERA that it "shall not supersede other provisions of the Education Code" (Gov't Code § 3540).

Further, the EERA specifies that matters not specifically enumerated as bargaining topics are not negotiable and left to the discretion of the employer. As noted earlier in the chapter, while the layoff of certificated teachers for lack of funds is listed as a negotiable item, the nonextension of their contracts is not. Thus, the arbitrator exceeded his authority in attempting to enforce a provision in a contract that required due process procedures for contract nonextensions (*Board of Education of the Round Valley Unified School District v. Round Valley Teachers Association*, 1996).

The California Supreme Court relied on its *Round Valley* decision to rule in 2012 that provisions in a collective bargaining agreement relating to the conversion of a public school to a conversion charter school are not arbitrable if they conflict with the Education Code. Education Code Section 47611.5 states that the approval or denial of a charter petition is not to be controlled by collective bargaining agreements. The case involved provisions in the collective bargaining contract between the United Teachers of Los Angeles and the Los Angeles school district that the union argued the school district failed to follow, such as providing the complete charter to employees and providing them and the union time to review it.

The Supreme Court determined that it was unclear whether these provisions actually conflicted with the Education Code. As a result, it sent the case back to the trial court for further deliberations. The Court pointed out that there would be no conflict if following the procedures "would neither control the approval or denial of a charter petition nor delay or obstruct the charter petition approval process." The Court added that, if arbitration does occur and the arbitrator, in applying the collective bargaining provisions, imposes obligations on the district that run counter to the Education Code or otherwise violate public policy, the arbitration award would be invalid (*Board of Education of the Round Valley Unified School District v. Round Valley Teachers Association*, 1996).

Generally, if a matter is arbitrable, the chances of overturning an arbitration award are slim. A case in point involves the Bonita Unified School District's effort to overturn an arbitrator's decision against bypassing progressive discipline to terminate a classified employee.

In that case, the school district provided the employee with a notice of termination and suspension without pay for a number of reasons, including incompetence, dishonesty, insubordination, and immoral conduct. The collective bargaining agreement with the California School Employees Association (CSEA) provided that the district could not terminate a classified employee without first following specified "progressive discipline" procedures — including verbal warnings, written warnings, and a letter of reprimand. However, the agreement permitted the district to bypass the progressive discipline procedures if the offense was sufficiently serious.

The agreement provided that, in accord with Education Code Section 45113 (e), whether the school district may bypass the progressive discipline procedures could be submitted to final and binding arbitration. CSEA challenged the district's determination to arbitration to determine whether the alleged offenses were sufficiently serious. If so, the arbitrator would become the district's hearing officer for a termination hearing, with the board having the right to accept, reject, or modify the hearing officer's findings and recommendations.

However, the matter never reached a hearing on the merits of the dismissal because the arbitrator found a lack of evidence to support many of the charges against the employee, thus leading to a conclusion that the offenses were not sufficiently serious to warrant bypassing progressive discipline. The district vacated that decision, citing a provision of Section 1286.2 of the California Code of Civil Procedure that permits overturning arbitration awards when the arbitrator exceeds his or her powers.

The union and the employee filed suit. Both the California trial court and court of appeal ruled against the district. The appellate court noted that school boards, like courts, have very limited statutory grounds to overturn arbitration awards. Here the arbitrator was well within his authority to determine what constitutes "serious" for purposes of bypassing progressive discipline (*California School Employees Association v. Bonita Unified School District*, 2008).

Unfair labor disputes. Occasionally during the contract, an unfair labor dispute will arise that will require the involvement of the PERB and even the courts. For example, a dispute over the use of the school district's internal mail system arose in the San Leandro Unified School District. The San Leandro Teachers Association (SLTA) filed a lawsuit against the San Leandro governing board because the board refused to permit it to circulate a newsletter that included a section discussing support for SLTA-endorsed governing board candidates. A second newsletter pertaining mostly to employment issues included a sentence urging bargaining unit members to volunteer to phone or walk in support of the candidates. The PERB dismissed the unfair labor charge on the basis of Education Code Section 7054, which prohibits use of school funds, services, supplies, or equipment for political endorsements. The union then appealed the PERB's decision to the superior court.

The trial court decided in favor of the union. However, a California court of appeal overturned that decision, citing Education Code Section 7054. The school's mail system, the judges observed, can be viewed as both a service and as equipment. The union argued that Section 3543.1(b) of the Educational Employment Relations Act gives it the right to contact employees through institutional bulletin boards, mailboxes, and other means of communication. The court agreed but noted that the provision conditions the right on "reasonable regulation." Here, denying use of the school district's mail system for political activity, as contrasted with employment matters, serves a valid public purpose and is reasonable.

The union also argued that the restriction violates its freedom of speech under the federal and California constitutions. The court rejected the argument, noting that the San Leandro internal mail system was not being operated as a public forum. Further, the union had other ways to communicate its political messages to its members, including leaving material in the faculty lounge and mailing newsletters to teachers' home addresses.

The union appealed and the California Supreme Court unanimously affirmed the decision in 2009, incorporating much of the appellate court's reasoning as its own. Noting that political speech is at the core of free speech protection in both the federal and California constitutions, the high court emphasized the narrowness of its ruling. The school could, the justices pointed out, open up its mailboxes for political endorsement literature as long as it is done on an equitable basis. And they noted that the court's ruling does not restrict a recognized union from using school mailboxes to urge members to become involved in elections and from engaging in public policy discussion in more general terms rather than engaging in one-sided endorsements (*San Leandro Teachers Association v. Governing Board of the San Leandro Unified School District*, 2009).

Organizational Security Arrangements

Organizational security arrangements are critically important to unions because they provide the union with the resources and protections to be effective. Union dues, one of the primary mechanisms to access resources necessary to provide services to unit members, and the "agency fee" have been the subject of significant litigation over the course of the past decades.

By way of background, the EERA required that, once a union is recognized as the "exclusive representative" of employees in the bargaining unit, each employee who chose not to be a dues-paying union member was required to pay a fair share service fee—also known as an agency fee or agency-shop fee—that was not to exceed the dues paid by union members (Gov't Code § 3546). Government Code Section 3546.3 permitted those having religious objections to either joining a union or paying a service fee to opt out of doing so. However, to prevent religious objections from providing bargaining unit members with an incentive to avoid paying anything at all, the law provided that the money must be routed to a non-religious charitable organization.

In 2003, a teacher in the Chino Valley School District filed a lawsuit against her union, contending that having to pay an amount equivalent to full union dues to a charitable organization while agency fee payers paid a lesser amount to the union constituted discrimination against religion and a denial of equal protection of the laws. The federal district court rejected her claim, noting that religious objectors are not in the same category as agency fee payers. Religious objectors received the full benefits of union representation without having to pay anything and, at the same time, got to advance the cause of their charities (*Madsen v. Associated Chino Teachers*, 2004).

Like exclusivity, service fees were designed to eliminate free riders. Since the union had a legal obligation to represent both members and nonmembers, it was only fair that nonmembers contributed their share of the union's costs. On request by the union, the public school employer was required to deduct the fee from the employee's salary and turn the amount over to the union, even without employee authorization (Educ. Code § 45061). The fee could include, but was not limited to, the cost of negotiation, contract administration, and similar activities germane to the collective bargaining process. It also included costs of union lobbying targeted at fostering collective bargaining negotiations and contract administration or securing benefits for union members outside the collective bargaining process. In 1989, the California Supreme Court excluded most such costs in the absence of specific statutory authority (*Cumero v. Public Employment Relations Board*, 1989). In 2000, the legislature provided that authority by adding Government Code Section 3546. Because the service fee was a large portion of what a regular union member pays, it was not uncommon for feepayers to decide to join the union so that they have a voice in union affairs. Once a union member, the person is obligated to maintain membership in good standing for the duration of the agreement. However, the member could terminate membership within a period of thirty days following the expiration of the agreement.

The organizational security arrangement could be rescinded by a majority vote of members in the bargaining unit if the voting request is supported by a petition signed by at least 30 percent of the membership (Gov't Code § 3546 (d)). The vote may be conducted only once during the term of the collective bargaining contract. The school district's governing board must be careful not to influence the rescission process lest an unfair labor charge be filed against it and the election blocked. This could occur, for example, if the school administration spoke out against the agency fee and/or refused to enforce it. Such a situation occurred in a dispute between the representative of classified employees and the governing board in the Mount Pleasant Valley Elementary School District some years ago (*Charles H. Allen et al., Petitioners-Appellants, and California School Employees Association and Pleasant Valley Elementary School District, Respondents*, 8 PERC P 15051 (1984)). If the vote was successful, the union could petition for the reinstatement of the organizational security arrangement by requesting another election to be held not earlier than one year after the rescission pursuant to a petition signed by at least 30 percent of the bargaining unit members, or the union may negotiate the matter.

Prior to being overturned by the United States Supreme Court in 2018 (discussed below), the fair share service fee had been the source of significant controversy.

Much of the controversy has centered on the use of the money—especially lobbying activities that the nonunion payee objects to.

In its *Cumero* decision, the California Supreme Court faced this question in a case involving a teacher who objected to having to support any union expenses beyond those incurred in the negotiation and administration of the contract. The court rejected the teacher's argument that having to support any lobbying to which he objected would violate his First Amendment rights. The court cited a 1977 U.S. Supreme Court decision, *Abood v. Detroit Board of Education*, in support of a distinction between lobbying to support collective bargaining activities and lobbying for ideological causes unrelated to collective bargaining. Only the latter violated the nonunion payee's First Amendment rights.

Second, the court agreed with the teacher that union organizational activities in other school districts to build union strength are too attenuated from the costs of negotiating contracts to be within the scope of an organizational security arrangement. But the court rejected the teacher's contention that the agency fee could be used by the local affiliate only to support its work and not to support its state and national affiliates. The court noted that the term *employee organization*, as defined in EERA, includes not only the bargaining agent but also "any person such an organization authorizes to act on its behalf." Because the local teacher union utilized the services of the California Teachers Association (CTA) and its national affiliate, the National Education Association, in representing its members, payment of a portion of the agency fee to them was permissible.

A related matter concerned nonunion members' access to information on how the agency fee was spent. Agency feepayers had a right to receive a rebate or fee reduction of the portion of the fee that was not used for its intended purposes. EERA required the public employer to provide the bargaining agent with the home address of each unit member, regardless of when the member begins employment, so that the union could comply with notification requirements set forth in a 1986 U.S. Supreme Court decision. In that decision, the Court ruled that the union had an obligation to provide nonmembers with an explanation of the basis of the agency fee, a reasonably prompt opportunity to challenge the amount of the fee before an impartial decision maker, and the establishment of an escrow account for the disputed amount pending the outcome of the challenge (*Chicago Teachers Association, Local No. 1 v. Hudson*, 1986). This correspondence became known as the "Hudson notice" and usually encompassed the most recently audited prior year broken down by major categories of expense, indicated chargeable and nonchargeable categories for nonmembers, and set forth the agency fee for the following year. If the union failed to issue a Hudson notice, it could be liable to nonconsensual feepayers. While employers had the responsibility to assure procedures that protect nonunion member rights, the Ninth Circuit has ruled that they were not required to assure that feepayers receive a Hudson notice before agency fees are deducted (*Foster v. Mahdesian*, 268 F.3d 689 (9th Cir. 2001), *cert. denied sub nom. Foster v. Garcy*, 535 U.S. 1112 (2002)). They could be liable, however, if they took adverse action against a feepayer because the feepayer challenged the union's handling of the matter.

Federal courts, including the U.S. Supreme Court, have issued significant decisions affecting agency fees. For instance, in 2007, the Supreme Court concluded that a state could require unions to seek permission from nonmembers before spending agency fees for political purposes. In that case, the Washington Education Association argued that imposing the consent requirement intruded on the union's First Amendment rights. The Court unanimously rejected the argument (*Davenport v. Washington Education Association*, 2007).

While California did not have such a requirement, the matter has surfaced in the past. In a related matter involving a California union, the U.S. Supreme Court ruled seven-to-two in 2012 that public sector unions must send agency feepayers a second Hudson notice in addition to an annual fee notice when adopting a temporary, midterm fee increase beyond what was projected for that year. This was a necessary step to avoid violating nonmembers' First Amendment rights by making them contribute to political causes to which they object.

Five members of the Court went further to rule that, rather than sending out notice giving nonmembers the right to opt out of the special fee, the notice must require that nonmembers affirmatively opt in. The effect was to make it harder for unions to secure nonmember support. The four dissenters viewed this as judicial overreaching because it could apply not to just special assessments but to regular annual agency fees as well (*Knox v. Service Employees International Union, Local 1000* 2012).

It also bears noting that the U.S. Court of Appeals for the Ninth Circuit considered whether a union could be required to provide nonmembers with a formal audit and ultimately rejected such a requirement. In that case, nonunion teachers in eight California school districts sued their local unions and the CTA, claiming that, in order to comply with the *Hudson* decision, unions must submit audited financial statements so that the nonmembers could confirm that their agency fees were being spent for authorized purposes.

At the time, the CTA required local unions to secure financial statements by an outside certified public accountant if their estimated annual revenue from membership dues and agency fees totaled $100,000 or more. If the amount were less than $100,000, the financial disclosure could be reviewed by a certified public accountant or audited by CTA staff auditors. If it were less than $50,000, the local union was only required to provide feepayers access to its check register and canceled checks, along with a form required by the IRS and another by the PERB.

The Ninth Circuit found fault only with the policy involving the smallest local unions. No outside reviewers verified the accuracy of the financial records, and only partial information was made available. The court noted that the unions do not provide fee payers access to such financial records as bills or inventories. The judges left it to the union and its state affiliate to devise a system that complied with its mandates (*Harik v. California Teachers Association*, 326 F.3d 1042 (9th Cir.), cert. denied sub nom. *Sheffield v. Aceves*, 540 U.S. 965 (2003)).

Despite auditing requirements and a well-developed body of case law governing agency fees, the topic of union membership and agency fees continued to arise as a major subject of litigation. For instance, in 2015, four dues-paying members of several teacher unions initiated litigation in a California federal district court contending that requiring them to join their union and pay dues forces them to support certain union political and ideological views with which they disagree in violation of their free speech rights. They argued that, if they choose not to pay union dues but only an agency fee, they would forfeit certain benefits available to dues-paying union members. The district court rejected the contention, noting that unions are not state actors and, thus, the First Amendment doesn't apply to them. The court noted that terms of dues-paying membership are determined not by the state but by the union (*Bain et al. v. California Teachers Association et al.*, 2015).

Around the same time, a case reached the United States Supreme Court involving California teachers who argued that requiring non-members in a public sector bargaining unit to pay an agency fee for union activities violates their First Amendment rights. Both the Ninth Circuit and the federal district court refused to rule on the matter, citing the *Abood* decision discussed above. In March 2016, the Supreme Court, in an equally divided decision, affirmed the lower court decisions without opinion. *Friedrichs v. California Teachers Association*, 2016.

However, in 2018, the United States Supreme Court found agency fees in public employment to be unconstitutional. Specifically, in *Janus v. American Federation of State, County and Municipal Employees*, Mark Janus, a state employee in Illinois, sued his union, AFSCME, arguing that a state law requiring nonmembers to pay an agency fee violated his First Amendment rights. Although the Court specifically found agency fees to be constitutional through its holding in *Abood* in 1977, the Court reversed its earlier position and, on this occasion, found the agency fee violated Mr. Janus and others' First Amendment rights. The Court reasoned:

Compelling individuals to mouth support for views they find objectionable violates that cardinal constitutional command, and in most contexts, any such effort would be universally condemned. Suppose, for example, that the State of Illinois required all residents to sign a document expressing support for a particular set of positions on controversial public issues—say, the platform of one of the major political parties. No one, we trust, would seriously argue that the First Amendment permits this.

California's response was swift. In fact, the Legislature responded to *Janus* before the Court issued its decision. Specifically, the Legislature passed four bills, Assembly Bill (AB) 119, Senate Bill (SB) 112, SB 285, and SB 866 intended to mitigate some of the significant anticipated impacts of *Janus*.

AB 119 and SB 112 require public employers to provide unions with access to employees during orientation sessions. In addition, AB 119 requires public employers to provide the union with each unit member's name; job title; department; work location; work, home, and personal cellular telephone numbers; personal e-mail addresses; and home addresses within 30 days of each new hire's employment with the employer and all employees' above noted information at 120-day intervals, unless the union and employer agree to different intervals.

The Legislature also passed SB 285, which was related to employer communications concerning union membership. In particular, SB 285 prohibits employers from discouraging employees from joining the union. In addition, SB 285 provided PERB with jurisdiction to hear and decide disputes related to alleged violations of SB 285.

Finally, in an effort to protect the union's access to dues, the Legislature passed SB 866. That legislation requires employers to deduct union dues in accordance with the union's instructions so long as the union certifies to the employer that it has obtained a dues authorization from the employee. SB 866 clarifies that the union shall not be required to disclose the authorization to the employer, unless a dispute arises related to the authorization. In exchange, the union is required to indemnify the employer for any employee claims related to the authorization.

FUTURE CHALLENGES

Both the National Education Association and the American Federation of Teachers are professional associations and unions. However, it seems fair to say that they have not been as successful as other trade unions in securing the professional interests of their members. For many trade unions representing professional employees, the collective bargaining agreement is intended to secure economic benefits and prevent the erosion of the employees' traditional influence over their work. Contemporary examples are the American Federation of Musicians, an AFL-CIO affiliate that includes most symphony orchestras in its membership; the Air Line Pilots Association, also an AFL-CIO affiliate that represents some 60,000 airline pilots in the United States and Canada; and Actors Equity, another AFL-CIO affiliate that represents 49,000 theatrical performers.

Teacher unions have become more aggressive in advancing the professional interests of their members through collective bargaining. For example, they have sought a voice for teachers in the development of the school curriculum. This reflects, in part, the nature of unions to continue to serve their members' interests and the growing concern about the quality of public schoolteachers and schools.

Teacher union advocates point out that having public policymakers, bureaucrats, and school administrators make decisions about curriculum standards and student assessment leaves out of the loop the valuable input of teachers who face students every day. Opponents contend that such assertions mask a union power drive that would stifle innovation. For the moment, the EERA gives California teacher unions the right to consult on, but not negotiate, educational objectives, course and curriculum content, and textbook selection. Union polling shows that many newer members are very interested in education reform issues. This is one of the reasons why the California Teachers Association (CTA), for example, has become involved in the implementation of the Quality Education Investment Act, as described in the previous chapter.

The area most troubling to teacher unions is the expansion of school choice through charter schools, particularly vouchers and tuition tax credits for private school attendance. Charter schools pose a dilemma for unions because, in many cases, teachers are among those who develop the charter petition and undertake the design of the school and its program. They both teach and oversee the operations of the school. Many teachers consider themselves part of the administration of the school and are not predisposed to unionize. Even if they desired to do so, would it be contrary to the EERA because, in effect, teachers would be sitting on both sides of the bargaining table?

According to a 2003 PERB decision, however, the fact that some members of the charter school bargaining unit may rotate into and out of management and supervisory roles cannot deny all members of the bargaining unit their rights under the EERA to organize (*Robert L. Mueller Charter School*). PERB held that the exclusion of eight certificated members of the charter school's thirteen-member leadership team from the bargaining unit would result in a unit consisting of just classroom teachers. Whether the eight should be excluded, however, was an issue left to future determination should the charter school challenge the ballot process.

More recently, the reversal of a PERB decision rejecting an unfair labor claim filed by three charter schoolteachers demonstrates how teachers often play different roles in charter schools. The dispute involved the contract termination of three teachers by the Journey Charter School in the Capistrano Unified School District. Journey is modeled on the Waldorf method of education that, among other things, encompasses a collaborative governance structure involving teachers, parents, and administrators.

In this case, two of the three teachers were members of the school's governing council. When complaints arose related to the school's operation, the two teachers were removed for a time as council members, an act that created dissension among other teachers and the parent community. Later, one of the teachers contacted the California Teachers Association (CTA).

In July 2006, all Journey teachers met to draft and sign a letter to the parents of Journey students regarding challenges the school faced and the school's departure from the collaborative governance model. A month later, the teachers voted to become affiliated with the CTA. The nonteacher members of the charter school's governing council then voted not to renew the three teacher contracts.

The CTA filed an unfair labor practice with PERB against the school claiming the school terminated the teachers because of their involvement with the CTA and in retaliation for writing the July letter, both protected activities. In a two-to-one decision, the PERB concluded that there was no credible evidence that the teachers had been fired because of involvement with the CTA and that the letter the teachers had written was not a protected act under the EERA because it did not deal with the interests of the teachers as employees.

The California Court of Appeal reversed PERB's decision, noting that PERB had not considered the unique role of the teachers in Journey Charter School. The court noted that in response to one of the teacher's letters, the parent-dominated council required all official communications with parents to be approved by the council. The court viewed this act as retaliatory because it affected the role of teachers as employees in the charter school setting, where they played a role in collaborative governance. The court stated, "Even assuming that complaints about the management structure of a school might not be viewed as addressing 'the teachers' interests as *employees*' in a traditional public school," and the judges observed, "it is difficult to conclude they do not do so in this case—or perhaps in any case involving a charter school" (p. 1089, emphasis in original).

Furthermore, the court found that only these three teachers were fired because the council believed they encouraged the other teachers to join the union. Thus, the letter was protected conduct under the EERA. Given its decision on the July letter, the appellate court did not reach the contention that the three teachers were fired because of their efforts to unionize with the CTA. Noting that the teacher contracts were terminated in violation of the EERA, the court returned the case to PERB for a decision consistent with the court's opinion (*California Teachers Association v. Public Employee Relations Board*, 2009).

While California law permits charter schoolteachers to unionize, relatively few have done so in schools that begin without a faculty union. Still, some charter school operators like Green Dot Public Schools, a network of charter schools in Los Angeles, have not opposed unionization of their teachers and have worked constructively to tailor the contract to the mission of the school.

The rapid growth of nonunionized charter schools threatens to erode the traditional union power base. It also raises the free-rider question in that unrepresented charter school employees benefit from union lobbying on behalf of public schools generally, particularly regarding funding. Partly for this reason, California teacher unions have been reluctant supporters of charter schools and have pressured the legislature to impose more regulations on them.

For example, these unions supported legislative efforts in 1998 to limit the number of charter schools, to require that charter schoolteachers be credentialed, and to require that half of all permanent teachers in a public school approve the school's conversion to charter school status. At the same time, unions advise their members to think carefully about moving to charter schools, where they may not have the job protections that unionization affords, and they strive to extend provisions in the existing contract to them. The expansion of charter schools affords unions the opportunity to address inevitable tension between some charter operators and their teachers. To be successful, unions will have to adapt to the different role that teachers often play in charter schools.

Adding to the complexity is the question of the status of teachers in a charter school operated by a private educational management organization (EMO). Suppose, for example, that a charter school recipient contracts with an EMO to provide instructional services. The EMO then hires the teachers to staff the school. Are these teachers the employees of the public charter school or of the private EMO? If the latter, a union seeking to represent them would have to do so under the terms of the National Labor Relations Act (NLRA), the law applicable to the private sector. This is so because the EERA applies only to public employees. The NLRA presents a new set of legal concerns for public sector unions, not the least of which is that unless the school substantially affects interstate commerce, it is not likely to be subject to the NLRA.

So far, there is little law on the question, though the matter has surfaced in California. In 2003, a regional director of the PERB ruled that the employees of a charter school remain public employees for purposes of the EERA, even though the operators of the school contended otherwise. In that case, a private nonprofit public benefit organization known as Options for Youth (OFY) sought and received a charter from the Victor Valley Union High School District in 1993 to operate learning centers for at-risk students. Employees of the school were hired by the board of directors, and the learning centers operated in leased commercial space. A majority of the school's twenty full-time teachers opted for representation by a teacher association, which sought to gain collective bargaining rights under the EERA. OFY opposed the move, claiming that the teachers were private, not public, employees and could organize only under the NLRA.

PERB began its analysis by noting that the NLRA excludes from the definition of "employer" a state or a political subdivision of a state. So, the key question was whether the charter school, despite being operated by a private nonprofit benefit corporation, remained a political subdivision of the state. PERB observed that, in 1971, the United States Supreme Court developed the "Hawkins test," a test for making this determination (*National Labor Relations Board v. Natural Gas Utility District of Hawkins County, Tennessee*, 1971). The Hawkins test requires that the entity is created directly by the state or administered by officials who are responsible for public officials or the general electorate.

To apply the test, PERB examined provisions of the Education Code creating charter schools and *Wilson v. State Board of Education*, a 1999 California court of appeal decision upholding the constitutionality of the Charter Schools Act. Both the statutes and the decision are discussed in some detail in Chapter 1. Based on his analysis, PERB concluded that charter schools, even those operated by nonprofit benefit corporations, are clearly part of the public school system and carry out educational functions under the auspices of the legislature and the public school district granting the charter.

Indeed, the OFY charter petition recognized this fact. Thus, there was no question that OFY Charter School was a political subdivision of the state. Nor was there any question that the charter school officials were fully accountable to the chartering entity, the State Board of Education, and the superintendent of public instruction. Thus, the teachers at the OFY charter school could organize under the EERA (*Options for Youth-Victor Valley, Inc. v. Victor Valley Options for Youth Teachers Association*, 27 PERC P 104 (2003)).

Following PERB's decision, Options for Youth sought to take the matter to court. However, to do so, the charter school had to obtain the PERB's consent, and the PERB did not grant it.

The matter remains subject to dispute, and future legal developments may occur, particularly if EMOs insist on a right to make their own personnel decisions independent of the entity granting the charter and the charter recipient. It should be noted that, in 2010, the Ninth Circuit rejected an Arizona charter schoolteacher's claim that his contract nonrenewal by an EMO operating the public charter school denied him due process of law under the Fourteenth Amendment to the U.S. Constitution. Though charter schools are public schools, the appellate court found that Arizona law did not directly impact the employment actions of EMOs to make them state actors. Thus, the EMO was not subject to constitutional constraints in making personnel decisions (*Caviness v. Horizon Community Learning Center*, 2010). This decision, when compared to PERB's above-noted analysis, sets up a potential dispute among jurisdictions that may lead to a decision by a higher authority.

Even more threatening to teacher unions are publicly funded vouchers and tuition tax credit programs that make the private educational sector available to many parents. The National Education Association, the American Federation of Teachers, and other public school teacher advocacy organizations are philosophically opposed to vouchers and tuition tax credits, which they see as threatening the ideal of universal public education.

Few private schools are unionized because most are too small to come within the terms of the NLRA and because the U.S. Supreme Court has ruled that the NLRA does not apply to private school religious faculty members (*National Labor Relations Board v. Catholic Bishops of Chicago*, 1979). Most private schools in California are religiously affiliated. The ruling does not preclude unions from seeking to unionize lay faculty at such schools.

Even if some unionization is possible in the private school sector, teacher unions would have to shoulder the costs of organizing teachers and negotiating and administering contracts in both the public and private sectors. Further, union influence on private school management likely would be reduced because private school boards, like charter school boards, are not popularly elected. Finally, the expansion of private school choice inevitably siphons students and teachers from public schools, thus reducing the traditional union power base. This, of course, is precisely what many voucher advocates hope will occur. For all these reasons and many others, unions oppose voucher and tuition tax credit programs.

Collective bargaining in education has led to a multitude of ideas and suggestions related to the future of unions in education. In some quarters, calls have been made for changes to the role of unions and the nature of the collective bargaining process in education to make both more compatible with the systemic changes occurring throughout public education. For example, it has been suggested that greater accommodation to nuances at the school site level would be realized by having the union negotiate a master contract with the school district regarding basic salary levels and benefits, and then a series of separate agreements at the campus level governing school operation.

Another recommendation suggests that unions should start charter schools. Operating charter schools and partnering with administrators in education reform initiatives require significant changes in how unions view themselves and perhaps in the legal framework governing unionization and collective bargaining. However, if public schooling continues to undergo structural changes, teacher unions will be hard-pressed not to adapt.

It is likely that the future will hold many other ideas for union representation of public school staff. It remains to be seen whether and to what extent these ideas will influence public education and existing procedures.

SUMMARY

Until the 1960s, California school district operation was essentially controlled by elected officials and school administrators. While teachers' unions had existed for many years, their role was limited. They had little clout to influence how educational decisions were made, including those affecting working conditions.

The enactment of the Brown Act in 1961 and the Winton Act in 1965 gave unions the right to meet and confer with public employers. While this was a significant step forward, it did not deprive the public employer of the right to have the final say. That changed for public schools with the enactment of the Educational Employment Relations Act (EERA) in 1975.

Modeled on the venerable National Labor Relations Act that had governed labor relations in the private sector since 1935, EERA enfranchises public school employees with the right to form and join unions; the right to select an exclusive bargaining agent; the right of the agent to negotiate a binding contract with the school district governing wages, hours, and other terms and conditions of employment; and the right to negotiate dispute settlement procedures.

Because unions had a lengthy history in California and engaged in significant lobbying efforts related to the right to bargain collectively, unionization proceeded rapidly. It was not long before the professional and classified staffs of most districts in the state were unionized.

Over the past thirty years, a vast body of law has developed around the process of determining bargaining units, certifying and decertifying unions, negotiating contracts, and settling disputes. Most of this law emanates from the regulations and rulings of the Public Employee Relations Board (PERB), the state agency charged with implementing and overseeing EERA. Given the technical nature of its work and the expertise it has developed over the years, PERB decisions are accorded significant deference by judges.

Aside from charter and private schools, the collective bargaining process has become ingrained in the operation of California schooling. To a large extent, the relations between educational employees and their employers are governed by the collective bargaining agreement. Through unions, employees have gained economic benefits and a greater influence in educational decision-making. Employers have benefited by having a body of law that regularizes day-to-day school operations. Both employers and employees benefit from having a mutually agreed-upon process for channeling and resolving disputes.

Collective bargaining is not without its problems and limitations. The process is time-consuming and expensive. Critics accuse unions of having too much influence at the bargaining table because, as powerful interest groups, they shape legislation and influence school board elections. Unions are said to be more concerned with serving their own interests than with reforming public education.

Unions argue that they have done more than any other organization in improving working conditions for teachers and other school employees who have been mistreated and underpaid in the past. They argue that until teachers and their representatives have a significant voice in the development of educational policy, efforts to improve schools will fall short.

Systemic reforms being touted for schooling will pose major challenges for unions and traditional collective bargaining. Teacher assessment, the growth of charter schools, the privatization of public schooling, and many other factors carry significant implications for how unions function in the future.

5 EMPLOYMENT

California's public school system relies on over 500,000 employees to perform the myriad tasks necessary to keep school doors open and students learning. The rights of these employees are a combination of state and federal statutes, regulations, and constitutional principles. This chapter focuses on the Education Code's specific provisions regarding the employment, classification, discipline, dismissal, release, and layoff of public school employees.

The Education Code's patchwork of statutes regarding public school employees is complicated and, at times, quite confusing. Even judges have found the Education Code employment statutes to be less than a model of clarity. For instance, in a 1992 California court of appeal decision regarding the Education Code's dismissal statute for teachers, the first sentence in the opinion reads, "In this case, we confront the formidable task of making sense out of the California Education Code" (*Woodland Joint Unified School District v. Commission on Professional Competence*, p. 229).

This chapter begins with a discussion of the different types of public school employees, focusing on the two main categories: certificated and classified. This sets the stage for reviewing due process of law and its application to employee discipline and dismissal. The procedures applicable to the discipline or dismissal of an employee are a function of the employee's category (i.e., certificated or classified).

Attention is then given to the process for non-reelecting certificated and dismissing classified employees during their probationary periods and prior to their attainment of permanent status. After obtaining permanent status, certificated and classified employees retain their employment until dismissal, layoff, resignation, or death. We detail the permissible circumstances for layoff after a brief word on the employment rights of administrators and a comment on the rights of public school employees regarding their personnel files. The final pages of the chapter concern the leave rights of public school employees and applicable antidiscrimination laws.

Unless otherwise noted, our discussion concerns the employees of a governing board in a school district with 250 or more average daily attendance (ADA). ADA measures student attendance for receipt of state funding. School districts with less than 250 ADA are subject to a number of different statutes governing the employment, discipline, and release of employees.

CLASSIFICATIONS AND CATEGORIES OF PUBLIC SCHOOL EMPLOYEES

There are two basic classifications of public school employees: certificated and classified. A certificated employee is an individual who is required to hold a credential issued by the California Commission on Teacher Credentialing (CCTC). The CCTC oversees the issuance, denial, suspension, and revocation of credentials. A teacher is the most common type of certificated employee. Counselors, school site administrators, and other administrators who are required to hold a credential are also certificated employees.

Classified employees are all other employees of the school district not specifically exempted by the Education Code from classified service. Classified employees include those who keep a school running through custodial services, grounds maintenance, cafeteria operation, instructional assistance, and the provision of administrative support. Classified employees also include supervisory management employees who oversee other classified employees (e.g., assistant superintendent of business, director of food services). Unlike certificated staff, classified employees do not provide service under a credential issued by the CCTC.

The distinction between certificated and classified employees is important for reasons beyond the employees' job duties. Certificated and classified employees have different employment, discipline, dismissal, and layoff rights. Important distinctions among employment rights also occur within the different types of certificated and classified employees. For example, a certificated employee in the employee's first year of employment as a probationary teacher may be released at the conclusion of the school year. The employee completes the current school year and does not return. This is known as non-reelection. Alternatively, if the same employee works with the school district beyond March 15 of their second consecutive year, the teacher becomes permanent at the start of the next school year and is entitled to a formal hearing, if the employee so desires, prior to dismissal. Non-reelection is no longer an option for the district to pursue.

Administrators also are critical to the daily operations of public schools. However, the generic term *administrator* does not constitute a third category of public school employees. While the employment terms and conditions of an administrator differ greatly from those of a certificated or classified employee, the administrator may nonetheless be a certificated or classified employee who is simply working in an administrative position. The administrator still retains any rights he or she accrued as a certificated or classified employee and, in the instance of a certificated administrator, may become a permanent teacher in the school district even if they never served as a teacher in that district. However, the school district's board of education retains discretion in reassigning the administrator to a classroom teaching position.

The vast majority of public school employees work for the governing board of a school district. Education Code Section 35160 and following sections set forth the general powers and duties of school district governing boards. The Education Code requires governing boards to employ certificated (§44831) and classified (§45103) employees. In addition to these two basic types of employees, governing boards also employ individuals in senior management positions (e.g., superintendent, assistant superintendent of human resources) and special consultants or experts. The latter include attorneys for legal services, architects, accountants, and any other service providers whose services are not otherwise in conflict with or preempted by law. This last catchall category of special consultants or experts is permissible under Education Code Section 35160.

Public school employees may also work for a county superintendent. A county board of education does not have hiring authority. The county superintendent, however, may permit its employees to assist the county board of education (Educ. Code § 1290 et seq.). A county superintendent may enter into a contract of employment with a certificated employee for a period not to exceed the end of the school year in which the county superintendent's term expires.

No contract of employment between a county superintendent and a certificated employee may exceed four years and six months. Certificated employees under contract with the county superintendent have the same rights with respect to a leave of absence, sick leave, and bereavement leave as do certificated employees working for a governing board (Educ. Code § 1294). Education Code Sections 44922 (part-time employment) and 44949 and 44955 (layoffs) also apply to certificated employees working for the county superintendent.

Public school employees also work for charter schools. As noted in Chapter 1, charter schools are public schools that are exempted from many state statutes and regulations. Unless charter schools voluntarily adopt the Education Code provisions related to employment that apply to the employees of governing boards, those requirements do not apply. These include the extensive classification systems, discipline and dismissal procedures, and leave rights that are addressed in this chapter. However, charter schools are nonetheless employers subject to a wide range of state and federal laws, including antidiscrimination laws. For example, charter schools are subject to the federal Americans with Disabilities Act and California's Fair Employment and Housing Act.

PROPERTY RIGHTS IN EMPLOYMENT

In 1972, the U.S. Supreme Court ruled that public schoolteachers have a protected property right in employment under the terms of the Fourteenth Amendment to the U.S. Constitution if the state gives them a "legitimate claim of entitlement" to it (*Board of Regents v. Roth*, 1972). The Fourteenth Amendment provides in part that no state (or political subdivision of the state, like a public school district) shall deprive a person of "life, liberty, or property, without due process of law." Thus, the dimensions of property rights in public employment are to be found in state law, local policies, collective bargaining agreements, and contractual provisions. Once a governmental entity has created a property right protected by the Fourteenth Amendment, it may not take that right away without providing the employee due process of law.

Employees who do not have property rights and are not protected by civil service rules or union contract are said to be employed "at will," which means that they serve at the pleasure of the employer. For example, Education Code Section 44953 states that substitute teachers may be dismissed at any time at the pleasure of the governing board. Because there is no expectation of continued employment in an at-will arrangement, the employee is not entitled to notice and a hearing before dismissal. Conversely, the employee need not give the employer any notice before leaving or resigning. The employment arrangement continues at the discretion of both parties. But as we will see, "at-will" employment, in its truest sense, does not exist in the public school setting, given that public agencies must have legitimate, nondiscriminatory reasons to release employees. However, for clarity, these employees do not enjoy the property interest described earlier.

The Education Code defines property rights for public school employees in California. Property rights vary, however, between certificated and classified employees and among different classifications of certificated and classified employees. The interrelationship between property rights and employee classification underscores the importance of properly determining a public employee's classification prior to initiating disciplinary action or dismissal.

CERTIFICATED EMPLOYEES

Credentials

A public school employee in a certificated position must hold an appropriate credential from the CCTC. The CCTC can issue two types of credentials: a teaching credential and a service credential. (See Chapter 2 for a more detailed discussion of teacher credentialing). The Education Code and Title 5 of the California Code of Regulations contain extensive statutes and regulations regarding credentials (Educ. Code § 44250 et seq.; Admin. Code, Title 5, § 80000 et seq.).

The holder of a Multiple Subject Teaching Credential may teach grades kindergarten through twelve, preschool, and adults in a self-contained classroom (the setting commonly associated with elementary schools). The holder of a Single Subject Teaching Credential may teach the same range of students in a departmentalized, rather than self-contained, classroom. Middle, junior high, and high schools commonly contain departmentalized classrooms. As the name implies, a Single Subject Teaching Credential is issued for a specific subject (e.g., art, English, or mathematics).

The most common types of service credentials include Administrative Services, Pupil Personnel Services, Health Services, and Clinical or Rehabilitative Services. An individual holding an Administrative Services Credential may work in the position of superintendent (although superintendents are not required to hold credentials), assistant superintendent, principal, or vice principal. The Pupil Personnel Services Credential will specifically authorize the holder to serve in the position of school counselor, school social worker, school child welfare and attendance services, or school psychologist. School nurses hold the Health Services Credential. The Clinical or Rehabilitative Services Credential will authorize its holder to perform a specific clinical or rehabilitative service (e.g., speech and hearing).

The CCTC may also issue emergency permits for an individual who has not completed all of the requirements for a credential (Educ. Code § 44300 et seq.). Emergency Multiple and Single Subject Permits are available for assignments of greater than thirty days. A school district seeking to employ an individual with an emergency credential must justify the need for the emergency credential to the CCTC (Educ. Code § 44300).

An individual with a bachelor's degree who passes the California Basic Educational Skills Test (CBEST) is eligible to receive an emergency Substitute Permit to perform day-to-day substitute teaching for no more than thirty days in any one assignment during the school year. Holding an emergency credential can have important implications for determining the classification of a certificated employee. This aspect of an emergency credential is discussed later in the chapter.

The CCTC issues a permit rather than a certificate to preschool teachers. An individual employed in a position requiring a child development permit for the instruction and supervision of children is "deemed to be employed in a position requiring certification qualifications" (Educ. Code § 8303). As an individual working in a position requiring certification qualifications, a preschool teacher receives most of the rights afforded to other certificated employees, with the exception of layoff rights. Education Code Sections 8295–8305 govern preschool teachers.

It bears noting that special education preschool teachers must hold teaching credentials (Educ. Code § 8360.3). In some instances, special education preschool teachers receive the same or similar rights as other teachers in non-preschool programs. In other instances, they receive rights aligned with the classified service. For instance, like teachers and pursuant to Education Code Section 8303(a), every employee "of a public or private agency in a position requiring a child development permit for the supervision and instruction of children . . . or in the supervision of a preschool program, shall be deemed to be employed in a position requiring certification qualifications." In contrast, like the former classified layoff provisions and pursuant to Education Code Section 8303(c), school districts "may lay off preschool teachers at any time during the school year for lack of work or lack of funds or may provide for the employee's employment for not to exceed 90 days." Further, "The order of layoff shall be determined by length of service. The employee who has served the shortest time shall be laid off first, except that no permanent employee shall be laid off ahead of a probationary employee. A permanent employee who has been laid off shall hold reinstatement rights for a period of 39 months from the date of layoff."

A credential cannot be issued to an individual who has been convicted of any of the following offenses: a sex offense as defined in Education Code Section 44010, a narcotics offense as defined in Education Code Section 44011, or a crime listed in Education Code Section 44424. These Education Code sections cross-reference the Penal Code. An individual who has been judicially determined to be a mentally disordered sex offender is also ineligible for a credential.

Classifications

In addition to a wide range of credentials, there are different statutorily recognized classifications of certificated employees. The property rights a certificated employee has derived from the Education Code are a function of the employee's classification. Property rights, in turn, drive the level of due process necessary for discipline and dismissal. Therefore, before a school district can determine how—or even if—it can discipline or dismiss a certificated employee, there must be a preliminary determination as to the employee's appropriate classification.

Determining an employee's classification can sometimes be difficult because there are circumstances in which an employee is hired in one classification and, through subsequent events, attains an entirely different classification. The Education Code recognizes four different categories of certificated employees: substitute, temporary, probationary, and permanent. Courts generally avoid identifying staff members as substitute or temporary unless they meet the strict statutory provisions that permit school districts to employ them as substitute or temporary employees. Courts treat the probationary and permanent classifications as the default classifications, depending on whether the employee has met the criteria to become permanent.

Of the four classifications, substitute affords an employee the least job protection. Throughout this section, we refer to certificated employees as *teachers* because they constitute the largest category of such employees.

Substitute. A substitute teacher generally provides day-to-day service in place of a regular school district employee who is absent from duty. Through the nature of their work, substitute teachers do not have an expectation of continued employment. In other words, there is no property right in continued employment with the school district.

A governing board may dismiss a substitute teacher "any time at the pleasure of the board" (Educ. Code § 44953). Of course, the board may not release a substitute for an unlawful reason, such as discrimination based on a protected status.

A school district may employ a substitute teacher after September 1 and for the remainder of the school year if no qualified regular employee of the district is available and the teacher consents to the substitute assignment (Educ. Code § 44917). Absent a written notice of release by the end of the school year, the teacher must be reemployed for the next school year in any vacant position.

A substitute teacher working in a certificated position at least 75 percent of the school year will be deemed to have served a complete school year as a probationary teacher if the individual is employed as a probationary teacher for the following school year (Educ. Code § 44918(a)). A substitute teacher serving in an on-call status to replace absent regular teachers of the district on a day-to-day basis does not attain probationary status solely by virtue of that day-to-day employment (Educ. Code § 44918(d)).

Temporary. Temporary employees are those persons working in positions requiring certification qualifications, other than substitute employees, who work for a school district on a temporary basis (Educ. Code § 44919). For example, a high school Spanish teacher may enter into a contract with a governing board to teach for a semester to replace a permanent teacher who is on leave. "At the time of initial employment," a school district must give a temporary certificated employee a written statement "clearly indicating the temporary nature of the employment" and the duration of the employment (Educ. Code § 44916). If a written statement does not indicate the temporary nature of the employment, the teacher is deemed a probationary employee. The presence or absence of the foregoing written notice is critical because an individual working in a probationary certificated capacity is accruing time toward permanent status.

In the 2003 California Supreme Court decision in *Kavanaugh v. West Sonoma County Union High School District*, the court interpreted the phrase "at the time of initial employment" in Section 44916 to settle a dispute over a teacher's classification. Alta Kavanaugh had applied for a position as an English teacher with the West Sonoma County Union High School District (West Sonoma County UHSD) for the 1999–2000 school year. Alta interviewed for and received the job. According to Alta, however, it was never made clear to her whether the position was temporary or probationary. A few weeks after Alta's first day of employment, West Sonoma County Union High School District's Board of Trustees ratified Alta's hiring as a teacher. Alta received a letter confirming her employment "as a temporary teacher" a few days after the West Sonoma County UHSD Board of Trustees meeting.

Near the end of the school year, West Sonoma County UHSD experienced financial difficulties. Alta and other temporary employees were released and not reemployed for the following school year. Alta challenged this decision in court, making a two-part argument. First, Alta argued that she was a probationary employee by default because she did not receive written notice of her temporary status "at the time of initial employment," as required by Section 44916. Second, she argued that because she was a probationary employee and did not receive notice of non-reelection, she was entitled to reemployment for the following school year.

The school district's failure to timely non-reelect a probationary employee automatically results in the rehiring of the employee for the next school year. Alta prevailed on both arguments. Because Alta did not receive written notice of her temporary classification "on or before her first day of paid service," the court concluded that she "must be considered a probationary employee as a matter of law" (p. 823). A school district that provides timely written notice of an employee's temporary classification and subsequent release may rehire and release the employee in a temporary classification for multiple consecutive school years (*McIntyre v. Sonoma Valley Unified School District*, 2012).

Similarly, an employee is considered probationary if the employee works even a single day before signing their employment contract, even if the contract was intended for a temporary position. This concept was exemplified in the case of Shanna Petersil, who was hired as a temporary certified employee by the Santa Monica–Malibu Unified School District in August 2008. Petersil worked a single day for the district before signing a contract identifying her as a temporary employee. In March 2009, the district sent a notice of non-reelection to Petersil and then rehired her as a temporary employee in July 2009. The district sent another notice of non-reelection to Petersil in March 2010. The notices referred to Petersil as a temporary employee and referenced the Education Code section permitting the release of temporary employees.

Petersil challenged her release by arguing that the notices of non-reelection were not sufficient because she was actually a probationary employee by virtue of working a single day before signing her temporary employment contract in 2008. Petersil further argued that, as a result of the untimely signing of her contract, the district did not issue sufficient notice of non-reelection as the non-reelection notices from the district only made reference to the Education Code section pertaining to the release of temporary employees.

The court found Petersil to be a probationary employee because she worked a day before signing the contract, which designated her as a temporary employee. However, the court found that the reference in the non-reelection notices to the incorrect code section did not invalidate the district's non-reelection notice. The court explained that Education Code Section 44929.21(b) merely requires that the probationary employee be notified of the board's decision to reelect or not reelect before March 15 of the second year of employment. In this case, the court found that the school district provided the notice requirements described in Section 44929.21 and upheld her release from employment (*Petersil v. Santa Monica-Malibu Unified School District*, 2013).

A temporary teacher may also attain probationary status with retroactive probationary credit for time served as a temporary employee if (1) the temporary teacher performs the duties normally associated with a teacher for at least 75 percent of the school year, and (2) the teacher is employed as a probationary teacher for the following school year. In this scenario, the teacher (who is now a probationary teacher) receives retroactive credit for the prior year of service as though the employee were serving as a probationary employee (Educ. Code § 44918(a)). This means the probationary teacher has one year of probationary service credit toward attaining permanent status. It also means that the teacher's seniority date, which is defined as the first date in paid probationary status, is also backdated to the first day of temporary employment in the year that was later converted to the first probationary year.

Education Code Sections 44909, 44917, 44919, 44920, and 44921 describe the types of temporary employees a school district may employ. Depending on the nature of the temporary employee's position, the employee will have different re-employment rights and, in some instances, the prospect of attaining permanent status after only three or four months. For example, Education Code Section 44919 describes the following two types of temporary employees who attain probationary status after working beyond the three- or four-month period for which the employees were hired:

- Three months: Individuals employed "to serve from day-to-day during the first three months of any school term to teach temporary classes not to exist after the first three months of any school team or individuals employed to perform any other duties which do not last longer than the first three school months of any school term."
- Four months: Individuals employed to "teach in special day and evening classes for adults or in schools or migratory population for not more than four school months of any school term."

Deviation from the specific criteria in the relevant code section can result in the "temporary" employee acquiring probationary credit. For example, a school district seeking to utilize Section 44920 to classify employees as temporary must ensure that the temporary employee is, as the section requires, replacing a certificated employee on leave or experiencing long-term absence. Deviation from this key requirement of Section 44920 prohibits the classification of the employee as temporary and affords the employee probationary credit (*Bakersfield Elementary Teachers Association v. Bakersfield City School District*, 2006).

As noted earlier, temporary employees who serve more than 75 percent of the school year in a position requiring certification and are hired as probationary employees for the next school year receive retroactive probationary credit for their service. This retroactive credit is not available to temporary employees serving in the previously noted three- or four-month positions. This distinction is critical because it requires the employee to work longer as a probationary employee before attaining permanent status (i.e., for an extra three or four months).

Education Code Section 44954 permits the release of a temporary employee at the "pleasure of the board" prior to the employee's completion of at least 75 percent of a school year. If a temporary employee serves more than 75 percent of a school year, the employee may be released with written notice of the "district's decision not to reelect the employee for the succeeding school year" and will be released at the conclusion of the current school year.

School districts may employ certificated employees in categorically funded programs, although categorical programs have decreased significantly following the implementation of the Local Control Funding Formula (discussed in Chapter 3) (Educ. Code § 44909). Certificated employees in these positions may be classified as temporary employees as long as the school district satisfies the very strict requirements described in Section 44909. In certain circumstances, however, they can obtain permanent status with a school district. Receipt of categorical funding, however, is contingent on the recipient school district adhering to the terms and conditions upon which the funding is made available. If the funding is no longer available, the school district is no longer eligible for the funding, or the funding dips below the costs associated with the teacher's compensation, how is a school district to classify the certificated employees who were hired to work in the program?

The 2002 California court of appeal decision of *Zalac v. Governing Board of the Ferndale Unified School District* addressed this question. Mary Jo Zalac was hired by the Ferndale Unified School District (Ferndale USD) to serve in the program. After Zalac's second year of employment, Ferndale USD was unable to meet certain statutory criteria for the program, and the program funding ceased. Ferndale USD decided nonetheless to retain Zalac and offered her a contract as a temporary teacher in essentially the same position. Zalac received two notices from Ferndale USD in March of her third year. The first notice said she would not be reemployed as a temporary teacher because of the loss of program funding. The second notice said she was going to be laid off under Education Code Section 44955. The layoff notice (which is not required for a temporary employee) was likely a precautionary effort by Ferndale USD in the event that Zalac was not actually a temporary certificated employee.

Zalac initiated a court action challenging her dismissal. She argued that the district had improperly classified her as a temporary employee, thus rendering her termination void. Prior to determining if Zalac was a temporary employee, the court addressed whether the program was a categorically funded program under

Section 44909. The court determined it was. The court then focused on the following language in Section 44909 to determine if Zalac was a temporary employee of the district:

> Service pursuant to this section shall not be included in computing the service required as a prerequisite to attainment of, or eligibility to, classification as a permanent employee unless (1) such person has served pursuant to this section for at least 75 percent of the number of days the regular schools of the district by which he is employed are maintained and (2) such person is subsequently employed as a probationary employee in a position requiring certification qualifications.

The court interpreted the section's language to mean that Zalac should be granted a year toward permanent status for each year she served in the program. Focusing on the district's decision to rehire Zalac, the court determined that she was rehired in her third year as a probationary employee, thereby retroactively granting her two years of service credit as a probationary teacher and affording her permanent status on the commencement of her third year of employment. Note the distinction between this result and the statutory analysis for a temporary teacher who serves 75 percent or more of the school year in a position requiring certification and is rehired as a probationary teacher. The latter receives only one year of credit as a probationary employee and must survive the entire subsequent year without a notice of non-reelection. Zalac's victory on this point was a hollow one, however, for the court upheld her layoff as an independent basis to sever her employment from the district.

Under *Zalac*, school districts must immediately decide whether to terminate certificated employees hired under a categorical funding program when the program no longer exists. Rehiring the employees for a subsequent year after the applicable categorical funding program expires may result in their attaining probationary or permanent status. A school district must strictly follow the requirements of Section 44909 to retain temporary classification for employees hired under that section. School districts that fail to follow those requirements may not classify the teacher as temporary, and the teacher may be deemed probationary.

It also bears noting that a 2012 California court of appeal decision held that "employees may be treated as temporary only if they are hired for the term of the categorically funded project and are terminated at the expiration of the categorically funded project for which they were hired" (*Stockton Teachers Association CTA/NEA v. Stockton Unified School District*, 2012). Meeting this requirement has proved challenging, as certain funds, such as Title I monies, do not end but fluctuate year to year.

Probationary. Prior to attaining permanent classification, a teacher must either serve as a probationary employee or receive retroactive credit for service as a probationary employee. A school district has an opportunity to evaluate an employee's performance during the employee's probationary period. This permits the district to make an informed decision as to whether the employee should attain permanent status.

Governing boards of school districts must classify as probationary employees "those persons employed in positions requiring certification qualifications for the school year, who have not been classified as permanent employees or as substitute employees" (Educ. Code § 44915). A key feature of probationary status is non-reelection. (Additional information related to non-reelection is found later in this chapter in the section titled Non-reelection and Dismissal of Probationary Teachers.)

Non-reelection permits a school district to notify a probationary teacher in writing that the teacher's service with the district will not continue into the next school year. The employment relationship ends at the close of the school year in which the notice is given, without any further action on the school district's behalf. On receipt of the written notice, the Education Code offers the probationary teacher no recourse. Non-reelection is not available for permanent teachers. This is why Marilyn Fleice and Lori Summerfield, each a teacher in separate cases reviewed later in this chapter, initiated legal actions to have a court grant them permanent status. While probationary status does not provide the job security of permanent status, it is still important because it is a precursor to permanent status.

Under certain circumstances, interns employed by school districts in certificated positions may attain probationary status. The Education Code recognizes three types of intern programs: preinternship teaching internships, school district internships, and university internships. While the Education Code is silent on the employment status of preinterns, it is unlikely that they are serving in a probationary position. Education Code Sections 44325 to 44328 govern school district internships. Education Code Section 44885.5 details the two circumstances in which a district intern is a probationary employee. First, an individual hired as a district intern is a probationary employee. Second, an individual who is not hired as a district intern may nonetheless become a probationary employee when the individual completes service in the intern program and is reelected in the next succeeding school year to a position requiring certification.

Can a school district alter the probationary status of a district intern through a contract identifying the intern as a temporary employee? The 2001 California court of appeal decision of *Welch v. Oakland Unified School District* answered this question in the negative. Melanie Welch was offered a teaching position by the Oakland Unified School District (Oakland USD) in September 1998. Welch was a participant in the Partnership Program at California State University. On Welch's behalf, Oakland USD applied for an internship Multiple Subject Teaching Credential with CCTC. Approximately one month later, the district issued her a contract of employment identifying her as a temporary teacher. The contract specified that either party could terminate the contract with fifteen days' notice.

Welch experienced difficulty in her employment with Oakland USD. According to her, the principal at her school introduced himself by explaining that the culture at the school was Christian and that Welch would "not fit in if Jesus talking bothered [her]" (p. 376). Welch alleged that she was later attacked by a student and threatened by a parent. After bringing her concerns to the principal, Welch alleged that he would "have [twenty] kids say [she] hit and kicked them" (p. 376).

In November 1998, Welch was placed on administrative leave for allegations regarding erratic behavior and hitting and kicking students. By February 1999, Oakland USD sent Welch a letter releasing her from her temporary employment contract. A temporary certificated employee generally may be released midyear unless a contract of employment provides otherwise.

Welch sued, arguing that she was improperly released. She claimed that, because she was an intern in a district internship program, she was a probationary, not temporary, employee. The district rested its argument on a narrow interpretation of Education Code Section 44885.5, which states in relevant part:

> Any school district shall classify as a probationary employee of the district any person who is employed as a district intern pursuant to Section 44830.3 and any person who has completed service in the district as a district intern . . . and is reelected for the next succeeding school year to a position requiring certification qualifications.

Oakland USD argued that a district intern is not a probationary employee until the intern is hired, completes a year of service, and is reelected for the next school year. The court disagreed, observing that the phrase "any person" in the statute preceded a second, separate manner in which a district intern could attain probationary status. Because Melanie Welch was employed as a district intern, she was a probationary employee. This entitled her to thirty days' notice and the right to a hearing for a midyear dismissal. The court concluded that the contract identifying her as a temporary employee was invalid. *Welch*, among other things, demonstrates the inability of a school district to contract around a certificated employee's appropriate classification under the Education Code.

A university internship is established by a school district in cooperation with an approved college or university. Education Code Section 44450 and following sections govern university internships. The intern serves under an internship credential issued by CCTC and cannot obtain permanent status while serving under the internship credential. A university intern obtains permanent status by completing the internship program, serving a complete school year, and being reelected for the next succeeding school year (Educ. Code § 44466). After completion of the university internship but prior to attaining permanent status, the intern is a probationary employee.

Permanent. Except for those in very small districts, a full-time teacher must serve for two consecutive school years as a probationary employee before becoming a permanent employee (Educ. Code § 44929.21(b)). In school districts with average daily attendance (ADA) of less than 250, a full-time certificated teacher must serve three consecutive years as a probationary employee before becoming a permanent employee (Educ. Code § 44929.23(a)). There are numerous other distinctions in the classifications of certificated employees for school districts with ADA less than 250 that are not addressed here. A probationary teacher who has served for at least 75 percent of a school year is deemed to have served a complete school year (Educ. Code § 44908).

A certificated employee serving in a "teaching position" for a county superintendent with 250 ADA or more must do so for two consecutive years before attaining permanent status (Educ. Code § 1296(b)). The county superintendent or county board of education designates those positions that qualify as teaching positions (Educ. Code § 1296(c)). These "teaching positions" may not necessarily be the same types of positions occupied by the probationary teachers of governing boards. Permanent status is generally not available for a certificated employee employed by a county superintendent with ADA of less than 250.

As noted earlier, one exception to these general rules regarding permanent status exists when a temporary employee serves for more than 75 percent of the school year and is subsequently hired into a probationary position. In this circumstance, the school district must retroactively count the employee's year of service as a temporary employee as though it were a year of service as a probationary employee. Permanent status, or "permanency" or "tenure," as it is sometimes referred to, is established only with the current employer. A school district's governing board may, but does not have to, extend permanent status to a newly hired teacher who established permanent status elsewhere in the state (Educ. Code § 44929.28).

May a school district grant permanent status to a teacher prior to the teacher's completion of two consecutive school years of service as a probationary employee?

The 1988 California court of appeal decision of *Fleice v. Chualar Elementary School District* addressed this question concerning Marilyn Fleice. Fleice taught for one year as a probationary teacher before she was given a contract by the Chualar Elementary School District (Chualar ESD) to work the next school year as a permanent employee. Fleice executed the contract. At the start of the next school year, a new superintendent took office. The superintendent decided that Fleice was not entitled to be a permanent teacher, notwithstanding the contract, because Marilyn did not complete two years of consecutive service as a probationary teacher. The superintendent corrected the mistake by sending Fleice a letter explaining that tenure was erroneously granted and that she was a probationary certificated employee. Fleice was not rehired for the following year.

Marilyn Fleice sued, seeking to compel Chualar ESD to rehire her as a permanent certificated employee. She argued that the Education Code did not prohibit the district from granting permanent status to an employee prior to completion of the employee's two-year probationary period. The court disagreed. Viewing the two-year probationary period as a mandatory prerequisite to attaining permanent status, the court concluded that the governing board did not have the power to grant Fleice early permanent status. Thus, the contract rehiring Fleice as a permanent certificated employee was not legally enforceable, and she had been properly reclassified as a probationary teacher subject to release through non-reelection.

Save for certain narrow exceptions, time spent serving under a "provisional credential" does not count toward attaining classification as a permanent teacher (Educ. Code § 44911). Is a provisional credential the same as an emergency credential? This was the question Lori Summerfield posed to a California court of appeal in 2002 (*Summerfield v. Windsor Unified School District*). Summerfield served as a certificated employee for the Windsor Unified School District (Windsor USD) under a series of emergency credentials from September 1996 to March 1998. In March 1998, the district informed her that she had successfully completed her probationary period and would be rehired as a permanent employee for the next school year. A month later, however, the governing board advised Summerfield that it believed her service under an emergency teaching credential did not count toward permanent employee status. Like Marilyn Fleice, Lori Summerfield was reclassified as a probationary teacher, worked another school year, and was thereafter released through non-reelection.

Summerfield filed a legal action requesting the court to order Windsor USD to grant her permanent status. She argued that the phrase "provisional certificates" in Section 44911 did not include emergency credentials. The court rejected Summerfield's argument, ruling that the phrase "provisional certificate" in Section 44911 means the same thing as an emergency credential. Because Summerfield did not satisfy any of the exceptions in Section 44911, the time she served under her emergency credentials did not count toward the attainment of permanent status. Although the district previously informed Summerfield that she attained permanent status, the court dismissed this by citing *Fleice* for the proposition that "it is well settled that the two-year probationary period for teachers is mandatory and may not be shortened by the advice or actions of a school district" (p. 240).

Once a probationary teacher completes the requisite number of consecutive school years of service, the teacher automatically attains permanent status upon the commencement of the next school year (*Vittal v. Long Beach Unified School District*, 1970). No action by the school district's governing board is required. Once elevated to permanent status, a teacher has a vested property right in employment (*Adelt v. Richmond School District*, 1967). Permanent teachers may be dismissed only for grounds specified in the Education Code and are afforded full due process rights, as discussed later in the chapter. A teacher attaining permanent status is entitled to continued employment with the school district until retirement, resignation, death, dismissal, or layoff. Probationary teachers like Marilyn Fleice and Lori Summerfield do not have these same rights and may be non-reelected prior to March 15 during their second year of probationary status. In effect, the property right ends at this time, and due process other than timely written notice of non-reelection is not required. It is primarily for this reason that school districts are well advised to carefully consider whether a certificated employee should ascend from probationary to permanent status.

Evaluation and Reassignment

The evaluation of teachers plays an important role in year-to-year retention, which may lead to permanent status, and in documenting employee performance for purposes of discipline or dismissal. Education Code Section 44660 and following sections, commonly known as the "Stull Act," set forth the guidelines a school district is to consider in developing and implementing an evaluation system for its teachers. While the Education Code delegates a fair amount of discretion to school districts in this process, all evaluation systems must have certain key features. The criteria used to evaluate teachers must be negotiated with the exclusive representative of the teachers' union.

Teacher evaluation is to be done on a uniform basis. For "compelling reasons," however, a governing board may use different evaluation criteria for teachers of certain schools within the district (Educ. Code § 44660). The statute does not provide further detail regarding these reasons. However, one potential example is attempting to impose a different evaluation system on teachers in a school receiving substandard test scores either by state or federal standards. The governing board must consider the advice of teachers within the district in developing an evaluation system. A school district may, by mutual agreement with the teachers' union, include objective standards from the National Board for Professional Teaching Standards or from the California Standards for the Teaching Profession in the evaluation criteria.

Education Code Section 44662 sets forth the minimum criteria by which a governing board must evaluate and assess teacher performance. These criteria include the instructional techniques and strategies used by the teacher, the teacher's adherence to curricular objectives, and whether the teacher has established and maintained a suitable learning environment. The performance of the teacher's students toward the standards of expected student achievement established by the governing board is another component of the evaluation. Student achievement may also focus on state-adopted academic content standards.

If a school district participates in the Peer Assistance and Review (PAR) program for teachers, the teacher's participation in PAR must also be made part of the teacher's evaluation (Education Code §44662(d)). PAR provides mentor-type assistance to permanent teachers whose evaluation results in a rating of "unsatisfactory performance." School districts are not required to participate in PAR. In the past, the state made funding available to those who participated in PAR, although that funding is no longer available. Education Code Section 44500 and the following sections detail PAR's requirements. PAR is also a mandatory subject of bargaining, and some school districts continue to include PAR in their collective bargaining agreements.

An evaluation must be reduced to writing and given to the teacher not later than thirty days prior to the end of the school year in which the evaluation occurred (Educ. Code § 44663). Prior to the last day of the school year, the evaluator and the teacher meet to discuss the evaluation. The teacher may issue a written response, which becomes a permanent attachment to the employee's personnel file. Special timelines regarding the evaluation of certificated noninstructional employees, such as administrators, are described in Education Code Section 44663(b). A teacher not performing his or her duties in a satisfactory manner is given an evaluation of unsatisfactory performance. The superintendent, or superintendent's designee, must meet with any teacher receiving an unsatisfactory performance, provide the employee with specific recommendations regarding areas that require improvement, and endeavor to assist the teacher to improve.

Education Code Section 44664 sets forth the frequency with which teachers must be evaluated. A probationary teacher is evaluated at least once every school year. A permanent teacher is evaluated at least once every other year. A permanent teacher receiving an unsatisfactory performance is evaluated annually until the employee receives a positive evaluation or is no longer employed by the district. A permanent teacher with ten years of service in a school district may be evaluated at least once every five years if the teacher satisfies certain requirements described in Education Code Section 44664 and both the teacher and the evaluator agree to an evaluation at least once every five years. A school district may exclude substitute teachers from evaluations. The evaluation process does not apply to teachers who are employed on an hourly basis in adult education classes.

Subject to the approval of the governing board, it is the superintendent's duty to assign all certificated employees of the district to the position in which they will serve (Educ. Code § 35035(c)). As a general rule, the superintendent has the power to transfer a certificated employee from one school to another when the superintendent concludes that the transfer is in the best interests of the district. A teacher does not have a vested property right in the location of the teaching assignment (*Bolin v. San Bernardino City Unified School District*, 1984). A collective bargaining agreement, however, can dictate a process for determining how employees are transferred (e.g., on the basis of seniority, with the least senior teacher transferred first).

Discipline of Probationary and Permanent Employees

Discipline consists of action against an employee short of dismissal. Save for egregious acts, the discipline of public school employees generally follows a format known as progressive discipline. An oral warning (which ideally is documented in some fashion) may precede a conference, which can escalate to a written warning. A stronger tone can be taken with a letter of reprimand. An unfavorable evaluation may command even more attention from the offending employee. Suspension, which is the last resort before dismissal, is technically available in many instances, yet often not worth the time and expense of the hearing an employee may request to challenge it.

The Education Code contains specific provisions concerning suspension and derogatory statements or comments entered into an employee's personnel file. The focus here is suspension, but the placement of a derogatory statement or comment in the personnel file is discussed later in this chapter. A governing board may negotiate the causes and procedures for disciplinary action, other than dismissal, including a suspension of pay for up to fifteen days with the exclusive representative of the employee's union (Gov't Code § 3543.2(b)). In this instance, a collective bargaining agreement governs the suspension process for both permanent and probationary teachers.

Absent a collective bargaining agreement, a school district is left with the relatively inflexible and cumbersome suspension provisions of the Education Code. A governing board may "suspend without pay for a specific period of time on grounds of unprofessional conduct" a permanent teacher (Educ. Code § 44932(b)). A governing board may also suspend a permanent teacher for "grounds of unprofessional conduct consisting of acts or omissions other than those specific in Section 44932," but the charge must specify the instances of behavior deemed to be unprofessional conduct, follow a notice of unprofessional conduct pursuant to Section 44938 issued at least forty-five days prior to the suspension, and satisfy other procedural requirements. Suspension of a probationary teacher is permissible for cause under Education Code Section 44932 or unsatisfactory performance under Education Code Section 44948.3, so long as the school district complies with certain procedural requirements prior to implementing the suspension.

Immediate suspension of a permanent teacher is only permissible based on written charges of immoral conduct, conviction of a felony or of any crime involving moral turpitude, incompetency due to mental disability, or willful refusal to perform regular assignments without reasonable cause (Educ. Code § 44939). The term *immoral conduct* includes, among other things, "egregious misconduct." Egregious misconduct includes certain sex offenses, drug offenses, and child abuse, neglect, and endangerment.

The immediate suspension may be implemented while dismissal charges are pending. Certificated employees may seek to reverse the unpaid suspension by filing a Motion for Immediate Reversal of Suspension, or MIRS, with California Office of Administrative Hearings. The MIRS process is an expedited, prehearing motion procedure that includes an administrative law judge's (ALJ) analysis of the charges to determine "whether the facts as alleged in the statement of charges, if true, are sufficient to constitute a basis for immediate suspension under this section" (Educ. Code § 44939(c)(1)). The ALJ's decision on the MIRS motion does not affect the ultimate outcome of any decision issued by a Commission on Professional Competence reviewing the certificated staff member's dismissal. The MIRS process is not available to certificated staff members charged solely with egregious misconduct.

Education Code Section 44942 contains a detailed process for the suspension and dismissal of a permanent certificated employee if the employee is "suffering from mental illness of such a degree as to render him or her incompetent to perform his or her duties." The expense and complexity of the process, which includes a panel of psychologists or psychiatrists to examine the employee, makes it a largely impracticable option for school districts. Dismissal or suspension for the alleged misconduct often may be based on dishonesty, immoral conduct, persistent failure or refusal to follow school laws or the school district's regulations, or evident unfitness for service under Education Code Section 44932.

A so-called *Skelly* conference is a prerequisite to the suspension of a certificated employee without pay. The conference is an informal meeting between the administration and the employee and takes its name from the 1975 California Supreme Court decision of *Skelly v. State Personnel Board*. The essence of *Skelly* is that a government employee is to receive written notice and an opportunity to respond prior to the deprivation of a property right. Loss of pay during a suspension constitutes the loss of a property right. A *Skelly* conference, in which the employee is apprised of the basis for the suspension and is given an opportunity to respond, thus satisfies due process of law prior to the suspension.

Non-Reelection and Dismissal of Probationary Teachers

If a probationary teacher of a school district with ADA of 250 or more does not receive a written notice of non-reelection by March 15 of the employee's second consecutive year of employment, the teacher is automatically reelected for the following school year and obtains permanent classification. A special non-reemployment, rather than non-reelection, process applies to probationary teachers in school districts with ADA of less than 250.

A governing board meeting must occur in which the board acts to non-reelect probationary teachers. The meeting may be held in closed session (i.e., with no members of the public or press or notice to the teacher) (*Fischer v. Los Angeles Unified School District*, 1999). Under the Ralph M. Brown Act, the board must properly notice the closed session in which this decision is made. After the closed session, the board's decision must be reported to the public. A notice of non-reelection must be given by personal notice or an equivalent means to the teacher. Service of the notice by certified mail is not sufficient where the notice is received after March 15 (*Hoschler v. Sacramento City Unified School District*, 2007). If a teacher evades receipt of a written notice of non-reelection, however, delivery of the written notice to an individual residing in the teacher's home or oral notice of the non-reelection to the teacher is sufficient where the teacher has actual knowledge of the district's decision to non-reelect (*Sullivan v. Centinela Valley Union High School*, 2011). The Education Code does not include hearing procedures to challenge the non-reelection. A probationary teacher may, however, challenge the non-reelection if the employee can prove the non-reelection was for an unlawful reason, such as race or sex discrimination or retaliation for union activity.

May a school district give written notice of non-reelection to a probationary teacher after March 15 during the employee's first year of employment? The 1987 California court of appeal decision of *Grimsley v. Board of Trustees* addressed this question. Sherilyn Grimsley was a first-year probationary teacher working for the district when she received a notice of non-reelection on April 23, 1984. The notice stated that her employment with the district would terminate on June 30, 1984. In the ensuing legal action, Grimsley argued that her non-reelection was invalid because it was issued after March 15. The court disagreed and held that non-reelection is permissible any time prior to March 15 of the probationary teacher's second consecutive year of employment. In a footnote, however, the court did note that a notice of non-reelection issued on June 29 for release on June 30 may well be unreasonable, given the teacher's reliance on continued employment until that time.

In addition to the non-reelection process, probationary certificated staff members may be terminated midyear. However, given the ease with which the governing board of a school district can non-reelect probationary teachers and the extensive requirements to implement a midyear probationary dismissal, it is quite rare for a midyear dismissal action to be undertaken against them. Education Code Section 44948.3 governs the dismissal of probationary teachers in a school district with ADA of 250 or greater. These employees may be dismissed during the school year for unsatisfactory performance determined under the Stull Act, but the district must comply with Education Code Section 44938, which provides for ninety-day notice of the unsatisfactory performance to permit the employee to correct his or her faults and overcome the grounds for the charge (*Achene v. Pierce Joint Unified School District*, 2009). Dismissal may also be for cause, as described in the next section.

Although the midyear probationary dismissal process is less extensive than the procedures related to the termination of a permanent teacher, the procedures may be costly, time-consuming, and burdensome. For instance, a probationary teacher must receive at least thirty days' prior written notice of dismissal. If the teacher is in the second year of employment, the written notice must be received no later than March 15. The notice must include a statement of the reasons for the dismissal and notice of the opportunity for a hearing. This is necessary because the teacher has a property right during the term of the contract (i.e., to complete the full term of the school year), a right that cannot be removed without due process of law. The notice of dismissal for unsatisfactory performance must include a copy of the teacher's evaluation. The teacher then has up to fifteen days to submit a written request for a hearing to the governing board. Failure to request a hearing within fifteen days after receipt of the dismissal notice results in a waiver of the right to a hearing. Although the Education Code provides a statute covering the dismissal of a permanent teacher, it does not contain a statute setting forth the requirements for the dismissal hearing of a probationary teacher. Hearing procedures, which the governing board develops, must comport with due process of law (e.g., notice, right to representation, right to testify, and right to call and question witnesses). A governing board may conduct the hearing or delegate the matter to an administrative law judge. If an administrative law judge conducts the hearing, a recommendation is given to the governing board. The governing board reviews the recommendation and makes its own decision regarding dismissal. Once again, the employee may appeal the decision on the grounds that the dismissal was unlawfully motivated.

Dismissal of Permanent Teachers

The Education Code limits the reasons for which permanent or probationary may be dismissed. Specifically, permanent and probationary teachers may be dismissed only for one or more of the specific causes set forth in Education Code Section 44932. These causes are as follows:

- Immoral conduct, including egregious misconduct (discussed later in this chapter)
- Unprofessional conduct
- Commission, aiding, or advocating the commission of acts of criminal syndicalism, as prohibited by Chapter 188 of the Statutes of 1919 or in any amendment to that chapter
- Dishonesty
- Unsatisfactory performance
- Evident unfitness for service
- Physical or mental condition unfitting him or her to instruct or associate with children
- Persistent violation of or refusal to obey school laws of the state or reasonable regulations prescribed for the government of the public schools by the State Board of Education or by the governing board of the school district employing him or her
- Conviction of a felony or of any crime involving moral turpitude
- Violation of Section 51530 or conduct specified in Section 1028 of the Government Code, added by Chapter 1418 of the Statutes of 1947
- Alcoholism or other drug abuse which makes the employee unfit to instruct or associate with children

The four most common grounds for dismissal include immoral or unprofessional conduct, unsatisfactory performance, evident unfitness for service, and persistent violation of or refusal to obey school laws or reasonable regulations.

Immoral or unprofessional conduct. Courts have defined immoral conduct for purposes of dismissal pursuant to Education Code Section 44932 as "that which is hostile to the welfare of the general public and contrary to good morals" (*San Diego Unif. Sch. Dist. v. Commission on Professional Competence*, 194 Cal. App. 4th 1454, 1466 (2011)). Courts have found immoral conduct where the actions constituted "wilful [*sic*], flagrant, or shameless conduct showing moral indifference to the opinions of respectable members of the community" (*Palo Verde Unified Sch. Dist. v. Hensey*, 9 Cal. App. 3d 967, 972 (1970)).

In 2014, AB 215 added "egregious misconduct" to immoral conduct for the purposes of teacher discipline. "Egregious misconduct" is defined "exclusively as immoral conduct that is the basis for an offense described in Section 44010 [sex offense] or 44011 [controlled substance offense] . . . or in Sections 11165.2 [neglect of a child] or 111.65.6 [child abuse or neglect], inclusive, of the Penal Code."

Unprofessional conduct, as its name implies, is conduct that violates the school district's expectations and requirements related to professionalism and appropriate behavior. Prior to initiating suspension and/or dismissal for unprofessional conduct, the school district is required to serve the certificated employee with a "45-Day Notice of Unprofessional Conduct" pursuant to Education Code Section 44938 (discussed later in this chapter).

In the case of immoral or unprofessional conduct, it must be established that the conduct undermined the teacher's effectiveness. This was the focus of the seminal ruling of *Morrison v. State Board of Education*, a decision of the California Supreme Court in 1969. That case involved a teacher who resigned when confronted with evidence of a private, consensual homosexual relationship. Although the relationship had not been known among students or teachers, the state revoked the teacher's credential. The court ruled in favor of the teacher, noting the absence of evidence that the relationship had negatively affected the teacher's performance. The court identified seven criteria to be used in assessing whether the teacher's conduct affects their fitness to teach. Known as the *Morrison* factors, these factors are as follows:

- "The likelihood that the conduct may have adversely affected students or fellow teachers"
- "The degree of such adversity anticipated"

- "The proximity or remoteness in time of the conduct"
- "The type of teaching certificate held by the party involved"
- "The extenuating or aggravating circumstances, if any, surrounding the conduct"
- "The likelihood of recurrence of the questioned conduct"
- "The extent to which disciplinary action may inflict an adverse impact or chilling effect upon the constitutional rights of the teacher involved or other teachers"

The inquiry is whether the teacher is fit to teach, considering these factors in the aggregate. Not all factors may be implicated in all cases, and the Commission on Professional Competence, which reviews any proposed teacher dismissal, is responsible for weighing the applicable factors in determining whether a teacher is fit to teach. (The role of a Commission on Professional Competence is found within the discussion of the dismissal process later in this chapter.)

Examples of the application of the Morrison factors can be helpful in understanding how they operate. For instance, the sexual harassment of female students by a teacher may constitute immoral conduct under the *Morrison* factors (*Governing Board of ABC Unified School District v. Haar*, 1994). Kenneth Haar was a certificated music teacher in a middle school. The school district initiated dismissal proceedings against Haar on the grounds that he engaged in immoral conduct by sexually harassing his female students. Allegations against Haar included touching a female student on the thigh; hugging a female student tightly until the student pushed him away; and, while dressed up as Santa Claus, indicating to female students that an extra raffle ticket for a drawing was available in return for a kiss. Kenneth Haar's dismissal was upheld by a California court of appeal because substantial evidence demonstrated that his conduct rendered him unfit to teach.

In applying the Morrison factors, the court found substantial evidence that the misconduct (1) adversely affected the students, (2) occurred in close proximity to Haar's dismissal, (3) was repetitive in nature, (4) lacked a justifiable motivation, and (5) constituted an extenuating and aggravating circumstance as it rose to the level of the physical harassment. Considering these factors in the aggregate, the court found that Haar's actions demonstrated his unfitness to teach.

The *Morrison* factors have also been applied to the causes of dishonesty as well as evident unfitness for service. For example, in a 2011 decision, a California appellate court interpreted the evident unfitness for service standard to uphold the dismissal of a teacher for his posting of graphic content soliciting sex on the internet via a Craigslist "men seeking men" page (*San Diego Unif. Sch. Dist. v. Commission on Professional Competence*, 2011).

In that case, Frank Lampedusa was a permanent teacher, was reported to do a generally good job, and was considered a candidate for a promotion to vice principal when an anonymous caller brought the posting to the attention of the school district. The posting included graphic nude pictures and communicated his desire to connect with other men for the purpose of having sex. Lampedusa's principal directed him to remove the posting, and he complied with that directive.

Shortly thereafter, the school district placed Lampedusa on administrative leave and served him with dismissal charges. He challenged the dismissal before the Commission on Professional Competence and prevailed. The Commission held that, because no students had seen the pictures, the posting had not interfered with Lampedusa's ability to serve as a role model and teach.

The school district appealed the Commission on Professional Competence decision and filed a petition for writ of mandate with the Superior Court of San Diego County. The court denied the petition, finding the district failed to show the Commission's findings were not supported by the weight of the evidence. The school district appealed again. This time, the court of appeals reversed and found Lampedusa's conduct constituted grounds for dismissal based up his evident unfitness to teach and immoral conduct.

The court noted that, contrary to the Commission's findings, a student and parent (the anonymous caller) saw the advertisement, and their observation had an adverse impact on students because of the graphic nature of the advertisement. The court also noted that Lampedusa attempted to shift the blame for his actions to parents and students by noting that they should not be accessing the advertisement. The court also took issue with Lampedusa's testimony before the Commission that he would post additional advertisements in the future but take care to censor the pictures more effectively.

The court also applied the *Morrison* factors and concluded that Lampedusa was unfit to teach by considering those factors in the aggregate. Specifically, because a parent and an educator viewed the ad, there was a subsequent adverse impact on Lampedusa's on-campus relationships. Also, substantial evidence demonstrated there was a high likelihood of recurrence of the conduct due to Lampedusa's unwillingness to acknowledge the inappropriateness of his actions, the fact that he had previously posted multiple ads soliciting sex on the internet, and his statement that he would continue to post ads soliciting sex online. Other factors that weighed in favor of Lampedusa's dismissal included the close proximity to the date of the incident to which he was served with the charges, the fact that he held both a secondary school credential and an administrative credential, and the lack of evidence suggesting that the disciplinary action would have any adverse impact or chilling effect on the constitutional rights of teachers.

The court concluded that the graphic nature of the conduct, in combination with Lampedusa's failure to accept responsibility for his actions, demonstrated an evident unfitness to teach and also constituted immoral conduct (*San Diego Unif. Sch. Dist. v. Commission on Professional Competence*, 2011).

It bears noting that the court's decision also included specific language related to the teacher's obligation to serve as a role model. Specifically, the court noted that certain professions inherently impose responsibilities and duties upon the individuals who enter those professions. The court reasoned that individuals who work as police officers, nurses, or schoolteachers serve as role models to those they serve.

Seeking to dismiss a teacher on the basis of unprofessional, but not immoral, conduct requires the school district to give the employee written notice, commonly labeled a "45-Day Notice of Unprofessional Conduct," specifying the nature of the conduct and the "behavior with such particularity as to furnish the employee an opportunity to correct his or her faults and overcome the grounds for the charge" (Educ. Code § 44938(a)). The written notice must also include the most recent evaluation. After issuance of the foregoing written notice, the school district must wait at least forty-five calendar days before filing a charge of unprofessional conduct to initiate the suspension and/or dismissal process. Teachers are therefore given an opportunity to understand the nature of their unprofessional conduct and change their conduct prior to the initiation of formal dismissal proceedings. School districts may not proceed with a teacher's suspension and/or dismissal for unprofessional conduct without first issuing a 45-Day Notice of Unprofessional Conduct (*Crowl v. Commission on Professional Competence of the Governing Board of San Juan Unified School District*, 1990).

Unsatisfactory performance. A 1995 amendment to Education Code Section 44932 substituted the phrase "unsatisfactory performance" for "incompetency." As in dismissal for unprofessional conduct, a teacher receives prior written notice of unsatisfactory performance. Commonly labeled a "90-Day Notice of Unsatisfactory Performance," the school district cannot initiate formal dismissal proceedings until ninety calendar days after the employee is given written notice of the unsatisfactory performance (Educ. Code § 44938(b)(1)). The written notice is in the same form and detail as described in the preceding section regarding unprofessional conduct (albeit with a description of the specific instances of behavior that constitute unsatisfactory performance).

Unprofessional conduct and unsatisfactory performance are the only grounds for dismissal requiring prior written notice to the teacher and a grace period for the teacher to alter conduct prior to initiation of a dismissal proceeding. Following issuance of either notice, the school district may proceed with suspension and/or dismissal charges after the forty-five-day period in cases of unprofessional conduct and the ninety-day period in cases of unsatisfactory performance. Such charges may be issued for up to four years following the conduct and/or performance issues described in those notices.

It bears noting that the school district may issue "dual notices" when the concerns at issue relate to both conduct and performance. In those circumstances, the school district will typically issue one document, often titled a "45-Day Notice of Unsatisfactory Performance and 90-Day Notice of Unsatisfactory Performance" addressing both areas.

Evident unfitness for service. In *Woodland Joint Union School District v. Commission on Professional Competence* the court considered when a certificated employee's conduct rises to the level of evident unfitness for service within the meaning of Education Code Section 44932(a)(5). In that case, the district sought to terminate a permanent English teacher. The district's dismissal charges were based on an allegation of evident unfitness for service and persistent refusal to obey school laws of the state or reasonable regulations. Writing sarcastic and belittling notes about students, insulting students in class, behaving rudely and contemptuously toward parents, displaying insubordination and disrespect toward administrators, and bullying and threatening other teachers were among the allegations supporting the charges of dismissal. A Commission on Professional Competence heard the charges and found the allegations not supported by the evidence and insufficient to justify dismissal. (*Woodland Joint Unified School District v. Commission on Professional Competence*, 1992).

The district challenged the commission's findings in a superior court action and requested a finding that the teacher's conduct demonstrated that he was temperamentally unfit to teach, so that his continued employment would pose a substantial danger to faculty, administrators, students, and parents. The superior court agreed, and the teacher appealed.

The first question for the court of appeal was whether the charge of "evident unfitness for service" is synonymous with the charge of "unprofessional conduct." The teacher argued that the charges were synonymous and that the district erred in not providing him with the forty-five-day written notice that must precede a charge of unprofessional conduct. Recall that failure to provide this notice for dismissal on the basis of unprofessional conduct effectively terminates the dismissal proceeding, thereby resulting in the teacher's reinstatement. The court first observed that the purpose of the notice requirement for unprofessional conduct is to allow the teacher to correct his or her conduct. After noting that no such requirement applies to dismissal for evident unfitness for service, the court held that "unlike 'unprofessional conduct,' 'evident unfitness for service' connotes a fixed character trait, presumably not remediable merely on receipt of notice that one's conduct fails to meet the expectations of the employing school district." Otherwise, the Education Code would also provide a teacher with prior written notice of conduct constituting evident unfitness for service to enable the teacher to alter his or her conduct. This teacher, at least in the opinion of the court, was not an individual who could change his conduct.

In upholding the teacher's dismissal, the court also clarified the role of the *Morrison* factors in a dismissal for evident unfitness for service. The teacher had argued that the court must apply the *Morrison* factors individually to each allegation. The court rejected the teacher's argument and approved an application of the *Morrison* factors to the evidence in the aggregate. In the words of the court, "when a camel's back is broken we need not weigh each straw in its load to see which one could have done the deed." If the application of the *Morrison* factors demonstrates unfitness for service in the aggregate, the only remaining question is whether the offensive conduct is the result of a defect in temperament, thus demonstrating evident unfitness for service.

Persistent violation of or refusal to obey school laws. School laws and regulations are taken from numerous sources, including statutes, regulations, and board policies. For instance, Title 5 of the California Code of Regulations contains the Rules of Conduct for Professional Educators. While these rules may not themselves be reasons for dismissal, they can be cited as evidence that the certificated employee is persistently violating or refusing to obey school laws. Some governing boards add to these provisions through their own code of ethics, employee handbooks, Board Policies, and/or Administrative Regulations. The code prohibits the following conduct:

- Failure to use professional candor and honesty required in letters and memoranda of employment recommendation.
- Withdrawal from professional employment without good cause.
- Unauthorized private gain or advantage from the use of confidential information relating to students or fellow professionals.
- Performance of duties when substantially mentally impaired for any reason, including alcohol or substance abuse. This rule also includes the assignment of such a person to perform duties.

- Harassment or retaliation against those who report actual or suspected wrongdoing.
- Failure to perform duties for a person because of discriminatory motives.

A teacher's failure to adhere to a goal in an evaluation may also constitute a persistent violation of or refusal to obey school laws or reasonable regulations. Such was the case with a teacher in the 1985 California court of appeal decision of *San Dieguito Union High School District v. Commission on Professional Competence*. In that case, the teacher's evaluation set forth a goal of "providing thorough lesson plans when absent, and calling early for a substitute when needed" (p. 353). The teacher failed to meet this goal. The court ultimately upheld the teacher's dismissal, noting that one substitute testified that for twelve of the seventeen times she had substituted in the teacher's classroom, she could not locate lesson plans. Absenteeism (in the form of an evident unfitness for service charge) was another ground on which the court upheld the teacher's dismissal.

The Dismissal Hearing Process

The dismissal hearing process starts with the filing of written charges with the governing board. Suspension or dismissal of a teacher may not generally be based on charges or evidence relating to matters occurring more than four years prior to the filing of charges (Educ. Code § 44944(a)). The California Supreme Court has ruled that a school district may seek to introduce evidence of wrongdoing from more than four years prior to the filing of charges where it can be shown that the employee induced the school district to avoid bringing charges within the four-year time period (*Atwater Elementary School District v. California Department of General Services*, 2007). In addition, evidence related to sexual conduct with a student or a minor and other limited forms of evidence outside the four-year period may be admitted in the dismissal hearing.

As noted earlier, teachers have a right to an informal *Skelly* hearing in instances where the dismissal charges include an immediate unpaid suspension. In those matters and before presented to the board, the school district will typically serve draft dismissal charges and provide the teacher with an opportunity to participate in a *Skelly* hearing with an administrator in the school district who was not involved in the investigation of the underlying conduct and/or development of the dismissal charges.

If the *Skelly* hearing officer upholds the charges and the Board of Education approves them, the school district will place the certificated employee on unpaid status. The employee may then file a Motion for the Immediate Reversal of Suspension, or MIRS, with the Office of Administrative Hearings (OAH) seeking an order to reinstate their pay. Review of the motion is limited to a determination of whether the facts alleged in the dismissal charges, if true, are sufficient to warrant immediate suspension. The decision on the MIRS is not dispositive of the facts and allegations ultimately at issue in the CPC hearing.

On receipt of the dismissal charge(s) that have been approved by the school district's governing board, the teacher has thirty days to request a hearing. Failure to request a hearing results in dismissal. If a hearing is requested, a formal process initiates, including the parties' required disclosures and prehearing discovery, and the CPC conducts the dismissal hearing. (The hearing procedures may be accessed at Education Code § 44930 et seq.)

Regarding cases based solely on egregious conduct, Education Code Section 44944.1 provides for a separate hearing process and contains particular features, including adjudication by OAH instead of the traditional CPC panel. In addition, evidence of certain sex offenses and child abuse that is more than four years old may be admitted at the hearing.

Teacher dismissal hearings involve high stakes for all parties. On the one hand, the teacher risks losing employment and potential disciplinary action against their credential in separate proceedings before the California Commission on Teacher Credentialing following the hearing. On the other hand, the dismissal process requires the school district to commit significant staff time and resources, including its own attorneys' costs, to litigate the matter. In addition, if the Commission on Professional Competence reverses the dismissal, the school district must pay the teacher's attorneys' fees and other costs (Education Code § 44944(f)(2)).

If the employee requests a hearing and the district does not rescind the charges, as it has the right to do under Education Code Section 44943, the district must proceed with the hearing and cannot unilaterally rescind the hearing without consequence (*Boliou v. Stockton Unified School District*, 2012). In *Boliou*, the district requested that the CPC vacate the hearing date prior to the commencement of the hearing after an unfavorable ruling on a prehearing motion filed by the employee, and the appellate court held that the district could not rescind the hearing request without prejudice. The court ordered the district to pay reasonable attorneys' fees to the employee under Education Code Section 44944(e)(2) because the CPC did not dismiss the employee.

The CPC is an ad hoc panel of three: One panel member is chosen by the teacher, one is chosen by the governing board, and the third is an administrative law judge. The members selected by the parties cannot be related to the employee or employed by the district. In addition, they must hold a valid credential and possess at least three years' experience within the previous ten years in the discipline of the employee (Education Code § 44944(c)(5)).

A majority vote of the CPC is required for dismissal. On petition by either party, judicial review of the CPC's decision may occur.

Layoff

School districts may lay off certificated and classified employees due to a lack of work and/or lack of funds. (Classified layoff procedures are described later in this chapter.) A detailed explanation of the layoff process is beyond the scope of this book, but the main contours of the process are described here.

The Education Code sets forth three circumstances in which layoffs of certificated employees are permissible: average daily attendance (ADA) layoffs, particular kinds of services (PKS) layoffs, and budget act/revenue limit layoffs.

Elimination of certificated positions is permissible through ADA layoffs if the ADA for the current year is lower than that in either of the previous two school years. Education Code Section 44955 details the process for determining if ADA layoffs are permissible. A mathematical formula is used to identify a percentage corresponding to the decline in ADA.

PKS layoffs, the far more commonly accessed form of layoffs, permit a reduction in certificated employees "whenever a particular kind of service is to be reduced or discontinued not later than the beginning of the following school year" and, in the opinion of the governing board, it becomes necessary to decrease the number of certificated employees in the district (Educ. Code § 44955(b)). Unlike ADA layoffs, PKS layoffs are not tied to a mathematical formula. PKS layoffs permit the governing board to eliminate certain positions in the district (e.g., elementary teachers, school psychologist, nurses) without demonstrating a decline in ADA.

Education Code Section 44955.5 governs layoffs for insufficient increase in revenue limit funding per average daily attendance (not increased at least 2 percent for the fiscal year). The time frame for a district making this determination is between five days after the enactment of the Budget Act and August 15 of the fiscal year to which the Budget Act applies. Contract termination of probationary and permanent certificated employees under this provision follow the provisions of Section 44955, except that the schedule of notice and hearing are as adopted by the governing board.

Regardless of the basis for the layoff and/or the classification of the employee (permanent or probationary), the same notice, procedure, and hearing rights extend to all certificated employees to whom the layoffs apply. Additionally, the layoff rights set forth in Education Code Sections 44979 and 44959 apply to teachers who hold provisional credentials (e.g., an emergency teaching permit) (*California Teachers Association v. Vallejo City Unif. Sch. Dist.*, 2007). Final written notice of layoffs, including the reasons for them, must be given to employees no later than May 15 of the school year in which the layoffs are being conducted. The layoff of a permanent teacher generally cannot occur while any probationary teacher, or any other teacher with less seniority, is retained to render a service the permanent teacher is certificated and competent to render.

If necessary, the governing board must reassign a certificated employee with such seniority to another position for which they are appropriately credentialed and qualified instead of terminating the employee through a layoff. If the reassignment requires a permanent teacher to instruct in an area for which the employee does not have a teaching credential or that is not in the teacher's major area of postsecondary study, the governing board must require the employee to pass a subject-matter competency test in the relevant area.

In the event of a tie between two certificated employees hired on the same date, the governing board must determine the order of termination based solely on the needs of the district and its students. These criteria are known as "tie-breaking criteria." In the event of a tie following the application of the tie-breaking criteria, the layoff is determined by lot.

A governing board has some discretion to deviate from the seniority-driven ordering of certificated employees in layoffs. This is known as "skipping" and is permissible in the following two instances (Educ. Code § 44955(d)):

- The district demonstrates a specific need for personnel to teach a specific course or course of study or to provide services authorized by a services credential with a specialization in either pupil personnel services or health for a school nurse, and that the certificated employee has special training and experience necessary to teach that course or course of study or to provide those services, which others with more seniority do not possess; or
- For purposes of maintaining or achieving compliance with constitutional requirements related to equal protection of the laws.

Opponents to the layoff procedures, specifically those related to seniority ("last in, first out," or "LIFO"), believe that it violates equal protection requirements and has a disproportionate impact on schools serving high percentages of low-income students in urban areas. A seminal lawsuit from the past is the California Supreme Court's 1992 decision in *Butt v. State of California*, 1992).

Butt involved the closure of schools in the Richmond Unified School District six weeks prior to the end of the school year because the district had run out of money. The California Supreme Court concluded that the closures deprived the students of basic educational equality and that the state has an obligation to prevent a district's budgetary problems from denying them that equality.

Equal protection as a challenge to layoffs rose again in 2011 when the parents of students in the Los Angeles Unified School District challenged disproportionate layoffs at three inner-city schools through a class action lawsuit. The plaintiffs obtained an injunction preventing the proposed layoffs at the three schools, and a settlement was subsequently reached that exempted the twenty-five lowest academically performing schools from layoff, among other protections. The court relied on Section 44955(d)(2) in approving the agreement by noting that the section permits districts to deviate from seniority-based layoffs by skipping certain teachers to maintain or achieve compliance with constitutional requirements related to equal protection of the laws. The decision, however, was struck down on procedural grounds, and the matter returned to the trial court for further proceedings (*Reed v. United Teachers Los Angeles*, 2012).

In 2014, the parties in *Reed* settled the matter and agreed that, in order to exempt teachers at the low-performing schools involved in the litigation from seniority-based layoffs across the district, the district must provide funding to attract, mentor, and retain teachers at these schools. The parties agreed each school would receive an additional assistant principal and counselor, a special education coordinator, and several mentor teachers. In the event of future layoffs, the settlement provided that the district must establish that its teacher training justifies exempting teachers at these schools.

Around that same time, nine public school students initiated another significant challenge to the layoff procedures based on, among other things, the equal protection clause of the California Constitution. This time, the student plaintiffs also challenged the two-year probationary period (Educ. Code § 44929.21) and teacher dismissal statutes (Educ. Code §§ 44934, 44938 (b)(1)–(2), 44944)

In that case, the plaintiffs argued that the statutes result in "grossly ineffective teachers obtaining and retaining permanent employment, and that these teachers are disproportionately situated in schools serving predominately low-income and minority students." In doing so, the plaintiffs argued that the statutes violate their fundamental right to equal educational opportunity. Significantly, the judge agreed and ruled that the challenged statutes fail to meet the strict level of judicial scrutiny necessary when they intrude on constitutional rights.

Two years later, a California appellate court reversed the trial court's decision for two notable reasons. First, the court found that the students who were assigned grossly ineffective teachers were not specifically identifiable for purposes of an equal protection challenge because the student groups vary from year to year. In effect, the subset of students is basically a random assortment. This is particularly true when, according to the trial court's findings, only one percent to three percent of California teachers are allegedly grossly ineffective.

Second, the court found that it is not the laws that assign poorly performing teachers to schools serving large numbers of low-income students and students of color but school administrators who decide which teachers are assigned to their schools and which teachers should be transferred to other schools. This so-called dance of the lemons results from staffing decisions where poorly performing teachers were repeatedly transferred from one school to another. The court concluded that declaring the statutes facially unconstitutional would not prevent administrators from continuing to assign ineffective teachers to schools serving mostly low-income students and students of color.

In August 2016, the California Supreme Court, by a 4–3 vote, declined to take up the matter, thus leaving the appellate court decision intact. The majority issued no opinion for the rejection. In his dissent, Justice Mariano-Florentino Cuellar noted:

> Beatriz Vergara and her fellow plaintiffs raise profound questions with implications for millions of students across California. They deserve an answer from this court. Difficult as it is to embrace the logic of the appellate court on this issue, it is even more difficult to allow that court's decision to stay on the books without review in a case of enormous statewide importance.

The appellate court ruling was later reissued to include the California Supreme Court's dissenting opinions (*Vergara v. State of California*, 2016).

It bears noting that proper employee classification is very important in ensuring the school district properly identifies those who will be subject to layoff. For instance, misclassification of a certificated employee as a temporary employee when the employee should have been considered probationary or attained permanent status can result in a hearing officer ordering changes to the school district's proposed layoff schedule.

The procedures school districts must follow when implementing layoffs are robust. Employees who receive layoff notices may request a hearing. The right to request a hearing extends to probationary employees as well (*Cousins v. Weaverville Elementary School District*, 1994).

Following receipt of a layoff hearing request, the employee may engage in certain expedited "discovery" with the school district and request information related to the layoff. Eventually, the employee has a right to a hearing before an administrative law judge (ALJ) appointed by the California Office of Administrative Hearings. From a practical perspective, those hearings typically occur in April, and parties are advised to request a hearing as quickly as possible to ensure that OAH can convene the hearing on the parties' preferred dates.

The ALJ conducts the layoff hearing and prepares a proposed decision containing findings of fact regarding the layoff and a recommendation as to its disposition. Generally speaking, the ALJ analyzes whether the school district complied with the procedural requirements described in the Education Code. The ALJ does not analyze the wisdom of the layoff and/or the Board of Education's rationale in implementing the layoff as those matters exceed the scope of the ALJ's jurisdiction. The ALJ issues a written decision to the school district on or before May 7. The decision is a recommendation to the Board of Education. The Board of Education must convene to discuss and adopt or revise the decision and issue final notice of layoff to the certificated employee no later than May 15.

After considering the findings of fact and recommended decision, the Board of Education makes the final decision related to the layoff. A permanent teacher who is laid off is placed on a thirty-nine-month reemployment list. The teacher is given preferential consideration for rehiring based in the order in which the employee was laid off. A permanent teacher may waive the right to reemployment for up to one school year. The process for a laid-off probationary teacher is similar, but reemployment preference is limited to a twenty-four-month period. Under a showing of specific need, however, a governing board may deviate from the general preference to rehire based on seniority. Education Code Sections 44956 and 44957 address reemployment rights for laid-off permanent and probationary certificated employees.

CLASSIFIED EMPLOYEES

Classified employees comprise the other primary classification of public school employees. While classified employees do not hold a credential, they enjoy rights that are similar to certificated employees in the areas of permanent status, discipline, dismissal, and layoff.

Categories

To review, the four main categories of certificated employees (substitute, temporary, probationary, and permanent). Classified employees also serve in different categories. The employment, discipline, termination, and layoff rights of a classified employee are a function of the employee's classification.

Technically, there are two very common categories of classified employees, permanent and probationary. An individual may serve in a classified position on a short-term basis or as a substitute employee, but these employees are not part of the classified service. Rounding out the classified service are individuals serving in senior management who do not require credentials, such as the school district's chief business official.

Slightly complicating the discussion is the existence of merit system school districts. In a merit system school district, the classified employees are subject to different rules and have different rights as compared to their counterparts in a nonmerit school district. The major differences are explained later in the chapter.

A classified employee attains permanent status after completion of a prescribed period of probation not to exceed six months or 130 working days, whichever is longer (Educ. Code § 45113). Prior to attaining permanent status, a classified employee is considered probationary unless the employee is serving in a short-term or substitute capacity.

A short-term employee is "any person who is employed to perform a service for the district, upon the completion of which, the service required or similar services will not be extended or needed on a continuing basis" (Educ. Code § 45103(d)(2)). A short-term employee is not part of the classified service of the school district. Prior to hiring someone in this capacity, the governing board, at a regularly scheduled board meeting, must identify the specific duties the employee will perform and the ending date of the employee's service.

An individual contract between the short-term employee and the governing board sets forth the terms and conditions of employment. Although the ending date of the short-term classified employee's service may be shortened or extended by the governing board, the ending date cannot exceed 75 percent of the school year. Seventy-five percent of the school year is defined in this section of the Education Code as "195 working days, including holidays, sick leave, vacation and other leaves of absence, irrespective of the number of hours worked per day" (Educ. Code § 45103(d)(3)).

A substitute employee is defined as "any person employed to replace any classified employee who is temporarily absent from duty" (Educ. Code § 45103(d)(1)). School districts may also hire one or more substitutes to serve in vacant positions for up to sixty calendar days so long as the school district is in the process of searching for a permanent employee to fill the vacancy. A collective bargaining agreement, however, may provide for a different period of time. A substitute employee is not part of the classified service of the school district.

A governing board may adopt a resolution designating certain positions as senior management of the classified service (Educ. Code § 45100.5). An individual serving in this capacity cannot obtain permanent status. The employment terms are a function of the employee's individual contract with the governing board. The Education Code limits the number of positions school districts may designate as senior management based on that school district's ADA (Educ. Code § 45108). School districts may request a waiver of that limit in order to expand the number and type of senior management positions.

In addition to short-term and substitute employees, the following noncertificated positions are not part of the classified service of a school district: apprentices, professional experts employed on a temporary basis for a specific project regardless of the length of employment, full-time students employed part-time, and part-time students employed part-time in any college work-study program or work education experience program (Educ. Code § 45103).

Evaluation and Discipline

The Education Code's guidelines for use in the evaluation of certificated employees is covered earlier. No similar provisions apply to the evaluation of classified employees. A governing board, however, must "prescribe written rules and regulations, governing the personnel management of the classified service" (Educ. Code § 45113(a)). These rules and regulations may include criteria for evaluation. The procedures for the evaluation are negotiable with the classified employees' union.

Despite the absence of evaluation provisions, it bears noting that the Education Code recognizes the importance of classified employees and their continued training. For instance, Education Code Sections 45390 and 45391 require the school district expending funds for the professional development of any school site staff to also consider the professional development needs of its classified employees. The professional development may be in any of a number of areas relevant to public schools, including working with at-risk youth, curriculum, and special education.

Unlike Education Code Section 44932, which sets forth rigid causes for discipline of certificated employees, the governing board is responsible for identifying causes for which suspension of a classified employee may be imposed. Such rules and regulations generally set forth a wide range of inappropriate behavior warranting suspension and/or dismissal. A collective bargaining agreement may also address the causes and procedures related to the suspension and dismissal of a classified employee.

As a general rule, misconduct occurring beyond two previous years or during the employee's probationary period cannot form the basis for discipline (Educ. Code § 45113(d)). However, misconduct may form the basis for discipline charges if the misconduct was concealed or not disclosed by the employee when it could be reasonably assumed that the employee should have disclosed the facts to the school district.

A governing board must also adopt procedures governing the suspension of classified employees, including informing the employee of the specific charges being brought and the employee's right to request a hearing. Notice of the specific charges must be in "ordinary and concise language of the specific acts and omissions upon which the disciplinary action is based" (Educ. Code § 45116). The notice must contain a statement of the cause for the disciplinary action. If a violation of a regulation or rule is involved, the rule or regulation also must be in the notice. Citing the rule or regulation without further detail as to the specific charges and cause for the disciplinary action is insufficient for imposing discipline.

A *Skelly* conference is required prior to placing an employee on an unpaid suspension. As we previously discussed, a *Skelly* conference is an informal meeting during which the charges against the employee are explained and the employee may respond. If the employee requests a hearing, the hearing will occur under the procedures adopted by the governing board (often a hearing with an impartial hearing officer) or, in some instances, pursuant to the terms of a collective bargaining agreement. Unless the collective bargaining agreement results in a final and binding hearing decision, the hearing results in a proposed decision the governing board may accept, reject, or modify.

Dismissal and Layoff

Dismissal of a permanent classified employee may occur only for cause pursuant to rule or regulation prescribed by the governing board. The same notice and hearing rights discussed for the suspension of a classified employee also apply to the dismissal of a permanent classified employee. This includes the necessity of specific charges, the right to a hearing, and a *Skelly* conference if suspension without pay is ordered. Education Code Section 45113(d)'s general prohibition against basing discipline on conduct occurring more than two years prior or before the employee attainted permanent status also applies to dismissal. Service of the charges by mail may not be sufficient to provide notice consistent with due process of law if the employee does not work the entire school year because the employee could be gone for an extended period of time and not receive the notice (*California School Employees Association v. Livingston Union School District*, 2007). Absent an unlawful motivating factor (such as retaliation against free speech), a probationary classified employee may be dismissed without notice or any other due process.

The layoff of classified employees is permissible for "lack of work or lack of funds" (Educ. Code § 45308). A layoff of classified employees is initiated by a resolution of the governing board. The governing board has the discretion to determine the positions or classifications subject to the layoff. As with the layoff of certificated employees, the order of the layoff is a function of seniority or, as the phrase is used in Education Code Section 45308, "length of service."

Length of service consists of all hours in paid status, whether during the school year, a holiday, recess, or during any period that a school is in session or closed, but does not include overtime pay. Under a collective bargaining agreement, length of service may be, and very often is, defined as the date of hire.

A collective bargaining agreement may also include bumping rights for more senior classified employees. Exercise of a bumping right permits a classified employee who would otherwise be laid off to bump a more junior employee. In some instances, the employee subject to the bump may be in a position that was not even within those positions or classifications originally subject to the layoff.

As an alternative to being laid off, a school district may permit a classified employee to accept a voluntary demotion or transfer or a reduction in hours. Special rules contained in Education Code Section 45117 govern the layoff of classified employees due to the expiration of a specially funded program.

Laid-off classified employees are placed on a reemployment list for thirty-nine months. Reemployment occurs in order of seniority. Classified employees accepting a voluntary demotion or reduction in hours have these same rights plus twenty-four additional months of eligibility on a reemployment list. Education Code Section 45298 governs the reemployment rights of classified employees in the context of a layoff or voluntary demotion or reduction in hours.

In the past, classified employees were entitled to only forty-five, then sixty, days' advance notice of their layoff. However, in 2022, the California Legislature adopted, and the Governor signed, legislation that provided permanent classified employees with layoff rights similar to those enjoyed by certificated staff.

Specifically, under the revised Education Code Section 45117, classified employees are now entitled to written notice of layoff for the coming school year for lack of work or lack of funds no later than March 15. Classified employees may request a hearing to challenge the layoff.

Classified employees who request a hearing are entitled to rights similar to those described above, which are related to certificated employee layoff hearings. For instance, they are entitled to, among other things, limited discovery and a hearing before an ALJ assigned by the California Office of Administrative Hearings (which typically occurs in April). Following the layoff hearing, the ALJ must issue a recommended decision to the Board of Education before May 7. The Board of Education must convene to discuss and adopt or revise the decision and issue final notice of layoff to the classified employee no later than May 15.

These described layoff procedures in no way limit the school district's right to release probationary employees during their probationary period for legitimate and non-discriminatory reasons. Education Code Section 45117(e)(1) clarifies that permanent employees who do not receive proper notice of layoff are deemed re-employed for the following school year. That subdivision defines "permanent classified employee[s]" to include "an employee who was permanent at the time the notice or right to a hearing was required and an employee who became permanent after the date of the required notice."

Merit System School Districts

In a merit system school district, a three-member personnel commission and a personnel director are responsible for the administration, regulation, discipline, and dismissal of classified employees. Education Code Section 45220 and following sections detail the various ways in which a school district may adopt the merit system. These include the vote of classified employees, the vote of the governing board of the school district and the county board of education, and the vote of the electorate of the school district.

The governing board of the school district appoints one member of the commission, and the classified employees of the school district appoint another. These two members of the commission choose the third member. The commission thereafter appoints a personnel director who is responsible for administering the classified employees of the district.

The commission is responsible for classifying all of the classified employees in the district. The governing board retains the power to prescribe the duties of the various positions. The commission also prescribes rules governing a wide array of items pertaining to the classified employees of the district. These include rules regarding applications, examinations, eligibility, appointments, promotions, demotions, vacations, discipline, leaves of absence, performance evaluations, and compensation within classifications.

If a collective bargaining agreement exists, the personnel commission rules must be consistent with the agreement (Educ. Code § 45261(b)). If there is a conflict between the collective bargaining agreement and rules, the agreement controls.

The personnel commission also makes recommendations to the governing board regarding salary schedules for the classified service. However, the governing board may approve, amend, or reject these recommendations (Educ. Code § 45268).

The commission also oversees the discipline of classified employees. Aside from promulgating the rules governing the discipline of classified employees, the personnel commission also hears appeals regarding the suspension, demotion, or dismissal of classified employees. The personnel commission may assign the dismissal hearing to a hearing officer who will issue a recommended decision for the commission's consideration.

ADMINISTRATORS

Administrators do not enjoy a property interest in their administrative assignment. However, they do enjoy a right to continued employment in the district. This means the administrator does not have the right to a due process hearing prior to reassignment to a nonadministrative position. However, administrators gain permanency in nonadministrative assignments and retain rights in those assignments, including previously held positions. As described in this section, the Education Code contains special notice provisions applicable to the release of certificated administrators, including certain high-level administrators such as assistant superintendents.

It bears noting that a school district's internal administrator reassignment policies and procedures may provide a due process right that would not otherwise exist, and that right may be enforced in state court (*Bernstein v. Lopez*, 2003). While the administrators in *Bernstein* were unsuccessful in federal court, they prevailed in state court after the judge determined that the school district violated due process of law by reassigning administrators to less well-paid teaching positions without following the district's own procedures for reassignment of administrators.

An administrator serves in an administrative position at the pleasure of the governing board. Education Code Section 44951 provides that these employees may be released (through written notice that they either may be or will be reassigned by March 15) for the following year. Absent written notice, the employee will continue in the position through the following school year and be once again subject to the prospect of release prior to March 15. Administrators who receive notice that they "may be" reassigned must receive final notice that they will be reassigned by May 15. The "may be" reassigned notice does not require approval by the Board of Education. However, the final notice that the employee will be reassigned must be approved by the Board of Education. The notice requirements also apply to the reassignment of an administrator to another administrative position.

Prior to reassignment to a teaching position, administrators also have a right to request the Board of Education provide a written statement including the reasons for the reassignment (Educ. Code § 44896). If the reason for the reassignment is incompetency, the employee is also entitled to an evaluation under the Stull Act.

Section 44951 does not apply to administrators who have a written contract specifying an ending date beyond the current school year. Section 44951 also does not apply to an administrator in a position funded for less than a school year or serving in an acting position.

Education Code Section 35031 governs the release or reassignment of superintendents, associate or assistant superintendents, or senior management employees who serve for a period of up to four years. A written notice of non-reemployment for these administrative employees must be provided forty-five days prior to the expiration of the employee's contract term. Failure to provide this notice in a timely manner results in the reelection of the employee for a subsequent term of equal length.

THE PERSONNEL FILE

The Education and Labor Codes govern the rights of public school employees regarding their personnel files. These rights are important because the personnel file often serves as the largest source of information and/or evidence for employee evaluation, discipline, and dismissal.

Labor Code Section 1198.5 permits an employee to inspect personnel records regarding either the employee's performance or any grievance concerning the employee. Similarly, Education Code Section 44031 provides an employee the right to inspect certain records in his or her file and receive notice and comment on any derogatory statement before the comment is entered into the personnel file. The employee also can attach his or her own response to the derogatory statement.

An employee without a credential has the right to access his or her numerical score on a written examination used to screen or qualify for a position. Subject to certain exceptions in Section 44031, an employee is entitled to copies of only those documents that he or she signs (Labor Code § 432). The employee's union, however, may have a right to examine the entire personnel file if the file is necessary and relevant to the representation of the employee in a grievance.

A school district's failure to observe these rules may frustrate or invalidate efforts to impose discipline or dismissal. In the 1979 California Supreme Court decision of *Miller v. Chico Unified School District*, Hal Miller was reassigned from administrator to teacher. The reassignment was based, in part, on numerous confidential memoranda that were never provided to Miller prior to the reassignment. Rather than reinstate Miller to his prior position, however, the court sent the case back to trial to determine if the absence of these documents from his personnel file was prejudicial (*Miller v. Chico Unif. Sch. Dist. Bd. of Ed.*, 1979).

PUBLIC SCHOOL EMPLOYEE LEAVE RIGHTS

A collection of state and federal statutes governs the leave rights of public school employees. These statutes consist of select provisions of the Education and Labor Codes, a state law entitled the California Family Rights Act (CFRA), and a federal law entitled the Family and Medical Leave Act (FMLA). The CFRA and FMLA are similar in many respects. To the extent either law affords an employee a greater benefit, the employee receives the greater benefit. See Appendix C for a reference to useful websites regarding the CFRA and FMLA.

Certificated and classified employees receive sick leave. Specifically, certificated employees receive ten days of sick leave each school year or a pro rata portion consistent with their part-time status. Certificated employees may access their sick days in any given school year before they accrue those sick days. Unused sick days accumulate from year to year and are available for use in later school years (Educ. Code § 44978.)

Classified employees who are employed full-time for the entire fiscal year are entitled to twelve sick days each school year. Part-time employees and those who do not work the entire fiscal year receive a pro rata portion of those twelve days. Classified employees may use their sick leave for that school year prior to accruing them, except that new employees may not access more than six days, or the pro rata amount to which they are entitled, before six months of service with the school district. Like certificated employees, classified employees' unused sick days accumulate from year to year and are available for use in later school years (Educ. Code § 45191).

Certificated and classified employees receive personal necessity leave. Personal necessity leave permits an employee to use sick leave pursuant to rules and regulations of the governing board or in certain statutorily defined circumstances (e.g., death or serious illness of a family member or an accident involving the employee's person or property). Unless a collective bargaining agreement specifies otherwise, certificated and classified employees are generally limited to seven days per school year of personal necessity leave. Education Code Section 44981 governs personal necessity leave for certificated employees. Education Code Section 45207 governs personal necessity leave for classified employees.

Certificated and classified employees also receive three paid days of bereavement leave, or five paid days if out-of-state travel is required, following the death of an immediate family member (Educ. Code § 44985, 45191). However, Government Code Section 12945.7 guarantees all employees up to five unpaid days of bereavement leave. Immediate family is defined as "the mother, father, grandmother, grandfather, or a grandchild of the employee or of the spouse of the employee, and the spouse, son, son-in-law, daughter, daughter-in-law, brother, or sister of the employee, or any relative living in the immediate household of the employee."

The Education Code permits school districts to provide additional days of paid bereavement leave and to expand the definition of "immediate family member" to include additional individuals. School districts are well advised to ensure their practices guarantee all employees the bereavement leave provided by the Education Code, including the three paid days and, at a minimum, the two additional unpaid days authorized under the Government Code.

Education Code Section 44043.5 permits the establishment of a catastrophic leave program. Under this program, school district employees may donate accrued sick and vacation leave to another employee for use when the employee or a member of the employee's family experiences a catastrophic illness or injury. A "catastrophic illness" or "injury" is an illness or injury expected to incapacitate the employee (Educ. Code § 44043.5(a)(1)). An illness or injury expected to incapacitate a member of the employee's family, which requires the employee to care for the family member for an extended period of time, is also a catastrophic illness or injury. An employee must exhaust all sick leave and other paid leave before accessing a catastrophic leave program. If a school district desires to establish a catastrophic leave program, the program's terms and conditions must be negotiated with the employees' union.

After exhausting all paid leave, certificated and classified employees become eligible for extended illness leave in the form of differential pay. For a period not to exceed five months, certificated and classified employees on an extended illness leave receive differential pay that is calculated by their salary minus the salary paid to their substitute replacement.

Education Code Section 44977 governs differential pay for certificated employees and permits them to access one five-month period of extended illness leave per "illness or accident." It also limits the extended illness leave to one leave period per school year but allows the certificated employee who does not access the entire five-month period in a school year to carry over the remaining month(s) at the beginning of the next school year.

Section 44977 makes clear that the certificated employee's sick leave and extended sick leave run consecutively and the extended illness leave commences once the certificated employee has exhausted all available and accrued sick leave. Finally, Section 44977 permits the school district to deduct the actual amount paid to the substitute employee or the amount that would have been paid to a substitute employee if the school district did not employ a substitute to cover the employee's absence.

Alternatively, Education Code Section 44983 permits school districts to adopt an extended illness leave system that guarantees certificated staff fifty percent of their pay rather than the difference between their salary and the amount paid to a substitute. Section 44983 specifically notes that Section 44977 shall not apply to school districts that adopt the fifty percent pay rule.

Additionally, Education Code Section 44977.5 provides additional differential pay benefits to a certificated employee in the form of up to 12 school weeks of maternity or paternity leave. Each certificated employee may receive only one twelve-week period per twelve-month period, and, to the extent that Section 44977.5 conflicts with an existing collective bargaining agreement, the section shall not apply until the expiration or renewal of the agreement. The birth of an employee's child and placement of a child with an employee in connection with the adoption or foster care of the child are included within the section's definition of maternity or paternity leave.

Education Code Section 45191 governs differential pay for classified employees but also permits the school district to adopt a system whereby classified employees receive 100 days of sick leave with classified employees receiving full pay while they access any sick leave and accrued sick leave, then fifty percent of their salary of the remaining 100 days of leave.

Unlike certificated employees and absent collective bargaining agreement language to the contrary, classified employees' extended illness leave runs concurrently with available and accrued sick leave. In addition, a classified employee's extended illness leave is not limited to the same "illness or accident," which may permit the classified employee to access extended illness leave in multiple school years to treat the same illness or accident. Finally, unlike certificated employees and absent collective bargaining agreement language to the contrary, (for school districts not adopting the fifty percent pay), differential pay includes the pay actually paid to a substitute and does not include a deduction in pay for monies that would have been paid to a substitute if the school district chose not to employ one.

Certificated and classified employees exhausting all paid leave, including differential pay, who remain unable to return to work are placed on a reemployment list. While on the reemployment list, the employee may return to a position for which the employee is qualified once the employee is medically able to do so. Certificated employees are entitled to return as soon as they are medically able to do so, while classified employees need not be returned to a position unless a vacancy exists.

Education Code Section 44978.1 governs the reemployment list for teachers. A probationary teacher may remain on a reemployment list for twenty-four months, and a permanent teacher may remain on the list for thirty-nine months. Education Code Section 45192 governs the reemployment list for classified employees and provides a thirty-nine-month reemployment right but does not distinguish between permanent and probationary status.

Therefore, when a permanent certificated employee resigns, they are entitled to return to permanent status if they are reemployed by the same school district within 39 months of their last day of paid service. (Educ. Code § 44931). With that said, does Section 44931 allow a teacher to return to permanent status if the employee was later rehired as a substitute teacher? The court answered this question in the 2014 case *Edwards v. Lake Elsinore Unified School District* and held that Section 44931 does not apply when the former permanent certificated employee is rehired as a substitute teacher (*Edwards v. Lake Elsinore USD*, 2014).

In that case, Lori Edwards served as a certificated employee of the Lake Elsinore Unified School District from the commencement of the 2003–2004 school year until July 2006, at which time she voluntarily resigned. In January 2007, she applied for reemployment with the district as a substitute teacher. Various records, including time sheets and retirement documents, were completed by Ms. Edwards, and the district referred to her as a substitute teacher.

Ms. Edwards alleged that the school district improperly classified her as a substitute teacher upon her rehire and should have classified her as a permanent certificated employee. She sought retroactive pay because the district ultimately classified her as a permanent certificated employee, effective August 2008.

Ms. Edwards first argued that she was a permanent employee because the district had not given her an employment contract identifying her as a substitute employee. The court, however, concluded that, because Ms. Edwards was hired as a substitute rather than a temporary employee, she was not entitled to a written employment contract under Education Code Section 44916 at the time of her reemployment in January 2007. The court also held that Ms. Edwards was not entitled to a written employment contract under Education Code Section 44909, which applies to certain categorically funded positions, because she was not hired to fill a categorically funded position.

Ms. Edwards next argued that Education Code Section 44918 entitled her to retroactive pay. The court disagreed and noted that Section 44918 merely provides for retroactive credit of one year of time served as a probationary teacher for a substitute teacher who works in a certificated position for at least 75 percent of the school year and is hired as a probationary teacher for the next school year. The court also rejected Ms. Edwards' argument that she was entitled to retroactive benefits under Section 44931 because the evidence established that she was rehired in January 2007 as a substitute employee and not as a permanent certificated employee.

FEDERAL AND STATE ANTIDISCRIMINATION LAWS

A number of state and federal antidiscrimination laws applicable to the private sector also apply to public school employers and their employees. Taken in the aggregate, these civil rights laws protect applicants, employees, and even former employees from discriminatory employment practices based on disability, gender, gender identity, gender expression, nationality, race or ethnicity, religion, sexual orientation, or any other characteristic that is contained in the definition of hate crimes set forth in Section 422.55 of the Penal Code, including immigration status. In certain areas, state law affords greater protection to public school employees than federal law.

Title VII

Title VII of the Civil Rights Act of 1964, commonly known as Title VII, is a federal antidiscrimination law governing private and public employers (42 U.S.C. § 2000e et seq.). The Equal Employment Opportunity Commission (EEOC) is the federal agency charged with promulgating regulations interpreting Title VII.

EEOC investigates allegations that an employer violated Title VII. Title VII applies to state and local government entities, which include the entire range of public school employers. Title VII prohibits employment practices or discrimination based on race, color, religion, sex, or national origin. In certain instances, these protections extend to job applicants, current employees, and even former employees.

Race or color discrimination includes discrimination based on associating with persons of another race. Title VII's prohibition against discrimination based on religion requires an employer to accommodate employees' religious beliefs or observations. This matter is discussed in Chapter 7. Sex discrimination includes discrimination based on pregnancy and extends to sex discrimination in which the offender and victim are the same sex. In addition, the United States Supreme Court has recognized that Title VII prohibits discrimination based on sexual orientation and gender identity (*Bostock v. Clayton County, Georgia*, 2020; see also https://www.justice.gov/crt/laws-we-enforce).

Sexual harassment is a form of sex discrimination that violates, among many other authorities, Title VII and includes a variety of circumstances such as unwelcome sexual advances, requests for sexual favors, or other verbal or physical conduct of a sexual nature that explicitly or implicitly affects an individual's employment, interferes with work performance, or otherwise creates an intimidating, hostile, or offensive work environment. The victim does not necessarily need to complain about the conduct to the employer and/or have to be the person harassed but may be anyone affected by the conduct. Unlawful sexual harassment may occur despite the absence of economic damage or loss of employment to the victim.

EEOC's regulations define national origin discrimination as "including, but not limited to, the denial of equal employment opportunities because of an individual's, or his or her ancestor's, place of origin; or because an individual has the physical, cultural, or linguistic characteristics of a national origin group" (29 C.F.R. § 1606.1).

Title VII case law contains a number of different discrimination theories. These include a straightforward allegation of discrimination against an individual (known as intentional discrimination or disparate treatment claim), an allegation that a facially neutral policy is having a discriminatory effect on a protected class and is not justified by a business necessity (known as a disparate impact or adverse impact claim), and an allegation of a regular policy or procedure of discrimination on a classwide basis (known as a pattern and practice or systematic disparate treatment claim). The theory of discrimination is important because it dictates the manner in which the plaintiff employee and defendant employer must present their respective cases to the court.

For example, if a school principal alleges that he was terminated based on race, he may need to prove the following to maintain a Title VII disparate treatment lawsuit:

1. He was a member of a protected class;
2. he was qualified for his position;
3. he was discharged; and
4. he was replaced by a person outside of the protected class.

If the principal can demonstrate each of these factors by a preponderance of the evidence (i.e., more than 50 percent of the evidence), there is an inference of discrimination, and the burden shifts to the employer school district to rebut the claim by demonstrating that there was a legitimate, nondiscriminatory reason for the adverse employment action. If the school district can make this showing, the burden then shifts back to the principal to demonstrate that the school district's reason was not the true reason for his termination but a pretext for discrimination.

Title VII requires an individual to file a charge with EEOC or the California Civil Rights Department (CRD; formerly the Department of Fair Employment and Housing) before bringing a legal action in court. Accessing a necessary intermediate administrative process prior to bringing suit in a court is referred to as exhaustion of an administrative remedy.

The charge must be filed with EEOC within 180 days after the employee knew or should have known of the allegedly discriminatory act. If a complaint is first sent to a state agency (e.g., pursuant to a parallel state employment antidiscrimination law), the complainant has 300 days, instead of 180 days, to file the complaint with the EEOC.

Once the EEOC completes its investigation, the charging party receives a right-to-sue letter. In some instances, the EEOC, or the CRD, if the complaint is made at the state level, may bring legal action on behalf of the complainant. If a lawsuit is to be filed by the employee, the employee must do so within ninety days after the issuance of the right-to-sue letter. Failure to first bring a charge alleging a violation of Title VII with EEOC or timely initiating a legal action after receipt of the right-to-sue letter may foreclose the aggrieved party from suing the employer in court.

A successful plaintiff in a Title VII lawsuit may be entitled to a range of remedies, including back pay, front pay, reinstatement, and compensatory damages. Title VII, like other civil rights statutes, contains a fee-shifting provision to encourage attorneys to represent individuals alleging employment discrimination. As a result, a prevailing plaintiff is also entitled to recover their attorneys' fees and costs. This operates as an exception to the general rule in America that each party bears its own costs in a lawsuit.

Americans with Disabilities Act and Section 504

The Americans with Disabilities Act of 1999 (ADA) and Section 504 of the Rehabilitation Act of 1973 (Section 504) are federal laws prohibiting discrimination on the basis of disability. ADA applies to public and private employers, while Section

504 applies only to recipients of federal funding. As public employers in receipt of federal funding, all public school employers are subject to ADA and Section 504. ADA and Section 504's antidiscrimination provisions also extend to certain students meeting the statutes' definition of disability (see Chapter 8). Our focus in this chapter is the application of these statutes to employment.

ADA and Section 504 provide essentially identical obligations to public school employers and rights to public school employees. Unless otherwise indicated, our reference to ADA also applies to Section 504. Effective January 1, 2009, the ADA Amendments Act of 2008 significantly revised the ADA and Section 504.

ADA's protections extend to a "qualified individual with a disability." ADA defines a disability as:

1. a physical or mental impairment that substantially limits one or more major life activities;
2. a record of such an impairment; or
3. being regarded as having such an impairment.

An individual who meets one of the foregoing criteria satisfies the ADA's definition of disability.

The first definition of disability contains multiple components. A physical or mental disability is broadly defined to include any physiological, mental, or psychological disorder. Major life activities include caring for oneself, performing manual tasks, working, lifting, bending, walking, seeing, hearing, speaking, breathing, learning, and working. Major life activities also include impairments of major bodily functions (for example, immune, neurological, circulatory, and reproductive systems). An individual may also be considered disabled even if his or her impairment limits a major life activity episodically or is in remission.

The phrase "a record of such impairment" means that the person has a history of, or has been misclassified as having, a mental or physical impairment that substantially limits one or more major life activities. (Note, the California Fair Employment and Housing Act, a similar state law, requires only that the physical or mental impairment "limit" a major life activity. The Fair Employment and Housing Act includes this distinction and is detailed later in this chapter.) The phrase "being regarded as having such an impairment" refers to an individual who is treated as though he or she has a physical or mental impairment that limits a major life activity even though the individual does not actually have the impairment. The ADA also prohibits retaliation, and its protections extend to nondisabled individuals that advocate on behalf of disabled individuals (*Barker v. Riverside Cty. Office of Educ.*, 2009). The ADA requires interpretation of the definition of "disability" in favor of broad coverage.

In determining whether an individual satisfies ADA's definition of disability, is the individual to be considered with or without corrective devices (for example, glasses for an individual with poor eyesight)? The ADA Amendments Act of 2008 provides that, except for ordinary eyeglasses or contact lenses, consideration of ameliorative measures is not permitted to determine if an impairment limits a major life activity.

Satisfying ADA's definition of disability is not the end of the inquiry to determine if ADA's protections apply to an employee. The individual must be a qualified individual with a disability. This aspect of ADA is unique to the employment context and does not apply to ADA or Section 504 issues for students. A qualified individual with a disability is "an individual with a disability who, with or without reasonable accommodation, can perform the essential functions of the employment position that such individual holds or desires" (29 C.F.R. § 1630.2(m)). Determining if an individual satisfies this definition is a fact-intensive inquiry.

An employer must make reasonable accommodations for qualified individuals with a disability. Reasonable accommodations include making existing facilities readily accessible, restructuring jobs, and acquiring or modifying equipment (29 C.F.R. § 1630.2(o)). For example, permitting a blind employee to bring a guide dog to work is a reasonable accommodation.

Employers do not have to provide an accommodation that will impose an undue hardship on the employer or pose a direct threat to the health or safety of the employee or others. An undue hardship is an action requiring significant difficulty or expense, although objections related to expense should be carefully analyzed as courts will often compare the expense associated with the accommodation against the school district's total operating budget (29 C.F.R. § 1630.2(p)). Interpretive guidance accompanying the ADA's regulations cites an example of a waiter with a disabling visual impairment requesting the employer nightclub to provide bright lights as a reasonable accommodation. The guidance concludes that this request will impose an undue hardship if the bright lights destroy the ambiance of the nightclub or make it difficult for patrons to view the stage show.

An employer is required to engage in an "interactive process" with an employee to determine whether a reasonable accommodation is necessary, and if so, the nature of the accommodation. The interactive process is a good faith dialogue between the employer and employee during which the employee shares the functional limitations of their condition and the parties work to identify potential reasonable accommodations. The employee is free to request accommodations and the employer is required to consider those requests in good faith, but the employer is typically ultimately responsible for identifying and offering reasonable accommodations. Employers are well advised to document all interactive process meetings and share them with the employee to confirm the parties' mutual understanding of the discussion during the interactive process meeting.

At times, the employer and employee may require input from a physician in, among other things, understanding the limitations and/or potential accommodations. Employers may make medically-related inquiries so long as those inquiries are job-related and consistent with business necessity. Employers are well advised to attempt to acquire any necessary medical information through the least invasive means first, such as discussions with the employee, before requiring information from the employee's treating physician or the potentially more invasive option of requiring the employee to submit to a fitness for duty examination with employer's doctor.

The EEOC enforces the ADA with the same powers, remedies, and procedures applicable to Title VII. An individual seeking to initiate a legal action against an employer under the ADA must first file a timely complaint with the EEOC, wait for a right-to-sue letter, and thereafter bring suit within ninety days of receipt of the letter. The time period for filing a complaint under Title VII also applies to the ADA.

An individual may demonstrate disability discrimination under the ADA with the same discrimination theories applicable to Title VII. For example, a plaintiff alleging wrongful termination in violation of the ADA must prove the following: He or she meets the ADA's definition of disability; he or she is able to perform the essential functions of the job, with or without reasonable accommodation; and he or she was terminated because of disability. A prevailing employee in an ADA action may generally seek and receive the same relief available under Title VII (for example, back pay, front pay, reinstatement, compensatory damages).

Fair Employment and Housing Act

The Fair Employment and Housing Act (FEHA) is a California law governing employment discrimination (Gov't Code § 12900 et seq.). FEHA applies to private and public employers. FEHA defines public employers as the State of California, cities, counties, local agencies, special districts, and any other political or civil subdivision of the state. Governing boards, county superintendents of schools, and charter school operators are subject to FEHA. FEHA, however, does not apply to nonprofit religious organizations or to corporations exempt from state and federal taxes.

FEHA's protections extend to both employees and job applicants. An applicant does not include a person who voluntarily, and without coercion, withdraws his or her application before being interviewed, tested, or hired.

FEHA's antidiscrimination provisions are broader than those in Title VII or the ADA. FEHA prohibits discrimination on the basis of age, ancestry, color, creed, denial of family and medical care leave, disability (mental and physical) including HIV and AIDS, marital status, medical condition (cancer and genetic characteristics), national origin, race, religion, sex, and sexual orientation.

With this in mind, can a female management math consultant be paid less than her male counterparts? In short, it depends on whether the reasons for the lower salary placement were based on her gender, a protected characteristic, or other non-discriminatory reasons, such as a large discrepancy in training and/or experience. This was the central issue in a matter involving Aileen Rizo, a Fresno County Office of Education math consultant, who filed a federal lawsuit maintaining that basing her current lower salary on her prior salary level violates (1) the federal Equal Pay Act (29 U.S.C. § 206(d), (2) Title VII of the 1964 Civil Rights Act, and (3) the California Fair Employment and Housing Act. The U.S. Court of Appeals for the Ninth Circuit focused only on the Equal Pay Act, since it had ruled previously that standards under Title VII are the same and since there was no assertion that equal pay standards under the California Fair Employment and Housing Act are any different than under federal law.

In this case, the county office of education asserted that while there was a pay differential, this was caused by Ms. Rizo's lower prior salary, not her gender. The Ninth Circuit returned the case to the trial court to determine if there was justification for the county office's claims that the prior salary differential was based on factors such as encouraging persons to leave previous employment and the judicial use of taxpayer dollars. Notably, the court recognized that, if prior salary alone was responsible for the differential, the Equal Pay Act has been violated (*Rizo v. Vovino*, 2017). (Note: Labor Code section 432.3(b) now prohibits employers from requesting salary information.)

FEHA differs from federal law (ADA) in the definition of disability. Recall that the ADA requires a mental or physical impairment to substantially limit one or more major life activities. FEHA, however, merely requires a physical or mental impairment to limit a major life activity. FEHA explicitly provides that the determination of whether a mental or physical impairment "limits" a major life activity is to be undertaken without regard to mitigating measures such as medications, assistive devices, or reasonable accommodations. FEHA contains a requirement on the exhaustion of administrative remedies like that in Title VII. Before bringing a legal action under FEHA, an individual must file a verified complaint with the CRD, wait for the CRD to investigate, and receive a right-to-sue letter.

SUMMARY

A public school employee's due process rights are a function of the employee's classification. Depending on the employee's classification, due process may range from informal communication that informs a substitute teacher that the substitute's services are no longer necessary to a lengthy dismissal proceeding before a Commission on Professional Competence for a permanent teacher.

Within the two primary classifications of certificated and classified employees, there is a stepladder series of subclassifications defining the employee's amount of process due prior to the deprivation of that employee's right in employment. The four classifications of certificated employees are substitute, temporary, probationary, and permanent. Substitute employees enjoy the least job protections, while permanent employees have the most. Substitute teachers serve at the pleasure of the governing board, and the release of temporary teachers is permissible with written notice and for legitimate, non-discriminatory reasons. The non-reelection process requires written notice to a second-year probationary teacher prior to March 15 of the teacher's year of employment. Otherwise, the teacher is reemployed for the subsequent school year and attains permanent status.

Classified employees are either probationary or permanent, although an individual may serve in a classified position in a substitute or short-term capacity. Like their certificated counterparts, permanent classified employees enjoy the most job protections, including the right to a formal hearing prior to dismissal.

The dismissal of permanent teachers may occur only for cause, as defined in the Education Code. The grounds of unprofessional conduct and unsatisfactory performance require advance written notice and an opportunity for the teacher to improve prior to initiation of dismissal proceedings. The dismissal and suspension of probationary teachers is quite rare because the midyear dismissal process can be cumbersome and time-consuming, but the non-reelection process for these individuals is relatively simple.

The Education Code sets forth a number of unique leave and reemployment rights for certificated and classified employees. Federal and state leave laws complement these rights.

Federal and state antidiscrimination laws also govern the rights of public school employees and the obligations of their employers. These laws prohibit discrimination on the basis of race, national origin, color, sex, religion, age, disability, and other classifications. To the extent a state law affords an employee a greater benefit than federal law does, the employee receives the benefit of the state law.

6 RIGHTS OF EXPRESSION

For many decades of public schooling, neither teachers nor students had constitutionally protected free speech rights at school. By the late 1960s, major judicial rulings had extended rights of expression to both. The decisions coincided with the expansion of civil rights in the wake of the 1954 school desegregation decision *Brown v. Board of Education of Topeka, Kansas*. Student activism of the 1960s added further stimulus. More recently, federal and state courts have retreated somewhat from the early decisions, but the core constitutional principles remain.

This chapter discusses the extent to which both educators and students have rights of expression within traditional public and charter schools and the implications for school administrators in making personnel and student discipline decisions. Because the right to freedom of the press and the right to association are closely associated with free speech, this chapter will encompass them as well.

EDUCATOR EXPRESSION RIGHTS

Speaking Out on Matters of Public Concern

In 1968, the U.S. Supreme Court considered a case involving an Illinois teacher who was dismissed after he wrote a letter critical of the school board's handling of a bond election. The letter was published in a local newspaper. The school board contended that Marvin Pickering owed his employer a certain amount of allegiance and that the letter writing was detrimental to the efficient administration of the schools. Pickering, in contrast, maintained that he had a First Amendment right as a citizen to comment on school board matters and that doing so should not compromise his position as a teacher. The First Amendment to the U.S. Constitution provides in part that Congress shall make no law "abridging the freedom of speech, or of the press; or the right of the people peaceably to assemble, and to petition the Government for a redress of grievances." As noted in the first chapter, the Fourteenth Amendment extends these provisions to states and their political subdivisions. The Illinois Supreme Court decided in favor of the school board. The *Pickering* case was appealed directly to the U.S. Supreme Court.

In a unanimous decision, the U.S. Supreme Court overruled the Illinois Supreme Court and decided in favor of Mr. Pickering (*Pickering v. Board of Education*, 1968). However, the Court recognized that both the school board and the teacher had credible arguments. The Court's task, wrote Justice Thurgood Marshall, was to "arrive at a balance between the interests of the teacher, as a citizen, in commenting upon matters of public concern and the interest of the State, as an employer, in promoting the efficiency of the public services it performs through its employees" (p. 568).

In this case, the justices found insufficient evidence to justify Mr. Pickering's dismissal. The Court observed that the bond election clearly was a matter of public concern and that teachers are the community members most likely to have informed and definite opinions on how funds allotted to schools should be spent. While it was true that the teacher's letter contained some false statements, the Court observed that the school board could easily have corrected them by writing its own letter to the newspaper. There was no evidence that Mr. Pickering's statements undermined his effectiveness as a teacher or disrupted the school. Likewise, there was no evidence that he had made false statements knowingly or recklessly.

Pickering is a seminal decision for public schoolteachers and for governing boards in both traditional public and charter schools, as well as in postsecondary education. For teachers, it clearly establishes the right to speak out on matters of public concern and not fear loss of employment. In fact, the California Supreme Court has ruled that any form of retaliation for the exercise of First Amendment rights is out of bounds. In the words of that court:

> Any sanction imposed for the exercise of protected First Amendment conduct must be viewed as having a chilling effect on speech and on the right of teachers to engage in those activities which are protected by the First Amendment. Lesser penalties than dismissal can effectively silence teachers and compel them to forego exercise of the rights guaranteed them by our Constitution (*Adcock v. San Diego Unified School District*, 1973).

For governing boards and administrators, *Pickering* establishes the necessity to assemble sufficient documentation to show that the exercise of free speech has been abused. This can be done by showing that the teacher's effectiveness has been significantly compromised, that school operation has been disrupted, or that false statements have been made knowingly or recklessly. Assertions that a teacher's speech "might" or "could" prove disruptive in some way rarely will suffice. This is because most judges give special weight to robust free speech in a democratic society.

Suppose Mr. Pickering voiced his comments at school during school hours. To what extent can a teacher exercise free speech on school grounds? A year after the *Pickering* ruling, the California Supreme Court considered a challenge to a directive from the Los Angeles City Board of Education that teachers cease circulating a petition on campus during noninstructional time. The petition related to public school financing.

In that case, the school district conceded that teachers have a right under *Pickering* to speak among themselves during duty-free periods about such issues. But the district contended that petitioning would be disruptive and hence not constitutionally protected.

The California high court disagreed. The justices observed that the governing board could not seriously argue that its teachers should be "unthinking 'yes men'" who never share ideas or fear to do so. The court unanimously ruled that the ban on the petition violated the teachers' free speech rights (*Los Angeles Teachers Association v. Los Angeles City Board of Education*, 1969). At the same time, however, the court noted that the school district could issue a regulation protecting teachers in faculty rooms and lunchrooms from unwelcome interruptions. Commonly labeled "time, place, and manner" rules, such restrictions are permissible because they do not constitute an outright ban on speech content but rather determine the conditions under which speech rights can be exercised.

A somewhat similar situation arose a number of years later in the San Diego Unified School District. In that instance, the California Teachers Association filed a lawsuit against the district's ban on the wearing of political buttons anytime during school hours. The school district relied on a provision of the California Education Code that permits, but does not require, school districts to regulate officer and employee political activity during working hours on school grounds and to restrict political activities in general (Educ. Code §§ 7050–7058). The law does permit the use of public resources to provide information to the electorate in a fair and impartial manner on bond issues or ballot measures.

The union argued that the school district restriction intruded on protected free speech. It cited both the First Amendment and Article I, Section 2 of the

California Constitution, which provides that "every person may freely speak, write and publish his or her sentiments on all subjects, being responsible for the abuse of this right. A law may not restrain or abridge liberty of speech or press."

The California appellate court ruled that neither the First Amendment nor Article I, Section 2 of the California Constitution limit the power of school authorities to dissociate themselves from political controversy by prohibiting employees from engaging in political advocacy in the classroom (*California Teachers Association v. Governing Board of San Diego Unified School District*, 1996). The judges wrote, "Most self-evident is the conclusion that when public schoolteachers and administrators are teaching students, they act with the imprimatur of the school district which employs them and ultimately with the imprimatur of the state which compels students to attend their classes" (p. 479).

Based on the foregoing, the court concluded that the district's ban on partisan political activity in that setting did not violate the teachers' rights of free speech. However, outside the classroom, the ban could not be enforced because it conflicted with the precedents set by the U.S. Supreme Court and the California Supreme Court in *Pickering* and *Los Angeles Teachers Association*, respectively, supporting the right of teachers to express their political opinions to each other.

In 1979, the U.S. Supreme Court unanimously ruled that a teacher who expresses views on matters of public concern privately—for example, in the principal's office—is also protected by the First Amendment (*Givhan v. Western Line Consolidated School District*). In that case, the school district terminated a junior high school English teacher's contract after she complained about school policies and practices she found racially discriminatory. The Court recognized that the supervisor–employee relationship may be of greater concern when private expression is involved. If the exercise of free speech impairs institutional efficiency, it may not be entitled to constitutional protection.

Finally, an interesting First Amendment dispute arose when a school board member in Washington State contended that he was removed as vice president by other board members because of his criticism of the school superintendent. The U.S. Court of Appeals for the Ninth Circuit rejected the lawsuit, noting that the board members themselves were exercising First Amendment rights when they made the decision. Such action is typical of the give-and-take of political bodies (*Blair v. Bethel School District*, 2010).

Mt. Healthy Test

In *Mt. Healthy*, the Ohio teacher Fred Doyle's two-year term contract was not renewed following his phone-in discussion on a radio talk show about the school's faculty dress code policy. While he was not entitled to either notice or a hearing under Ohio law, he requested a statement of reasons for the action. He received a letter from the superintendent explaining that the radio station incident was a factor in the decision.

Doyle promptly sued, claiming retaliation for the exercise of free speech. Both the federal trial and appellate courts supported his claim based on *Pickering*. However, the U.S. Supreme Court did not. The high court noted that the radio station incident was not the only incident involving Doyle. The record revealed that Doyle had argued with another teacher, culminating in Doyle's being slapped by the other teacher. Both were suspended for a short time. In other incidents, he had argued with cafeteria workers about the amount of spaghetti he had been served, referred to students as "sons of bitches," and made an obscene gesture to two female students when they failed to follow his directive.

Given this record, the Court observed that, although a teacher should not be denied tenure because of the exercise of constitutional rights, "that same candidate ought not to be able, by engaging in such conduct, to prevent his employer from assessing his performance record and reaching a decision not to rehire on the basis of that record, simply because the protected conduct makes the employer more certain of the correctness of the decision" (p. 286). Several years earlier, the California Supreme Court expressed the same sentiment, noting that while it would not permit school officials to mask an unconstitutional dismissal behind a statement of valid causes, it also would not allow an ineffective teacher to avoid dismissal by engaging in political activities (*Bekiaris v. Board of Education of City of Modesto*, 1972).

The U.S. Supreme Court sent the *Mt. Healthy* case back to the trial court for a determination of whether the governing board would have reached the same decision had it not considered Doyle's comments on the radio. Applying the so-called *Mt. Healthy* test, the trial and appellate courts later decided in favor of the governing board.

The significance of *Mt. Healthy* cannot be underestimated. The Ninth Circuit has articulated a two-part test for applying the *Mt. Healthy* principles. First, the school employee must show that the speech is constitutionally protected, a relatively easy task if it relates to a matter of public concern. Second, the employee must show that the exercise of free speech played a substantial role in a negative employment decision. This may not be an easy burden when there is little evidence, and especially when an employee is not entitled to either notice or a hearing, as in the case of the non-reelection of a probationary teacher.

In 2001, the Ninth Circuit upheld a lower court ruling against three members of the deputy superintendent's cabinet who contested their reassignments as retaliation for free speech. In that case, the employees were unable to overcome a two-year time lap between their speech charging the deputy superintendent with mismanaging federal funds and their reassignments. Nor were they able to establish convincingly that the central office administrator knew of the speech by one of the employees or was opposed to what the other two had said (*Keyser v. Sacramento City Unified School District*). Of course, in the *Mt. Healthy* case, Doyle had little trouble meeting this burden because the superintendent had sent him a letter telling him that the radio talk show incident played an important role in the contract nonrenewal, even though Doyle was not entitled to written notice of the reasons for the action. The lesson for school administrators, of course, is to avoid citing legally impermissible reasons, but ensure that all actions are supported by legitimate and nondiscriminatory reasons.

It also bears noting that, even when free speech does play a substantial role in a negative employment decision, the governing board still can prevail if it can show the existence of job-related deficiencies unrelated to the exercise of the protected right that would have resulted in the employee's release. To do this, the governing board should base their decision on the administrator's documented evidence related to the employee's performance and/or conduct deficiencies. Without it, the governing board may struggle to satisfy the *Mt. Healthy* test.

In 2006, the U.S. Supreme Court restricted public employee free speech rights by ruling 5–4 that employee speech on matters of public concern made pursuant to official duties is not constitutionally protected (*Garcetti v. Ceballos*). In that case, a Deputy District Attorney alleged that he suffered retaliation by his supervisor after he wrote an internal memo in his official capacity recommending dismissal of a case because of prosecutorial misconduct. He claimed that the memorandum involved a matter of public concern and thus was constitutionally protected.

The majority ruled that, even if the subject of the memorandum was a matter of public concern, it was written in the Deputy District Attorney's official capacity as an employee. At the same time, the Court recognized that public employees who make such statements outside their official duties may be entitled to constitutional protection. However, such might not be the case if the employee is in a policymaking position such as a school principal or superintendent.

The Ninth Circuit noted in a 1998 decision that "we are most doubtful that the Constitution ever protects the right of a public employee in a policymaking position to criticize her employer's policies or programs simply because she does not share her employer's legislative or administrative vision" (*Moran v. State of Washington*, p. 850). The case involved a deputy insurance commissioner who was dismissed on the basis of philosophical differences with the insurance commissioner.

The deputy commissioner argued unsuccessfully that the dismissal violated her free speech rights.

The U.S. Supreme Court in *Ceballos* added two other caveats to its ruling. First, the justices rejected the contention that employers may curtail employee free speech rights on the job by creating excessively broad job descriptions. Second, the justices observed that speech related to scholarship or teaching may be treated differently. However, the majority seemed to focus on academic freedom at the public college and university level, not in K–12 public schools where academic freedom exists to a much lesser extent.

Several years later, the U.S. Supreme Court considered the extent to which public employee testimony in judicial or administrative hearings is protected by the First Amendment. In that case, Edward Lane, an Alabama community college administrator, was hired on a probationary basis to direct a statewide training program for underprivileged youth. Mr. Lane dismissed Suzanne Schmitz, an Alabama State Representative who was employed by the training program but regularly did not report to work.

Mr. Lane's action triggered considerable public attention and prompted an FBI investigation into Ms. Schmitz's employment based on public corruption concerns. Eventually, Mr. Lane testified before a federal grand jury and later trial against Schmitz about his reasons for firing Ms. Schmitz. Subsequently when the training program experienced budget shortfalls, Mr. Lane was one of twenty-nine probationary employees who were dismissed by Steve Franks, the new community college president.

Mr. Lane sued alleging that his dismissal was in retaliation for his grand jury and trial testimony. Both the trial and the appellate courts relied on *Garcetti v. Ceballos* to reject the lawsuit because Mr. Lane's speech, even if considered a matter of public concern, was based on what he had learned as an employee pursuant to his official duties.

The U.S. Supreme Court overturned this portion of the appellate court decision, ruling that the First Amendment protects public employees from retaliation for providing truthful sworn testimony under oath even if the content of the speech is learned while acting as an employee. This is so because sworn speech "is a quintessential example of speech as a citizen" and is protected by *Pickering v. Board of Education* when it is based on a matter of public concern. Further, there was no evidence that Mr. Lane's testimony was false or erroneous or undermined his effectiveness as an employee (see the *Pickering* discussion above regarding when free speech even on matters of public concern loses its protection) (*Lane v. Franks*, 2014).

It is important to note that the California Constitution broadly protects public employee free speech rights. Furthermore, when a California public employee speaks out about possible wrongdoing, the Whistleblower Protection Act comes into play, as described later in this chapter. Given the legal implications, school administrators may wish to consult counsel before penalizing employees for what they say on the job.

Complaints About Working Conditions

In the *Pickering* and *Mt. Healthy* decisions, the U.S. Supreme Court focused on speech relating to matters of public concern. Are employees likewise protected when they complain about their own working conditions? Sheila Myers was employed as an Assistant District Attorney in New Orleans serving at the pleasure of the district attorney, meaning that she had no contract and hence no expectation of continuing employment. She became disgruntled over a decision to transfer her to prosecute cases in another section of the criminal court. Believing that others also were unhappy about such matters, she constructed a questionnaire and circulated it to fifteen coworkers. The questions centered on office morale, levels of trust in various supervisors, the transfer policy, and the need for a grievance committee. When Harry Connick Sr., the district attorney (and father of the well-known singer by the same name), learned of her action, he considered it insubordinate and terminated her employment. Ms. Myers filed suit, contending that she was being penalized for exercising free speech. Both the trial and appellate courts ruled in favor of Ms. Myers based on the *Pickering* decision. The U.S. Supreme Court agreed to hear the case.

Once again, as in *Pickering*, the Court was faced with balancing the interests involved. But this time, in a closely divided opinion, it struck the balance in favor of the employer, distinguishing between speech on matters of public concern and on matters of internal office concern (*Connick v. Myers*, 1983). Although the former is entitled to constitutional protection, the latter is not. On balance, the Court found the questionnaire focused on internal matters. It also observed that Ms. Myers circulated the questionnaire both at lunch and at other times during working hours, thus undermining the efficiency of the workplace.

In 1997, a California court of appeal handed down a decision that is instructive on how state courts apply the *Pickering*, *Givhan*, and *Connick* precedents to speech by school employees (*Kirchmann v. Lake Elsinore Unified School District*). The case involved a secretary in the school district's facilities department. The secretary's supervisor directed her to draft a memo to the superintendent recommending that a particular architectural firm be chosen as project manager for future construction projects. Concerned that a consultant to the firm had been involved in its selection, the secretary faxed a notice from her home to the unsuccessful bidders about the appearance of a conflict of interest and suggesting they attend the board meeting to question the matter. After learning of the fax, the secretary's superiors sought her suspension for thirty days, a recommendation accepted by the governing board following an administrative hearing. The secretary challenged her suspension as retaliation for the exercise of free speech.

The appellate court first considered whether the secretary's fax addressed a matter of public concern under the *Pickering* decision or a matter relating to her working conditions under *Connick*. The judges noted that courts in California have been protective of public employee speech critical of governmental operations and that California Government Code Section 81000 and following sections prohibit conflicts of interest by governmental employees and consultants. This being the case, the secretary's fax addressed a matter of public concern. It did not matter that her fax was not aired in public, because *Givhan* protects privately expressed speech on public issues. Nor did it matter that the secretary may have sent the fax because she sought revenge against her supervisor for a threatened layoff. If the speech addresses a matter of public concern, the motive behind its utterance is irrelevant.

Noting that free speech on matters of public concern can lose its protection under the *Pickering* rationale if abused, the judges next examined whether this was the case. They did not find the fax to be knowingly or recklessly false. The secretary's action did not undermine her relationship with her supervisor or the consultant, because no unusual level of loyalty to either was demanded. If the superior–subordinate relationship had been that critical, the judges observed, the district would have sought to reassign the secretary to another position or terminate her employment rather than give her a short-term suspension. Nor was there evidence of any significant disruption of the project manager selection process. Finally, the fact that the secretary was only suspended and not terminated does not diminish her right to protected free speech. As the court noted, "If the speech is protected, any sanction, whatever its severity, is prohibited" (p. 281). While the case was decided before the U.S. Supreme Court's 2006 *Garcetti v. Ceballos* decision, that ruling may not have applicability to the situation here because the secretary sent the fax on her own time away from work and the scope of her duties was not discussed. A 2008 decision of the U.S. Court of Appeals for the Ninth Circuit is instructive on this point. The case involved an Idaho school security employee whose position was eliminated after he wrote a letter at home to his school administrators expressing concerns about the lack of adequate security measures on campus. In overturning the trial court decision against the employee, the Ninth Circuit noted that whether an employee is speaking within the scope of employment is a mixed question of law and fact. Here there was evidence the employee was addressing concerns beyond his duties as a security specialist and thus acting as a citizen. The case was sent back to the trial court for further proceedings (*Posey v. Lake Pend Oreille School District No. 84*, 2008).

Similarly, a middle school special education teacher who managed a school district's Educational/Behavioral Disorders program challenged her dismissal as retaliation for speaking negatively to school administrators and parents about the program. In upholding the trial court's rejection of her claims, the Ninth Circuit cited the U.S. Supreme Court's *Garcetti v. Ceballos* decision in noting that the comments were made within the scope of her employment and thus not protected by the First Amendment (*Coomes v. Edmonds School District No. 15*, 2016).

Notably, the judges acknowledged that the teacher's job description encompassed both up-the-chain complaints and speaking to parents. Therefore, her complaints embedded in a chain of emails to both were unprotected. The Ninth Circuit did not address how encompassing a job description can be, a matter that the U.S. Supreme Court justices cautioned against. The judges also sidestepped the teacher's assertion that speaking to her union about the matter was constitutionally protected as made outside the scope of her employment since she had not argued that point. Whether her complaints may have been protected under Washington State law also was not addressed, and the case returned to the trial court on this issue. As noted herein, employee speech may receive greater protection under state law than under the First Amendment.

It also bears noting that an employee's speech is not protected by the First Amendment when they speak out as a public official to students within the scope of their employment. This was exemplified in the case of a Bear Creek High School campus supervisor who claimed that she had a First Amendment right to direct students to video record a police arrest of a Black Female student they had taken to the ground during a fight between students and nonstudents in the school parking lot. The supervisor allegedly yelled that the arrest "was police brutality" and "bullshit" before she told students to video record the incident. The court concluded that the campus supervisor was speaking as a public official to students within the scope of her employment and thus there was no violation of her First Amendment rights when school officials reprimanded her and recommended termination of her employment for escalating the turmoil (*Toney v. Young*, 2017).

Expression Through School Channels

When employees communicate through school-maintained channels of communication, their free speech rights are subject to much greater control than when speaking face-to-face. This is because the school can control its own channels of communication. One of the key rulings to this effect is a 1983 U.S. Supreme Court decision involving a challenge to a collective bargaining agreement between an Indiana school district and its recognized teachers' union granting the union exclusive access to an interschool mail system. In that case, another union argued that the restriction violated the First Amendment (*Perry Education Association v. Perry Local Educators' Association*).

The Court decided in a narrow 5–4 ruling that the school mail system is not automatically a public forum available to teachers, their associations, and others to disseminate information. A public forum is a place for virtually unrestricted communication. Street corners and parks are prime examples of public forums. To enforce a content-based exclusion in this setting, the government must have a compelling reason that is very precise in its application (judges term this as being "narrowly tailored" to serve the state's substantial interest). For example, a municipality might be able to curtail an inflammatory racist speech on a public street corner if the harangue threatens imminent lawless action. The municipality would argue that it had a compelling interest in preventing a riot and that its action was very precise (or "narrowly tailored") because it applied to only a single speaker.

At the opposite end of the spectrum from the open forum is the closed forum. A closed forum is governmental property that is traditionally not a place for public communication. A prison is a good example. The Court in *Perry* viewed the public school mail system to be inherently a closed forum under school district control unless the school has opted to convert it into a "limited open forum." A limited open forum accommodates certain types of communication but not other types. For example, a school district could choose to open its mail or e-mail system to certain types of communication—say, announcements by community organizations—but not to commercial advertising. Once the communication system is open to certain categories of information, however, the school cannot discriminate within categories. Thus, if community organizations like a local garden club have access to make announcements of their meetings through the school communication system, the school would have difficulty denying access to an LGBTQ+ community organization for a similar purpose.

In the *Perry* case, the rival union argued that once the school permitted the recognized teachers' union to use the school mail system, it had to permit rival unions to do so too. But the majority noted that there was a difference between the recognized union and its rivals. When the teachers' union was selected as the exclusive bargaining agent, it became the official representative of all teachers in the school system on matters relating to the collective bargaining contract. Its status had become quite different from those of rival labor organizations. Permitting the recognized bargaining agent to use the interschool mail system to communicate with teachers about relations between labor and management did not create a limited open forum for competing labor organizations. The majority noted that these entities still could communicate with teachers through school bulletin boards, meetings on school property after hours, and outside of school.

The *Perry* ruling was cited in a 1996 case involving the open session of a school board meeting in the Moreno Valley Unified School District. Like many districts, the school board's policy specified that no oral or written presentations in open session could include charges or complaints about district employees, whether or not such employees were identified. A parent and president of a statewide organization identified a middle school principal and the district superintendent during remarks she made about parent complaints during an open session. She was ejected from the meeting and later filed suit, contending the restriction was a violation of free speech. The federal judge agreed (*Baca v. Moreno Valley Unified School District*).

Under the California open meeting law, known as the Brown Act, school board meetings are open to the public, and the public has a right to address the school board on matters related to school affairs (Gov't Code § 54954.3). The open session thus constitutes a limited open forum. While the governing board can confine the discussion to school business under *Perry*, the judge noted that it cannot restrict speech within that category unless it can establish a compelling interest for doing so and can show that its action was narrowly tailored to serve that interest.

In *Baca*, the court found no compelling interest to prevent criticism of the named school officials. Wrote the judge: "It is difficult to imagine a more content-based prohibition on speech than this policy, which allows expression of two points of view (laudatory and neutral) while prohibiting a different point of view (negatively critical) on a particular subject matter (District employees' conduct or performance)" (p. 730). The court was not persuaded that the employees' ability to bring defamatory actions against their attackers under California law rendered them inappropriate for the meeting because comments at open sessions of board meetings are absolutely privileged. The constitutionally protected right of members of the public to speak freely to elected officials at board meetings takes precedence.

Even though they are employees, teachers have the same right to address the school board and cannot be penalized for doing so. A provision of the Education Code gives all school employees this right (Educ. Code § 44040). The U.S. Supreme Court likewise has ruled that a teacher has a constitutional right to speak out during the open session of a school board meeting. The case arose when a member of a Wisconsin teachers' union was permitted to speak at a school board meeting on a matter involving the union; the union later filed an unfair labor practice claim against the district, claiming that only the union could speak to the board about employment matters (*City of Madison v. Wisconsin Employment Relations Commission*, 1976).

The lesson of *Perry* and *Baca* is that whether a school-maintained channel of communication is open to free speech to any extent depends upon state law and governing board policy. If a limited open forum has been created, then school authorities cannot discriminate within the categories of speech that are allowed.

It bears noting that the use of social media, and in particular public comments on social media accounts related to school district business, including otherwise private accounts, has become a topic of intense litigation in the recent past. For instance, on March 15, 2024, the U.S. Supreme Court issued a decision in two cases (*Lindke v. Freed* ("*Freed*") and *O'Connor-Ratcliff v. Garnier* ("*Garnier*")) concerning public officials' interactions with the public via social media. Both cases considered whether public officials' removal of the comments from members of the public and blocking them from the public officials' social media accounts violated their First amendment right to free speech. As described in greater detail below, in *Freed*, the Court established a legal test for determining when actions taken by a public official on social media infringe on a member of the public's First Amendment rights. The Court remanded both the *Freed* and *Garnier* cases to the lower courts for review under the standard set forth in *Freed*.

In *Freed*, Kevin Lindke sued James Freed, a city manager who removed Lindke's Facebook comments and blocked future comments on his public Facebook page, under 42 U.S.C. Section 1983, which, "provides a cause of action against '[e]very person who, under color of any statute, ordinance, regulation, custom, or usage, of any State' deprives someone of a federal constitutional or statutory right" (*Lindke v. Freed*, 2024). Lindke argued that Freed's limitations violated his First Amendment right to free speech in a public forum. The Sixth Circuit Court of Appeal concluded that Freed did not violate Lindke's First Amendment rights because he privately maintained his Facebook page and did not do so as part of his official duties.

In *Garnier*, Christopher and Kimberly Garnier sued O'Connor-Ratcliff and T. J. Zane, two members of the Poway Unified School District Board, after the pair blocked them from viewing and posting comments on their Facebook pages and Twitter accounts. The Ninth Circuit Court of Appeal concluded that O'Connor-Ratcliff's and T. J. Zane's limitations violated the Garniers' First Amendment rights because, among other things, they used their accounts to communicate information related to Board activities to the public.

The claims raised in *Garnier* were substantially similar to those in *Freed*. However, the courts reached different conclusions, which resulted in the U.S. Supreme Court consolidating and considering both matters.

As a threshold matter, the Court noted that Section 1983 is "designed as a protection against acts attributable to a State, not those of a private person." As such, the Court first analyzed whether Freed's actions on Facebook constituted a state action or the actions of a private citizen. The court developed the following two-part test for making this determination:

A public official who prevents someone from commenting on the official's social media page engages in state action under §1983 only if the official both:

1. possessed actual authority to speak on the State's behalf on a particular matter, and

2. purported to exercise that authority when speaking in the relevant social media posts.

If the public official is found to have engaged in "state action" through their social media, then restricting public access to view or comment upon those state actions violates the individual's First Amendment right to free speech.

The Court noted that whether the public official was exercising their authority in an official capacity becomes relevant once it has been determined that the public official had "actual authority" to speak on behalf of the State. It is not enough to establish that the public official has *some* authority to speak on behalf of the agency. Rather, the plaintiff must establish that, "the alleged censorship [is] connected to speech on a matter within [the public official's] bailiwick." The power to speak on behalf of the State can be established through "statute, ordinance, regulation, custom, or usage."

The Court noted that a public official "may have the authority [speak on behalf of the State] on social media even if the law does not make that explicit." Therefore, the public official, "must have actual authority rooted in written law or longstanding custom to speak for the State. That authority must extend to speech of the sort that caused the alleged rights deprivation. If the plaintiff cannot make this threshold showing of authority, he cannot establish state action."

If the plaintiff establishes that the public official has actual authority to speak for the State, the analysis then turns to whether the public official's social media actions purport to "exercise that authority." First, the court considers whether the social media account appears to be an official or personal account. Next, the court analyzes whether the specific social media posts in question appear to purport this authority.

If the account is clearly labeled as "personal" or "official" that fact will weigh heavily in a determination on how the posts are categorized. Labeling an account as "personal" means the public official, "would be entitled to a heavy (though not irrebuttable) presumption that all of the posts on his page were personal." However, if the account is not clearly labeled as "personal" or "official," the determination of authority will depend on the content of the individual posts. The Court also noted that additional factors could also imply that a post or account is "official," such as using government staff or resources to create posts or administer accounts.

Ultimately, public officials are subject to liability if they meet both factors set by *Freed*. Determining whether a public official holds authority to speak for the state or whether their social media post purports to exercise that authority requires a highly fact-sensitive analysis that depends on the circumstances of each case. However, the Court has provided in their opinion guidelines to follow to protect against this potential liability:

1. Public officials should clearly label all social media accounts as "personal" or "official."

2. A "personal" label does not "insulate government business from scrutiny by conducting it on a personal page." If government business is clearly being conducted on a personal page, it may still be considered "official." However, "a post that is compatible with either a "personal capacity" or "official capacity" designation is "personal" if it appears on a personal page."

3. Any posts to a personal account should not conduct any formal business, set policy, or be an official or exclusive avenue of communication with the public (e.g., a council meeting cannot be hosted on a personal social media account; a personal account cannot be the only means of receiving comments on a proposed regulation).

4. Removing comments only creates liability for those specific posts. However, if blocking a member of the public from the account restricts access

to any post on the account, then every post on the account is subject to scrutiny as to whether it is an "official" communication. Therefore, public officials should be discerning when blocking members of the public from the entire account.

Use of Electronic Communication Devices

Teachers are increasingly using the school's and their own electronic communication devices (ECDs) to communicate with students about assignments, projects, and other matters. It is expected that the future of teaching will continue to incorporate greater use of technology, including artificial intelligence. At the same time, educators need to be aware of the dangers of misuse, particularly misuse away from school.

A good illustration of this issue is a Connecticut high school teacher who set up a MySpace account after students invited him to view their MySpace pages. The teacher, Jeffrey Spanierman, used his MySpace account to communicate with students about homework, to learn more about his students so he could relate to them better, and to conduct casual conversations with them. Over time, the conversations became more personal and revealing. His profile page included a picture of him when he was about the same age as his students, pictures of some of his students, and several pictures of naked men with inappropriate comments below them. Once aware of the profile page, school officials advised him to remove the page, which he did. But then he started another that was similar. His contract was not renewed. The teacher filed a federal lawsuit, contending, among other things, that the action violated his First Amendment right to engage in free speech outside of school on his own ECDs.

The federal judge agreed with Spanierman that the U.S. Supreme Court's *Garcetti v. Ceballos* decision did not apply because he was speaking outside the scope of his employment. Additionally, the judge noted that a poem on the teacher's MySpace profile expressing the teacher's opposition to the Iraq War was constitutionally protected free speech. However, the judge agreed with the school district that Spanierman's interactions with students undermined his professionalism and would cause disruption at school. Indeed, some students maintained that they were uncomfortable with what Spanierman was saying. Thus, the school's concerns outweighed the teacher's free speech rights and the contract nonrenewal was justified (*Spanierman v. Hughes*, 2008).

While the activities of public school teachers and other employees on their own time and away from school is normally not the school district's concern, conduct that affects their ability to effectively perform their essential job functions may affect their employment status with the school district. Thus, it is important for educators to understand the following:

- What is said on the internet and on social media platforms can be, and often is, disseminated instantaneously. Thus, it is important to understand the privacy protections and potential impacts on one's employment when communicating on platforms such as Facebook, Instagram, X (formerly known as Twitter), and other platforms.
- Despite privacy protections, little prevents persons on social media from forwarding pictures, videos, and message to others so that what one says can become widely known and potentially undermine the employee's effectiveness.
- Communicating with students on the school issued technology should relate only to legitimate school business. Some school districts may require that all teacher electronic communication with students other than family members be done through the school's e-mail and/or approved communication system.

Educator Association Rights

The right of association is anchored both in constitutional and in statutory law. The U.S. Supreme Court long has supported the right of teachers to join groups and causes without fear of losing their jobs. For instance, in *Shelton v. Tucker*, a case decided by the U.S. Supreme Court in 1960, the Court concluded that this right had been violated by an Arkansas statute requiring teachers as a condition of continued employment to file annually an affidavit listing every organization they belonged to or regularly supported during the previous five years (*Shelton v. Tucker*). Wrote Justice Potter Stewart for the Court, "It is not disputed that to compel a teacher to disclose his every associational tie is to impair that teacher's right of free association, a right closely allied to freedom of speech and a right which, like free speech, lies at the foundation of a free society" (pp. 485–486). Stewart added, "The vigilant protection of constitutional freedoms is nowhere more vital than in the community of American schools" (p. 487). There are less intrusive means, noted the Court, for the state to inquire into the fitness and competency of its teachers.

To some degree, the right of association overlaps with the right of privacy. Teachers have a right to their own lifestyle outside of school. The California

Supreme Court ruled as much in a 1969 decision (*Morrison v. State Board of Education*). *Morrison* involved a teacher with a virtually unblemished record, but his lifetime teaching credential was revoked because he had engaged in private homosexual acts with a consenting adult outside of school some years earlier. As discussed in more detail in Chapter 10, the court ruled that a public schoolteacher cannot be dismissed for lifestyle behavior unless evidence is presented showing unfitness to teach. (Please see additional information concerning the Morrison factors in Chapter 5.)

Neither free speech nor the right to associate is absolute. In a free speech case with overtones of associational rights, the Ninth Circuit decided against a teacher who aggressively advanced his religious beliefs to students in and out of class. The teacher complained that the school principal directed him not to discuss religion or to attempt to convert students to Christianity while meeting with students on campus, including lunch and before and after school. For reasons discussed in Chapter 7, the appeals court found that the restriction was appropriate in light of the school's interest in avoiding advancing religion (*Peloza v. Capistrano Unified School District*, 1995).

The right of association in the context of labor organizations is a well-established statutory right in California. One of the purposes of the Educational Employment Relations Act is "to promote the improvement of personnel management and employer–employee relations within the public school systems in the State of California by providing a uniform basis for recognizing the right of public school employees to join organizations of their own choice" (Gov't Code § 3540). Please see the discussion concerning unions and collective bargaining in Chapter 4.

Whistleblowing

The term *whistleblowing* refers to reporting unlawful activity in the workplace to appropriate authorities. Like most states, California has enacted a statute that protects public employees who "blow the whistle" on improper governmental activities. The California Whistleblower Protection Act, which is found in California Government Code Section 8547 and following sections, apply to schools pursuant to a 2000 statute bearing the ungainly title of the Reporting by School Employees of Improper Governmental Activities Act (Educ. Code § 44110 et seq.).

In essence, the Reporting by School Employees of Improper Governmental Activities Act provides that school employees and other persons who disclose improper governmental activities in good faith may not be subject to retaliation for doing so by school employees acting in their official position. The term *school employee* exempts from liability persons elected by popular vote, persons appointed by the Governor, management employees, and confidential employees, but a California court of appeal has ruled that management employees who are acting as supervisors are not exempt (*Conn v. Western Placer Unified School District*, 2010).

In *Conn,* the court considered the claims raised by a probationary teacher who sued her school district and certain employees for allegedly denying her permanent status in retaliation for her disclosure that the district was not properly evaluating certain students for special education services. The appellate court ruled that the principal, director of personnel, and the superintendent were not exempt from the teacher's whistleblower claim under the management employee category because they exercised supervisory authority in recommending that her contract not be extended. However, the case was ultimately dismissed because the teacher was unable to establish that her comments amounted to any violations of law.

The statute encompasses both illegal orders and improper governmental activities. An "illegal order" means a directive that is contrary to federal, state, local law, rule, or regulation or a directive to work outside the scope of employment in conditions that would unreasonably threaten the health or safety of employees or the public. "Improper governmental activity" encompasses a work activity by a school district or employee that violates a state or federal law or regulation including, but not limited to, corruption, malfeasance, bribery, theft of government property, fraudulent claims, fraud, coercion, conversion, malicious prosecution, misuse of government property, or willful omission to perform a duty. "Improper governmental activity" also includes activities that are economically wasteful or involve gross misconduct, incompetency, or inefficiency. Reports of alleged wrongdoing must be directed to an appropriate official agent, such as a school administrator, member of the governing board, county superintendent of schools, or superintendent of public instruction.

School employees who believe they have suffered actual or threatened reprisal for exercising their whistleblower rights may file a written complaint with their supervisor, school administrator, or governing board and also may file a claim with local law enforcement. In addition to the school district's potential liability, those who intentionally interfere with the right of an employee to report alleged wrongdoing in good faith may be subject to criminal penalties, including a fine of not more than $10,000 and a jail term of not more than one year.

Civil damages may also be imposed if the injured party has notified local law enforcement when filing the complaint with the district. Intentional interference with an employee's whistleblowing rights may result in disciplinary action by the school employer, including termination of employment. Finally, the statute provides that it does not diminish any rights that employees have under a collective bargaining agreement or any other state or federal law.

It also bears noting that the California Labor Code provides similar protections. For instance, Labor Code Section 1102.5 prohibits employers from placing limitations on employees' ability to report violations to government agencies or law enforcement. Further, Labor Code Section 1102.6 provides the applicable framework for litigating and adjudicating Section 1102.5 whistleblower and retaliation claims. As described by the California Supreme Court in *Lawson v. PPG Architectural Finishes*, 2022, when a plaintiff raises a 1102.5 claim, Section 1102.6 first "places the burden on the plaintiff to establish, by a preponderance of the evidence, that retaliation for an employee's protected activities was a contributing factor in a contested employment action." Second, after "the plaintiff has made the required showing, the burden shifts to the employer to demonstrate, by clear and convincing evidence, that it would have taken the action in question for legitimate, independent reasons even if the plaintiff had not engaged in protected activity." The Lawson decision represents a significant departure from the three-part burden shifting standard established under the McDonald Douglas test when analyzing whistleblower and retaliation claims.

As with the *Mt. Healthy* decision discussed earlier, nothing precludes a school district from taking an adverse action against a school employee who exercises whistleblower rights if there are other reasons unrelated to the whistleblowing to justify the action. Thus, ineffective employees and/or those who engage in misconduct cannot use the whistleblower act to shield themselves from an adverse personnel action.

STUDENT EXPRESSION RIGHTS

Traditionally, school officials have stood *in loco parentis* with regard to students, meaning they have the same right to control students in school that parents have to control them at home. Accordingly, the old maxim that "children are to be seen and not heard" essentially applied to the status of student free speech. But in 1969, this all changed. In one of its most important education law decisions, the U.S. Supreme Court advised that "it can hardly be argued that either students or teachers shed their constitutional rights to freedom of speech or expression at the schoolhouse gate." (*Tinker v. Des Moines Independent Community School District*, 1969, p. 506). That decision begins our discussion of student expression and associational rights.

Face-to-Face Communication

Christopher Eckhardt, John Tinker, and Mary Beth Tinker, secondary students in the Des Moines School District, were involved with their parents in the peace movement during the Vietnam War. To publicize their objections to the war and their support for a truce, the students opted to wear black armbands to school in December 1965. Learning that this might be the case, school officials announced a policy that anyone who came to school with an armband would be asked to remove it, and if he or she failed to do so, the student would be suspended from school. Undeterred, the trio wore their armbands to school. All were suspended and did not return until after the planned period for wearing armbands had ended. In addition to these students, eleven-year-old Hope Tinker and eight-year-old Paul Tinker also wore armbands to their elementary school. Because the suspension rule applied only to the secondary students, the elementary school students were not suspended. Instead, their teachers took advantage of the opportunity to engage the elementary students in a discussion about dissent in a democratic society.

A year after *Pickering v. Board of Education* (1968), and in one of the last decisions of the progressive Court headed by Chief Justice Earl Warren, former governor of California, the justices voted 7–2 to uphold the right of students to wear their symbolic armbands in school as a form of free speech (*Tinker v. Des Moines Independent Community School District*, 1969). The Court did not confine student expression to any particular part of the campus. A student's speech rights "do not embrace merely the classroom hours," wrote Justice Abe Fortas for the majority. Fortas added: "When he is in the cafeteria, or on the playing field, or on the campus during the authorized hours, he may express his opinions, even on controversial subjects like the conflict in Vietnam" (pp. 512–513). At the same time, the Court recognized that the public school is not the equivalent of the public park. The environment must be conducive for teaching and learning. Accordingly, a student loses the right of free speech if the student materially disrupts the school or substantially interferes with the rights of others. The majority cited with approval a 1966 ruling by the U.S. Court of Appeals for the Fifth Circuit in which that court had upheld a school prohibition against the wearing of "freedom buttons" after students at an all-Black high school in Mississippi engaged in boisterous distribution of the buttons by trying to pin them on others, throwing buttons through windows, and refusing to attend class (*Blackwell v. Issaquena County Board of Education*, 1966). Conversely, in the *Tinker* case, the school had no convincing evidence that any disruption had taken place.

In addition to the material disruption/substantial invasion of the rights of others condition on the exercise of student free speech, the Court's decision pertained only to the three named secondary school students. The majority never mentioned the two elementary students. Consequently, there are few decisions supporting free speech rights at the elementary level. In one of the few, a majority of all the judges assigned to the U.S. Court of Appeals for the Fifth Circuit ruled in 2011 that elementary school students have the same right as secondary school students to engage in private nondisruptive speech (*Morgan v. Swanson*). The long-running case involved a prohibition on elementary students in the Plano school district near Dallas discussing or distributing tickets to religious events or distributing candy canes and the like with attached religious messages during winter-break classroom parties and other school events. However, the students were allowed to distribute nonreligious material. The school district later revised the policy prohibiting the distribution of any materials in classrooms during school hours except at three annual parties. Elementary students could distribute materials with religious or nonreligious messages at other designated times on campus. The Fifth Circuit upheld the new policy.

The majority in *Tinker* clearly opted for a view of the secondary school as a marketplace of ideas. Writing for the Court, Justice Fortas phrased it this way:

> In our system, state-operated schools may not be enclaves of totalitarianism. School officials do not possess absolute authority over their students.... In our system, students may not be regarded as closed-circuit recipients of only that which the state chooses to communicate. They may not be confined to the expression of those sentiments that are officially approved (p. 511).

Expressing quite a different view, Justice Hugo Black in dissent observed that "one may, I hope, be permitted to harbor the thought that taxpayers send children to school on the premise that at their age they need to learn, not teach" (p. 522). For Black, the school is a place for the inculcation of the values, skills, and knowledge that the community wishes students to learn. These two perspectives on the purpose of school—to serve as a marketplace of ideas or to inculcate community values and beliefs—underlie much of the tension in the case law in this area and continue to dominate dialogue among educators as well.

The *Tinker* decision robustly protects interstudent communication. Because students are not employees, their rights of expression are not confined to matters of public concern but can encompass matters of personal interest including those involving the school. In 2006, the Ninth Circuit ruled in an Oregon case that high school basketball players have a First Amendment right to sign a petition requesting resignation of their coach and voicing complaints about the coach at a meeting with school officials. However, refusal to board a team bus even if viewed as free speech materially interfered with the school's ability to compete effectively in a game and thus was not constitutionally protected (*Pinard v. Clatskanie School District 6J*, 2006). *Pinard* established a three-part test for First Amendment retaliation. The plaintiff must show that (1) he or she was engaged in a constitutionally protected activity, (2) the defendant's actions would chill a person of ordinary firmness from continuing to engage in the protected activity, and (3) the protected activity was a substantial or motivating factor in the defendant's conduct.

California law adds a higher layer of protection that may not be seen in many states. The California Supreme Court has reiterated that the same standards applied in Tinker with respect to free speech rights in schools also apply under the California Constitution (*Bright v. Los Angeles Unified School District*, 1976, p. 455). Additionally, California Education Code Section 48907 gives public school students in California traditional public and charter schools a broad right of free speech and free press, including access to bulletin boards, distribution of printed material including petitions, and the wearing of buttons and insignia. Citing both the First Amendment and Article 1, Section 2 of the California Constitution, Education Code Section 48950 gives California public and private secondary school students, except those in private schools controlled by religious organizations, the same rights of expression on school grounds that they enjoy off campus. This section also gives them the right to seek a court order against enforcement of a school rule that violates this provision. School officials may impose reasonable time, place, and manner regulations. No protection is given to harassment, threats, or intimidations that are not constitutionally protected. The question, of course, is when does speech fall into this category so as not to be entitled to constitutional protection? Much speech is intended to be disputatious. Sections 48907 and 48950 both prohibit negative employment actions against school employees who support student expression rights.

In 1996, the Ninth Circuit provided clarification on when students may be disciplined for making threats (*Lovell v. Poway Unified School District*, 1996, p. 372). The case involved a tenth-grade student in the Poway Unified School District who had spent several hours trying to get her schedule changed. When she met with her counselor for what she thought was the last time, the counselor told the student that the classes she wanted were overloaded. There was some apparent confusion as to what transpired next, whether the student responded about shooting "someone" or the counselor. Even though the student apologized for her behavior, the student was given a three-day suspension. She and her parents challenged the discipline as a violation of her right to free speech under the First Amendment and California Education Code Section 48950.

The lower court decided in favor of the student. However, the Ninth Circuit reversed, opting to believe the counselor. The judges agreed that threats of physical violence, whether made on or off campus, are not protected by the First Amendment; two of the three agreed that threats are not protected by Section 48950 of the Education Code either (*Lovell v. Poway Unified School District*, p. 372). The judges noted that in light of violence prevalent in many schools, school officials are justified in taking student threats against faculty and students seriously. A few years later, the Ninth Circuit noted:

> Although schools are being asked to do more to prevent violence, the Constitution sets limits as to how far they can go. Just as the Constitution does not allow the police to imprison all suspicious characters, schools cannot expel students just because they are "loners," wear black and play video games. Schools must achieve a balance between protecting the safety and well-being of their students and respecting those same students' constitutional rights (*LaVine v. Blain School District*, 2001, p. 987).

In this case, however, the appeals court did uphold the temporary expulsion of a troubled student who had written a threatening poem that he showed to his English teacher. The action, the appeals court concluded, did not violate the student's right to expression but rather was based on concern for the safety of other students. But the appeals court did disallow any mention of the incident in the student's records.

These cases raise the question of when a student's statement is a "true threat," unprotected by the First Amendment. The U.S. Supreme Court appears to have eased the analysis, although legal opinions vary. In *Counterman v. Colorado* (2023), a challenge made by a criminal defendant, the justices held that the State must prove that the defendant had some *subjective* understanding of his statement's threatening nature, but . . . the First Amendment demands no more than a showing of recklessness." It remains to be seen how this approach may be applied in a school setting.

Although some conduct such as the wearing of armbands or peaceful picketing is a form of expression, conduct that is only tangentially related to expression may not be. In a situation that had a sad ending, several middle school students in the Ontario-Montclair Unified School District left school without permission to walk by themselves to another school to participate in a protest against immigration policies. The school was on lockdown, however, and no one was there. Later, the students walked home. The assistant principal confronted the students two days later, advising them that their absences were unexcused and that they would be precluded from participating in an end-of-the-year school celebration as a result. One of the students went home and shot himself. He later died. In his suicide note, he mentioned, among other things, the confrontation with the assistant principal. Later, a lawsuit was filed against the principal and the district claiming, among other things, violation of First Amendment rights. The Ninth Circuit agreed with the trial judge that enforcing a content-neutral policy of disciplining truancies and leaving campus without permission cannot be overcome by student First Amendment rights. "To hold otherwise," the judges noted, "would be to allow 12- to 14-year-old students to leave school without the permission of their parents or school authorities to engage in any claimed First Amendment activity, no matter the danger" (*Corales v. Bennett*, 2009, p. 568). The appellate court affirmed the trial judge's dismissal of the case on all claims.

In 1986 the U.S. Supreme Court once again visited student free speech. But this time a much more conservative Court headed by Chief Justice Warren Burger drew back from its rigorous protection of student free speech in *Tinker*. The case, involved a Washington State high school student, Matthew Fraser (*Bethel School District v. Fraser*, 1986). The audience was a voluntary assembly of high school students brought together to hear nominating speeches for student body officers. Fraser's speech contained abundant sexual metaphor for a candidate that he supported—for example, "I know a man who is firm—he's firm in his pants, he's firm in his shirt, his character is firm—but most . . . of all, his belief in you, the students of Bethel, is firm" (p. 687). The speech was every bit as successful as Fraser had intended. Indeed, Fraser was later elected by write-in vote to give the high school graduation speech. However, the school administration suspended Fraser, who thereafter filed suit contending that his First Amendment rights had been violated. Both the federal trial court, and the Ninth Circuit decided in his favor under the *Tinker* ruling because there was little evidence of any significant material disruption or interference with the rights of others. But the majority on the U.S. Supreme Court ruled that student speech that is lewd, profane, or indecent is not entitled to any constitutional protection at all. Viewing the school as a vehicle for inculcating community values, Chief Justice Burger pointed out that one of its most important functions was to teach students to speak in civilly acceptable ways.

In 2007, the high court, by a 5–4 margin, rejected a Juneau, Alaska, student's claim that his holding up a sign with the words "Bong Hits 4 Jesus" during released time to view an Olympic parade passing in from of the high school is protected by the First Amendment (*Morse v. Frederick*). Five justices agreed with the school principal that the sign evidenced support for drug use and held that such speech is not constitutionally protected. But the decision was very narrow. Chief Justice John Roberts, who wrote for the majority on the First Amendment issue, refused to endorse the school's position that any student speech viewed as plainly offensive enjoys no constitutional protection. Two justices who agreed that the speech in this case was not protected drew the line at extending the ruling to other forms of student expression. "I join the opinion of the Court," Justice Samuel Alito wrote, "on the understanding that the opinion does not hold that the special characteristics of the public schools necessarily justify any other speech restrictions" (p. 423). Justice Anthony Kennedy agreed with him. It is important to note that both the California Constitution and Education Code are more supportive of student expression rights than are the rulings of the U.S. Supreme Court. Whether a California court would rule similarly today on the "Bong Hits" sign is questionable.

Expression Targeting Protected Identities

California has a hate-crime statute outlawing force or threat of force that intimidates, oppresses, or threatens a person's exercise of protected rights because of the person's race, color, religion, ancestry, national origin, disability, gender, or sexual orientation or perception of having one or more of these characteristics (California Penal Code § 422.6). A subsection prohibits defacing, damaging, or destroying property of any person on these grounds. At the same time, the statute specifies that no person is to be penalized for speech alone; it must be shown that the speech threatened violence against a specific person or group and that the speaker had the apparent ability to carry out the threat. A subsection prohibits defacing, damaging, or destroying property of any person on these grounds. At the same time, the statute specifies that no person is to be penalized for speech alone; it must be shown that the speech threatened violence against a specific person or group and that the speaker had the apparent ability to carry out the threat.

A student sought to overturn his delinquency conviction under this statute for using a permanent black marking pen to write a racial slur on the classroom door of his school's only Black teacher at the school and "Kill the [racial slur]" on a concrete post outside the music building where Black students congregated (*In re Michael M.*, 2001). The student first argued that the school door and the concrete post were the property not of the targeted persons but of the school. The California court of appeal chose to construe the statute broadly so that ownership is not required. Wrote the judges, "As long as the property is regularly and openly used, possessed, or occupied by the victim so that it is readily identifiable with him or her, it falls within the statutory scope" (p. 16).

The student next argued that the mere scrawling of the words on the door and concrete post did not constitute a credible threat of violence but was instead protected free speech. The appellate court noted that the California Supreme Court had ruled earlier that the statute is targeted at conduct that results from hate speech, not hate speech itself (*In re M.S.*, 1995). Here, the words had a violent connotation. The teacher testified that she was shocked, felt belittled, and was fearful of entering her classroom. The court noted that the words could reasonably be interpreted as a direct, violent threat. Thus, the speech had lost its protection and could be grounds for the conviction.

The courts of the Ninth Circuit have generally allowed schools to discipline arguably protected political speech targeting protected identifies on two grounds under *Tinker* (1969): (1) it impinges the rights of the targeted student "to be secure and to be let alone" (p. 508), or (2) it may be reasonably forecast to incite violence and thereby cause substantial disruption.

For example, in *Harper v. Poway Unified Sch. Dist.* (2006), the Ninth Circuit found a student could be disciplined for wearing a shirt saying, "Homosexuality is shameful." The plaintiff's speech was not protected by *Tinker* because it impinged the rights of others to be secure and left alone. The court limited its holding to instances of "derogatory and injurious remarks directed at students' minority status such as race, religion, and sexual orientation" (p. 1183). Judge Kozinski dissented and argued there was no evidence plaintiff harmed rights of others and majority was censoring offensive views because they were offensive.

Another shirt case occurred at Live Oak High School, which had a history of racial violence between white and Hispanic students. On Cinco de Mayo in 2010, a group of white students wore American flag shirts. After being informed by other students there might be a fight, the principal told the students to cover up the shirts and sent them home with an excused absence when they refused. Under those circumstances, the Ninth Circuit found the principal responded properly to anticipated violence and substantial disruption of school activities (*Dariano v. Morgan Hill Unified Sch. Dist.*, 2014).

Finally, in *Castro v. Clovis Unified Sch. Dist.* (2022), a California district court addressed an incident in which a student tweeted a picture of a Black classmate captioned by a racial slur on the school's graduation day while on campus. After being informed by another student, the principal gave the perpetrator his diploma but did not allow him to walk at graduation. The court found that, although no substantial disruption could reasonably be forecast from the tweet, the plaintiff had impinged the rights of the other student by invading her right to be secure and left alone.

Expression Through Electronic Communication Devices

In recent years, students increasingly communicate at school through their own wireless electronic devices, such as mobile phones and tablets. Misuse includes students receiving calls during classes, text messaging during examinations, and taking and transmitting photos that invade student privacy. In accordance with California Education Code Section 48901.5, school officials can regulate the use of such electronic communication devices (ECDs) at school, school-sponsored activities, and at other times when students are under the supervision of school employees. The law also provides that no student shall be prohibited from possessing or using such a device if a licensed physician and surgeon determines it is essential to the health of the student and used for that purpose.

As we noted in Chapter 2, school control over student expression on the internet is greatest when students are using school computers and other devices, given their agreement to abide by the district's acceptable use policy (AUP). But this control is considerably less when students use their own ECDs at home to communicate about school matters.

However, a student's free speech rights may be lost if the student goes too far in criticizing the school and its constituents on his home computer and engages in behavior considered threatening. But case outcomes vary. A good illustration of a decision in the district's favor involves an eighth-grade student in upstate New York who used AOL Instant Messaging (IM) software on his parents' home computer to create a small icon of a pistol firing a bullet at a person's head (*Wisniewski v. Board of Education of Weedsport Central School District*, 2007). Above the head were dots representing splattered blood, and below it were the words "Kill [name of the student's English teacher]." The student sent IM messages displaying the icon to some fifteen members of his IM "buddy list." The icon came to the attention of one classmate who gave a copy to the English teacher. The school board imposed a semester-long suspension of the student. The case ended up in federal court after the student and his parents contested the suspension as violating the student's rights of free speech. Both the trial and federal appellate courts rejected the contention. As the appellate court judges noted, "There can be no doubt that the icon, once made known to the teacher and other school officials, would foreseeably create a risk of substantial disruption within the school environment" (p. 40). But compare an example from a district in Oregon of a student making what seems to be a threat but to the court was protected speech (*Burge v. Colton School District*

53, 2015). The student posted on Facebook "haha [teacher] needs to be shot." The court held that the student speech was not serious and no disruption could be reasonably forecast. Thus, the law is unresolved and suggests that the analysis is fact based but also varies from court to court.

Statutory law is filling part of that void. "Cyberbullying" involves communication through an electronic device such as a telephone, wireless telephone, computer, or pager (Cal. Educ. Code § 48900). Bullying, including by electronic means, may subject the student to discipline, at least in California. To prevail against free speech claims, school officials must document carefully the harm created by a student's use of these devices. In most cases, that harm must include a clear threat.

School Regulation of Off-Campus Speech

Early free speech cases, such as *Tinker* (1969) and *Fraser* (1986), occurred firmly on school grounds. But the proliferation of electronic devices allowing off-campus speech to have on-campus consequences has prompted schools to increasingly seek to discipline students for off-campus speech.

The U.S. Supreme Court finally addressed off-campus speech for the first time in *Mahanoy Area School District v. B. L. Levy*, (2021). B.L. failed to make the varsity cheer squad and was particularly piqued that a freshman had made it instead. While with a friend in a Coca Hut, she posted on Snapchat "Fuck school fuck softball fuck cheer fuck everything." The Supreme Court declined to endorse the Third Circuit's crisp rule that "pure" off-campus speech (such as that in this case) received the same First Amendment protection as speech of adults. Neither did it set forth a "broad, highly general First Amendment rule" as to where the special characteristics of the school environment ended, and the adult First Amendment began.

It articulated three reasons for diminished (but not nonexistent) school control over off-campus speech. First, schools rarely stand in loco parentis with respect to off-campus speech because discipline off-campus is the province of the actual parents. Second, school regulation of off campus speech would effectively put students under permanent surveillance. Third, schools themselves have an interest in protecting unpopular expression, especially when it takes place off campus (pp. 2045–2046). Schools therefore had much less authority to restrict off-campus speech where the "special characteristics" did not exist. Overall, the Court found that the student's interest in free expression outweighed the school's interest in restricting speech. The student's speech, though offensive, was not targeted at any student or staff personally and did not cause substantial disruption.

Following that decision, the Ninth Circuit concluded that Mahanoy was consistent with the nexus test it had already laid out in *McNeil v. Sherwood School District*

88J (2019) and therefore decided to continue using it in *Chen Through Chen v. Albany Unified School District* (2022). Plaintiffs Epple and Chen at Albany High School created a private Instagram account shared only with their select friends. They shared racist content, including a noose and scenes of lynching. When news of the private account spread to the rest of the school, teachers reported classes were disrupted and many of the targeted students missed school. There were also protests and rallies before the School Board expelled the plaintiffs.

The Ninth Circuit upheld the disciplinary action, emphasizing that the historical context of KKK terrorism would make the posts deeply upsetting and intimidating. Moreover, individual students were targeted, and the posts could not be construed as contributing to the marketplace of ideas. The case neatly combined the two kinds of student speech least likely to be protected: speech threatening violence and speech threatening protected identities. Finally, the school had carefully documented the harm caused by the speech: targets felt "'devastated,' 'scared' and bullied,'" their grades suffered, they missed school, and one was withdrawn by her parents (p. 721). This enabled the school to make a credible showing of substantial disruption in addition to the fact that the extreme racism severely invaded the rights of the targeted students, one of the two *Tinker* criteria.

At least in some circumstances, schools may punish speech that occurs between students going to and from school, even if school is not in session. C.R. and his friends sexually harassed two students with disabilities shortly after the end of school while they were walking home from school (*C.R. ex rel. Rainville v. Eugene School District 4J*, 2016). The incident took place on a path a few hundred feet from the school's property line. The court hesitated to create a general rule and limited its holding to the facts by noting the close temporal and spatial proximity to the school. Under either the foreseeability or nexus test, the sexual harassment impinged the rights of the disabled students to be "secure and to be left alone" and was thus punishable under *Tinker* (p. 508).

Reinforcing earlier decisions that threats are a special category under free speech, the Ninth Circuit in *McNeil v. Sherwood School District 88J* (2019) adopted a "flexible and fact-specific" nexus test to determine when discipline was justified. The court listed three relevant considerations to consider based on the totality of the circumstances: "(1) the degree and likelihood of harm to the school caused or augured by the speech, (2) whether it was reasonably foreseeable that the speech would reach and impact the school, and (3) the relation between the content and context of the speech and the school" (pp. 707–708). Although this test is somewhat vague, the court laid down a clear rule covering the current facts: There is always a sufficient nexus between the speech and the school when the district "reasonably concludes it faces a credible, identifiable threat of school violence." The court had no doubt the test was met, pointing to the student's gun collection, specific threats against the school, a hit list of students and one former staff, panicked reactions from students on list and their parents, and widespread media coverage.

A much earlier case in 2010 demonstrates that school officials face a dilemma in dealing with off-campus student misuse of ECDs that is not an issue when the misuse occurs on campus or with campus equipment (*J.C. ex rel. R.C. v. Beverly Hills Unified School District*). In J.C., parents filed a lawsuit seeking to overturn a two-day suspension for a video using profanity toward another student, among other objectionable comments. Since the student C.C. produced the video outside of school, the federal district court found the district could not discipline the student, thus overturning the suspension but not allowing money damages. The judge concluded that *Tinker v. Des Moines School District* (1969) requires material or substantial disruption of school activities, and the school had not demonstrated that.

First, it must be established that it was foreseeable to the student communicator that what was communicated would become knowledgeable at school. Second, there must be evidence that the communication caused material disruption and/or substantial interference with the rights of others. These terms are emphasized because student expression off campus on the student's own time using the student's personal ECD is strongly protected free speech. Yet, failing to intervene when students at school are the victims of cyberbullying, sexting, and other forms of electronic abuse occurring outside of school may result in lawsuits filed by victims. It is a particularly difficult area for school administrators, who must make often quick decisions on the seriousness of a perceived threat.

Expression Through School Channels

Two years after the *Fraser* (1986) decision, the U.S. Supreme Court was faced with a challenge to school administrator censorship of a school-sponsored student newspaper (*Hazelwood School District v. Kuhlmeier*, 1988). The matter arose when the school principal in a Missouri school district decided that two articles in *Spectrum*, the high school newspaper, should not be published. One dealt with the impact of divorce on students and the other on the experiences of three pregnant, unwed high school students. The editor of the paper, Cathy Kuhlmeier, filed suit, contending that the deletion of the articles violated the First Amendment freedom of the press. The Supreme Court began by reaffirming the *Tinker* ruling that students have First Amendment rights at school. But in quoting from that ruling, the majority in the 6–3 ruling did not cite Justice Fortas's comments about student rights in the classroom. Rather, the Court was careful to limit its affirmance of *Tinker* to interstudent communication occurring elsewhere on campus. Here, by contrast, the student communication was flowing through a channel of communication operated by the school—the student newspaper.

While evidence was conflicting, the majority concluded that the school had not converted the newspaper into an open forum for student expression. Had it done so, the censorship would have been harder to justify. As a closed forum, the newspaper remained under the control of school authorities. Writing for the majority, Justice Byron White observed that educators can control the contents of school-sponsored publications, theatrical productions, and other expressive activities that are part of the school curriculum and supervised by school personnel "to assure that participants learn whatever lessons the activity is designed to teach, that readers or listeners are not exposed to material that may be inappropriate for their level of maturity, and that the views of the individual speakers are not erroneously attributed to the school" (p. 271). The only justification for the control is that it addresses legitimate pedagogical concerns. Applying that rationale to the censorship of *Spectrum*, the Court deferred to the judgment of the principal, noting that he had legitimate concerns that the articles were not well written and did not sufficiently shield the identity of students.

As we have noted, California law is somewhat more supportive of student free speech rights than the First Amendment. In according students the right to exercise freedom of speech and of the press, Education Code Section 48907 specifically includes the right of expression in official school publications "whether or not such publications or other means of expression are supported financially by the school or by use of school facilities." In other words, by statute, school-sponsored publications are limited public forums open for student free expression. The statute provides that student editors of school publications are responsible for assigning and editing the news, editorial, and features content of their publications. While school officials can preview what is being written in school-sponsored publications, they can exercise content control only on narrow grounds. These encompass expression that is obscene, libelous, or slanderous; that so incites students as to create a clear and present danger of the commission of unlawful acts on school premises or the violation of lawful school regulations; or that threatens substantial disruption of school operations. The fact that school officials might disagree with the viewpoints being expressed is not grounds for censorship. School officials have the burden of showing justification "without undue delay" prior to any limitation of student expression under these conditions.

The application of this statute to school-sponsored newspapers was the focus of an important 1988 California appellate court ruling (*Leeb v. DeLong*). The case arose after the school principal of Rancho Alamitos High School in the Garden Grove Unified School District prohibited distribution of the April Fools' Day edition of the student newspaper, a decision upheld by the superintendent. The principal particularly was concerned about an article titled "Nude Photos: Girls of Rancho" in which it was stated that a future issue of *Playboy Magazine* would carry nude photos of Rancho Alamitos students. The article was accompanied by a photo showing five fully clothed female students standing in line, purportedly with applications in hand. The principal believed the article and photo would damage the girls' reputations and the reputation of the school. The father of one of the girls threatened legal action if the article were published. The principal also felt that the April Fools' Day disclaimer in the paper was too inconspicuous to be noticed and that, because time was short, he had no choice but to ban distribution of the entire issue following his review.

The student editor filed suit, arguing that the limited prior review authorized by California Education Code Section 48907 is contrary to Article I, Section 2 of the California Constitution. The trial court ruled in favor of the school district, and the student editor appealed. While the appellate court affirmed the lower court ruling because the passage of time had rendered printing of the newspaper moot and because the student did not challenge the lower court's finding that the article was defamatory, the judges discussed the limits of school board censorship. The court recognized that, while *Hazelwood* (1988) does not apply in California and while public publishers do not have the same extensive authority over their publications as do private publishers, the school does not lose all authority to regulate student expression in school-sponsored newspapers. The court noted that Education Code Section 48907 gives school officials the right to preview for limited purposes what students want to include in school-sponsored publications.

The court refused to accept the student's argument that any form of prior review is unconstitutional. The limited use of prior review authorized by Section 48907 serves a valid purpose, the judges observed, in that the school would be vulnerable to defamation suits if it could not preview what students write. This in turn could cause the school to discontinue school-sponsored publications. Accordingly, Section 48907 does not violate the state constitution by permitting school officials to censor expression from official school publications that they believe reasonably will contain actionable defamation, meaning that the targeted expression contains a false statement likely to harm the reputation of another or hold that person up to shame, ridicule, or humiliation.

However, the threat of a lawsuit is not enough to justify suppression, the judge wrote. There must be a factual determination of potential liability. If public officials are targets of the article, the court advised that actual malice would have to be established. Actual malice means that students deliberately intended to commit an injury by including statements they know to be false or with reckless disregard as to their truth or falsity. School officials may not censor "as a matter of taste or pedagogy" (*Leeb v. DeLong*, 1988, p. 502). The judges also rejected the principal's contention that prepublication censorship could be justified by concerns over tarnishing the school or district reputation, adding that "the mere reputations of government entities may never be defended by censorship in a society governed by the governed" (p. 503). While the court did affirm the lower court decision against the student, it required the district to implement a set of procedural guidelines providing for a speedy opportunity to be heard and a swift procedure for administrative review in exercising prior review as mandated by Section 48907.

Editorials written by students in school-sponsored school newspapers often address controversial issues that can upset the school community. However, school officials need to be aware that controversy alone is insufficient to justify censorship. A case in point involves an editorial written by Andrew Smith, a Novato High School student, in the high school newspaper, *The Buzz*, in which he spoke out critically against illegal immigration (*Smith v. Novato Unified School District*, 2007). Among other things, he stated: "If they can't legally work, they have to make money illegal way [sic]. This might include drug dealing, robbery, or even welfare," and "Criminals usually flee here in order to escape their punishment" (p. 512). He ended his editorial by writing: "I feel like there has to be some major reforms in immigration policy. I just hope it happens before our country rots from within" (p. 521). The acting principal of the school reviewed and approved *The Buzz* before it was distributed. The editorial upset students and their parents, resulting in an assembly to discuss the matter. At the meeting, the principal apologized for misinterpreting board policy in allowing publication of the editorial but warned that the school would not tolerate any retaliation against Andrew. Without reading the editorial, the superintendent ordered that all undistributed copies of *The Buzz* be retrieved and, together with the principal, sent a letter home with all students in which they stated that the editorial shouldn't have been printed. They maintained that student rights of expression under board policy are limited to maintain an orderly school environment and protect the rights, health, and safety of all members of the school community. The student filed suit, alleging that these comments violated his right to free expression, pointing to Education Code Section 48907. The trial court rejected the claim, but a California court of appeal reversed.

The appellate court noted that under Section 48907 student expression is protected unless it incites students to engage in unlawful acts or disrupt school operation. While the article was disrespectful and unsophisticated, it did not incite students to engage in such actions and thus was protected speech. While the court applauded school officials for holding the assembly and found no fault with distancing the school from Andrew's comments, their statement that the editorial shouldn't have been printed violated Section 48907. The court also disapproved of the superintendent's intent to retract undistributed copies of *The Buzz*. The judges advised that, "when faced with offensive student speech, school districts must proceed cautiously with due regard to the valuable rights at stake, rather than reacting impulsively because of protest about the speech" (p. 527). The U.S. Supreme Court later refused to hear the case.

While the grounds for content censorship are very narrow under California law, nothing precludes school officials from assigning a low grade to a student whose article is poorly researched or sloppily written. Further, the inclusion of a disclaimer would advise readers that the contents of a school-sponsored publication do not bear the school's imprimatur.

Unofficial publications in the form of printed materials that students want to distribute on school grounds cannot be previewed. The prior review procedure of Education Code Section 48907 that was the focus of the court's attention in *Leeb v. DeLong* (1988) applies only to official school publications. In the case of unofficial publications, school officials can only impose reasonable time, place, and manner regulations and discipline students for violating them. Because the school in this instance is merely a place of distribution, it has no legal responsibility for content of the materials. The *Leeb* court noted that "the power to regulate time, place, and manner expression cannot be converted into a right to control content" (p. 501).

In sum, by virtue of Education Code Section 48907, California public school students are entitled to greater free expression rights in school-sponsored publications than is true in most other states. School control over content is limited, and the procedures for exercising it are spelled out. In *Ariosta v. Fallbrook Union High School* (2009), for example, the school principal censored two articles from the student newspaper, *The Tomahawk*, one critical of the superintendent's conduct during San Diego's 2007 wildfires and another of abstinence-only education. *The Tomahawk*'s faculty adviser opposed the censorship, and in response, the principal shut down the newspaper and cancelled the journalism class. However, once the students and faculty adviser sued and moved for a preliminary injunction, the district quickly settled because of the strong protections of Section 48907. It agreed to restore *The Tomahawk*, run the articles uncensored, and pay $27,500.

At the same time, because the statute concerns only students, the school district's control over the access of nonstudents to school publications and the content of what they wish to convey is greater, as long as the publications remain closed forums to outsiders. Even in this instance, however, the school cannot engage in viewpoint discrimination by permitting expression on only one side of an issue. For example, while a school could not censor from the school-sponsored newspaper a well-written story about birth control penned by one of its high school students, it might very well exclude an advertisement by a birth control clinic in the advertising section of the paper if that section were operated as a closed forum and no ads were permitted on the subject of procreation and birth control under *Planned Parenthood of Southern Nevada, Inc. v. Clark County School District (1991)*. This Ninth Circuit holding on a Nevada case has never been directly applied to California (although it could be), so whether a California case would come out the same way is uncertain. The issue remains complicated, however; for this reason, school publication policies and practices should be carefully reviewed with the school attorney.

Student Dress, Grooming, and Uniforms

In 1971 the U.S. Court of Appeals for the Ninth Circuit rejected the claim advanced by a high school student and a community college student that they have a First Amendment right to have long hair (*King v. Saddleback Junior College District*). However, in making the contention, neither student explained what the expression was. The appellate court discussed possible sources of such a right other than the First Amendment but noted a lack of consensus among judges generally as to what it might be: "No doubt their confusion is fostered by the tenuous nature of the right asserted," the judges mused (p. 938). Finding no interference with a significant constitutional right, the court ruled against the students.

The same year, a California court of appeal addressed the issue. (*Montalvo v. Madera Unified School District Board of Education*, 1971). The case involved a fourteen-year-old student who was suspended from school for three days because he refused to cut his hair in conformity with the school's rule regarding hair length for males. Like their federal counterparts in the *King* case, the state appellate judges were wary of anchoring a student's right to personal grooming in the First Amendment. Nor did they feel comfortable equating it to a right of marital privacy. However, they did find a right to personal grooming in the word *liberty* of the Fourteenth Amendment. But the judges in this case were reluctant to give personal grooming much weight, opting to defer to the judgment of school officials. "At most," wrote the judges, "hair style is an indefinite and vague expression of personality, individuality or of an idiosyncrasy much like the color or style of clothes or deportment" (pp. 600–601). All that is necessary to justify controlling the length and style of hair is a legitimate concern on the part of the school administration relating to the educational process. The judges found such an interest in maintaining discipline and protecting the health and safety of students. The court pointed to testimony that long hair might subject a male student to danger in a shop class or to razzing from other students, testimony that clearly dates the case. The trial court's decision in favor of the school district was upheld.

California Education Code Section 35183 recognizes that "gang-related apparel" is hazardous to the health and safety of the school environment and gives governing boards the authority to ban it through a dress code policy. At the same time, the statute acknowledges the difficulty of identifying constantly changing gang attire and gang affiliation and suggests the adoption of a school uniform as an alternative. No particular style of uniform is described. The statute leaves this detail to the school principal, staff, and parents. Adoption of a dress code banning gang attire or instituting a school uniform, according to Section 35183, does not violate the students' free speech rights under Education Code Section 48950.

In 2008, the Ninth Circuit confronted the constitutionality of mandatory student uniforms. The case arose when several Nevada students contended that the uniforms established by their schools in conformity with a school district policy violated their rights of expression and free exercise of religion. The court ruled against the students by a 2–1 vote in *Jacobs v. Clark County School District* (2008). The policy, the majority observed, had nothing to do with prohibiting a particular form of "pure speech," like the restriction in *Tinker* against armbands protesting the Vietnam War. Rather the policy prohibited all forms of "expressive conduct" via dress and thus warranted a less searching level of judicial scrutiny than used for viewpoint-based speech restrictions like the one in *Tinker*. The majority was a little troubled by the fact that the school district did permit uniforms to display school logos on clothing but concluded this was less for purposes of expressing a viewpoint than for an identifying mark. The court also noted that students still had the right to engage in interstudent communication during the school day, publish articles in school newspapers, join student clubs, and dress as they like outside of school. So, could students in the Nevada district wear armbands on their school uniform protesting the uniform policy? While the majority did not address the matter, it appears from the ruling that any form of communication on a school uniform other than the school logo would be impermissible. The dissenting judge argued that the majority's rationale was inconsistent with *Tinker* and contrary to its own *Chandler v. McMinnville School District* (1992) ruling permitting students to wear pro-teacher buttons on their clothing.

In 2014, the Ninth Circuit returned to school uniforms in another Nevada case and addressed lingering issues from *Jacobs* (2008). In *Frudden v. Pilling* (2014), the uniform policy had two key differences from that of *Jacobs*. First, the uniform had to display the motto "Tomorrow's Leaders." Second, the policy exempted students wearing uniforms of "nationally recognized youth organizations, such as Boy Scouts or Girl Scouts, on regular meeting days." The court found these policies had to be evaluated under strict scrutiny because the motto was compelled speech and the exemption for nationally recognized youth organizations was content based. Three years later, the Ninth Circuit reversed the District Court's finding that the policies survived strict scrutiny (*Frudden v. Pilling*, 2017). How applicable these decisions are to California traditional public and charter schools is uncertain in light of Education Code Section 48907 that protects the right of students to wear buttons, badges, and other insignia and that makes no mention of a school uniform policy.

While lawsuits always are possible over dress code restrictions, especially those attempting to define and prohibit gang-related attire, a uniform policy in California schools is less likely to result in litigation. This is so because Section 35183 provides that "the governing board shall provide a method whereby parents may choose not to have their children comply with an adopted school uniform policy." Presumably, those who are likely to bring lawsuits would avail themselves of the opt-out opportunity. The statute also provides that if a uniform policy is adopted, it may not be implemented without less than six months' notice to parents and without the availability of resources to assist economically disadvantaged families.

Right of Association

In 1981, the U.S. Supreme Court handed down an important First Amendment decision pertaining to student associational rights on a public college campus. This decision led directly to an important federal statute extending associational rights to public secondary school students. In *Widmar v. Vincent* (1981), the question arose as to whether the University of Missouri, which had made its facilities available to registered student groups, could refuse to accommodate a student religious group that wished to meet for worship and religious discussion. Writing for the Court in this 8–1 decision, Justice Lewis F. Powell observed that by accommodating student groups, the university had created a limited public forum and, having done so, could not discriminate among them on the basis of speech content. While the university contended that the separation of church and state provision in the

First Amendment known as the establishment clause (the focus of our attention in Chapter 7), as well as a similar provision in the Missouri Constitution, required that it not permit religious groups to practice their religion at a public university, the Court disagreed. Wrote Justice Powell: "Having created a forum generally open to student groups, the university seeks to enforce a content-based exclusion of religious speech. Its exclusionary policy violates the fundamental principle that a state regulation of speech should be content-neutral" (p. 277).

Congress extended the ruling in *Widmar v. Vincent* to public secondary school student groups when it enacted the Equal Access Act (EAA) in 1984. Originally intended to apply only to student religious groups, the statute makes it unlawful for any secondary school receiving federal funding to "deny equal access or a fair opportunity to, or discriminate against, any students who wish to conduct a meeting within that limited open forum on the basis of religious, political, philosophical, or other content of the speech at such meetings" (20 U.S.C. § 4071(a)). Under the EAA, a limited open forum exists when the school allows one or more non-curriculum-related student groups to meet on campus during noninstructional time. The U.S. Supreme Court defined the term *non-curriculum-related* when it upheld the EAA in *Board of Education of Westside Community Schools (Dist. 66) v. Mergens* in 1990, a decision discussed in more detail in Chapter 7. A group is directly related to the curriculum if the subject matter of the group is taught, if the subject matter of the group concerns the curriculum as a whole, if participation in the group results in academic credit, or if participation is related to a specific course. If the secondary school accommodates one or more groups that do not fall into any of these categories, then it has created a limited open forum under the act and must accommodate all similar groups that wish to meet. As we shall see in Chapter 7, the courts have considerably expanded this holding to provide First Amendment protections to student religious groups.

In *Mergens* (1990), the school argued that it had a closed forum because it permitted only curriculum-related groups to meet. But using the Court's definition, the justices concluded that the scuba diving and chess clubs, as well as a service group that worked with special education classes, were not curriculum related. Thus, the school had a limited open forum, and Bridget Mergens's religious club had a right to meet on campus during noninstructional time. The same would be true for any other student-initiated group that desired to meet.

Some noncurricular student groups can be quite controversial. Such was the case with the Gay-Straight Alliance (GSA) that sought to meet under the EAA at the El Modena High School in the Orange Unified School District (*Colin ex rel. Colin v. Orange Unified School District,* 2000). Anthony Colin and a friend decided to form the club after Matthew Shepard, a Wyoming youth, died following a brutal assault motivated at least in part by his homosexuality. The purpose of the club was to raise public awareness and promote tolerance by providing a safe forum for discussion of issues related to sexual orientation and homophobia. Colin found a faculty member to sponsor the group and submitted a club constitution in compliance with school policy. While the school had a limited open forum, school officials had their doubts and forwarded the application to the school board. While the application was pending before the board, the group was not allowed to participate in a one-day informational fair about student groups. Nevertheless, over fifty students signed a petition in support of the club. Administrators tried to get the students to change the club's name and to steer its mission away from sexual orientation. The school board denied the club's application because it allegedly infringed on the school's teaching of sex education. The students sought an injunction under the EAA to overturn the board's decision.

In a carefully reasoned opinion, the federal district court granted the injunction. The judge rejected the school's novel argument that because the GSA was curriculum related, the school could refuse to recognize it. The club's mission was not concerned with the physiology of sex education. Even if it were, it would be inconsistent for the governing board to exclude the club and at the same time teach sex education. Moreover, the court observed that the board did not have authority to foreclose access to the campus because a group's speech content may relate to the curriculum in some way: "The only meetings that schools subject to the Act can prohibit are those that would 'materially and substantially interfere with the ordinary conduct of educational activities with the school'" (p. 1146). There was no evidence that a community gay and lesbian support group controlled the GSA contrary to the terms of the EAA. Efforts by the administration to change the name and mission of the club violated the group's speech and associational rights. Furthermore, the court noted that the board's delay and discrimination against the students ran counter to legislation prohibiting discrimination based on sexual orientation in public schools (Educ. Code § 200).

Prior to 2023, the Ninth Circuit held that public schools could deny official recognition to clubs that discriminated in their membership based on protected characteristics in contravention of school discrimination policies (see *Truth v. Kent Sch. Dist.* (2008), which allowed a Washington school district to deny recognition to a student club that allowed only Christian students to be members). However, the Ninth Circuit in 2023 overruled its precedents in *Fellowship of Christian Athletes v. San Jose Unified School District Board of Education*. The court held that the First Amendment required the school to recognize a Christian club that limited its membership to Christians and did not allow homosexuals. (See a more detailed discussion of this in Chapter 7).

In summary, the right of older students to associate has become clearly established. While the public secondary school may find the content of expression objectionable, even contrary to the mission of the school, it has little authority to intervene once a limited public forum has been created. To this extent, the school is a marketplace of ideas. However, the authority of the state and the school over what transpires in the classroom is quite a different matter.

EXPRESSION RIGHTS IN THE CLASSROOM

Teacher Academic Freedom

The exact dimensions of a public schoolteacher's "right to teach," often known as academic freedom, remain unclear. Academic freedom has been mentioned in several U.S. Supreme Court rulings but never explicitly defined.

For instance, in *Epperson v. Arkansas* in 1968, Justice Abe Fortas observed for the Court that "it is much too late to argue that the State may impose upon the teachers in its schools any conditions it chooses" (*Epperson v. Arkansas*, 393 U.S. 97, 107 (1968)). *Epperson* involved a challenge by a teacher to an Arkansas statute prohibiting the teaching of evolution in the state's public schools. Noting that the ban was motivated by a preference for the biblical view of the origin of man, the Court declared the statute an unconstitutional advancement of religion. In his concurring opinion in that case, Justice Potter Stewart recognized that, while a state could decide that only one foreign language should be taught in its schools, he doubted that a state could punish a teacher for asserting in the classroom that other languages exist.

Similarly, in *Ambach v. Norwich*, the U.S. Supreme Court considered whether a New York statute denying teaching credentials to noncitizens who do not intend to apply for citizenship violated the Equal Protection Clause of the Fourteenth Amendment. Writing for the majority, Justice Lewis F. Powell described the Court's decision to uphold New York State's right to deny public school teaching certificates to noncitizens that "in shaping the students' experience to achieve educational goals, teachers by necessity have wide discretion over the way the course material is communicated to students" (*Ambach v. Norwick*, 1979).

In 1973, the California Supreme Court considered whether a school district could non-reelect a probationary teacher because he read a theme containing objectionable language to his tenth-grade English class (*Lindros v. Governing Board of Torrance Unified School District*). The teacher, who also was a Catholic priest on leave from his church, asked his class to write a short paper on a personal emotional experience. To illustrate what he had in mind, he read a story he had written entitled "The Funeral." The story concerned one of the teacher's former students at a predominately Black high school in Watts who died of a heroin overdose. In his poignant and moving story, the teacher used the phrase "white mother-fuckin Pig." Teachers had considerable authority to select supplementary instructional material at the high school, and the teacher had not consulted school administrators before reading the story. Books with similar terms were available in the school library. Though no students or parents complained, the teacher's contract was not extended because of the incident, and he later challenged his non-reelection.

In a divided decision, the California Supreme Court ruled in favor of the teacher. The court distinguished between the use of profane words in a classroom and their inclusion in teaching material. The judges noted that such words have long been used to convey emotion in works of literature. "In sum, we could not impose upon teachers of writing, as a matter of law, that they must tell and teach their students that in depicting the jargon of the ghetto, the slum, or the barrack room, characters must speak in the pedantry of Edwardian English" (p. 536). It is important to note that the court did not specifically rule that the teacher had an academic freedom right to read the story with the offensive terms. Rather, the court based its decision on the lack of good cause for the board not to extend his contract.

Courts continue to wrestle with the dimensions of teacher classroom speech. In 2001 the U.S. Court of Appeals for the Ninth Circuit ruled that Proposition 227, requiring English-learners be taught in English, does not violate teacher rights. The California Teachers Association contended that the requirement that teaching be "overwhelmingly" in English in English-immersion classrooms and that "nearly all" classroom instruction be given in English in sheltered English-immersion classes is vague and has a chilling effect on teacher classroom free speech. Wrote the two judges in the majority, "Here, in the context of curriculum presentation, it is the state's pedagogical interests that take clear precedence over the teacher's First Amendment interests" (*California Teachers Association v. State Board of Education*, 2001). But the appeals court did not delineate what First Amendment rights a public schoolteacher has in the classroom.

Two 2011 decisions of the U.S. Court of Appeals for the Ninth Circuit provide somewhat different perspectives on the dimensions of public schoolteacher academic freedom rights. In one, the court held that the Poway Unified School District did not violate a high school math teacher's free speech rights by directing him to remove from his classroom two large banners with highlighted references to God and "the Creator" because a public schoolteacher is not speaking as a private citizen in the classroom but as the spokesperson for the district. Thus, under the U.S. Supreme Court's *Pickering v. Board of Education* ruling, the school district has the authority to control what a teacher expresses in that setting. The implication, of course, is that teachers have very little, if any, academic freedom. Here, the district had the authority to ensure that its employees not promote religion contrary to the establishment clause of the First Amendment. The teacher argued that other teachers at the high school had messages with religious themes posted in their classrooms, for example, a Tibetan prayer flag. However, the court noted that they were not intended to promote religion but were used for secular purposes (*Johnson v. Poway Unified School District*).

In the other, a different three-judge panel of the same court supported a measure of academic freedom for public school teachers. In that case, a high school student challenged comments he viewed as antireligious expressed during class by his AP European history teacher. Because the student had graduated, the judges did not rule on this contention. However, they did reject his claim for damages and in the process noted that the U.S. Supreme Court has long supported robust exchange of ideas in education. They pointed out that having a frank discussion about the role of religion in history is an integral part of any advanced history course. Doing so fosters student critical thinking and analytical abilities. At the same time, the court recognized that teachers must be sensitive to students' personal beliefs. In a key comment, the court observed, "[W]e must be careful not to curb intellectual freedom by imposing dogmatic restrictions that chill teachers from adopting the pedagogical methods they believe are most effective" (*C.F. ex rel. Farnan v. Capistrano Unified School District*). The U.S. Supreme Court later refused to hear both decisions.

In a matter tangential to academic freedom, a Los Angeles Unified School District high school teacher attached postings to a bulletin board across the hall from his classroom that took a general anti–gay and lesbian approach. His action was in response to a bulletin board the school established in recognition of Gay and Lesbian Awareness Month. Faculty and staff were permitted to post materials on the board, subject to the oversight of the school principal. Because the teacher's postings were contrary to the message the school wished to convey, the principal directed the teacher to remove his postings. The teacher, Robert Downs, filed a lawsuit against the district, contending that the school had created a free speech forum and that he should be allowed to present an alternative view. The school countered that its bulletin boards are not free speech forums but rather are reserved for messages that the school wishes to communicate. The case is interesting because it pits a teacher's speech claims against the speech claims of the school.

Here, the U.S. Court of Appeals for the Ninth Circuit upheld the school district's actions by finding that it was speaking as the educator through the bulletin board. The school had not opened this channel of communication to general discussion and had not opted to let Downs speak as its representative. Thus, the school could insist that its teachers convey the school's chosen curricular message. Downs could advance his own views on his own time, but not "when he is speaking as the government, unless the government allows him to be its voice" (*Downs v. Los Angeles Unified School District*). The court did not specifically address the extent to which Downs could advance his personal views in face-to-face discussions with students and other teachers on campus. Given the case law, he should do so with caution.

While there is no academic freedom right to determine a student's grade, California teachers have been given significant authority to do so under state law. Education Code § 49066 provides that a teacher's grade can be changed only if it is based on clerical or mechanical mistake, fraud, bad faith, or incompetency and then only in consultation with the teacher. In a 2001 ruling, a California appellate court determined that conduct grades are included within the statutory term *grade* for purposes of Section 49066 and can be changed only for the reasons listed in the statute (*Las Virgenes Educators Association v. Las Virgenes Unified School District*).

In that case, a principal revised a teacher's assigned conduct grades after the teacher failed to alert parents as required by district policy. The court noted previous decisions that "NM" (meaning "no mark") and "W" (meaning "withdrawal") fall within the term *grade*. Because failure to notify a parent is not among the reasons listed to change a teacher's grade, the principal was without authority to do so. While the principal could not change the grade, the principal could hold the teacher responsible for failing to follow district policy. When parents request changes in student records including grades, the teacher who awarded the grade must be given an opportunity to provide their rationale for the grades and, to the extent practicable, included in all discussions related to the changing of the grade (Educ. Code § 49070). If the parent is unsuccessful, the parent may file an objection that becomes part of the student's record.

While the right of a teacher to teach is not well established in case law and is significantly confined by state curriculum content standards, teachers must have some discretion to address the needs of their students. Teachers and administrators are well advised to review school governing board policy, teacher handbooks, and the collective bargaining agreement to determine the extent to which they may introduce supplementary materials into their classrooms, lead students in discussing controversial subjects, and invite outside speakers. When in doubt, it may be wise to consult with the immediate supervisor to better understand any expectations and requirements.

Student Classroom Expression

The U.S. Supreme Court was quite clear in holding in its 1969 *Tinker* decision that student rights of expression encompass the classroom. But in later decisions the Court drew back from this position. As noted earlier, in its 1986 *Bethel School District v. Fraser* decision, the Court embraced the concept that the purpose of public schools is to inculcate community values and beliefs, not to permit unfettered student free speech. And two years later in *Hazelwood School District v. Kuhlmeier*, the Court indicated that school officials have the authority to determine what manner of speech is inappropriate in the classroom and other venues controlled by the school. While provisions of the California Education Code strongly support student speech rights on campus, as described earlier, they do not expressly include the classroom (Educ. Code §§ 48907, 48950). Further, they do not deny school personnel the right to impose reasonable time, place, and manner regulations on the exercise of student speech. Thus, student expression could be confined to a classroom discussion period and not permitted during a lecture or demonstration. Additionally, any student speech that creates material disruption or substantially interferes with the rights of other students is not constitutionally protected. For example, a student who desires to speak out about the recall election process in California during a physics class would not be entitled to do so, because the speech would clearly disrupt the teaching of physics.

A 1995 California appellate court ruling sheds light on the extent of student classroom expression rights (*Lopez v. Tulare Joint Union High School District*). The case involved students in Valley High School (a continuation school in the district) who had produced a video in their fine arts class addressing problems of teenage parenting. The video was to be shown to students and parents and entered in an off-campus film competition. Entitled *Melancholianne* after the name of the baby, the film depicted a day in the life of teenage parents in a dingy, unkempt motel room. The father had just been released from prison after serving time for raping another girl. The dialogue included considerable profanity (e.g., *shit, ass, pimp, fuck*), which the students maintained added realism because it was the language they heard every day. The fine arts instructor agreed. But the principal found the language highly offensive and educationally unsuitable. Relying on an administrative regulation dealing with school publications, he directed that it be removed from the script. Among other things, the regulation specified that school publications must reflect professional standards of English grammar and journalistic writing style and must not include profanity, defined as language that would not be used in area newspapers. The school board backed the administration; the students, with assistance from the American Civil Liberties Union, filed a lawsuit contending that the censorship violated their expression rights.

Two of the three appellate court judges accepted the premise that the video was an official school publication, a position that the students and their attorneys apparently did not contest. Thus, the provisions of Education Code Section 48907 applied. As noted earlier, this statute gives public school students broad rights of free speech and press, subject to limited school oversight. The court noted that the statute requires school governing boards to have a written publication code and to review official school publications to make sure that professional standards of English and journalism are followed. Here, the court held that school officials were acting in accordance with Section 48907 when they refused to permit profanity to be included in the video. Further, the judges pointed out that this section of the Education Code does not violate the California Constitution. As an official school publication, the video was a limited public forum subject to the control of the school to achieve a specific purpose. Here the purpose was to teach students not to use profane and vulgar language. Nor did the suppression of the speech violate Education Code Section 48950, which gives secondary school students the same free speech rights at school that they have off campus. This is so because that section expressly indicates that it does not limit or modify the provisions of Section 48907.

The third judge reached the same conclusion but by a different route. He concluded that *Melancholianne* was not an official school publication. Thus, all the discussion about journalistic standards and prior review of school publications under Section 48907 did not apply. Instead, he viewed the case as one pertaining to student expression within the classroom. Rather than viewing the classroom as an open forum for the exchange of ideas, as had the justices in *Tinker*, this judge viewed the classroom as a closed forum subject to school control. Hence, school officials could prevent students from using profanity in the film because doing so served a legitimate pedagogical purpose.

Given the different perspectives expressed in the *Lopez* case, the degree to which student classroom expression is protected remains unclear. Classroom expression that may involve threats against others is subject to particularly careful scrutiny in light of the recent history of school violence.

SUMMARY

Because public school employees owe some degree of allegiance to their employer, their free speech rights at school are limited. They can speak out on matters of public concern outside the scope of their employment and be free from retaliation so long as they do not abuse the right. However, they have no constitutional entitlement to complain about working conditions. The manner and extent to which they can do so are determined by school policy and union contracts. The school's interest in controlling the curriculum generally takes precedence over a teacher's claim to academic freedom in the classroom. Some districts explicitly accord teachers the right to choose supplemental teaching materials, to engage students in discussing controversial topics, and to invite speakers to their classes. Others, however, retain tight control over classroom teaching, in part to ensure that the state's curriculum content standards are implemented and that student achievement targets are met. Thus, it is important for educators to determine what the policy and practices are in their districts and follow them. When uncertain, the best strategy is to ask the supervisor.

As a corollary to the right to speak, school employees have a constitutional right to associate with others. This encompasses the right to join and participate in organizational affairs and to engage in lifestyle activities. Like freedom of speech, however, the right to associate is not absolute. This is particularly true when educators use electronic communication devices to engage in social interaction with students. If such activity disrupts the learning environment or undermines the employee's effectiveness, the employee's job may be in jeopardy.

Because students are not employees, they do not owe the same allegiance to their schools as do employees. Therefore, their expression rights are more extensive. At the same time, however, because the school is a place for learning, speech that creates material disruption or significantly invades the rights of others is not constitutionally protected. Students who use their own electronic communication devices on and off campus in ways that harm other students can be subject to discipline, but the burden is on school officials to justify doing so.

California law is even more protective of free speech for public school students, giving them broad access to school channels of communication such as bulletin boards and school newspapers. The law even goes so far as to say that both public and nonreligious private secondary school students' expression rights are as extensive in school as outside of school. However, federal and state judicial decisions provide little constitutional protection for student speech that is profane, indecent, or threatening to the safety of others. As we have seen, judicial deference to school board authority over classroom instruction has undercut student expression rights in this setting.

The school can impose reasonable time, place, and manner rules that channel when and how student speech can be exercised. While the school has a right to preview what students wish to express in school-sponsored channels of communication such as the school newspaper, its authority under California law to engage in content censorship is quite limited. The school does have a broader right to regulate student dress and grooming, but even here expression rights may surface. Indeed, the wearing of symbolic armbands was what triggered the U.S. Supreme Court's *Tinker v. Des Moines Independent Community School District* ruling.

The student right of association is safeguarded by the federal Equal Access Act, which gives non-curriculum-related student groups broad access to secondary schools that receive federal financial assistance. The rights of elementary students to free speech and association are less well defined. This is understandable, given their age and maturity level.

THE SCHOOL AND RELIGION

Education and religion have long been intertwined. Before there were public schools, religious private schools provided most formal education in America. Enacted in 1787, two years before the ratification of the U.S. Constitution, the Northwest Ordinance set aside lands for public education, noting, "Religion, morality, and knowledge being necessary to good government and the happiness of mankind, schools and the means of education shall forever be encouraged."

Even after the public common school system began to take shape in the nineteenth century, religion was an integral part of schooling. Much of the early public school curriculum was focused on religion. The famous McGuffey Readers, introduced in 1836 and used by millions of students until the mid-twentieth century, drew heavily on Protestant religion. In fact, the Protestant character of public schools drove many Catholics to start their own parochial school systems in the late nineteenth century. Over the years, America has become more religiously diverse. Today, some 145 million Americans are affiliated with over 200 different religious denominations. Increasing religious heterogeneity within public schools generated conflict and litigation after World War II that has continued unabated to the present. Gradually, a body of law has developed governing many manifestations of religion in public education. It is this body of law that we discuss in this chapter, beginning with a review of applicable constitutional law.

FEDERAL AND CALIFORNIA CONSTITUTIONAL LAW

No Government Establishment of Religion

The writers of the Constitution knew from their experiences that government involvement in religion inevitably generates conflict. If government were to prefer one religion to another, the question arises, "Whose religion?" If religion in general were favored over nonreligion, then nonbelievers and those holding secularized belief systems would be penalized. Seeking to avoid such problems, the founders included a provision in the First Amendment of the U.S. Constitution preventing Congress from making laws "respecting an establishment of religion." By virtue of the Fourteenth Amendment, the provision applies to states and political subdivisions of states like school districts and charter schools. Exactly what the establishment clause means in practice, however, has long been the subject of debate.

To some, the establishment clause merely prohibits government from setting up a state church similar to the Anglican Church in England. To others, the word *an* before "establishment of religion" indicates that the clause was intended to prevent government involvement with any one or all religious denominations. The latter approach has been characterized as maintaining a "wall of separation between church and state." The wall metaphor originated in a letter President Thomas Jefferson sent to the Danbury Baptist Association in 1802. The U.S. Supreme Court first used the phrase in its 1879 decision holding that, while Mormons have a right to believe in polygamy, Congress can ban its practice (*Reynolds v. United States*). The Court again referred to the wall metaphor in its first prominent ruling involving religion and education (*Everson v. Board of Education*, 1947). What is interesting about the latter decision is that, after citing Thomas Jefferson to exclaim how stringent the establishment clause is, the five-justice majority found no bar to the use of public funds to underwrite bus transportation for students attending parochial schools. Writing for the majority, Justice Hugo Black observed that the purpose of the New Jersey legislation was to get students safely to and from school, regardless of what type of school they attended. The four dissenters viewed the aid program as tax support for religion because it furthers the mission of these schools to provide religious training and teaching.

Continued uncertainty as to how to apply the establishment clause is evident in later decisions. In 1948, one year after the *Everson* decision, the Court ruled against a released-time program whereby religious instruction was given to public school students on school premises during the school day (*McCollum v. Board of Education*). Four years later, the Court upheld a released-time program that allowed public school students to leave school during the school day to receive religious instruction off school grounds (*Zorach v. Clauson*, 1952). Justice Black, who had written for the Court in the *Everson* and *McCollum* decisions, found this degree of accommodation unconstitutional and dissented.

As time went on, the Supreme Court developed criteria for deciding when a law violates the establishment clause. In *Lemon v. Kurtzman* (1971), the Court established a three-part test. The criteria of constitutionality were as follows:

1. A secular, as contrasted with a sectarian or religious, governmental purpose,
2. A primary effect that neither advances nor inhibits religion, and
3. No excessive entanglement of government with religion.

Over the years, the Court did not apply the *Lemon* test consistently and frequently undermined or tinkered with it, particularly in cases involving government assistance to religious institutions. For example, in *Agostini v. Felton* (1997), the Court combined the effect and entanglement prongs and upheld Congressional funding to pay public school teachers to teach secular subjects at private religious schools (overturning *Aguilar v. Felton* (1985), a case decided only twelve years earlier). Even as the lower courts continued to rely on *Lemon* to resolve conflicts over religion in public schools, the Court's conservative justices repeatedly sought to kill it, with Justice Scalia lambasting it as "like some ghoul in a late-night horror movie that repeatedly sits up in its grave and shuffles abroad, after being repeatedly killed and buried" (*Lamb's Chapel v. Center Moriches Union Free School District*, 1993, p. 398).

With more conservative appointments after 2000, the Supreme Court has emphasized the protection of free exercise, with its critics saying this has been at the expense of the establishment clause. In *Town of Greece v. Galloway* (2014), Justice Kennedy upheld town meetings beginning with sectarian prayers, holding that the establishment clause had to be interpreted with "reference to historical practices and understandings" and history showed sectarian prayers commonly opened legislative sessions at the time of the Founding. In the landmark *Kennedy v. Bremerton School District* (2022) decision, the Supreme Court finally overruled *Lemon*. Justice Gorsuch's opinion, discussed in the section on school prayer, found that there was no conflict between the free exercise and establishment clauses and public school employees had a broadly protected First Amendment right to pray privately. A year later, *Groff v. DeJoy* (2023) recognized the abrogation of *Lemon* and also expanded the private prayer rights of public employees, this time for a postal carrier in the context of Title VII.

The California Constitution also has provisions restricting government involvement with religion. Article I, Section 4 provides in part that "the Legislature shall make no law respecting an establishment of religion." Article XVI, Section 5 states:

Neither the Legislature, nor any county, city and county, township, school district, or other municipal corporation, shall ever make an appropriation, or pay from any public fund whatever, or grant anything to or in aid of any sectarian sect, church, creed, or sectarian purpose, or help to support or sustain any school, college, university, hospital, other institution controlled by any religious creed....

This section has particular relevance for both direct and indirect forms of aid to religious private schools, a matter discussed in the last section of the chapter.

Protection for Free Exercise of Religion

While both federal and state constitutions have limits on governmental involvement with religion, they also recognize the fundamental right of individuals to exercise their religious beliefs freely. Religious freedom is a central tenet of our society. Many of the colonists who left Europe for the new country did so to escape religious persecution. To prevent repression in America, the founders provided in the First Amendment that Congress is not to make laws prohibiting the free exercise of religion. The Fourteenth Amendment added after the Civil War extends the same prohibition to states and their political subdivisions.

The system the founders designed guarantees that all religions can flourish. This includes secularized belief systems because the word *religion* in the free exercise clause has been interpreted more broadly than in the establishment clause. Judicial decisions involving the establishment clause generally have confined the term *religion* to theistic belief systems, that is, to those that relate to a supreme being. For this reason, the argument that schools are promoting a "religion of secularism" by not teaching theistic religion has not been generally accepted. As defined in the dictionary, *secular* means "not sacred or ecclesiastical." At the same time, however, schools cannot ignore theistic religion to the point that they become religion-free zones. As the U.S. Supreme Court noted in its well-known 1963 decision against state-mandated prayer in public school, "We agree of course that the State may not establish a 'religion of secularism' in the sense of affirmatively opposing or showing hostility to religion, thus 'preferring those who believe in no religion over those who believe'" (*School District of Abington Township v. Schempp*, 1963, p. 225). Confinement of the term *religion* to theistic beliefs for purposes of the establishment clause does not preclude complaints from parents and students that public schools are promoting nonmainstream belief systems like Wicca or Satanism through the curriculum. We have occasion to examine some of these cases later in this chapter.

While secularism is not a religion under the establishment clause, the U.S. Supreme Court has recognized that it does fall within the definition of religion in the free exercise clause. The 1961 ruling to this effect involved a state requirement that public officers must declare a belief in God to hold public office. Such a requirement, the Court unanimously ruled, violates the individual's right to freedom of conscience, noting that the free exercise clause encompasses nontheistic beliefs "such as Buddhism, Taoism, Ethical Culture, and Secular Humanism and others" (*Torcaso v. Watkins*, 1961, p. 495 n. 11). Were it otherwise, the argument could be made that religion is being favored over nonreligion, a violation of the establishment clause. The Court recognized this by ruling in 1965 that a conscientious objector who expressed skepticism about the existence of God but who did acknowledge a belief in and devotion to goodness and virtue for their own sakes was entitled to an exemption from the military draft. Writing for the majority, Justice Tom Clark concluded that "the beliefs which prompted his objection occupy the same place in his life as the belief in a traditional deity holds in the lives of his friends, the Quakers" (*United States v. Seeger*, 1965, p. 187).

The validity of a belief system is beyond the purview of public officials. As the Supreme Court ruled long ago:

> Freedom of thought, which includes freedom of religious belief, is basic in a society of free men. It embraces the right to maintain theories of life and of death and of the hereafter which are rank heresy to followers of orthodox faiths. Heresy trials are foreign to our Constitution. Men may believe what they cannot prove. They may not be put to the proof of their religious doctrines or beliefs (*United States v. Ballard*, 1944, p. 886).

As long as a belief system is sincere, government officials may ask no more.

The California Constitution has a provision protecting free exercise of religion as well. Article I, Section 4 states in part that "free exercise and enjoyment of religion without discrimination or preference are guaranteed." Because most litigation over free exercise of religion has occurred in federal courts, the California provision has not been relied upon as often.

MANIFESTATIONS OF RELIGION ON CAMPUS

Judicial rulings reveal the many ways that religion manifests itself on the public school campus. In some instances, the manifestations violate the constitutional principles previously discussed, and in other instances, they do not. In this section, we include decisions illustrating the impermissible.

The Pledge of Allegiance

Education Code Section 52720 permits use of the Pledge of Allegiance during required daily patriotic exercises in public schools. Instruction promoting an understanding of such terms as *pledge, republic,* and *indivisible* and the understanding of the pledge also satisfies the requirement. If such instruction focuses on the words of the pledge, then the giving of the pledge must be included (Educ. Code § 52730). However, when the exercise is conducted, all students cannot be required to participate. This is because the U.S. Supreme Court ruled in 1943 that the First Amendment prevents a public school from compelling anyone to salute the flag. Writing for the majority in that case, Justice Robert Jackson observed, "[W]e think the action of the local authorities in compelling the flag salute and pledge transcends constitutional limitations on their power and invades the sphere of intellect and spirit which is the purpose of the First Amendment to our Constitution to reserve from all official control" (*West Virginia State Board of Education v. Barnette*, 1943, p. 642).

The pledge of allegiance became the focus of considerable attention in California in 2004 when the U.S. Supreme Court issued an opinion in *Elk Grove Unified School District v. Newdow*. An elementary student's father had filed a lawsuit contending that Congress violated the establishment clause by adding the phrase "under God" to the pledge in 1954. But the court sidestepped addressing the issue because the father lacked custody of his daughter. An attorney and avowed atheist, the father found a way to continue the litigation. The matter ended in 2010 when the U.S. Court of Appeals for the Ninth Circuit ruled that Congress did not violate the establishment clause when it added the words. Rather, the purpose was to inspire patriotism, not to promote religion (*Newdow v. Rio Linda Union School District*). The two judges in the majority reached this decision following a review of the context within which the change was made, noting that the purpose was to recognize the religious history of the United States in the same way as the national motto "In God We Trust" does on U.S. currency. The court also ruled that California Education Code Section 52720 permitting use of the pledge during daily patriotic exercises in public schools is constitutional. In a lengthy dissent, Judge Stephen Reinhardt asserted that while the majority's decision might be pleasing to the public, it cannot mask the fact that Congress's addition of "under God" clearly violates the first sentence of the First Amendment that "Congress shall make no law respecting an establishment of religion." Reinhardt was one of two judges who struck down the pledge in an earlier ruling on the matter.

School Prayer

In the early 1960s, the U.S. Supreme Court handed down two decisions involving prayer in public schools that have generated controversy to this day. In 1962, the Court ruled that this prayer composed by the New York State Board of Regents for reading in the public schools violated the establishment clause: "Almighty God, we acknowledge our dependence upon Thee, and we beg Thy blessings upon us, our parents, our teachers, and our Country" (*Engle v. Vitale*, 1962, p. 425). That the prayer was nondenominational and that its recitation could be voluntary made no difference. The majority concluded:

> We think that the constitutional prohibition against laws respecting an establishment of religion must at least mean that in this country it is no part of the business of government to compose official prayers for any group of American people to recite as a part of a religious program carried on by government.

A year later, the Court struck down without comment a Pennsylvania statute mandating the daily reading of ten verses from the Bible at the beginning of the school day (*School District of Abington Township v. Schempp*, 1963). The readings were done by either student volunteers or homeroom teachers. While recognizing the important role of religion in American life, as it had done the year before in the *Engle* case, the Court found the practice a violation of the establishment clause.

Some commentators have argued that these decisions in essence removed religion from the public schools. They cited Justice Potter Stewart's dissent in *Schempp* in support of the contention. Stewart noted that compulsory education so structures a child's life that "if religious exercises are held to be an impermissible activity in schools, religion is placed at an artificial and state-created disadvantage" (p. 313). He argued that permission should be granted for those who want to exercise their religious beliefs at school. If such accommodation is not granted, then "a refusal to permit religious exercises thus is seen, not as the realization of a state neutrality, but rather as the establishment of a religion of secularism, or at the least, as government support of the beliefs of those who think that religious exercises should be conducted only in private" (*Id.*). As we have noted, clearly public schools cannot become religion-free zones because, as Stewart noted, this would place the state in a position of hostility to religion. The question thus becomes, how can prayer be accommodated in the public schools without either overly promoting it or being hostile to it? Following these two U.S. Supreme Court rulings, lower courts have struggled to find a workable rationale. The dividing line that has emerged separates school-sponsored or endorsed prayer from private prayer and religious exercise. The former is impermissible. The latter is not.

School-sponsored or endorsed public prayer. Clearly, school-sponsored public prayer at the beginning of the school day is unconstitutional. What about a period of silent meditation? In 1985, the U.S. Supreme Court was faced with an Alabama statute that required a moment for "silent meditation or prayer" at the start of the school day (*Wallace v. Jaffree,* 1985). The majority was concerned about the legislature's amending an earlier statute to include the phrase "or prayer." Based on legislative testimony, the majority viewed the addition as a subtle way to get around the Court's prayer decisions, rejecting Chief Justice Warren Burger's assertion in dissent that the addition was merely an effort to let schoolchildren know that prayer was an option. Without a secular legislative purpose, the statute was unconstitutional. But writing for the six-justice majority, Justice John Paul Stevens observed, "The legislative intent to return prayer to the public schools is, of course, quite different from merely protecting every student's right to engage in voluntary prayer during an appropriate moment of silence during the school day" (p. 59). In other words, setting aside a time for silent meditation would, by itself, not violate the Constitution. The U.S. Court of Appeals for the Eleventh Circuit so ruled with regard to Georgia Moment of Quiet Reflection in Schools Act (*Bown v. Gwinnett County School District,* 1997). The Fourth Circuit, in Brown v. Gilmore (2001), similarly upheld a Virginia statute providing for a minute of silence for students to "meditate, pray, or engage in any other silent activity" because the legislature articulated both secular and nonsecular purposes for the statute and teachers did not actively lead students in prayer as in *Jaffree.* California does not have a similar statute.

Sometimes it is difficult to know what is school sponsored and what is not. In 1981 the U.S. Court of Appeals for the Ninth Circuit ruled that an Arizona school principal's allowing the student council to open voluntary school assemblies with prayer constitutes impermissible government endorsement of religion (*Collins v. Chandler Unified School District*). The student council selected a student from the student body, and the student was free to choose the prayer and manner in which it was delivered. The appeals court observed that school endorsement of the practice conveys a subtle message to impressionable students. Furthermore, nonconsenting students were forced either to listen to the prayer or to forgo attending an important school function.

Seeking to avoid a problem with sponsorship under the establishment clause, a Texas school district attempted to convert a brief time during pregame ceremonies of home football games into a free speech forum for an "invocation and/or message" to solemnize the event, to promote good sportsmanship and student safety, and to establish the appropriate environment for competition. According to the policy, the high school student council was to conduct an election to determine whether to have a message or invocation and, if so, to elect a student from a list of volunteers to deliver it. The school board viewed turning the matter over to the student council as a "circuit breaker" between the school and religious endorsement. The policy further provided that any message or invocation had to be nonsectarian and nonproselytizing. The U.S. Supreme Court struck down the policy in 2000 as lacking a secular purpose (*Santa Fe Independent School District v. Doe*). The six-justice majority first rejected the district's contention that the comments delivered during this period constituted private student speech and thus were beyond the thrust of the establishment clause, which applies only to government. Rather, the justices considered the invocation and/or message to be public speech because it was authorized by the government to take place on school property at a school-sponsored event. The district had not created a true free speech forum for private speech because only one student could speak during the entire semester and then could give an invocation or message only for the limited purpose of solemnizing the event. The Court viewed the words *invocation* and *solemnize* as evidence of the school's support for religion. Indeed, the school district had a long history of incorporating religion into its program. The justices also were troubled by the student council majority vote process, viewing it as a means of stifling minority views and assuring that only one viewpoint was expressed. After this decision, it appears dubious whether a school district could create a free speech forum prior to a special-purpose school event like an athletic contest. Even doing so before the opening of school would require some artful drafting by the school attorney. Note that the court in *Bremerton* further refined the parameters.

In *Marsh v. Chambers* (1983), the Supreme Court upheld prayers before the convening of legislative bodies, and in *Town of Greece v. Galloway* (2014), it endorsed sectarian prayers before town meetings. Armed with these precedents, the Chino Valley Unified School Board argued its practice of beginning sessions with a prayer, usually by a local clergyman but sometimes by a Board member or student was allowable. However, in *Freedom from Religion Foundation, Inc. v. Chino Valley Unified School District Board of Education* (2018), the Ninth Circuit declined to extend the "legislative prayers" exception to the school board meetings on several grounds. First, it found that the prayers were not the sort that the legislative prayer exception contemplated, where "solemnizing and unifying" prayers were directed to adult lawmakers who could come and go freely. Rather, these prayers took place in front of many children whose attendance was not truly voluntary. Second, the Board meetings were not solely a venue for policymaking, but also a location for student discipline and recognizing extraordinary student achievement. Finally, in addition to the opening prayers, the Board meetings contain frequent preaching to the community and Bible readings that distinguished them from the Town of Greece's legislative meetings.

Private prayer and religious exercise. It is quite clear that both students and teachers have a right on their own to engage in nondisruptive private prayer during the school day. As described in Chapter 6, neither students nor teachers shed their constitutional rights at the public schoolhouse gate under the U.S. Supreme Court's 1969 *Tinker v. Des Moines Independent Community School District* decision. As the U.S. Court of Appeals for the Eleventh Circuit put it in a decision dealing with an Alabama student prayer statute, "so long as prayer is genuinely student-initiated, and not the product of any school policy which actively or surreptitiously encourages it, the speech is private and protected" (*Chandler v. Siegelman*, 2000, p. 1317).

This right extends to groups of students as well. For example, as long as it is not disruptive, nothing precludes students from holding a prayer rally around the school flagpole or engaging in group prayer at a lunch table in the school cafeteria. Similarly, students can distribute religious literature on the school campus because handing out literature is a form of free speech. At the same time, the school has the right to limit the time, place, and manner of such distribution to prevent disruption of normal school activities. School officials could, for example, require student distributors to identify themselves and restrict distribution to a table outside the school cafeteria during certain times of the school day. The U.S. Department of Education issued guidelines in 2003 providing that students have a right to engage in private prayer in schools receiving federal financial assistance. The guidelines give as examples reading Bibles or other religious literature, saying grace before meals, and praying or studying religious materials with other students when not engaged in school activities or instruction. According to the guidelines, teachers too can meet with each other before school and during lunch for prayer or Bible study, provided they are not acting in their official capacities. However, the Seventh Circuit has ruled that a school district can prevent teachers from holding organized prayer meetings on campus before the school day begins, so long as this time is restricted to school business (*May v. Evansville-Vanderburgh School Corporation*, 1986). The case involved an Indiana elementary school that refused to permit Evangelical Christian teachers from using the campus before the school day began for praying, singing, and reading the Bible. The appeals court commented that the school is not inherently a public forum and that, to be able to hold the prayer meetings, the teachers had to establish that the school had opened its campus to meetings on subjects other than school business during this time.

This they could not do. While it is possible to reconcile the guidelines and the court ruling—informal communication is permitted while organized meetings on closed campuses are not—it is important to note that when there is a conflict between judicial law and administrative guidelines, the former takes precedence.

Public school employees cannot be penalized for their religious beliefs. A case in point is a Ninth Circuit ruling in favor of an Idaho elementary school principal who challenged his reassignment to a teaching position because he opted to educate his children at home for religious reasons (*Peterson v. Minidoka County School District No. 331*, 1997). While the school district was concerned that the homeschooling decision would engender a loss of confidence in the principal by teachers and parents, that concern and supporting evidence were not sufficiently compelling to override the exercise of the principal's religious beliefs and his liberty right to determine the education of his children. It would have been different, the court noted, if the principal's action was not motivated by a religious belief but by lack of confidence in the district's educational program, or if there were other job-related reasons unrelated to the principal's rights to justify the reassignment.

While teachers generally have a right to discuss religious matters on the public school campus, there are some limits. Recall that teachers as public officials must remain neutral when addressing religion with students. In 1994 the Ninth Circuit upheld a school district's directive that a teacher refrain from attempting to convert students to Christianity or initiating conversation about the teacher's religious beliefs with students at any time during the school day, given the teacher's penchant for proselytizing. The appeals court commented that "the school district's interest in avoiding an Establishment Clause violation trumps [the teacher's] right to free speech" (*Peloza v. Capistrano Unified School District*, 1994, p. 522). Two years later the same court ruled that a complete ban on religious advocacy anywhere in the workplace imposed by a department in the California Department of Education was not justified, because the employees performed no educational functions and did not interact with students or other nonemployees (*Tucker v. State of California Department of Education*, 1996). However, the result is different if the employee regularly interacts with outsiders. Daniel Berry's duties as a social services employee included assisting unemployed clients in their transition out of welfare programs. The Ninth Circuit found he could be restricted from discussing religion with clients and displaying religious decorations in his cubicle where he met with clients (*Berry v. Department of Social Services*, 2006). (See also *Johnson v. Poway Unified School District* (2011) (could forbid teacher from displaying large religious banners in classroom)).

Kennedy v. Bremerton School District (2022) is the Supreme Court's most important public schools establishment clause case in decades, and greatly expands the definition of permissible "private" prayer by school employees. According to Justice Gorsuch's majority opinion, Joseph Kennedy, the football coach at Bremerton High School, knelt at midfield after games to offer a quiet prayer during a period when school employees were free to speak with a friend or attend to other personal matters. His prayers were offered when students were otherwise occupied, such as with singing the school fight song. Kennedy initially prayed alone but was eventually joined by many players. Kennedy also began incorporating short religious motivational speeches with his prayer when others were present. Kennedy stopped the religious motivational speeches when directed to by the district but refused to stop praying at the fifty-yard line after games. According to Gorsuch, Kennedy's prayer was doubly protected by the First Amendment: both by the Free Speech clause and Free Exercise clause. The court rationalized that in forbidding Kennedy from praying during a time in which employees were free to check e-mail or attend to other secular matters, the school burdened Kennedy's religious speech because it was religious. The district's policies were therefore not neutral and generally applicable and needed to be evaluated under strict scrutiny.

The school tried to argue Kennedy's midfield prayers were coercive because students were joining only because they did not wish to lose playing time or be singled out by the coach. While Gorsuch agreed that coerced religious activity would be forbidden by the original meaning of the establishment clause, he found no evidence that students were actually coerced and that absent evidence of coercion, visible religious speech by school officials was protected. The dissent heavily disputed the majority's version of the facts, finding that Kennedy's prayers were far from quiet, but public, filmed by local news, and disruptive to the extent the school made arrangements with local police and placed robocalls to remind parents the field was not open to the public. Moreover, the dissent argued the postgame prayers were inescapably coercive even if the prayers were not explicitly required. Players looked to their coaches as role models and depended on their approval for tangible benefits like playing time. The record demonstrated social pressure, with several players reporting joining the prayers not because of their belief but because they wanted to follow their coach and teammates. Finally, Kennedy told the district he began his prayers alone and that players followed over time until a majority joined him.

According to the dissent, this showed coercive pressure at work. Although the full impact of *Kennedy* is not yet clear, three major conclusions are apparent: First, the *Lemon* test is well and truly dead, replaced by a historical-originalist test in which courts must draw the line between permissible and impermissible according to history and faithfully reflect the understanding of the founding fathers. Second, the definition of private prayer has expanded significantly. Last, the majority has also altered the previous implicit standard of one where the *possibility* of coercion of schoolchildren violated the establishment clause to one in which only *proven* coercion will violate the establishment clause.

Religion in the Classroom

As seen from a review of the case law in this section, teaching about religion in a public school classroom is entirely appropriate; but promoting it is not. This distinction is evident in a 1980 U.S. Supreme Court ruling that displaying a religious symbol like the Ten Commandments in the classroom is impermissible (*Stone v. Graham*, 1980). It did not matter that private contributions underwrote the cost of implementing the statute, nor that the statute required a notation on the display to the effect that "the secular application of the Ten Commandments is clearly seen in its adoption as the fundamental legal code of Western Civilization and the Common Law of the United States." In an unsigned opinion, five justices wrote that the statute lacked a secular purpose because the Ten Commandments is undeniably a sacred text in the Jewish and Christian faiths and because several of the commandments address religious duties of believers (e.g., worshiping the Lord God alone, avoiding idolatry, not using the Lord's name in vain, and observing the Sabbath Day). Recently, several states, including Louisiana, Arkansas, and Texas, have either passed a law mandating the posting of the Ten Commandments in classrooms or are in the process of doing so. These cases are working their way through the courts. Watching this series of challenges to existing judicial law is advised. However, the Court recognized that the Ten Commandments can be included as a topic of study within the school curriculum. In 2005, the U.S. Supreme Court distinguished displaying the Ten Commandments in public school classrooms from displaying them on other government property, noting that *Stone* "stands as an example of the fact that we have 'been particularly vigilant in monitoring compliance with the Establishment Clause in elementary and secondary schools'" (*Van Orden v. Perry*, 2005, p. 691).

Teachers need to be sensitive to the wearing of religious attire in the classroom. School districts must reasonably accommodate the wearing of religious attire under Title VII of the 1964 Civil Rights Act but not to the point of imposing an undue hardship. In addition, employees have rights of free speech and the free exercise of religion. At the same time, however, the school must ensure that it and its employees remain neutral with regard to religion. This is especially true in elementary grades, where students are highly impressionable. It thus becomes a matter of balancing the interests of the school in avoiding the advancement of religion and the rights of employees to exercise their religious beliefs. While the wearing of a small religious symbol such as a cross or a Star of David would be appropriate, the wearing of an extremely large cross or a Star of David that lit up periodically might not be.

Teaching about religion. Despite the claims of many critics, the U.S. Supreme Court did not remove religion from the public schools when it struck down school-sponsored prayer in the 1960s. In fact, the Court was careful to protect it. In the 1963 *Schempp* ruling, Justice Tom Clark, who wrote the opinion, noted that "it might well be said that one's education is not complete without a study of comparative religion or the history of religion and its relationship to the advancement of civilization. It certainly may be said that the Bible is worthy of study for its literary and historic qualities" (p. 225). He added, "Nothing we have said here indicates that such study of the Bible or of religion, when presented objectively as part of a secular program of education, may not be effected consistently with the First Amendment."

Section 51511 of the California Education Code similarly recognizes that religion can be incorporated in the curriculum. It states:

> Nothing in this Code shall be construed to prevent, or exclude from the public schools, references to religion or references to or the use of religious literature, art, or music or other things having a religious significance when such references or uses do not constitute instruction in religious principles or aid to any religious sect, church, creed, or sectarian purpose and when such references or uses are incidental to or illustrative of matters properly included in the course of study.

In essence, both the U.S. Supreme Court and the California Legislature permit the school to teach *about* religion but not teach religion. The philosophy is that teaching religion is the province of the home, the church, and the private religious school. Despite the simplicity of this guideline, however, schools have run into legal challenges over incorporation of religion in the curriculum.

Charter schools have not escaped litigation over allegations of impermissible advancement of religion. Parents in Michigan filed suit in federal court against the Vanguard Charter School Academy in Grand Rapids and its operator, National Heritage Academies, contending among other things that the elementary school permitted parents to pray on school grounds, permitted distribution of religious materials in student folders, and taught morality from a religious perspective. They were unsuccessful on all counts (*Daugherty v. Vanguard Charter*

School Academy, 2000). With regard to permitting parents to pray on campus, the school had set aside a room for parents to meet during and after school hours. The fact that a "Moms' Prayer Group" had access to the room did not violate the establishment clause, the judge noted, because other parent groups also were allowed to meet there. Further, the room was off-limits to students, and meetings were held behind closed doors. The inclusion of religious materials from community groups in student folders did not impermissibly advance religion, because announcements from other community groups also were included. The school's Moral Focus Curriculum, the judge noted, did not mention religion. The use of words and concepts that happen to coincide with tenets of religion did not render the curriculum unconstitutional.

Though dismissing all the claims in *Daugherty*, the federal judge noted that federal courts are more sensitive to allegations of establishment clause violations at the elementary level because of the age and impressionable nature of the students. For example, the court observed that allowing parents to read Bible stories to students during classroom time was "questionable." What helped the school avoid liability in this case was the school's development of a set of First Amendment guidelines intended to prevent unconstitutional conduct by teachers and excessive entanglement with religion.

The matter of teaching creation-science came before the U.S. Supreme Court in 1987 (*Edwards v. Aguillard*). The case involved a statute enacted by Louisiana bearing the ungainly title "The Balanced Treatment for Creation-Science and Evolution-Science in Public School Instruction Act." The thrust of the statute was to require that whenever evolution was taught in the public school curriculum, the science associated with creation had to be taught. Proponents labeled it a way of promoting academic freedom by teaching all the information relating to the origins of man. Opponents viewed it as a confining measure restricting academic freedom by permitting only two views to be taught. They considered it an effort to infuse a fundamentalist Christian perspective into the teaching of science. By a 7–2 vote, the Court agreed with the opponents. The justices ruled that Louisiana's creation-science act lacked a secular purpose. The majority noted that "teaching a variety of scientific theories about the origins of humankind to school children might be validly done with the clear secular intent of enhancing the effectiveness of science instruction" (p. 594). But rather than add to the science curriculum, the creation-science act served to discredit evolution by advancing a particular religious view. A few years later, creation-science came before the Ninth Circuit when the teacher in the *Peloza* decision discussed earlier in this chapter alleged that by being required to teach only evolution in his science classes, he was being forced to proselytize "evolutionism" to his students under the guise of its being a valid scientific theory. The teacher contended that the school district was establishing a religion by teaching only evolution. The appellate judges affirmed the lower court's rejection of the claim, noting that neither the U.S. Supreme Court nor any court within the Ninth Circuit has ever held that "evolutionism" or secular humanism are "religions" within the meaning of the establishment clause. The judges pointed out that evolution is a biological concept holding that higher life-forms evolve from lower ones and is not religious (*Peloza v. Capistrano Unified School District*, 1995).

Months before the *Peloza* (1994) decision, the Ninth Circuit rejected a claim that the school was advancing the Wicca belief system by permitting its teachers to use *Impressions*, a series of fifty-nine books containing some 10,000 literary selections and classroom activities (*Brown v. Woodland Joint Unified School District*, 1994). Of particular concern to the parents were selections they contended promoted witchcraft and that asked students to discuss witches or create poetic chants. This, they contended, amounted to advancement of the Wicca religion. Assuming, but not ruling, that Wicca is a religion, the appeals court rejected the claim. Merely reading and discussing witches does not have the effect of advancing religion. "If an Establishment Clause violation arose each time a student believed that a school practice either advanced or disapproved of religion," the judges wrote, "school curricula would be reduced to the lowest common denominator, permitting each student to become a 'curriculum review committee' unto himself or herself" (p. 1379). The court expressed more concern about having students act out rituals but noted that the activities in this case were drawn from a secular source and used for a secular purpose. The appeals court also rejected the parents' claims under the California Constitution. It noted that because no California decision indicates that the state's establishment clause in Article I, Section 4 is stricter than its federal counterpart, California courts would uphold use of the challenged selections from *Impressions*.

In *California Parents for the Equalization of Educational Materials v. Torlakson* (2020), a coalition of Hindu parents challenged the California State Board of Education history standards for sixth and seventh graders. The parents' principal objections to the standards were that (1) Hinduism was portrayed as a mere "belief system," while other religions were described as having a divine origin; (2) the Aryan invasion theory of Indian history was portrayed as true, following mainstream scholarship but contrary to the assertions of Indian nationalists; and (3) the caste system was discussed as a religious rather than a social system. The Ninth Circuit noted that plaintiffs were motivated by a sincere belief that the educational materials disparaged Hinduism in comparison to other religions, but that the materials had to be interpreted from the perspective of a reasonable observer. An objective, reasonable observer would find the material "entirely unobjectionable," and even isolated passages implying hostility toward religion would not violate the establishment clause unless they were the "principal or primary effect." Additionally, the court found that the plaintiffs did not have a Free Exercise claim because their allegations at most suggested the standards contained material offensive to their religious beliefs. But the fact that public school curriculum contradicted their religion was not a free exercise violation because there was no actual burden on the profession or exercise of religion. Overall, the standards reflected a balanced, constitutional approach to major world religions.

A California court of appeal ruled that incorporation of yoga in physical education for elementary students in the Encinitas Union School District did not advance religion contrary to the establishment clause in Article I, Section 4 of the California Constitution. The court noted that when the program was initiated, some parents complained that it was advancing Hinduism. The program was funded by a grant from the K. P. Jois Foundation, which promotes Ashtanga yoga as explained in Hindu texts. The district responded by revising the program to remove features that could be construed as religious (e.g., Sanskrit language, Ashtanga tree poster, guided meditation scripts). Character quotations from religious figures were replaced with those from famous persons like Babe Ruth and Dr. Martin Luther King. The appellate court noted that while a reasonable person might know that a grant from the Jois Foundation was linked to Hinduism, that same person "would also be aware that, as *implemented*, the District's yoga program was clearly *not* Ashtanga eight-limbed yoga" (p. 890). The yoga teachers were from the district, and the district itself was not involved with the Jois Foundation. The latter's involvement in the program other than funding it was in assisting the district in ensuring that yoga teachers would be proficient teaching yoga poses to students (*Sedlock v. Baird*, 2015).

A coalition of seventeen national religious and educational organizations has developed six guidelines that remain very helpful in deciding what public schools can and cannot do in incorporating religion into the instructional program (C. C. Haynes, *A Teacher's Guide to Religion in the Public Schools*, First Amendment Center, 1999). The guidelines for teaching about religion are set forth in the following list:

- The school's approach to religion must be academic, not devotional.
- The school may strive for student awareness of religion but should not press for student acceptance of any one religion.
- The school may sponsor study about religion but may not sponsor the practice of religion.
- The school may expose students to a diversity of religious views but may not impose any particular view.
- The school may educate about all religions but may not promote or denigrate any religion.
- The school may inform the student about various beliefs but should not seek to confine him or her to any particular belief.

Student religious papers and presentations. As noted in Chapter 6, school officials have considerable authority to control the content of the curriculum and what transpires in the classroom. Occasionally, disputes arise over the desire of students to write papers and give presentations on religious topics. The general pattern of federal judicial decisions to date is to defer to the judgment of educators. Two venerable decisions from the U.S. Court of Appeals for the Sixth Circuit, whose jurisdiction extends to Michigan, Ohio, Kentucky, and Tennessee, are illustrative. The first involves a second grader in a Michigan public school who wanted to show to her classmates a videotape of herself singing a proselytizing religious song during a church service. The teacher had started a "VIP of the Week" program to afford each child an opportunity to gain confidence and experience in verbal communication by telling the class about the child's interests and what the child considers important.

After viewing the videotape, the teacher told the child that the videotape could not be shown. The teacher concluded that showing the video would not satisfy the purpose of the VIP program by giving the student an opportunity to talk before the class, and if other students brought videos, she would have to spend considerable time viewing them to see if they were suitable. She also feared that the religious message of the video would convey a message of school endorsement. The parents filed a lawsuit, contending the denial violated their child's First Amendment rights of expression and free exercise of religion. The trial court ruled in favor of the district, as did the Sixth Circuit, relying on *Hazelwood School District* and noting that the school can exercise content control over the classroom as long as the classroom is not an open forum and a legitimate pedagogical purpose justifies the control.

The second decision involved a ninth grader who planned to write a paper on the life of Jesus after indicating she was going to write her paper on drama. The teacher did not approve the new topic and gave the student a failing grade when the student chose not to write a paper. The trial court dismissed the lawsuit, and the Sixth Circuit affirmed the judgment. The appellate court noted that teachers should have wide latitude in giving assignments and awarding grades. Here the teacher had legitimate reasons for her action. "So long as the teacher limits speech or grades speech in the classroom in the name of learning and not as a pretext for punishing the student for her race, gender, economic class, religion, or political persuasion," the judges noted, "the federal courts should not interfere" (*Settle v. Dickson County School Board*, 1995, p. 155).

Guidelines issued by the U.S. Department of Education in 2003 under the No Child Left Behind Act seem to be less deferential to educators than the federal courts. The guidelines state:

> Students may express their beliefs about religion in homework, artwork, and other written and oral assignments free from discrimination based on the religious content of their submissions. Such home and classroom work should be judged by ordinary academic standards of substance and relevance and against other legitimate pedagogical concerns identified by the school.

Thus, "if a teacher's assignment involves writing a poem, the work of a student who submits a poem in the form of a prayer (e.g., a psalm) should be judged on the basis of academic standards (such as literary quality) and neither penalized nor rewarded on account of its religious content (U.S. Department of Education, 1993)." In California, the dearth of case law suggests that following the guidelines is a sensible approach absent a specific legal opinion. While federal guidelines do not have the legal weight of statutes or judicial decisions, noncompliance could result in sanctions including the loss of federal funding.

Holiday Observances and Religious Music

The leading case on holiday programs in public schools is a 1980 decision from the U.S. Court of Appeals for the Eighth Circuit, whose geographic jurisdiction encompasses several midwestern states (*Florey v. Sioux Falls School District*). The case involved a school district policy advising teachers on how to address holidays that have both a religious and secular basis such as Christmas, Easter, Passover, and Hanukkah. The policy permitted teachers to recognize the religious nature of the holidays through references to art, music, literature, and religious symbols. The policy had been developed by a representative committee of various faiths in the community. In a 2–1 decision, the appeals court found the new policy had a secular purpose, did not advance religion, and did not excessively entangle the school and its teachers in religion.

The dissenting judge found the holiday program too closely tied to the Christian and Jewish faiths. His commentary has more relevance today now that nontraditional and many different belief systems are increasingly represented in school districts (p. 1324). While there are practical limits, the more encompassing a school district or charter school's holiday observance program is of faiths represented in the community, the more likely it will avoid criticism or legal action.

Sometimes lawsuits also involve religious music in school programs and events. The U.S. Court of Appeals for the Ninth Circuit confronted such a case involving a student in Washington State who sought to perform an instrumental version of "Ave Maria" at her high school graduation (*Nurre v. Whitehead*, 2009). The year before, the school district had received complaints from graduation attendees when it allowed the student choir to sing a vocal piece with references to "God," "heaven," and "angels." So, when the Wind Ensemble chose "Ave Maria," district officials directed that a secular piece be performed instead. The Ninth Circuit, whose jurisdiction encompasses Washington State, recognized that instrumental music without lyrics is a form of protected speech. And the school district did not challenge the student's assertion that a limited public forum existed at graduation because it allowed students to select musical pieces. The question was whether the district was justified in denying the selection of "Ave Maria." The Ninth Circuit held that the district did have such authority. In a key passage, the majority noted that "we confine our analysis to the narrow conclusion that when there is a captive audience at a graduation ceremony, which spans a finite amount of time, and during which the demand for equal time is so great that comparable nonreligious musical works might not be presented, it is reasonable for a school official to prohibit the performance of an obviously religious piece" (p. 1095). The majority found that the district's action served a secular governmental purpose, was neutral on the subject of religion, and did not constitute excessive entanglement with religion The U.S. Supreme Court refused to hear the case on appeal.

Graduation Prayer and Religious Speeches

In a seminal 1991 decision, the California Supreme Court ruled that school-sponsored invocations and benedictions at a high school graduation ceremony violate the state constitution (*Sands v. Morongo Unified School District*). The high court construed one of the three state constitutional provisions it considered, Article XVI, Section 5 as prohibiting "*any* official involvement that promotes religion" (italics in original). In short, the California Constitution asserts a very strong separation of church and state.

The next year, the U.S. Supreme Court came to the same conclusion regarding the U.S. Constitution in a case involving a middle school student who contested her principal's asking a rabbi to give a nondenominational invocation and benediction at her graduation ceremony (*Lee v. Weisman*, 1992). The majority in this 5–4 ruling viewed the principal's involvement in inviting the rabbi to give the prayer and then advising him to deliver a nondenominational prayer as impermissible government endorsement of religion. It made no difference that the prayer was nondenominational. Writing for the majority, Justice Anthony Kennedy noted, "The suggestion that government may establish an official or civic religion as a means of avoiding the establishment of a religion with more specific creeds strikes us as a contradiction that cannot be accepted" (p. 590). The majority also ruled that the prayer placed psychological coercion on nonbelievers. The fact that the student did not have to attend the graduation ceremony did not erase the coercion, because few students would choose to miss such an important event in their educational career. In his dissent, Justice Antonin Scalia decried the lack of sensitivity the majority exhibited toward the wishes of the majority of parents, students, and others attending graduation. But Justice Anthony Kennedy countered, "While in some societies the wishes of the majority might prevail, the Establishment Clause of the First Amendment is addressed to this contingency and rejects the balance urged upon us" (p. 596).

Can school officials turn the matter of invocation and benediction over to students and let them decide whether to have a prayer and, if so, to select someone to give it? In 2000, the Ninth Circuit dismissed a lawsuit filed against the Oroville Union School District after the district refused to permit the co-valedictorian to give a religious presentation and another student to give a sectarian invocation (*Cole v. Oroville Union High School District*). The pair subsequently delivered their proselytizing presentations in defiance of the directive. The Ninth Circuit ruled that the refusal to permit both the proselytizing invocation and valedictory speech was necessary to avoid breaching the establishment clause. The appeals court observed that the graduation ceremony is held on district property, financed with district funds, and only selected students are allowed to speak. The principal retains supervisory control and has final authority to approve speech topics. The school broadcasts the speech over a public address system. Given the control the school has over the graduation ceremony, allowing the student to give such a valedictory speech would constitute government endorsement of religion and have a coercive effect on nonbelievers. The two students were free to pray and promote their beliefs outside of school. In another case with nearly identical facts, the lawyer for the student graduation speaker suggested that the district could provide a disclaimer stating that the views of the student speakers do not represent those of the school district. But the school officials chose instead to excise offending portions of the speech. The student was permitted to distribute the unedited version of the speech outside the graduation ceremony. The student later filed suit against the school district and its officials, alleging violation of his First Amendment rights. As in the *Cole* decision, the Ninth Circuit affirmed the lower court's decision in favor of the district. "Although a disclaimer arguably distances school officials from 'sponsoring' speech, it does not change the fact that proselytizing amounts to a religious practice that the school district may not coerce other students to participate in, even while looking the other way," said the court (*Lassonde v. Pleasanton Unified School District*, 2003, pp. 984–985).

U.S. Department of Education guidelines provide the following:

> Where students or other private graduation speakers are selected on the basis of genuinely neutral, evenhanded criteria and retain control over the content of their expression . . . that expression is not attributable to the school and therefore may not be restricted because of its religious (or anti-religious) content. (U.S. Department of Education, *Guidance on Constitutionally Protected Prayer and Religious Expression in Public Elementary and Second Schools*, 2023)

The guidelines go on to assert that school officials may use disclaimers to clarify that such speech reflects the views of the speakers, not the school. In light of the Ninth Circuit rulings, the key phrase in the guidelines appears to be "retain control over the content of their expression." These rulings indicate that, because the graduation ceremony is a closed forum controlled by the school, the speakers do not retain such control.

Access of Religious Groups to Campus

Student religious groups and the Equal Access Act. Constitutional law precludes a public school from recognizing a student religious group as a school-sponsored organization. This is clear from a 1977 California appellate court ruling (*Johnson v. Huntington Beach Union High School District*). The court ruled that permitting a voluntary student Bible club to meet on the campus during the school day as a recognized student club with a faculty sponsor would have the primary effect of advancing religion and would create excessive entanglement between the school and religion.

As we discussed in Chapter 6, Congress enacted the Equal Access Act (EAA) in 1984, making it unlawful for any public secondary school that receives federal funding and has a limited open forum to deny any noncurricular-related group access to the campus during noninstructional time to engage in various forms of speech. In 1997 the Ninth Circuit ruled that noninstructional time includes an activities period during the day when classes do not meet. In that case, the appeals court ruled that a student religious club could meet at this time because other clubs were allowed to do so. Accommodating the club in this way does not constitute impermissible advancement of religion (*Ceniceros v. Board of Trustees of the San Diego Unified School District*).

In a later ruling, the Ninth Circuit permitted a student religious group to meet during "student/staff time" when individual student tutoring takes place (*Prince v. Jacoby*, 2002). While agreeing that the EAA does not require this degree of accommodation, two judges on the three-judge panel held that because the school district had permitted officially recognized Associated Student Body clubs to meet during this period, it could not engage in viewpoint discrimination under the First Amendment by preventing the student religious club and similar student-sponsored clubs from doing so. The dissenting judge argued that permitting a student group to conduct religious activities during instructional time violates the establishment clause. The *Prince* ruling is discussed in more detail later in this section.

In 1990, the U.S. Supreme Court upheld the EAA against a charge that it violates the establishment clause as applied to student religious groups that seek access under its terms to a public secondary school (*Board of Education of Westside Community Schools v. Mergens*). The Court ruled that the EAA does not violate the establishment clause because it does not extend just to student religious groups but to all groups regardless of the content of their speech. Further, the speech that is being protected by the EAA is private, not government, speech. Writing for the majority, Justice Sandra Day O'Connor added, "We think that secondary school students are mature enough and are likely to understand that a school does not endorse or support student speech that it merely permits on a nondiscriminatory basis" (p. 250).

The EAA requires that noncurricular groups must be student initiated. School personnel are prohibited from sponsoring their meetings and may be present at religious meetings only in a nonparticipatory capacity. The EAA also prohibits the district and its personnel from influencing the form or content of prayer or other religious activity or from requiring any person to participate in prayer or other religious activity. The school retains authority to maintain order and discipline and to ensure that student attendance is voluntary. School personnel may be asked to serve in a custodial role at meetings unless the content of the speech at such meetings conflicts with their beliefs. Nonschool persons may not direct, conduct, control, or even regularly attend activities of student groups. The school may restrict the times outsiders may attend meetings or deny access altogether.

Noncurricular student groups have access to the school media, including the public address system, school paper, and bulletin boards, to announce their meetings if the school grants similar groups access. The Ninth Circuit's *Prince* decision mentioned earlier addressed the extent to which this must be permitted for religious groups. The case involved the World Changers, a student religious group addressing issues of concern to students from the Gospel of Jesus Christ. The Spanaway Lake High School in Washington State had a policy distinguishing Associated Student Body (ASB) clubs from those clubs meeting under the terms of the EAA. Unlike ASB clubs, EAA clubs at the school did not have access to ASB funding, did not appear in the yearbook, could not meet during student or staff time, could not publicize events as extensively at school, and did not have the same access to school supplies, use of audiovisual equipment, and school vehicles for field trips. The World Changers challenged this as a form of discrimination under both the EAA and the First Amendment.

In a lengthy decision, the Ninth Circuit first discussed whether the school had violated the EAA. The court noted that the Spanaway Lake High School student council, not the school, controls the budgeting process for student groups and generates funds from sale of ASB cards and from fundraising events. Likewise, ASB-generated funds are used to produce the yearbook. Denying student religious groups access to ASB funding and making them pay for appearing in the school yearbook is a violation of the EAA. The court held that denial of the same access to the public address system and bulletin boards as ASB clubs also violates the EAA. However, as discussed earlier, the court ruled that the student religious club does not have a right under the EAA to meet during student and staff time, because instruction occurs then. Nor do non-ASB groups have a right under the EAA to school supplies, audiovisual equipment, or vehicles.

While such benefits are not available under the EAA, two members of the three-judge panel then went further to decide that they nevertheless must be provided because it would be a form of First Amendment viewpoint discrimination to deny them. In the words of the majority:

> Spanaway Lake High School has created a limited public forum in which student groups are free to meet during student/staff time, as well as to use school vehicles for field trips, to have priority for use of the AV equipment, and to use school supplies such as markers, posterboard, and paper (*Prince v. Jacoby*, 2002, p. 1091).

Therefore, without a compelling reason, the high school could not deny World Changers (and any other non-ASB group) the right to meet during student and staff time and have access to these benefits without violating the First Amendment. The majority rejected the school's claim that accommodating World Changers in this way would put the school in the position of advancing the religious mission of the club and thus violate the establishment clause. Treating World Changers in the same way as any other student club ensures neutrality, the majority noted. The fact that school supplies and school vehicles involve public funds rather than ASB student funds did not alter the outcome. Any concern the school might have about conveying the perception of endorsing the World Changers' religious mission could be dispelled "by making it clear to students that a club's private speech is not the speech of the school" (p. 1094). The dissenting judge agreed with the school district that allowing World Changers to meet during student and staff time and giving or lending the group supplies, AV equipment, and transportation on school vehicles advances its religious mission and thus violates the establishment clause.

The *Prince* decision applies to California and other states within the geographic jurisdiction of the Ninth Circuit. The decision seems to have blurred the distinction in *Mergens* between noncurricular and curricular student clubs by permitting both to meet during student/staff time and to benefit from nonschool funds controlled by the student council. It may be that a more direct form of public funding would breach the federal or state constitution.

In another case originating in Washington State, the Ninth Circuit sided with the school district when the district backed its Associated Student Body (ASB) Council's refusal to grant a charter to a student religious club called Truth (*Truth v. Kent School District*, 2008). Without the charter, the club could not be a recognized student club at the school. The club divided its membership into three categories: attendees, nonvoting members, and voting members. Becoming an attendee or nonvoting member was contingent on a student's complying in good faith with Christian character, Christian speech, Christian behavior, and Christian conduct as described in the Bible. To be a voting member or an officer, a student had to sign a "statement of faith" requiring an affirmation that the student believes "the Bible to be the inspired, the only infallible, authoritative Word of God." The member also had to pledge that he or she believes "that salvation is an undeserved gift from God" and that only by "acceptance of Jesus Christ as my personal Savior, through His death on the cross for my sins, is my faith made real" (p. 639).

ASB and the school district require equal educational treatment without regard to race, creed, and other statuses. *Creed* encompasses religious beliefs. The Ninth Circuit agreed with the school district and lower court that Truth's membership requirements violated the school district's nondiscrimination policies and were not protected by the First Amendment. The court also found such action consistent with the terms of the Equal Access Act because the district's action in denying access to Truth was not based on the club's religious speech but rather on its discriminatory membership criteria. The court noted that two other Bible clubs at the school receiving ASB recognition did not have membership requirements at odds with the district's nondiscrimination policies. However, the case was sent back to the trial court for a determination if Truth could prove its contention that other clubs were granted exemptions from the nondiscrimination policy while it was not because of its religious character and speech. Later, the U.S. Supreme Court overruled this decision but not on grounds relating to religion. Then in 2010 the high court affirmed a Ninth Circuit decision that relied on *Truth* in upholding the decision allowing the University of California, College of the Law, San Francisco to reject the application of the Christian Legal Society for status as a recognized student organization because it barred students based on religion and sexual orientation (*Christian Legal Society v. Martinez*).

This approach changed dramatically in 2023. The "accept all-comers" rule in *Truth* as a condition for approving student organizations was overturned by the Ninth Circuit Court of Appeals in *Fellowship of Christian Athletes v. San Jose Unified School District*. In this case, the Fellowship of Christian Athletes sought to form a club at Pioneer High School. The school refused on the grounds the club required a belief in Christianity and excluded homosexuals, contrary to its "all-comers" policy. However, the Ninth Circuit majority noted that the school allowed secular clubs like the Senior Women club and South Asian Heritage Club to maintain discriminatory membership requirements. The school also conceded that a hypothetical Republican Club would be approved even if it required members adhere to the Republican platform. Additionally, the record showed the school was motivated by hostility to religion, including labeling FCA members as "charlatans" who "chose darkness" and "perpetuated ignorance." Therefore, the school's policy was not neutral and generally applicable, but unconstitutionally singled out religion for disfavor. Going forward, public schools will not be able to refuse recognition to religious clubs, even ones that use discriminatory membership criteria.

Teaching about religion in a public school classroom is entirely appropriate; but promoting it is not. This distinction is evident in a U.S. Supreme Court ruling that displaying a religious symbol like the Ten Commandments in the classroom is impermissible (*Stone v. Graham*, 1980). It did not matter that private contributions underwrote the cost of implementing the statute, nor that the statute required a notation on the display to the effect that "the secular application of the

Ten Commandments is clearly seen in its adoption as the fundamental legal code of Western Civilization and the Common Law of the United States" (p. 41). In an unsigned opinion, five justices wrote that the statute lacked a secular purpose because the Ten Commandments is undeniably a sacred text in the Jewish and Christian faiths and because several of the commandments address religious duties of believers (e.g., worshiping the Lord God alone, avoiding idolatry, not using the Lord's name in vain, and observing the Sabbath Day). However, the Court recognized that the Ten Commandments can be included as a topic of study within the school curriculum. In 2005, the U.S. Supreme Court distinguished displaying the Ten Commandments in public school classrooms from displaying them on other government property, noting that *Stone* "stands as an example of the fact that we have 'been particularly vigilant in monitoring compliance with the Establishment Clause in elementary and secondary schools'" (*Van Orden v. Perry*, 2005, p. 691).

Community use policies. The U.S. Supreme Court ruled unanimously in 1993 that the First Amendment prevents a school district from denying a religious group access to its facilities if it permits other organizations to use them under the terms of a community use policy (*Lamb's Chapel v. Center Moriches Union Free School District*). In effect, the district has created a limited open forum. As described in Chapter 6, a limited open forum accommodates certain categories of expression but not others. With regard to those categories of expression that are permitted, there can be no discrimination based on the viewpoints being expressed.

Subject to conditions set forth in the statute and the rules and regulations of the governing board, California's Civic Center Act provides that school districts may allow community groups to use their buildings and grounds for recreational, educational, political, economic, artistic, or moral activities including the conduct of religious services by churches that have no suitable meeting place (Educ. Code § 38130 et seq.). School districts are required to authorize the use of their facilities or grounds to nonprofit organizations, clubs, and associations such as the Girl Scouts and Boy Scouts that promote youth and school activities when an alternative location is not available (Educ. Code § 38134). In effect, public school districts in this state are limited open forums under the terms of the Civic Center Act.

The basic principles involved in administering a limited open forum surfaced in a 1999 Ninth Circuit decision. The case centered on whether the Downey Unified School District's refusal to post a local businessperson's sign containing the text of the Ten Commandments on a fence surrounding the high school's baseball field was a violation of the First Amendment. The district permitted commercial advertisements for fund-raising purposes but excluded ads it deemed inappropriate for the secondary school. Accordingly, advertisements promoting alcohol and taverns were refused, as was a Planned Parenthood advertisement. Additionally, the district asserted that permitting the posting of a sign with the Ten Commandments would violate the establishment clause and might cause disruption.

In upholding the lower court's ruling in favor of the district, the Ninth Circuit ruled that the district had not designated the fence as a public forum for any form of expressive activity. Rather, it had created a limited open forum that excluded certain categories of speech. Accordingly, the district had to cite only a reasonable basis for excluding the Ten Commandments sign. It had done so by citing its desire to avoid disruption and the possibility of litigation that would undercut the purpose of posting ads in the first place. The district's action did not constitute viewpoint discrimination because it limited posting to commercial advertisements, and the contested sign was not commercial. Nor did the district's decision to stop posting advertisements altogether in response to the litigation constitute viewpoint discrimination (*DiLoreto v. Downey Unified School District Board of Education*, 1999). A few months earlier, a California court of appeal had ruled similarly in the case with regard to the state constitution. That court held that posting the advertisement would have violated Article I, Section 4, preventing establishment of religion and that the refusal to do so did not violate either the free exercise of religion provision in that section or the free speech provision of Article I, Section 2 (*DiLoreto v. Board of Education*, 1999).

The wording of community use policies is critical for determining what kinds of communication and activity are allowed on public school grounds and what are not. The Good News Club was a private Christian organization for children ages six to twelve and wanted to hold after-school meetings in the school cafeteria.

The U.S. Supreme Court decided in a 6–3 decision that the exclusion of the Good News Club constituted impermissible viewpoint discrimination under the First Amendment (*Good News Club v. Milford Central School*, 2001). The majority noted that the district had established a limited open forum by permitting outside groups to meet on school facilities for educational and recreational purposes. The Court found no establishment clause justification for the district permitting secular organizations to address character and moral development but denying access to organizations addressing the same concerns from a religious perspective. The meetings were to be held after school, not sponsored by the school, and not limited just to Good News Club members.

The majority rejected the school's concern about conveying a message of religious endorsement to impressionable children. The relevant audience was parents, not children, because parents had to give permission for their children to participate. Further, the meetings were not held in an elementary school classroom but in a combined high school resource room and middle school special education room. Because the meetings were held after school, no students or teachers were present. The Good News Club instructor was not a teacher, and the students were from six to twelve years old. Excluding the club, the Court observed, could be perceived as a message of hostility toward religion.

The Ninth Circuit later applied the *Good News Club* precedent to an Oregon school district that similarly excluded the Good News Club from holding meetings after school at an elementary school serving children from kindergarten through grade three. Pursuant to a state law similar to California's Civic Center Act, the district had adopted a policy encouraging the use of school buildings at no cost for educational and recreational purposes. A number of groups met at the elementary school after school hours, including the Birth-to-Three program, Cub Scouts, and the Upper Willamette Youth sports program. With one modification, the Ninth Circuit affirmed the lower court's decision in favor of the Child Evangelism Fellowship of Oregon, which had applied as a sponsor of the Good News Club. The appeals court observed that requiring teachers to hand out permission slips puts them in the position of advancing the religious mission of the club. This would be a violation of the establishment clause. However, teachers could hand out the club's brochures just as they did for other organizations (*Culbertson v. Oakridge School District No. 76*, 2001).

Just two years later, the Ninth Circuit revisited the matter of community use policies. The decision in *Hills v. Scottsdale Unified School District No. 48* (2003) illustrates the complexity of designing and administering such policies. In this case, the district had a policy and practice of allowing nonprofit outside groups to distribute or display brochures and other promotional literature to students. But material of a commercial, political, or religious nature was not allowed. Hills, the organizer of a nonprofit summer camp, sought to advertise his camp by distributing a flyer at the district's elementary schools. In the flyer, he described the courses to be offered, including two addressing religious subjects. Both courses emphasized coming to know Jesus Christ and the importance of Bible reading. The school district halted the distribution and then permitted it with the addition of a disclaimer. Later, it changed its mind and again disallowed distribution until Hills changed the brochure to, among other things, remove descriptions of the Bible classes. Hills filed suit, contending that the district's actions violated his rights to freedom of speech and religious exercise.

The Ninth Circuit found the application of the district's community use policy flawed. Based on testimony of school officials, the judges concluded that the district had created a limited open forum for community announcements that were intended to notify students and their parents of extracurricular activities or issues of general interest to all students. Having done so, a refusal to permit Hills to circulate his camp brochure constituted viewpoint discrimination. The judges noted that the district had conceded that summer camps are permissible subjects and so too the Bible if taught as history or literature. Thus, the district could not refuse outright to permit Hills to distribute the brochure.

However, the judges noted that the district could exercise some control over the contents of what Hills intended to communicate. For example, the court noted that the district could restrict some of the phrasing that exhorted the reader to involve children in religious observance. Said the court, "The District cannot refuse to distribute literature advertising a program with underlying religious content when it distributes quite similar literature for secular summer camps, but it can refuse to distribute literature that itself contains proselytizing language." The court added, "The difference is subtle, but important" (p. 1053). A concern that the court did not address is whether there may be a violation of the establishment clause when school officials begin reviewing the contents of religious materials and deciding what is and what is not permissible.

Given the Civic Center Act, school districts in California appear not to have the option of declaring their facilities and grounds to be closed to outside nonprofit groups that promote youth and school activities. But governing boards do have the authority to develop rules and regulations governing their use. Therefore, it is important to consider legal implications when drafting a community use policy and advising school officials on how to enforce it so that violations of free speech and free exercise of religion do not occur. In deciding the *Hills* case, the Ninth Circuit recognized the complexity of the matter but agreed with the observation of the Seventh Circuit that "The school's proper response is to educate the audience rather than squelch the speaker. . . . Schools may explain that they do not endorse speech by permitting it" (*Hedges v. Wauconda Community Unit School District No. 118*, 1993, pp. 1299–1300).

Religiously Based Exemptions

The California Education Code has several provisions dealing with religiously based exemptions. Public school students are exempt from school attendance for, among other things, observance of a religious holiday or ceremony or attendance at religious retreats (Educ. Code § 48205). Attendance at the latter is limited to four hours per semester. Governing boards have the discretion to give students excused absences for receiving moral or religious instruction off school grounds with the consent of their parents for up to four days a month (Educ. Code § 46014). The

U.S. Supreme Court has upheld such released-time programs (*Zorach v. Clauson*, 1952). A California court of appeal ruled similarly with respect to the state constitution in 1947 (*Gordon v. Board of Education of the City of Los Angeles*). Teachers have the right to opt out of school district evaluations and surveys that ask about religious beliefs (Educ. Code § 49091.24). Teachers also may opt out of teaching weekend classes if doing so would conflict with their religious beliefs or practices (Educ. Code § 44824).

The extent to which parents can rely on religion to seek exemptions for their children from public school programs and activities has generated litigation. In 1985, the Ninth Circuit faced the question whether a school district's refusal to remove the novel *The Learning Tree*, by Gordon Parks, from the sophomore English literature curriculum violated the free exercise rights of an objecting parent (*Grove v. Mead School District No. 354*). The book looks at the world through the eyes of a Black teenage boy from a working-class family. The appeals court noted no significant intrusion on the student's religion because she had been given an exemption from reading the book. Additionally, she could leave the class when the book was discussed, although she chose not to do so. The judges pointed out that if everything objectionable to someone had to be eliminated from the public school curriculum, nothing would be left. The parents also argued that including the book violated the establishment clause because it advanced secular humanism. The court rejected the contention, noting that *The Learning Tree* was religiously neutral. The key to the outcome in this case was the fact that the student had been given an exemption. In Chapter 1, we discussed how the Old Order Amish were successful in convincing the U.S. Supreme Court that their religious beliefs and practice justified exempting their children from school attendance beyond the eighth grade, an exemption that has not been accorded to other belief systems (*Wisconsin v. Yoder*, 1972). More recently, the U.S. Supreme Court has ruled that the free exercise of religion, which was the basis of the *Yoder* decision, cannot provide an exemption from a neutral and generally applied law (*Employment Division, Department of Human Resources v. Smith*, 1990). But what about the *Yoder* decision, which provided an exemption from the compulsory school law for the Old Order Amish, based on their religion? The Court avoided overruling *Yoder* by pointing out that *two* rights were involved in that case—the parent's right to control their child's upbringing *and* the religious beliefs of the Old Order Amish—thus constituting a "hybrid" claim.

The hybrid claim has received a mixed reception from federal appellate courts. For example, the Tenth Circuit observed in 1998 that merely invoking the parental rights doctrine in combination with a free exercise claim will not suffice (*Swanson*

v. *Guthrie Independent School District*). "Whatever the *Smith* hybrid-rights theory may ultimately mean," the judges wrote, "we believe that it at least requires a colorable showing of infringement of recognized and specific constitutional rights, rather than the mere invocation of a general right such as the right to control the education of one's child" (p. 700). The case involved the Oklahoma parents of a homeschooled student who argued that the school district's refusal to permit the child to attend part-time violated their rights. The appeals court rejected the contention.

Citing this ruling, the Ninth Circuit decided against Nevada parents who cited parental rights in combination with the Individuals with Disabilities Education Act (IDEA) in support of a reimbursement claim for speech therapy services for their homeschooled child with a disability (*Hooks v. Clark County School District*, 2000). The Ninth Circuit noted that IDEA leaves to the states the question of whether home education constitutes a private institution for purposes of receiving IDEA services and that parents do not have the right to pick and choose the services they wish from a school district.

In summary, there is no assurance that religion can provide the basis for an exemption to activities that public schools require of all students, even when coupled with parental rights. Parents who strongly oppose the experiences of their children within public schools on religious grounds may enroll their children in religious private schools. The problem for most families, however, is the high cost of private education.

Transgender Students, Public Schools, and Religion

California Education Code Section 220 says no person shall be subjected to discrimination on the basis of, among other categories, "gender, gender identity, and gender expression." Section 221.5 additionally states that pupils will be allowed to participate in sports and use facilities consistent with gender identity, irrespective of gender listed on the pupil's records. Finally, guidelines issued by the California School Boards Association in October 2022 states that schools are required, with rare exceptions, to "respect the limitations that a student places on the disclosure of the student's transgender status and consider the student's privacy rights and safety associated with this information, including not sharing that information with the student's parents." These strong protections have seen considerable litigation, although little published precedent at the present time.

In May 2024, Jurupa Valley High School in Riverside County settled for $360,000 a lawsuit filed by a former teacher who says she was fired because she stated she would refuse to use students' preferred pronouns, to allow them to use the locker room matching their gender identity, or to "withhold information" from parents about their child's gender identity. The teacher never actually took these actions. However, she was fired after making social media posts some students found offensive and refusing, based on her Christian beliefs, to curb her posting and follow district policy on transgender students. As part of the settlement, the teacher agreed to not seek future employment with the district.

Partly in response to such lawsuits, California Attorney General Rob Bonta sued Chino Valley School Board for adopting a policy that requires parents be informed if a pupil identifies as a gender other than that on official records. Chino Valley's policy is contrary to current California law but could be viewed sympathetically by a more conservative Supreme Court, depending on how broadly it interprets the right of parental control in *Pierce v. Society of Sisters*. This lawsuit is still pending as of 2024.

In *Regino v. Staley* (2023), the Eastern District of California dismissed a lawsuit by a parent challenging the school's policy of not disclosing gender transitions by pupils to parents. The court found that there was no precedent establishing a fundamental parental right to knowledge of a pupil's gender transition and the California's policy was supportable on a rational basis.

Issues relating to gender identity and particularly transgender students should be watched carefully as the law on this topic is very fluid presently.

AID TO RELIGIOUS PRIVATE SCHOOLS

In many states with sizable numbers of private schools and legislatures populated by their graduates, efforts have long been made to channel public funding to private schools. As discussed at the beginning of the chapter, the U.S. Supreme Court's first major case involving religion and education dealt with a New Jersey statute underwriting the cost of bus transportation to private schools (*Everson v. Board of Education*, 1947). Rather than seeing this program as advancing the religious mission of the private school, the majority of justices viewed it as a pupil benefit program. The state was doing nothing more than assuring that all students got to and from school safely. A California court of appeal took the same position a year earlier in upholding a similar state law against a charge that it violated the state constitution (*Bowker v. Baker*, 1946).

Currently, California Education Code Section 39808 permits the governing board of a school district to provide transportation to students attending private schools upon the same terms, in the same manner, and over the same routes as public school students. However, the statute does not permit providing transportation reimbursement money to parents or guardians of students attending private schools. In addition, Education Code Section 37253 permits districts to offer supplemental instruction in core academic areas at various times, including the summer. The attorney general has advised that private school students can be permitted to attend during the summer because the primary beneficiaries are the students and parents, not the private schools. However, the attorney general issued a word of caution that doing so should not substantially benefit private schools by, for example, relieving them of having to provide courses (70 Op. Atty. Gen. 282, 1987).

Direct Aid Programs

Beyond police and fire protection and student transportation, private schools in California receive few direct financial benefits from the state. The U.S. Supreme Court upheld a New York law authorizing public school authorities to lend secular textbooks free of charge to private school students (*Board of Education v. Allen*, 1968). But a similar effort failed in this state before the California Supreme Court in 1981 (*California Teachers Association v. Riles*). Wrote the judges in a unanimous decision, "It is not the meaning of the First Amendment which is critical to our determination, but section 8 article IX and section 5 of article XVI of the California Constitution" (p. 311). Those provisions require that public funds must be spent for public schools and specifically prohibit appropriations that help support or sustain schools controlled by religious organizations. Unlike police and fire protection, the court found that the provision of textbooks would advance the educational mission of the religious private school and thus be clearly unconstitutional.

Direct aid cases have come before the U.S. Supreme Court, and the Court has responded over the years with rulings that often seem contradictory. Two such rulings well portray the current stance of the Court regarding direct assistance to religious and nonreligious private schools. In 1997 the Court in a 5–4 ruling upheld the use of public school teachers to deliver remedial instruction to educationally at-risk children on the premises of private schools under Title I of the Elementary and Secondary Education Act, overturning an earlier ruling to the contrary. The majority noted that the aid was not being used to advance the religious mission of the private schools (*Agostini v. Felton*). A number of California private schools have students who receive Title I services in this manner. In deciding this case, the justices modified the guidelines for deciding direct aid cases. First, there must be a secular purpose. Then it must be determined whether the aid has the effect of advancing religion. To determine the latter, three criteria must be addressed: whether the aid results in government indoctrination, whether it defines recipients by reference to religion, and whether it creates excessive entanglement between government and religion.

The Court used these criteria three years later to uphold the lending of educational materials such as computer hardware and software, library materials, and reference and curriculum materials to private schools under the Education Consolidation and Improvement Act of 1981 (*Mitchell v. Helms*, 2000). Chapter 2 of that law permits the federal government to channel funds to state educational agencies, and through them, to local education agencies. The local educational agency uses the funds to purchase the materials and then loans them to both public and private schools. The program was deemed secular because it provides money for both public and private education. In providing the key fifth vote to the majority, Justice Sandra Day O'Connor observed that the program only loans the materials to the private schools and requires that the materials must be secular, neutral, and nonideological. Thus, Chapter 2 money never reaches the coffers of religious schools. The other four justices in the majority, however, went further to maintain that even if the materials were used for sectarian purposes, that would not violate the establishment clause. In effect, this approach would eliminate the distinction between direct aid and indirect aid and permit unrestricted expenditure of public money in private religious schools.

More recent cases prove this point. In 2017, U.S. Supreme Court ruled against the state of Missouri, finding that the state violated the free exercise clause when it excluded a religious school from a grant program for playground resurfacing (*Trinity Lutheran Church of Columbia, Inc.*). In the Court's opinion, Chief Justice Roberts very narrowly limited the holding to playground resurfacing, something that does not come up often and is unlikely to recur in that manner. But it opened the door.

Indirect Aid Programs Through Vouchers and Tax Credits

Indirect aid does not raise the same constitutional concerns as direct aid because funding arrives at religious and other private schools via the decisions of other than the government. The U.S. Supreme Court relied on this rationale to breathe new life into the voucher movement by upholding the Pilot Project Scholarship Program for children in the failing Cleveland public school system against a challenge that it constituted impermissible aid to religious private schools in violation of the establishment clause of the federal constitution (*Zelman v. Simmons-Harris*, 2002). While parents had a choice of out-of-district public schools, none chose to participate. Ninety-six percent of the scholarship recipients enrolled in religious private schools. The majority in the 5–4 decision found the fact that parents had a range of choices encompassing traditional public schools, magnet schools, and charter schools and that funding flowed through parents to the private schools diminished concern about advancing religion. Writing for the majority, Chief Justice Rehnquist cited earlier rulings in observing that,

> where a government aid program is neutral with respect to religion, and provides assistance directly to a broad class of citizens who, in turn, direct government aid to religious schools wholly as a result of their own genuine and independent private choice, the program is not readily subject to challenge under the Establishment Clause (p. 652).

Thereafter, voucher measures were introduced in a number of state legislatures. However, about one-third of the states including California have strict provisions against the establishment of religion in their state constitutions. The possible continued viability of these provisions came before the Supreme Court in two recent cases.

But in 2020, Chief Justice Roberts wrote for the majority in *Espinoza v. Montana Department of Revenue*, finding that the state excluding a private religious school from a scholarship program that was open to private school students was discriminatory. Then in 2025, the U.S. Supreme Court split 4–4 as to whether the state of Oklahoma could approve a Catholic charter school and support it from public funds previously restricted to public schools (including nonsectarian charter schools). Because there was no clear majority, the underlying decision against allowing this expansion held. But expect more challenges similar to this.

As noted in Chapter 1, Californians decidedly voted down voucher initiatives on two occasions. In other states, legislatures have looked at individual income tax credits as a way of enabling parents to enroll their children in private schools. It is argued that income tax credits are more likely to be considered private, not government, money and thus less vulnerable to state constitutional attack than are state-funded vouchers. Because they are not government funds, tax credits are less likely to be accompanied by restrictive regulatory measures imposed on private schools.

A general tuition tax credit has a distinct advantage over the individual tax credit. Any taxpayer, including corporations, can obtain a tax credit for making contributions to a tuition scholarship fund. As a result, the amount of accumulated money is likely to be much greater. In 2006 the Arizona Legislature expanded its individual tuition tax credit program to encompass a general tuition tax credit program whereby businesses can donate up to a certain level for private school tuition grants handed out by school tuition organizations (STO). An Arizona court of appeals upheld the program in 2009 against a number of challenges (*Green v.*

Garriott, 2009). Whether there will be any interest in a similar program in California and how it might fare in the state courts remains to be seen.

As the battles over state initiatives demonstrate, any program that expands school choice to encompass private schools will encounter strong views on both sides of the question.

SUMMARY

Conflict over the role of religion in public schooling is unlikely to abate any time soon. For this reason, school leadership should check for current case law before making decisions. While this chapter has covered many facets of religion and schooling, several key points are worth repeating.

First, while public schools cannot promote prayer, nothing precludes students from engaging in nondisruptive private religious discussion and prayer outside of classroom instructional time. The same is true of employees, though teachers and others in direct contact with students need to be especially circumspect in not conveying the impression of religious endorsement.

Second, schools can teach about religion but cannot teach religion. The incorporation of religious materials, artifacts, and music in the instructional program and during holiday observances is appropriate as part of a secular program of instruction. Whether students can write papers and give presentations on religious topics depends on the purpose of the assignment. If such topics would serve the goals of the lesson plan, then students cannot be denied the opportunity to do so lest the school and its officials portray hostility toward religion. However, in accord with Ninth Circuit rulings, student speeches on religious topics at graduation ceremonies, along with an invocation and benediction, breach the separation of church and state in both the federal and California constitutions.

Third, aside from several statutory exemptions (such as sex education), parents generally do not have a right to exempt their children from curricular activities to which they object on religious grounds when those activities are required of all students as part of a secular program of instruction.

Finally, while public schools cannot sponsor student religious organizations, such organizations have a right under the federal Equal Access Act as noncurricular groups to meet on campus during noninstructional time at public secondary schools and may have a similar right at public elementary schools under the terms of the district and school's community use policy. Religious organizations may be allowed access to a school's campus and facilities under the terms of the California Civic Center Act and in compliance with a school district's community use policy.

Private schools receive few benefits from the state of California. One of these is that school districts have the discretion to provide transportation to children attending private schools and to include them in a supplementary summer school program. Federal assistance to religious private schools that is routed through state, county, and local educational agencies for the education of certain categories of students does not violate the establishment clause of the First Amendment. Giving parents publicly funded vouchers for tuition expenses at religious private schools in combination with other choice programs is permissible under the federal Constitution but not under the California Constitution. How the California Legislature and judiciary will respond to efforts to privatize public education will likely remain a contentious and litigious subject.

8 STUDENTS WITH DISABILITIES

Federal special education law brought sweeping changes to public education, a matter historically often left to the states. This chapter explores the events and movements spurring federal special education law into existence, followed by the extensive statutes and rules of special education under federal and state law. The chapter covers a discussion of what is meant by a free appropriate public education (FAPE), and how students are located, referred for initial evaluation, and determined eligible for special education under the Individuals with Disabilities Education Act (IDEA). The role, composition, and requirements of individualized education program (IEP) teams are detailed and precede an explanation of the contents of an IEP. A comment on behavior-related plans and services, mental health services, transition plans and services, and private school students follows. An overview of the impact of the Americans with Disabilities Act (ADA) and Section 504 of the Rehabilitation Act of 1973 (Section 504) concludes the chapter. This chapter is not the final word on these topics but an introduction to their general contours and requirements. Readers desiring greater specificity should reference the resources noted in the appendix and consider consultation with experienced legal professionals.

Special education law is an amalgamation of hundreds of pages of statutes, regulations, judicial and administrative decisions, and administrative guidance.

SPECIAL EDUCATION LAW

A Brief History

Federal and state laws afford special education students numerous protections and entitlements that are not available to general education students. Among these are a guarantee for a particular type and level of education (depending on identified needs), numerous procedural safeguards, and recourse to an administrative hearing process to challenge any aspect of the educational program offered by the school district. To those first encountering these laws, a simple question may arise: Why does special education law exist?

In 1970, it has been estimated that United States public schools excluded 1 in 5 children with disabilities—and that number likely is low. Congress acted under its Spending Clause power, providing funding for states if they agreed to develop a plan for children with disabilities and then implement it. That law, the 1970 Education of the Handicapped Act (EHA) conferred upon students an enforceable substantive right to public education in participating states, meaning states that received the funding must comply with the provisions of the Act.

At about the same time, two important cases were heard in federal District Courts: *Pennsylvania Association of Retarded Children (PARC) v. Commonwealth of Pennsylvania* (1972) and *Mills v. Board of Education of the District of Columbia* (1972). In 1972, the two respective courts found that children with disabilities often were either served poorly, frequently segregated from more typical children, or not educated at all. PARC and Mills are considered the definitive cases where disability law for children in public schools began to emerge. Both cases had far-reaching effects, establishing what is called the "zero-reject principle."

The zero-reject principle has continued to guide the law relating to children with disabilities in states receiving federal funds. Simply stated, it means that every child with a disability has a right to an education, regardless of the severity of the disability. Note that theoretically the federal guarantee applies only to participating states, but every state has long accepted the funding. Additionally, many states have their own guarantee as found in the state's own statutes. Thus, all children with identified disabilities and corresponding needs must be educated.

The minor plaintiffs in *PARC* did not have access to a public education because they were "mentally retarded." Under Pennsylvania law at the time, the state board of education was not obligated to educate any child whom a public school psychologist certified as uneducable or untrainable. After such a certification, the state's burden to care for the child shifted to the Department of Welfare, which had no obligation to provide any educational services. These children had no place in a Pennsylvania public school.

The plaintiffs in *PARC* argued that this and other similar Pennsylvania laws violated the due process and equal protection clauses of the U.S. Constitution. The plaintiffs argued that due process was denied because their children were excluded from a public education without any notice or a hearing to challenge the exclusion.

The equal protection argument was aimed at the state's current practice of providing a public education to nondisabled children while denying that education to mentally retarded children. *PARC* ended in a judicial consent decree repealing the exclusionary laws and practices at issue. A consent decree is an agreement between parties that is approved and enforced by the court. This ensures compliance. The historical significance of *PARC* extends beyond its then-immediate impact on Pennsylvania law. Some of the key terms and conditions in the *PARC* consent decree influenced Congress in its deliberation and drafting of the nation's first federal special education law years later.

Mills also dealt with the exclusion of children with disabilities from public education. The named plaintiff, Peter Mills, was in the fourth grade when he was identified by the principal as a "behavior problem." Without a full hearing or review, Peter was approved for exclusion from public education without any other publicly funded educational alternatives. Unlike *PARC*, laws already existed in the District of Columbia providing for the education of children with disabilities and due process protections prior to their removal from school. The board of education, as it admitted in court, simply failed to follow these laws. In response to the plaintiffs' due process and equal protection arguments, the defendants made a single argument: We do not have the money to provide special education. The court made short work of this defense, noting that limited financial resources must be spread equitably among all students.

The court ordered the board of education to provide "each child of school age a free and suitable publicly supported education regardless of the degree of the child's mental, physical, or emotional disability or impairment" (p. 878). The order forbade the practice of exclusion from public school without a hearing and set the board of education to the task of notifying thousands of parents that their children, regardless of their disability, were entitled to a public education. To this end, newspaper and radio advertisements ran for weeks after the decision.

PARC and *Mills* brought reforms to the school districts within Pennsylvania and the District of Columbia. Nationwide, however, there was no uniformity among state laws in how children with disabilities were, if at all, educated. All of this changed in 1975 with passage of the Education for All Handicapped Children Act (P.L. 94-142) (EAHCA or, more commonly, simply EHA). Congressional findings preceding the EHA noted the widespread nature of the circumstances litigated in *PARC* and *Mills*. The House Report accompanying the EHA's enactment set out the grim statistics. In 1974, over 1.75 million children with disabilities did not receive any educational services (H.R. Rep. 94–332, p. 11). Of those attending school, approximately 2.5 million were not receiving appropriate services and were "left to fend for themselves in classrooms designed for education of their nonhandicapped peers" (*Board of Education v. Rowley*, 1982, p. 191, discussed in depth below). Millions of children with disabilities "were either totally excluded from schools or [were] sitting idly in regular classrooms awaiting the time when they were old enough to 'drop out'" (H.R. Rep. No. 94-332, p. 2).

To address these inequities, the EHA made federal money available to states in return for a promise to abide by the EHA's requirements. Many of the EHA's core requirements came from *PARC* and *Mills*. School districts were charged with locating and evaluating students for receipt of special education services. The EHA guaranteed eligible students a free appropriate public education (FAPE), comprised of special education and related services. The requirement of individualized education program team meetings for making decisions regarding a child's special education program was codified into the law. The IEP team was required to detail the student's educational program in a written document entitled "individualized education program." Parental involvement in their child's special education program was mandated. Special education students were to be placed with their nondisabled peers to the maximum extent appropriate. The EHA contained a procedural framework to ensure parent participation and timely compliance with the law's requirements. Parents also were given an administrative hearing process for bringing grievances regarding their child's educational program.

Congress enacted the EHA to remedy the inequalities in public education facing disabled children and their families. In signing the EHA in 1975, however, President Gerald Ford acknowledged some of the concerns that had been raised regarding the expense and administrative burden of this new law:

> Unfortunately, this bill promises more than the federal government can deliver.... Everyone can agree with the objective in the bill—educating all handicapped children in our nation. The key question is whether the bill will really accomplish that objective.

President Ford's concerns remain as pressing today as they did over four decades ago. Despite authorizing federal funding up to 40 percent, Congress has never appropriated more than 20 percent to the states. The funding shortfall is absorbed by states and local school districts. Some special educators and school administrators feel as though the majority of their time is spent not educating but performing the myriad administrative tasks necessary to ensure compliance with IDEA's procedural requirements. Disagreements between parents and school districts are increasingly subject to timely and expensive litigation, both at the administrative and federal court levels.

These criticisms are shaping the modern debate over IDEA, which Congress last reauthorized in 2004 with the passage of the Individuals with Disabilities Education Improvement Act of 2004 (IDEA 2004). It took two more years before the U.S. Department of Education's Office of Special Education and Rehabilitative Services published new regulations for IDEA 2004—one indication of the mixed views on almost every element of the statute and regulations.

Sources of Special Education Law

Reflecting on the structure of school law as described in Chapter 1, we can divide the sources of special education law into three categories: statutory, administrative, and judicial law. At the federal level, IDEA is the vehicle through which Congress seeks to "open the doors of public education to handicapped children." IDEA sets forth the rights of eligible students, their parents, and the obligations of covered public entities for every aspect of special education law. The U.S. Department of Education (USDOE) publishes comprehensive regulations interpreting IDEA. The complete text of IDEA and its implementing regulations can be found in Title 20 U.S. Code, Section 1400 and following sections, and in the Code of Federal Regulations, Chapter 34, Part 300. The Office of Special Education Programs (OSEP) provides administrative guidance on how to interpret IDEA. OSEP's opinion may be relied on as persuasive, but not binding, legal authority by courts.

At the state level, California Education Code Section 56000 and following sections contain parallel provisions to IDEA. Title 5 of the California Code of Regulations contains specific regulations enacted by the State Board of Education (SBE) detailing the implementation of various provisions of the Education Code. The Office of Administrative Hearings (OAH) conducts administrative hearings applying these state and federal laws to disputes between parents and school districts. Unlike judicial decisions, OAH decisions do not create legal precedent binding other OAH administrative law judges (ALJ), although the hearing office presumably has guidelines for ALJs to follow. OAH decisions are considered nonbinding, persuasive authority by OAH administrative law judges in future hearings. OAH decisions can be appealed to state and federal district courts in California, and then further in the federal system all the way to the U.S. Supreme Court.

IDEA applies to each state that receives federal funding under the statute. IDEA's coverage thereafter extends to all political subdivisions of the state that are involved in the education of children with disabilities. These include the state educational agency, local educational agencies, state schools for children with disabilities, and state and local juvenile and adult correctional facilities. School districts are understandably the primary public entity subject to IDEA's requirements.

Charter schools that are deemed a local educational agency (LEA) are also directly responsible for complying with IDEA. Education Code Sections 47640 and 47641 define when a charter school is a LEA for purposes of IDEA responsibility. The key inquiry is whether the charter school elected to be a LEA in its petition for establishment or renewal of its charter (Educ. Code § 47641(a)). As a LEA, a charter school is essentially an independent entity for purposes of complying with IDEA and attendant Education Code sections. A charter school that is not a LEA is deemed a "school of the district" of the LEA that granted the charter (Educ. Code § 47641(b)). In this latter situation, the school district granting the charter remains responsible for ensuring the charter school's IDEA compliance (e.g., funding educational programs and being subject to a due process hearing when a dispute arises). The SBE also can grant a charter to a charter school but delegate oversight of the charter school to a school district. In this situation, the school district must ensure the charter school's adherence to IDEA.

IDEA's procedural and substantive rights extend to a child with a disability and the child's parent. The California Education Code uses the phrase "individual with exceptional needs" in lieu of "child with a disability." Unless otherwise noted, the words *school district* or *school districts* are used in this chapter for purposes of referring to any public agency within California covered by IDEA. Students who qualify for special education under IDEA are referred to as IDEA-eligible, special education students, or children with disabilities.

The Language of Special Education

Special education has its own language populated with acronyms. Parents and schools do not refer to a free appropriate public education, but a FAPE. Instead of individualized education program team meetings, IEP team meetings is the phrase typically heard. The following is a brief explanation of the most common acronyms and terms encountered. Further detail and context regarding each term are provided throughout the chapter.

- Individuals with Disabilities Education Act (IDEA): The federal law governing all aspects of special education and requiring public school districts to provide eligible students with a free appropriate public education or FAPE. IDEA's precursor was EHA and EAHCA.
- Free appropriate public education (FAPE): Special education and related services that are provided at public expense, under public supervision, meet the standards of the state educational agency, and are in conformity with the student's individualized education program.

- Special education: Specifically designed instruction, at no cost to the parents, that meets the unique needs of a student with a disability.
- Related services: Related services encompass a wide variety of supportive services that are necessary for a student to benefit from the student's educational program. These services may include transportation, occupational therapy, speech and language therapy, counseling, as only a few examples.
- Child with a disability: A student who meets one or more of thirteen defined categories in IDEA (e.g., a specific learning disability, autism) and by reason of the student's disability needs special education and related services.
- Parent: A natural parent, legal guardian, a person acting in the place of a parent if the individual is legally responsible for the child's welfare, a surrogate parent, or at times, a foster parent.
- Individualized education program: The master document that charts a student's educational program. An IEP contains a description of a student's educational needs, goals for the year, progress on goals from the previous year if applicable, and, among other items, the nature and type of special education and related services for the student.
- IEP team: The group of individuals responsible for developing, reviewing, or revising an IEP for a child with a disability. IEP teams have both mandatory and discretionary team members.
- Independent educational evaluation (IEE): Parents disagreeing with a school district's evaluation of their child may request an independent evaluation at public expense. The school district is responsible for funding the IEE unless it requests a due process hearing without unnecessary delay and demonstrates to the hearing officer that its evaluation was appropriate.
- Extended school year (ESY): ESY is a continuation of a student's special education and related services beyond the traditional school year to prevent regression.
- Due process hearing: An administrative hearing that can be requested by either a parent or school district. A common issue is whether a FAPE was offered or provided.
- Stay put: When a parent files for a due process hearing, a student generally remains in the student's last agreed-upon and implemented educational placement. The student's stay put placement maintains the educational status quo pending completion of the due process hearing and subsequent appeals. The exceptions to stay put are incidents involving weapons, drugs, or serious bodily injury.

FREE APPROPRIATE PUBLIC EDUCATION (FAPE)

Special education students have an entitlement to a FAPE under IDEA. FAPE has a procedural and substantive aspect. The procedural component of FAPE refers to the procedural requirements that a school district must follow in developing, providing, and revising the substantive component. Procedural elements of FAPE include, among other things, notice requirements, timelines, the composition of the IEP team, and the development of the IEP. The substantive component of FAPE is the student's educational program, which consists of special education and related services.

Procedural Component

Congress placed emphasis on both the procedural and substantive aspects of FAPE. If school districts follow the procedural requirements of the law, Congress reasoned, the substantive requirement of making FAPE available would be met. There are a seemingly infinite number of ways in which school districts can commit a procedural violation. Among these potential procedural violations are significantly missing a timeline, failing to provide adequate written notice, not having a mandatory IEP team meeting member at an IEP team meeting, or not drafting the IEP document in conformity with the IDEA. However, a procedural violation does not always equate to a denial of a FAPE.

The U.S. Court of Appeals for the Ninth Circuit held that only procedural violations that result in a "loss of educational opportunity" or "seriously infringe the parents' opportunity to participate in the IEP formulation process" are a denial of FAPE (*W. G. v. Board of Trustees of Target Range School District No. 23*, 1992). There must be some demonstrable harm to the student's education or the parents' opportunity to participate in the IEP process for a procedural violation to rise to the level of a denial of a FAPE. In other words: No harm, no foul.

IDEA permits an OAH administrative law judge to determine that a procedural violation is a denial of a FAPE only if the violation:

- "Impeded the child's right to a [FAPE]";
- "Significantly impeded the parents' opportunity to participate in the decisionmaking process regarding the provision of a [FAPE] to the parents' child"; or
- "Caused a deprivation of educational benefits" (20 U.S.C. § 1415(f)(3)(E)(ii)).

An understanding of what it means to impede a child's right to a FAPE will likely continue to evolve over time through OAH and court decisions interpreting this aspect of IDEA.

Substantive Component

FAPE is statutorily defined as special education and related services that are provided at public expense under public supervision and direction, without charge; meet the standards of the state educational agency; include preschool, elementary school, or secondary school education; and are provided in conformity with an appropriate IEP. IDEA is silent on the level of education FAPE requires. Should a special education student be entitled to a basic level of services, to the best possible program that focuses on maximizing the student's potential, or something in between? The U.S. Supreme Court took up this question in special education's most famous case: *Board of Education of Hendrick Hudson School District v. Rowley* (1982).

Amy Rowley was a deaf student attending elementary school. After a short trial period, the school district proposed, and parents accepted, an offer that Amy be placed in regular kindergarten with an FM hearing aid. This proved successful for Amy. At the IEP meeting for first grade, the district proposed a continuation in a regular class with an FM hearing aid, one hour of instruction per day from a tutor for the deaf, and instruction from a speech therapist for three hours per week. Amy's parents asked the school administrators to provide a qualified sign-language interpreter for all of Amy's academic classes. The school district initially provided the requested interpreter to assess her needs. After two weeks, the interpreter concluded that Amy did not need his assistance. Parents were adamant about the need for the interpreter, but the district did not believe Amy needed that service. The school district then discontinued the interpreter. Amy's parents offered to trade out some of the other offered services, but the district did not agree. Note that it would be very difficult for the district to agree to drop a service that it believed was required based on her needs. The resulting impasse ended up with Amy's parents initiating an administrative hearing, followed by an administrative appeal, federal district court trial, and federal appellate court trial. Amy's case eventually made it to the U.S. Supreme Court. Amy's parents urged the high court to find, as the federal district and appellate court had, that FAPE requires school districts to "maximize the potential of each handicapped child commensurate with the opportunity provided nonhandicapped children." Carefully examining the legislative history of EHA, the Court disagreed in a 5–3 split.

The majority concluded that the EHA confers a "basic floor of opportunity" onto eligible students and not the potential maximizing services Amy and her parents sought. But that opportunity must be meaningful. "The Act's legislative history shows that Congress sought to make public education available to handicapped children, but did not intend to impose upon the States any greater substantive educational standard than is necessary to make such access to public education **meaningful**. The Act's intent was more to open the door of public education to handicapped children by means of specialized educational services than to guarantee any particular substantive level of education once inside" ((p. 177(b), emphasis added)).

Because Amy performed better than the average child in her class and was easily passing from grade to grade, the majority held that she did not require a sign-language interpreter to receive a FAPE. The importance of *Rowley* cannot be overstated; until *Endrew F.* in 2017, it was the definitive legal standard that school districts throughout the nation had to meet to provide FAPE or make FAPE available. The latter (making FAPE available) refers to those students who are never enrolled by their parents in the school district's offered program.

In *Endrew F. v. Douglas County School District* (2017), the U.S. Supreme Court revisited the amount of educational progress required under the free appropriate public education (FAPE) standard for the first time since the Court's decision in *Rowley*.

The case concerned a young man, Endrew F., who was eligible for special education under the category of autism. He attended Douglas County School District in Colorado from preschool through the fourth grade. Believing that the IEP offered by the district for fifth grade did not offer FAPE, his parents filed an administrative due process hearing against the district. They were unsuccessful, and then appealed that decision in federal district court, and subsequently to the Tenth Circuit Court of Appeals. The administrative law judge, federal district court, and the Tenth Circuit Court of Appeals all found that the IEPs developed for Endrew by the District were reasonably calculated for Endrew to make some progress, which they defined as "merely more than *de minimis*." *De minimis* is a Latin term for trivial.

The U. S. Supreme Court did not agree, reversing the Tenth Circuit Court of Appeals. The Court held that a FAPE requires that an IEP be reasonably calculated to enable the child to make appropriate educational progress *in light of the child's circumstances* and that sufficient progress means a level of benefit greater than "merely more than *de minimis*" (pp. 402–403, emphasis added). The Court declined to establish a bright line rule as to what constitutes appropriate progress but did note that a FAPE requires a school district to design a program that allows the student to advance appropriately from year to year, attain IEP goals and make progress in the general curriculum. The Court also acknowledged that grade level advancement may not be a realistic goal for all children with IEPs but that these children are nonetheless entitled to an educational program that is "appropriately ambitious in light of the [child's] circumstances" (p. 403). Thus, the IEP must be designed for those children to make meaningful progress.

The Court's decision does not appear to fundamentally alter the legal analysis of a FAPE in California as the Office of Administrative Hearings has for many years required that a child receive "meaningful" educational benefit and that the child's unique, disability-related needs are to be considered in determining whether meaningful educational benefit was attained.

A school district's special education program for a student must satisfy four elements to constitute a FAPE.

1. Be designed to meet the student's unique educational needs;
2. Be reasonably calculated to provide the student with some educational benefit;
3. Be provided in conformity with the student's IEP; and
4. Be in the least restrictive environment or LRE.

The U.S. Court of Appeals for the Ninth Circuit endorses the educational benefit standard articulated in *Rowley* (*J.L. v. Mercer Island School District*, 2010).

Appropriate administration and interpretation of assessments play a key role in the first element. If, for example, a student is not assessed in all areas of suspected disability (as IDEA requires), the IEP team may not be aware of one or more of the student's unique needs. The same result can occur if a student is appropriately assessed but the IEP team does not offer any services to address one of the student's unique needs resulting from the student's disability. A special education program that is not designed to meet a child's unique needs does not constitute a FAPE and will in all likelihood be determined inappropriate to some degree by OAH. Once a student's unique needs have been identified, the second element is whether the special education student's program is reasonably calculated to provide some educational benefit. As noted in *Rowley*, FAPE does not require the absolute best or "potential maximizing" education for the student. But as refined in *Endrew F.*, a FAPE does require that an IEP be designed for the child to make educational progress in light of the child's individual needs.

A number of judicial decisions have further defined FAPE. As the Ninth Circuit ruled in 1987, the correct inquiry is not whether the student may obtain more benefit from the placement preferred by the parents but whether the school district's placement is reasonably calculated to provide the student with some educational benefit (*Gregory K. v. Longview School District*). The phrase "some educational benefit," however, has substance. De minimis or trivial educational benefit will not satisfy the *Rowley/Endrew F.* standard (*Walczak v. Florida Union Free School District*, 1998). The limitations imposed by the student's disability are taken into consideration when determining whether some educational benefit has been conferred (*Mrs. B. v. Milford Board of Education*, 1997). A 1999 Ninth Circuit decision refers to an IEP as a "snapshot," in which a review of its appropriateness focuses on what "was, and was not, objectively reasonable . . . at the time the IEP was drafted" (*Adams v. Oregon*, p. 1149). Under *Adams*, hindsight is irrelevant in determining the appropriateness of an educational placement.

The third element pertains to implementation of a student's IEP. A failure to implement parts of a student's IEP, however, is not necessarily a denial of a FAPE. Rather, the failure must be material. The services a school provides must fall significantly short of the services required by a student's IEP to constitute a material failure (*Van Duyn v. Baker School District*, 5J, 2007). One factor that is considered in determining whether a material failure to implement occurred is the progress, or lack thereof, of the student.

The fourth element of FAPE, the LRE, warrants separate discussion.

FAPE and the Least Restrictive Environment (LRE)

The LRE is both part of FAPE and its own distinct concept. A student cannot receive FAPE unless the student is in the LRE. IDEA's LRE requirement has two related aspects. First, school districts must ensure that "to the maximum extent appropriate, children with disabilities . . . are educated with children who are not disabled" (20 U.S.C. § 1412(a)(5)(A)). Second, the "removal of children with disabilities from the regular education environment occurs only when the nature or severity of the disability of a child is such that education in regular classes with the use of supplementary aids and services cannot be achieved satisfactorily." The last part of the definition, the use of supplementary aids and services, is an area that is easy to forget but critical to meeting the statute. In essence, absent extraordinary circumstances, to meet the requirement a school must identify and try supplementary options before considering a more restrictive placement for any part of the day.

Given the wholesale exclusion in *Mills* and *PARC*, it is not surprising that Congress sought to include special education students with their general education peers. As the second aspect of LRE indicates, however, there are circumstances in which a special education student cannot receive a satisfactory education in the regular education environment and a more restrictive setting is appropriate. In the context of LRE, restrictiveness is primarily a function of the degree to which the special education student is educated with nondisabled peers. For example, spending the entire school day in a special day class that contains no nondisabled students is far more restrictive than attending a special day class for two periods of the school day and spending the remainder of the school day in the general education setting. The definitive ruling addressing LRE for California came from the Ninth Circuit in 1994 (*Sacramento City Unified School District, Board of Education v. Holland*) and remains good law today.

In this case, Rachel Holland's parents, citing the IDEA's LRE requirement, wanted their daughter to be placed in a general education classroom for the entire school day. Taking note of Rachel's moderate mental retardation and her forty-four IQ, the school district denied her parents' request. From the school district's perspective, Rachel was too severely handicapped to benefit from a full-time placement in a general education classroom. Over the next four years the school district and Rachel's parents argued their respective positions to an administrative hearing officer, federal district court, and the Ninth Circuit Court of Appeals. The school district lost at every level.

For *Holland*, the federal district court was charged with interpreting IDEA's directive to educate disabled children "to the maximum extent appropriate" with their nondisabled peers. The federal district court created a four-factor balancing test to determine whether a full-time placement in a general education classroom would be appropriate for Rachel, and the Ninth Circuit affirmed both the decision and the test. The four factors are as follows:

1. the educational benefits of placement full-time in a regular class;
2. the nonacademic benefits of such placement;
3. the effect the student has on the teacher and children in the regular class; and
4. the costs of mainstreaming the student

In applying *Holland*, OAH routinely rejects school district arguments that a student will receive a better education in a special day class as opposed to a general education classroom. The appropriate inquiry, as OAH states, is whether the student can receive a satisfactory education in a general education classroom with the use of supplementary aids and services. Supplementary aids and services cover a wide range of items, such as classroom accommodations and modifications, behavior plans, or the provision of a full-time, one-to-one aide. IDEA requires school districts to appropriately use these aids and supports to enable a special education student to be educated with the student's nondisabled peers to the maximum extent appropriate.

However, the LRE mandate is not so strong as to overcome the student's entitlement to an appropriate education or FAPE. If a student cannot receive a satisfactory education in a general education classroom (e.g., the classroom placement does not address the student's unique needs and provide some educational benefit), even with supplementary aids and services, the student may be placed in a more restrictive setting without violating the IDEA's LRE mandate. IDEA requires the education of children with disabilities with nondisabled peers only to the "maximum extent *appropriate*" (emphasis added).

CHILD FIND, REFERRAL, ASSESSMENT, AND ELIGIBILITY

School districts must affirmatively seek out students who may be IDEA-eligible, undertake comprehensive assessments, notice and convene initial IEP team meetings to determine whether the students qualify for special education, and make FAPE available for those students who are children with disabilities under IDEA. Parental notice and consent are integral components of this process. Notwithstanding the important role of parents in the education of their children, a school district's obligations under IDEA remain the same regardless of how involved or uninvolved parents may be regarding their child's special needs.

Child Find and Referral for Initial Assessment

Under IDEA's child-find provision, school districts are under an affirmative obligation to identify, locate, and assess all children residing within the district's geographical boundaries who may need special education and related services. A school district's child-find obligations are not relieved if a parent does not request a special education evaluation for the parent's child. The duty to identify, locate, and assess also extends to children who are not attending a public school. .

Since school districts are under an obligation to get the word out about the availability of special education, some creativity is needed. Neither IDEA nor the Education Code details what public schools in California must do to fulfill their child-find obligation. For students already attending public schools, a teacher referral system coupled with notices to parents about the availability of special education is typical. To reach private school students, some school districts use media advertisements and website notices. Some school districts go a step further and mail notices regarding the availability of special education directly to private schools within the school district's geographical area.

School districts are required to conduct child find for children *attending* private schools located within the geographical boundaries of the district, whether or not the children and their parents reside within the district boundaries. If assessment of a child is warranted, the school district where the child is attending school must undertake the assessment, determine whether the child is eligible for services, and, if the parents do not desire services for the child, develop an individual services plan (ISP) for the child (34 C.F.R. § 300.131(a)).

A referral for special education need not be made until "after the resources of the regular education program have been considered, and where appropriate, utilized" (Educ. Code § 56303), unless a parent requests that the child be assessed for special education. Sometimes, parents are not sophisticated and may not use formal language for their request. The 2004 IDEA added some language that is favorable to school districts (*see* 20 U.S.C. §§ 1414(a)(1)(C)(ii); *id.* at 1414(a)(1)(D)(ii)). Regardless, the wise approach is to assume a parent request meets the requirements and offer an assessment plan or prior written notice on the reasons the district declines.

Further, if a parent makes a verbal request for an assessment, the school district would be required to assist the parent with placing the request in writing. Ideally, the request will contain a brief reason for the referral and the parent's reason for the request (e.g., "my child seems to be failing most classes" or "my child melts down in the classroom every day and cannot complete his assignments").

When a child begins to struggle (whether academically or emotionally), a school district should begin documenting the resources of the regular education program that were considered or modified (if any), as well as a description of the results of any interventions tried.

There are, of course, instances in which a child is referred by an outside agency for a special education assessment. Consideration should be given to Section 3021(a) of California Code of Regulations, Title 5, which states that all referrals "shall initiate the assessment process."

The decision to assess for special education eligibility triggers the first of many procedural rights for the student under IDEA. Education Code Section 56321 details the procedural requirements concerning assessment. The school (or district if the child is not yet attending a school in the district) must provide the parent with a proposed assessment plan within fifteen days of receiving the request or referral. The proposed assessment plan must be accompanied by a document explaining the procedural safeguards available to the parent under IDEA. The procedural safeguards include many parent rights and some protections for school districts. IDEA's implementing regulations detail the necessary components of the procedural safeguards notice. A school district need only provide a parent with a notice of procedural safeguards one time per year and in the case of assessment, the first occurrence of a state complaint or due process hearing, when a decision is made to make a removal that constitutes a disciplinary change in placement, or on the request of the parent (Educ. Code § 56301(d)(2)). Both an obligation to inform parents of their rights and a deadline requiring completion of a task within a set time are recurrent themes throughout IDEA. The former provides parents with the knowledge to understand their rights; the latter with the assurance that educational issues are addressed in a timely manner.

Initial Assessment

A school district's failure to conduct its own assessment may result in a denial of FAPE. That is well-documented by the Ninth Circuit Court of Appeals in the 2016 decision in *Timothy O. v. Paso Robles Unified School District*. In *Paso Robles*, the court held that the School District should have suspected autism for the child, the district's failure to conduct autism assessment could not be excused by district's possession of a third party report on the child's autism, and that the district's failure to conduct its own autism assessment of the child denied the child a free appropriate public education.

The Ninth Circuit addressed whether a school district could be excused from conducting its own assessment of a child in the area of autism because the district received an autism report for the child completed by an evaluator from another agency, the Regional Center. The Ninth Circuit held that the School District could not and that by doing so the district denied the child, Luke, a free appropriate public education. The decision emphasizes the importance of school districts conducting their own appropriate assessments of children.

A failure to assess in an area of suspected disability is a procedural violation of the IDEA. The IDEA states that a procedural violation in and of itself, however, does not deny the child a FAPE. Rather, to deny the child a FAPE, the violation must seriously impair the parents' opportunity to participate in the formulation of the child's IEP, result in the loss of educational opportunity for the child, or cause a deprivation of the child's educational benefits. The Ninth Circuit determined that the district's failure to assess Luke for autism was a substantial procedural violation that both deprived him of educational benefit and substantially hindered his parents' participation in the IEP process.

The lesson of the case is clear. If a school district is on notice that a child is suspected of having a disability, the district must conduct its own IDEA-compliant assessment of the child in the areas of suspected disability, convene an IEP meeting, and consider the assessment report at an IEP team meeting.

On a related topic on the timing of the initial assessment, the Ninth Circuit found that even a four month delay in assessing a child may not be a procedural violation relating to a denial of FAPE. *D.O. v. Escondido Union School District*, 2023.The case had gone back and forth, with the ALJ finding for the district and then the District Court finding for the parent. Finally, the Ninth Circuit found for the district, and the case concluded. These cases are very fact-specific and in the case of D.O., the facts as suggested by the district implied that the parent had not cooperated fully or at least, not quickly, and thus the burden was not on the district. That argument proved persuasive. However, schools should not rely on a long delay always having this result, especially when the statute requires an assessment plan within 15 days of the request or appropriate notice.

Prior to conducting an assessment, the school must provide the parent with the proposed assessment plan and the accompanying procedural safeguards notice, along with a cover letter that explains the school district cannot assess without the parent's written consent. This plan is typically a single page and contains a description of the areas in which the school district desires to assess the child. Sometimes, a district may identify a few of the assessment tools, but that is not required. Historically, the assessment plans were very detailed, but schools realized that assessors might identify additional assessments as a result of the initial round, and any change or addition needed to go back through the process (notice and signatures, for example). Because that can be time consuming, districts at least in California now uniformly use a one-page simple document.

Should a parent exercise her parental discretion to refuse consent for the proposed assessment plan, the district may need to request a hearing to seek an order to assess the child without parental consent. Parents may find this surprising, but in such a case the school district has a very real quandary. Once it is determined that a student requires an assessment, not to proceed puts the district at risk of being found denying FAPE.

Education Code Section 56320 and following sections detail the requirements of an assessment plan, assessments, related assessment reports, and the follow-up IEP team meeting. An assessment plan must be in terms easily understood by the general public, must be in the parent's primary language or mode of communication (unless to do so is not feasible), must explain the types of assessments to be conducted, and must state that no IEP will result from the assessment without the parent's consent. A school district does not have to identify every specific assessment tool that may be used in the assessment. Some assessment plans contain a short list of potential assessment tools. As noted, an explanation of the parent's procedural rights and safeguards must accompany the assessment plan.

Assessment must occur in "all areas of suspected disability." The school personnel undertaking the assessment must be qualified to administer their respective portions of the plan; use assessments that are not racially, culturally, or sexually discriminatory; and administer the assessments in the student's primary language as heard at school. In addition to these statutory requirements, school districts in California are prohibited from using intelligence tests with students who are Black, regardless of parental consent (*Larry P. v. Riles*, 1984). In *Larry P.*, the court found that the use of intelligence tests with Black students was inaccurate due to a cultural bias in the tests and led to racially discriminatory overinclusion of Black students in classrooms for educable mentally retarded students. IDEA permits the use of nonstandardized assessment tools. School districts therefore are not obligated to use intelligence tests even with non-Black students (*Ford ex rel. Ford v. Long Beach Unified School District*, 2002).

Only a credentialed school psychologist can administer tests of intellectual or emotional functioning. No single procedure can be used as the sole criterion for determining either eligibility. The individuals assessing the child must prepare written reports noting, among other items, whether the student may need special education and related services; the relevant behavior noted during any observations; the relationship between the observed behavior and academic and social functioning; and, where appropriate, a determination concerning the effects of environmental, cultural, or economic disadvantage. To the extent protocols are completed with information specific to the child, these documents are pupil records, and in California the parent has a right to a copy of those records, notwithstanding any concerns on the district's behalf regarding potential copyright infringement regarding the publisher of the test(s) to which the protocol(s) relate (*Newport-Mesa Unified School District v. State of California Department of Education*, 2005).

An IEP team meeting to discuss the child's eligibility under IDEA must be held within sixty days after the school district's receipt of the parent's written consent to the assessment plan. School breaks in excess of five days are not calculated as part of the sixty-day period. The parent can also agree in writing to a longer period of time. Copies of all written reports and documentation of the determination regarding eligibility must be given to the parent when the IEP team meeting is held. If the parent disagrees with a school district's assessment, they can request an independent educational evaluation (IEE) at public expense.

The process for an initial assessment contains many of the procedural requirements that reoccur throughout IDEA: notice of a proposed action, attendant notice to a parent regarding his or her rights, parental consent, minimum criteria for the action undertaken by the school district, and the imposition of specific time lines.

Eligibility

After signing the assessment plan, the parent typically meets with a school psychologist and nurse, or fills out information to assist the professionals with their assessments. The information will include medical history and health issues or concerns. The psychologist may provide a questionnaire to complete regarding the child's behavior at home. The psychologist also gives the child a number of tests. After both the nurse and psychologist conclude their interviewing and testing, an IEP team meeting will be held to determine whether the child qualifies for special education. The parent must receive a written notice from the school for the IEP team meeting. The notice contains a suggested time, location, and date of the meeting, but the parent may request a different time. The law requires that the meeting be held at a mutually agreed-upon time and place. The notice also lists the other individuals who will be attending and states the purpose of the meeting. The parent should return the notice back to the school district after signing it. Sometimes, it can take a number of tries to arrive at a date that works for the school and the parent. However, the school cannot simply proceed with the meeting; the parent's schedule must be accommodated if it is reasonable. Reasonable typically means the hours of a standard business day, which raises challenges for schools as teachers typically are not required to remain on campus until 5:00 p.m. Nevertheless, it is critical for the school to arrive at a mutual agreement with the parent for the meeting day and time, because the law requires parent attendance.

  An IEP team meeting must be held to determine whether the student is eligible for special education under IDEA. If the student is found eligible, the IEP meeting will be referred to as the initial IEP. The IEP team will have agreed upon one or more of the thirteen defined disability categories in IDEA *and* that the disability "requires instruction, services, or both, which cannot be provided with modification of the regular school program." Consideration of both elements is critical. For example, a student with a diagnosis of attention deficit hyperactivity disorder (ADHD) can, if other criteria are met, be evaluated as having an "other health impairment," which is one of IDEA's defined disability categories. Another student with ADHD may be able to access the curriculum successfully in a general education classroom with accommodations such as preferential seating, extra time for testing, and a homework contract to ensure timely completion of assignments. If these adjustments to the general education classroom are sufficient, this student with ADHD may not qualify for special education under IDEA despite being evaluated as satisfying one of the disability categories.

When determining eligibility, the school should be mindful of services that the student is already receiving at the school, as evidenced by the outcome of a rehearing for *L.J. by and through Hudson v. Pittsburg Unified School District* (2017). The School District had determined that while L.J. met three disability categories, he did not demonstrate a need for special education because he performed reasonably well. But the court noted that "the School District had already been providing L.J. with special services, including counseling, one-on-one assistance, and instructional accommodations" (p. 999). Thus, LJ was entitled to an IEP.

The age criterion for special education in Part B of IDEA is three to eighteen years of age (or up to age 22 for students who have not graduated or who will not graduate with a diploma). However, a child may qualify for early intervention under Part C of IDEA. School districts' IDEA obligations began at the transition to age three, with services under Part C the responsibility of California's extensive Regional Center system. Prior to age three, the school district must assess the children qualifying for this early intervention, determining whether they qualify for special education and if so, the IEP process is the same as for older children. Education Code Section 56426.9 details school districts' obligations for transitioning children with disabilities into a public education program at age three. A student's eligibility for special education ends on receipt of a high school diploma or after the end of the current fiscal year in which the student reaches age twenty-two, if the student has not earned a diploma. In the latter case, a student may receive a certificate of completion on or about age 22. A student may also cease to be eligible if they do not continue to meet one of IDEA's defined disability categories or to need special education.

IDEA contains thirteen categories by which a student may qualify as a child with a disability. The thirteen categories are (1) autism; (2) deaf-blindness; (3) deafness; (4) emotional disturbance; (5) hearing impairment; (6) intellectual disability; (7) multiple disabilities; (8) orthopedic impairment; (9) other health impairment; (10) specific learning disability; (11) speech or language impairment (California uses "language or speech disorder"); (12) traumatic brain injury; and (13) visual impairment. Specific requirements for each category are detailed in the

Code of Federal Regulations, Title 34, Section 300.8 and the California Code of Regulations, Title 5, Section 3030. Of note are California's revised definitions of autism and specific learning disability to conform to federal law.

School districts must provide the written report of any assessments to the parent at the IEP meeting, if not before. While there is no duty to provide it ahead of time, best practice is to do so as that gives the parent time to review it prior to the discussion at the meeting. School staff also receive a copy of the report at the meeting. The case manager (often the school psychologist or resource teacher) describes the testing and interviews that were completed to write the report.

The IEP team discusses whether the student meets the definition of a child with a disability under IDEA. The report often includes various disability categories and how the student may qualify for them (or not).

As noted earlier, the IDEA sets forth two criteria for a child to be determined eligible for special education services: the child must meet one or more of the IDEA's eligibility categories (e.g., autism, specific learning disability, etc.) and, by reason thereof, require special education and related services. Of note is a pair of Ninth Circuit cases amending and superseding the first District Court decision, with the Appeals Court ultimately finding that the student exhibited a need for special education in part based on repeated hospitalizations and suicide attempts and that the district failed to disclose critical information to the parent. Thus, student was eligible under IDEA and should have been found eligible (*L.J. by & through Hudson v. Pittsburgh Unified Sch. Dist.*, 2017).

Independent Educational Evaluation (IEE) and Reevaluation

There are three distinct types of assessments that may be considered by the IEP team. The first, discussed earlier in this chapter, is the district's assessment in all areas of suspected disability. The second is an Independent Educational Evaluation (IEE), in essence a second opinion. A parent has the right to obtain an IEE, at public expense, if the parent disagrees with a school district assessment (Educ. Code § 56329(b)). The parent has the right to choose the assessor. The school district can either agree to fund the IEE or without unnecessary delay request a due process hearing before OAH to demonstrate that the school's evaluation was appropriate. If OAH determines that the school's evaluation was appropriate, the school district does not have to pay for an IEE. Finally, parents may obtain private assessments through their medical insurance or other methods such as private payment, in which case the parents cover the cost. If a parent does have a private assessment that they wish to share with the IEP team, then they provide it to the school case manager. That is important because IDEA requires the IEP team to consider any private assessments. The district may choose not to accept the findings of a private assessment after due consideration. A parent is only entitled to one IEE in each area assessed by the school district per assessment period. The individual performing the IEE must be a qualified professional.

Special education students must be reevaluated at least once every three years. Conversely, a student cannot be assessed more than one time per year unless the parent and school district agree. A three-year reevaluation is referred to as a triennial. A reevaluation must conform to all of the requirements of the initial evaluation. A special education student's needs may change before his or her triennial is due. In these instances, reevaluation can occur if conditions warrant reevaluation. The individuals comprising a student's IEP team can meet or communicate informally to determine whether conditions warrant reevaluation. An IEP team meeting is not required to determine whether reevaluation is warranted nor to develop an assessment plan.

THE IEP PROCESS

No single document is more critical to the education of a special education student than the student's individualized education program. An IEP operates as a road map to a special education student's educational program; all individuals working with the student must consult it. There is a specific process to create an IEP, beginning with the team meeting. Education Code Section 56340 and following sections contain the requirements for both IEP team meetings and IEPs.

IEP Team Meetings

The initial IEP must be developed through a properly noticed and convened IEP team meeting. For as long as the student remains eligible for special education under IDEA, all key decisions regarding the educational program will occur through an IEP developed or revised in an IEP team meeting. A parent and school district may agree in writing to amend a student's IEP without convening a meeting after the student's annual IEP team meeting is held.

IEP team meetings must be held at least once annually to review a special education student's educational program, when the student demonstrates a lack of anticipated progress, when the parent requests an IEP team meeting, and for purposes of discussing school district assessments. A student who has already been found eligible for special education under IDEA must have an IEP in effect at the beginning of each school year.

An IEP team meeting includes both mandatory and discretionary team members. Mandatory IEP team members are required by law to attend an IEP team meeting. Discretionary IEP team members are not required to attend but may be invited by either the parent or the school district.

California Education Code Section 56341 requires that an IEP team meeting *must* include the following individuals:

- Not less than one general education teacher of the student, if the student is participating in the general education environment. If the team is considering whether a student may be participating in general education when they are not currently placed in that setting, then a general education teacher.
- No less than one special education teacher of the student.
- An administrative representative from the school district.
- If applicable, an individual who undertook an assessment of the student on the school district's behalf. Otherwise, an individual who is knowledgeable about the assessment procedures used, familiar with the assessment results, and qualified to interpret the instructional implications of the assessment results must attend. That individual may be one of the other team members (meaning a member may serve a dual role).
- At least one parent of the student, unless the school district is unable to convince the parent to attend after multiple attempts.
- If applicable, a representative of the student's group home or an individual named by the court to hold education rights.
- Whenever appropriate, the student.

A parent and school district may consent to a mandatory IEP team member not attending the meeting. The parent must agree to the nonattendance in writing, and if the absent team member's area of curriculum is going to be modified or discussed, that team member must submit written input into the development of the IEP to the parent and IEP team prior to the meeting.

Either the parent or school district may invite individuals who have knowledge or special expertise about the student to attend the IEP team meeting. These individuals are the discretionary IEP team members. The determination of whether an invitee has such knowledge or special expertise is made by the party inviting the individual to be a member of the IEP team. Discretionary IEP team members typically include independent experts or assessors, therapists, and legal representatives. Discretionary IEP team members may not include media. (85 Ops. Atty. Gen. 406, 2002). These individuals, the attorney general reasoned, do not have the requisite knowledge or special expertise required for an individual to be a discretionary member of an IEP team.

A parent must be notified of an IEP team meeting early enough to ensure an opportunity to attend (Educ. Code § 56341.5(b)). Many school districts opt for the unofficial "ten-day rule" and give notice of IEP team meetings ten days in advance. If all parties are in agreement, however, an IEP team meeting can be held on as little notice as possible. Even with sufficient notice, if a parent cannot attend on the requested date, then the law requires the school to work with the parent until they mutually agree on a date and time. Typically, the school provides a written notice to the student's parent or guardian; e-mail is acceptable so long as the parent and school generally communicate that way. The notice must specify the purpose, time, and location of the meeting and the attendees. The law does not require written notice. A telephone call conveying the same information is sufficient. To avoid confusion and to document compliance, school districts often use written notice. Because an IEP team must be held at a mutually agreed-upon time and place, a school district generally defers to a parent's schedule. A school district, however, cannot force a parent to attend an IEP team meeting. School officials must carefully balance the parent's right to participate in an IEP team meeting with the district's obligation to develop an IEP regardless of any disagreement between the student's parent and the school district.

If the parent refuses to attend an IEP team meeting (as opposed to merely requesting another meeting date or time), the school district must document multiple efforts to encourage attendance and then convene the meeting (Educ. Code § 56341.5(h)). Both the parent and school district have the right to make an audio recording of an IEP team meeting if notice of the intent to record is given at least twenty-four hours prior to the meeting. If, however, the school district initiates the notice of intent to record and the parent or guardian refuses to attend or objects to recording, the school district cannot record. Depending on the relationship between the parent and the school district, audiotape recordings of IEP team meetings may be standard practice but should never be assumed.

School districts may not unilaterally alter an IEP. To do so constitutes a denial of FAPE, because the parent or parents are mandatory members of the IEP team and must be involved in any changes (*M.C. v. Antelope Valley Union School District*, 2017).

IEP Contents

IDEA and attendant California Education Code sections set forth the minimum requirements of an IEP. The particular format of the document is left to each school district. While there may be hundreds of different formats for IEPs throughout California, all IEPs must, at a minimum, contain the following:

- Present levels of educational performance. Present levels of performance include, among other items, academic skills (reading, math, writing), social emotional skills, and physical abilities.
- The student's needs as identified through assessment and input from parents and team members.
- Measurable annual goals. Under Education Code Section 56345(a), annual goals may include short-term objectives related to meeting the student's needs that result from the student's disability to enable the student to be involved in and progress in the general education curriculum, and to meeting each of the student's other educational needs that result from the student's disability. Short-term objectives to support goals are not required unless the student is taking alternate assessments aligned to alternate achievement standards.
- Special education instruction, related services, and special factors, including accommodations. The instruction and services, and a statement of program supports for school personnel, must be provided for the student to advance appropriately toward attaining the annual goals, to be involved and progress in the general curriculum, to participate in extracurricular and other nonacademic activities, and to be educated and participate with other students with disabilities and nondisabled students.
- An explanation of the extent, if any, to which the student will not participate with nondisabled students in general education.
- Any accommodations necessary for the student to participate in state- or districtwide assessments. If the IEP team determines that the student will not participate in such assessments, the IEP team must note why assessment is not appropriate and how the student will be assessed.
- The projected date for the beginning of special education instruction and/or services, including the anticipated frequency, location, and duration of those services.
- Appropriate objective criteria, evaluation procedures, and schedules for determining, on at least an annual basis, whether the annual goals are being achieved.
- One year before the student reaches age eighteen, a statement that the student has been informed of his or her rights that will transfer to the student upon the student's turning eighteen.

- A statement of how the student's progress toward annual goals will be measured.
- A statement of how the student's parents will be informed of the student's progress.

Depending on the student's needs, additional IEP requirements contained in Education Code Section 56345 may apply.

IEP goals are drafted by the IEP team to focus on the student's educational needs. Goals are written for implementation over a one-year period, which also coincides with the requirement that the IEP be reviewed at least annually.

To the extent possible, IDEA requires goals to be written to meet each of the student's identified needs. Often, a student may need multiple goals for one need (such as reading). Goals must be measurable, and best practice dictates that a data-driven baseline be identified with regular monitoring of goal progress at specific points throughout the year. IEPs reach the one-year mark at different times throughout the year, depending on the date of the initial IEP. For example, if the IEP team meets in December, the goal should be written to be met by December of the following year.

Goals are not all academic in nature. Special education students may require goals addressing areas of need that are not academic. However, these goals must address needs that are having an impact on the student's education. For example, a special education student may have goals addressing social skills, behavior, attention, school attendance, and any number of other educational needs resulting from the student's disability. The provision of related services is also accompanied by goals specific to the need being addressed by the service (e.g., an articulation goal for the provision of speech and language therapy).

The number and type of goals in an IEP are dependent on the unique needs of the student in question. Accurately identifying all the needs of a special education student through the assessment process is therefore an important and necessary step to drafting appropriate goals. It is important to note that an inappropriate or incomplete assessment may lead to a detrimental domino effect on the student's special education program.

Special Education and Related Services

An important part of the process is the IEP team discussing the type of special education and related services to make available to the student, including the location (e.g., general education class, resource specialist program, special day class, speech therapist).

Parents may have specific programs in mind, such as a specific type of reading program. So long as the program offered by the school district can meet the student's needs, the school decides the methodology.

Put another way, school districts have the discretion to choose the methodology that will be used with a special education student as long as that approach is appropriate, and provides FAPE, for the student. The U.S. Supreme Court has been clear that "once a court determines that the requirements of [IDEA] have been met, questions of methodology are for resolution by the States" (*Board of Education v. Rowley*, p. 208). A similar rule applies to the personnel that school districts can choose to implement a special education student's program. If the chosen individual is qualified and can appropriately implement the service in question, school districts are free to exercise their discretion regarding who is chosen to work with the student (*Gellerman v. Calaveras Unified School District*, 2000). In *Gellerman*, a parent unsuccessfully argued that only the aide who worked with her autistic son at home could meet his classroom needs.

Special education is specially designed instruction without cost to parents that meets the unique needs of the student. Special education also includes related services when the services are necessary for the student to benefit educationally from the student's instructional program. Related services includes both specialized instruction and services. The list of related services in the Education Code is not exhaustive, and it includes audiological services, orientation and mobility services, instruction in the home or hospital, physical and occupational therapy, vision services, specialized driver training instruction, counseling and guidance, psychological services, parent counseling and training, specially designed vocational education and career development, and recreation services. A common related service is transportation, which may be necessary depending on the student's needs.

A wide variety of related services may be necessary for special education students, depending on their needs. However, IDEA makes it clear that medical services are available for diagnostic and evaluation purposes only. However, the U.S. Supreme Court's definition of unavailable medical services is very narrow. The 1984 case *Irving Independent School District v. Tatro* made that clear. In *Tatro*, the parents of an eight-year-old child with spina bifida requested that the school district empty their daughter's bladder every three to four hours through a process called clean intermittent catheterization (CIC). The process takes a few minutes and can be taught to a layperson in an hour. The school district argued that CIC was a medical service and therefore not a related service under IDEA. The high court disagreed, holding that the medical exclusion to related services applies only to those services that must be performed by a physician or a hospital. The Supreme

Court reiterated this clear exception in *Cedar Rapids Community School District v. Garrett F. (1999)*, in which the school district was ordered to provide a student paralyzed from the neck down with, among other things, a full-time nurse, suction of a tracheotomy tube, assistance with eating and drinking, and placement in a reclining position for five minutes each hour.

Purchasing medical equipment is not the responsibility of the school district. Note that cochlear implants are not required to be provided by the district, but learning how to use them to hear better in the classroom may be (20 U.S.C. § 1401(26)(A-B)).

Despite the compelling nature of the disputes in *Tatro* and *Garrett F.*, cases such as these are quite rare. Rather, parents and school administrators more typically find themselves debating the necessity of an additional thirty minutes of speech and language therapy a week, provision of less common services such as vision or sound therapy, or the necessity of a particular placement to receive the services.

Extended School Year (ESY)

ESY services are available beyond the regular school year to prevent certain special education students from regressing beyond a point where they cannot obtain the level of self-sufficiency and independence (such as educational progress) they would otherwise be expected to retain when school resumes. This is referred to as "regression and recoupment." ESY services are made available during the summer months for students on a traditional academic calendar and during extended breaks for students on a year-round calendar. ESY maybe part of a school district's obligation to provide FAPE. For example, some children with autism receive services that extend through part of the school district's winter break. California's regulations describe the type of student that requires ESY services:

> Such individuals shall have handicaps which are likely to continue indefinitely or for a prolonged period, and interruption of the pupil's educational programming may cause regression, when coupled with limited recoupment capacity, rendering it impossible or unlikely that the pupil will attain the level of self-sufficiency and independence that would otherwise be expected in view of his or her handicapping condition. (5 C.C.R. § 3043).

Behavior-Related Assessments and Plans

IDEA does not define the terms "functional behavioral assessment" (FBA), "behavioral intervention services and modifications," or "behavioral intervention plan" (BIP). It does not even require an FBA or a BIP to be written or to be a component of the IEP. That ambiguity makes it more difficult for states to develop legally sufficient components in an IEP when behavior is at issue. IDEA does require consideration of behavior "in the case of a child whose behavior impedes the child's learning or that of others" (20 U.S.C. § 1414(d)(3)(B)(i)) and for changes in placement greater than ten days (*id.* at § 1415(k)). IDEA also does not specify the type of information the IEP team must consider in determining the BIP, other than "to the extent appropriate . . . the general education teacher is required to participate in the determination of appropriate positive behavioral interventions and supports, and other strategies" (§ 1414(d)(3)(C)).

The short provisions in federal law constitute the entire requirement in the IDEA statute for dealing directly with serious behavior problems that arise. What the terms "functional behavioral assessment" or "behavioral intervention plan" mean, and how they are to be implemented, is left to the individual states. Note that California uses the term "functional analysis assessment," or FAA, instead of the term in federal law, "functional behavior assessment," or FBA. For many years as required by the Education Code and Title 5 of the Code of Regulations, California utilized industry best practices for dealing with behaviors. But effective July 1, 2013, Assembly Bill (AB) 86 went into effect, aligning the state's Education Code and Title 5 regulations with the much more minimal federal requirements of the IDEA. AB 86 also adds language to the Education Code addressing the use of emergency behavioral interventions such as physical restraint (codified as Educ. Code § 56521.1).

What remains? California school districts must consider strategies, including positive behavioral interventions and supports, in circumstances in which a student's behavior impedes his or her learning or that of others (Educ. Code § 56341.1(b)(1)). That consideration should include someone trained in behavior techniques, although that is not a requirement. If behavior needs have been identified, the IEP team should develop goals and offer accommodations and services as appropriate to address a wide range of behaviors that are impeding learning.

A plan seeking to address a serious behavior problem that significantly interferes with the implementation of the goals and objectives of a student's IEP is a behavioral intervention plan (BIP). It is not necessary for the IEP team to wait until there is overt aggression or recurring behaviors that might result in disruption to student learning, or even in rare instances, self-injury or property destruction. Behaviors that impede learning of a special education student, even those as seemingly minor as not completing homework consistently or excessive talking and shouting out to get attention, should be included in the IEP.

Comments to IDEA indicate that an FBA is a process that searches for an explanation of the purpose behind a problem behavior. An FBA may be an assessment requiring parental consent or a review of existing data by the IEP team. An FBA can consist of record review and consultation among school district employees, or it can take the form of a more in-depth evaluation requiring parental consent. Neither IDEA nor the Education Code mandates an FBA before developing a behavioral intervention plan, except for students who are being removed; then, the law requires an FBA if one has not previously been completed. Sound educational practice makes it advisable for some level of record review or evaluation before developing a behavior plan. An FBA can also play an important role in the discipline of a special education student, as discussed more fully in Chapter 9.

Mental Health Services

In some instances, the needs of a special education student may require mental health services or placement in a residential facility. Effective July 1, 2011, mental health services and residential placement are the responsibility of the school district. Previously, these obligations were undertaken by the State Department of Mental Health, but the passage by the California legislature of Assembly Bill 114 in 2011 terminated the department's obligations. Subsequently, some school districts have hired their own personnel to address the mental health needs of IDEA-eligible students, while other districts have contracted with counties to provide these same services.

Placement

A continuum of program options must be available to meet the needs of a special education student. These program options must include, but are not necessarily limited to, all or any combination of the following: a general education program; resource specialist program (RSP); related services; special classes and centers; nonpublic, nonsectarian schools; residential treatment centers; state special schools; itinerant instruction; instruction using telecommunication; and instruction in the home, in hospitals, and in other institutions (Educ. Code § 56361). Recall the LRE discussion and take note of how the continuum of program options goes from the least (general education program) to the most restrictive environment (home or hospital setting).

In the context of special education, a nonpublic school (NPS) is a private school that has been certified by the California Department of Education (CDE) to contract directly with school districts. That placement may then be included as the IEP placement. A private school that is not certified by the CDE is simply a private school. There are NPSs outside of California; in some instances, a student may be able to receive a FAPE only in an NPS outside of California, thereby obligating the school district to fund the placement. A school district may also have a shortage of a particular related services provider. The school district can contract with a nonpublic agency (NPA) to provide the related services to special education students. An NPA is a private company that is certified by the CDE to provide services to special education students. Absent a waiver from the CDE, school districts cannot prospectively contract with a school or agency that is not certified as an NPS or NPA (Educ. Code § 56366(d)). Office of Administrative Hearings (OAH) administrative law judges (ALJ) are also prohibited from ordering prospective placement or services with a school or agency that is not certified (Educ. Code § 56505.2(a)). Nothing in the law prohibits such placements as part of a settlement agreement, however.

Under IDEA, an IEP team meeting is a collaborative effort whereby all team members work together to determine the appropriate placement for a student. The IEP team is to consider the continuum of placement options and reach agreement on the placement that is appropriate (or makes FAPE available) for the student.

At the end of the IEP team meeting, regardless of whether the parents and the school district IEP team members agree or disagree, the school district must present the parents with a formal written offer of placement. In 1994, the Ninth Circuit held that one purpose of a written offer of placement is to permit the parents to seriously consider the school district's offer (*Union School District v. Smith*). At a minimum, a formal written offer of placement should note the school site, classroom(s), and related services (including type, frequency, and location) being made available to the student. A failure to make a formal written offer of placement is a procedural violation that may constitute a denial of a FAPE.

Parents also have the right to observe and have an expert of their choosing observe the placement made available by the school district. If a parent seeks an IEE, the parent's independent assessor is entitled to observe the parent's child in the school district's offered placement to the extent the district's assessors did so or to the extent such observation is permissible under the district's assessment procedures (Educ. Code § 56329(b)). Section 56329(b) has been interpreted to permit observation of a school district's placement by a parent's selected expert regardless of whether an IEE was being sought (*Benjamin G. v. Special Education Hearing Office*, 2005).

TRANSITION PLANS, THE AGE OF MAJORITY, EXITING SPECIAL EDUCATION, AND REVOCATION OF CONSENT

Transition Planning and Age of Majority

IDEA does not focus solely on a special education student's educational program during the time the student attends school. There is also an emphasis on preparing the student for independent living and life after special education services under IDEA cease. To this end, transition plans are created for students. Education Code Section 56345.1 details the requirements of transition plans.

At sixteen years of age, or younger if determined appropriate by the IEP team, a student's IEP must contain a plan detailing the transition services the student is to receive. The specific legal requirements of a transition plan focus on both academic and functional achievement. The statute refers to a "coordinated set of activities" designed to promote movement from school to postschool activities, including (as appropriate) postsecondary education, vocational education, integrated employment (including supported employment), continuing and adult education, adult services, independent living, and community participation. The district is responsible for these to age twenty-one or twenty-two, depending on the student's birthdate.

IDEA requires the IEP for a student who is sixteen years of age or older to contain "appropriate measurable postsecondary goals based on age appropriate transition assessments related to training, education, employment, and where appropriate, independent living skills" as well as the "transition services (including courses of study) needed to assist the child in reaching those goals" (20 U.S.C. § 1414(d)(1)(A)(i)(VIII)).

Once a student is eighteen years of age, the student (unless there is a conservatorship) holds his or her own educational rights. The district must explain this to the student prior to the eighteenth birthday. The school district is also required to provide both the student and the student's parents with a copy of the procedural safeguards on or before the student's eighteenth birthday. Despite the age at which educational rights transfer to a student, the age of majority in and of itself has no impact on eligibility for special education services.

Exiting Special Education

There are three circumstances in which a special education student is no longer eligible for services under IDEA. First, the termination of special education eligibility turns on either age or the receipt of a high school diploma. A special education student receiving a high school diploma is no longer eligible for services under IDEA. However, a student receiving a certificate of completion remains eligible for services under IDEA. Special education students may continue to receive services until they are twenty-two. A school district does not have to evaluate a special education student before terminating services if the student receives a high school diploma or "ages out" of eligibility.

Second, a special education student may no longer meet one of the thirteen eligibility categories or demonstrate the need for special education and related services. While many of the eligibility categories are based on permanent disabilities, other categories do present an opportunity for students to improve in the relevant area so that they do not continue to qualify for special education. A school district must undertake an evaluation of a special education student before determining that the student is no longer eligible for special education under IDEA. These are rare, because often a student is performing successfully *because of the provision of special education services*. Thus, removing services must be considered with the utmost care.

Third, parents also have the right to revoke consent to their child's receipt of special education services pursuant to Education Code Sections 56021.1 and 56346. Once consent is revoked the student is no longer entitled to the benefits and protections of IDEA. A school district must honor a parent's request to revoke consent to special education services, and the district cannot use a due process hearing to override the revocation. However, hearing decisions have made it clear that should a parent refuse services, the district cannot later be held for failures during the period when services were not allowed. School districts are not required to delete records related to the prior provision of special education services to the student.

PRIVATE SCHOOL STUDENTS AND IDEA

We have already seen that a school district's child-find obligations extend to students in private schools. But do students in private schools have an entitlement to a FAPE? The answer, like so much in special education law, depends. There are two general categories of private school students: (1) students placed by a school district in a private, nonpublic school (commonly referred to as an NPS) certified by the California Department of Education (CDE); and (2) students placed by their parents in an NPS or private school (not certified by CDE). The second category can be further divided into (a) students placed by their parents in an NPS or private school when the parents dispute the school district's offer of FAPE and (b) students placed by their parents in an NPS or private school when the parents make a personal choice, such as a religious private school, and do not dispute the school district's offer of FAPE. The Education Code prohibits school districts, but not parents, from placing students in a private school that is not certified as an NPS.

Some special education students are placed by a school district in an NPS for the student to receive a FAPE. This is an IEP placement and included in the document. These students clearly have an ongoing entitlement to FAPE. The students have been placed at the NPS to receive FAPE. Placement in an NPS by a school district is permissible only if the school district itself does not have an appropriate public education program for the student (Educ. Code § 56365(b)).

The last category of students pertains to those special education students placed by their parents at an NPS or private school when the school district's offer of FAPE is not in dispute. A private school student in this latter category does not have an individual entitlement to special education and related services and thus has no recourse to a due process hearing. This group of students is rare because the parents must pay the NPS or private school expenses. To avoid potentially falling into this subgroup of privately placed students, some parents maintain their child in a private school or NPS and summarily disagree with any IEP offered by the school district to leave open the possibility of reimbursement through a due process hearing. A private school student can request an individual services plan (ISP) to receive services in an amount proportionate to the student's share of federal funding. This generally amounts to some consultation but not to direct services, as it is virtually impossible to compute a figure.

DUE PROCESS HEARINGS

A key concern in *PARC* and *Mills* was the lack of recourse available to children who were prohibited from attending a public school. These children were deprived of due process of law because there was no mechanism available to challenge their exclusion. The Education for All Handicapped Children Act (EHA) and its modern-day equivalent, IDEA, have changed all of this dramatically. Virtually every aspect of a special education student's program can be challenged in a due process hearing before an impartial hearing officer.

IDEA contains its own administrative hearing process in which both parents and school districts can request a hearing regarding identification, evaluation, placement, or the provision of FAPE. In California, the Office of Administrative Hearings (OAH) currently oversees due process hearings. Due process hearings are governed by a combination of state and federal laws and regulations (34 C.F.R. § 300.507 et seq.; Educ. Code § 56500 et seq.; and 5 C.C.R., § 3080 et seq.).

Due process hearings are somewhat more informal in comparison to proceedings in a court, but they most closely resemble a "bench trial," meaning there is no jury. The hearing officer takes a more active role in the proceeding, sometimes asking their own questions. A request for a due process hearing, in the form of a letter or legal complaint, needs only to note the name of the student, the address of residence, a description of the nature of the problem (including facts relating to the problem), and a proposed resolution of the problem to the extent known. A request for a due process hearing must be made within two years from the date the party initiating the request knew, or had reason to know of, the facts underlying the basis for the request.

However, school districts should be conscious of the "knew or should have known" requirement for the two-year limitation to file for a due process hearing. If a parent challenges the statute of limitations due to an alleged ignorance of the events leading to the denial of FAPE, the hearing officer or court will need to make a determination about the parent's knowledge of the matter and the timing of that knowledge (*Avila v. Spokane School District 81*, 2017).

A party in California may not have a due process hearing until a notice that meets the above-noted requirements is filed with OAH. IDEA further provides that the hearing request will be deemed sufficient unless the party receiving the request notifies the other party and the hearing office within fifteen days that the request is not sufficient. IDEA thereafter requires the hearing officer to make a determination regarding whether or not the hearing request contains the requisite information. A party is not permitted to raise issues at the due process hearing that were not raised in the hearing request without the agreement of the other party. However, the Administrative Law Judge (ALJ) hearing the matter frequently reframes the issues during a pre-process called the Pre-Hearing Conference (PHC).

After a school district receives a due process hearing request, the district must send a written notice to the parent within ten days, unless one has already been provided. The law refers to this as Prior Written Notice (PWN). The PWN must contain:

> "(A) a description of the action proposed or refused by the agency;
> (B) an explanation of why the agency proposes or refuses to take the action and a description of each evaluation procedure, assessment, record, or report the agency used as a basis for the proposed or refused action;
> (C) a statement that the parents of a child with a disability have protection under the procedural safeguards of this subchapter and, if this notice is not an initial referral for evaluation, the means by which a copy of a description of the procedural safeguards can be obtained;
> (D) sources for parents to contact to obtain assistance in understanding the provisions of this subchapter;
> (E) a description of other options considered by the IEP Team and the reason why those options were rejected; and
> (F) a description of the factors that are relevant to the agency's proposal or refusal."

(20 U.S.C. § 1415(c)(1))

IDEA also requires a parent to respond in writing to a hearing request filed by a school district. The parent must specifically address the issues raised in the school district's hearing request.

Before going to hearing, the parties are encouraged to resolve their dispute through mediation. The Office of Administrative Hearings makes mediators available at no cost to assist the parties in resolution through settlement. IDEA contains a provision to encourage resolution through settlement when a parent files for due process. This is called a "resolution session." There is no such requirement when a district files for due process. Under this provision, a school district is required to respond to a due process hearing request filed by a parent by convening a meeting with the parents and relevant members of the IEP team within fifteen days. The school district cannot have an attorney present unless an attorney accompanies the parent. If a settlement agreement is executed during the resolution session, either party has three business days to void the agreement. The school district and parent can agree in writing to waive the resolution session and consider more formal mediation.

California Education Code Section 56346 requires a school district to initiate a due process hearing if the district determines that a component of the proposed special education program to which the parent does not consent is necessary to provide a FAPE to the child. Is failure to do so a denial of FAPE in itself? The Ninth Circuit determined that Los Angeles Unified School District's failure to initiate a hearing for a year-an-a-half was unreasonable and denied the child a FAPE because the goal of Section 56346 is to ensure that placement disputes are resolved promptly (*I.R. v. Los Angeles Unified School District*, 2015). While there may be some flexibility, a lengthy delay is not acceptable.

Stay-Put During Hearing

From the date a due process hearing is requested to the time of final adjudication, including appeals, a student generally has a right to remain in the student's last agreed-upon and implemented IEP placement, unless the school district and the parent agree otherwise or an exception applies. (20 U.S.C. §1415(j)). This placement is referred to as "stay-put." Stay-put is the maintenance of the status quo for the student's educational placement

The contents of an IEP or settlement agreement may have unintended consequences for a student's stay-put placement. For example, an IEP naming a specific individual as a service provider may convince an OAH administrative law judge to obligate the school district, which otherwise has discretion in choosing personnel, to continue the provision of services by the named individual. Likewise, a settlement agreement's provision of a service or placement on a temporary basis may become a student's stay-put placement if the language in the agreement does not specify the temporary nature, often including a date certain, of the placement of service. Systemwide administrative changes such as school closures and furlough days, however, are not subject to stay-put. The U.S. Court of Appeals for the Ninth Circuit rejected the argument of parents that stay-put prohibited the State of Hawaii from shortening the 2009–2010 school year by seventeen days through a combination of shortened school days and furlough days to address a fiscal crisis (*N.D. et al. v. Hawaii Department of Education*, 2010).

There are three exceptions to stay put: weapons, drugs, and serious bodily injury. IDEA pulls the definitions from other federal statutes. The standard for weapons is low, while the standard for bodily injury is quite high, with the standard for drugs more complex (20 U.S.C. §1415(k)(7)(B-D)). When an exception applies, the school district need not maintain the current placement. In those cases, the district may unilaterally place the student in an interim alternative education setting (IAES) for forty-five days. The placement can be extended by another forty-five days if a new placement is not decided upon or the hearing has not concluded with a decision issued. However, the student still has a right to FAPE in the IAES. (34 C.F.R. § 300.532(b)(3)).

The law allows one other option for the district. A hearing officer or a court may allow the LEA to remove a child in serious cases, but the LEA must prove that the child, remaining in their current placement, is substantially likely to cause injury to themselves or others (20 U.S.C. §1415(k)(3)(B)(ii)(II).

Due Process Rights

The process begins when one party files a request for a hearing. The filing party should include their issues and proposed resolutions. Ten days before the hearing, the opposing party must provide a written response. If the party who receives the filing believes it is insufficient, they may file a Notice of Insufficiency (NOI) with OAH within fifteen calendar days. Note that the NOI is not meant to litigate the issues, but rather to bring to attention if the complaint is unclear or vague. An ALJ will make a determination based on the notice requirements. If an NOI is granted, the party who filed the hearing request has leave to amend.

Clarification of the issues occurs through a prehearing telephone conference (PHC), in which the parties and/or their attorneys discuss the issues and hearing process, including proposed witnesses, with the ALJ.

Unlike a civil trial, a due process hearing has no discovery phase during which each party can depose (question under oath) witnesses and request documents.

However, either party may request a subpoena duces tecum, a court order that requires the other party to provide documents or other evidence or to require a person (such as a school staff) to appear at the hearing.

The entire administrative record is usually composed of the student's educational records and perhaps some independent assessments. All of the documentary evidence a party intends to rely on must be given to the opposing party at least five business days before the hearing commences. A list of witnesses, including their general areas of testimony, must also be exchanged at least five business days prior to the hearing.

Parties to a due process hearing may be accompanied by an attorney if notice is given ten days prior to the hearing. Once the hearing convenes, the party requesting the hearing typically puts on its case first. The party seeking relief in a due process hearing bears the burden of persuasion (i.e., the burden of proving their claim(s) by a preponderance of the evidence) (*Schaffer v. Weast*, 2005).

Regardless of the outcome of the hearing, hard feelings may last for years on both sides. The hearing may damage the relationship between a student and their family and the school district even though both parties must work together for the student's education for many years to come. Beyond the emotional toll of a hearing, there is the financial cost. The prospect of further litigation in federal court only compounds these costs. Thus, if issues can be worked out through mediation prior to the hearing, costs may be much lower and relationships may not have the same level of negative effects.

There is also an option for an Expedited Hearing, in cases where parties feel they cannot wait for the longer hearing process (such as when a student is expelled or out of school for another reason). An expedited hearing is scheduled for 20 days after the initial petition is filed, and the decision must be rendered within ten days after the conclusion of the hearing. Parties may mediate, but the hearing will not be delayed while that occurs. There is a resolution session if a parent files for the hearing, and it must be held within seven days (resolved within 15 days).

Due Process Remedies

The most common remedies sought in a due process hearing by parents are reimbursement for educational expenses already incurred, reimbursement for an independent educational evaluation or IEE, compensatory education, and/or a specific placement or related service to be ordered prospectively. There is no damages remedy under IDEA, meaning that a parent may not receive monetary compensation for pain, suffering, or emotional distress. The most common remedies for a school district are an order that the district's offer constituted FAPE, that a district may assess the student over the parent's objection, or that the district's assessment was appropriate. A remedy may order that a student remain in general education or special education or require a district to revise the IEP.

Compensatory education. IDEA grants a court the power to grant such relief as the court determines is appropriate. OAH administrative law judges have broad powers to remedy a finding that a school district did not provide a FAPE by ordering compensatory education. The purpose behind such an order is to replace the lost educational opportunity that accompanies the denial of a FAPE.

A simple example of compensatory education is a single related service like speech and language therapy. Here is an example: if the school district erred in not assessing a student's receptive communication skills when it appeared the student had serious issues, then an administrative law judge may find that the student should have received speech and language therapy, but did not. Then, the judge may award compensatory education in the form of speech and language therapy for an amount of time to be determined by the judge. In calculating the amount of compensatory education, the judge does not have to undertake a one-to-one calculation. The judge can exercise discretion to award an amount that is, within the words of the Ninth Circuit, reasonably "designed to ensure that the student is appropriately educated within the meaning of the IDEA" (*Parents of Student W. v. Puyallup School District No. 3*, p. 1497, 1994).

Reimbursement for educational expenses. A parent seeking to obtain reimbursement for educational expenses must satisfy two criteria. First, during the time period in which the educational expenses were incurred, the school district did not provide or make available a FAPE. Second, the educational services obtained by the parents must be designed to meet the student's unique needs and provide the student with educational benefit. Does this mean that a parent must meet the FAPE standard to which school districts are held? No. The U.S. Supreme Court has ruled that it is immaterial if the student was at a private school not certified by the state (*Florence County School District Four v. Carter*, 1993). The court reasoned that a parent cannot be expected to know all the nuances of private placements. The U.S. Court of Appeals for the Ninth Circuit has held that parents need not show that a private placement furnishes every special service necessary to maximize their child's potential but merely demonstrate that the placement provides educational instruction designed to meet the unique needs of the handicapped child, supported by such services as are necessary to permit the child to benefit from instruction (*C.B. v. Garden Grove Unified School District*, 2011). The impact of these cases is that, if a school district does not provide or make a FAPE available, a parent may well obtain reimbursement for educational services that would not constitute a FAPE if provided by a school district. Additionally, there is no prerequisite that a student receive special education and related services from a school district pursuant to an IEP before parents initiate a due process hearing to challenge an IEP made available by the district and seek recovery of expenses resulting from a private placement selected by the parents (*Forest Grove School District v. T.A.*, 2009).

While expert witnesses may be critical to a parent or school district to obtain a favorable decision from OAH, expert fees are not recoverable as a cost by a prevailing parent in a due process hearing (*Arlington Central Unified School District Board of Education v. Murphy*, 2006).

Attorneys' Fees

Parents who prevail in a due process hearing may recover their attorneys' fees. IDEA contains a fee-shifting provision to encourage attorneys to represent the class of individuals protected by the law: children with disabilities, especially those who cannot possibly afford legal assistance (20 U.S.C. §1415(i)(3)). School districts usually cannot recover attorneys' fees. Attorneys' fees to parents in due process hearings may be extensive. Depending on the length and complexity of the due process hearing, a prevailing parent may be entitled from $25,000 to in excess of $200,000. The attorneys' fees that may result from a hearing can significantly exceed the cost of the educational services at issue. For better or worse, IDEA's attorneys' fees provision has had a profound impact on the number of due process hearings, the decisions parties to a hearing make for or against settlement, and the financial costs school districts must consider in ensuring compliance with IDEA.

In 1994, the Ninth Circuit held that a "prevailing party for the purpose of awarding attorney's fees [under IDEA] is a party which succeed[s] on any significant issue in litigation which achieves some of the benefit the parties sought in bringing the suit" (*Parents of Student W. v. Puyallup School District*, p. 1498 (quoting *Hensley v. Eckerhart*, 1983)). A parent does not need to prevail on all issues to be considered a prevailing party. A parent, however, must obtain more than merely technical or de minimis (minimal) relief to be a prevailing party entitled to attorneys' fees.

It is not unusual for OAH to issue a decision in which the student prevails on some, but not all, of the issues. If the student was represented by an attorney, the degree of the student's success is used as the criteria to determine the amount of attorneys' fees and costs that are properly recoverable (*Aguirre v. Los Angeles Unified School District*, 2006). For example, if a student seeks 100 hours of compensatory education and is awarded fifty, the school may be able to argue that attorneys' fees and costs should be less than the amount requested. However, it can be very difficult to separate an attorney's time when there are multiple overlapping issues.

Thus, a hearing officer may award the entire amount requested even when the parent did not prevail on all issues.

There are additional grounds for reducing or denying an award of attorneys' fees. A school district can issue a written offer of settlement at any time more than ten days before the due process hearing begins. If the offer is not accepted within ten days and the relief finally obtained by the parents is not more favorable than the offer, the parents cannot obtain attorneys' fees and related costs subsequent to the school district's issuance of the offer. Parents can avoid the limiting effect of a written offer of settlement if they are substantially justified in rejecting it. An award of attorneys' fees is not available for attendance at an IEP team meeting unless the meeting is ordered by OAH or a court. Attorneys' fees can be reduced or denied if the parent acts unreasonably during the proceeding, the hourly rate for attorneys' fees being sought is unreasonable, and/or the time spent on legal services was excessive.

Parents may be "substantially justified in rejecting an offer" when the parent obtains more relief when proceeding to the hearing after the statutory offer. The risk to the parent is whether or not the court decides that the parent did obtain more relief, especially when the case has multiple issues and the parent does not prevail on each one—which is typical in special education hearing decisions in California. When there is a dispute on whether the parent was justified, often the issue ends up back in court. In *T.B. v. San Diego Unified School District* (2015), the Ninth Circuit found that the parents were justified and thus entitled to attorney fees.

In 2004, when IDEA was reauthorized, Congress added a provision that would allow for an award of reasonable attorneys' fees to a prevailing school district "against the attorney of a parent, or against the parent, if the parent's complaint or subsequent cause of action was presented for any improper purpose, such as to harass, to cause unnecessary delay, or to needlessly increase the cost of litigation" (20 U.S.C. § 1415(i)(3)(B)(i)(III)). As long as the parents present evidence that, if believed by the fact finder, would give them relief, the case is not per se frivolous and will not support an award of attorneys' fees (*R.P. v. Prescott Unified School District*, 2011). In a different vein, the Ninth Circuit reversed a District Court's award of attorney fees to the district in a matter involving IDEA and Section 504, because the court believed the parent's claims were not frivolous but rather poorly claimed, pled, and argued. The court did affirm the fees awarded under Section 1983 and the ADA in the same case, however (*C.W. v. Capistrano Unified School District*, 2015).

SECTION 504 AND THE AMERICANS WITH DISABILITIES ACT (ADA)

This section is designed as an introduction to Section 504 of the Rehabilitation Act of 1973 (Section 504) and the Americans with Disabilities Act (ADA). A complete discussion is beyond the scope of this chapter. Indeed, entire books have been written about Section 504 and the ADA.

Often, Section 504 and the ADA may overlap with facts in a case brought under IDEA. Noteworthy is a 2016 case, *A.G. v. Paradise Valley Unified School District No. 69*, where the Ninth Circuit determined that the parents' consent to implementation of the IEP does not bar claims for damages under Section 504 and the ADA. Likewise, a school district's compliance with obligations to a deaf or hard-of-hearing student does not necessarily establish compliance with the ADA. The Ninth Circuit determined that a court reviewing an alleged violation of the effective communication regulation under Title II of the ADA and IDEA must analyze the allegations separately. While it is true that a school district's offer of accommodations under an IEP may well comply with IDEA and Title II, nevertheless the court must separately review the actions under each statute (*K.M. ex rel. Bright v. Tustin Unified School District*, 2013).

Section 504 of the Rehabilitation Act of 1973

Section 504 is an antidiscrimination law that applies to all recipients of federal funding, such as California public schools, but also includes any private schools or entities that receive federal funds (e.g., grants, student loans). Covered entities are prohibited from discriminating against an individual on the basis of disability. A school district may also be required to provide educational services to students who qualify as individuals with a disability under Section 504. Effective, January 1, 2009, the ADA Amendments Act directly impacts interpretation and application of Section 504.

An individual with a disability, or handicapped person as the phrase is used in Section 504, is "any person who (i) has a physical or mental impairment which substantially limits one or more major life activities, (ii) has a record of such an impairment, or (iii) is regarded as having such an impairment" (34 C.F.R. § 104.3(j)(1)). Only students in the first category have a right to educational services. The latter two categories are aimed at preventing discrimination on the basis of disability. Section 504's coverage is not limited to students. Section 504's impact on employment in public schools is discussed in Chapter 5.

The first category for eligibility has three requirements. A student must have (1) a physical or mental impairment (2) that substantially limits (3) one or more major life activities. A student must be assessed by a school district before being found eligible under Section 504, but the assessment need not be as comprehensive as an assessment for an IEP. In fact, many schools simply use data and assessments in the school record, in addition to teacher comments. A school district does not have to assess all students for whom a referral for assessment is made and may inform a parent of its decision to refuse assessment. Section 504's implementing regulations contain an illustrative, but not exhaustive, list of qualifying physical and mental disorders. These disorders include "any physiological disorder or condition" or "any mental or psychological disorder." The variety of qualifying physical or mental impairments is seemingly infinite. Eligibility under Section 504 also requires that the physical or mental impairment substantially limits one or more major life activities. Major life activities are defined as "functions such as caring for one's self, performing manual tasks, walking, seeing, hearing, speaking, breathing, learning, and working" (34 C.F.R. § 104.3(j)(2)(ii)). This list also is not exhaustive, and the ADA Amendments Act of 2008 provides that major life activities include "the operation of a major bodily function, including but not limited to, the function of the immune system, normal cell growth, digestive, bowel, bladder, neurological, brain, respiratory, circulatory, endocrine, and reproductive functions" (42 U.S.C. § 12102(2)(B)).

Section 504 does not define the phrase "substantially limits." In the context of the major life activity of learning, the phrase has been interpreted by the Office for Civil Rights (OCR), which enforces Section 504, to require an important and material limitation (*Pinellas County (FL) School District*, 1993). Like the criteria for eligibility under IDEA, the presence of a disability is not sufficient in and of itself to confer coverage to a student under Section 504. A student diagnosed with attention deficit disorder who nonetheless made academic progress was not substantially limited in the major life activity of learning (*Worth County Schools*, 1997). When determining whether a student meets Section 504's eligibility criteria, a school district should compare the student's performance to that of the average student in the general population (*Bercovitch v. Baldwin School*, 1998). The ADA Amendments Act of 2008, however, notes that the definition of disability (i.e., whether an individual is eligible for the protections of the ADA and Section 504) "shall be construed in favor of broad coverage ... to the maximum extent permitted by the Act" (42 U.S.C. § 12102(4)). The ADA Amendments Act of 2008 may therefore expand eligibility beyond the contours established by prior case law and guidance from the OCR.

What role do mitigating measures (such as medication or glasses) play in determining whether a student is eligible under Section 504? The ADA Amendments

Act of 2008 reverses existing case law from the U.S. Supreme Court by providing that the determination of whether an impairment substantially limits a major life activity is to be made without reference to the effects of mitigating measures (42 U.S.C. § 12102 (4)(E)(i)). Ordinary eyeglasses or contact lenses are an exception and "shall be considered in determining whether an impairment substantially limits a major life activity" (42 U.S.C. § 12102 (4)(E)(ii)).

We know that IDEA-eligible students are entitled to FAPE. But what services are available to a student who is not eligible for services under IDEA but is covered by Section 504? According to Section 504's implementing regulations, school districts must also provide a FAPE to qualifying students under Section 504. But is this the same FAPE that IDEA requires? Perhaps, but probably not.

Section 504 defines the provision of an appropriate education as either regular or special education and related aids and services that are designed to meet individual educational needs of handicapped persons as adequately as the needs of nonhandicapped persons. It is difficult to conceive of any student who requires special education under Section 504 yet is not eligible for special education services under IDEA. In other words, if Section 504 requires a school district to provide special education to a Section 504 student, that student should actually be an IDEA-eligible student receiving special education services under IDEA. However, if there is a Section 504–eligible student who requires special education yet does not satisfy one of IDEA's thirteen eligibility categories, then the student would have an entitlement to special education services under Section 504. One, but not the only, way to satisfy Section 504's definition of an appropriate education is to develop an IEP for a student in conformance with IDEA. School districts can also develop a Section 504 Plan. A Section 504 Plan is a written document noting the educational services, accommodations, and modifications a student receives under Section 504. Federal law does not require the plan to be written, but common sense, sound practice, and district policies mean that these plans are typically written.

Section 504 does not have a due process hearing system like that of IDEA. However, school districts are required to develop an internal hearing process to address complaints. An allegation of noncompliance regarding Section 504 can also be filed with the OCR. The OCR will investigate the allegation and issue a written letter of findings. Corrective action may be ordered by the OCR. A lawsuit may be filed in federal court under a Section 504 claim. The Ninth Circuit has held that the FAPE requirement under Section 504 is separate and distinct from the FAPE requirement under IDEA (*Mark H. v. Lemahieu*, 2008). In a subsequent ruling in the same case, the Ninth Circuit also held that the parents could seek money damages against the school district under Section 504 based on an alleged failure by the district to provide necessary services to the parents' children (*Mark H. v. Hamamoto*, 2010). The ruling is significant because, as mentioned earlier, money damages are not available under IDEA. To the extent a plaintiff alleging a violation of Section 504 seeks relief available under or based on an alleged violation of IDEA, the plaintiff must first utilize IDEA's administrative hearing process before pursuing Section 504 allegations in a civil lawsuit (*Payne v. Peninsula School District*, 2011). This concept was further explained by the U.S. Supreme Court in *Fry v. Napoleon Community School* (2017). *Fry* established that a plaintiff seeking relief that is also available under the IDEA must first exhaust the IDEA's administrative procedures. But recall that money damages are not available under IDEA. If a plaintiff prevails in litigation on a Section 504 claim, attorneys' fees may be available.

When exiting a student from special education, it is wise to hold a Section 504 team meeting to determine whether the student qualifies as an individual with a disability under Section 504. The Section 504 team reviews the recent assessment reports that were used to exit the student from special education. There may be some disagreement as to whether the deficit substantially limits a major life activity. If the team agrees that the student meets Section 504 criteria, the plan should contain accommodations and modifications that the student should receive in the general education classroom (e.g., preferential seating, extra time on tests, and the like). Note that services such as counseling or even speech and language, while not common, may be included in a 504 plan.

Americans with Disabilities Act (ADA)

Application of the ADA to an entity, public or private, is not contingent on the receipt of federal funding. The most relevant portion of the ADA for our discussion is Title II, which prohibits public entities from discriminating on the basis of disability. Title I, which prohibits discrimination on the basis of disability in employment, is reviewed in Chapter 5.

Title II applies to school districts in California. The ADA uses the same three-part test contained in Section 504 (e.g., physical or mental impairment that substantially limits one or more major life activities, a record of such impairment, or regarded as having such an impairment) to define the word disability. Title II's protections extend to a "qualified individual with a disability," which means:

> An individual with a disability who, with or without reasonable modifications to rules, policies, or practices, the removal of architectural, communication, or

transportation barriers, or the provision of auxiliary aids and services meets the essential eligibility requirements for the receipt of services or the participation in programs or activities provided by a public entity. (42 U.S.C. § 12131(2))

Take note of the definition's reference to reasonable "modifications." Reasonable "accommodations" are reserved for Title I of the ADA in the employment context. Also note the series of items following the phrase "with or without." These are the areas in which Title II may require a school district to undertake a specific action to ensure access to a program or activity for a student who meets the definition of a qualified individual with a disability. A school district, however, is not required to modify a rule, policy, or procedure if making the modification would fundamentally alter the nature of the service, program, or activity. Detailed regulations governing school districts' obligations concerning architectural barriers, transportation, communication, and the provision of auxiliary aids and services are in 28 C.F.R. §36.301 and following sections.

OCR enforces Title II of the ADA. Like Section 504, an allegation regarding a school district's noncompliance with the ADA will trigger an OCR investigation that will result in a letter of findings. A lawsuit also may be filed in federal court alleging a violation of the ADA. To the extent a plaintiff alleging a violation of the ADA seeks relief available under or based on an alleged violation of IDEA, the plaintiff must first utilize IDEA's administrative hearing process before pursuing ADA allegations in a civil lawsuit (*Payne*, 2011). Attorneys' fees are available under the ADA to a prevailing plaintiff.

SUMMARY

The Individuals with Disabilities Education Act (IDEA) is a comprehensive statutory scheme governing the education of children with disabilities. A school district must identify, locate, and assess all children residing within the district's geographical boundaries who may need special education and related services. To receive services under IDEA, a child must meet one of IDEA's disability categories and, by reason thereof, need special education and related services. If a child satisfies both of these criteria, the child is entitled to a free appropriate public education (FAPE).

FAPE has a procedural and substantive component. Not all procedural violations, however, constitute a denial of a FAPE. The substantive component of FAPE requires a school district's educational program to be designed to meet the student's unique educational needs, be reasonably calculated to provide the student with some educational benefit, be provided in conformity with the student's individualized education program and be in the least restrictive environment (LRE). FAPE's substantive component does not require a potential maximizing program. In this regard, school districts need only provide an educational program that is reasonably calculated to offer some educational benefit appropriate in light of the child's circumstances (*Endrew F.*, 2017).

A special education student's educational program is created by an IEP team during an IEP team meeting. An IEP team includes both mandatory (e.g., parent, general and special education teachers, administrator) and discretionary (e.g., an independent assessor, a related service staff, or an attorney) team members. An IEP team meeting must be held at least annually. IEP team meetings also must be held if requested by a parent, if there is a lack of anticipated progress, or if assessments need to be reviewed.

A special education student's IEP functions as a road map to the student's educational program. An IEP must include present levels of educational performance; measurable annual goals; special education instruction and services and program modifications; an explanation of the extent, if any, the student will not participate with nondisabled peers in general education; any modifications necessary for the student to participate in state- or districtwide assessments; the projected date for the beginning of special education services, including the anticipated frequency, location, and duration of those services; appropriate objective criteria, evaluation procedures, and schedules for determining, at least on an annual basis, whether goals are being achieved; a statement of how a student's progress toward goals will be measured; and a statement of how a student's parents will be informed of the student's progress.

Special education is specifically designed instruction without cost to the parents that meets the unique needs of the student. Special education also includes related services when necessary for the student to benefit from the student's academic program. A wide variety of related services are available. However, medical services are available only for diagnostic and evaluation purposes. School districts do not have to provide a related service if it can only be performed by a physician or hospital. Some special education students receive extended school year (ESY) services over the summer to prevent regression.

An IEP must also address a student's behavior when the behavior impedes the learning of the student or others. A behavior intervention plan (BIP) can address serious behavior problems that significantly interfere with implementation of the goals and objectives in the student's IEP. A BIP is the product of a functional behavioral assessment (FBA), which is a detailed, systematic series of observations and data resulting in a comprehensive report regarding the behavior at issue.

California uses the term Functional Analysis Assessment (FAA); it is synonymous with the federal FBA. Both the FAA and the BIP are required when a student with an IEP has a change of placement for ten days or greater.

A continuum of placement options must be available to meet a special education student's needs. All placement decisions must consider IDEA's LRE mandate, which requires that to the maximum extent appropriate, children with disabilities are educated with children who are nondisabled; and the removal of children with disabilities from the regular education environment occurs only when the nature and severity of the disability is such that the education in regular classes with the use of supplementary aids and services cannot be achieved satisfactorily. IDEA's LRE presumption does not supersede FAPE. Depending on a student's needs, placement in a more restrictive environment may be necessary for the student to receive a FAPE.

The due process hearing system is available to address special education disagreements between parents and school districts. The Office of Administrative Hearings (OAH) oversees due process hearings. Virtually every aspect of a student's educational program can be challenged in a due process hearing. A school district must maintain the child in the child's stay-put placement for the duration of the due process hearing and any subsequent appeals, absent three possible exceptions. A prevailing parent may be entitled to attorneys' fees, and in very limited instances a school district may obtain an entitlement to attorneys' fees against a parent and the parent's attorney.

Section 504 and the Americans with Disabilities Act (ADA) prohibit discrimination on the basis of disability and provide eligible students with affirmative rights. A student who is determined not to be eligible for services under IDEA may meet the eligibility criteria under Section 504 and the ADA. A student who is an individual with a disability under Section 504 (or a qualified individual with a disability under ADA) may be entitled to special services and accommodations. FAPE is required under a 504 Plan, but it is not as rigorous as that required under an IEP. In the context of Section 504, these services and accommodations can be implemented through a Section 504 plan.

9 STUDENT DISCIPLINE

Article I, Section 28 of the California Constitution specifies that all public school students and staff have the "inalienable right to attend campuses which are safe, secure, and peaceful." In Chapter 2, we discussed laws that restrict outsiders from disrupting school activities. In this chapter, we focus on student discipline. We begin our discussion with the importance of effective and legally defensible student discipline rules. Then we explore the acts for which a student may and must be disciplined. We address informal types of discipline, suspension, and expulsion. The constitutional and statutory requirements for imposing discipline are included in the discussion. We then examine in some detail the expulsion process, its components, and the power to expel, which is vested in the governing board. An explanation of the expulsion appeal process follows. Relevant case law and opinions of the California Attorney General are interspersed throughout.

We have also included a discussion of the Individuals with Disabilities Education Act's (IDEA) requirements for the discipline of students who qualify, or are suspected to qualify, for special education. We recommend reading Chapter 8 before reading this chapter in the context of students with disabilities.

THE IMPORTANCE OF STUDENT DISCIPLINE RULES

Student rules do more than merely inform students as to what conduct is impermissible. When written and implemented consistently and effectively, student rules provide order. In the wake of a 1982 U.S. Supreme Court decision, courts generally defer to the judgment of school officials on the development, interpretation, and application of student rules (*Board of Education of Rogers, Arkansas v. McCluskey*). The case involved a student who challenged the school board's reliance on a rule against drug use to expel him for drinking. The lower courts agreed that the rule was flawed and overturned the youth's expulsion. But the Supreme Court reversed the judgment, noting that "the District Court and the Court of Appeals plainly erred in replacing the Board's construction of [the rule] with their own notions under the facts of the case" (p. 971). Because alcohol can be classified as a drug, the school board was within its discretion to apply the rule as it had. As we have noted in earlier chapters, however, judges do not hesitate to become involved when student rules intrude on constitutionally protected behavior. Perhaps the best example is the seminal 1969 U.S. Supreme Court ruling in *Tinker v. Des Moines Independent Community School District*, discussed in Chapter 6. In that case, the school instituted a rule against the wearing of symbolic black armbands and then used it to suspend several students who did so. The Supreme Court held that the suspensions were unconstitutional because they deprived the students of their freedom of speech under the First Amendment.

The fact that judges normally do not second-guess educators on the development and use of student discipline rules does not mean that rule development should be taken casually. The better the rules are constructed, the more likely the courts will uphold them. A few simple illustrations will demonstrate the point. Consider a rule that states "disruptive offenses include gum chewing." Is the intent of the rule to prohibit only gum chewing that is disruptive, or all gum chewing? If the school intends to ban gum chewing, the rule should state that gum chewing is not permitted in school. Otherwise, the rule is ambiguous, and students will not know exactly what behavior is acceptable. Similarly, a rule providing that "students may be placed in an alternative education setting for insubordination to school personnel" invites uncertainty because *insubordination* is not likely to be well understood by a majority of students. A more precise and less authoritarian way of stating the rule is to say that "students may be placed in an alternative education setting for failing to follow the directives of school personnel." Here are several guidelines and suggestions for improving the quality of student discipline rules:

- Conduct periodic audits of the student code of conduct.
- Delete rules that deal with trivial matters and are not worth the cost of enforcement. Use oral directives instead.
- Make sure that rules are understandable to students. For example, elementary school rules will be worded differently than secondary school rules.
- Make sure rules are worded carefully so they do not intrude on constitutionally protected behavior (e.g., rules pertaining to campus rallies or the distribution of student literature).

- Exercise special care in developing and applying rules to govern off-campus student behavior (e.g., use of the internet). Link off-campus discipline to the legitimate interests of the school.
- Make sure that students know the rules by distributing them every year and discussing them in homeroom classes.
- Enforce the rules consistently and fairly.

All public schools in California publish a student code of conduct. Education Code Section 35291 requires school districts to prescribe rules for student discipline. At least every four years, public schools may review the rules and adopt new rules if necessary (Educ. Code § 35291.5). In developing rules under Section 35291.5, schools are to involve parents, teachers, administrators, school security personnel, and, for junior and senior high schools, students. Governing boards may prescribe procedures for giving continuing students written notice of the rules at the beginning of each school year and to transfer students when they enroll. Every school employee has the responsibility to see that the rules and discipline procedures are enforced.

Rules also serve a necessary constitutional purpose. The presence of clearly defined rules is a prerequisite to due process. The Fourteenth Amendment to the U.S. Constitution provides that no state (the public school is a political subdivision of the state) shall deprive any person of life, liberty, or property without due process of law. Article I, Section 7(a) of the California Constitution contains a similar provision. Due process requires that students first be on notice of what behavior will subject them to sanctions. Fundamental fairness requires no less.

The school campus is a microcosm of society. A school campus without order is like a society on the verge of rebellion and anarchy. Rules, however, have limits. School violence and disharmony among students can still occur despite the most meticulously written and equitably enforced rules. And when this occurs, discipline must be administered. California has developed a comprehensive set of student discipline requirements, and it is to them we now turn.

CALIFORNIA'S LEGAL FRAMEWORK FOR STUDENT DISCIPLINE

Student discipline is governed by Education Code Section 48900 and following sections. In some instances, consideration must also be given to local school district policy, the state and federal constitutions, and IDEA. Chapters 6 (Rights of Expression) and 10 (Public Access, Privacy, and Student Search and Seizure) detail the relevant constitutional issues. Judicial decisions and California Attorney

General opinions interpreting these statutes and constitutional provisions complete the legal framework for student discipline.

Who Can Discipline

Classroom teachers, principals or superintendents, and the school district's governing board all have the power to discipline a student under the Education Code. Teachers can suspend students from class for specified misbehavior or impose other related forms of discipline, although this rarely occurs without consultation with school administration (Educ. Code § 48910). The principal or superintendent can suspend students and recommend expulsion (Educ. Code § 48900). While the school district's governing board can also suspend a student, only the governing board can order an expulsion (Educ. Code §§ 48912, 48915).

A principal's designee may also discipline students. A principal may designate, in writing, one or more administrators at the school site as his or her designee to assist with disciplinary procedures. If there is no administrator in addition to the principal, a certificated employee can be the principal's designee. An additional backup employee may also be identified for imposing discipline if neither the principal nor a principal's designee is available. The names of all individuals identified as a principal's designee must be on file in the principal's office. Education Code Section 48911(h) details the requirements for classifying an individual as a principal's designee. Section 48911 also applies to the disciplinary actions of a site principal at a nonpublic school (NPS) in which a special education student is enrolled (Educ. Code § 48911.5). A NPS is a private school that has been certified by the California Department of Education to provide an educational program to special education students.

Education Code Section 48910(a) permits a teacher to suspend a student from class for the day of the offense and the following day. The teacher must immediately report the suspension to the local school site principal and send the student to the principal or principal's designee. A parent–teacher conference must be scheduled as soon as possible following the suspension. Instead of issuing a suspension, a teacher may send the student to the principal's office. During the classroom suspension, the student may not be placed in another class scheduled at the same time but may continue to attend other classes during the day with other teachers.

Due Process of Law

Before exploring the specific grounds for suspension and expulsion, it is necessary to comment on due process of law. As noted, the Fourteenth Amendment to the

U.S. Constitution prohibits a public school from depriving any person of property without due process of law. Is attending a public school a property right under the Fourteenth Amendment, and if so, what process is due prior to deprivation of that right (e.g., discipline resulting in removal from school)? In 1975, the U.S. Supreme Court took up this question in the context of short-term suspensions in the case of *Goss v. Lopez*.

In 1971, Dwight Lopez was a student attending Central High School in Columbus, Ohio. During February and March 1971, there was widespread student unrest at Central High School and other schools within the Columbus Ohio Public School System (CPSS). Dwight was suspended for ten days in connection with a disturbance in a lunchroom resulting in damage to school property. Dwight maintained he was an innocent bystander, noting that at least seventy-five other students were suspended on the same day. Dwight was not given an opportunity to respond to the charges resulting in his suspension.

Dwight and eight other students suspended in a similar manner brought a legal action against the CPSS alleging that a suspension without a hearing was unconstitutional under the Fourteenth Amendment. The Court agreed. The Court held that through the compulsory schooling law, public education is a state-created property right under the Fourteenth Amendment, invoking the necessity of due process of law prior to deprivation. Focusing on the length of the suspension (ten days), the Court held that due process of law requires that a student be given oral or written notice of the charges and, if the student denies the charges, an opportunity to present his or her side of the story. Significantly, the Court did not require school districts to provide full adversarial hearings for suspensions of up to ten days. However, the Court did note that longer suspensions (e.g., more than ten days) and permanent removal from school through an expulsion may require more formal procedures.

When students are asked to repeat a course or are retained in the same grade for the next year, are they entitled to procedural due process as in *Goss v. Lopez*? The purpose of procedural due process essentially is to elicit truth. When academic decisions are made, truth normally is not in question. Test score performance, grades, and consultations with the student and the student's parents reveal the reason for these actions.

Thus, a *Goss v. Lopez*-type hearing is not necessary for academic disputes.

Whether procedural or substantive, there must be a deprivation of a liberty or property interest for due process to be required under the federal constitution. Does a student have such an interest in extracurricular and athletic activities? In the first California appellate decision to consider the matter, the answer insofar as the federal constitution is concerned was no. But the court was less certain in the context of the California Constitution (*Ryan v. California Interscholastic Federation—San Diego Section,* 2001). In this ruling, the court was faced with a case involving a student from Australia who was determined by the California Interscholastic Federation (CIF) not to be eligible for interscholastic football because he had already completed eight semesters of schooling beyond initial enrollment in the ninth grade. Established in 1914, CIF was recognized by the legislature in 1981 as a voluntary, nonprofit organization responsible for administering interscholastic athletics in California secondary schools under a set of eligibility rules and complaint procedures (Educ. Code § 33353 et seq.; see also § 35179 et seq.). CIF also determined that the student was not eligible under the Federation's transfer rule because his family had not changed their Australian residence. The student challenged the decision as a violation of his due process rights under both the federal and California constitutions.

Citing a long line of federal court decisions, the California court of appeal held that participation in interscholastic sports, like being a class officer or acting in a school play, is a privilege, not a right, under the Fourteenth Amendment. Thus, a *Goss v. Lopez*-type hearing is not required when a student is denied an opportunity to participate. The student also argued that his constitutionally protected Fourteenth Amendment liberty right to a good reputation was damaged by CIF's ruling that the district's head football coach had violated the Federation's undue influence rule in working with the student. But the court was not supportive, noting that the U.S. Supreme Court has ruled that reputation becomes a protected liberty only when the person's reputation is stigmatized by public officials in the context of loss of a significant state-conferred benefit, such as employment or welfare. Here the student's athletic ineligibility did not rise to this level. Further, the court questioned how the student's reputation had been damaged over a matter involving the coach.

With regard to the California Constitution, the court recognized that the state Supreme Court had ruled in 1979 that neither a liberty right nor a property right has to be involved for a person to invoke the due process clause of Article 1, Section 7(a) (*People v. Ramirez*). However, the amount of process due depends on the nature of the statutorily conferred benefit or interest that is at stake. If the benefit is minor, then informal due process will suffice prior to deprivation. But if the benefit is significant, then more formal due process becomes necessary. In this case, the appellate court could not identify what statutorily conferred benefit was at stake. While students have a constitutionally protected right not to be charged for participating in extracurricular activities and on athletic teams as part of a free public education, there is no statutory entitlement to participate. The judges noted that, even if some procedural due process were necessary in this case, CIF's eligibility rules and internal appeal process satisfied it.

The requirements of due process under the federal constitution as identified in *Goss v. Lopez* and particularly under the more supportive California Constitution account for the due process procedures set forth in Section 48900 and following sections of the California Education Code for student discipline.

TYPES OF DISCIPLINE

School discipline can be divided into three categories: discipline short of suspension, suspension, and expulsion. All three categories are important for the maintenance of order and control in a public school. It is the latter two categories, however, that invoke the Education Code and both the informal and formal procedures noted in *Goss v. Lopez* (1975). Corporal punishment is not among the disciplinary options available as it is explicitly prohibited by Education Code Section 49001.

Discipline Short of Suspension

Education Code Section 48925(d) defines which types of discipline are not considered suspension. These types of discipline include reassignment to another education program or class at the same school, where the student will receive continuing instruction for the duration of the school day as other students in the same grade level; referral to a certificated employee designated by the principal to advise students (e.g., a counselor); and removal from class, but without reassignment to another class or program, for the remainder of the class period without sending the student to the principal or the principal's designee. Removal of a student from a particular class cannot occur more than once every five school days. These low-level types of discipline may be helpful for teachers and administrators who must maintain order on a daily basis. They are a function of school district policy and do not invoke the statutory requirements of the Education Code. For special education students, implementation of behavior management techniques in an individualized education program (IEP) or reassignment of a student's classroom per an IEP does not constitute a suspension. Chapter 8 addresses behavior plans and IEPs.

Suspension

The Education Code's grounds for suspension are a catalogue of inappropriate student conduct. Column A of Table 9.1 lists the acts for which suspension may or shall (must) be imposed. These are all the acts contained in Education Code Sections 48900, 48900.2, 48900.3, 48900.4, and 48900.7. We have included the statutory citations for offenses in cell A3 of Table 9.1 because they are specifically referenced elsewhere in the discipline statutes. Readers need to keep in mind,

TABLE 9.1
Disciplinary Acts and Consequences

Column A	Column B	Column C	Column D
Student Act (Acts are specified in Educ. Code Sections 48900–48900.4, 48900.7, and 48915)	School Administration Response to Act	Finding to Recommend Expulsion to Governing Board	Final Action If Governing Board Adopts Recommendation from Expulsion Hearing
A1	**B1**	**C1**	**D1**
Possessing, selling, or otherwise furnishing a firearm. Possession must be verified by a school district employee.	Immediate suspension and mandatory recommendation for expulsion.	Student committed the act.	The governing board must order expulsion of the student. The governing board *may* suspend enforcement of the expulsion order.
Brandishing a knife at another person.			
Unlawfully selling a controlled substance listed in the Health and Safety Code.			
Committing or attempting to commit a sexual assault as defined in Subdivision (n) of Section 48900 or committing a sexual battery as defined in Subdivision (n) of Section 48900.			
Possession of an explosive.			
A2	**B2**	**C2**	**D2**
Causing serious physical injury to another person, except in self-defense.	The student *may* be suspended for a first-time offense if (1) The student is determined to have committed an act violating Section 48900(a)–(e); or (2) through his or her presence the student causes a danger to persons or property or threatens to disrupt the instructional process.	Student committed the act. Other means of correction are not feasible or have repeatedly failed to bring about proper conduct, and/or due to the nature of the act, the student's presence creates a continuing danger to the physical safety of the student or others.	The governing board *may* order expulsion. If the governing board orders expulsion, the governing board *may* suspend enforcement of the expulsion order.
Possession of any knife or other dangerous object of no reasonable use to the pupil.			
Unlawful possession of any controlled substance listed in the Health and Safety Code, except for the first offense for the possession of not more than one avoirdupois ounce of marijuana, other than concentrated cannabis, or possession of over-the-counter medication or medication prescribed by a physician for the student.			

(Continued)

TABLE 9.1
(Continued)

Column A	Column B	Column C	Column D
Robbery or extortion. Assault or battery, as defined in Penal Code Sections 240 and 242, upon any school employee.	Otherwise, suspension can be imposed only when other means of correction fail to bring about proper conduct. The student must be recommended for expulsion unless inappropriate due to the particular circumstances.		
A3 Caused, attempted to cause, or threatened to cause physical injury to another person(Educ. Code § 48900(a)(1)). Willfully used force or violence upon the person of another, except in self-defense (Educ. Code § 48900(a)(2)). Possessed, sold, or otherwise furnished any firearm, knife, explosive, or other dangerous object, unless, in the case of possession of any object of this type, the pupil had obtained written permission to possess the item from a certificated school employee, which is concurred in by the principal or the designee of the principal(Educ. Code § 48900(b)). Except for possession or sale of a firearm or possession of an explosive (see A1) or possession of a knife or other dangerous object of no reasonable use to the student (see A2).	**B3** The student *may* be suspended for a first-time offense if (1) The student is determined to have committed an act violating Section 48900(a)–(e); or (2) through his or her presence the student causes a danger to persons or property or threatens to disrupt the instructional process. Otherwise, suspension can only be imposed when other means of correction fail to bring about proper conduct. The student may be recommended for expulsion.	**C3** Student committed the act. Other means of correction are not feasible or have repeatedly failed to bring about proper conduct, and/or due to the nature of the act, the student's presence creates a continuing danger to the physical safety of the student or others.	**D3** The governing board *may* order expulsion. If the governing board orders expulsion, the governing board *may* suspend enforcement of the expulsion order. (Note: Education Code Section 48915 does not specifically reference Education Code Sections 48900(d)–(q) and (s) or 48900.7. No court has addressed the possible implications of this omission. However, some school districts have taken a conservative approach by still requiring the findings noted in cell C3 before ordering expulsion.)

Unlawfully possessed, used, sold, or otherwise furnished, or been under the influence of, any controlled substance listed in the Health and Safety Code, an alcoholic beverage, or an intoxicant of any kind (Educ. Code § 48900(c)). *Except for unlawful sale (see A1) or possession (see A2) of a controlled substance.*

Unlawfully offered, arranged, or negotiated to sell any controlled substance listed in the Health and Safety Code, an alcoholic beverage, or an intoxicant of any kind; and either sold, delivered, or otherwise furnished to any person another liquid, substance, or material and represented the liquid, substance, or material as a controlled substance, alcoholic beverage, or intoxicant (Educ. Code § 48900(d)). *Except for unlawful sale (see A1) or possession (see A2) of a controlled substance.*

Committed or attempted to commit robbery or extortion (Educ. Code § 48900(e)). *Except for committing robbery or extortion (see A2).*

Caused or attempted to cause damage to school property or private property (Educ. Code § 48900(f)).

Stole or attempted to steal school property or private property (EDUC. Code § 48900(g)).

Possessed or used tobacco, or any products containing tobacco or nicotine products, including, but not limited to, cigarettes, cigars, miniature cigars, clove cigarettes, smokeless tobacco, snuff, chew packets, and betel. However, this section does not prohibit use or possession by a student of his or her own prescription products (Educ. Code § 48900(h)).

Committed an obscene act or engaged in habitual profanity or vulgarity (Educ. Code § 48900(i)).

Unlawfully possessed or unlawfully offered, arranged, or negotiated to sell any drug paraphernalia, as defined in Section 11014.5 of the Health and Safety Code (Educ. Code § 48900(j)).

Disrupted school activities or otherwise willfully defied the valid authority of supervisors, teachers, administrators, school officials, or other school personnel engaged in the performance of their duties (Educ. Code § 48900(k)). Exception, as amended in 2020: A school may not suspend any pupil enrolled in kindergarten or any of grades 1 through 5, for disrupting school activities or otherwise willfully defying the authority of schoolteachers, administrators or other school personnel, and those acts shall not constitute grounds for a pupil enrolled in kindergarten or any of grades first through twelfth, inclusive, to be recommended for expulsion. This change effectively eliminates the ability of schools to expel a student for disruption of school activities or willfully defying authority.

Knowingly received stolen school property or private property (Educ. Code § 48900(l)).

Possessed an imitation firearm. "Imitation firearm" means a replica of a firearm that is so substantially similar in physical properties to an existing firearm as to lead a reasonable person to conclude that the replica is a firearm (Educ. Code § 48900(m)).

Harassed, threatened, or intimidated a pupil who is a complaining witness or a witness in a school disciplinary proceeding for the purpose of either preventing that pupil from being a witness, retaliating against that pupil for being a witness, or both (Educ. Code § 48900(o)).

Unlawfully offered, arranged to sell, negotiated to sell, or sold the prescription drug Soma (Educ. Code § 48900(p)).

Engaged in, or attempted to engage in, hazing as defined in Education Code Section 48900(q).

Engaged in bullying, including communications made in writing or by means of an electronic act (Educ. Code § 48900(r)). Electronic act includes a communication originated, created, or transmitted on or off the school site. However, school personnel still must carefully evaluate discipline for an electronic act that occurs off site to ensure that any disciplinary action does not violate the free speech rights of the offending student.

Aiding or abetting, as defined in Penal Code Section 31, the infliction or attempted infliction of physical injury to another person may result in suspension of the offending student. However, a student who has been adjudged by a juvenile court to have committed, as an aider and abettor, a crime of physical violence in which the victim suffered great bodily injury or serious bodily injury will be subject to discipline under Education Code Section 48900(a) (Educ. Code § 48900(s)).

Committed sexual harassment (inapplicable to students enrolled in kindergarten and grades 1 to 3, inclusive) (Educ. Code § 48900.2).

Caused, attempted to cause, threatened to cause, or participated in an act of hate violence as defined in Education Code Section 233(e) (Educ. Code § 48900.3).

Intentionally engaged in harassment, threats, or intimidation, directed against school district personnel or students, that is sufficiently severe or pervasive to have the actual and reasonably expected effect of materially disrupting classwork, creating substantial disorder, and invading the rights of either school personnel or students by creating an intimidating or hostile educational environment (Educ. Code § 48900.4).

Made terroristic threats against school officials, school property, or both (Educ. Code § 48900.7).

however, that these sections of the Education Code are frequently amended. Thus, it is advisable to consult a current copy of the Education Code in conjunction with studying this table.

A1 details the particular circumstances under which an act in Section 48900 requires immediate suspension. All the particular circumstances in this section are derived from an act or acts in Section 48900. For example, brandishing a knife is a combination of Section 48900(a)(1) (attempting to cause or threatening physical injury to another person) and Section 48900(b) (possession of a knife). Section 48915(a) also sets forth particular circumstances based on an act or combination of acts in Section 48900 (such as assault or battery on any school employee).

The general rule is that a suspension must be imposed only when other means of correction fail to bring about proper conduct (Educ. Code § 48900.5). Other means of correction include, but are not limited to, a conference with the student and the student's parents, referral to a counselor or psychologist, the development of an individualized behavior plan, enrollment in an anger management program, assignment to an after-school program that addresses specific behavioral issues, or community service (to be discussed in the following pages).

While suspension for a first-time offense is typically not an option, certain acts permit, and may require, suspension regardless of whether other means of correction may bring about proper conduct—for example, if a student

- is determined to have committed an act violating Section 48900(a)–(e) as set forth in cell A3 of Table 9.1, or
- through his or her presence causes a danger to persons or property or threatens to disrupt the instructional process (cells B2 and B3).

Additionally, immediate suspension must occur for a student determined to have committed certain acts listed in cell A1. Either the principal or district superintendent must determine whether the student did the act for which suspension may, or must, be imposed.

Implementation of a suspension requires the informal notice and meeting requirements discussed in *Goss*. At the time of a student's suspension, a school employee must make a reasonable effort to contact the student's parent in person or by telephone. A report of the suspension, including the cause for the suspension, must be sent to the school district's governing board or superintendent consistent with district policy. Certain acts require the principal or principal's designee to inform the appropriate law enforcement agency prior to suspension (Educ. Code § 48902). Law enforcement reporting is required for acts that may violate Penal Code Sections 245 (assault with a deadly weapon or force likely to produce great bodily injury), 626.9 or 626.10 (possession of weapons on campus), and Education Code Section 48900(c)–(d) (controlled substances, alcohol, intoxicants, and lookalike substances). A principal or principal's designee reporting to law enforcement a potential violation of Penal Code Section 245 or Education Code Section 48900(c)–(d) may not be held civilly or criminally liable unless a knowingly false report is made or the report is made with a reckless disregard for the truth.

Consistent with *Goss*, the Education Code generally requires a suspension to be preceded with an informal conference among school administration, the student, and whenever practicable the school employee who referred the student for discipline. Parents must respond without delay to a request to meet with school administrators regarding their child's behavior. At the conference, the student is informed of the evidence against them and is given an opportunity to present the student's side of the story. However, if an "emergency situation" exists, a student may be suspended without an informal conference. An emergency situation is defined here as a situation determined to constitute a clear and present danger to the life, safety, or health of other students or school personnel (Educ. Code § 48911(c)). A student subject to a suspension in an emergency situation must receive an informal conference within two school days of the suspension unless the student waives his or her right to the conference or is unable to attend. Since parents hold the students' education rights until age eighteen, school personnel should not rely on a student waiver but should confirm that a student's parent agrees to waive the right to a conference.

May a student suspected of sexual harassment learn the names of his accusers during the informal presuspension meeting? No. In *Granowitz v. Redlands Unified School District (2003)*, Evan Granowitz was given a five-day suspension for sexual harassment. During the presuspension conference, Evan and his father, an attorney, requested the names of the students who had accused Evan. The principal did not disclose the names of these individuals, due to the nature of the accusations. Evan served his suspension and graduated. A few months later Evan, with his father as his attorney, sued the school district and the principal alleging a denial of due process of law. The principal was sued in his individual capacity and found liable by the superior court in excess of $100,000 under a federal statute known as 42 U.S.C. § 1983 that is discussed in Chapter 12.

The school district appealed and prevailed on all issues. The principal, in the appellate court's view, gave Evan all the process he was due under *Goss*. Citing the confidentiality provision in Education Code Section 48918(f) for expulsion hearings, which permits witnesses to remain anonymous to avoid psychological harm, the court also upheld the principal's decision not to identify these individuals in the suspension process.

A single suspension cannot exceed five consecutive school days in California (Educ. Code § 48911). As a general rule, a student cannot be suspended for more than twenty school days in one school year (Educ. Code § 48903(a)). The two exceptions to the limit of twenty school days pertain to a student who has his or her suspension extended or who transfers to another school (including a continuation school), in which case the limit is thirty days. Note that suspensions extended as a result of additional facts likely require a repeat of the notice and opportunity to be heard on the new facts. The school may extend the suspension of a student committing an act resulting in a recommendation for expulsion while the expulsion is being processed (Educ. Code § 48911(g)). An extension of a suspension can occur only if it has been determined, following a meeting in which the student and the student's parents are invited to participate, that the student's presence at school or at an alternative school placement would cause a danger to persons or property or a threat of disrupting the educational process. This meeting can be held with the informal conference that generally precedes a suspension. A thirty-school-day limit on suspensions applies to a student who enrolls in or is transferred to another regular school, an opportunity school or class, or a continuation education school or class (Educ. Code § 48903(a)). A school district may, but does not have to, count suspensions a student received in another school district toward the foregoing limitations on the length of suspensions.

While there is no appeal of a suspension, a school district's governing board may meet to consider suspension of a student prior to issuance of the suspension, although this seldom occurs as due process does not require it. The governing board's meeting can be in closed session if holding a public hearing would result in the disclosure of private student information (as defined in Education Code § 49073 et seq.). Prior to holding a meeting for this purpose, the governing board must inform the student and the student's parents if he or she is eighteen years of age, in writing of the intent of the governing board to hold a closed session. Within forty-eight hours of this notice, a student may make a written request for a public meeting. If disclosure of private student information would occur in a public meeting, however, a closed meeting may be held.

Traditional suspensions are not the only options available as discipline for acts that do not warrant expulsion. Instead of suspension from school, a student may be required to perform community service on school grounds outside of school hours (Educ. Code § 48900.6). With written parental consent, a student may be required to perform community service off school grounds. Community service includes, but is not limited to, work in the areas of outdoor beautification; community or campus betterment; and teacher, peer, or youth assistance. Community service is not an option if the student is suspended pending expulsion.

Instead of suspension from school, a student may be ordered to a supervised suspension classroom for the entire period of the suspension (Educ. Code § 48911.1). A supervised suspension classroom is not available if expulsion proceedings have been initiated or the student poses an imminent danger or threat to the campus, students, or staff. During imposition of a supervised suspension classroom, the student remains separated from other students at the school site. A parent must be notified in person or by telephone when the parent's child is assigned to a supervised suspension classroom. Written parental notice is required when a student is assigned to a supervised suspension classroom for longer than one class period.

Interestingly, a teacher may also require a student's parent to attend school with a student suspended from a class (Educ. Code § 48900.1). Such unusual punishment is reserved for violations of Education Code Sections 48900(i) (obscene act, habitual profanity, or vulgarity) or 48900(k) (disrupting school activities). School districts may adopt a policy to require parent attendance. The parent attends the class from which the student was suspended. The policy shall take into account reasonable factors that may prevent compliance with a notice to attend. The attendance of the parent or guardian shall be limited to the class from which the pupil was suspended. The policy must require the parent to meet with a school administrator after the classroom visit.

Expulsion

The same acts that qualify a student for suspension can also result in a recommendation for expulsion. There are three classes of offenses for which a recommendation for expulsion is permissible. The acts in cell A1 of Table 9.1 require a recommendation for expulsion. The acts in cell A2 require a recommendation for expulsion unless such a recommendation is inappropriate under the circumstances. A school administrator may recommend expulsion for a student determined to have committed an act in cell A3. As Table 9.1 indicates, a recommendation for expulsion from a school administrator is the first step in the expulsion process. The other three steps are detailed in the following subsections.

Mandatory recommendation for expulsion. A student committing an act described in cell A1 of Table 9.1 must be immediately suspended and recommended for expulsion.

Possession of a firearm requires an employee of the school district to verify the student's possession of the firearm. Student possession of a firearm on school grounds is permissible if prior written permission is obtained from a certificated employee (e.g., a teacher), and the permission is concurred in by the principal or principal's designee (Educ. Code § 48915(c)(1)). Most likely due to the unfortunate and tragic school shootings of recent years, the authors are not aware of any contemporary instances in which a school district has allowed a student to possess a firearm on a school campus under this provision of the Education Code. Further, possession of a firearm on a school campus would also have to comply with the Gun-Free School Zone Act (Penal Code § 626.9). Under this criminal law, a school district superintendent, his or her designee, or equivalent school authority must give written permission for a student to possess a firearm in a school zone.

Does a student impermissibly have possession of a firearm if he or she finds the weapon on campus and is merely delivering it to school officials for disposal? No. A 1997 California Attorney General opines that "possession" requires a student to knowingly and voluntarily have direct control over a firearm and does not include brief possession solely for the purpose of delivery to school officials (80 Ops. Atty. Gen. 91). Possession of an imitation firearm may, but does not have to, result in mandatory suspension and expulsion.

The Education Code defines a knife as "any dirk, dagger, or other weapon with a fixed, sharpened blade fitted primarily for stabbing, a weapon with a blade fitted primarily for stabbing, a weapon with a blade longer than three and one-half inches, a folding knife with a blade that locks into place, or a razor with an unguarded blade" (Educ. Code § 48915(g)). The term *explosive* has the same meaning as the phrase "destructive device" as described in Section 921 of the Title 18 of the United States Code (Educ. Code § 48915(h)). The U.S. Code provides a broad definition of the phrase "destructive device," which includes, among other items, a bomb, grenade, any similar device, and a weapon capable of expelling a projectile (save for a shotgun). Although a shotgun is not considered a "destructive device," it is still prohibited as a firearm.

These are not the only instances in which a school administrator has to cross-reference another statute to determine whether a student has committed an act warranting expulsion. For example, drug offenses reference the Health and Safety Code and the prohibition against sexual assault and battery reference the Penal Code. The entire California Code is available on the internet at www.leginfo.ca.gov or in a law library. In the following list, we comment on the Health and Safety and Penal Code sections relevant to acts that mandate a recommendation for expulsion:

- A recommendation for expulsion is mandated for a student who is determined to have unlawfully sold a controlled substance listed in Chapter 2 (commencing with Section 11053) in the Health and Safety Code (Educ. Code § 48915(c)(3)). Health and Safety Code Section 11053 and the pertinent following sections contain an exhaustive list of controlled substances ranging from the commonly known (opium, cocaine, marijuana) to the obscure (Levoalphacetylmethadol).

- A recommendation for expulsion is mandated for a student who is determined to have committed or attempted to commit a sexual assault as defined in Sections 261, 266c, 286, 288, 288a, or 289 of the Penal Code or committing a sexual battery as defined in Section 243.4 of the Penal Code (Educ. Code § 48915(c)(4)). These provisions of the Penal Code supply detailed definitions of a wide range of acts, from touching a person against his or her will for purposes of sexual gratification to rape.

May a school district enforce a "zero tolerance" policy mandating an immediate suspension and recommendation for expulsion for a student who committed an act other than those described in cell A1 of Table 9.1? This was the issue a California court of appeal addressed in a 2004 decision (*T.H. v. San Diego Unified School District*). T.H. was a twelve-year-old student who engaged in three fighting incidents during the school year. Under the district's zero-tolerance policy, a school principal or designee was required to suspend and recommend for expulsion all students who were "involved in three or more incidents of fighting that inflicts injury or trespassing within one year" (p. 538). After her third fighting incident, T.H. was immediately suspended and recommended for expulsion.

After reviewing the evidence, the expulsion panel determined that T.H. violated the regulation. The panel also noted that T.H. had been suspended on five previous occasions for acts ranging from sexual harassment to inflicting physical injury. The panel determined that expulsion was appropriate because other means of correction were not feasible and T.H.'s continued presence at school caused a physical danger to T.H. and others. As we discuss later in the chapter, these additional findings must be made for a student committing acts in cells A2 and A3 of Table 9.1 if the expulsion hearing is to result in a recommendation of expulsion to the governing board. T.H. brought a legal action challenging the zero-tolerance policy.

In relevant part, T.H. argued that the policy violated the Education Code by removing the principal's statutory discretion to not recommend expulsion. Recall that only those acts in Education Code Section 48915(c) (as detailed in cell A1 of Table 9.1) entirely remove a principal's discretion in recommending expulsion. The offense described in the district's regulation is not among the acts in Education Code Section 48915(c). T.H. argued that, except for those acts described in Education Code Section 48915(c), a principal must always be able to exercise discretion in determining whether or not to recommend expulsion. The appellate court did not agree with T.H. The court held that the Education

Code's imposition of a mandatory recommendation for expulsion to certain acts did not preclude a school district from applying a mandatory recommendation for expulsion to other acts (e.g., three or more instances of fighting that inflict injury in the case of T.H.).

Mandatory recommendation for expulsion unless inappropriate. A determination that a student has committed an act described in cell A2 of Table 9.1 mandates a recommendation for expulsion unless it would be inappropriate due to the circumstances or alternative means of correction would address the misconduct. If the latter, then the principal or superintendent must make the determination as soon as possible so the student does not lose instructional time. Assault or battery, as defined in Sections 204 and 242 of the Penal Code, on any school employee is one of the particular circumstances warranting expulsion (unless inappropriate due to the circumstances) in cell A2. Penal Code Section 240 defines an assault as an unlawful attempt, coupled with a present ability, to commit a violent injury on the person of another. Penal Code Section 242 defines a battery as any willful and unlawful use of force or violence upon the person of another.

Another particular circumstance in cell A2 is possession, not sale, of a controlled substance (Educ. Code § 48915(a)(3)). The previously noted definition of a controlled substance (which was discussed in the context of selling a controlled substance) also applies to the possession of a controlled substance.

While the acts in cell A2 are still quite serious, the California Legislature has given school administrators some discretion in recommending expulsion. The initial recommendation for expulsion, however, is a distinct and separate step from the findings necessary for the expulsion hearing to result in a recommendation for expulsion to the governing board. Cell C2 of Table 9.1 notes the additional findings necessary to expel a student for committing an act in cell A2. We discuss these additional findings next.

Discretionary expulsion. A student determined to have committed one of the remaining acts in Education Code Section 48900 may be recommended for expulsion. A student cannot be expelled for committing one of the acts described in cells A2 and A3 of Table 9.1 unless there is a further determination of either of the following as delineated in cells C2 and C3:

- Other means of correction are not feasible, or have repeatedly failed to bring about proper conduct; or
- due to the nature of the act, the presence of the pupil causes a continuing danger to the physical safety of the student or others (Educ. Code § 48915(b) and (e)).

The Education Code does not require either of the preceding determinations prior to a principal or superintendent making a recommendation for expulsion. However, the expulsion hearing cannot result in a recommendation for expulsion to the governing board without such a determination. If a school administrator does not consider this issue prior to making a recommendation for expulsion, the school district may terminate the expulsion proceedings prior to the hearing. For example, a student with no prior disciplinary record who violates Education Code Section 48900(l) (receiving stolen property) will most likely be suspended and not recommended for expulsion. This is because the absence of prior discipline is evidence that other means of correction may be feasible, and there have not been any prior attempts to bring about proper conduct. Additionally, receiving stolen property is not an act that typically causes physical danger to the student or others. An entirely different result may occur in our hypothetical if the act of receiving stolen property is replaced with a violation of Education Code Section 48900.7 (terroristic threats against school officials).

Certain subdivisions of Section 48900 cross-reference the Health and Safety and Penal Codes. Education Code Sections 48900(c)–(d) reference the same Health and Safety Code definition of a controlled substance. Education Code Section 48900(n) references the same Penal Code definition of sexual assault and battery discussed earlier in this chapter. Expulsion may also be recommended for a student who is determined to have unlawfully possessed or unlawfully offered, arranged, or negotiated to sell any drug paraphernalia, as defined in Section 11014.5 of the Health and Safety Code (Educ. Code § 48900(j)). Section 11014.5 defines the term *drug paraphernalia* broadly as follows:

> All equipment, products and materials of any kind which are designed for use or marketed for use, in planting, propagating, cultivating, growing, harvesting, manufacturing, compounding, converting, producing, processing, preparing, testing, analyzing, packaging, repackaging, storing, containing, concealing, injecting, ingesting, inhaling, or otherwise introducing into the human body a controlled substance in violation of this division.

Drug paraphernalia includes devices designed for preparing, testing, and measuring controlled substances (e.g., kits, testing equipment, and scales).

Education Code Section 48900.2 permits discretionary expulsion for sexual harassment, which is defined in Education Code Section 212.5 as follows:

> Unwelcome sexual advances, requests for sexual favors, and other verbal, visual, or physical conduct of a sexual nature, made by someone from or in the work or educational setting, under any of the following conditions:

(a) Submission to the conduct is explicitly or implicitly made a term or a condition of an individual's employment, academic status, or progress.
(b) Submission to, or rejection of, the conduct by the individual is used as the basis of employment or academic decisions affecting the individual.
(c) The conduct has the purpose or effect of having a negative impact upon the individual's work or academic performance, or of creating an intimidating, hostile, or offensive work or educational environment.
(d) Submission to, or rejection of, the conduct by the individual is used as the basis for any decision affecting the individual regarding benefits and services, honors, programs, or activities available at or through the educational institution.

Swift school district action against student-on-student sexual harassment does more than maintain the integrity of the educational setting and the dignity of students. It can also be an important defense to a civil rights lawsuit against a school district and its employees, based on an alleged failure to adequately address student-on-student sexual harassment. Chapter 11 explores the issue of school district and school district employee liability for student-on-student sexual harassment.

Discipline for an Act Not on School Grounds

A student may be suspended and/or expelled for an act that does not occur on school grounds. A student may be disciplined for an act relating to a school activity or attendance that occurs while on school grounds; while going to or coming from school; during lunch period, whether on or off campus; and during, or while going to or coming from, a school-sponsored event (Educ. Code § 48900(s)). These circumstances in which discipline is permissible for an act not on school grounds are illustrative rather than exhaustive.

Can a student be disciplined for an act occurring on a campus the student is not attending? Yes. A 1991 California court of appeal decision upheld a governing board's decision to expel a student for an altercation on a campus the student was not attending (*Fremont Union High School District v. Santa Clara County Board of Education*). In *Fremont*, Matthew was attending an alternative program when he went to a comprehensive high school campus within the district. Matthew was not taking any classes at the high school. On the high school campus, he used a stun gun on another student. Expulsion proceedings led to the governing board voting to expel Matthew for possessing a dangerous object without permission while on a district campus and causing, attempting to cause, or threatening to cause physical injury to another person. Matthew appealed the expulsion order to the county board of education. The county board reversed the order to expel because

Matthew was not attending his own school or engaged in his own school activity when he used the stun gun. The school district petitioned a court to reverse the county board and prevailed. The court held that as long as the prohibited act is related to school activity or attendance within the district, discipline is permissible.

However, the off-campus behavior must have some legitimate relation to the school's interests and must not involve constitutionally protected activity. That protected activity is a high bar. Education Code Section 44807 extends the discipline authority of school personnel to student conduct on the way to and from school. Thus, should a fight break out at an off-campus bus stop, the school could have authority to discipline the guilty students. But suppose students at the bus stop were to distribute a newspaper of their own making that is highly critical of the school principal. Because expression is involved, school officials would have a harder time justifying disciplinary action. As we noted in Chapter 6, for expression to be ground for discipline, school officials must be prepared to show that it creates material disruption or substantial interference with the rights of others. In this scenario, if an investigation established that the distribution of the newspaper interfered with students boarding or exiting the bus, discipline might then be warranted.

Or consider a situation where student athletes engage in drinking at a private residence following a football game. In this situation, the disciplinary arm of the school may not reach far enough to suspend or expel the students for violating the school's rule against drinking. As the U.S. Court of Appeals for the Fifth Circuit noted some years ago, "the width of a street might very well determine the breadth of the school board's authority" (*Shanley v. Northeast Independent School District*, 1972, p. 974). Students engaged in wrongdoing off campus are within the jurisdiction of the police and, of course, their parents. In our drinking scenario, the school could conceivably remove the athletes who consumed alcohol from the team if they had signed training rules committing them not to consume alcohol on or off campus during the season. Unlike compulsory schooling, participation in extracurricular activities is considered a privilege, not a right, and can be conditioned in this way. Of course, an investigation would be necessary to identify those students who had in fact been drinking.

Increasingly, school administrators are reviewing student communication occurring electronically whether by text or a social network on the internet to determine whether the communication warrants discipline. Education Code Section 48900(r) contains a detailed definition of what is commonly known as cyberbullying. Bullying is defined as any severe or pervasive physical or verbal act or conduct, including communications by means of an electronic act, directed at one or more pupils, and of such a nature that can be reasonably predicted to have the effect of one or more of the following: place the pupil in fear of harm to his or her person or property; cause a reasonable pupil to experience a substantially detrimental effect on his or her mental or physical health; cause a reasonable pupil to experience substantial interference with his or her academic performance; or cause a reasonable pupil to experience substantial interference with his or her ability to participate in or benefit from the services, activities, or privileges provided by a school.

The term *electronic act* includes, but is not limited to, a message, text, sound, video, image, or post on a social media site with such features as a "burn page" of another student, an impersonation of another student, or a false profile of an actual student—all for bullying purposes. Transmission can be made by such electronic communication devices as a telephone, cell phone, computer, or pager. The statute also includes a prohibition on cyber sexual bullying, which "means the dissemination of, or the solicitation or incitement to disseminate, a photograph or other visual recording by a pupil to another pupil or to school personnel by means of an electronic act that has or can be reasonably predicted to have" a similar effect on the victim, including a "photograph or other visual recording . . . that includes "the depiction of a nude, semi-nude, or sexually explicit photograph or other visual recording of a minor where the minor is identifiable from the photograph, visual recording, or other electronic act."

Involuntary Transfer

Education Code Section 48432.5 permits the involuntary transfer of a student to a continuation school. The governing board of each high school must adopt rules and regulations for the involuntary transfer of students. If a transfer is initiated, the student and the student's parents must be given written notice of their right to request a meeting with a designee of the district superintendent prior to the transfer. At the meeting, the student and the parents are to be informed of the specific facts and reasons for the transfer. The meeting must also permit the student and the parents an opportunity to inspect all documents relied on, question any evidence and witnesses presented, and present evidence on the student's behalf. A student may bring a representative and/or witnesses to the meeting with the superintendent's designee.

An involuntary transfer must be based on a finding that the student committed an act in Education Code Section 48900 or has been habitually truant or irregular in attendance at school. Generally, an involuntary transfer can be imposed only when other means of correction fail to bring about school improvement. However, a student may be involuntarily transferred the first time the student commits an act in Education Code Section 48900 (see cell A3 in Table 9.1) if the principal determines that the student's presence causes a danger to persons or property or threatens to interrupt the educational process. Additionally, a 2014 California Court of Appeals case held that Section 48432.5 does not require exhaustion of all other means of correction. The court also explained that an involuntary transfer to a continuation school does not affect a student's interest in an education because the transfer does not deny the student enrollment at a public school, rather it is simply a different school site (*Nathan G. v. Clovis Unified School District*.

A decision to involuntarily transfer a student to a continuation school must be in writing, state the facts and reasons for the decision, and be sent to the student and the student's parents. The written notice must also indicate whether the decision to involuntarily transfer the student is subject to periodic review and the procedures for review. None of the individuals involved in making a final decision to involuntarily transfer a student may be staff at the school where the student is currently enrolled. The involuntary transfer must not extend beyond the end of the semester following the semester during which the acts leading directly to the involuntary transfer occurred. A governing board with an adopted procedure for yearly review of an involuntary transfer may extend the time period for review of the transfer.

A student convicted of a violent felony or misdemeanor under the provisions of the Penal Code may be transferred to another school if the student and the victim of the crime are enrolled in the same school (Educ. Code § 48929). This new law requires the district's governing board to first adopt a policy that gives the student and the student's parent or guardian a right to request a meeting with the principal or designee, requires prior attempts to resolve the conflict through dispute resolution measures and counseling, and describes the process for the board's consideration. Additionally, the policy must be included in the district's annual notice to parents and guardians of their rights and responsibilities.

Dismissal from a Charter School

Charter schools are subject to some, but not all, of the laws applicable to traditional public schools. Education Code Section 48918, which provides for an expulsion hearing, does not apply to students in charter schools. The pertinent charter school case, *Scott B. v. Board of Trustees of Orange County High School of the Arts* (2013), involved a student who brought a knife to school. The board moved to dismiss the student, and the student appealed under California expulsion statutes. However, the court recognized that there is a difference between being expelled and being dismissed, finding that Scott was dismissed and therefore not entitled to the procedural protection of an expulsion hearing. The court observed that Scott was free to immediately enroll in his traditional public school of residence upon being dismissed from the charter school. Such is not the case for an expelled student attempting to enroll in a different high school. This is perhaps unrealistic as it is difficult to see a public high school immediately accepting him, because bringing a knife to that school likely would have resulted in an expulsion, Nevertheless, the court's decision is frequently used by charter schools.

THE EXPULSION PROCESS

Education Code Section 48900 details the acts qualifying a student for suspension and/or expulsion. Education Code Section 48915 notes the particular circumstances when a student committing an act in Section 48900 may or must be recommended for expulsion. Section 48915 also notes whether a governing board may or must order expulsion for a particular act. Education Code Section 48918 governs the expulsion hearing. We can conceptualize the expulsion process in four components.

The first component requires a determination by a principal or superintendent that a student has committed an act warranting expulsion. As previously noted, the administrator may or may not have discretion in recommending expulsion. The second component of the process is the expulsion hearing. The hearing may result in no recommendation for expulsion, which terminates the entire process, or a recommendation for expulsion made to the governing board. The third component of the expulsion process occurs when the governing board considers the recommendation from the hearing. The governing board must review the evidence from the hearing and determine whether to adopt the recommendation for expulsion through a vote. Depending on the findings and the offense, the governing board may or may not be able to exercise discretion in voting for expulsion. The final component of this process is the enforcement of the expulsion order. The governing board, in its discretion, may suspend enforcement of the expulsion order.

Recommendation for Expulsion

The expulsion process starts when a principal or superintendent determines that a student has committed one of the acts in Education Code Section 48900 warranting expulsion and thereafter recommends expulsion. As noted previously, a recommendation for expulsion may be discretionary or mandatory, depending on the particular circumstances. Because expulsion from school implicates the student's property right to attend school, a formal expulsion hearing is held. Note the distinction between the relatively formalized components of an expulsion hearing, which are detailed next, and the informal notice and meeting that accompany a suspension.

The Expulsion Hearing

Education Code Section 48918 details the rules governing expulsion procedures and hearings. Special rules applicable to an expulsion hearing for committing or attempting to commit sexual assault or battery are set forth in Section 48918.5. An expulsion hearing must be held within thirty days after the principal or superintendent determines that the student has committed an expellable offense. A student may request a postponement of an expulsion hearing in writing. The first request for a postponement must be granted for a period not to exceed thirty days. The school district's governing board may, but does not have to, grant additional postponement requests. If a postponement is granted, the reason for the postponement must be included as part of the record when the expulsion hearing is conducted.

Is a student entitled to any educational instruction after the recommendation for expulsion but before the expulsion hearing? No, unless the student is eligible for special education and related services under IDEA. Chapter 8 addresses special education in detail. We comment at the end of this chapter on the educational programming a special education student must receive while awaiting an expulsion hearing. General education students do not have a similar entitlement. Under Education Code Section 48913, a teacher of any class from which a student is suspended *may* require the student to complete assignments and tests missed during the suspension. The Education Code contains no other reference to the educational instruction to be provided to a general education student pending the student's expulsion hearing. A school district's governing board, however, may adopt a policy requiring a student awaiting an expulsion hearing to receive homework or other work.

Written notice of an expulsion hearing must be sent to the student's parent in their native language at least ten calendar days prior to the start of the hearing. The notice must include the following:

- the date and place of the hearing;
- a statement of the specific facts and charges on which the proposed expulsion is based;
- a copy of the disciplinary rules of the district that relate to the alleged violation;
- a notice of the parent's obligation to inform the next school the student may attend of the basis of the expulsion for an act in cell A3 of Table 9.1; and

- a notice of the student or parent's opportunity to appear in person or be represented by an attorney or nonattorney adviser, to inspect and obtain copies of all documents to be used at the hearing, to question all other evidence presented, and to present oral and documentary evidence on the student's behalf, including witnesses.

The school district or student may request subpoenas from the governing board to compel the attendance of percipient (individuals with firsthand knowledge) witnesses. A request for a subpoena may be made before the hearing starts or after its commencement. The governing board is not required to issue a subpoena. Does this mean a governing board can always refuse to issue subpoenas for expulsion hearings? No, according to a 2003 California court of appeal decision (*Woodbury v. Brown-Dempsey*). In *Woodbury*, six students were alleged to be involved in a number of very inappropriate acts occurring in the football squad's locker room. The decision details the graphic allegations and circuslike atmosphere of the expulsion hearing. Prior to the start of the expulsion hearing, the students requested the governing board to issue subpoenas for numerous witnesses, including some current district employees. The governing board denied the request, noting that it had never issued subpoenas in the past. Current district employees, however, were voluntarily made available for the expulsion hearing.

The students were expelled by the governing board and went to court to challenge the expulsion. The students argued, and the trial court agreed, that the Education Code imposes a mandatory duty on the governing board to issue subpoenas on request and that a failure to issue the subpoenas was a denial of due process. The school district appealed. The appellate court held that while the governing board is not required to issue a subpoena in response to every request, the governing board cannot act arbitrarily by refusing to exercise discretion in considering a request for subpoenas. Despite the board's procedural error, the appellate court found no miscarriage of justice and denied the expelled students' demand that subpoenas be issued for certain witnesses. The lesson of *Woodbury* is that although a governing board does not have to issue a subpoena, consideration should at least be given to the request for one.

A school district, through the superintendent or superintendent's designee, may object to the issuance of a subpoena. The governing board can meet in closed or open session, if requested by the student, to consider an objection to the issuance of a subpoena. The governing board's decision regarding an objection to the issuance of a subpoena is final.

Expulsion hearings are closed to the public unless the student makes a written request for an open hearing five days before the start of the hearing. The school district's governing board, a hearing officer, or an impartial hearing panel of three or more certificated persons may conduct the hearing. The hearing officer may be from the county office of education or the Office of Administrative Hearings, which provides hearing officers for a variety of administrative hearings throughout the state. If an impartial administrative panel conducts the expulsion hearing, no individual on the panel may be a member of the district's governing board or employed on the staff of the school in which the student is enrolled.

Is a student denied a fair hearing if all members of the administrative panel are teachers employed by the school district? No, according to a 1982 California Supreme Court decision (*John A. v. San Bernardino City Unified School District*). John was expelled from school for his involvement in a fight after a football game. The county board of education adopted the governing board's expulsion order, and John sought court intervention to overturn the expulsion. Among other arguments, John urged the court to reverse his expulsion because teachers have a "built-in bias in disciplinary matters against students" (p. 308). To the court, potential bias in and of itself was not sufficient to reverse the expulsion. If fairness requires a total absence of preconception in the mind of the judge, the court wrote, "'no one has ever had a fair trial and no one ever will' because all have attitudes which affect them in judging situations" (p. 309). Because none of the administrative panel members were on the staff of the school where John was enrolled (as required by the Education Code) when the fight occurred, John's argument was rejected and his expulsion upheld.

Unlike criminal and civil proceedings, expulsion hearings are not subject to the technical rules of evidence. Evidence is considered relevant and admissible in an expulsion hearing if it is the kind of evidence on which reasonable persons are accustomed to rely in the conduct of serious affairs. Testimony by a student witness in an expulsion hearing is privileged, like testimony in court (Educ. Code § 48918.6). This means student witnesses can testify without fear of subsequent legal action for defamation of character. Section 48918.6 was enacted in response to an incident where a student was sued for defamation after reporting another student's comment that he wanted to kill people. Although the lawsuit was dismissed, the reporting student and her family incurred approximately $40,000 in legal expenses.

An expulsion hearing resembles an informal trial, with each side presenting opening statements, documentary evidence, questioning witnesses, making legal arguments if appropriate, and concluding with a closing statement. A record of the hearing must be made that is clear enough to permit a reasonably accurate and complete written transcription. In criminal law, evidence obtained in violation of the Fourth Amendment of the Constitution of the United States is inadmissible under the exclusionary rule. The Fourth Amendment prohibits unreasonable searches (e.g., a search without reasonable cause). The question of whether the exclusionary rules apply to expulsion hearings arose in a 1984 California court of appeal decision (*Gordon J. v. Santa Ana Unified School District*). Gordon was approached by the vice principal of his high school and asked to turn out his pockets. The vice principal's suspicions were based on what the court characterized as "stale information, previous misbehavior, and the student's unusually heavy use of a public telephone" (p. 532). Marijuana was found in Gordon's pocket. Gordon was expelled for a year and challenged the expulsion in court. Gordon argued that because he was searched in violation of the Fourth Amendment, the evidence obtained during the search should not have been used against him in a disciplinary proceeding. While the court agreed that the vice principal did not have sufficient cause for a lawful search of Gordon's pockets, the court declined to extend the exclusionary rule to high school disciplinary proceedings. A student may therefore be disciplined on the basis of evidence obtained in violation of the Fourth Amendment, though this area of the law remains murky, and school officials are advised to have reasonable cause to conduct a search. The law regarding student searches is discussed in Chapter 10.

If an allegation of committing or attempting to commit sexual assault or battery is the basis for the expulsion hearing, special rules may be used for questioning of the complaining witness. The complaining witness must be given five days' notice prior to being called to testify and is allowed to have up to two adult support persons present. Evidence of specific instances of the complaining witness's prior sexual conduct is presumed inadmissible, absent a determination that extraordinary circumstances exist requiring the evidence to be heard. Prior to determining whether such evidence may be heard, the complaining witness must be given notice and an opportunity to present opposition to the introduction of the evidence. Under no circumstances is reputation or opinion evidence regarding the sexual behavior of the complaining witness admissible.

Regardless of the act at issue in the expulsion hearing, there is another unique circumstance in which a witness may not have to testify in the usual manner. A hearing officer, administrative panel, or governing board may determine that the disclosure of either the identity of a witness or the testimony of that witness would subject the witness to an unreasonable risk of psychological or physical harm. In this scenario, the testimony of the witness is introduced through a sworn declaration examined solely by the hearing officer, administrative panel, or governing board. A copy of the declaration is given to the student with the name and identity of the witness redacted. The use of a declaration under these circumstances is also appropriate even if a subpoena is issued for the witness to testify at the expulsion hearing.

The individual or group of individuals charged with determining whether expulsion is warranted at the conclusion of the hearing may meet in closed session for deliberation. However, if any other individual is admitted to the closed session aside from the hearing officer, administrative panel, or governing board (as the case may be), the student, the student's parent, and legal counsel may also attend the closed-session deliberations.

If an expulsion hearing is conducted before a hearing officer or administrative panel, a recommendation regarding whether to expel must be made to the governing board within three days after the hearing's conclusion. If expulsion is not recommended, the expulsion proceedings are terminated, and the student is immediately returned to a classroom instructional program, a rehabilitation program, or any combination of these programs. The superintendent or superintendent's designee determines the student's placement after consultation with school district personnel, including the student's teachers and the student's parent(s). A decision not to recommend expulsion is final.

Final Determination by the Governing Board

If a hearing officer or administrative panel recommends expulsion, findings of fact in support of the recommendation must be prepared and submitted to the governing board. If the governing board itself conducts the expulsion hearing, a decision regarding whether to expel must be made within ten school days. For a hearing held by a hearing officer or administrative panel, a decision to expel by the governing board must be made within forty school days after the date of the student's removal. In either situation, the student may make a written request to delay the decision.

Failure to observe the applicable ten- or forty-day time period does not invalidate a governing board's decision to expel a student (*Board of Education v. Sacramento County Board of Education*, 2001). In *Sacramento County Board of Education*, the governing board expelled a student for possession of a pipe bomb. Due to a summer break occurring after the expulsion hearing but before the governing board's vote to expel, there was disagreement as to whether the forty-day period was met. Adopting the student's position, the county board of education to which the expulsion order had been appealed reversed the expulsion order after determining that the governing board took longer than forty days to issue an expulsion order. The governing board petitioned a court to reverse the county board of education. The court agreed with the governing board, holding that a failure to adhere to the forty-day period does not invalidate an order to expel.

The findings of fact and recommendation submitted to the governing board can be based only on evidence from the expulsion hearing. The governing board can accept a recommendation for expulsion in one of two ways. First, the governing board can accept the recommendation based on a review of the findings of fact and recommendation submitted by the hearing officer or administrative panel. Education Code Section 48918(f) requires a decision by a governing board to expel a student to be "based upon substantial evidence relevant to the charges adduced at the expulsion hearing or hearings." Although hearsay evidence is admissible in an expulsion hearing, an expulsion cannot be based solely on hearsay evidence. Alternatively, the governing board can order a supplementary hearing. If the supplementary hearing results in a recommendation for expulsion, the governing board can adopt the recommendation.

As in the initial decision to recommend expulsion, a governing board may or may not be able to exercise discretion in ordering expulsion. As noted in cell D1 of Table 9.1, a governing board must order expulsion for a student who commits an act described in cell A1. All other offenses in column A permit the governing board to exercise discretion in determining whether to order expulsion as noted in cells D2 and D3. To order expulsion for all acts aside from those in cell A1, a governing board must determine both that the student committed both the act and either of the following, as noted in cells C2 and C3:

- Other means of correction are not feasible or have repeatedly failed to bring about proper conduct, and
- due to the nature of the act, the presence of the student causes a continuing danger to the physical safety of the student or others.

This is the same analysis that occurs during the expulsion hearing to determine whether a recommendation for expulsion to the governing board can be made for an act aside from those included in cell A1.

A written notice of the governing board's decision to expel must be sent to the student's parent and be accompanied by:

- Notice of the right to appeal the expulsion to the county board of education
- Notice of the educational alternative placement to be provided to the pupil during the time of expulsion
- Notice of the obligation of the parent or student to inform the student's next school of the basis for the expulsion acts listed in cell A3

The expulsion order is then placed in the student's record and sent to any California public elementary, middle, or high school in which the student subsequently enrolls. After adopting a recommendation for expulsion, a governing board may suspend enforcement of the expulsion. Suspension of an order to expel is detailed later in this section.

A governing board must maintain a record of each expulsion, including the cause for each expulsion. The Education Code refers to this record as a "nonprivileged, disclosable public record" (Educ. Code § 48918(k)). A federal law, entitled the Family Educational Rights and Privacy Act (FERPA), however, classifies this type of record as personally identifiable information that cannot generally be disclosed unless a specific provision of FERPA permits disclosure (e.g., court order, subpoena, written consent for disclosure, and so on). A school district's receipt of federal funding is conditioned on compliance with FERPA. In response to a request for an expulsion record, should a school district release the record and risk a loss of federal funding, or not release the record and violate Section 48918(k)?

A California court addressed this query in a 2002 decision, in which, the school district received a request for expulsion records and did not release the records (*Rim of the World Unified School District v. Superior Court*). In *Rim of the World Unified School District*, the school district reasoned that the terms of FERPA, as a federal law, controlled over Education Code Section 48918(k), which is a state law. The court agreed with the school district because Section 48918(k) presents an "obvious obstacle to accomplishing Congress' purpose and objectives in enacting FERPA" (p. 1399). The court also declared that Education Code Section 48918(j), requiring the governing board to announce an expulsion order in open session violated FERPA. Violating Sections 48918(j) and 48918(k) to adhere to FERPA is the appropriate choice for a school district faced with our initial question.

A determination by a governing board to expel a student does not necessarily mean the student will be expelled. A governing board may suspend enforcement of an order to expel. Education Code Section 48917 governs suspension of an order to expel. Suspension of an order to expel is a probationary reprieve for the student. During suspension of the expulsion order, the student is on probationary status and on a rehabilitation plan. The suspension cannot exceed one year and may require the student to enroll in a different school, class, or program that is "deemed appropriate for rehabilitation" of the student. The suspension order can include a rehabilitation program mandating parent involvement. Refusal or failure of a parent to abide by this requirement, however, cannot be considered by a governing board to determine whether the student satisfactorily completed the rehabilitation program. May enforcement of an expulsion order based on one of the acts mandating expulsion (such as possession of a firearm, brandishing a knife, or the like) be suspended? Yes, according to a 1997 California attorney general opinion (80 Ops. Atty. Gen. 85). It is therefore possible for a student to avoid the implementation of an expulsion order for even the most serious acts.

When a student is under a suspended expulsion, they may have their probationary status revoked for committing any of the acts in Education Section 48900 or violating any of the district's rules and regulations governing student conduct. Revoking the suspension of an expulsion order may result in the student being expelled pursuant to the terms of the original expulsion order. A student who successfully completes the student's rehabilitation assignment must be reinstated to a school of the district (assuming the student was placed elsewhere as part of his or her rehabilitation program) and may have all records of the expulsion proceeding expunged from his or her record. A governing board's decision to suspend an order to expel does not affect the time period and requirements for filing an appeal of the expulsion order.

Postexpulsion Educational Programming

A student expelled for one of the acts listed in cell A1 of Table 9.1 must be placed in a program that is appropriately prepared to accommodate students who exhibit discipline problems (Educ. Code § 48915(d)). The program cannot be at a comprehensive elementary, middle, junior, or senior high school, nor at the school site the student attended when he or she committed the offense warranting expulsion. If a student is being expelled for any other act (cells A2 and A3 of Table 9.1), the student generally must also be referred to a program of study that meets this requirement. In the case of a student expelled for an act in cells A2 or A3 of Table 9.1, however, a county superintendent of schools may certify that an alternative program of study is not available away from a comprehensive campus. Thus, the student may be permitted to attend a comprehensive campus for the duration of his or her expulsion. The governing board may also require a student who is expelled for a drug or alcohol offense to enroll, with the permission of the student's parent(s), in a county-supported drug rehabilitation program prior to readmission (Educ. Code § 48916.5). And, as with suspension, a school district may require a student to perform community service on school grounds outside of school hours in lieu of expulsion or a portion thereof (Educ. Code § 48900.6).

A plan of rehabilitation must accompany a student's expulsion order (Educ. Code § 48916(b)). Section 48916(b) suggests, but does not require, the following elements for a plan of rehabilitation: "periodic review as well as assessment at the time of review for admission," and "recommendations for improved academic performance, tutoring, special education assessments, job training, counseling, employment, community service, and other rehabilitative programs." The governing board must also provide a description of the readmission process to a student for whom expulsion is ordered.

Readmission Following Expulsion

Education Code Section 48916 governs readmission of a student after expulsion. For a student expelled for an act in cell A1 of Table 9.1, the governing board must set a date one year from the expulsion on which to review readmission of the student to a district school. On a case-by-case basis, an earlier date for review may be set. For all other acts resulting in an expulsion, the governing board must set a date for reviewing readmission not later than the last day of the semester following the semester in which the expulsion occurred. A student expelled during summer session, or the intersession period of a year-long program, must have the student's review for readmission set by the governing board no later than the last day of the semester following the summer session or intersession period in which the expulsion occurred.

A school district's governing board must adopt rules and regulations establishing a procedure for the filing and review of requests for readmission. A governing board must readmit a student who completes the readmission process unless the governing board determines that the student did not meet the conditions of the student's rehabilitation plan or continues to pose a danger to campus safety or to other students or employees of the school district. If readmission is denied, the governing board must determine whether the student is to remain in the current alternative educational program or attend another program, which may include a placement serving expelled students such as a county community school. A denial of readmission must be accompanied by written notice to the student and the student's parent(s) describing the reasons for the denial and a determination of the educational program for the student. The student must enroll in the educational program chosen by the governing board unless the parent(s) elect to enroll the student in another school district.

Appeal of an Expulsion Order

After a governing board orders an expulsion, a student has thirty days to file an appeal with the county board of education. Education Code Sections 48919 to 48924 govern the appeal of an expulsion order. A student on probationary status under a suspended expulsion order may not challenge revocation of the student's probationary status and the subsequent implementation of the expulsion order if the student did not appeal the expulsion order. The appeal must be heard within twenty school days. The appeal is heard by the county board of education, or in a class one or class two county, by a hearing officer or impartial administrative panel. An appeal heard by a county board of education results in a final decision by the county board of education. An appeal heard by a hearing officer or impartial administrative panel, however, results in a recommendation to the county board of education regarding the appeal. Like the governing board's role in the expulsion process, the county board of education has the final say on an expulsion appeal.

The time period for calculating the time to file an appeal starts on the day the governing board votes to expel the student. A request for an appeal by a student must be accompanied by a simultaneously written request to the school district for a copy of the written transcripts and supporting documents from the expulsion hearing. The school district must provide the student with the requested documents within ten school days. The student then files these documents with the county board of education. The student must pay for the cost of the transcript unless the student's parent certifies that he or she cannot reasonably afford the cost of the transcript because of limited income or exceptional necessary expenses. If the student pays for the cost of the transcript and the expulsion is reversed on appeal, the school district must reimburse the student for the cost of the transcript.

A county board of education must adopt rules and regulations for expulsion appeals. Regardless of whether the county board of education, a hearing officer, or an administrative panel hears an expulsion appeal, the rules and regulations must detail and explain the following:

- requirements for filing a notice of appeal
- setting of a hearing date
- furnishing of a notice to the student and the governing board regarding the appeal
- furnishing of a copy of the expulsion hearing record to the county board of education
- procedures for the conduct of the hearing
- preservation of the record of the appeal

Hearing officers and administrative hearing panel members may not be members of the governing board of the school district or employees of the school district from which the appeal is filed. A hearing officer or member of the administrative panel that oversaw the expulsion hearing cannot hear the appeal. Three school days after the hearing officer or administrative panel hears the appeal, a recommended decision, including any findings or conclusions required for that decision, must be sent to the county board of education.

The county board of education's review of the governing board's decision to expel is limited to four questions:

- Whether the governing board acted without or in excess of its jurisdiction
- Whether there was a fair hearing before the governing board
- Whether there was a prejudicial abuse of discretion in the hearing
- Whether there was relevant and material evidence that, in the exercise of reasonable diligence, could not have been produced or that was improperly excluded at the hearing before the governing board

A proceeding without or in excess of jurisdiction "includes, but is not limited to, a situation where an expulsion hearing is not commenced within the time periods prescribed by this article, a situation where an expulsion order is not based on the acts enumerated in Section 48900, or a situation involving acts not related to a school activity or attendance" (Educ. Code § 48922(b)). An abuse of discretion is established "(1) if school officials have not met the procedural requirements for an expulsion, (2) the decision to expel a pupil is not supported by the findings prescribed by Section 48915," or (3) if the "findings are not supported by the evidence" (Educ. Code § 48922(c)(1)–(3)). However, determination of an abuse of discretion does not result in an automatic reversal of the expulsion order. The county board of education must also determine that the abuse of discretion was prejudicial, meaning that it unfairly tainted the expulsion decision.

The county board of education has four options after its review of the underlying hearing and decision by the governing board: remand to the governing board for reconsideration or adoption of required findings, order a new hearing, affirm the expulsion, or reverse the expulsion. The county board of education may remand the matter to the governing board for reconsideration, or they can order a new hearing if the county board of education finds that "relevant and material evidence exists which, in the exercise of reasonable diligence, could not have been produced or which was improperly excluded at the hearing" (Educ. Code § 48923(a)). If reconsideration is ordered, the student may be readmitted to school pending the reconsideration. A new hearing must conform to the requirements of Education Code Section 48918 discussed earlier. If the county board of education determines that the decision of the governing board is not supported by the findings required by Section 48915, but evidence supporting the findings exists in the record of the proceedings, the county board of education must remand the matter to the governing board for adoption of the required findings. A remand for adoption of the required findings does not result in an additional hearing for the student; however, the final action of the governing board to expel on adoption of the required findings must be taken consistent with Education Code Sections 48918(j)–(k) as judicially interpreted. Subsections (j) and (k) contain the notice requirements discussed previously and the governing board's obligation to maintain a record of each expulsion.

Otherwise, the county board of education must enter an order either affirming or reversing the decision of the governing board. If the county board reverses the governing board's decision to expel the student, the county board of education may direct the governing board to expunge the records of the school district of any references to the expulsion action. A reversal of the expulsion also requires that the expulsion is deemed not to have occurred. A county board of education can remand or reverse a governing board's decision to expel only for the circumstances noted earlier in this section. In 1997, the California attorney general opined that a decision by the county board of education to reverse a governing board's decision for any other reason is an abuse of discretion (80 Ops. Atty. Gen 91). Does the governing board have any recourse if the county board of education reverses the governing board? Yes: the 1997 attorney general opinion also concludes that the governing board may seek judicial review of the county board of education's decision.

DISCIPLINE AND SPECIAL EDUCATION

Additional care and attention must be given to the discipline of students who are, or are suspected of being, eligible for special education services under the Individuals with Disabilities Education Act (IDEA). IDEA, a comprehensive statutory scheme governing the rights of children with disabilities and the duties of school districts in educating these children, is discussed in detail in Chapter 8. Because special education law contains numerous unique terms, phrases, and concepts, readers should consult, or perhaps read in its entirety, Chapter 8 prior to reading this section.

For purposes of completing the discussion of student discipline, it is important to note the additional rights IDEA affords students who are, or are suspected of being, eligible for special education services. The key inquiry to determine whether these additional rights apply in a given situation is whether the discipline will result in a "change in placement," generally but not always a removal of ten days or more. Schools must conduct an IEP meeting, called a Manifest Determination meeting, to consider whether a student's behavior is a manifestation of their disability. If not, the student can be disciplined in the same manner as a general education student. However, if the discipline will result in a change in placement, special procedures detailed more fully in upcoming subsections must be followed.

Different Types of Disciplinary Removals

Understanding when a change in placement occurs can be challenging, but the easiest method to understand this is to look at the number of days out of school. The removals can be broken down as a short-term removal of ten days or less; a series of short-term removals of more than ten cumulative days; a series of short-term removals of more than ten cumulative days; and long-term removals of more than ten consecutive school days.

When is a special education student "removed" under the law? A special education student may be "removed" when the student cannot continue to progress in the general curriculum, receive the services in the student's individualized education program (IEP), and/or participate with nondisabled children to the extent the student would in the student's current placement. A removal can include a bus suspension because an inability to get to school prevents a student from receiving the services in the student's IEP. A school district is required to provide an alternative form of transportation to a student at no cost to the parent if the student is excluded from bus transportation and transportation is specified in the student's IEP (Educ. Code § 48915.5(c)). Removals can be problematic if they interfere with the provision of FAPE and are not in conformance with current law.

Short-Term Removals

Suspensions are the most common short-term removals. Parents may be surprised that a student with an IEP can be suspended, but the law supports that. Similar to regular education students, special education students who are suspended (ten days or less) may be treated as any other student. However, school districts do have to provide educational services to students with an IEP on the eleventh day of the student's disciplinary removal. The educational services made available must constitute a free appropriate public education (FAPE).

Long-Term Removals

Long-term removals can result from a series of short-term removals that constitute a change in placement, or a single removal of more than ten consecutive school days (34 C.F.R. § 300.536(a)(1)–(2)). A special education student in a long-term removal is entitled to receive educational services that constitute a FAPE. A series of short-term removals may, in the aggregate, constitute a pattern of removals that is considered a change in placement. A pattern may result because of factors such as the length of each removal, the total amount of time the student is removed, and the proximity of the removals to each other. A school district can also consider whether the child's behavior in the most recent removal was similar to behavior demonstrated in prior removals (34 C.F.R. § 300.536(a)(2)(ii)). If the behaviors are not substantially similar, the school district could consider this to be a factor mitigating against a determination that a change in placement occurred. Determining when such a pattern of removals exists is no easy task. Some school districts might choose to provide services on the eleventh day to err on the side of caution.

If a dispute arises regarding a long-term removal, a parent may request a due process hearing. The "stay-put" provision generally requires the school district to maintain the student in his or her last agreed-upon and implemented placement until completion of the hearing and any subsequent appeals or the parties agree otherwise (34 C.F.R. § 300.518).

If a removal constitutes a change in placement, there are three steps that a school district must undertake before further disciplining a special education student. First, the school district must immediately notify the student's parents of the disciplinary action and provide a copy of IDEA's procedural safeguards to the parents. Second, the school district must conduct a manifestation determination IEP meeting (i.e., determine whether the student's behavior was a manifestation of the student's disability). The manifestation determination must be conducted within ten school days of the decision to change the placement of the student. Third, the IEP team must review the behavior intervention plan if one exists, or create one if it does not. This may require a functional behavioral assessment (FBA) (34 C.F.R. § 300.530).

Steps two and three often occurs in a single meeting (the manifestation determination meeting) that should be held immediately, but no later than ten school days after the date the school district decides to impose a removal that results in a change in placement (34 C.F.R. § 300.530). The meeting's purpose is twofold: to prevent disciplining a student for behavior that is a result of the student's disability and to determine whether any changes need to be made to the student's IEP to address behavioral concerns.

A manifestation determination does not try to determine why a student committed a particular act. Rather, the inquiry focuses on the relationship between the student's behavior and the student's disability. The basic premise is that a student should not be disciplined if the student's behavior is a result of the student's disability.

A special education student's conduct is a manifestation of the student's disability if

- the conduct in question was caused by, or had a direct and substantial relationship to, the child's disability; or
- the conduct in question was the direct result of the local educational agency's failure to implement the IEP.

If the members of the manifestation determination meeting determine that the behavior in question was a manifestation of the student's disability, no disciplinary action can result. Alternatively, if the determination of the meeting is that the student's behavior was not a manifestation of the disability, disciplinary rules applicable to general education students apply. In this latter scenario, all disciplinary and special education records must be sent to the final person (e.g., the principal for an expulsion) or entity (the governing board for an expulsion) charged with making a decision regarding discipline for the student.

IDEA does not define FBA. An FBA can consist of a file review or a formal assessment and is undertaken to determine why a student is engaging in inappropriate behavior. The members of the manifestation determination meeting may conclude that an FBA is warranted because of the student's behavior. IDEA requires an FBA no later than ten school days after imposing the change in placement if the student does not have an existing IDEA BIP. Failure to timely complete an FBA may result in a reversal of the school district's disciplinary action by an OAH hearing officer (*A.G. v. Paradise Valley Unified School District No. 69*, 2016).

Interim Alternative Educational Settings and a *Honig* Injunction

Federal law permits school districts to order a special education student to an interim alternative educational setting (IAES) for up to forty-five school days if the student carries a weapon to school or to a school function, knowingly possesses or uses illegal drugs, sells or solicits the sale of a controlled substance, or has inflicted serious bodily injury on another while at school or at a school function (34 C.F.R. § 300.530(g)). A special education student committing one of these acts can be ordered to an IAES regardless of whether the act was a manifestation of the student's disability; however, the school must still complete the Manifest Determination meeting requirement (even if the student is already removed)

Aside from weapons offenses, drug offenses, or infliction of serious bodily injury, a hearing officer may order a student into an IAES for up to forty-five school days if certain criteria are met. To obtain such an order, a school district must show that maintaining the current placement of the student is substantially likely to result in injury to the child or others.

A school district may believe that a special education student presents a substantial risk of injury (to the student or others), yet not be able to meet the criteria for implementing an IAES or obtaining an administrative order to change the student's placement. A court order, referred to as a *Honig* injunction, can be sought by a school in order to change a student's placement (*Honig v. Doe,* 1988). A school district must demonstrate that maintaining the student in his or her current placement is substantially likely to result in injury to the student or to others. If it agrees with the school district, the court will issue an injunction permitting the school district to change the student's placement.

Students Not Yet Identified as Special Education Students

The foregoing disciplinary procedures also can apply to general education students who are not yet identified as special education students. If a school district is "deemed to have knowledge" that a general education student is a child with a disability under IDEA, the procedures applicable to disciplining special education students subject to a category three or four removal apply to the student (34 C.F.R. § 300.534). This inquiry also is referred to in terms of whether the school district has a "basis of knowledge." IDEA's implementing regulations identify the following circumstances in which a school district is deemed to have knowledge that a student is a child with a disability:

- The parent of the child has expressed concern in writing to personnel of the appropriate educational agency that the child is in need of special education and related services.
- The parent of the child has requested an evaluation of the child.
- The teacher of the child, or other personnel of the school district, has expressed specific concerns about a pattern of behavior demonstrated by the child directly to the director of special education of the agency or to other supervisory personnel.

A school district is not deemed to have knowledge that a student is a child with a disability if the child's parent has not permitted an evaluation by the school district to determine special education eligibility, the child's parent has refused special education services, or the child has been evaluated and determined not to be eligible for special education services under IDEA.

The Office of Administrative Hearings (OAH), which adjudicates special education disputes in California, can conduct an expedited due process hearing to determine whether a school district had a basis of knowledge that prevents the school district from disciplining the student as a general education student. A determination that a basis of knowledge exists will result in an order returning the student to his or her prior placement unless the parties agree otherwise.

SUMMARY

Student discipline rules are necessary for the maintenance of order in public schools. The acts for which suspension or expulsion is permissible are in Education Code Section 48900. Section 48900 and following sections were enacted in response to the U.S. Supreme Court's decision in *Goss v. Lopez*. *Goss* notes the type of due process required by the Fourteenth Amendment to the U.S. Constitution prior to discipline resulting in a removal from school. Suspensions of ten days or less require an informal conference and an opportunity for the student to present the student's interpretation of the events at issue. Removals from school in excess of ten school days require the more formalized procedures of an expulsion hearing.

Table 9.1 details those acts for which a student may or must be suspended and/or expelled. While Section 48900 details all of the grounds for which suspension and/or expulsion are permissible, Section 48915 notes the particular circumstances for which immediate suspension and/or a mandatory recommendation for expulsion are required. These are described in cell A1 and mandate immediate suspension and recommendation for expulsion. A secondary category of acts, detailed in cell A2, mandates expulsion unless inappropriate under the circumstances. All remaining acts listed in cell A3 vest discretion in school administrators on whether to recommend expulsion. Suspension for a first-time offense is not appropriate unless the student violates Education Code Section 48900(a)–(e), the student's presence causes a danger to persons or property or threatens to disrupt the instructional process, or the student commits one of the acts mandating expulsion. Nontraditional disciplinary options are also available to school administrators. These include supervised classroom suspensions, requesting parents to attend school with their child, an involuntary transfer, and community service.

All acts aside from those in cell A1 of the table require an additional finding of one of the following before the governing board can order expulsion: Other means of correction are not feasible or have repeatedly failed to bring about proper conduct; or, due to the nature of the act, the presence of the student causes a continuing danger to the physical safety of the student or others. The governing board reviews the findings of the individual or panel conducting the expulsion hearing and must order an expulsion of a student who commits one of the acts in cell A1.

The governing board may exercise discretion in ordering expulsion for all other acts. The governing board may also suspend an order to expel. A student may pursue an appeal of an expulsion order with the governing board or the county board of education, if the matter has moved to that entity.

The Individuals with Disabilities Education Act (IDEA) contains its own requirements for the discipline of a special education student resulting in a change of placement. A change of placement may occur through a series of separate removals that are more than ten school days in the aggregate for similar acts or through a single removal for longer than ten school days. For a change in placement, a school district must notify the parents and provide a copy of the IDEA's procedural safeguards, conduct a manifestation determination (which determines whether the student's behavior was a manifestation of the student's disability), and convene an individualized education program (IEP) team meeting to discuss behavior interventions. Certain offenses (drugs, weapons, and inflicting serious bodily injury) permit a school district to place a special education student in an interim alternative educational setting (IAES). A school district can also petition a court or the Office of Administrative Hearings (OAH) to change a special education student's placement, but the student still has a right to FAPE.

10 PUBLIC ACCESS, PRIVACY, AND STUDENT SEARCH AND SEIZURE

The law requires that the public's business must be conducted in public. Yet, while the public has access to governing board meetings and to the records that are generated through the business of operating schools, some matters are shielded from view. Both federal and state laws provide a cloak of privacy for students and parents. What employees do on their own time is largely beyond the purview of the school unless that off-duty conduct impairs their ability to perform their essential job functions (see our discussion in Chapter 5 for additional information). And while school officials must maintain a safe environment for learning, students have a constitutional right to be free from unreasonable searches and seizures. Balancing the needs of the public against the privacy interests of students, parents, and employees is no easy task, but it is one that courts have had to address. In this chapter, we describe the applicable law to identify which aspects of school operation are governed by public access laws, those matters remaining private, and the kinds of searches and seizures that may be conducted without violating student rights.

PUBLIC ACCESS

While federal and state law offers a cloak of privacy for families and students, state law brings the affairs of government out into the open. Article 1, Section 3 of the California Constitution states, "The people have the right of access to information concerning the conduct of the people's business, and, therefore, the meetings of public bodies and the writings of public officials and agencies shall be open to public scrutiny."

Open Meetings Under the Brown Act

Passed in 1953, the Ralph M. Brown Act begins by noting that "public commissions, boards and councils and other public agencies in this state exist to aid in the conduct of the people's business. It is the intent of the law that their actions be taken openly and that their deliberations be conducted openly" (Gov't Code § 54950). To this end, California courts have interpreted the law broadly and the exceptions to open meetings narrowly.

The Brown Act applies to the governing boards of traditional public schools and certain subsidiary bodies of the governing board. In addition, most agree that the Brown Act applies to charter schools. It also applies to the board of a nonprofit benefit corporation that is created by an elected body to exercise delegated power or that receives funds from the elected body and includes a member of that body as a voting member on its governing board. Thus, nonprofit benefit corporations formed to operate charter schools must comply with the Brown Act.

The Education Code stipulates that governing board meetings are to be conducted in accord with the terms of the Brown Act (Educ. Code § 35145 et seq.). This is true for both monthly and quarterly board meetings as well as those held at other times.

In conformity with the Brown Act, the Education Code specifically provides that agendas must be posted, minutes taken and made available to the public, and members of the public able to place matters within the subject matter jurisdiction of the school district on the board agenda. If the matter does not directly relate to school business, the board has discretion not to include it (*Mooney v. Garcia*, 2012, 2012). In addition, every agenda for regular meetings must provide members of the public an opportunity to address the board on agenda items of interest to them. In contrast, members of the public may comment only on maters included on the agenda at special meetings. This does not preclude a board's hearing testimony on matters not on the agenda, provided that no action is taken on the matter being addressed.

Several court decisions have indicated that the open portion of a governing board meeting constitutes a limited open forum; as a result, the authority of governing boards to control what persons say is curtailed. A case in point involves two parents in the Vista Unified School District who challenged a governing board bylaw permitting the board president to terminate a presenter's comments if the presenter persists, after being warned, to engage in improper conduct or remarks (*Leventhal v. Vista Unified School District*, 1997). At a board meeting, the parents attempted to address the qualifications and performance of the school superintendent, including his social relationship with a board member. At one point the board member responded, triggering an animated exchange. The board president cut the parents off, noting that personnel criticisms could not be made in a public board meeting. Later, the parents filed a lawsuit in federal court, contending the restriction violated their First Amendment right of free speech.

The federal judge noted that under both the Brown Act and the Education Code, open board meetings are limited open forums, meaning that they are open to public comment on matters within the subject matter of the jurisdiction of the governing board. As such, the district's interests in controlling public commentary "cannot outweigh the public's fundamental right to engage in robust public discourse on school issues" (p. 957).

The school board argued that a provision of the Brown Act permitting closed sessions for personnel matters specifically lists hearing complaints or charges against an employee unless the employee requests a public session. Thus, the school board president acted appropriately in limiting criticism.

The court disagreed. The court noted that the Brown Act favors open meetings, and the personnel exception under Government Code Section 54957 cannot preclude a person from raising personnel issues in public session. The board can then deliberate about them in closed session. In effect, the privacy rights of district employees cannot supersede the First Amendment rights of members of the public.

Further, the court noted, permitting a board member to criticize members of the public who address the board but then prohibiting the latter from responding is a form of viewpoint discrimination (*Baca v. Moreno Valley Unified School District*, 1996). Because there was no disruption of the public meeting, the board president was in error when he terminated the parents' right to speak. The court left open the possibility of channeling calls for actual disciplinary action against an employee to closed session under the personnel exception of the Brown Act.

Key provisions. While the Brown Act, interpretive law, and administrative opinions are quite extensive, a few of the more salient features are summarized here. First, public meetings must be open and public; though, as described later, the board may go into executive session (commonly labeled "closed session") for specific purposes after announcing in open session the intention to do so. Meetings must be held within the boundaries of the district or the charter school's serving area except in certain situations (e.g., to interview a potential employee from another district). Meetings must be held in facilities that accommodate persons without reference to race, religion, color, national origin, ancestry, sex, and disability and that do not require a payment or purchase from attendees. An agenda describing each item of business or discussion for both open and executive sessions must be posted in an accessible location and on the governing board's website, if it has one, at least seventy-two hours before a regular meeting. If requested, the agenda must be made available in appropriate alternative formats for persons with disabilities and include information about accommodations for them at the meeting. While agenda items need not be described in detail, they should be understandable to the average citizen.

Special meetings of the governing board may be called at any time by the board president or by a majority of the board (Gov't Code § 54956). This requires a twenty-four-hour written notice both to board members and the media describing the time and place of the meeting and the business to be transacted or discussed. The notice also must be posted in a place accessible to the public at least twenty-four hours prior to the special meeting and on the governing board's website, if it has one. No other business may be conducted at a special meeting beyond that described in the notice.

Emergency meetings are permitted when some crippling activity or disaster strikes. In this event, the media who have so requested are to be notified by telephone at least one hour prior to the emergency meeting in lieu of the twenty-four-hour notice and posting requirement for special meetings. If telephone service is not available, the media are to be notified of the purpose and actions taken at the meeting as soon as possible. Emergency meetings may be held in executive session if agreed to by two-thirds of those members present or, if less than two-thirds are in attendance, by unanimous vote. After the meeting, the minutes must be posted for at least ten days in an accessible place.

"Adjourned meetings" are meetings that have been adjourned or re-adjourned to a different time. A notice of adjournment must be conspicuously posted on or near the door where the meeting was held within twenty-four hours of adjournment. Both regular and special meetings may be adjourned.

The governing board may use video teleconferencing to receive public comment or testimony and to deliberate. However, board members may not use technological devices or otherwise communicate among themselves to reach a collective concurrence (Gov't Code § 54952.2). The California Attorney General has advised that this provision precludes the use of e-mail for this purpose (84 Ops. Atty. Gen. 30, 2001). If video teleconferencing is used, the agenda must be posted at all teleconference locations, and a quorum of the governing board must participate from within the boundaries of the district.[1]

---

[1]Certain Brown Act provisions become inoperative and replaced by other provisions on January 1, 2026. Readers would be well advised to analyze Government Code Sections 54950–54963 when reviewing the Brown Act information described in this paragraph.

A member of the public does not have to sign a register or provide other information as a condition of attendance. If an attendance sheet is circulated during the meeting, there must be an indication that signing it is voluntary. Audio and videotaping of open sessions are permitted unless disruptive. An official audio or videotape of the session is a public record available for inspection without charge, though it may be destroyed by the school district after thirty days. Broadcasting of open meetings is permissible unless it would prove disruptive. There is no requirement that minutes or recordings must be made during closed sessions.

Government Code Section 54957.9 provides that if a meeting is willfully interrupted and order cannot be restored by removing disruptive persons, the members of the governing board may order the room cleared and continue in session. The media must be allowed to attend, except for those who are involved in the disruption. The governing board may establish a procedure for readmitting persons not responsible for the disruption.

Similarly, the Board president or other presiding officer may order the removal of individuals who are "disrupting" the meeting (Gov't Code § 54957.95). *Disrupting* means engaging in behavior during a meeting that actually disrupts, disturbs, impedes, or renders infeasible the orderly conduct of the meeting and includes, but is not limited to, failing to comply with regulations adopted by the Board pursuant to Section 54954.3 (concerning public comment), and behavior that constitutes use of force or a true threat of force. Prior to removing an individual, the president or other presiding officer must warn the individual that their behavior is disrupting the meeting and that their failure to cease the behavior may result in their removal. Except for individuals who use or threaten force (who may be immediately removed), the Board president or other presiding officer may remove the individual only if they do not "promptly" cease their disruptive behavior.

Although the First Amendment protects robust interaction among members of the public and board members during an open session, its protection is not unlimited. A case in point involves the arrest of an attendee after he dumped bags of garbage on the floor of a multipurpose room in an elementary school where the governing board meeting was being held. The incident occurred during the portion of the meeting reserved for public comments. The speaker had sought to demonstrate how derelict the school was in preventing high school students in the district from littering neighborhoods surrounding the campus. He did take the precaution of spreading a tarp on the floor and donning gloves before opening the bags and pouring their contents on the tarp. Some of the contents spilled out onto the floor. The principal of the elementary school was present and warned the speaker that the room would be used as the school's cafeteria the next day.

The meeting was adjourned and the police called. Meanwhile, the speaker continued talking to the audience and dumping trash. The police advised that they were without authority to make an arrest, whereupon the superintendent made a citizen's arrest of the speaker for willfully disturbing a public meeting. The speaker filed a lawsuit against the district, its board members, and its superintendent for, among other things, violating his First Amendment rights.

The appellate court affirmed dismissal of the lawsuit. It noted that the speaker was arrested for violating California Penal Code Section 403, which provides in part that anyone who willfully disturbs or breaks up any lawful assembly or meeting is guilty of a misdemeanor. The California Supreme Court interpreted this statute narrowly in 1970 to pertain to disruptive actions, not to the content of the speech. Here, the appellate court agreed with the jury that the speaker had exceeded the limit of the law when he dumped the garbage. His actions were not a legitimate part of the meeting but rather had become a significant impairment of it (*McMahon v. Albany Unified School District*, 129 Cal. Rptr. 2d 184 (Cal. App. 1 Dist. 2002), *cert. denied*, 540 U.S. 824 (2003)).

Commonly labeled the "Greene Act," Education Code Section 35147 provides that meetings of school site councils and advisory committees, including the English learner parent advisory committee, advisory committees convened related to the LCAP, districtwide advisory committees related to bilingual education, and other committees, must be open to the public and members of the public given a chance to address agenda items. Notice of the meetings must be posted at the school or other appropriate place accessible to the public at least seventy-two hours before the meeting. The notice must specify date, time, and location and include an agenda. Action cannot be taken on matters not on the school site agenda unless those present unanimously vote to take immediate action on a matter that came to their attention after the agenda was posted. Questions or brief statements made at meetings by members of the council, committee, or public that do not significantly affect students or employees or that can be resolved informally need not be included on the agenda. If a person complains about a violation of these procedures, the matter is to be reconsidered at the next meeting following an opportunity for public comment. Finally, any materials provided to any committee covered by the Greene Act must be made available in accordance with the terms of the California Public Records Act.

Defining open meetings. The term *open meetings* as used in the Brown Act applies both to gatherings at which action is taken and to meetings where deliberation takes place. Thus, an informal luncheon where school board members talk among themselves about school matters is governed by the act. However, advisory committees composed solely of board members and consisting of less than a quorum are not legislative bodies subject to the terms of the act unless they are standing committees (Gov't Code § 54952(b)). For example, meetings of an ad hoc advisory committee comprised solely of less than a quorum of board members to advise the full board of qualifications of candidates for appointment to a vacant board position are not open to the public (*Henderson v. Los Angeles City Board of Education*, 1978).

A 1993 California appellate court decision sheds some light on the scope of the open meetings portion of the Brown Act. That decision relates to a case involving complaints to a school board related to a recently adopted reading series known as "Impressions." In accordance with board policy, two committees were appointed, one to review the merits of the complaints and a second to hear testimony from the first committee and then make a recommendation to the board about retaining the series. During this time, district staff members sent board members information about the work of the committees, including the views of the director of instruction about the issue. A quorum of board members met with members of the school's curriculum council to view a videotape relating to censorship and to be brought up to date on parent complaints. The curriculum council was overseeing the work of the two committees. The school board eventually voted in open session to retain the series after hearing all sides to the issue. Parents upset about the way the matter was handled filed suit. Among their arguments were that the two committees should have held their deliberations in public session and that the board violated the Brown Act by viewing the videotape with the curriculum council.

The court ruled that the two committees were subject to the Brown Act. Government Code Section 54952 provides that the term *legislative body* includes a "commission, committee, board, or other body of a local agency, whether permanent or temporary, decisionmaking or advisory, created by charter, ordinance, resolution, or formal action of a legislative body." The fact that the superintendent and his staff actually set up the committees and appointed their members was irrelevant because they were acting under a formal board policy dealing with complaints about instructional materials.

The court also agreed with the parents that, because a quorum of the board viewed the videotape with the curriculum council, the viewing constituted a "meeting" under the Brown Act. In addition to viewing the tape, the board engaged in discussion with members of the council.

The court noted that the Brown Act is not limited to gatherings where a quorum of board members takes some form of formal action. Deliberative gatherings are included as well. However, the transmission of information by district staff to members of the governing board did not involve communication among board members or any collective action and so did not violate the act. Whether the board's violations of the Brown Act tainted its decision reached in open session to continue the "Impressions" reading series was a matter to be determined by the trial court (*Frazer v. Dixon Unified School District*, 1993).

Exceptions to open meetings. The Brown Act includes several of exceptions to holding government meetings in open session. Among them are real property transactions discussed with the governing board's negotiators, provided the property being discussed and the persons with whom the negotiators will deal have been announced in open session (Gov't Code § 54956.8). Another exception is conferring with legal counsel in closed session on existing or anticipated litigation (Gov't Code § 54956.9). The attorney general has advised that this exception encompasses discussing and taking action on proposed settlement of lawsuits (75 Ops. Atty. Gen. 14, 1992). The attorney general also has advised that a school board member may not publicly disclose information that was received and properly discussed in closed session concerning pending litigation unless authorized by law to do so (80 Ops. Atty. Gen. 231, 1997).

The personnel exception specifies that closed sessions are permissible for considering the "appointment, employment, evaluation of performance, discipline, or dismissal of a public employee or to hear complaints about or charges brought against the employee by another person or employee unless the employee requests a public session" (Gov't Code § 54957). The purpose of the personnel exception is to protect employees from public embarrassment and to permit free and candid discussions of personnel matters by members of the governing board. But the scope of the exception is limited, as noted by case law analyzing it.

For example, a principal in the Los Angeles Unified School District sued, contending that the superintendent and area superintendent had violated the personnel exception when they commented critically to newspaper reporters about the principal's handling of disturbances at his high school. The comments were later reported in the *Los Angeles Times*. The appellate court affirmed the trial court's dismissal of the lawsuit. Both courts found the personnel exception inapplicable because the newspaper comments were not the equivalent of a personnel evaluation. The appellate court added that the principal's argument "turns the Brown Act on its head, because the general purpose of the Brown Act is to *increase* public awareness of issues bearing on the democratic process" (emphasis in original). Citing the *Leventhal* decision discussed earlier, the judges noted that the personnel exception must be read narrowly (*Morrow v. Los Angeles Unified School District*, 2007).

Additionally, the degree to which the personnel exception limits what board members can discuss in closed session was addressed in a 2001 California court of appeal ruling. The case involved a school governing board's indication on several meeting agendas that closed meetings would be conducted to evaluate the superintendent's performance. Plaintiffs contended that the board violated the Brown Act by discussing only the form to be used for evaluation during the closed session and not the superintendent's performance, then later taking action to find the evaluation sufficiently positive to renew the superintendent's contract. The appellate court rejected the contention. The judges noted that performance evaluations, as used in Section 54957, may be confined to a particular aspect of job performance and may include discussion of the means of evaluation. Similarly, providing the superintendent with positive feedback about the evaluation during closed session is part of the evaluation process (*Duval v. Board of Trustees*, 2001).

When the governing board decides to hold a closed session on a specific complaint or charge against an employee, the employee is entitled to written notice within twenty-four hours of the right to have the matter held in open session. The employee does not have a right to appear in closed session and participate in the Board's discussion of the matter in closed session. Rather, their right is limited to require the Board to hear the complaint or charge in open session.

As noted in Chapter 5, governing boards may non-reelect probationary teachers for any legitimate, nondiscriminatory reason and without a hearing. Does a negative evaluation of a probationary teacher constitute a specific complaint or charge sufficient to give the teacher the right to a twenty-four-hour notice to request an open meeting? No, according to a 1999 California court of appeal ruling. According to the court, the twenty-four-hour requirement pertains only to specific complaints and not to employee appointment, employment, evaluation of performance, discipline, or dismissal. The evaluations of the teachers in this case did not fall into the specific complaint category. Rather, they were evaluations of performance (*Fischer v. Los Angeles Unified School District*, 1999).

By contrast, a high school football coach who also was a permanent teacher in the District successfully claimed that the Vista Unified School District's governing board violated his rights when it voted in closed session to remove him from his coaching assignment with no loss in pay. The California Interscholastic Federation (CIF), which supervises interscholastic athletic competition in California in consultation with the California Department of Education, ruled that the coach had used undue influence in the enrollment of an Australian student to play football. CIF placed the school's athletic program on probation, suspended its membership in the federation, and ordered the school district to review the matter and take whatever actions it deemed appropriate with regard to the coach.

The school board scheduled a special closed meeting to address these matters. One of the items on the agenda was "public employee discipline/dismissal/release." The coach alleged that the board violated the Brown Act when it did not inform him within twenty-four hours of specific complaints against him in the form of presentations at the meeting by the school superintendent and an associate superintendent who also served as CIF board chair. The appellate court agreed. The court reasons that, when the school officials presented the CIF undue influence finding against the coach to the governing board, it evolved into a specific complaint or charge against him by another person or employee. This triggered the twenty-four-hour notice, which would have given him a chance to clear his name and avoid disciplinary action. Thus, the court concluded that the board violated the act (*Bell v. Vista Unified School District*, 2000). It is apparent from this decision and several similar decisions that, when deliberation strays from personnel evaluation to discuss specific complaints and possible disciplinary action, the twenty-four-hour notice requirement will be invoked.

Another important exception to public meetings is that of conducting closed sessions for conferring with the district's labor negotiators regarding salaries, salary schedules, and fringe benefits. However, prior to going into executive session, the governing board must disclose the identities of its representatives in open session (Gov't Code § 54957.6). The attorney general has advised that a county board of education may not meet in closed session under this section to consider salaries or compensation paid in the form of fringe benefits to certificated or classified employees of the county superintendent because, while the county board has an interest in the ultimate results of negotiation, the superintendent, and not the board, is the employer (85 Ops. Atty. Gen. 77, 2002).

Following the closed session, the board must reconvene in public session to disclose the actions taken in closed session and the votes of each member present (Gov't Code § 54957.1). The governing board may, but is not required to, designate an employee to take minutes at the closed session. The minutes, which could be in the form of an audio recording, are confidential and available only to governing board members or a court if litigation ensues. Absent approval of the governing board, no person may disclose to an unauthorized person confidential information that has been presented in a closed session dealing with selected matters such as real estate, pending litigation, personnel matters, and salaries (Gov't Code § 54963). An exception is if the person questions the propriety or legality of the action taken.

Enforcement. The statute provides that every governing board member who attends a meeting where action is taken in violation of the Brown Act and intentionally deprives the public of information to which they are entitled is guilty of a misdemeanor (Gov't Code § 54959). The Brown Act also provides for civil actions against the governmental entity. If a member of the public or the media believes a violation has occurred or may occur, the person first must contact the entity, its representative, its superior agency if there is one, or the district attorney to resolve the matter within 90 days of the alleged violation (*Ingram v. Flippo*, 1999). The entity then has thirty days to cure and correct the alleged violation and/or issue an unconditional commitment to the complaining party.). If the entity fails to do so, the next step is to seek an injunction to prevent or stop a violation (Gov't Code § 54960). The Brown Act also authorizes courts to invalidate an entity's action and declare it null and void (Gov't Code § 54960.1). If the entity fails to act and its prior conduct violated the Brown Act, an injunction may be sought to reverse the action. A party who successfully sues to enforce the Brown Act may be entitled to reimbursement of their attorneys' fees from the entity.

The Public Records Act

Modeled on the federal Freedom of Information Act, the California Public Records Act (PRA) provides that any public record in the possession of a governmental body must be disclosed unless specifically exempt (Gov't Code § 7922.525). The first section of this statute conveys its intent: "In enacting this chapter, the Legislature, mindful of the right of individuals to privacy, finds and declares that access to information concerning the conduct of the people's business is a fundamental and necessary right of every person in this state" (Gov't Code § 7921.000).

The term *person* is broadly defined in the statute to include any natural person, corporation, partnership, limited liability company, firm, or association. In 2007, a California court of appeal ruled that the term encompasses a public agency and its attorney seeking disclosure of public records held by another public agency. The case involved an effort by the City of Long Beach and its attorney to seek records from the Los Angeles Unified School District relating to a school construction project that they were concerned could affect Long Beach (*Los Angeles Unified School District v. Superior Court*, 2007).

Disclosable public records are open to inspection at all times during regular office hours. On request for copies of records, agencies have ten days to determine whether the information sought is disclosable and, if so, to issue an initial response to the requestor informing them of the estimated date and time when the records will be made available. Agencies may extend the initial response deadline by an additional 14 days (for a total of 24 days to issue the initial response) if "unusual circumstances" exist. "Unusual circumstances" include the following:

1. The need to search for and collect the requested records from field facilities or other establishments that are separate from the office processing the request.
2. The need to search for, collect, and appropriately examine a voluminous amount of separate and distinct records that are demanded in a single request.
3. The need for consultation, which shall be conducted with all practicable speed, with another agency having substantial interest in the determination of the request or among two or more components of the agency having substantial subject matter interest therein.
4. The need to compile data, to write programming language or a computer program, or to construct a computer report to extract data (Gov't Code § 7922.535).

Agencies may charge a fee for making copies, but the fee must be limited to the direct cost of duplication or to an amount permitted by another statute, if applicable (*North County Parents Organization v. Department of Education*, 1994). Any information that is exempted from disclosure may be redacted. Exact copies are required unless it is impracticable to do so.

Public record means "any writing containing information relating to the conduct of the public's business prepared, owned, used, or retained by any state or local agency regardless of physical form or characteristics" (Gov't Code § 6252(e)). The term *writing* includes just about every form of communication, including documents, text messages, emails, videos, pictures, and many others. If records are maintained in an electronic format, they must be made available in that same format.

The PRA permits persons to seek a court order to enforce their rights under the statute. Those who prevail are entitled to court costs and attorneys' fees, but if the claims are deemed frivolous, requestors must pay the agency's costs and attorneys' fees (Gov't Code § 7923.115(b)).

The legislature's concern about protecting privacy is evident in the numerous exemptions from disclosure. The burden is placed on the agency to establish that a requested record falls into one of the exceptions when denying access. Exempted records that pertain most directly to public schools include routine preliminary drafts and memoranda not retained by the school and of little interest to the public, records pertaining to pending litigation, personnel records (but not employment contracts and certain discipline records related to "well-founded and substantial" allegations) that if released would constitute a clearly unwarranted invasion of personal privacy, test questions and examination data, and computer software developed by the school district (but not the public information stored on computers).

Case law provides useful guidance regarding the exemptions. For example, in 2006 a California appellate court ruled that the personnel record exception does not prevent the disclosure of an investigatory file pertaining to allegations of student verbal and sexual harassment by a school superintendent. The case involved the superintendent of the Dunsmuir Joint Union High School District, who resigned pursuant to a resignation agreement negotiated by his attorney and the district's attorney.

Among other things, the agreement provided that the board would not release any documents in the superintendent's personnel file without the latter's approval. The investigatory report containing written summaries of numerous interviews was placed in a sealed envelope in the file.

Concerned about a possible "sweetheart deal," the publisher of a newspaper sought release of the investigatory report. Overruling the trial court, the California court of appeal held that the report must be released because, although the superintendent as a public official has a right of privacy in his personnel file, that right is not absolute.

The public also has an interest in knowing how the school board responds to allegations of misconduct by the district's chief administrator. Here, that interest far outweighed the privacy concerns of the board and superintendent. Accordingly, the investigatory report and supporting documents had to be released but with the names of any students, parents, staff members, and faculty members redacted (*BRV, Inc. v. Superior Court*, 2006).

Similarly, in *Marken v. Santa Monica-Malibu Unified School District*, the court denied a high school math teacher's request for preliminary injunction by concluding that the public's right to know about the teacher's prior violation of the district's sexual harassment policy outweighed the teacher's privacy interest in shielding the information from disclosure. In 2012, Ari Marken, a teacher at Santa Monica High School, was accused of sexually harassing a student. Subsequently, the school district placed Mr. Marken on home assignment while it investigated the allegations.

Following the investigation, the district issued a written reprimand to Mr. Marken and returned him to work. A couple of years following the incident, Michael Chwe, a parent, requested the documents pertaining to the investigation of Mr. Marken under the California Public Records Act. In an effort to keep the documents private, Mr. Marken filed a complaint for injunctive relief, alleging that the Public Records Act did not authorize disclosure of his personnel records and would violate his privacy rights. The court disagreed and found the public's interest in the disclosure of the information outweighed Mr. Marken's privacy interest. Notably, the court found that records related to complaints that are "substantial and well-founded" must be disclosed in response to a Public Records Act request (*Marken v. Santa Monica-Malibu Unified Sch. Dist.*, 2012).

Access to other personnel information is limited. For instance, the home addresses and telephone numbers of school and county district employees are exempt from disclosure to anyone other than a family member or agent, an officer or employee of another education entity, an employee organization, and health benefit plan employees (Gov't Code § 7928.300). In addition, documents that assess a local agency's vulnerability to a terrorist attack or similar criminal act that are intended for closed-session deliberation are also exempt from disclosure.

In 1999 the legislature added several sections to the PRA describing information collected pursuant to various state and federal statutes that may be exempt from disclosure. The purpose of this extensive list is to assist public agencies and members of the public in deciding what must be released and what must not be. The legislature intends that any statutory changes that exempt information in a public record from disclosure will be added to the list in the future.

The education-related items that are exempt from disclosure include information demonstrating proof of majority support submitted by an employee organization to the Public Employment Relations Board, student records protected by provisions of the Education Code, disclosure of witness testimony presented in closed session during a student expulsion hearing under Education Code Section 48918, student personal information conveyed to school counselors under Education Code Section 49602, teacher credentialing information submitted to the California Commission on Teacher Credentialing under Education Code Section 44341, and certified school personnel examination results under Education Code Section 44289.

The statute also has a catchall provision that permits a public agency to refuse to disclose records that, on the facts of a particular case, would not serve the public interest (Gov't Code § 7922.000). Specifically, agencies may withhold requested information when the public's interest in nondisclosure significantly outweighs the public's interest in disclosure. The burden is on the agency to establish the justification in writing. This provision has been relied on to justify refusal to release the identities of confidential law enforcement informants and the governor's daily appointment schedule.

Similarly, Poway Unified School District sought to rely on the pending litigation and catchall exceptions to withhold a claim form requested by the media. A claim form is the first step in a lawsuit under the California Tort Claims Act. In that case, the claim form contained information about an incident in which a high school student was sodomized with a broomstick as part of an initiation ritual. The form was submitted by one of the perpetrators, who sought to sue the district. The victim's identity previously had been revealed in juvenile court proceedings attended by the media, and the victim had participated in a press conference to announce the settlement of his lawsuit against the district. (In a related case, the court overruled the victim's objections to having the amount of the settlement released to the press because the public has a right to know how public funds are spent (*Copley Press, Inc. v. Superior Court*, 1998)). The perpetrators also had consented to release of their confidential juvenile court records and files because they wanted to publicize a pattern of hazing at the high school.

The school district sought to have the claim form exempted from disclosure to a local newspaper, though the newspaper had a policy of protecting the identity of juvenile offenders and the victims of sex crimes. The trial court ordered the claim form to be released, with information about the students involved redacted. The school district appealed. The appellate court upheld the lower court's decision that claim forms do not fall within the exception for nondisclosure of records pertaining to pending litigation. Nor did protecting the privacy of those involved justify refusing to release the claim form under the catchall provision of Section 7922.000. Because the students' privacy interests already had been diminished by their own actions and because the district could still delete identifying information, the court concluded that the claim form must be released. The appellate court also rejected the school district's contention that the claim form constitutes a protected educational record under the Family Educational Rights and Privacy Act, a federal law discussed in some detail later in the chapter, as defying "logic and common sense." (*Poway Unified School District v. Superior Court*, 1998).

The increased use of personal accounts, such as text messages and personal e-mail accounts, has complicated public agency efforts to respond to PRA requests, particularly when those agencies do not have access to the personal accounts containing those messages. In *City of San Jose v. the Superior Court of Santa Clara*, 2 Cal. App. 5th 508 (2017), the California Supreme Court considered whether and to what extent public agencies are required to search employees' and other officials' personal items and accounts, such as cell phones and e-mail addresses, when responding to PRA requests.

In that case, a citizen requested emails and text messages, "sent or received on private electronic devices used by the mayor, two city council members, and their staffs." The city disclosed communications through its own telephone numbers and e-mail addresses, but did not disclose information transmitted through private accounts because those accounts were outside the city's custody and control. The citizen sued claiming that the city violated the PRA by failing to produce communications maintained on private devices and in private accounts.

In reviewing the citizen's claim, the Court specifically analyzed whether "writings concerning the conduct of public business are beyond the [PRA's] reach merely because they were sent or received using a nongovernmental account." In analyzing that question, the Court noted that the PRA requires it to broadly construe laws that further the public's right of access and narrowly construe those that limit that right of access. The Court also noted that the PRA requires agencies to disclose all records "unless the Legislature has *expressly* provided to the contrary." (Emphasis in original.)

The Court explained that, in order to qualify as a public record under the PRA, the communication must include the following attributes: "(1) a writing, (2) with content relating to the conduct of the public's business, which is (3) prepared by, *or* (4) owned, used or retained by any state or local agency" (emphasis in original).

In analyzing the first element, the Court first noted that written communication has increased significantly with the rise of electronic communications including those writings describing "fleeting thoughts and random bits of information, with varying degrees of import, often to broad audiences." The Court conceded that "the line between official communication and an electronic aside is now sometimes blurred."[2]

Regarding the second element, the Court noted that not every writing produced by a public employee is subject to review and disclosure and noted that, to qualify as a public record, "a writing must 'contain[] information relating to the conduct of the public's business.'" The Court conceded that whether a writing relates to the public's business "will not always be clear." The Court compared two contrasting examples—one involving a statement to a spouse that a coworker "is an idiot," which likely would not relate to the public's business, with a second reporting an

---

[2] It bears noting that the PRA does not limit strictly records to writings, but also includes audio and video recordings, computer data, and other forms of information.

employee's mismanagement of an agency project, which likely would be subject to disclosure. The Court noted that, to qualify as a public record, the writing:

> must relate in some substantive way to the conduct of the public's business. This standard, though broad, is not so elastic as to include every piece of information the public may find interesting. Communications that are primarily personal, containing no more than incidental mentions of agency business, generally will not constitute public records.

Regarding the third element, the Court reviewed whether communications through private accounts constitutes those "prepared by any state or local agency." The Court concluded, among other things, that the Legislature's use of the word "official" throughout the PRA demonstrates an awareness that individuals, rather than the agency, may possess records that qualify as public records under the PRA.

Regarding the fourth element, the Court closely considered the city's argument that communications through personal accounts are not "prepared, owned, used, or retained by any state and local agency" and, thus, are not disclosable. The Court ultimately concluded, "a city employee's communications related to the conduct of public business do not cease to be public records just because they were sent or received using a personal account. Sound public policy supports this result."

The Court then described several policy considerations related to the use of private accounts. The court noted, "If communications sent through personal accounts were categorically excluded from CPRA, government officials could hide their most sensitive, and potentially damning, discussions in such accounts." The Court also noted that the PRA includes several exceptions to disclosure, all which focus on the content of the records, rather than their location or medium.

The Court then provided guidance regarding conducting searches for public records that may be maintained in private accounts. The Court noted that, once the agency receives a PRA request, it is required to communicate with the custodian of records related to that request. The Court continued:

> As to requests seeking public records held in employees' nongovernmental accounts, an agency's first step should be to communicate the request to the employees in question. The agency may then reasonably rely on these employees to search *their own* personal files, accounts, and devices for responsive material. (Emphasis in original.)

The Court then analyzed court authority under the Freedom of Information Act (the federal counterpart to the PRA) and Washington state's public records act. Under both authorities, the Court noted that employees may complete affidavits demonstrating that they do not possess responsive and disclosable records. The Court specifically held:

> We agree with Washington's high court that this [affidavit] procedure, when followed in good faith, strikes an appropriate balance, allowing a public agency 'to fulfill its responsibility to search for and disclose public records without unnecessarily treading on the constitutional rights of its employees.'

Notably, the Court continued:

> We do not hold that any particular search method is required or necessarily adequate. We mention these alternatives to offer guidance . . . and to explain why privacy concerns do not require categorical exclusion of documents in personal accounts from CPRA's 'public records' definition.

School districts that receive PRA requests for information sent via personal devices and/or personal accounts would be well advised to immediately forward the request to the applicable employee(s) and/or Board members and request they produce all responsive and disclosable information as quickly as reasonably possible. Of course, the school district will not (and is not required to) review those personal devices and/or accounts, but should prepare an affidavit that may be completed by each employee and/or Board member. The affidavit could include standard responses that could be acknowledged by the employee and/or Board member, such as:

> I have no records which are responsive to the request.

> I have disclosed all records in my possession which are responsive to the request within the attached records.

> I have included all records in my possession which are responsive to the request within the attached records, but have redacted exempt information and/or information that is not responsive to the request.

> I have personal records that may be responsive to the request, but for the reasons noted below, I am withholding those records because they are exempt from disclosure since they are unrelated to my position with the school district.

PERSONAL PRIVACY

Personal privacy, as a matter of federal constitutional law, has its roots in a series of U.S. Supreme Court rulings beginning in 1965. That year, the Court struck down a state ban on the use of contraceptives by married couples as intruding on the right of privacy (*Griswold v. Connecticut*). The Court later extended the decision to encompass unmarried persons (*Eisenstadt v. Baird*, 1972). Thirty years later, the U.S. Supreme Court relied on the *Griswold* decision to invalidate a Texas law criminalizing same-sex intimate relations among consenting adults (*Lawrence v. Texas*, 2003). However, in 2022, the Court rolled back previous expansion of the right to privacy as it relates to access to abortion" (*Dobbs v. Jackson Women's Health Organization*).

Because privacy is not a specifically enumerated right in the U.S. Constitution, the Supreme Court justices inferred it from other provisions of the U.S. Constitution, most notably the word *liberty* in the due process clause of the Fourteenth Amendment ("nor shall any state deprive a person of life, liberty, or property without due process of law"). In addition to privacy, the justices similarly have protected marriage, procreation, and parental rights. These interpretations remain a matter of some contention among textualists, who argue that judges should stick to the written words, and originalists, who look toward a historical understanding, as shown in the Dobbs decision. In California, inference is unnecessary because the state constitution specifically mentions privacy. Article I, Section 1 states: "All people are by nature free and independent and have inalienable rights. Among these are enjoying and defending life and liberty, acquiring, possessing, and protecting property, and pursuing and obtaining safety, happiness, and privacy."

Minors also have privacy rights. The U.S. Supreme Court struck down a restriction on the sale or distribution of contraceptives to minors under the age of sixteen in 1977 (*Carey v. Population Services, International*). In writing for the Court a year earlier that the right to an abortion extends to minors, Justice Harry Blackmun observed: "Constitutional rights do not mature and come into being magically only when one attains the state's defined age of majority. Minors, as well as adults, are protected by the Constitution and possess constitutional rights" (*Planned Parenthood of Central Missouri v. Danforth*, 1976, p. 74). In 1997 the California Supreme Court relied on the right of privacy in the state constitution to hold that a minor cannot be required to secure permission from her parent or guardian before seeking an abortion, even if there is resort to a court if the parent or guardian refuses (*American Academy of Pediatrics v. Lungren*). In this section, we review exactly what rights of privacy employees and students have in the context of public schooling.

Employee Lifestyle

Years ago, it was not unusual for schoolteachers to be dismissed because the school board disapproved of their behavior out of school. A teacher could jeopardize their employment by obtaining a divorce or by not going to church. Additionally, a few governing boards in parts of the country even sought to terminate the contracts of teachers for cohabitation outside of marriage. For the most part even then, these efforts were unsuccessful. More recently but rare, some school boards have sought to discipline or terminate teachers for their sexuality or gender identity. Basically, however, what a school employee does outside of school is beyond the control of school authorities unless the behavior is so notorious as to jeopardize the employee's effectiveness on the job and there is evidence to support the contention.

An important ruling on teacher personal behavior came from the California Supreme Court in 1969. In *Morrison v. State Board of Education*, a case discussed in more detail in Chapter 5, the court was confronted with a schoolteacher's challenge to the termination of his credential by the California State Board of Education for unfitness to teach. The teacher resigned when confronted with evidence of a private, consensual homosexual relationship. The court ruled that, in the absence of any evidence that his behavior had rendered him unfit to teach, the state board's action was unwarranted. In other words, there must be a connection between the actions and the responsibilities of an employee. The California high court revisited the matter nearly ten years later when the board of education of the Long Beach Unified School District sought to terminate a veteran elementary teacher who had been arrested for allegedly engaging in homosexual solicitation in a public restroom (*Board of Education of Long Beach Unified School District v. Jack M.*, 1977). Though no charges were ever filed against the teacher, the school board maintained that his behavior had rendered him unfit to teach. In rejecting the school board's arguments, the justices noted that the teacher's behavior was not known to his students, that he had testified he would not engage in such behavior again, and that he had not improperly influenced his students.

However, California courts sometimes distinguish *Morrison* and *Jack M.* when the teacher's lifestyle activities, posted by the teacher onto the internet, become known by students and parents. In 2008, an exemplary tenured teacher solicited sexual relations by posting pornographic pictures and sexually explicit text multiple times on an adult website (*San Diego Unified School District v. Commission on Professional Competence*, 2011). Although the teacher did not state his name or employer, a parent found the posting and anonymously told the school. The court of appeal determined the explicit postings, seen by members of the school community, sufficiently impaired him for service as a teacher.

A teacher's claim to privacy must yield in the face of a compelling state interest. This is clear from a 1981 court of appeal decision involving a teacher in the Los Angeles Unified School District who refused to secure a chest X-ray contrary to the requirement of Education Code Section 49406 (*Garrett v. Los Angeles City Unified School District*, 1981). The California court of appeal noted that chest X-rays for teachers and even students are constitutional as a health measure for the protection of society in general. Note that under Subsection (i) of the statute, a religious objection may provide an exemption from the requirement.

Several state statutes support the right of privacy and lifestyle behavior. The California Fair Employment and Housing Act prevents discrimination on several grounds, including marital status and sexual orientation. Education Code Section 49091.24 gives teachers the right to refuse to participate in surveys that address personal values, sexual orientation, political views, religious beliefs, and family life.

One section of the Education Code provides that no recording devices are permitted in classrooms without the permission of both the teacher and the principal (Educ. Code § 51512), although another provision of the Code permits teachers to audio record themselves in the interest of improving their teaching without the prior approval of the principal or other school official (Educ. Code § 44034). Interestingly, a California court of appeal ruled in 1999 that a videotape that students had secretly made in a classroom and turned over to the school board for use in a disciplinary action against the teacher did not violate this provision (*Evens v. Superior Court*). The judges rejected the teacher's claim that the taping intruded on the teacher's privacy, noting that classroom teaching by its nature is sufficiently open that a teacher must always expect public dissemination of what transpires there. Nor did the school board's use of the purloined tape violate the California Invasion of Privacy Act (Penal Code § 630 et seq.). Except for limited law enforcement purposes, that statute restricts the use of eavesdropping via electronic devices and techniques without consent of all parties.

Student Lifestyle

Students also have lifestyle rights. In 2007 the legislature reworded and broadened state antidiscrimination law by enacting a bill entitled the California Student Civil Liberties Act (Educ. Code § 200 et seq.). Section 200, which was amended in 2018, reads:

> It is the policy of the State of California to afford all persons in public schools, regardless of their disability, gender, gender identity, gender expression, nationality, race or ethnicity, religion, sexual orientation, or any other characteristic that is contained in the definition of hate crimes set forth in Section 422.55 of the Penal Code, including immigration status, equal rights and opportunities in the educational institutions of the state."

The statute applies to private schools as well, except those controlled by religious organizations whose tenets are in conflict with the application of the statute (Educ. Code § 221).

Courts have relied on both constitutional and statutory provisions to protect student lifestyle rights. A federal district court in California ruled in 2003 that removing an eighth-grade student from her physical education class and making her sit in the principal's office because she told her teacher and fellow students that she is a lesbian constituted a violation of the equal protection clause of the Fourteenth Amendment to the U.S. Constitution. Accordingly, school officials were not entitled to immunity from her lawsuit (*Massey v. Banning Unified School District*). In 2007 another federal district court recognized that students have a constitutional right to express their sexuality at school. However, the right does not protect all expressive conduct of their lifestyle. In this case, a female student was suspended for openly and repeatedly engaging in kissing with another female student, making out, and groping. The judge upheld the suspension. Nor was there a violation of the student's equal protection rights because heterosexual students engaging in the same behavior would have been treated similarly. The court also recognized that students have a right under both the federal and California constitutions to informational privacy about their sexual identity. Here, however, the principal's disclosure to the mother that the student had been kissing another girl did not violate that right because the principal was merely following through with his statutory responsibility to give the mother a factual explanation for the basis of the suspension (*Nguon v. Wolf*).

Federal and California courts have not been certain as to whether students have a privacy right regarding gender identity. Recently in September 2024, a California superior court struck down a school district's policy requiring school employees to notify parents any time their student requests to use a different name or pronouns than that on their official records (*California v. Chino Valley Unified School District*). Alternatively, a federal court in California granted a preliminary injunction to stop another school district's policy that would discipline staff if they disclosed a student's requested gender identity (*Mirabelli v. Olson*). Those two cases are "unpublished" meaning they can only be cited in very rare circumstances.

In late 2024, the Ninth Circuit heard arguments in *Regino v. Staley*, in which a parent sought to stop the school board's policy that would prohibit disclosure of a student's changed gender identity to the student's parents. In April 2025, the court remanded the case back to the lower court, stating the latter had used the incorrect legal standard, among other reasons. In July 2024, Governor Newsom signed AB 1955 into law, which prohibits school districts from creating policies that require disclosure of a student's sexual orientation, gender identity, or gender expression, to any person—including their parents—without the student's consent.

Students' privacy rights may also be limited when students post publicly on social media or internet forums. A provision was added to the Education Code requiring school districts, county offices of education, and charter schools to inform parents of programs they propose to use to monitor their students' social media activities and to collect and store the data and postings (Educ. Code § 49073.6). Many schools seek to gather this information to help prevent bullying, sexting, school violence, and student suicide. An opportunity for public comment must be provided at a regularly scheduled board meeting before such a program is adopted. Presumably to deter litigation over invasion of personal privacy, the statute gives students and their parents the right to examine information collected about them from social media and to make corrections or deletions. To protect student privacy over the long term, all such information must be destroyed within one year after the student turns eighteen or is no longer enrolled. This legislation applies as well to third parties hired by the governing board to undertake this task.

Another provision added to the Education Code protects student privacy rights when schools enter into a contract with third parties to provide services including those that are cloud-based for digital storage, management, and retrieval of student records (Educ. Code § 49073.1). The law does not apply to existing contracts in effect before January 1, 2015, when the new law went into effect until their expiration, amendment, or renewal.

As digital learning becomes increasingly incorporated in school instructional programs, more federal and state laws protecting parent, student, and teacher privacy are likely to be enacted.

Student Records and Surveys

Student records. The Family Educational Rights and Privacy Act (FERPA) is a federal law that applies to any educational institution receiving federal funding (its provisions can be found in 20 U.S.C. § 1232g). Basically, the law gives parents access to, and the right to challenge, the content of their children's school records. It also restricts the release of personally identifiable information contained in student records without permission of the parents or eligible student. FERPA rights transfer to a student when the student reaches eighteen or attends a postsecondary educational institution (hence the term *eligible student*). However, parents continue to have access if the student is financially dependent on the parents for federal income tax purposes. The term *parent* includes a natural parent, guardian, or any person acting as a parent in the absence of a parent or guardian. Even if the parent does not have custody of the child, the parent has access to student records unless contrary to a court order.

Each school year, the school must notify parents and students over eighteen of their right to inspect the student's education records, seek an amendment to those portions believed to be inaccurate or misleading or a violation of the Act, consent to disclosure of personally identifiable information, and file a complaint with the Family Policy Compliance Office in the U.S. Department of Education. FERPA regulations require effective notice to persons with disabilities and to non-English speakers. While fees can be charged to make copies of records on an ability-to-pay basis, educational agencies may not charge a service fee to retrieve the requested document.

An education record consists of records maintained by the school, or by a party acting for the school, regardless of where they are kept. They encompass the classroom as well as student involvement in videoconferences and internet communication sessions outside the classroom. The records can be in writing; in print; or in the form of a video- or audiotape, film, microfilm, or microfiche. Notes about particular students kept in the sole possession of school personnel for their own use and not revealed to anyone other than a temporary substitute are not within the definition and thus do not have to be disclosed. Also falling within this category are records maintained by a law enforcement unit of the school. While parents have a right of access to information about their children, they do not have access to information about other children. In general, a parent who asks to see a surveillance videotape of his student acting up on the school bus would not be entitled to view the tape if it includes the images of other students. But the parent would be entitled to see an official evaluation form on the child's misbehavior completed by the bus monitor and used as the basis for disciplinary action. In guidance issued in 2017, the U.S. Department of Education stated that parents may have the right to view video or written statements that are in a child's disciplinary record (and thus an educational record) "so long as the information in these records cannot be segregated and redacted without destroying its meaning." Otherwise, the educational institution must separate and redact as necessary information pertaining to other students.

The U.S. Supreme Court ruled in 2002 that a teacher having students grade each other's papers in class and call out the results does not violate FERPA (*Owasso Independent School District v. Falvo*). This is so because the term *education record* refers to records maintained by the school; until grades are entered into a teacher grade book, they are not within the definition, said the court. Also not within the definition are records of the school's law enforcement. Information in these records can be revealed or withheld without violating FERPA.

Personally identifiable information cannot be disclosed in any form without prior written consent from the parent or eligible student. This information encompasses the student's name, family member names, addresses, Social Security number, personal characteristics that would identify the student, date and place of birth, biometric records such as fingerprints and handwriting, and similar traceable information. While parents and eligible students can waive their FERPA rights, as in the case of confidential recommendations for college or employment, the waiver must be a knowing one, that is, voluntary and with full knowledge of what is being waived. The school must maintain a record of every person who requests or obtains access to a particular student's record, except for the student's parents and school officials.

Directory information falls into a different category with regard to disclosure. Directory information consists of information in an education record that would not be considered a significant invasion of privacy if revealed. It includes such general information as a student's name, photograph, weight, and height, and so on. Through local policy, school districts can define what they mean by directory information. This information can be routinely included in school directories, athletic rosters, and the like without seeking permission from the parent or eligible student, provided that the school gives parents annual notice and an opportunity to request that such information not be released without prior written consent. This typically occurs at the beginning of the school year with other notices. Schools must continue to honor requests made by former students when enrolled that directory information not be released unless they rescind the opt-out.

FERPA and its implementing regulations provide a long list of exceptions to nondisclosure. Chief among them is disclosure of student records to others within the school or school district who have a legitimate educational interest in the information so long as the records directly relate to that interest. For example, it would not violate the act if a supervisor included the names of students in a memorandum to a teacher following a classroom observation because the teacher needs to know which students are not being well served. Among the other more notable exceptions is disclosure to another educational institution the student wishes to attend, to accrediting bodies, to organizations that are conducting research on testing and instructional programs, and to law enforcement personnel. In this connection, the California attorney general has advised that a school district may permit the district attorney to view a school bus videotape of an assault of one student on another for law enforcement purposes without parental consent, court order, or subpoena (84 Ops. Atty. Gen. 146, 2001). FERPA also permits release of student records to appropriate persons in an emergency situation when necessary to protect the health or safety of the student or other persons. Thus, it would not violate the act to release to police officers the records of a student who threatens to blow up the school. However, a California court of appeal has ruled that the portion of Education Code Section 48918 requiring that formal action to expel a student be taken during the open session of a governing board meeting violates FERPA and is null and void (*Rim of the World Unified School District v. Superior Court*, 2002). The same is true of making the student's expulsion record available to anyone who asks for the information. Even a probation department request for those types of records is generally held to require a court order.

The Individuals with Disabilities Education Act (IDEA) provides additional protection for these students. Parents have a right to receive copies of the child's eligibility report and related documentation, as well as the individualized education program (IEP), at no cost. There are specific time lines for providing parents with this information. Parents also have the right to have their representatives inspect and review the education records on their behalf. The details of this law are discussed in Chapter 8.

What happens if a schoolteacher or official violates FERPA? The U.S. Supreme Court has ruled that the sole remedy for FERPA violations involves administrative sanctions imposed by the U.S. Department of Education (*Gonzaga University v. Doe*, 2002). Individuals whose information was disclosed in violation of FERPA are not able to obtain a remedy directly from the school. In rare instances, these sanctions could include loss of federal funding. Additionally, it should be noted that an employee who violates the act could be subject to discipline by the educational institution.

California law tracks the provisions of FERPA and goes beyond them to some extent (Educ. Code § 49060 et seq.). Under state law, if parents are divorced or legally separated, only the parent having legal custody of the child may challenge the contents of the child's record, offer a written response to a record, or consent to release of records to others unless there is a written agreement to the contrary. The annual notice to parents about the district's policy on student records includes a long list of components. Among them are types of records the school keeps and their location, the person responsible for the maintenance of each record type, the location of the log of those requesting or receiving student records, the costs for reproducing records, the school's policies for reviewing and expunging records, the procedures for challenging the content of the pupil's records, the cost charged to the parent for reproducing copies of the records, and what constitutes directory information (Educ. Code § 49063). Another section provides that while a school can charge for copying, it may not charge for up to two transcripts of former students or up to two verifications of various former student records (Educ. Code § 49065). It also may not charge for retrieving records.

As seen in Chapter 1, parents in California have an absolute right of access at both public and private schools to student records during school hours and within five days of making a request (Educ. Code § 49069). Any editing or withholding of records is prohibited. In conformity with FERPA, the Education Code describes the due process procedures to be followed when parents challenge the content of their child's education records (Educ. Code § 49070). Basically, within thirty days of filing a request to challenge the contents of a student's record, the parent is entitled to meet with the superintendent or designee and the school employee who recorded the information. If the superintendent denies the request, the parent can appeal to the governing board within thirty days of the denial, whose decision is final. The parents can file an objection to the decision, which becomes part of the student's school record.

Among other provisions of note, Education Code Section 49602 provides that personal information conveyed by a student over the age of twelve to a school counselor is confidential and cannot become part of the student's record without the student's permission. Nor can it be revealed, even to the student's parents, except in narrow circumstances as described in Chapter 12 regarding legal liability of school counselors. Education Code Section 45345 prohibits an instructional aide from giving out personal information about a student to anyone other than a teacher or administrator in the school. Section 49068 requires the transfer of student records to a new public or private school on request. These records may not be withheld because of any charges or fees owed by the student or parent. Section 49072 permits parents to file a written statement or response in their child's record about any disciplinary action taken against the child. Following the McKinney-Vento Homeless Assistance Act (42 U.S.C. § 11434a(2)), California Education Code Section 49073 was amended to restrict the release of directory information regarding a homeless student, as defined by the McKinney-Vento Act, without the written consent of a parent of the student when the student reaches eighteen years old or attends a postsecondary educational institution.

Section 49073.5 states that the legislature's intent is to minimize the release of student telephone numbers in the absence of parental consent because of harassment concerns. This would appear to have bearing on the school's use of directory information. Section 49076 includes a student who is sixteen or older and has completed tenth grade as one of those who have access to records under the legitimate educational interest exception to nondisclosure without parental consent. If the student is both homeless and unaccompanied as defined by the McKinney-Vento

Act, then this section permits a student aged fourteen or over to have access to their school records. These records can also be released to an individual who completes the Caregiver's Authorization Affidavit as provided in Family Code Section 6552 and signs the affidavit for the purpose of enrolling a minor in school. Section 49076 also permits school districts to participate in interagency computerized data systems that contain student information, provided the systems are secure so that unauthorized personnel cannot gain access and privileged or confidential information is not disclosed.

Finally, Section 49079 requires school districts to inform a student's teachers based on information contained in school records or obtained from law enforcement that within the past three years the student has engaged in, or is reasonably suspected of having engaged in, a suspendable or expellable offense other than the use or possession of tobacco. Failure to do so is a misdemeanor, punishable by confinement in county jail of up to six months and a $1,000 fine. The teacher is prohibited from disseminating this information to anyone else.

Student surveys. Shortly after it was enacted, FERPA was amended to give parents and guardians the right to inspect instructional material and request exemptions from material they found objectionable for their children (20 U.S.C. § 1232 h). Now known as the Protection of Pupils Rights Amendment (PPRA), the act applies to hard copy or electronic or digital instructional material other than tests used in applicable programs.

The term *applicable program* means a program administered or funded by the U.S. Department of Education and its secretary. For programs to which it does apply, the act restricts the use of surveys to gather information on such topics as political affiliations, mental or psychological problems of the student or student's family, sex behavior of family members, critical appraisals of family members, legally recognized privileges such as lawyers or physicians, religious practices, and income without prior consent of the parent or eligible student. The act requires districts to develop policies in consultation with parents to implement it.

California law tracks PPRA. Education Code Section 49091.12, part of a chapter entitled the Education Empowerment Act of 1998, provides that a student may not be compelled to affirm or disavow any worldview, religious doctrine, or political opinion. Nor may students be given a behavioral, mental, or emotional evaluation without written parental consent. Education Code Section 69091.18 provides that neither the student's family nor the student can be asked to participate in an assessment of home life, any form of parental testing, a nonacademic home-based counseling program, a parent training program, or a family education service plan. Education Code Section 51513 states that no test, questionnaire, survey, or examination with questions about student or family personal beliefs or practices in sex, family life, morality, and religion can be administered in public school unless the parent or guardian has given written consent.

STUDENT SEARCH AND SEIZURE

Since the late 1970s, California public school students have been protected from unreasonable searches and seizures by the state constitution and then later by the federal constitution as well. In recent years, drug trafficking and violence at school have increased the vigilance of school officials over student behavior. Whenever possible, school officials seek to take preventive action to keep the school safe. Inevitably, doing so raises questions of how far they can go without violating student search-and-seizure rights. The judicial decisions discussed in this section provide good insight into what school officials can and cannot do.

Student Searches

We begin with a discussion of the standards laid down by the U.S. and California supreme courts for conducting legally valid student searches. We then examine how lower courts have applied the standards in specific situations to gain a better understanding of how school officials can go about conducting a legally valid student search.

Standards. The U.S. Supreme Court first faced the question of student searches in a New Jersey case involving a student who denied that she had been smoking in the girls' restroom contrary to school rules (*New Jersey v. T.L.O.*, 1985). A teacher discovered the girl, T.L.O., and a companion apparently doing so and herded the two girls to the office. There, the other girl confessed, but T.L.O. did not. The principal, Theodore Choplick, demanded to see T.L.O.'s purse. When Choplick looked inside, he found a pack of cigarettes. He also spotted a package of cigarette rolling papers, raising his suspicions about possible drug involvement. He searched further and found a small amount of marijuana, a pipe, a number of empty plastic bags, a substantial amount of money, a list of names of students who owed T.L.O. money, and two letters implicating the student in drug dealing. His suspicions confirmed, he turned the student over to the police. T.L.O. was suspended from school and later declared delinquent in juvenile court and placed on probation. She sought to overturn her conviction by arguing that the purse search violated her right under the unreasonable search provision of the Fourth Amendment to the U.S. Constitution. That provision, which applies to the states and their political subdivisions through the Fourteenth Amendment, reads:

The right of the people to be secure in their persons, houses, papers, and effects, against unreasonable searches and seizures, shall not be violated, and no Warrants shall issue, but upon probable cause, supported by Oath or affirmation, and particularly describing the place to be searched, and the persons or things to be seized.

The U.S. Supreme Court first observed that the Fourth Amendment applies to searches of public school students. That question answered, the next question for the justices was whether the standards for a lawful search require school officials to establish probable cause and obtain a warrant from a judge in conformity with the wording of the Fourth Amendment. In other decisions, the Supreme Court has permitted exceptions to the probable cause/warrant requirements when exigent circumstances exist. These exceptions include a search incident to lawful arrest, a search conducted by police pursuant to a stop and frisk for weapons, and a consensual search. The State of New Jersey argued that the need to maintain a safe educational environment is so compelling that any search of student personal property brought into the school is justified. Writing for the majority, Justice Byron White noted that the Court had ruled to this effect with regard to prisoners but observed, "We are not yet ready to hold that the schools and the prisons need be equated for purposes of the Fourth Amendment" (p. 742).

The Supreme Court set forth two standards for a search of a public school student to conform to the Fourth Amendment. First, there must be *reasonable cause*, justified at its inception, to believe that a student has violated a school rule or a law. Second, the search that is conducted must be reasonable—not *excessively intrusive*—in light of the age and gender of the student and the nature of the infraction. Applying the standards to the search that Choplick conducted of T.L.O.'s purse, the Court observed that the principal had reasonable cause to suspect the student had been smoking, based on the teacher's report. Thus, the initial search of her purse met the reasonableness standard. When Choplick was conducting this search, he spotted the cigarette rolling papers. The Court previously had ruled that evidence "in plain view" during a search can be used against a person even though the evidence was not suspected of being there. Because the rolling papers were in plain view during the initial cigarette search, they justified the second, more intrusive search resulting in discovery of the drug paraphernalia. The search of T.L.O.'s purse was therefore lawful. The Court upheld her delinquency conviction.

A few months after this decision, the California Supreme Court reached a different decision in a case involving the search of a student's calculator case (*In re William G.*, 1985). In the *T.L.O.* decision, the U.S. Supreme Court had observed in a footnote that a state constitution might confer greater rights on students, but the New Jersey courts had not relied on its state constitution in that case. In *In re William G.*, the California Supreme Court did so. It pointed out that a student's right to be free from unreasonable searches emanates both from the Fourth Amendment and from Article 1, Section 13 of the California Constitution, which is nearly a word-for-word repeat of its federal counterpart. In addition, the justices noted the relevance of Article 1, Section 1 of the state constitution for protecting privacy. The California Supreme Court observed, "Homage to personhood is the foundation for individual rights protected by our state and national Constitutions. The privacy of a student, the very young or the teenager must be respected" (pp. 125–126). The justices applied these provisions to the case at hand.

The facts of the *William G.* case are relatively simple. At Chatsworth High School in Los Angeles, assistant principal Reno Lorenz confronted William G., a sixteen-year-old student, and two male companions walking through the campus. Wondering why the students were not in class, Lorenz walked toward them. As he did so, he noticed William G. was carrying a small black bag, later identified as a vinyl calculator case, that had an odd-looking bulge. The students' attention was focused on the bag. The assistant principal's suspicions were aroused, and he asked William G. why he was not in class. The student responded that his classes were over for the day. As he spoke, the student placed the case to his side and then behind his back. Lorenz asked what William G. had in his hand and received the reply, "Nothing." The student added, "You can't search me" and "You need a warrant for this." Lorenz took William G. to the office. There Lorenz forcefully took the case and unzipped it. Inside he found marijuana and drug paraphernalia. Lorenz contacted the police, who placed the student under arrest. The juvenile court refused to accept William G.'s argument that the evidence was illegally obtained, and the student appealed.

Viewed from the perspective of the federal and state constitutions, the California Supreme Court concluded, the search violated the student's rights. The search was not based on articulated facts but rather on a hunch. Lorenz had no reason to believe that William G. was involved in drug dealing, and there was no evidence of exigent circumstances requiring an immediate nonconsensual search. This point is important because, in a situation where school officials have reason to believe a student has a concealed weapon, they may well have no alternative to conducting a nonconsensual search. The search of William G. being illegal, the evidence obtained from it could not be used in the juvenile court. The student's conviction of delinquency was overturned.

The California Supreme Court sidestepped the issue of the standards to be applied when school security officers or law enforcement officials are involved in the search. The U.S. Supreme Court had done the same in *T.L.O.* However, the California courts of appeal have stated that school officials include school resource officers for the purposes of applying the reasonable suspicion standard (*In re William V.*, 2003). The California Supreme Court also did not discuss whether evidence seized in an illegal search could nevertheless be used against the student in a school disciplinary proceeding as contrasted with a criminal prosecution, noting in a footnote that the matter had not been raised in the case.

However, the year before, a California court of appeal ruled that the exclusionary rule did not apply in student disciplinary proceedings and that marijuana seized in what turned out to be an unjustified search could be used to suspend the student from school (*Gordon J. v. Santa Ana Unified School District*, 1984). How strong a precedent this case presents today is questionable, given that it was decided before both the *T.L.O.* and *In re William G.* decisions. Clearly, aside from emergency situations, it is always wise for administrators to have articulated facts justifying a student search and then to make sure the search is not excessively intrusive on student privacy. The lesson learned from the *In re William G.* decision is that the California constitution is more protective of the student right to be free from searches and seizures than is the federal constitution, even when the searches are of school property assigned to students.

General searches are more problematic because they run counter to the purpose of the Fourth Amendment. That amendment was included in the Bill of Rights because the American Founders wanted to eliminate the capricious searches the colonists had experienced at the hands of the British. Still, general searches have been permitted where the expectations of personal privacy are limited and the needs of government substantial. A good illustration is a search conducted at an airport. The U.S. Supreme Court confronted the general search issue in 1995 in a case involving random, unannounced drug testing of public school athletes (*Vernonia School District v. Acton*). The school district in that case had experienced a serious drug and alcohol problem among its students. The district asserted that the leaders of the drug culture in the school were student athletes and instituted a general drug-testing program to combat it. The program required a written consent form from parents. Without the written consent, a student would not be able to participate in the school's athletic team. One student, Wayne Acton, and his parents refused to sign the consent form, arguing that it violated their Fourth Amendment rights. The Ninth Circuit agreed. The Supreme Court reversed that decision. The *Vernonia* decision is important because it sets the standards for a lawful student drug test under the federal constitution.

The Supreme Court first observed that students who voluntarily participate in interscholastic sports have a diminished expectation of privacy. "School sports are not for the bashful," wrote Justice Antonin Scalia for the majority. At the same time, the school's interest in curtailing illicit drug use among students and protecting student athletes from injury is significant. The drug-testing policy minimally intruded on student privacy. Female students produce samples in an enclosed bathroom stall within earshot of a school official of the same gender. Male students do so at a urinal with a school official standing at some distance behind them. The samples are sent to a laboratory with a nearly 100 percent accuracy rate. The laboratory does not know the identity of the students and sends the results to the superintendent. Only school administrators have access to the testing results, which are not kept for more than one year. Significantly, the consequences of a positive test are limited. A student who tests positive must undergo a second test. If the result again is positive, the student is given an option of participating in a six-week assistance program or being suspended from athletics for the remainder of the season and the next season. A second offense results in a similar penalty, while a third offense results in suspension for the remainder of the season and the next two athletic seasons. Students were neither expelled nor turned over to the police.

A few years later, the high court extended the *Acton* ruling to a similar general drug testing encompassing students participating in all extracurricular activities. The case involved Lindsay Earls, a high school student in an Oklahoma school district who was a member of several nonathletic extracurricular activities including the show choir, the marching band, and the National Honor Society. While the district's drug-testing policy covered all extracurricular activities, in practice it applied only to competitive extracurricular activities such as band, choir, pompom, cheerleading, Future Farmers of America, Future Homemakers of America, and athletics. For the same reasons advanced in the *Acton* decision, the majority upheld the policy (*Board of Education v. Earls*, 2002).

In sum, the standards for legally permissible individualized searches of public school students and school property assigned to students arising from these decisions require articulated facts of alleged wrongdoing and a search that is not excessively intrusive on student privacy. A general search is permissible in the context of student drug testing of student athletes and those participating in extracurricular activities so long as there is ample justification, personal privacy is given measured protection, samples are not compromised on the way to testing, and sanctions are tailored to the offense. We now examine how these standards have been applied to a variety of searches conducted in California public schools.

Individual searches. In 2004, a state court recognized the continuing validity of *In re William G.* in a case involving the search of a student's purse. Lisa G., a San Diego High School student, and several other students were disruptive in class (*In re Lisa G.*). The teacher told the students to sit down and focus on their work. Lisa requested permission to go to the bathroom. The teacher refused, unaware of information from the school nurse that the student should be permitted to use the bathroom on request because of a medical condition. Becoming more agitated and insistent, Lisa walked to the classroom door. The teacher attempted to block her from leaving, but Lisa pushed the teacher aside and left the classroom. The student could not reenter the classroom because the door was locked. At the end of class, the teacher decided to write a discipline referral for Lisa. However, the teacher did not know Lisa's name. When the student left the classroom, the teacher took Lisa's purse for safekeeping. The teacher decided to open the purse in hopes of finding identification information. She found a knife and called security. Lisa was arrested and subsequently declared a ward of the state and placed on probation. Lisa sought to suppress the evidence used against her as a violation of her Fourth Amendment right to be free from unreasonable searches. The California court of appeal found the search little different from the one in *In re William G.* As in that case, there was no justification for the search. The fact that the student had been disruptive in class was irrelevant. In a key passage, the judges pointed out that "[m]ere disruptive behavior does not authorize a school official to rummage through his or her students' personal belongings" (p. 166). Thus, the search was unreasonable, and the evidence resulting from it had to be suppressed. Without the evidence, there was no evidence to support Lisa's conviction of possession of a knife on school grounds. Whether it would have made any difference if the student had just been disciplined internally is not clear. The best advice is always to have reasonable cause—meaning clearly articulated facts—before conducting student searches.

In its *In re William G.* ruling, the California Supreme Court did not distinguish between searches of school property assigned to students and searches of student possessions. In an important passage, the justices wrote, "Neither indiscriminate searches of lockers nor more discreet individual searches of a locker, a purse or a person, here a student, can take place absent the existence of reasonable suspicion. Respect for privacy is the rule—a search is the exception" (p. 126). A California appellate court followed this directive in 1995 in upholding a locker search triggered by a call from a parent on a Wednesday to the school's vice principal, informing him that the previous Friday night her son saw another student with a pistol at the high school football game. Fearing for her son's safety, the parent asked for confidentiality. Based on the tip, the vice principal and security guard searched the student's locker the next day but found nothing except books. A short time later they saw the student place his backpack in the locker. They waited a few minutes and then searched the locker a second time. During this second search, they found a loaded handgun in the student's backpack.

The student sought to overturn his conviction as a delinquent minor by arguing that the initial locker search was unjustified because the tip came from an anonymous source and was too remote in time. The second locker search, he contended, was completely without cause. The appellate court disagreed. The tip was not anonymous, and, even if it had been, that would be but one factor to weigh regarding reasonable cause. The court also rejected the argument that the information about the weapon was stale because it was based on an incident occurring five days earlier outside of school. With regard to the second search, the judges observed that school officials reasonably could conclude that a student who brings a gun to school will keep it in a locker, in a backpack or purse, or on his or her person. The judges advised:

> School officials should investigate reports that particular students are carrying firearms onto campuses by the minimal intrusion of checking the contents of a student's locker. Such a minimal intrusion is justified particularly when school officials observe the student putting a backpack, a likely place for carrying a gun, into a locker. (*In re Joseph G.*, p. 906)

Thus, the second search of the locker and the backpack, which was in plain view, was justified. Whether a school could condition student use of its lockers and desks by having students consent to periodic unannounced inspections remains unclear.

In 2003 a federal district court in California provided additional guidance for conducting individualized searches on public school campuses (*United States v. Aguilera*). The case involved a nonstudent who argued that his conviction for possessing a sawed-off shotgun on a public school campus should be overturned because school security personnel could not rely on the relatively lax *T.L.O.* standards to conduct the search. The court rejected the contention, noting that the purpose of the *T.L.O.* ruling was to provide a safe school environment and "must surely encompass the conduct of non-students who pose a threat to that environment" (p. 1209). The court also observed that reliance on an anonymous tip to conduct a search satisfies the reasonable cause standard of *T.L.O.* as long as the tip is reliable. In this case the anonymous tip came from the mother of a student, who had observed the youth with a gun tucked into his shorts walk past her car and toward the campus and who then used her cell phone to alert the office staff. In the view of the court, the tip exhibited "sufficient indicia of reliability" to provide reasonable suspicion.

A 2010 California court of appeal decision elaborates on search standards when police officers and school administrators collaborate. The case involved a narcotics officer who learned from a confidential informant that a student was carrying illegal drugs in his pants (*In re K.S.*). The narcotics officer passed the information on to the police officer assigned to the school. That officer in turn informed the vice principal. The vice principal decided that she needed to conduct a search in the interest of school safety but was concerned about her own safety and asked the narcotics officer, who had come to the school, and another police officer to accompany her. The student was in a physical education class at the time, so the vice principal went to the student's locker, had it unlocked, and found a plastic bag containing several Ecstasy pills in the student's trousers. The evidence was turned over to the police and used in a juvenile proceeding. Because both the decision to conduct the search and the actual search were done by the vice principal, the *T.L.O.* reasonable cause standard was appropriate, and the student's motion to suppress the evidence was denied. Another California court of appeal further provided that this relaxed standard applied to backup officers called by a school resource officer when the school resource officer reasonably believed a student had a gun on campus (*In re K.J.*, 2018).

What about conducting a search of another student's locker where the student in question may have stored illicit items? This arose in the Richmond High School in West Contra Costa Unified School District when a female student alerted campus security officers that student T.H. shot someone on a city bus the day before and she had heard that he had taken the weapon to school. The campus security officers alerted the police. One of the campus security officers noted that T.H. did not spend time at his locker but rather at one of the nearby lockers and had done so with his girlfriend on the day of the shooting at a time when students were required to be in class or at lunch. The campus security officers knew that students often store illicit items in other students' lockers. When the campus security officers opened this particular locker, nothing was found. They then searched other lockers in the area where T.H. had been seen. In one of these lockers assigned to student J.D. they found the butt of a sawed-off shotgun along with papers containing T.H.'s name.

When police officers questioned J.D. after reading him his Miranda rights, J.D. admitted the weapon belonged to him. In a delinquency proceeding, J.D. challenged the search of his locker as a violation of his privacy rights. The appellate court rejected the argument, noting that student privacy concerns need to be balanced against the need for campus safety. Here there was reasonable cause for school officials to search J.D.'s locker, knowing that students often stored illicit items in lockers assigned to other students and that T.H. had frequented the locker area where the weapon was found (*In re J.D.*, 2014).

Searching lockers and asking students to empty their pockets or purses is quite different from conducting a search of students themselves. In 2009 the U.S. Supreme Court stated that an underwear search of a student was unreasonable as there was no indication of danger to other students or that the student was hiding evidence of wrongdoing in her underwear (*Sanford Unified School District No. 1 v. Redding*). Although the Supreme Court did not prohibit strip-searches of students in any case, such searches are not permissible in California. Education Code Section 49050 prohibits searches involving the removing or rearranging of the clothing of a student to permit visual inspection of "the underclothing, breast, buttocks, or genitalia of the pupil." Body-cavity searches are likewise outlawed. Given the reluctance of many judges to condone excessively intrusive searches of students and the thrust of this California Education Code section, personally intrusive searches should be left to parents and to law enforcement except in the most exigent circumstances, when maintaining student safety is at risk.

So far, limited case law exists regarding searches and seizures of student electronic devices such as cell phones, tablets, and laptops at school. If the students are using school-owned electronic communication devices (ECDs), then the terms of the acceptable use policy they and their parents signed must be followed. The same is true of teachers. However, if they are using their own ECDs, then there is more extensive privacy protection. One informative ruling regarding the latter comes from a federal district court in Pennsylvania holding that a student's right to freedom from unreasonable seizures is not violated when his or her cell phone is confiscated after the student uses the device contrary to a school rule (*Klump v. Nazareth Area School District*, 2006). However, the court refused to dismiss the student's Fourth Amendment unreasonable search claim against school officials for searching his phone for alleged drug activity by checking text messages and voice mail. Nor was there justification for school officials to call other students whose numbers were listed on the cell phone to determine whether these students might be involved in drug matters.

In California, an assistant principal at Antioch High School became concerned about suspicious behavior of two students who were not in class, one of whom was suspected of bringing a firearm to school but then discarding it in a campus trash can. The two students were taken to two adjoining rooms in the vice principal's office for questioning. Meanwhile, the firearm was found and taken to the office. Another student was observed walking back and forth by the office. The administrators were concerned, as they did not yet know who brought the firearm to school. The student was directed to enter the office but did not do so. He was escorted back to the office. The administrators noticed that he was fidgety and reaching down into his pocket. Concerned that he had a concealed weapon in his clothing and was resisting their checking, they took him to the ground. The cell phone was found. Concerned that this student was communicating with one of the other two students detained in the office about the firearm since they knew each other and had argued earlier that morning, one of the administrators removed the phone from the student's pocket to keep him from manipulating it. The student had turned off the cell phone. So the assistant principal plugged it into a USB cable, which brought it back on line. The assistant principal viewed the student's collection of text messages and photographs showing him holding the firearm that later was recovered from the trash can.

When questioned about his potential involvement in the gun incident by a second vice principal, the student became irate and screamed profanities. According to this assistant principal, he said "Those are my photos. You can't do that." After becoming belligerent, the student was subdued by campus supervisors. The Antioch police were contacted. When the student contested the cell phone search at a juvenile court hearing as a violation of his Fourth Amendment rights, the judge rejected it and declared the juvenile a ward of the state. The California appellate court concurred with the ruling, noting that the discovery of a firearm and its magazine cartridge on school property coupled with the student's connection with the other two students in the office fell within the reasonable grounds for a student search. "This is particularly true," wrote the judges, "when one considers the gravity of the situation that initially gave rise to the search—the discovery of a firearm and magazine on school grounds." (*In re Rafael C.*, 2016).

The police are required to read persons under arrest their *Miranda* rights, based on the famous 1966 U.S. Supreme Court *Miranda v. Arizona* decision: "You have a right to remain silent. Anything you say can be used against you in a court of law. You are entitled to an attorney. If you cannot afford one, an attorney will be appointed to represent you." Are these rights required before searching a student? In a 1988 decision, a California appellate court ruled in the negative, following a long line of similar rulings by courts in other parts of the country. The case involved an Oakland middle school student, Corey L., who consented to being searched after the school principal had learned from three students that someone on the school grounds had drugs. One of the three identified Corey L. as possessing cocaine. The principal found two baggies containing what turned out to be cocaine. The student said someone else had given them to him and denied that he intended to sell it on campus. A month earlier, the principal suspected Corey L. was involved in drug dealing because the student had a large amount of cash without credible explanation. The police were summoned, and Corey L. was arrested. The student sought to suppress the evidence against him by arguing that the principal should have read him his *Miranda* rights. The principal had not done so.

The court rejected the contention, noting that *Miranda* comes into play after a person is taken into police custody and does not apply to student questioning by school officials. The court observed, "Questioning of a student by a principal, whose duties include the obligations to maintain order, protect the health and safety of pupils and maintain conditions conducive to learning, cannot be equated with custodial interrogation by law enforcement officers" (*In re Corey L.*, p. 361).

Group searches. Suppose a school administrator suspects that some members of a group of students have contraband but is unsure exactly which ones. Can the administrator subject them all to a search? This was the question before a California court of appeal in a case involving the detention and subsequent search of a group of students in connection with a confrontation between rival gangs at Grant High School in the Los Angeles Unified School District (*In re Alexander B.*, 1990). The dean of students heard yelling and noticed one group of students running toward another group. He separated the two groups and ordered them to the office. An unidentified boy in one of the groups said, "Don't pick on us; one of those guys has a gun," gesturing to a third group of five or six students who had been egging the others on from the sidelines. The dean directed an officer from the district's police department who had been standing nearby to check the third group of students for a weapon. The officer ordered the third group to sit on the curb while he began searching each student. One of the students refused to comply with the officer's order to remain sitting. When the student attempted to leave, the officer wrestled the student to the ground. As he did so, the officer noticed a black handle sticking out from the student's belt. A machete knife and scabbard were removed from inside the student's trouser leg. The student sought to overturn an order declaring him a ward of the juvenile court by arguing in part that the evidence was the product of an illegal search.

The court of appeal rejected the student's contention. Here, the district police officer had received information from the dean that someone in the group reportedly was in possession of a weapon. Given the need to provide students with a safe school environment, "a cursory search of appellant and others in his group for dangerous weapons was not only reasonable, it was constitutionally compelled" (p. 1576). The fact that the search was focused on five or six students rather than a particular student was immaterial. The officer had acted appropriately in deterring the student from attempting to leave and conducting the search.

There are two noteworthy comments to make about this case. First, the court did not decide the standards to be followed had the police officer conducted the search on his own volition or had ordered the dean of students to do so. The general assumption is that when the police initiate a search the standards are higher. However, if the police officer is assigned to the school, then the police officer may conduct searches under the relaxed *T.L.O.* standards just like a school administrator or security officer paid by the school (*In re William V.* 2003). Second, in a later decision discussed in the next section, the California Supreme Court distinguished searches from seizures, noting that brief detentions of students do not require reasonable cause. Thus, it would not have been necessary for the district police officer to show reasonable cause to detain either the group of students or the student who attempted to leave.

Employing drug-detecting sniffer dogs to search for drugs in school is not uncommon. In a 1999 decision, the Ninth Circuit set a limit on the use of such dogs (*B.C. v. Plumas Unified School District*). The case involved a sniffer dog search at Quincy High School in the Plumas Unified School District. School officials ordered students out of their classroom; as the students exited, they passed a drug-sniffing dog. The students waited while the dog entered the room to sniff their desks and belongings. The students again walked past the dog as they returned to their room. No drugs were found. One of the students, B.C., filed suit. After reviewing the law in other jurisdictions, the Ninth Circuit ruled that the use of sniffer dogs to sniff students is a search under the Fourth Amendment. Further, it is offensive and intrudes on personal privacy. Agreeing that school officials have an important, even compelling, interest in deterring drug use, the judges noted that relying on a sniffer dog to conduct a random, suspicionless search of students as they left and reentered the classroom was unreasonable in the absence of any evidence that there was a drug crisis or even a drug problem at the high school. Thus, the search of B.C. was unconstitutional.

Note that the appeals court did not rule out the use of sniffer dogs to conduct a general search of students if there were documented evidence of a major drug problem at school. Recall that the Supreme Court allowed random drug testing of students participating in athletics and extracurricular activities in part because there was a drug crisis articulated by the school district. In the absence of such a showing, sniffer dogs can be used only to search a particular student based on individualized suspicion. The judges differentiated sniffer dog searches of objects from searches of persons. Thus, it appears that sniffer dogs can be used to sniff lockers, desks, and cars without violating student rights.

To keep campuses and school events weapon free, schools often employ walk-through and handheld metal detectors to conduct general searches. The California attorney general has advised that these searches are similar to administrative searches conducted at airports and at courthouses and only minimally intrude on student privacy (75 Ops. Atty. Gen. 155, 1992). Further, the attorney general found their use consistent with provisions of the Education Code permitting school employees to remove injurious objects from students (Educ. Code § 49330 et seq.). The term *injurious object* means something that is capable of inflicting substantial bodily harm. School personnel may notify parents and have the option of notifying law enforcement. School officials can turn the object over to the parents or to the student at the end of the day if the object can be lawfully possessed off school grounds. The attorney general also advised that the use of metal detectors is consistent with provisions of the Education Code requiring the school site council or school safety planning committee to develop a comprehensive school safety plan (Educ. Code § 32280 et seq.). In short, the compelling interest to secure safety outweighs the minimal intrusions on personal privacy.

A California court of appeal has upheld the use of metal detectors to protect students and staff from weapons at school (*In re Latasha W.*, 1998). The metal detectors were used randomly in conformity with the high school's written policy. If a detector was triggered, the student was asked to open his or her jacket or pockets to reveal the source. When Latasha W. opened her jacket, a knife with a blade longer than two-and-one-half inches came into view. The student sought to overturn her conviction in juvenile court, arguing that the knife was the product of an illegal search. She was unsuccessful. While noting an absence of cases dealing with such searches in California, the appellate court reviewed decisions elsewhere and found that metal detector searches have been upheld in the absence of individualized suspicion. Given the substantial interest of the school in keeping guns and knives off campus coupled with the minimally intrusive nature of the search, the court found that the random, general use of metal detectors did not violate student rights. The judges noted no other effective way for the school to achieve a weapon-free environment.

Later the same court (different judges) cited *Latasha W.* in holding that not only are completely random weapons searches of students entering school groups permissible but that a nonstudent also has a lesser right of privacy than a student who is properly on school grounds (*People v. Jose Y.*, 2006). The case involved a pat-down search of a student from another high school who was taken to the security office and searched by a police officer assigned to the school. During the search the officer discovered a knife. The nonstudent contended that because the pat-down search violated his rights, his being placed on probation for violating a Penal Code provision against possessing a locking blade knife on school property should be tossed out. The court of appeal rejected the student's motion.

A California court of appeal decision cited the *Latasha W.* decision when upholding a high school policy providing that students who leave campus and return during the school day are automatically subject to a search (*In re Sean A*, 2010). The case arose when an assistant principal asked Sean, who said he had left campus to retrieve a notebook and returned, to empty his pockets. A plastic bag containing Ecstasy pills materialized. The assistant principal contacted the police, and Sean was arrested. He later sought to overturn a juvenile court decision placing him on probation for possessing a controlled substance by arguing the search was illegal. In a 2–1 decision, the appellate court rejected the contention, noting once again the importance of keeping schools safe. Further, all students and parents were informed of the search policy. The dissenting judge found the reasonable suspicion standard for individualized student searches set forth by both the U.S. and California supreme courts was not met. Because further litigation is likely on this issue, school officials should obtain legal advice before instituting or following a similar general search policy.

Occasionally, school districts will consider conducting general Breathalyzer searches to check student consumption of alcohol. Breathalyzer searches are more intrusive than metal detector searches, especially when a tube is inserted in one's mouth for exhalation of breath. Some years ago, a federal district court in Oregon upheld a Breathalyzer search that police conducted of students embarking on a field trip after one student became ill and admitted drinking and another student passed out after the school bus had left school. The vice principal had the bus turn around and head for the police station. All students were given Breathalyzer tests. The court found that police had probable cause to conduct the Breathalyzer search of the student who tested positive for alcohol and later filed the lawsuit, thus sidestepping application of the *T.L.O.* standards (*Juran v. Independence Oregon Central School District 12J*, 1995).

In sum, the case law relevant to California tells us that group searches of public school students are permitted when there is reasonable suspicion that someone in the group possesses contraband. The search must not be excessively intrusive in light of the circumstances. When students refuse to comply with the request for a search or when a particularly invasive search is necessary, the best policy is to contact law enforcement and let them handle the search. Any contraband they find usually will be admissible for a juvenile or criminal prosecution and also can be used in the school's administrative discipline procedures. General administrative searches using metal detectors are permitted when there is a need to conduct them. The use of sniffer dogs to detect drugs on school property also is permitted as long as the dogs are not used to sniff students. How much justification would be necessary to allow dogs to sniff students in a general manner is not known. In part, the answer will depend on the degree to which the dogs intrude on the students' zone of personal privacy.

Student Seizures

Both the federal and California constitutions prevent unreasonable seizures as well as searches. What is an unreasonable seizure? The leading ruling on the issue comes from the California Supreme Court in a case involving a fourteen-year-old male student, Randy G., who was spotted by a campus security officer in an area on campus where students were not permitted to congregate (*In re Randy G.*, 2001). When the student saw the security aide, he fixed his pocket nervously, leaving some of the lining sticking out. The aide thought the student acted very paranoid. Together with another security official, the aide went to the classroom where Randy G. had gone and asked him to step outside to the hallway. The aide asked the youth if he had something on him. He said he did not. Asked if he would consent to a pat-down search, Randy G. replied in the affirmative. The search produced an illegal knife. The student argued in juvenile court that use of the knife against him should be excluded because the ten-minute detention in the hallway amounted to a seizure without reasonable cause.

The justices first observed that minors are compelled to be in school, and while they are there, school officials have a responsibility to keep them safe. During the school day, students are ordered to be in various places at various times. Stopping a student to ask a question does not intrude on the student's liberty any more than these requirements do. Because a seizure is less intrusive than a search, the same reasonable suspicion standard does not apply. "Detentions of minor students on school grounds do not offend the Constitution," the justices unanimously concluded, "so long as they are not arbitrary, capricious, or for the purposes of harassment" (p. 525). In the *B.C. v. Plumas Unified School District* case discussed in the previous section, the Ninth Circuit similarly rejected the student's argument that by requiring him to stand with others in a nearby snack bar area while the drug-detecting dog sniffed the room, school officials had violated his Fourth Amendment right to be free from unreasonable seizures. Such a brief detention, the court noted, does not fall within the terms of the Fourth Amendment.

In making its ruling in the *In re Randy G.* case, the California Supreme Court did not differentiate between school administrators and school security personnel.

The title "security officer" itself is not constitutionally significant, the justices noted, so long as the latter are not acting as law enforcement officers. The court did not comment here on what the appropriate standard would be for seizures of students conducted by school personnel on campus or at school-sponsored events in conjunction with or at the behest of law enforcement agencies.

A federal district court in California later followed the same line of thinking evidenced by the California Supreme Court in its *In re Randy G.* ruling in a case involving a three-hour office detention of a student after numerous students reported that she had possessed and used drugs during the day (*Bravo ex rel. Ramirez v. Hsu*, 2005). An earlier search of her backpack, pockets, and shoes had revealed no drugs. The federal judge accepted the school's assertions that the detention served to prevent disruption, discipline the student, and prevent possible drug distribution and use. The federal judge expressed some impatience with the lawsuit, noting, "It is ironic and unfortunate that [school officials] were dragged into federal court and required to defend themselves against a civil rights lawsuit for simply doing their duty" (p. 1204). The case was dismissed.

Not all detentions, however, will automatically pass judicial inspection. In 2003, the Ninth Circuit was confronted with an odd case involving a vice principal who taped a second-grade student's head to a tree as a disciplinary measure (*Doe v. Hawaii Department of Education*, 2003). The student had been sent to the school official for fighting. The vice principal told the child to stand against the wall for punishment. If the child did not stand still, the vice principal said he would take the student outside and tape his head to a tree. The official carried through with his threat. The child was released when a fifth grader came on the scene and told the vice principal what he was doing was wrong. The child, through his parents, later filed suit against the Hawaiian Department of Education (all schools in Hawaii constitute one district operated by the department) and the vice principal. The Ninth Circuit ruled that the taping constituted an unreasonable seizure under the Fourth Amendment, noting, "Taping [the student's] head to a tree for five minutes was so intrusive that a fifth grader observed it was inappropriate" (p. 910). The case was sent back to the trial court to determine the extent to which the vice principal could be held liable.

SUMMARY

The Brown Act mandates public access to meetings of the governing board and many of its committees when deliberation or action takes place. Members of the public have the right to comment at these meetings as well. The act permits closed meetings but only in specific situations. The Education Code tracks the Brown Act and goes beyond it to some extent by requiring that school site councils and advisory committees must be open to the public. Likewise, the Public Records Act tilts in the direction of disclosing government documents that are not specifically exempted from disclosure. Among the exceptions are personnel records that would constitute a clearly unwarranted invasion of personal privacy if released.

Although the law generally requires that the public's business must be conducted in public, neither school employees nor students and their families lose their right to personal privacy. The Education Code protects the privacy rights of teachers in several specific situations, and other statutes protect teacher lifestyle choices. The support for student and family privacy rights is well anchored in both federal and state law, especially in the context of school records and the use of surveys and questionnaires.

While concerns about student drug use and violence on campus have increased, students have a right to be free from unreasonable searches and seizures under constitutional law. Aside from general drug-testing programs administered to students participating in extracurricular activities and metal detector searches for concealed weapons, school officials may search students only if they have reasonable cause to do so and the searches they conduct are not excessively intrusive. Though individualized suspicion is preferred, group searches are permissible when there are grounds to believe that someone in the group is in possession of contraband. Group searches are also sometimes permitted when they are minimally intrusive and are conducted for student safety. Personally intrusive searches intended to permit visual inspection of underclothing and private body parts are outlawed by the California Education Code. While students have asserted that being detained for questioning by school officials is a seizure and requires reasonable cause, both state and federal courts have rejected the contention.

It is evident from the privacy and search-and-seizure cases discussed in this chapter that this area of the law requires careful balancing of student rights with school interests. Given continuing concern about school safety, judges will continue to be called on to redress the balance. School authorities are best advised to monitor legal developments carefully.

11　RACE AND GENDER DISCRIMINATION

According to the California Department of Education, California's public school population of 5.8 million students is racially diverse. In 2023–2024, 56.1 percent was Hispanic or Latino, 20.3 percent white, 9.9 percent Asian, 4.9 percent Black, and 2.2 percent Filipino. Approximately three-quarters of the population is now composed of students of color, with Hispanic or Latino students being the most rapidly growing segment.

The fact that the population is racially diverse does not mean that each school reflects the state's student demographics. In fact, quite the opposite is true. In the state's large metropolitan areas, urban districts that serve mostly low-income students of color are surrounded by suburban school districts that are much more heterogeneous by race and class or, in some cases, are predominantly white with higher incomes. Race and class isolation in public schools remains among the most problematic and contentious public policy issues. The law in California for dealing with it is complex and confusing, reflecting crosscurrents in the thinking of judges, legislators, and voters.

This chapter begins with a review of federal desegregation law, then concentrates on California law. Included is a discussion of the consequences of racial isolation and why educators seek to integrate schools by both race and class, followed by gender discrimination and the current state of the law regarding single-sex programs and schools. Finally, because racial and gender harassment are forms of discrimination, the final section discusses both federal and California law targeted at their elimination.

RACIAL DISCRIMINATION

Racial Discrimination Under Federal Law

In 1954, the U.S. Supreme Court first recognized the right of students to be free from government-imposed racial segregation in *Brown v. Board of Education of Topeka, Kansas*. A unanimous Court held that the separation of children by race, even into buildings of equal quality, deprives minority children of equal educational opportunities. According to the Court, the act of separating nonwhite students "solely because of their race generates a feeling of inferiority as to their status in the community that may affect their hearts and minds in a way unlikely ever to be undone" (p. 494). Therefore, separate facilities are "inherently unequal," and as a result they violate the equal protection clause of the Fourteenth Amendment, which prevents any state from denying "to any person within its jurisdiction the equal protection of the laws."

Beginning in the mid-1960s, the Court sanctioned increasingly intrusive federal court involvement in local educational administration for the purpose of eradicating racially segregated schools. For example, the Court held that once a judge finds that a school purposefully engaged in discriminatory acts, the judge may redefine attendance zones and compel busing programs to integrate the schools (*Swann v. Charlotte-Mecklenburg Board of Education*, 1971).

In 1964, the federal government joined the Supreme Court in condemning governmental racism with the passage of the monumental Civil Rights Act. Two key provisions of the act are Title VI, which prohibits discrimination on the basis of race, color, or national origin by recipients of federal funds, and Title VII, which prohibits discrimination by public and private employers on the basis of race, color, national origin, religion, and sex. Title VI is most significant today because of the remedies it provides for the harassment of protected classes as discussed in more detail later in this chapter. Title VII plays an important role in employment law and is discussed in Chapter 5.

Despite the initial zealousness after *Brown*, the scope of the developing federal law was curtailed in the mid-1970s. Though the language of *Brown* was expansive enough to encompass de facto segregation (segregation due to societal factors) as well as de jure segregation (government-imposed segregation), the Court had never explicitly stated in the ruling whether de facto segregation alone was sufficient to prove a violation of the Constitution. It was not until 1973 that the Court clarified that *Brown* applied only to situations of government-sanctioned segregation.

In *Keyes v. School District No. 1*, the Court held that a plaintiff trying to prove a violation of the equal protection clause by unlawful racial segregation has to show "not only that segregated schooling exists but also that it was brought about or maintained by intentional state action" (p. 198). Shortly thereafter, the Court expanded its emphasis on intent, holding that desegregation plans may not involve schools outside the desegregating district unless those schools also had engaged in de jure segregation (*North County Parents Organization v. Department of Education*, 1994). As a result of these decisions, de facto segregated school districts are beyond the reach of the equal protection clause.

The Court also has retreated from its early support for judicial intervention in the local administration of de jure segregated schools. The remedy for such purposeful segregation—court oversight and involvement in school board decisions—had always engendered considerable controversy because of the judicial intrusion into local affairs. Following the Court's decision in *Brown*, some school districts operated under continual judicial supervision because of decades-old findings of de jure segregation. The districts return to self-control only when the supervising court determines they have become "unitary," a status indicating that the district has successfully eradicated all traces of the prior segregation. In the 1970s, a declaration of unitary status was difficult to obtain, particularly because the standard was so ill defined. Several Supreme Court decisions, however, have eliminated much of this uncertainty.

In 1976, the Court held in *Pasadena City Board of Education v. Spangler* that a desegregation court order should not be modified to account for de facto demographic changes occurring after the creation of the order. In 1991 the Court held that once all "vestiges of past discrimination [have] been eliminated to the extent practicable," a court should terminate its supervision of a school district (*Board of Education of Oklahoma City Public Schools v. Dowell*, 1991). One year after the Court decided *Dowell*, it unanimously held that a court may declare certain aspects of a district's operation unitary before the entire district has reached that stage (*Freeman v. Pitts*, 1992). In short, a supervising court has the authority to reduce its role in school district affairs as the district makes progress toward unitary status.

In 2007, the Court ruled 5–4 that admitting or rejecting public school students based solely on their race is unconstitutional. But the lineup of the justices' opinions in deciding this case did allow for a measure of affirmative action to further racial integration. For instance, *Parents Involved in Community Schools v. Seattle School District No. 1* involved two school districts, one in Seattle and one in metropolitan Louisville (Jefferson County), Kentucky. Seattle, which had never engaged in racial segregation, adopted a school choice plan for its ten high schools and used race as a tiebreaker to further diversity if more students sought to attend a school than there were places. The Jefferson County system continued to use race in assigning students to school to achieve racial balance after a desegregation court order had ended. In striking down the use of race in both districts, four of the five justices in the majority agreed that any use of race in public school assignment is unconstitutional.

Justice Anthony Kennedy, who agreed with the four justices that the use of race by Louisville and Seattle violated the equal protection clause, did not endorse total exclusion of race in student assignment and refused to sign on to this aspect of the majority opinion. In his view, public schools have a compelling interest in avoiding racial isolation and addressing the problem of resegregation. To this end, he noted that race could be considered in choosing sites for new schools, drawing attendance zones, allocating resources for special programs, and targeted recruiting of both students and teachers. Given that four justices disapproved of any use of race in student assignment and four justices took the opposite position, Justice Kennedy's opinion carries significant weight.

Racial isolation in education is increasing for a variety of reasons including demographic changes, housing patterns, the termination of desegregation court orders, and less interest in racial integration. The Civil Rights Project/Proyecto Derechos Civiles at UCLA published a study in 2007 on the extent of racial isolation in public schools in the United States. Among the findings in *Historic Reversals, Accelerating Resegregation, and the Need for New Integration Strategies* is one showing that in 1968 when school desegregation got under way, 77 percent of Black students attended a school that was predominately nonwhite. In 1988, that figure dropped to 63 percent, but by 2005 had climbed to 73 percent. In 2005–2006 the average Black or Latino student attended a school that was less than one-third white, while the average white student attended a school that was 77 percent white. There is also a significant overlap between race and socioeconomic status. In 2005–2006, the study shows that 84 percent of students received free or reduced-price lunches at schools with less than 10 percent white students. By contrast, only 18 percent of students received free or reduced-price lunches at schools with less than 10 percent Black and Latino students.

The overlap between race and poverty is important because statistics demonstrate that income is related to student achievement. The higher a family income level, the higher the student achievement. For example, according to statistics released by the College Board in 2023, students from families earning less than $53,263 a year averaged 891 points out of a potential 1600 points on the combined

Evidence-Based Reading and Writing section and the math section of the Scholastic Aptitude Tests (SATs). In contrast, students from families earning more than $100,113 a year averaged 1148 points. Isolation by class is as significant a concern in California as isolation by race and ethnicity.

Segregation in schools remains another pressing issue effecting California schools. A 2021 study by UCLA found that California was the most segregated state for Latinos, with roughly 58% of Latino students attending "intensely segregated schools." Additionally, the study found that "more than half of the state's Black students [were] concentrated in just 25 of the state's 1,000 school districts."

Segregation contributes to the racial student achievement gap in California. For example, in 2022, 40 percent of Black and Native American students and more than 33 percent of Hispanic students performed in the lowest level in math on the National Assessment of Educational Progress (NAEP), a standardized achievement test administered by the U.S. Department of Education to a cross section of students in all states, while only 14 percent of white students performed in the lowest level. Similarly, white students scored above the state average in reading while their Black and Latino peers scored an average of 37 and 29 points, respectively, lower on that portion of the NAEP. A similar student performance gap is evident on the California Standards Tests (CST). Students from low-income families also performed lower than those from higher income families on both NAEP and the CST.

Statistics like these carry immense implications for educators struggling to ensure that all students reach proficiency or higher levels on state standardized achievement tests. These statistics also stimulate efforts to increase the proportion of resources spent on schools populated by low-income students of color and to foster integration across racial and socioeconomic lines in these schools in the interest of providing an achievement-oriented peer group in all schools and of fostering student socialization.

Racial Discrimination Under California Law

Historical perspective. Though long considered among the most educationally progressive states, California does not have an unblemished record regarding racial segregation in public schooling. In 1860, the legislature passed a law providing public schooling for white children but excluding Black children, ", Mongolians, and Indians." The law did permit district governing boards to establish separate schools for educating these minority children. A few years later, the legislature deleted *Mongolians* from the provision for separate schooling, thus denying

Chinese American students, most of whom lived in San Francisco, any form of public education.

In 1874 in the case of *Ward v. Flood*, the California Supreme Court confronted a challenge to the separate education of Black children. The father of Mary Ward, an eleven-year-old Black child, filed suit after a San Francisco school principal refused to admit her to the neighborhood school. The principal of the school, Noah Flood, maintained that he was following state law and that the Black school to which Mary was assigned provided her with an equal education. The father contended that the exclusion of his daughter constituted a badge of servitude contrary to the Thirteenth Amendment and violated the Fourteenth Amendment equal protection clause.

The California high court rejected the first contention out of hand, noting no relationship between exclusion from a school and forced slavery. As to the equal protection argument, the justices cited with approval an 1849 Supreme Judicial Court of Massachusetts ruling that racially segregated schooling was no different from educating students separately by age, gender, and special needs. When the U.S. Supreme Court issued its notorious 1896 *Plessy v. Ferguson* ruling that "separate but equal" public facilities (including schools) do not violate the federal constitution, it cited a number of state court decisions in support of this position, including *Ward v. Flood*.

Though a historical anachronism from a racial perspective, *Ward v. Flood* did declare public education to be a vested right under state law that had to be provided equally to all children. This prompted the legislature to remove the white-children-only provision from the school law in 1880 and delete the provisions for separate schools for other races.

When the San Francisco school district attempted to exclude a Chinese American student from its public schools a few years later, the California Supreme Court cited the statutory change to require her admission (*Tape v. Hurley*, 1885). In 1890 the California high court declared that a Black student could not be directed to attend a Black school in the Visalia school district because state law no longer permitted racial segregation in public schools (*Wysinger v. Crookshank*, 1890). However, in both decisions, the court recognized that the legislature could change the status quo and opt for racially separate schools should it choose to do so.

In fact, after the *Tape* ruling, the California Legislature amended the statute to permit school districts to establish separate schools for children who are Native American and those of "Mongolian or Chinese descent." If separate schools were not established, then a school district was required to admit the students into its regular schools. These provisions were not removed until 1947. Redress in federal court was unavailing, particularly after the U.S. Supreme Court permitted Mississippi to classify Chinese students as "colored" so that they had to attend Black schools (*Gong Lum v. Rice*, 1927). Interestingly, the California Legislature did not permit separate schools for Japanese Americans until 1921, but by then most of these students were already attending white schools and continued to do so. The combination of increasing numbers of Chinese students in San Francisco and the costs of maintaining separate schools eventually forced the governing board to end segregated schooling in the city.

While California never sanctioned separate schooling for Latino students, local officials routinely segregated them based on language deficiencies. It was not until 1947 that segregation of Mexican American students based on claims of language deficiency ended. In *Westminster School District v. Mendez*, the court considered claims raised by students of Mexican descent in several Los Angeles area school districts who argued in federal court that such segregation violated the equal protection of the laws under both the California and U.S. constitutions. In affirming the federal trial court's decision against the district, the U.S. Court of Appeals for the Ninth Circuit first noted that the legislature had not authorized the segregation of Mexican students. In fact, a state law at the time allowed admission of Mexican children to California schools. Thus, the judges held that the California Supreme Court's ruling in *Ward v. Flood* and the U.S. Supreme Court's later ruling in *Plessy v. Ferguson* did not apply, thus sidestepping the question of state-sanctioned racial segregation in public schools.

Among those urging the appeals court to confront the matter head on were Thurgood Marshall and Robert Carter of the National Association for the Advancement of Colored People (NAACP), who filed an amicus brief in the case and a few years later would successfully argue *Brown v. Board of Education of Topeka, Kansas* before the U.S. Supreme Court. Because the state did not authorize segregation of Mexican students, the Ninth Circuit ruled that the actions of local school officials in doing so were unconstitutional (*Westminster School District of Orange County v. Mendez*, 1947). Following this decision, the California Legislature eliminated all references to racially separate public schools in the attendance law. However, as will become clear in the following sections, concern about racial segregation in California public schools has never abated.

Remedying racial isolation regardless of cause. In 1963, the California Supreme Court addressed the segregation of the Pasadena schools in a major shift in California school law away from the trend of the developing federal law. In July of 1961, a junior high school in Pasadena withdrew from its district, leaving its students in need of a new school. Many of the students and their families, who were predominately white, did not want to be included in the attendance zone for the nearest junior high school, which had a student body of predominately students of color. In response to political pressure, the school district redefined the school zones to allow the white students to attend a more distant, primarily white school. A thirteen-year-old Black student objected to the maintenance of the new zoning system because it led to the denial of his application to transfer out of his primarily minority school.

The California Supreme Court found that the redrawing of attendance zones to maintain the demographic status quo qualifies as de jure segregation. While relying primarily on the *Brown* decision, the court also cited State Board of Education regulations to the effect that "the right to an equal opportunity for education and the harmful consequences of segregation require that school boards take steps, insofar as reasonably feasible, to alleviate racial imbalance in schools regardless of its cause" (*Jackson v. Pasadena City School District*, 1963).

Although the *Jackson* decision clearly established an affirmative obligation of school officials to integrate schools, the impact of the decision on the daily lives of administrators was highly uncertain due to a technical aspect of the ruling that rendered it merely advisory rather than binding law. Because of this ambiguity, the California political community had to contend with the divisive issues left unresolved by *Jackson*.

Developing a coherent plan to address racial imbalances in student populations proved to be a difficult task. The controversy surrounding policies of forced integration through means such as busing or rezoning divided much of the population of California. The state legislature sought to respond to the will of the voters, but the temporary nature of any political majority made efforts at lawmaking short lived.

In 1970, the legislature declared that schools could not require "any student to be transported for any purpose or for any reason without written permission of the parent or guardian" (Educ. Code § 1009.5). The apparent purpose of this statute was to eliminate the forced busing of students to achieve racial integration in schools. The California Supreme Court found such a purpose to be unconstitutional and construed the statute as simply preventing students from being forced to use school-provided transportation without parental consent (*San Francisco Unified School District v. Johnson*, 1971). In 1971, the same year the California Supreme Court decided *Johnson*, the state legislature made an abrupt about-face and enacted the Bagley Act, which effectively codified the *Jackson* doctrine by placing the responsibility on school officials to operate racially integrated schools and gave the California Department of Education enforcement power.

However, the Bagley Act was short lived. One year following its enactment, the people of California approved by referendum Proposition 21 (now Educ. Code § 35351), which repealed the Bagley Act. Proposition 21 also attempted to effectuate the real purpose of Section 1009.5 by denying school officials the power to assign students to schools on the basis of their racial or ethnic identity. Once again, however, the California Supreme Court blocked the legislature's efforts.

Specifically, in *Santa Barbara School District v. Superior Court*, the court held that the repealing of the Bagley Act was constitutional. However, the court concluded that the portion of the proposition preventing school authorities from using racial classifications for student assignments was unconstitutional as applied to districts experiencing either de jure or de facto segregation (*Santa Barbara School District v. Superior Court*, 1975). The court found that the fatal flaw in Proposition 21 and its predecessor, Section 1009.5, was their failure to exempt the use of racial classifications by schools remedying past segregation. Without this exemption, the laws interfered with a school board's ability to remedy a violation of federal law.

Education Code Section 35351, which remains on the books, thus appears to have limited applicability in the racial context. The statute has been expanded to prohibit assigning students to schools on the basis of disability, gender, gender identity, gender expression, nationality, race or ethnicity, religion, sexual orientation, or any other characteristic that is contained in the definition of hate crimes set forth in Section 422.55 of the Penal Code, including immigration status.

In 1976, the California Supreme Court reentered the fray with a seminal decision that established the limits as well as the reach of *Jackson*'s affirmative obligation to integrate schools. In that case, the court analyzed the claims of a class of nonwhite students in the Los Angeles Unified School District who had filed a lawsuit in 1963 against the school district to force the integration of its schools. It was undisputed that the district's schools were segregated—in 1968, a significant number of student bodies within the district's schools were either 90 percent minority or 90 percent white. After several years of unsuccessful settlement negotiations, a trial, and appeals, the case came before the California Supreme Court. The court affirmed the *Jackson* ruling by this time explicitly noting that Article I, Section 7(a) of the California Constitution mandating equal protection of the laws requires all public school districts to undertake "reasonably feasible steps to alleviate school segregation, regardless of its cause" (*Crawford v. Board of Education of the City of Los Angeles*, 1976).

The court noted that, by ignoring its responsibility to integrate its schools as required by *Jackson*, the Los Angeles district had violated the state constitution. But the court's opinion emphasized that the obligation does not impose on school districts a duty to ensure that their schools reflect the ethnic makeup of the district as a whole. The court found "nothing inherently invalid in the fact that percentages of various racial or ethnic groups may vary, even significantly, in different schools throughout a school district, or even that a particular minority group may be completely unrepresented in a particular school" (p. 740). Rather, school authorities are charged under the California Constitution with taking "reasonable and feasible steps" to address racially segregated schools, which are "schools in which the minority student enrollment is so disproportionate as realistically to isolate minority students from other students and thus deprive minority students of an integrated educational experience" (p. 739).

The *Crawford* court added that whether a school is unconstitutionally segregated will depend on a fact-intensive inquiry sensitive to the circumstances of each case, with acknowledgment of the limited resources available to a school district to adopt corrective measures. Factors that should be considered include the racial makeup of the student body, faculty, and staff, as well as community attitudes toward the schools. Additionally, the court emphasized that the primary responsibility for compliance with the constitutional mandate and that the determination of corrective measures should rest with school administrators. California courts should not intervene in the desegregation process, regardless of the efficiency of the district's plans. Only on a finding that a district has failed to take any reasonable steps to ameliorate segregation may a trial court step in and order the district to follow certain guidelines or adopt certain procedures. Once a trial court has intervened, however, the *Crawford* court emphasized that the judge may use his or her full equitable powers to formulate a desegregation plan.

Limits on busing. Three years after *Crawford* invoked the equitable power of the intervening courts, those powers were drastically reduced by California voters. Proposition 1, which passed in 1979 and became part of Section 7(a) of Article I of the California Constitution, successfully did what Proposition 21 had failed to achieve seven years earlier. Specifically, it removed from state courts the ability to require schools to implement busing and student reassignment plans unless such remedies are necessary to comply with federal law. In effect, the constitutional amendment prevents courts that are addressing situations of de facto segregation from requiring the use of what is considered by some as one of the most effective tools to desegregate schools. With this law, the voters clearly indicated their discontent with the broad and potentially intrusive power of the state judiciary that *Jackson* and *Crawford* had authorized.

In 1982, the California Supreme Court confronted a case requiring it to clarify how Article I, Section 7(a) interacts with the *Jackson* doctrine. A group of parents and taxpayers filed suit against the Oxnard Union High School District, claiming that the district's procedure for complying with *Jackson* was inadequate. To support their contentions, they noted that the district had declared a school not segregated whose student body was 86 percent white and 14 percent students of color. In considering the case, the California Supreme Court rejected the contention that the "antibusing" aspect of Article I, Section 7(a) reduced the extent of the *Jackson* obligation. While the constitutional amendment reduces the power of judicial intervention in desegregation cases, it does not prevent school administrators from *voluntarily* implementing desegregation measures to comply with *Jackson* and *Crawford*. Specifically, the court stated that "the amendment neither releases school districts from their state constitutional obligation to take reasonably feasible steps to alleviate segregation regardless of its cause, nor divests California courts of authority to order desegregation measures other than pupil school assignment or pupil transportation" (*McKinney v. Oxnard Union High School District Board of Trustees*, 1982).

The court then applied the *Jackson* and *Crawford* criteria to the situation at Oxnard Unified. Noting the emphasis in *Crawford* on deferring to localized decision making, the court upheld the district's conclusion regarding the segregated status of its schools, stating that "the admittedly substantial disparity between minority and white racial percentages at Camarillo High School was not 'so disproportionate as realistically to isolate minority students from other students in the district'" (p. 553).

Three months after the court issued the *McKinney* decision, the U.S. Supreme Court upheld the constitutionality of the Proposition 1 amendment to Article I, Section 7(a). The Court clarified that "having gone beyond the requirements of the Federal Constitution, the State was free to return in part to the standard prevailing generally throughout the United States" (*Crawford v. Board of Education of the City of Los Angeles*, 1982). In other words, a state is not legally obligated, having placed the bar of state constitutionality higher than the bar of federal constitutionality, to forever maintain such a position. As applied to California, state desegregation law generally does require "more" than federal desegregation law because of the *Jackson* and *Crawford* holdings. But with respect to busing and pupil reassignment, state and federal law are congruent.

Limits on affirmative action and racial balancing. In 1996, California voters again altered the tenuous balance of state desegregation law, this time with even more restrictive results. Proposition 209, which passed by a vote of 54 percent, added Section 31 to Article I of the California Constitution prohibiting any governmental entity, including public schools, from discriminating or granting preferences on the basis of race as well as sex, color, ethnicity, or national origin in public employment, public education, or public contracting. However, very limited bona fide occupational qualifications based on sex are allowed in these areas if absolutely necessary to performing the job effectively.

In 1997, the Ninth Circuit affirmed the initiative's constitutionality (*Coalition for Economic Equity v. Wilson*). As a result of Section 31, school administrators may not adopt any racially discriminatory or preferential measures unless they are ordered to do so by a court enforcing the federal prohibition of de jure segregation. There is a small but significant exception to this rule. The amendment grandfathered in existing court orders and consent decrees requiring schools to desegregate, so school districts under continuing court supervision are unaffected by the new law. A good illustration is the rejection of a lawsuit filed against the Los Angeles Unified School District for student assignment to its magnet schools. A California appellate court ruled that the 1981 final court order ending the superior court's supervision of the district's plan required the district to continue to consider race in magnet school assignment to ameliorate the effects of segregation (*American Civil Rights Foundation v. Los Angeles Unified School District*, 2008). For districts without ongoing court orders, the effect of the amendment is more uncertain.

In 2002, a California appellate court examined the effect of Section 31 on the intradistrict transfer statute. In that case, a taxpayer in Huntington Beach objected to the racial and ethnic balancing component of the local district's transfer policy. Under the policy, transfers in and out of the "ethnically isolated" Huntington Beach High School could occur on a one-for-one basis only, meaning that a white student residing in the attendance area could transfer out only if another white student transferred in; and a minority student residing outside the attendance area could transfer in only if another minority student transferred out. The taxpayer viewed this as a form of racial discrimination. The California appellate court agreed, finding that the transfer policy "creates different transfer criteria for students solely on the basis of their race" (*Crawford v. Huntington Beach Union High School District*, 2002). The court then concluded that the racial and ethnic balancing requirement, which would allow for a policy like the one at Huntington Beach Unified, amounts to a granting of racial preferences in violation of Section 31 of the California Constitution. The court pointed out that the California Constitution has changed since the California Supreme Court decided the *Jackson* and *Crawford* cases and that Section 31 now controlled.

The U.S. Court of Appeals for the Ninth Circuit was more hesitant in considering the transfer request of a teacher at Van Nuys High School in Los Angeles to a similar position at another school in the district. The faculty transfer policy of the Los Angeles Unified School District would not permit him, as a white teacher, to move to a school with more than a specified percentage of white faculty members. The teacher sued in federal court, claiming the policy was a violation of Section 31 of the California Constitution. The federal district court held that the transfer policy at Los Angeles Unified did not give preferential treatment to or discriminate against a racial group. The policy required only that school faculty remain within a specified number of percentage points above or below the districtwide percentage of minority faculty members. The district court reasoned that the policy did not prefer one race of teachers over another.

Furthermore, the district court noted that Los Angeles Unified is exempted from the operation of Section 31 because it continued to operate under a court order mandating it to comply with *Jackson* and desegregate its schools to the extent feasible. The teacher appealed to the U.S. Court of Appeals for the Ninth Circuit.

The Ninth Circuit found the question presented a closer one than the trial court had believed it to be. The transfer policy could not definitively be declared neutral because although it erects both a minimum and a maximum applicable to each racial group, such that the policy's macroscopic effect (i.e., keeping whites and nonwhites in balance) touches both groups with equal force, "its microscopic effect—denying a transfer to a teacher who would upset that balance—operates to exclude an individual from a position based on his race" (*Friery v. Los Angeles Unified School District*, 2002, p. 1123).

The Ninth Circuit did not find the *Huntington Beach* decision controlling, because the student transfer policy in that case limited the transfers of white students out of a particular high school and of nonwhites into the school but did not apply to the transfer of nonwhites out and the transfer of white students in. By operating only in one direction, the Huntington Beach policy did not apply to each racial category equally. Because no California court decisions clarified whether the type of teacher transfer policy employed by the Los Angeles district constitutes preferential treatment, the Ninth Circuit submitted the question to the California Supreme Court and held up further proceedings in the case.

The Ninth Circuit also expressed reluctance to follow the California court of appeal's conclusion in *Huntington Beach* that *Jackson* and *Crawford v. Board of Education* have been diminished by the enactment of Section 31. "[T]he safer course," the judges observed, "is to seek an authoritative resolution of this question from the California Supreme Court" (p. 1124). The judges added that the Ninth Circuit is bound by the decisions of the California intermediate courts on matters of state law "only to the extent that the California Supreme Court would likely reach the same conclusions" (p. 1124). In a similar vein, the judges were uncertain whether Los Angeles Unified remained sufficiently under court order to fall within the exception to Section 31 and asked for clarification on this matter as well.

Subsequently, the California Supreme Court refused to take up the request from the Ninth Circuit. The Ninth Circuit eventually sent the entire matter back to the trial court in 2006 to determine whether Friery even had standing to file the lawsuit. The case was dismissed when Friery failed to continue the litigation.

Interestingly, the use of race as one factor in admissions to the Corinne A. Seeds University Elementary School, operated as a research laboratory by the University of California at Los Angeles Graduate School of Education, has survived judicial challenge. To ensure a student body appropriate for conducting research on issues relevant to children in urban settings, the school's admissions committee considered various factors in deciding whom to enroll, including race, ethnicity, gender, and family income.

In a 2–1 decision, the Ninth Circuit upheld the policy. The majority concluded that the research mission of the laboratory school provided the requisite compelling governmental interest to justify the consideration of race and ethnicity in admissions decision making (*Hunter ex rel. Brandt v. Regents of University of California*, 1999). The majority was influenced by the testimony of expert witnesses regarding the importance of using race as a factor in admissions decision making to fulfill the school's research mission.

The parents who initiated the lawsuit in federal court after their daughter was denied admission to the laboratory school also filed a lawsuit in state court, arguing that the racial preference policy violated the Section 31 embodiment of Proposition 209 in the California Constitution. A few years after the Ninth Circuit issued its decision in *Hunter*, a California court of appeal affirmed a trial court's decision that the parents' state law action should be dismissed. In an unpublished opinion—which has very limited value as legal precedent—the court noted that as a tuition-supported, selective-admissions-based laboratory school operated by UCLA, the school did not meet the definition of public school contained in Section 31 (*Hunter v. Regents of the University of California*, 2001 (unpublished)). Thus, Section 31 does not invalidate the laboratory school's admissions process.

The fact that this is a laboratory school limits the reach of these judicial decisions. This is significant for California charter schools, which are considered public schools, not laboratory schools, and are therefore prohibited by Section 31 from granting racial preferences. Despite this restriction, charter schools are required by the Education Code to address in their charter petition "the means by which the school will achieve a racial and ethnic balance among its pupils that is reflective of the general population residing within the territorial jurisdiction of the school district to which the charter petition is submitted" (Educ. Code § 47605(c)(5)(G)). In their efforts to comply with this statute, charter schools, just like traditional public schools, may not implement race-conscious admissions policies.

In summary, it is clear from this review that the state courts, the state legislature, and the voters have played equally significant roles in shaping desegregation law in California since the early 1960s. See a capsule summary of the major developments in Table 11.1. The apparent divide between popular political sentiment and judicial interpretation of the state constitution through the 1960s and 1970s produced a legal landscape that has become complex and in many ways contradictory. Although *Crawford* offered guidance to school officials in defining the extent of their obligation under state law regarding de facto segregation, Propositions 21, 1, and 209 have chipped away at the strength of the *Jackson* and *Crawford* opinions.

Finding other means of fostering diversity. Section 31 of Article I of the California Constitution explicitly prohibits the use of race for affirmative action purposes in the absence of a court order. It is thus not possible for a public school to set aside a certain percentage of its student enrollment for students of various races. Are there other ways that charter schools and traditional public schools can achieve a racially diversified student body? Perhaps. Some school districts and charter schools are using what the law calls "nonsuspect classifications" like family income, parent education, geography, targeted recruiting, and admission by lottery to ensure that their student bodies reflect at least to some extent the racial and ethnic composition of the communities within which they operate. In this way, the social and educational benefits of diversity are preserved without engaging in impermissible racial discrimination, although any kind of assignment system, including altering neighborhood attendance zones, is likely to generate controversy.

An illustration of a student assignment policy that survived judicial scrutiny is one crafted by the Berkeley Unified School District. At the elementary level, the plan at issue in the lawsuit had parents rank-order three of eleven schools for their children. The district then assigned students to reflect parent preferences but within constraints of six priority categories: students currently attending the school who live within the school's attendance zone, students attending the school who live outside the zone, siblings of students currently attending the school, school district residents not attending the school who live within the zone, school district residents not attending the school who live outside the zone, and nonresidents wanting an interdistrict transfer. Students in each of these six priority categories were given a diversity rating of one, two, or three for their planning area of four to

TABLE 11.1
Major Developments in California Desegregation Law

Year	Development	Content	Significance
1963	*Jackson v. Pasadena City School District*	California Supreme Court supports efforts to alleviate racial imbalance in public schools regardless of cause.	Unclear to what extent school officials must take action to alleviate racial imbalance.
1972	Proposition 21 amends the Education Code	Denies school officials the power to assign students to schools on the basis of race or ethnicity.	Limited ability of school officials to comply with *Jackson*.
1975	*Santa Barbara School District v. Superior Court*	California Supreme Court holds the portion of Proposition 21 prevent-ing use of student assignment based on race unconstitutional.	Restores the use of racial classifications for student assignment.
1976	*Crawford v. Board of Education of the City of Los Angeles*	California Supreme Court affirms *Jackson* that equal protection clause of California Constitution requires school districts to undertake reasonably feasible steps to alleviate racial segregation regardless of cause.	Court suggests but does not dictate the means by which integration is to be accomplished. Places primary responsibility on school administrators and directs judges to become involved only as a last resort.
1979	Proposition 1 amends Section 7(a) of Article I of the California Constitution	Limits state courts from requiring busing or student assignment to bring about integration unless necessary to comply with federal law.	Limits use of two significant tools for integrating school districts.
1982	*McKinney v. Oxnard Union High School District*	California Supreme Court rules that Proposition 1 does not curtail voluntary use of busing and student assignment by school districts.	Clarifies that school districts can continue to use busing and student assignment if they choose to do so. However, federal courts disapprove their use unless necessary to comply with a court order.
1996	Proposition 209 adds Section 31 to Article I of the California Constitution	Prevents government entities from discriminating or granting preferences on the basis of race.	Ends affirmative action measures unless required to comply with a court order.

six city blocks based on the average household income for the planning area, the average adult education for the planning area, and the percentage of students of color in the planning area. All students in a planning area received the same diversity score regardless of their individual race. Students from each of the categories then were assigned proportionately to individual schools. The goal was to have each school reflect the racial and socioeconomic diversity of its attendance zone.

The high school attendance plan had students rank-order their choice of six academic programs at the district's single high school. Students were assigned a one, two, or three diversity category based on the average household income, average adult education, and percentage of students of color in their planning area. The district then determined the number of students who could enroll from the three diversity categories in each academic program to match the diversity of the high school as a whole. A computer randomly selected students for each program and assigned them to their highest-ranked program choice where there were openings.

The California court of appeal agreed with the trial court that as crafted, the student assignment plan did not violate Proposition 209. The proposition, the judges noted, prohibits unequal treatment of particular persons or groups of persons but does not prohibit the collection and consideration of community-wide demographic factors. Further, the district did not use the race of an individual student or student group in student assignment. Rather, the district reviewed the racial composition of a neighborhood to determine its social diversity and then, based on the degree of diversity, assigned students to schools. White students and students of color from the same neighborhood received the same diversity rating and same treatment (*American Civil Rights Foundation v. Berkeley Unified School District*, 2009). While well crafted, the Berkeley plan at issue in this case is not readily applicable to many California school districts that encompass extensive geographic regions and/or are largely composed of one race.

GENDER DISCRIMINATION

Under English common law, women could not own property or enter into contracts. The American founders simply assumed that voting rights would not include women. Women did not gain the right to vote until the Nineteenth Amendment was ratified in 1920, and they only relatively recently have gained entry into the top echelons of corporate and nonprofit organizations and the government.

Originally proposed in 1923, the Equal Rights Amendment (ERA) proposed to amend the United States Constitution by guaranteeing equal rights for all citizens and prohibiting discrimination on the basis of sex. The ERA read, "Equality of rights under the law shall not be denied or abridged by the United States or any State on account of sex" and would have authorized Congress to enact enforcement legislation.

The ERA was amended in 1943 and eventually passed the House of Representatives and Senate in 1972. Although amendments generally must be ratified by three-fourths of all states (i.e., thirty-eight states) within seven years, Congress extended the ratification deadline to 1982. Only thirty-five states ratified the ERA by 1982.

It bears noting that, although the United States Constitution was not amended to include the ERA, the California Constitution includes similar protections. Specifically, Article 1, Section 8, of the California Constitution states, "A person may not be disqualified from entering or pursuing a business, profession, vocation, or employment because of sex, race, creed, color, or national or ethnic origin." We discuss this constitutional provision in detail below.

Constitutional Dimensions

For much of its history, the U.S. Supreme Court paid little attention to gender discrimination. It was only in the early 1970s that the Court began to question the constitutionality of gender-based classifications.

The Equal Protection Clause of the Fourteenth Amendment, which the Court had interpreted to forbid racial classifications in the school desegregation cases discussed earlier, was the logical starting point for the Court's analysis. In its first case recognizing gender discrimination as grounds for invalidating a statute, the Court held that the government may not treat similarly situated men and women differently merely because of archaic stereotypes, even if doing so would promote administrative convenience in some cases (*Reed v. Reed*, 1971). Holding otherwise would permit the continuation of "romantic paternalism" that, as the Court noted in a similar case, "put[s] women, not on a pedestal, but in a cage" (*Frontiero v. Richardson*, 1973).

Despite their determination that gender qualifies for constitutional protection, the justices did not initially agree on whether gender classifications merit the same level of protection as racial classifications. Several justices considered gender to be innately different from race because of the physical differences separating men and women, thus necessitating that there be some situations in which state actors can constitutionally take account of gender-based differences.

In a series of several decisions, the Court established that governmental gender classifications merit close review, though they are not as disfavored as racial classifications. Under no circumstances may gender be used to perpetuate stereotypes or foster the legal, social, or economic inferiority of women. Gender preferences, however, that seek to compensate women for past inequities may receive slightly less stringent review by courts. Regardless of the purpose, all such classifications must serve important governmental objectives by means that are substantially related to the achievement of those objectives.

Two important decisions illustrating the scope of protection afforded gender arise in the context of higher education. In 1982, the Supreme Court considered the gender-based admissions policy at an all-female Mississippi school for nursing. A male applicant who was refused admission because of his gender sued the school, claiming that its policy violated the Fourteenth Amendment's equal protection clause. The Supreme Court agreed. Writing for the Court, Justice Sandra Day O'Connor stated that "the party seeking to uphold a statute that classifies individuals on the basis of their gender must carry the burden of showing an 'exceedingly persuasive justification' for the classification" (*Mississippi University for Women v. Hogan*, 1982). In this case, the state had failed to show that its stated purpose for the restrictive admissions policy, compensating women for generations of educational discrimination, was the real justification for the policy. The Court also found that the policy did not actually help women overcome their stereotyped roles, because women already had considerably more opportunities than men in the nursing profession.

In 1996, the Court refined the standard it had set out in *Mississippi University for Women*. At issue was the Virginia Military Institute's (VMI's) refusal to admit women to its rigorous educational program designed to produce "citizen-soldiers" (*United States v. Virginia*, 1996). Virginia argued that the presence of women would require accommodations so extreme as to destroy the unique educational program. The state's alternative school for women, a gentler and less prestigious program than what was offered at VMI, fell far short of comparability. The lack of a comparable alternative, together with the historical exclusion of women from opportunities in higher education, led the Court to find that Virginia had failed to show that it had an "exceedingly persuasive justification" for its gender-based admissions policy at VMI. The Court also emphasized that Virginia's stated purpose for providing the two single-sex programs was merely formulated after the challenge began and was not the actual motivation that had prompted the state to set up the two-school system.

In 1974, the Court of Appeals for the Ninth Circuit struck down an admissions policy at the prestigious Lowell High School in the San Francisco Unified School District seeking to achieve gender diversity by setting higher admissions requirements for female applicants than for male applicants. The school district instituted the policy to ensure the numerical equality of male and female students in entering classes. The court rejected the school's contention that gender diversity is necessary for a quality education because the school had failed to provide any proof to support its claim. The school, therefore, could not meet the required showing under the equal protection clause of the Fourteenth Amendment that the gender-specific admissions policy substantially furthered the school's purpose of enhancing the education provided (*Berkelman v. San Francisco Unified School District*, 1974).

School athletic programs receive considerable attention for their impact on students of different genders and are subject to the same constitutional constraints as the academic programs discussed earlier. Title IX, which governs many of the details of these programs, will be discussed in depth in the following section of this chapter. In 1982, a class of male high school students in Arizona sued the Arizona Interscholastic Association (AIA), seeking access to their high schools' all-female interscholastic volleyball teams. AIA had a policy preventing male students from playing on all-female teams, though female students were allowed to play on all-male teams for noncontact sports.

In that case, the Ninth Circuit held that AIA is subject to the strictures of the Fourteenth Amendment because its activities are closely intertwined with the state. The court then noted that while male students in Arizona may have less access to interscholastic all-female volleyball teams, they do not have less access to interscholastic sports teams overall. AIA supported its policy of forbidding male students from participating in all-female volleyball teams by citing the history of discrimination against female students in athletic activities. Because male students could potentially overwhelm the all-female team and reduce the opportunities for the female team members to play, the court upheld the policy (*Clark v. Arizona Interscholastic Association*, 1982).

Later, AIA authorized interscholastic competition among male-only volleyball teams, but the school where Clark's brother, the lead plaintiff in the earlier AIA case, played had none. The brother then sought to participate on the female team. As before, the Ninth Circuit found past discrimination against women justified the female-only restriction (*Clark v. Arizona Interscholastic Association*, 1989).

In light of this case law, school districts must carefully consider the constitutionality of policies involving gender-based classifications. Such policies must, at the least, seek to further important—potentially even exceedingly persuasive—governmental objectives by means substantially related to those objectives. Further, those objectives cannot be formulated after the fact. Rather, they must be real expressions of the district's purposes in establishing the policies.

The California Constitution has both an equal protection clause and, as noted above, a provision that has been construed as the equivalent of the unsuccessful Equal Rights Amendment. The equal protection clause is found in Article I, Section 7(a). As discussed in Chapter 3, it was used in the school finance case, *Serrano v. Priest* (1976), to strike down the California foundation program that permitted substantial interdistrict disparities in per-pupil expenditures.

The gender-equality provision, which is similar to the ERA, is included Article I, Section 8, which states that "a person may not be disqualified from entering or pursuing a business, profession, vocation, or employment because of sex, race, creed, color, or national or ethnic origin." State judicial decisions have concluded that government classifications in these areas are suspect and must represent the narrowest and least restrictive means by which the statute's objectives can be achieved. And, as discussed in the race section of this chapter, Proposition 209, now codified as Article I, Section 31 of the California Constitution, prohibits discrimination and preferential treatment on the basis of gender as well as race, color, ethnicity, and national origin in public education, public employment, and public contracting, though bona fide qualifications based on sex are allowed if reasonably necessary for normal operation. Thus, although school districts must provide equal educational opportunities to both males and females under Article I, Section 8, they cannot engage in affirmative action efforts that prefer one gender over another under Section 31.

The door remains open for single-sex schooling under federal and state constitutional law, though proponents of such schemes will have to be prepared to withstand searching judicial inquiry into their motives and into the comparability of the programs offered. Consider in this context California's Single Gender Academies Pilot Program, enacted in 1996 (Educ. Code §§ 58520–58524). Its purpose is to increase the diversity of the state's public educational offerings by making single-gender academies available to those pupils of each gender who because of their unique educational needs will benefit from single-gender education. The statute requires that if a particular program or curriculum is available to one gender, a similar opportunity shall be available to those pupils of the other gender, though tailored to the differing needs and learning styles of each. Only a handful of schools were started before funding cutbacks curtailed further development. The availability of evidence supporting the justification for a school's gender-based policies appears to be essential.

Title IX and Its Regulations

Title IX of the 1972 Education Amendments provides in part that "no person in the United States shall on the basis of sex, be excluded from participation in, be denied the benefits of, or be subjected to discrimination under any education program or activity receiving federal financial assistance" (20 U.S.C. § 1681). The Office for Civil Rights (OCR) is charged with implementing and enforcing the law.

Education Code Section 270 requires that the thrust of its regulations be posted on the California Department of Education's website. The OCR is authorized to impose sanctions on funding recipients, including the loss of federal money. In addition to OCR enforcement, victims of discrimination may file lawsuits under Title IX and its implementing regulations against school districts and private schools receiving federal funds, seeking both injunctive relief and, if discrimination is intentional, compensatory damages.

In 2005, the U.S. Supreme Court ruled that third parties who suffer retaliation may also file lawsuits (*Jackson v. Birmingham Board of Education*, 2005). The case involved a high school basketball coach who complained about unequal treatment of the girls' basketball team. He sued the school district, alleging retaliation against him in the form of negative evaluations and removal from coaching. The removal cost him supplemental pay. The case was returned to the trial court to determine whether the coach could prove his claims.

Title IX applies primarily to students in public schools and in private schools receiving federal funds. Gender discrimination in employment discrimination and harassment falls under Title VII of the 1964 Civil Rights Act, as discussed in Chapter 5 on employment. An organization qualifies as receiving federal funds if any part of it receives "scholarships, loans, grants, wages or other funds" that are "payment to or on behalf of students admitted to that entity, or extended directly to such students for payment to that entity." Whether the district receives the money for educational purposes directly from the government or indirectly through its students is irrelevant. The same is true of Section 504 of the Rehabilitation Act of 1973, the Age Discrimination Act of 1975, and Title VI of the Civil Rights Act of 1964 by virtue of a federal law known as the Civil rights Restoration Act of 1987. Title IX excludes from its coverage the admissions policies of single-sex public high schools that have been single sex since their establishment as well as parochial schools that espouse religious principles contrary to the intent of the statute.

Title IX is most often cited in its application to school athletic programs. Schools subject to Title IX must ensure that their athletic programs offer equal opportunities for athletic participation, in essence creating gender equity. Though this requirement does not necessitate equal funding, a failure to provide necessary financial support for one gender's athletic programs is considered as a factor in determining whether a school has violated its Title IX obligations.

Additional factors in the Title IX analysis include the variety of sports and competition opportunities offered and whether they accommodate each gender's level of interest, the provision of equipment, game times and practice times, funding for travel expenses, coaching and academic tutoring opportunities, compensation for coaches and academic tutors, the quality of locker rooms, and the available facilities, housing, dining, and medical attention.

In a class action lawsuit filed by female students attending Castle Park High School in the Sweetwater school district, the federal district court found that many of these factors had been violated for years, particularly in the context of the boys' baseball team and the girls' softball team. In ruling against the district, the judge observed, "Equal athletic treatment is not a luxury. It is not a luxury to grant equivalent benefits and opportunities to women. It is not a luxury to comply with the law. Equality and justice are not luxuries. They are essential elements which are woven into the very fabric of this country. They are essential elements now codified as Title IX" (*Ollier v. Sweetwater Union High School District*, 2012).

On appeal, the U.S. Court of Appeals for the Ninth Circuit closely analyzed the federal district court's opinion. In a lengthy decision, the Ninth Circuit affirmed the federal district court decision. In doing so, the Court of Appeals adopted the three-part test set forth by the Office of Civil Rights in 1979 to determine compliance with Title IX in the context of athletics: (1) whether participation opportunities for male and female students are provided in numbers substantially proportionate to their respective enrollments, (2) whether the institution can show a history and continuing practice of athletic program expansion demonstrably responsive to the developing interest and abilities of the number of the underrepresented sex, or (3) whether it can be demonstrated that the interest and abilities of the underrepresented sex in athletics have been fully and effectively accommodated by the present program when the institution cannot show a continuing practice of athletic program expansion (*Ollier v. Sweetwater Union High School District*, 2014). Title IX does not prevent schools from operating single-sex sports teams if members are selected on the basis of competitive skill or if the team plays a contact sport. Contact sports include boxing, wrestling, rugby, ice hockey, football, basketball, and other sports involving bodily contact. For noncontact sports, schools may offer teams to one gender and not to the other, but they must allow students of the excluded gender to try out for such teams if opportunities in that particular sport have previously been limited for students of that gender. Scholarships must be made available to students of each gender on an equal basis in proportion to the number of students of each sex participating in interscholastic or intercollegiate athletics.

Federal regulations permit voluntary single-sex classes and extracurricular activities in nonvocational public schools to improve student educational achievement or needs. The excluded sex must be provided substantially equivalent single-sex and coeducational classes or extracurricular activities. Periodic evaluations are to be conducted to ensure that student needs are being met and that single-sex classes and extracurricular activities are justified.

Federal regulations also permit single-sex schools, including schools within schools, provided that the excluded sex is offered a substantially equal single-sex school or coeducational school. Nonvocational charter schools are exempt from this provision. Additionally, schools subject to Title IX may not discriminate on the basis of pregnancy, childbirth, false pregnancy, termination of pregnancy, or marital status unless the student volunteers to attend a comparable educational program separate from other students.

It also bears noting that the Education Code requires schools to publish information related to Title IX on their websites. Specifically, all California public and charter schools as well as private schools receiving federal funds, are required to post on their website specific information about Title IX. That information must include the name of the Title IX coordinator, rights provided by Title IX, responsibilities of the school under Title IX, how to file a complaint and how it will be investigated, and a link to the U.S. Department of Education Office for Civil Rights website (Educ. Code § 221.61). A public school that does not have a website must post the information on the school district or county office of education website.

California's Sex Equity in Education Act

Known as the Sex Equity in Education Act, Education Code Sections 221.5 through 231.5 require that elementary and secondary school classes and courses, including those that are nonacademic and elective, to be conducted without regard to the sex of students. The Sex Equity in Education Act also allows students to participate in school programs and activities and to use school facilities consistent with how they view their gender regardless of the gender listed on school records. Exceptions are sex education and HIV/AIDS prevention classes.

Similar to Title IX, the Act requires equal opportunities for male and female students in school-sponsored athletic programs. School districts may not utilize state funds for sports programs that do not provide male and female students with equal opportunities and equal use of facilities (Educ. Code § 221.7). Educational institutions may not exclude students from participation in equivalent athletic programs on the basis of their gender (Educ. Code § 230). Schools may meet this obligation in several ways: (1) by providing opportunities for the participation of male and female students in proportion to their respective enrollments; (2) by showing a history and continuing practice of program expansion responsive to the underrepresentation of a particular gender where there has been a history of such underrepresentation; or (3) by demonstrating that the interests and abilities of the underrepresented gender have been fully and effectively accommodated in the present athletic program when the educational institution cannot show a history or continuing practice of program expansion to encourage participation. Any cuts in the athletic budget must be in compliance with both state and federal gender equity laws.

Traditional public and charter elementary and secondary schools participating in competitive athletics are also required under the Sex Equity in Education Act to report at the end of the year student athletic participation data by gender (Educ. Code § 221.9). These data encompass the enrollment of the school by gender, the number of boys and girls who participate in athletics, and the number of boys' and girls' teams classified by sport and by competitive level. The data must be posted for at least three years on the school's website or if no website on the district's or charter operator's website. The purpose is to call attention to gender gaps as the first step in addressing them for the purpose of increasing the benefits of competitive athletics for female students.

It also bears noting that the California's Sex Equity in Education Act broadens protections to students who are transgender or gender nonconforming. For example, the Act permits students to use restroom facilities that are consistent with how they view their gender. Programs and activities for purposes of the protections afforded students under the Sex Equity in Education Act include athletic teams and competitions (Educ. Code § 221.5).

In the recent past, significant legislation and litigation has addressed the extent to which school staff may disclose a student's LGBTQ+ status to their parents. For instance, Assembly Bill No. 1955 (2024) requires, among many other things, that the California Department of Education develop materials to support parents, guardians, and families of LGBTQ students and periodically update those materials to reflect changes in law.

AB 1955 states that public school staff "shall not be required to disclose any information related to a pupil's sexual orientation, gender identity, or gender expression to any other person without the pupil's consent unless otherwise required by state or federal law" (see also Educ. Code § 220.3). AB 1955 further prohibits local education agencies, including school districts, from enact[ing] or enforce[ing] any policy, rule, or administrative regulation that would require an employee or a contractor to disclose any information related to a pupil's sexual orientation, gender identity, or gender expression to any other person without the pupil's consent, unless otherwise required by state or federal law.

AB 1955 states that the provisions described in this paragraph do not represent a change in law, but are declaratory of existing law. (See also Educ. Code §§ 220.3(b) and 220.5(b).)

The issue of whether and to what extent school staff may or must disclose students' LGBTQ status to their parents and policies related to the same has become the subject of several significant legal challenges. At the time of publication, courts have reached inconsistent conclusions on this topic and appeals are underway. It is strongly recommended that readers familiarize themselves with the current state of the law in this area is unsettled at the time of publication of this book.

RACIAL AND GENDER HARASSMENT

Harassment on the basis of race and gender is a form of discrimination and is outlawed under both federal and California law.

Racial Harassment Under Title VI

Ending racial segregation nationally and in California under the terms of the equal protection clauses of both the federal and state constitutions is only part of the story. This section examines how Title VI of the 1964 Civil Rights Act has become an important means of combating racial harassment in public schooling. Chapter 5 discusses how Title VII of the same act has targeted discrimination on the basis of race, color, religion, sex, and national origin in public and private employment.

Title VI of the 1964 Civil Rights Act provides that "no person in the United States shall, on the ground of race, color, or national origin, be excluded from participation in, be denied the benefits of, or be subjected to discrimination under any program or activity receiving federal financial assistance" (42 U.S.C. § 2000 d). As with Title IX, the OCR in the U.S. Department of Education has developed a set of administrative rules for implementing Title VI and has the power to levy sanctions against entities for violations, including curtailing federal funding. Because virtually all public and many private schools receive some form of federal funding, the consequences of violating the act are real.

In addition to OCR enforcement, victims of discrimination may file lawsuits under Title VI and its implementing regulations against school districts and private schools receiving federal funds, seeking both injunctive relief and compensatory damages. Lawsuits may be filed against public school personnel as individuals under 42 U.S.C. Section 1983, a matter discussed in Chapter 12.

To be successful in either case, plaintiffs must show an intent to discriminate. The U.S. Supreme Court has ruled that merely establishing that some action has a racially discriminatory impact is insufficient to trigger a violation under both the equal protection clause and Title VI (*Washington v. Davis*, 1976) and under Title VI's implementing regulations (*Alexander v. Sandoval*, 2001). This does not mean that activities having an unintentional discriminatory effect are always immune to judicial challenge under Title VI. Some federal agencies, including the Department of Education, have enacted implementing regulations that prohibit recipients of federal assistance from engaging in activities that have a disparate impact on different racial groups (34 C.F.R. § 100.3(b)(2)). Though individuals may not sue on the basis of these regulations, the federal agencies that have established them may impose sanctions (*Alexander v. Sandoval*, 2001).

In a 1998 decision, the Ninth Circuit identified the conditions for establishing a viable racial harassment claim under Title VI. The case involved Black parents who objected to having their children read *The Adventures of Huckleberry Finn*, by Mark Twain, and the short story *A Rose for Emily*, by William Faulkner, in public school ninth-grade English class. The parents filed suit, asserting that the requirement was discriminatory and created a racially hostile environment at school. The trial court dismissed their complaint, and the parents appealed. As discussed in Chapter 6 ("Rights of Expression"), the court concluded that use of the books in class did not constitute a violation of Title VI but rather served the interests of the school in exposing students to classic literary works and the interests of the students in reading them. But the judges were sufficiently concerned about the alleged racial harassment that they permitted this part of the lawsuit to proceed.

The complaint alleged that after reading the books, white students repeatedly called the Black students a racial slur, and racist graffiti were scrawled about the school. Though the Ninth Circuit could find no reported decision applying Title VI to student-to-student racial harassment, it did so in this case. Drawing on U.S. Department of Education guidelines, it laid out three conditions for peer racial harassment to violate Title VI.

First, it must be established that a racially hostile environment exists. This requires a showing that the harassment is sufficiently severe that it interferes with the ability of targeted students to obtain an equal benefit from schooling. Second, it must be established that the district knew or should have known about the racially hostile environment. Third, it must be shown that the district was deliberately indifferent to the need to take action to stop the harassment. Here, the complaint met all three tests, and the matter was sent back for trial (*Monteiro v. Tempe Union High School District*, 1998).

A 2002 racial discrimination claim filed in state court by two Black students at Tamalpais High School against the Novato Unified School District over racial harassment occurring at a basketball game was not successful because the school district had taken action in response to the harassment. Before the game at San Marin High School, a number of San Marin students arrived in costumes, some racist in character. At least one student wore an Afro wig, and others had blackface. During the warm-up period, some of the students chanted the n-word. School officials intervened to stop the racist comments, but the racial slur again was hurled at a Tamalpais player during the game.

Following the game, officials in the Novato district conducted an investigation and followed that up with letters of apology to the Tamalpais students. The two students bringing the lawsuit asserted that school officials knew of a long-standing racially hostile environment at San Marin High School and had failed to redress the situation effectively. They cited racial slurs directed to the only Black teacher at the school, a slave day when some students wore chains and torn clothing with brown shoe polish on their faces, and display of the Confederate flag in the school yearbook. The two students argued that the response of district personnel to the basketball incident was inadequate and constituted deliberate indifference under Title VI.

In an unpublished but instructive decision, the California court of appeal carefully examined the efforts that San Marin High School and school district officials took following the basketball game. They noted a number of actions in addition to the letters of apology. These included a nine-point plan to address racial issues, a diversity advisory committee, a policy on expected student behavior, and an equity plan designed to stop discrimination before it starts by teaching civility and acceptance.

As a result of these and other actions, the court found that the district was not deliberately indifferent. Similarly, claims filed against several school administrators in their individual capacities under 42 U.S.C. Section 1983, a federal civil rights law discussed in Chapter 12, were dismissed because the administrators had not been deliberately indifferent (*Malcolm W. v. Novato Unified School District*, 2002 (unpublished)).

In addition to missed educational opportunities and negative publicity, these cases demonstrate that failing to take steps to eliminate racial harassment can result in liability for both the district under Title VI and individual school personnel under Section 1983, as well as sanctions imposed by the federal government.

Sexual Harassment and Abuse Under Title IX

This chapter already examined gender discrimination and equity issues in public schools from the perspective of both federal and state law. This section analyzes how Congress and the courts have addressed sexual harassment and abuse under Title IX of the 1972 Education Amendments and its implementing of federal regulations.

To provide an effective remedy for victims of sexual harassment and abuse, the U.S. Supreme Court ruled in 1992 that victims can file their own lawsuits against school districts (*Franklin v. Gwinnett County Public Schools*, 1992). This case involved a female student who alleged that she was harassed and pressured into sexual intercourse by one of her male teachers. She sought monetary damages. The Court recognized that monetary damages may compensate a victim in a way that administrative sanctions imposed on the school district cannot, but the justices did not specify the conditions under which a district could be liable for employee-on-student sexual harassment. The answer was forthcoming six years later in the case of *Gebser v. Lago Vista Independent School District*, 1998).

Gebser was a fourteen-year-old high school student who was in a sexual relationship with her fifty-two-year-old social studies teacher over a six-month period. None of the encounters occurred at school. The parents of two other students complained to the high school principal that the teacher had made inappropriate sexual remarks in class. The principal spoke to the teacher, who claimed he did not believe his comments were offensive but he apologized and stated that but he would not let it happen again. The principal did not report the allegation to the school superintendent. After the pair was discovered in a wooded area, the teacher was terminated and his teaching credential revoked. He also served jail time on a charge of attempted sexual assault. Gebser sued the school district under Title IX, asserting that the teacher had used his position at school to sexually assault her and that the district should be accountable for the acts of its employees.

In this case, the Supreme Court established two factors for determining school district liability under Title IX: notice and deliberate indifference. First, the matter had to be reported to a school official who has authority to institute corrective measures; and second, the official has to be deliberately indifferent (failed to act when there is a complaint). Here, the district was not liable because the court found that there was inadequate evidence whether the school district had actual or constructive notice that the teacher was having a sexual relationship with a student.

Gebser argued that she did not know what to do about the continued harassment because the district had failed to provide her with a copy of its Title IX procedures. The Court did not find liability on this basis but did note that the U.S. Department of Education could impose sanctions on the district for failing to comply with its Title IX administrative regulations. Further, the Court noted that nothing precludes the student from seeking remedies under state law and suing school personnel individually for damages under 42 U.S.C. Section 1983.

In 1999, the Supreme Court confronted a case involving prolonged sexual harassment of a female student by one of her fifth-grade male classmates. The mother of the student alleged that the male student attempted to touch her daughter inappropriately, made vulgar statements such as "I want to get in bed with you" and "I want to feel your boobs," rubbed his body against her, and placed a doorstop in his pants.

The complaint claimed that school officials took no effective action. Only after three months of reported harassment was the daughter permitted to change her classroom seat so she wouldn't be next to the male student. The complaint further alleged that the girl's high grades had dropped, she wrote a suicide note, and she told her mother she did not know how long she could keep the student off her. The incidents ended when the male student pleaded guilty to sexual battery. The Supreme Court ruled in *Davis v. Monroe County Board of Education* (1999), that peer-on-peer sexual harassment is covered by Title IX and that the district may be liable if the harassment is reported to an official who has authority to take corrective action (presumably this could be the teacher as well as the campus administrator), the response is unreasonable in light of the circumstances, and the harassment was severe, pervasive, and objectively offensive.

Same-sex student peer harassment falls within the parameters of Title IX, just as it does with 42 U.S.C. Section 1983. A case in point involves an eighth-grade student in the Antioch Unified School District who was beaten severely on the way home by a fellow male student who taunted him about being homosexual, due in part to the fact that the victim's mother was a transgender female.

According to the allegation, the boy and his mother repeatedly reported harassing behavior of students to school district officials, but the school district failed to act. The boy asserted that the district knew that his attacker was violence prone. He also asserted that the attack left him so emotionally impaired and fearful of his safety as to deny him access to equal educational opportunities. The federal district court ruled that same-sex harassment is actionable under Title IX and refused to dismiss the case against the school district (*Ray v. Antioch Unified School District*, 2000).

Sexual Harassment and Abuse Under the California Education Code

California law both mirrors Title IX and goes beyond it. Education Code Section 220 and following sections prohibit public and private educational institutions from discriminating against persons on the basis of gender, gender identity, and gender expression as well as disability, nationality, race or ethnicity, sexual orientation, or any other characteristic that falls within the definition of hate crimes under Section 422.55 of the Penal Code. Private schools are exempt from this requirement if compliance would violate their religious tenets.

Section 210.7 defines *gender* to include a person's gender identity and gender expression whether or not related to a person's biological sex. In other words, transgender persons are accorded equal rights in the state's schools. For example, while it may be possible in some states to prevent a male dressed as a female from attending the school prom, this could not occur in California.

Education Code Section 231.5, part of the Sex Equity in Education Act, requires educational institutions to have a written policy on sexual harassment as part of its general operating procedures. The policy is to be provided to new employees and students and is to be prominently displayed at the school site and administration building. It is to include information on where to obtain information about reporting charges of sexual harassment and seeking remedies.

Education Code Section 234 and following sections known as the Safe Place to Learn Act requires the California Department of Education to ensure that all schools have adopted a policy prohibiting intimidation and bullying as well as discrimination and harassment based on all of the characteristics set forth in Education Code 220. The policy is to be posted in staff lounges and student government meeting rooms. School personnel must take immediate steps to enforce the policy when such behavior is observed. The policy is to include a timeline to investigate and resolve complaints. Known as "Seth's Law," the Safe Place to Learn Act was expanded in 2012 to encompass a broad definition of gender following pervasive harassment and bullying of a thirteen-year-old who was gay in the Tehachapi Unified School District, resulting in his tragic suicide.

In 2008 a California court of appeal ruled that under Education Code Section 262.4 money damages for violating these sections may be available to plaintiffs (*Donovan v. Poway Unified School District*, 2008). The case involved sustained harassment against two students who were gay by their peers in the Poway Unified School District that resulted in their cutting classes and eventually enrolling in a home-study program. Holding that the standards for seeking damages under

Section 220 are the same as under Title IX, the appellate court ruled that there were adequate grounds for the jury to conclude that the district had actual notice of the harassment and was deliberately indifferent to taking action to stop it, thus denying the two students access to equal educational opportunities. Significantly, the two students had kept detailed logs chronicling the numerous antigay peer harassment incidents they encountered at school and their reports to school administrators. The $300,000 damage award under Section 220 was upheld.

It also bears noting that a parent may proceed in a lawsuit related to bullying even though the student no longer attended school in the district. In one case, a court determined that, because there is a manifest public interest in enforcing anti-discrimination and anti-bullying laws in public schools, a California court of appeal permitted the parent of a special needs child who no longer attended the public school where the bullying had occurred to seek damages from the District. The court reasoned that, as a citizen and taxpayer, the parent had standing to seek enforcement of these laws (*Hector F. v. El Centro Elementary School District*, 2014).

California Unruh Civil Rights Act

In a dramatic effort to eradicate societal discrimination, the California legislature enacted the Unruh Civil Rights Act in 1959. Its key provision now states:

> All persons within the jurisdiction of this state are free and equal, and no matter what their sex, race, color, religion, ancestry, national origin, disability, medical condition, genetic information, marital status, sexual orientation, citizenship, primary language, or immigration status are entitled to the full and equal accommodations, advantages, facilities, privileges, or services in all business establishments of every kind whatsoever. (Civil Code § 51(a)).

The term *sex* includes, but is not limited to, pregnancy, childbirth, or medical conditions related to pregnancy or childbirth and encompasses a person's gender. *Gender* means sex, and includes a person's gender identity and gender expression. *Gender expression* means a person's gender-related appearance and behavior whether or not stereotypically associated with the person's assigned sex at birth.

The phrase *business establishments* appears to encompass public and private schools, though courts are divided. For a claim to be viable, it must be established that the discrimination was arbitrary or intentional. Practices that have an unintentional disparate impact on a class of persons are not actionable. Penalties include both compensatory damages and injunctive relief and can encompass both entities and individual employees. Punitive damages also are available.

In the schooling context, litigation under the Unruh Act has been limited, in part because the act deals only with equal access to establishments and in part to the availability of other remedies for discrimination. One important decision is *Nicole M. v. Martinez Unified School District*. After her daughter was allegedly sexually harassed and assaulted in school, the student's mother filed a lawsuit in federal court, advancing a number of federal and state claims. The student contended that the actions taken by the principal were so inadequate as to constitute a violation of her civil rights. She cited suspension of her attacker for one day and the placement of one of the worst perpetrators in a class to which she had been reassigned. Following the mandate of the California Supreme Court to apply the Unruh Act "in the broadest sense reasonably possible," the federal judge concluded that, if true, the lack of effective action may have deprived the student of the advantages and privileges of a public education. The school district argued that the Unruh Act had not been applied to claims of sexual harassment, but the judge could see no reason why it should not be (*Nicole M. v. Martinez Unified School District*, 1997).

The judge also permitted the lawsuit against the school district to proceed under Title IX and against the school principal individually under 42 U.S.C. Section 1983. For reasons discussed in the next chapter, the federal judge rejected the portion of the lawsuit contending that the school district and principal were liable under the California Tort Claims Act. The case was set for trial to determine whether the allegations were true and whether they amounted to intentional discrimination.

A year after the *Nicole M.* ruling, another case arose in the context of racial harassment. In that case, an Black high school student sued the Santa Barbara Unified High School District and various school officials after she was subjected to repeated racial harassment. Among other things, the student alleged that several students placed a drawing on her desk of a Black person hanging from a tree by rope. The student's name, combined with a racial slur, was written next to the body. The student contended that her teacher merely excused her from class and that school administrators did little to protect her. The student also contended that a racially hostile environment existed at the high school, noting that the NAACP had petitioned the district two years before to do something about it. The federal judge dismissed the student's claims under the Tort Claims Act. But he refused to do so under the Unruh Civil Rights Act, noting that, as in *Nicole M.*, the student had advanced sufficient allegations of a racially hostile environment to warrant a trial (*Davison v. Santa Barbara High School District*, 1998).

In 2009 a California court of appeal ruled that the Unruh Act does not apply to religious private schools and therefore the decision of the California Lutheran

High School to expel two female students for their same-sex relationship does not constitute discrimination on the basis of sexual orientation under the Act. The court relied on an earlier California Supreme Court decision declining to extend the Unruh Act to the Boy Scouts and similar charitable, expressive, and social organizations. The appellate court viewed the California Lutheran High School as similar to the Boy Scouts as an expressive social organization whose primary function is inculcation of its values rather than a business establishment (*Doe v. California Lutheran High School,* 2009).

SUMMARY

In 1954, the U.S. Supreme Court declared in *Brown v. Board of Education of Topeka, Kansas* that government-sanctioned racial segregation in public schools was unconstitutional. It soon became apparent that this goal could not be achieved simply by ending de jure segregation because of the legacy of harm suffered by generations of schoolchildren. To compensate them and to ensure equality of opportunity, the U.S. Supreme Court directed that steps be taken to integrate previously segregated schools. But the question arose as to whether this requirement applied to all racially segregated schools, not just those in the South where most schools were segregated. In 1974, the U.S. Supreme Court answered in the negative. Only where it could be proven that schools had practiced racial segregation could such a remedy be imposed. The result was a system of racially integrated schools in the South but not necessarily elsewhere. In the decades thereafter, the enthusiasm of federal judges to pursue racial integration waned. Many districts resegregated as judicial oversight came to an end.

The California experience has been somewhat different. The California Supreme Court did not distinguish between forced segregation and segregation by circumstance. Rather, beginning in the 1970s, school districts were required to take effective action to address racial isolation regardless of cause. Public opposition resulted in constitutional amendments limiting the use of busing, pupil assignment, and affirmative action to achieve this goal.

These limitations, coupled with the retreat of federal courts from vigorously pursuing the cause of integration, have prompted school officials to resort to creative ways of reducing racial isolation. These include the development of thematic choice schools in racially isolated areas and assigning students to schools based on socioeconomic and geographic factors. In the case of charter schools, which have a statutory responsibility to achieve a racial and ethnic mix reflective of the general population of the district within which they are located, focused recruitment in underrepresented areas is an oft-employed effort. Despite efforts to overcome it, racial and economic isolation in California's public schools remain.

Racial and gender harassment is strictly forbidden under both federal and California law. All schools should take preventive action to avoid lawsuits by informing both personnel and students about Title IX, Education Code Section 220, and the Unruh Act and by emphasizing their commitment to enforcing these laws.

12 LEGAL LIABILITY

The threat of lawsuits and legal liability are serious concerns for educators. In this chapter, we examine the extent to which school districts, board members, and employees can be held legally accountable in California state and federal courts. We do not discuss all legal claims but focus on those involving personal injury and civil rights because these are the most prevalent in public schools. The matter is quite complex. To make the discussion more understandable, we provide numerous illustrations drawn from judicial decisions. We begin by discussing liability under California law, then turn to examine liability for federal wrongs. The clear message from this review is that the best way to avoid legal liability is to know and follow the law.

LIABILITY UNDER CALIFORNIA LAW

Before we examine California law specifically, we need to point out that when Congress enacted the No Child Left Behind Act in 2001, it also enacted the Paul D. Coverdell Teacher Protection Act (20 U.S.C. § 7941). This federal law is intended to shield school employees and individual members of a governing board from liability in state court for maintaining order and ensuring safety at school. It applies to states like California that receive federal assistance and that have not elected to be exempt from the act.

Specifically, the law extends immunity protection when school employees or individual board members take action in conformity with federal, state, and local laws to control, discipline, expel, or suspend a student or maintain order or control in the classroom or school (20 U.S.C. § 7946). However, the immunity is carefully conditioned. There is no immunity if school personnel are not acting within the scope of their employment or if they engage in willful or criminal misconduct, gross negligence, reckless misconduct, or flagrant indifference to the rights of the individual. Nor is there any immunity for crimes of violence, sexual offenses, violations of civil rights, or acts or omissions occurring while alcohol or drug impaired. Nothing precludes a school or other governmental entity from filing a civil suit against a teacher or other school official. The act also does not apply to cases involving harm caused by the use of a motor vehicle, nor to those involving the imposition of corporal punishment.

The Coverdell Act was a response to the flurry of lawsuits against school officials that arose after the student shootings at Columbine and other high schools. However, as we will see in the ensuing discussion, its application in California is limited because state law already broadly protects school employees and governing board members.

California Tort Claims Act

The standards relating to liability of California governmental entities and their employees for damages under state law are set forth in the California Tort Claims Act (Gov't Code § 810 et seq.). School districts and charter schools are considered governmental entities. However, it remains unclear whether a charter school is sufficiently independent from the school district granting the charter to constitute a separate legal entity subject to being sued in its own right. The California attorney general has opined that such independence is lacking, though pursuant to the terms of the charter, the school may exercise such independent legal rights as to sue and be sued (81 Ops. Atty. Gen. 140, 1998). If charter schools are operated as nonprofit benefit corporations, Education Code Section 47604 provides that the chartering authority—school district, county board of education, or state board of education—will not be liable "for the debts or obligations of the charter school, or for claims arising from the performance of acts, errors, or omissions by the charter school" if the chartering authority has complied with all oversight responsibilities required by law. In other words, the charter school would be the focus of the lawsuit and would bear any liability. Of course, this provision does not preclude the inclusion of the chartering authority in a lawsuit. Whether the entity has performed all of its oversight responsibilities will be question of fact. County boards of education and county superintendents are considered governmental entities because the Education Code assigns governing duties to both (*Ross v. Campbell Union School District*, 1977).

While the Tort Claims Act encompasses a range of actions for damages beyond those commonly known as torts, we are primarily concerned with the latter. A tort is a civil wrong for which a court will award money damages. There are all kinds of torts, including libel, slander, maintaining a nuisance, and negligence. Negligence is the most common tort in the context of personal injury. It means that a person who has a legal duty toward another and fails to carry out the duty can be held liable for damages to the injured person if the failure was a substantial factor in causing he injury (what is termed "proximate cause" in the law).

Because the Tort Claims Act specifies the situations when California governmental entities, officials, and employees can be held liable, its key provisions relating to personal injuries are summarized in Table 12.1 in the context of public school employees and school districts. These same provisions may apply to charter schools and their employees. It is important to note that the Tort Claims Act does not apply to private schools and their employees. Private schools can be held liable for torts just like any private entity. Other provisions of the act will be referenced in the ensuing discussion. The act has a claims presentation requirement that necessitates submitting a written claim to the school district before legal action can be initiated for damages. The claims requirement, however, does not apply to charter schools operated by nonprofit benefit corporations because they do not meet the definition of a public agency (*Knapp v. Palisades Charter High School*, 2007). Many provisions of the Tort Claims Act are quite detailed, and only the general thrust of their contents is conveyed here. Readers will find it useful to consult the table periodically while reading this chapter.

A few key points emerge from reviewing the Tort Claims Act. First, as specified in Sections 820 and 820.2 of the Government Code, school employees are shielded from personal injury lawsuits when they are using discretion in carrying out their responsibilities. Because most acts of school employees are discretionary in the sense of their choosing among a variety of courses of action, the law provides a strong shield against employee liability. However, remember that we are discussing state, not federal, law. Immunity under state law does not extend to claims involving federal law.

Second, if the employee is immune, the district bears no liability unless otherwise provided by state law under Section 815.2 (see Table 12.1). If the employee is not immune, then the district bears the liability. The assumption of liability by the employer is called *vicarious liability* or *respondeat superior*, meaning that the district is held accountable for the acts of its employees. The purpose of the respondeat superior doctrine is to spread the risk for losses caused by employees through

TABLE 12.1
Key Provisions of the California Tort Claims Act as Set Forth in the Government Code
(worded in the context of school districts and employees)

Sections 820 and 820.2	A school employee is liable for an injury proximately caused by the employee's act or failure to act as would a private person, *except* when the employee is exercising discretion, whether or not such discretion is abused, unless otherwise provided by statute.
Section 820.8	A school employee is not liable for an injury caused by the act or failure to act of another person, unless otherwise provided by statute.
Section 822	A school employee is not liable for money stolen from his official custody, unless the loss was attributable to the employee's negligent or wrongful act or failure to act.
Section 825	Upon timely request, a school district must pay defense costs and any judgment against the employee arising out of an act or omission of the employee acting within the scope of employment. The employee must reasonably cooperate in the defense of the claim. A school district is not liable for punitive damages intended to punish the transgressor for acting recklessly or with malice or deceit. However, the district may choose to pay punitive damages assessed against an employee of the district when the latter is deemed liable.
Section 815.2	A school district is liable for injury proximately caused by an act or failure to act of an employee of the district if the employee was acting within the scope of his/her employment. However, if the employee is immune, the district bears no liability unless otherwise provided by state law.
Section 815.4	A school district is liable for injury caused by an independent contractor, except if the district would not have been liable for the injury had it been caused by the act or failure to act of a district employee.
Section 815.6	If a school district is under a mandatory duty imposed by law designed to protect against the risk of a particular kind of injury, the district is liable for an injury caused by its failure to carry out the duty, unless it can establish that it acted with reasonable diligence.
Section 820.9	School board members are not held liable for injuries caused by the act or failure to act of the school district.
Section 835	Unless otherwise provided by statute, a school district is liable for injury caused by a dangerous condition of its property if the dangerous condition resulted either from the negligence of its employees or from the district's failure to correct a known dangerous condition.
Section 831.7	Neither a school district nor its employees are liable to any person who participates in a hazardous recreational activity, including any person who assists the participant, or to any spectator who knew or reasonably should have known that the hazardous recreational activity created a substantial risk of injury to himself or herself and was voluntarily in the place of risk, or having the ability to do so failed to leave, for any damage or injury to property or persons arising out of that hazardous recreational activity. "Hazardous recreational activity" means a recreational activity conducted on property of a school district that creates a substantial, as distinguished from a minor, trivial, or insignificant, risk of injury to a participant or a spectator.

insurance and to provide greater assurance of compensation for victims. In effect, vicarious liability becomes a cost of doing business.

Third, as policy makers, school board members enjoy broad immunity for their acts under Section 820.9.

In the following sections, we examine how these and other provisions of the Tort Claims Act have played out in California courts in the context of public schooling.

Injury to students on campus. Under the terms of the California Tort Claims Act, the district is vicariously liable for the acts of its employees when they are acting in the scope of their employment and not undertaking a duty imposed by the Education Code. Thus, for example, when the California Education Code charges employees with the duty to supervise students and they fail to do so, the district can be liable under Section 815.2 because there is no discretion not to supervise students. A case in point is a 1993 California appellate court decision involving a ten-year-old student who was struck in the eye by a dirt clod during unsupervised recess when the student and others were throwing dirt clods at each other (*Lucas v. Fresno Unified School District*). The court ruled that the district was liable because school employees had failed to carry out the requirement of Education Code Section 44807 that students are to be supervised while on the school playground. This section of the Education Code imposes a duty to discipline students for misconduct occurring while going to and from school, on the playgrounds, and during recess. When the duty is breached, the Tort Claims Act provides the means for those injured to seek redress from the school district.

If supervision is provided but inadequate, liability may result. A provision of the California Code of Regulations requires principals to provide supervision by certificated employees for students who are on school playgrounds "during recess and other intermissions and before and after school" (5 C.C.R. § 5552). One case involved an elementary school that offered a supervised after-school playground program free of cost (*J. H. v. Los Angeles Unified School District*, 2010). Students could come and go voluntarily. Students were told to stay on a portion of the school campus where the program was offered, but there were no clear defining boundaries. On the day in question, four second-grade students wandered off the area to an unlocked storage shed. There, one student was sexually assaulted. The four students were known to be members of a group called the "kissing club." At the time, the one supervisor assigned to the playground program was supervising 113 students. A California court of appeal overturned the trial court's dismissal of the case, noting that the duty to supervise students on school premises is well established and particularly important in the context of immature elementary students.

Here, the presence of only one supervisor, the large number of young children to be supervised, and accessibility of children to the unlocked shed raised questions about whether the duty of care owed the children was breached and whether that breach was a proximate cause of the student's injuries. The case was sent back to the trial court for further proceedings.

Similarly, a school district may be held liable when school employees fail to use reasonable care in protecting students from injury by nonstudents on school grounds. A high school student wrestler in the Stockton Unified School District sued his school district, school principal, and wrestling coach when he was assaulted by a nonstudent in an unsupervised school restroom where he was changing his clothes before wrestling practice (*Leger v. Stockton Unified School District*, 1988). The California court of appeal noted that the defendants owed him a duty of reasonable care under Education Code Section 44807 and that he did not have to establish that prior acts of violence had occurred in the restroom to warrant some degree of supervision. The fact that it was unsupervised was enough to establish a claim. The case was sent back to the trial court for a determination of liability, a matter to be determined by the facts and the provisions of the Tort Claims Act.

The *Leger* case is interesting because the court drew from practices in private schools to define the extent of liability under the Tort Claims Act. The statute specifies that a public employee is liable for his acts or omissions "to the same extent as a private party" (Gov't Code § 820). Therefore, both the employee and the public entity are entitled to any defenses that a private employee or employer might assert. Noting that private schools have a duty under the law to supervise if school officials reasonably could anticipate that it is necessary, the court concluded that, had the public school employees been in the private sector, they would have been liable if the facts alleged by the student turned out to be true.

There is a consensus among judges that the duty to supervise is not so high as to require schools to be absolute insurers of the physical safety of students. This would require schools to be operated as lockdown prisons. However, such a duty does exist when students constitute a threat of foreseeable harm to other students. In a 2003 ruling, a California court of appeal was confronted with a lawsuit seeking damages from the school district for an assault committed during the school day on one high school student by another student in a restroom (*Thompson v. Sacramento City Unified School District*). The perpetrator, Damascus, had a record of disciplinary problems in elementary and middle school. He had been expelled from the middle school for fighting. After he was admitted to high school, his disciplinary infractions lessened. There were no incidents of threatening or violent behavior toward others, though the day before the assault, Damascus had an argument with a female student and was accused of setting fire to a bulletin board poster. He was told that failure to undergo anger management would result in a three-day suspension. The next day, Damascus and another student heard a rumor that the victim, Thompson, was carrying marijuana. The pair lured Thompson into the restroom and asked him to empty his pockets. The youth refused and ran out of the restroom. The fight broke out a few feet outside.

The appellate court found that the principal did not owe a duty to Thompson to immediately suspend Damascus from school following the argument the previous afternoon with the female student and the poster-burning allegation. These incidents were not related to Thompson. Indeed, the court noted that Damascus apparently did not know Thompson. Nor was there any evidence that the restroom or the area immediately outside it were known areas of danger. In fact, a school monitor had just passed the restroom before the incident occurred and immediately returned to the area when the fight broke out. Thus, there was insufficient causation to link the prior incidents involving Damascus to the assault on Thompson. The school principal had exercised reasonable care in supervising students. Dismissal of the lawsuit was upheld.

Liability in a failure-to-supervise case is especially likely when special education students are involved because of their special needs. This is the teaching of a 2003 California appellate court decision involving the sexual assault of a fifteen-year-old male special education student by another male special education student with a history of disciplinary problems (*M.W. v. Panama Buena Vista Union School District*). The act occurred in a boy's bathroom at approximately 7:15 a.m. The gates of the junior high school were unlocked at 7 a.m., but direct supervision did not begin until 7:45 a.m. Parents were not informed of the lack of supervision during the early-morning hours. Indeed, the victim's mother believed that her son was being supervised. School officials knew the victim to be vulnerable to teasing during this period because he frequently retreated to the office to escape it. Given the circumstances, the court of appeal in a 2–1 ruling found it foreseeable that the special education student was at risk for a physical or sexual assault. It affirmed a jury award against the district in the amount of $2.4 million under the California Tort Claims Act. To reduce the risk of liability, a school should either preclude students from coming on campus before the opening of school or be prepared to provide supervision if students are allowed on campus prior to this time. The same holds true at the end of the day.

Education Code Section 49079 imposes a mandatory duty on school districts to inform teachers about students who have engaged in, or are reasonably suspected of having engaged in, suspendable or expellable acts except the possession or use of tobacco within the previous three years. Section 815.6 of the California Tort Claims Act provides that a governmental entity may incur liability for breach of a mandatory duty imposed by statute if the failure to carry out the duty was the proximate cause of an injury and the entity did not exercise due diligence. Does this include warning teachers about a student's potential for future violence, and if there is no warning is the school district liable? The Vacaville Unified School District sought to overturn a jury award against it on this basis after a ninth-grade male student attacked the cocaptain of the volleyball team, breaking her jaw and inflicting severe and permanent injuries (*Skinner v. Vacaville Unified School District*, 1995). The victim claimed that the district was negligent in failing to warn the physical education teacher of the student's propensity to violence. There was no question that school administrators had not warned the teacher, although they knew that the ninth grader had a history of fighting.

The appellate court found the question "very close." While the ninth grader had not inflicted injury on other students and had not been expelled prior to the incident, the court concluded that the evidence supported the jury finding that school administrators had breached their duty under the statute to notify the teacher of the student's record of fighting. However, the district's failure to warn the teacher was judged not to be the proximate cause of the injury. The teacher already knew that the student could be a problem and had been keeping her eye on him. Because any additional information from the district may not have made a difference, the appellate court found insufficient evidence to support the jury finding of causation. The judgment against the district was overturned. Even though the district avoided liability in this instance, the lesson is clear. School officials must always inform teachers of students with discipline problems stemming from suspendable or expellable acts.

Can a school district be liable under Section 815.6 of the Tort Claims Act when school officials fail to ensure that students never will be subjected to corporal punishment? This was a question facing another California appellate court in a case involving parents who contended that their special education child had been subjected to beatings by his teacher in addition to physical, psychological, and verbal abuse (*Clausing v. San Francisco Unified School District*, 1990). In their lawsuit, the parents claimed that the school district had breached its mandatory duty under Education Code Sections 49000–49001, which prohibit the use of corporal punishment in public schools. The parents construed these provisions to mean that the district had a mandatory duty to see that corporal punishment never was used. The appellate court decided against the parents, pointing out that the corporal punishment statutes "do *not* create any mandatory, affirmative duty on the part of public schools and school districts to take action or carry out measures to ensure that students are never subjected to corporal punishment by teachers" (pp. 80–81, emphasis in original). Acceptance of the parents' position, the court noted, would transform the prohibition on corporal punishment into a requirement that schools take affirmative action to protect students from ever being disciplined in this way. This would subject schools to civil liability and damages at great cost.

That the legislature did not intend this to be the case, the judges noted, is apparent from reading another provision of the Tort Claims Act providing that public entities are not liable for injuries caused "by failing to enforce any law" (Gov't Code § 818.2). The parents also argued that the California Constitution gave them grounds to sue the school district. They cited Article I, Section 28, requiring that all public school students "have the inalienable right to attend campuses which are safe, secure, and peaceful," as well as Article I, Section 1, protecting the right of privacy. The appellate court again decided against the parents. Section 28 does not provide a damages remedy. As for Article I, Section 1, the court held that it supports a cause of action seeking only an injunction against alleged privacy violations, not one seeking money damages.

The outcome in the *Clausing* case does not mean that educators can use corporal punishment or violate a student's right to a safe school environment or to privacy without consequences. For example, a teacher who uses corporal punishment in violation of the statute and district policy may be liable to the student injured because the teacher would be acting outside the scope of employment. The district may be liable if it condones the use of corporal punishment. While Education Code Section 44807 does give educators the same degree of physical control over a student that a parent has as a matter of law, it provides no immunity from criminal prosecution or criminal penalties if the physical force exceeds that reasonably necessary to maintain order, protect property, safeguard students, or maintain conditions conducive to learning. Further, school administrators who fail to halt inappropriate use of physical force or corporal punishment as well as teachers who use it as a discipline technique are in danger of disciplinary action from their employers for failure to follow state law. The thrust of the *Clausing* decision is that the district does not have a mandatory duty under the provisions of the Education Code to prevent such actions from ever happening. In fact, in some situations, physical force may be necessary to protect a student from harm and shield the district and its personnel from liability. Education Code Section 49001 does permit a reasonable amount of force necessary to prevent physical injury to persons or damage to property, for self-defense, and to divest a pupil of weapons and dangerous objects. If school officials do not use force in such situations and a student is injured as a result, there could be liability against both the school district and its personnel.

Liability when school employees act outside the scope of their employment. Under Sections 820 and 820.2 of the California Tort Claims Act, employees are shielded from liability when they are acting within the scope of their employment and are using appropriate discretion in carrying out their responsibilities. And if employees are immune, so too are districts under Section 815.2 of the act, unless otherwise provided by state law. Discretion means choosing among a range of alternatives and making a decision. Employees are entitled to immunity even if the decision actually made was not effective. School administrators, for example, who responded to a student's sexual harassment and assault claim by allegedly suspending the perpetrator for one day and taking other actions that were not effective, were exercising discretion and hence immune from liability under the Tort Claims Act (*Nicole M. v. Martinez Unified School District,* 1997). However, lawsuits often involve numerous causes of action. As we noted in Chapter 11, administrators in the *Nicole M.* case were not immune from liability under California's Unruh Civil Rights Act. Further, the judge in that case cited case law in California indicating that the exercise of discretion means making a decision about what is just and proper under the circumstances (*Kemmerer v. County of Fresno,* 1988). Thus, as a matter of taking preventive action, school employees should exercise care in making discretionary decisions.

If employees are not acting in the scope of their employment, the district bears no liability unless state law specifies otherwise. The California Supreme Court ruled in 1989, for example, that a district is not vicariously liable under the Tort Claims Act for a teacher's allegedly sexually assaulting a fourteen-year-old student at the teacher's home (*John R. v. Oakland Unified School District*). The student was participating in a district-sanctioned work-experience program supervised by his teacher at the time of the assault. The court found the relationship between the teacher's act and his employment too attenuated for the district to be liable. Were it otherwise, the Supreme Court noted, the risk of a lawsuit would force school districts to foreclose all informal interaction between teachers and their students.

A California appellate court relied on the *John R.* decision to rule that a school district could not be liable under the Tort Claims Act for an alleged sexual molestation on a five-year-old student by her teacher because such an act is not encompassed within the teacher's scope of employment (*Kimberly M. v. Los Angeles Unified School District,* 1989). Similarly, a janitor who sexually assaulted a student in the janitor's office was not acting within the scope of his employment. The alleged assault was judged not incident to his employment and could not be reasonably foreseen by the district under the facts of the case (*Alma W. v. Oakland Unified School District*, 1981). In circumstances like these, when employees acting outside the scope of their employment injure students, the employees themselves will be the target of the lawsuit and possible criminal penalties and cannot rely on the district to defend them or pay any judgment against them. Nor can they depend on a professional insurance policy to shoulder a judgment against them. Parents of a third grader who was sexually abused by her teacher tried to secure a judgment against the Horace Mann Insurance Company, which issued the man an educator's employment liability policy (*Horace Mann Insurance Company v. Analisa N.*, 1989). The court of appeal agreed with the insurance company that sexual abuse was not encompassed within the policy. Wrote the judges: "We cannot fathom a more personal activity less related to the goal of education than [the teacher's] acts" (p. 64).

It is important to note that these state court rulings cannot shield the school district from lawsuits in federal court based on Title IX, as discussed in Chapter 11. It also is important to note that more recent decisions indicate that if district officials are negligent in hiring or supervising employees who injure students, the district may be liable. This is most apt to occur in the context of sexual abuse. The leading decision was handed down by the California Supreme Court in 2012. The case involved a guidance counselor who drove the fourteen-year-old student home from school and spent long hours with him on and off high school premises, including the student's home, over a period of many months (*C.A. v. William S. Hart Union High School District*). The counselor performed various sexual acts on the student and required him to perform similar acts on her. Relying on its earlier *John R.* decision, the high court agreed with the appellate court that the counselor was not acting in the scope of employment when this occurred and thus the district bears no liability under the Tort Claims Act for her actions. However, the high court disagreed with the appellate court that the district could not be liable on other grounds. If it could be shown that district administrators were negligent in using reasonable measures of hiring, supervising, and retaining the counselor to protect students from foreseeable harm, then liability attaches under Section 815.2 of the Tort Claims Act (look again at Table 12.1). This is so because students have a right to a safe schooling environment and because school administrators and supervisors, like teachers, have a duty to provide it. However, the justices noted that establishing the link between administrator action and the harm may be difficult, because the final hiring and firing decision is left to others. Even if such negligence is established, the greater share of fault ordinarily will lie with the employee who engaged in the misconduct.

A few years earlier, the California high court had ruled that liability can extend to previous school districts in these situations if the references they supplied on behalf of former employees are flawed. The decision involved a student who allegedly was sexually assaulted by an administrator in her school (*Randi W. v. Muroc Joint Unified School District*, 1997). The student sued the school district, along with a number of other school districts that had previously employed the administrator. She argued that the previous employers were negligent because they had written glowing recommendations of the administrator's performance, yet knew he had a history of sexual misconduct with students. In a detailed analysis, the court ruled that the writer of a letter of recommendation owes a duty to third parties not to misrepresent the facts in describing the qualifications and character of a former employee if making the misrepresentations would present a foreseeable risk of physical injury to third persons. Absent a foreseeable risk of physical injury, no duty of care exists. The court found that the recommendations in this case contained misleading half-truths indicating the administrator to be fit to interact with female students, even though prior experience with the administrator indicated otherwise. The student's complaint thus constituted an exception to the general rule excluding liability for nondisclosure.

Based on this ruling, it is important to be honest in recommendations. An administrative regulation issued by the California Commission on Teacher Credentialing specifies that a certificated person is not to sign a letter or memorandum to be used as a positive letter of reference that intentionally omits significant facts relating to the fitness of the employee for future employment or includes those that the writer does not know to be true. The rule does not pertain to statements that reflect personal opinions (5 C.C.R. § 80332). Truth is always a defense—a point underscored by California Civil Code Section 47(c), which provides a privilege against defamation suits for recommendations made without malice. A superintendent was successful in defeating a libel action against him on this basis by a teacher who discovered the superintendent's candid comments about her qualifications for future employment in a letter the superintendent had written (*Manguso v. Oceanside Unified School District*, 1984). The court of appeal ruled that the qualified privilege applies in such a situation unless there is substantial evidence of hatred or ill will, or without a reasonable belief that the comments are true, or of improper intent. Some attorneys advise that in the absence of a reference release form signed by the employee authorizing the employer to provide employment information to prospective employers, the best way to avoid the threat of litigation is to stick to established facts.

Occasionally, school administrators will file lawsuits seeking damages for defamation of character. The chances of success are slim. A lawsuit filed by a former charter school superintendent against the Anti-Defamation League (ADL) and its officers for libel over the contents of a letter posted on its website provides a good illustration (*Ghafur v. Bernstein*, 2005). The letter had been sent to the state superintendent of public instruction (SPI) calling for an immediate suspension of Gateway Academy's funding and urging an investigation of religious instruction and of the school's link to the Islamic terrorist organization Al-Fuqra. At the time, the SPI was investigating newspaper reports that Gateway was having students study Islam and charging tuition at certain of its multiple school sites contrary to state law. Later, the Fresno Unified School District, the chartering authority, terminated the charter for fiscal mismanagement. After the termination, the ADL posted on its website the letter it had sent to the SPI. The charter school superintendent contended that the contents were maliciously false and defamatory in stating that the charter school director was a member of the virulently anti-Semitic Islamic extremist group and in linking the official and the charter school to a terrorist organization.

The appellate court agreed with the trial court that the letter sent to the SPI was privileged under the "anti-SLAPP" (Strategic Lawsuit Against Public Participation) law (Civil Proc. § 425.16). That law was enacted to give courts more authority to reject lawsuits over speech on public matters. The court also agreed that the charter school superintendent, like her counterparts in the public schools, was a "public official." This means that to prevail against ADL on the website-posting issue, the charter school superintendent would have to show that the statements in the letter were made with knowledge of their falsity or with reckless disregard for their truth. This so-called "actual malice" test comes from *New York Times v. Sullivan*, a famous 1964 U.S. Supreme Court decision intended to protect freedom of the press (it has been applied to California public school teachers as well). Whether or not the charter school superintendent could show actual malice behind the letter posting was addressed in a section of the opinion that was not published.

Injury to student athletes and cheerleaders. Education Code Section 44807 places responsibility on teachers to supervise students on the way to and from school, on the playground, and at recess. California courts have recognized that the primary assumption of risk that student participants must shoulder when they engage in many extracurricular and athletic events lessens employee liability in these instances and, through them, the liability of the district. For example, a high school student was not successful when he sued both his wrestling coach and the school district after the student broke his arm during an exhibition with the coach on the use of the control hold (*Lilley v. Elk Grove Unified School District*, 1998). The student tried to brace himself by jamming his arm into the wrestling mat. The appellate court concluded that the type of injury the student suffered is an inherent risk of wrestling. The court did not accept the student's contention that Section 44807 precludes application of the primary assumption of risk doctrine to extracurricular sports. If otherwise, instructors would fear requiring their students to stretch beyond their present level of performance.

Because head injuries often result in serious harm to students and liability for schools, the California Legislature has enacted a law providing that athletes suspected of having sustained a concussion or head injury during an athletic activity outside the regular school day are to be immediately removed from the activity for the remainder of the day and not permitted to return until evaluated by a licensed health care provider (Educ. Code § 49475).

In 2014 the legislature added Section 35179.5 to the Education Code restricting school districts, charter schools, and private schools from conducting more than two full-contact practices per week for high school or middle school football teams during the preseason or regular season. A practice includes a team camp session. The full-contact portion of a practice is not to exceed 90 minutes in a day. No full-contact practice is to be held during the off-season, meaning a period extending from the end of the regular season until 30 days before the commencement of the next regular season. The California Interscholastic Federation (CIF) is urged to develop rules to implement these provisions.

Education Code Section 49475 also was amended to provide that if a licensed health care provider—meaning one trained in concussion management—determines that a student athlete has sustained a concussion or head injury, the athlete is to complete a graduated return-to-play protocol of no less than seven days under supervision of the provider. The CIF is urged to work with the American Academy of Pediatrics and the American Medical Society for Sports Medicine to develop implementing procedures.

In 2017, the Eric Paredes Sudden Cardiac Arrest Prevention Act was enacted, requiring the State Department of Education (SDE) to post on its website information and training information about sudden cardiac arrest and encourages all schools to do the same. In addition, each year before a student participates in an athletic activity whether governed by the California Interscholastic Federation or not, the public or private school that conducts the athletic activity must have the parent or guardian of participating students acknowledge receipt of the information posted on the SDE's website about sudden cardiac arrest symptoms and warning signs. Athletic personnel are to remove any student who passes out or faints while participating in or immediately following an athletic activity. The student is not to be allowed to participate until cleared to return in writing by a physician and surgeon or a nurse practitioner or physician assistant knowledgeable in this area. In addition, coaches are to complete the sudden cardiac arrest training course posted on the SDE website and to retake it every two years. For details, see Education Code Section 33479 and following sections.

The same assumption of risk discussed in the *Lilley* decision applies to cheerleaders. A cheerleader who was injured when she attempted an acrobatic activity known as "the cradle" claimed inadequate supervision in her lawsuit against the district (*Aaris v. Las Virgenes Unified School District*, 1998). The cradle requires two cheerleaders to form a base and then launch a third cheerleader into the air. After the flyer touches her toes, she is caught by the base cheerleaders. Denning, the injured student, had been part of the base and was hurt when the elevated cheerleader fell on her. Denning had attended a cheerleading camp, had been given safety instruction, and had received instruction in how to do a gymnastic stunt. She maintained that the coach failed to protect her from harm, especially because she was having trouble learning how to do the stunt and was afraid that she might get hurt. She argued that because students had not mastered the stunt, the coach's duty of care was greater in this instance. The district countered that students who participate in athletic activities must assume the risk of being injured and that no greater duty of care was required here. The appellate court agreed. A coach is not an insurer of the student's safety and cannot be liable unless the coach were to increase the risk of harm over and above that inherent in the sport. Here, there was no evidence that the coach had increased the risk of harm. The appellate court concluded that ruling to the contrary would fundamentally alter the nature of high school cheerleading, perhaps ending it altogether.

In 2003, the California Supreme Court expanded on the discussion about assumption of risk in sports activities. The case involved a fourteen-year-old competitive swimmer, Olivia Kahn, who broke her neck when she dived into a shallow pool just prior to a swim meet at Mount Pleasant High School in the East Side Union High School District (*Kahn v. East Side Union High School District*). The student had a strong fear of diving. In response, her coach had assigned her to the first leg of the relay in previous swim meets where she could start from inside the pool. But on the day of the accident, he told Olivia that she would not be swimming the first leg of the relay. The student alleged that she pleaded with the coach to change the rotation. But he did not do so. Before the relay race began and apparently without her coach's knowledge, the student practiced shallow dives with two fellow swimmers. The accident occurred on the third dive. Through her mother, Olivia sued the coach and the school district. In upholding the trial court's dismissal of the case, the court of appeal in a 2–1 decision noted that there is a primary assumption of risk when students voluntarily participate in sporting events. The risk is inherent if its elimination would alter the fundamental nature of the activity. Diving, the court concluded, is an integral part of competitive swimming. Either eliminating it or requiring deeper pools would fundamentally alter the sport. Therefore, a student must assume the risk of diving in shallow pools if the student wishes to participate in competitive swimming.

The California Supreme Court disagreed and sent the case back to the trial court for further proceedings against the coach. The student did not appeal the trial court's decision to dismiss the case against the school district. The high court pointed out that in 1992 it had ruled that the standard of liability of a sports participant for an injury to a coparticipant is if the participant "intentionally injures another player or engages in conduct that is so reckless as to be totally outside the range of the ordinary activity involved in the sport" (*Knight v. Jewett*, p. 17). In a lengthy review of a number of lower-court rulings on the matter, the justices concluded that the same standard should be applied to coaches. The supreme court noted that Olivia presented evidence that the coach failed to provide training to Olivia in shallow-water diving, had lulled her into a false sense of security by telling her she would not have to dive at competitions, and had breached that promise. The coach disputed these assertions. To resolve whether the coach had acted recklessly, a trial would have to be conducted. The importance of the ruling is the California Supreme Court's articulation of the standard for determining when a coach can be liable for accidents resulting in student injury. It is clear that, although there is a primary assumption of risk when students participate in competitive athletics and that nothing precludes a coach from encouraging students to go beyond their current level of competence, a coach has a duty of care reasonably to prepare students to engage in the activity so that the risk of harm is not heightened.

But it is important to note that when a student injury is *not* attributable to participating in the athletic activity, the standard of care exercised by the school and its personnel is the same as for students generally. Thus a California appellate court refused to dismiss a case filed by a middle school student's parents when the student was struck in the mouth by a golf club swung by another student during a physical education class. The court noted that in California a prudent standard of care has been imposed for injuries occurring during PE classes or physical exercise free periods, which are part of the curriculum. Being hit in the head by a golf club is not an inherent risk in the game of golf. Rather, it relates to such matters as the size of the class (in this case, fifty-four students), staffing, and similar matters.

The case was remanded to the trial court to determine whether the parents could establish that the class was disorganized and poorly supervised (*Hemady v. Long Beach Unified School District*, 2006).

As discussed in more detail later in the chapter with regard to injury to nonstudents, Section 831.7 of the Tort Claims Act provides immunity for districts and employees when persons engage in hazardous recreational activities on school property. Does this provision apply to student athletes who are injured? In the first California case confronting this question, the court of appeal in a 2–1 decision responded in the negative. The facts of the case are particularly wrenching. A high school gymnast, Omar, was working out one evening during the off-season at the school gymnasium while it was open for community use. His coach was assisting him. He was practicing a maneuver on the high bar called a "front catch" in which the gymnast swings forward and, at the top of the arc, lets go of the bar, performs a somersault, and catches the bar on the way down. Omar missed catching the bar and fell, landing on his neck. He was rendered a quadriplegic and died shortly thereafter.

The school district and Omar's coach argued that they were immune from liability because the student was engaged outside of school hours in a hazardous recreational activity, not a school-directed extracurricular activity. The appellate court disagreed. The judges began by noting that school-sponsored extracurricular athletic activities that are under the supervision of school personnel are not hazardous recreational activities. If they were so considered, schools would be immune for negligent supervision for a whole range of contact sports. The majority noted that school districts have a duty to supervise students at school-sponsored athletic activities, even if the events occur after school hours and during the off-season. Here, the coach ran a structured practice for members of the gymnastics team during the community recreational program. At the time of the accident, Omar was practicing on school equipment under the supervision of the coach, who had suggested he learn the catch maneuver. There was no question, the majority concluded, that Omar was engaged in a school-sponsored and supervised activity at the time of the injury. The case was sent back to the trial court for a determination of the amount of damages the district owed Omar's family. The dissenting judge agreed that school-sponsored extracurricular activities are not hazardous recreational activities, but he preferred to have the jury decide whether the activity in question was in fact school sponsored (*Acosta v. Los Angeles Unified School District*, 1995).

In a case decided the same year as *Acosta*, a fourteen-year-old student sought recovery from the school district after he suffered a double fracture of his right arm during a soccer match conducted during school hours as part of the school's physical education program. The school district sought immunity under the hazardous recreational activity provision of the Tort Claims Act, contending that the student had voluntarily placed himself at risk and knew or reasonably should have known that such an injury might occur in a bodily contact sport like soccer. The student argued that he was engaging in a compulsory class when the accident occurred and had no choice but to participate. The court of appeal agreed with the student, noting that a body contact sport incorporated into a physical education class during the school day is not a recreational activity, however hazardous it might be. Under Education Code Section 44807's duty to supervise students, it was up to a jury to determine whether there was negligence in supervision and what damages, if any, were due the injured student (*Iverson v. Muroc Unified School District*, 1995).

While students must assume some degree of assumption of risk when they participate in dangerous athletic activities as noted in the *Lilley* decision discussed on this page, that assumption does not eliminate the general requirement of providing student supervision. This point was made by a California court of appeal in a nonathletic case involving a middle school student who was seriously injured when forced to perform a flip by another student while engaging in break dancing in an unsupervised classroom (*Jimenez v. Roseville City School District*, 2016). The court noted testimony that teachers were not to leave classrooms unsupervised and that students had been told not to perform flips. The court also noted testimony from the teacher that he did not think it was necessary to tell the school administration that he had opened his classroom for early morning physical activity to help them prepare for a talent show and had them sign a release form [not clear what this stated], was unaware of the no-flipping directive, and left his classroom only briefly. Given that the injury to the student could have been caused by failure to enforce the no-flipping rule, lack of informing teachers about it, and/or negligent classroom supervision, the appeals court returned the case to the trial court. The lesson is for school administrators to make sure that teachers are fully aware when new student rules are made and that students are not left in unsupervised classrooms where physical activity can spiral into bodily harm.

Is there liability when students don't learn? Educators often wonder whether they and the school district can be held liable if a student does not learn. Outside the context of special education, the answer to date is generally no. Under special education law, a school district can be taken to an administrative hearing and perhaps beyond into federal court if a student does not receive meaningful educational benefit. For regular education students, the first and most famous case involving what later cases refer to as "educational malpractice" is *Peter W. v. San Francisco Unified School District*, decided in 1976. The student in that case argued that the district had failed in its duty to provide him an adequate instruction in basic academic skills. As a result, when he graduated from high school, he could be employed only as a manual laborer. The appellate court was not supportive, noting the complexity of the teaching-learning process: "Unlike the activity of the highway or the marketplace, classroom methodology affords no readily acceptable standards of care, or cause, or injury" (p. 860). Due to the absence of criteria to isolate the contribution of the school to a student's learning from the myriad other factors that affect it, the court dismissed the lawsuit.

In 2006, the California Supreme Court cited the *Peter W.* ruling in upholding a lower court's decision throwing out the portion of a lawsuit filed by parents who contended that the distance learning charter schools operated by One2One Learning Foundation failed to teach their children (*Wells v. One2One Learning Foundation*). However, the high court noted that nothing in *Peter W.* precludes a claim that a school operator failed to provide equipment and supplies, failed to employ appropriately credentialed teachers, violated rules governing independent study, or charged improper fees. Claims like these do not involve a court in determining educational quality or results. The parents in this case had filed their claim against the charter school operator under the California False Claims Act (Gov't Code § 12650 et seq.). That law provides civil penalties against anyone who knowingly presents a false claim to a government entity for payment or approval.

Basically, the False Claims Act (FCA) is intended to protect the treasury from those who seek to defraud the government. Here the parents claimed that the charter schools, their operator, and the authorizing school districts bilked the state out of some $20 million in average daily attendance (ADA) money. The high court agreed with the lower court that charter schools operated as nonprofit benefit corporations are "persons" under the FCA and can be held liable for defrauding the state or school district for three times the amount of damages, costs of the lawsuit to recover the money, and civil damages up to $10,000. However, the court concluded that the legislature did not intend to permit such lawsuits against school districts; the authorizing districts could not be sued. The high court also ruled that the parents could sue the charter schools and their operators under the California Unfair Competition Act to seek restoration of lost money or property (Bus. & Prof. Code § 17200 et seq.). Thus the lawsuit was allowed to go forward under both laws.

Injury to students off campus. In addition to requiring teachers to hold students strictly accountable for their conduct on the playground and at recess, Education Code Section 44807 extends the responsibility to students going to and from school. But it does not mean that teachers must supervise students on their way to and from school, for clearly this would be an impossibility when students are not riding school buses. Rather, it is intended to give teachers the authority to discipline students who misbehave on the way to and from school (e.g., the grudge fight that occurs on the way home).

Education Code Section 44808 provides that no school district, city or county board of education, county superintendent of schools, or their officers or employees shall be responsible or liable for student conduct and safety off school property *unless* they have undertaken to provide transportation to students to and from school premises, have undertaken a school-sponsored activity off school premises, have otherwise specifically assumed such responsibility or liability, or have failed to exercise reasonable care under the circumstances. If transportation is provided, it encompasses procedures for providing reasonable care to students boarding or exiting the vehicle (*Eric M. v. Cajon Valley Union School District*, 2009). The Education Code provision of "or have failed to exercise reasonable care under the circumstances" generally has been construed as pertaining to one of the previously listed undertakings. Only a few courts have viewed it as an independent source of liability. When a school district assumes responsibility for students when they are off campus, the statute provides that the district, board, or employee is liable or responsible for the conduct or safety of the student only when the student is or should be under the immediate and direct supervision of an employee.

A number of cases have focused on the application of Section 44808. One of the earliest dealt with a student who decided to play hooky from summer school and left without anyone's knowledge (*Hoyem v. Manhattan Beach City School District*, 1978). The student was struck by a motorcycle at an intersection and seriously injured. Was the district liable? The district claimed that it was not because the accident happened off campus, and it had not assumed responsibility for students when they were off campus. In this case, the California Supreme Court recognized that while school districts are not insurers of their students' safety, they do have a legal duty to exercise reasonable care in supervising students. The court avoided the problem of deciding how much supervision a district must bear for off-campus behavior. Here, the problem was whether the district had exercised reasonable care in preventing students from leaving school in the first place. The court sent the case back to the trial court to determine whether the district had exercised the degree of care that a reasonable person would have exercised in the same circumstances. The district tried to argue that its duty to supervise a voluntary summer school should be less than during the regular school year, but the court rejected the assertion. The judges observed:

Since at least the days of Huck Finn and Tom Sawyer, adults have been well aware that children are often tempted to wander off from school, and a jury might well conclude that defendants could have reasonably foreseen that this temptation might be especially strong during the summer session when a student's friends might not be in school (p. 8).

More recent cases have limited district liability under this section. In one, a teacher who was driving home from school encountered some of his students along the way (*Torsiello v. Oakland Unified School District*, 1987). When he stopped to talk to them, one of the students climbed on the rear bumper of the teacher's van and was injured when the teacher drove off. The court found that the teacher had not assumed responsibility for the off-campus conduct of the students and thus the district was not liable. In another case, school officials strongly encouraged a student to attend a nonprofit summer camp in the Sequoia National Forest for low-income, at-risk students (*Ramirez v. Long Beach Unified School District*, 2002). The school district provided applications and general information about the camp. The school superintendent was a camp board member. The youth's mother repeatedly asked about camp safety and was ensured by school personnel that the camp was safe. But the facts indicated otherwise. The youth drowned when swimming during a backpacking outing at the camp. There were no life jackets or other emergency equipment, and camp counselors were not trained in lifesaving techniques. The mother sued the school district. The school district was judged not liable under Section 44808 because the camp program was not a school-sponsored activity. While the district may have encouraged his participation, the youth was not required to attend the camp and received no credit for doing so. The school district did not provide transportation or assume responsibility for the youth's safety at the camp. No one at the camp was employed or supervised by the district, and the district did not formulate the camp's program. In 2006, an appellate court upheld the dismissal of the portion of a lawsuit against the Lake Tahoe Unified School District filed by parents of a student who was killed after being struck by a drunk driver when she was crossing a street to reach a designated bus stop (*Bassett v. Lakeside Inn, Inc.*). While the court observed that the superintendent has the authority to designate bus stops and that their location could amount to a dangerous condition of public property as described in the following discussion, Section 44808 limits the district's liability. The student was not on school property when the accident occurred and not under the direct supervision of the school.

Education Code Section 44808.5 exempts districts and employees from liability when high school students are allowed to leave school grounds during the lunch period with parental permission. Another exemption encompasses voluntary field trips and excursions. In addition to describing the conditions under which field trips can be conducted, Education Code Section 35330 specifies that "all persons making the field trip or excursion shall be deemed to have waived all claims against the district, a charter school, or the State of California for injury, accident, illness, or death occurring during or by reason of the field trip or excursion." This provision encompasses lawsuits against school employees acting within the scope of their duties of employment as well (*Casterson v. Superior Court*, 2002). Immunity also applies to any school, district, or county office of education that is a significant participant in the field trip (*Sanchez v. San Diego County Office of Education*, 2010). Education Code Section 35331 requires governing boards conducting field trips and excursions to provide medical and hospital services for participating students. Some districts have parents sign a statement to make them aware of this statute. If the field trip is out of state, all adults, including parents and guardians of participating students, are required to sign a statement waiving such claims.

While district and employee liability are thus restricted when students leave school grounds for lunch and field trips, Education Code Section 48900(s) gives districts the authority to discipline students at these and other times such as going to and from and during school-sponsored activities.

Injury to nonstudents. It is the last day of school, and student exuberance is high at the high school. When the final bell sounds, students flock to their cars. The high school has two parking lots. One is a main lot under adult supervision, and the second is an overflow lot that is not. A car driven by a sixteen-year-old student (who has never been a discipline problem at the school), peels out of the overflow parking lot. The car jumps the curb and strikes a pedestrian who is walking along the sidewalk. The injured pedestrian sues the school district, claiming the district breached its duty to protect him. Is the district liable?

The injured pedestrian, Frederick Hoff, first argued that under common law—meaning the precedents established by the courts over time—a special relationship exists between the school district and the student, Jason Lozano, who was driving the car. This special relationship imposes a duty on school district personnel to protect Hoff from the acts of Lozano. Hoff argued that the district is liable under the Tort Claims Act for its employees' negligence because school personnel failed to supervise Lozano as he exited the parking lot. The California Supreme Court recognized that state law long has imposed a duty on school personnel to supervise the conduct of students at all times on school grounds and to enforce rules and regulations necessary for their protection. The standard of care imposed on school personnel in carrying out this duty is one of ordinary prudence. But the duty runs to protect students, not to nonstudents like Hoff who are injured off campus.

Hoff sought to strengthen his argument by pointing out that the law recognizes a special relationship between parent and child, such that the parent has a duty to protect innocent third parties from foreseeable danger inflicted by the child. Because school officials stand in loco parentis with regard to their students, Hoff contended, they have the same duty. The concept of in loco parentis means, literally, "in place of the parent." Traditionally, the law has recognized that the in loco parentis doctrine gives educators considerable authority to control students at school. The concept has been eroded somewhat as students have gained such rights as freedom of speech and due process. This is particularly true at the secondary school level. Nevertheless, the in loco parentis doctrine remains viable, and Hoff argued here that school employees had breached it by not supervising the overflow parking lot. But the justices did not agree. Parents have a duty to protect third parties from the acts of their children only when there is foreseeable danger and can face liability when they do not do so. Because Lozano had not been a discipline problem at school and school officials had no reason to question his driving ability, there was no in loco parentis responsibility placed on school personnel to protect Hoff from Lozano.

Hoff next contended that the California Education Code requires the district and its employees to supervise students on and off school grounds, and when they are negligent in doing so, the district is liable under the Tort Claims Act for injuries sustained by innocent third parties. Hoff maintained that teenage automobile driving on school grounds is the most dangerous activity that students can engage in and thus is within the ambit of Education Code Section 44807, requiring teachers to supervise students on campus and going to and from school. Because teachers did not supervise Lozano, the district is vicariously liable. The California Supreme Court did not support Hoff's contention, noting that Section 44807 requires teachers to enforce those rules and regulations necessary for the protection of students. It is not intended to protect nonstudents who are not on school property against the risk of injury. Further, Hoff could not rely on this provision to sue the school district directly under the Tort Claims Act for failure to carry out a mandatory duty because Section 44807 places the duty on teachers and not districts.

Hoff additionally argued that the district had assumed responsibility for supervising the main parking lot and thus under Education Code Section 44808 was responsible for student driving into and out of school parking lots. As noted earlier, that provision imposes liability on the district and employees if they have assumed responsibility for student conduct and safety off campus. But the California high court did not agree that supervising the main parking lot signified a district decision to assume responsibility for a student's off-campus conduct. The accident did not happen in the parking lot. In any event, the district had not assumed any responsibility for students driving in the overflow parking lot. Thus, all of Hoff's arguments were rejected (*Hoff v. Vacaville Unified School District*, 1998). His only recourse was to attempt to hold Jason Lozano and his parents responsible.

The *Hoff* decision constitutes an important precedent in California on district liability for injuries sustained by nonstudents. A California court of appeal later relied on *Hoff* to reject a lawsuit against the coach of the Chico High School Ski and Snowboard Team over a snowboarding accident. The accident occurred when an eighteen-year-old member of the team was snowboarding at a high rate of speed down a run at Mammoth Mountain Ski Area. The student allegedly was racing his friends, looking back several times to see where they were, and was unable to swerve before slamming into an adult skier who had just completed the run, causing severe injuries to her. In addition to suing the student, the adult skier sued the coach and the Chico school district, among others. Citing *Hoff*, the appellate court noted that the coach had no reason to think the student required close and direct supervision; the student had never been reckless before. Therefore, the coach owed no duty to protect innocent third parties from injury. Because the coach was immune under the Tort Claim Act, so was the school district under Section 815.2. However, the court ruled that there was a question whether the student had acted recklessly and sent the case back for trial on that issue (*Lackner v. North*, 2006).

These decisions are instructive regarding liability to third parties resulting from the acts of students. First, school authorities have a well-recognized responsibility to supervise and protect students, and if they believe that students are dangerous, the duty extends to protecting third parties. For example, if school officials have reason to believe that a student is alcohol or sleep impaired after attending an all-night prom, they would have a duty under common law as set forth in the *Hoff* decision to prevent the student from driving. Similarly, if the coach in the *Lackner* case had reason to believe that the student would maneuver the snowboard recklessly on the ski slope, the coach would have had a duty to prevent him from doing so. Failure in either case to protect innocent third parties could be viewed as negligence and, if the proximate cause of the injury, could result in liability. Second, if school officials assume responsibility under Education Code Section 44808 for supervising students when they are off campus and then do not exercise reasonable care, they may be liable for injuries sustained by third parties.

Under the Tort Claims Act, school districts and their employees enjoy considerable immunity from liability for injuries sustained by nonstudents who participate in hazardous recreational activities on school premises (Gov't Code § 831.7). This provision is intended to offer protection from lawsuits when members of the public use public facilities after hours, on weekends, or during vacations. The statute defines a hazardous recreational activity as creating a substantial risk of injury to participants or spectators. The statute includes a long list of activities that fall within this definition, including trampolining and sports that involve bodily contact. The statute does not provide immunity from liability if the entity or employee knows about a dangerous condition that cannot be assumed to be inherent in the activity and provides no warning, if a specific fee is charged to engage in the activity, if the structure or equipment is not in good repair, if the public entity or employee recklessly or with gross negligence promotes participation in the activity, or if gross negligence by the entity or employee is the proximate cause of the injury.

Despite the exceptions, the provision does give considerable immunity to both school districts and employees. For example, the Oakland Unified School District was entitled to immunity when Yarber, a member of the public, was injured in an after-hours adult basketball game at a junior high school gymnasium (*Yarber v. Oakland Unified School District*, 1992). Yarber and others had rented the gym and had played there before. He was injured when the impact of another player propelled him against an unpadded concrete wall. He sued the district. The district claimed immunity from liability under the hazardous recreational activity provision. The appellate court agreed with the district, noting that playing basketball in a full-court game is a body contact sport and that being struck by another player and running into obstacles near the court are inherently part of the game. Yarber should have been aware of the unpadded wall, especially because he had played basketball in that gym before. The district was under no obligation to warn him of the hazard.

Dangerous condition of school property. Section 835 of the Tort Claims Act provides that a school district can be liable when a dangerous condition of its property causes injury. The condition must be caused either by the negligence of employees (e.g., failure to install protective guards on shop equipment) or by a known condition that the district did nothing to correct. A case in the latter category involved two elementary students in the Conejo Valley Unified School District who were injured when a car driven by a parent jumped the curb in a parking lot designated as the student pickup area (*Constantinescu v. Conejo Valley Unified School District*, 1993). The parking lot originally had been used as a bus loading zone. It was quite small and badly congested, in part because the school had ended staggered dismissal times. The driver of the car had just spoken with another driver, asking her for room to park. When she returned to her car and began to maneuver it into the space, the car rapidly lurched forward over the curb, striking the students. The parents of the injured students settled their claims against all defendants except the school district, which sought dismissal of the case.

The jury found that the district knew that the pickup area was dangerous but had not taken corrective action. The district was found liable, and it appealed. The California court of appeal affirmed the judgment. The court noted that principals at the school had complained over the years to district officials about hazardous congestion in the parking lot. Two experts had testified that, though no accidents had occurred in the past, the lot was an "accident waiting to happen." Thus, it could be foreseen that the impact of a driver's negligence would be exacerbated because of the congested space. The court wrote, "Where a public entity has actual or constructive notice [i.e., should have known] of a dangerous condition, it has a duty to take reasonable steps to protect the public from the danger even if such dangers are not necessarily created by the entity." Because a special relationship existed between the district and its students requiring a heightened duty to make the school safe, the district was negligent in not erecting barriers or taking other corrective measures (p. 739). Liability over dangerous conditions of school property is particularly likely when children with special needs are involved.

The condition of property must have something to do with the injury for there to be liability under this section of the Tort Claims Act. If the property is merely the site of the injury, no liability will incur. A student who props his bike against the school's chain-link fence so he can climb on it to pick oranges from a tree on the other side and is injured when the bike slips cannot recover damages from the school district because the fence did not constitute a dangerous condition of public property (*Biscotti v. Yuba City Unified School District*, 2007). The court observed, "The lesson learned," is that tort law does not protect [the student] from the consequence of his careless decision" (p. 557).

Conversely, if the condition of property increases the risk of injury, the district may incur liability. The Tort Claims Act provides as much even when the injury occurs on adjacent property not controlled by the school (Gov't Code § 830). An appellate court ruled in 2003 that if an open schoolyard gate encourages students to cross the street at an unguarded crosswalk with a history of "near misses" rather than walk to an intersection with a traffic light some distance away, the school can be liable for injuries sustained when a student is struck by a car in an adjacent crosswalk (*Joyce v. Simi Valley Unified School District*). The principal had ordered the fence opening to facilitate student entry to the junior high school. It would make no difference if the gate itself was not physically defective, or if the driver of the car was negligent. The appeals court upheld a damage award of over $2.8 million against the district.

Some years earlier, another court held that an opening in a school fence through which two boys gained access to the school playground after hours did not subject the school district to liability (*Bartell v. Palos Verdes Peninsula School District*, 1978). Once on the playground, one of the boys was killed when he fell while playing a version of crack-the-whip while on his skateboard. The district was judged not liable because the opening in the fence merely allowed access to the area. The only thing that was dangerous was the activity of the boys. This seems to be a narrow distinction, and different juries and judges may reach different outcomes. In any event, the best way to avoid litigation is to prevent injuries. This could have been accomplished in these cases simply by closing the gate and fixing the hole in the fence.

Waivers of liability. Waivers are only useful when they are explicitly worded. This is the teaching of a 1990 ruling involving the San Diego Unified School District. A high school student was injured during a campus hypnotism show sponsored by the Parent, Teacher, and Student Association (PTSA) at a fund-raiser. The student's father had signed a release form permitting his daughter to participate and waiving all liability against the PTSA, its members, the high school, and the school district. Both the student and her father signed another form indemnifying the hypnotist and any third parties from liability in connection with the show. The student had seen the show the previous year and wanted to participate. During the show, she was injured when she slid from her chair to the floor several times. The court of appeal first ruled that waivers of liability are not contrary to public policy. Without them, many school-sponsored activities and events could not be held at all. While a minor can disaffirm a previously signed contract, such is not the case when the contract is signed on the student's behalf by her parent. In this case, there was a binding agreement. However, the wording was vague. There was no language regarding bodily injury or negligence. Nor was there any language indicating that the child could not recover for bodily injury. Given the ambiguity in the agreement, the district could not rely on it to have the case dismissed. The matter was returned for trial (*Hohe v. San Diego Unified School District*).

For a waiver to be valid, the person signing it must be aware of what is being given up. This poses a challenge to drafters. As the court noted in the *Hohe* case:

A valid release must be simple enough for a layman to understand and additionally give notice of its impact. A draftsman of such a release faces two difficult choices. His Scylla is the sin of oversimplification and his Charybdis a whirlpool of convoluted language which purports to give notice of everything but as a practical matter buries its message in minutiae (p. 650).

What was missing from the *Hohe* waiver was an explicit indication that both the parent and the daughter were giving up the right to sue, even if the sponsors and actors were negligent and the student physically injured as a result.

Counselors and the duty to warn. In 1976, the California Supreme Court issued an important decision that has implications for counselors and psychologists. In *Tarasoff v. Regents of the University of California*, the court had to consider the extent to which confidentiality protects the doctor–patient relationship. The case involved a lover's quarrel between two students at the University of California at Berkeley. The situation confronted health officials at the institution with a difficult choice. They could maintain confidentiality with the male student, who said he intended to kill his girlfriend, or they could break the confidentiality and warn the intended victim. They chose not to warn the girlfriend. Two months later, the boyfriend murdered Tatiana Tarasoff. The girl's parents sued the doctors and the university. The university and the health officials asserted they owed no duty of reasonable care to Tarasoff and were thus immune from liability under the Tort Claims Act. A majority of the justices disagreed, ruling that when a therapist knows or should know that his patient presents a serious danger of harm to another person, the therapist has a duty to use reasonable care to protect the intended victim from harm. The cloak of confidentiality between doctor and patient cannot insulate the therapist from liability. As the court noted, "The protective privilege ends where the public peril begins" (p. 27).

Education Code Section 49600 specifies the functions of certificated school counselors. Included among them are student personal and social counseling. In these instances, students often reveal sensitive information. Are counselors protected by a shield of confidentiality, or can they be liable for not disclosing information that may pose a threat to others? Education Code Section 49602 delineates what must be kept confidential and what must be revealed. The statute provides that personal information disclosed by a student who is twelve years old or older is confidential and that the counselor is not to be subjected to any civil or criminal liability for nondisclosure. The same is true of confidential information disclosed to the counselor by a parent or guardian of a student who is twelve years old or older. Information is not to become part of the student's record without written consent of the person who disclosed it and may not be revealed to anyone.

The statute then goes on to list exceptions to nondisclosure. They include reporting of child abuse or neglect, communication between the counselor and psychotherapists or other health providers for student referral purposes, and disclosure to persons specified in a written waiver signed by the student and kept in the student's file. Two exceptions to confidentiality specifically track the *Tarasoff* ruling. The first permits reporting information to the principal or parents of the student when the counselor has reasonable cause to believe that disclosure is necessary to avert a clear and present danger to the student or other persons in the school community. The second permits disclosure to the principal, the student's parents, or other persons outside the school when the student indicates that a crime involving personal injury or significant property loss has been or will be committed. However, the statute prohibits disclosure of information to the parents of the student when the counselor has cause to believe that the disclosure would result in a clear and present danger to the health, safety, or welfare of the student. Note that disclosure is left to counselor discretion. The California attorney general has advised that if a counselor opts not to disclose the information about student pregnancy-related or abortion-related information to the parent or school principal and the student later suffers harm, the counselor is not liable for negligence under the Tort Claims Act. Nor is the school district vicariously liable. Conversely, if the counselor does notify the parent or school principal, doing so does not violate the student's privacy rights (94 Ops. Att. Gen. 111, 2011). The statute does require school counselors to disclose confidential information to law enforcement agencies pursuant to a court order when necessary to aid in the investigation of a crime or for purposes of testifying in an administrative or judicial proceeding.

It is important to note that the federal Family Educational Rights and Privacy Act provides that disclosure of personally identifiable information about students and their families for health or safety emergency reasons does not violate the act. In addition, California Civil Code Section 48.8 provides immunity from defamation liability for reporting information to a public or private school official that a person has threatened to use a firearm or other deadly weapon on school property. Liability occurs only if there is clear and convincing evidence that the report was made with knowledge of its falsity or with reckless disregard for the truth or falsity.

In 2013, two male high school students in the Grossmont Union High School District reported to a school counselor that they were being verbally and physically abused by their mother (*Cuff v. Grossmont Union High School District*). Some years before, the mother had been given sole legal and physical custody of the two boys. Later, she had allowed the father to move back into the home so he could take care of the sons while she was at work. In accord with the Child Abuse and Neglect

Reporting Act (CANRA), the school counselor as a mandated reporter submitted a child abuse report to Child Welfare Services and to the school's resources officer based on what the boys had told her. According to the counselor, she was advised to give a copy of the child abuse report to the boys' father, who had transported the boys to school, and to allow the father to take the boys to the sheriff's department. The father instead took the boys and the report to the courthouse where he sought to be awarded custody of his sons. The family court later rejected his claim, affirming the mother's right to sole legal and physical custody. Subsequently, the mother sued both the school counselor and the school district under the Tort Claims Act, alleging a violation of her right to privacy under CANRA when the counselor gave the boys' father a copy of the child abuse report. The trial court dismissed the lawsuit, and the mother appealed.

The court of appeal overruled the trial court, pointing out that in the interest of privacy protection, the CANRA expressly prohibits a mandatory reporter from disclosing a suspected child abuse report to someone like the boys' father who is not one of the individuals or entities identified in Section 11167.5 of the Penal Code. Thus, the counselor was not exercising discretion under Section 820.2 of the Tort Claims Act when she released the suspected child abuse report to the boys' father. The appellate court also ruled that the trial court's granting summary judgment to the school district was improper because the district could be vicariously liable for the counselor's conduct under Section 815.2 of the Tort Claims Act.

A word about insurance. Education Code Section 35208 requires school districts to secure liability insurance for themselves, their board members, and their employees for personal injury, property damage, and death. In lieu of securing insurance, districts can provide protection from their own funds. One way or another, employees are indemnified when they are acting within the scope of their duties of employment. Additionally, Section 32220 and following sections require school districts to ensure that members of athletic teams have specified amounts of insurance protection for medical and hospital expenses resulting from accidental bodily injuries, including those experienced while being transported to and from athletic events under the auspices of the district or a student body organization. The term *athletic team* includes team members, school bands, cheerleaders, team managers, and others involved in athletic activities, but it does not include student rooting sections or spectators unless the district so chooses. The expense of the insurance is to be paid by the district, funds of the student body, or parents, guardians, or other persons. However, if parents, guardians, or persons having charge of an athletic team are not able to pay the costs, then districts assume this responsibility. Section 32221.5 requires a written notice regarding insurance sent to members of school athletic teams to include a statement regarding no-cost or low-cost local, state, or federally sponsored health insurance programs. If 15 percent or more of the covered groups speak a primary language other than English, the notice must be translated in accord with Education Code Section 48985.

An area of particular concern to administrators and teachers is transporting students in private automobiles to and from school events. If an accident occurs due to the negligence of the school employee, is the district or the employee liable? The first question is whether the school employee is acting within his or her scope of employment when the accident occurred. If not, then the school employee's insurance company will have to pay; or, if the insurance coverage is inadequate, the employee personally will be responsible. For example, a teacher would have a difficult time arguing that he was acting within the scope of his duties of employment when driving students to school as part of a neighborhood carpool or transporting students to their homes from a movie theater on a Saturday night.

But suppose a teacher is transporting students in his car to a school event in compliance with an administrative directive to do so. As the result of negligent driving, the teacher's car strikes a pedestrian, causing serious injury. Can the teacher seek indemnification from the school district when the pedestrian files suit? The California Insurance Code requires that California drivers must carry liability insurance. Thus, the teacher is protected by his own insurance, subject to policy limits. The teacher also is protected by the school district's insurance because every school district must provide insurance for its employees. Section 11580.9 of the Insurance Code specifies that when two or more policies provide coverage for the same vehicle, the owner's policy is the primary insurer and the other policy or policies are secondary. Thus, in our hypothetical, the teacher's insurance will bear the initial burden and, if the settlement or judgment is more than the policy limit, the school district's insurance will provide the remainder. Nothing precludes the school district from satisfying its obligations under the Tort Claims Act in this way. Districts routinely advise employees to make sure that they have adequate liability insurance coverage for their vehicles and to advise their insurance companies that the vehicle might be used while on the job.

Recall that the Tort Claims Act also requires the school district to defend the employee in any legal action as well, as long as the employee is acting within the scope of employment. Where liability involves motor vehicles, the Insurance Code provides that defense costs are shared between the primary and secondary insurers. If the employee is not acting within the scope of employment, then the district has no responsibility either to defend the employee or to pay any judgment. Sometimes there may be a dispute about this, and the district's legal representative may decline to represent the employee. In this event, the employee will have to shoulder his or her own legal costs through a personal or professional insurance policy or through personal funds. As a matter of preventive action, it is always wise to check on the extent of insurance coverage under both personal and district policies before accidents happen and to make any necessary adjustments.

Fair Employment and Housing Act

As we discussed in Chapter 5, the California Fair Employment and Housing Act (FEHA) prohibits a broad range of discrimination and harassment in public and private employment. After exhausting the administrative remedies specified in the statute, victims can sue both employers and individual employees for money damages.

The California Supreme Court discussed the relationship between FEHA and the Tort Claims Act in a 1995 decision involving a superintendent whose contract was not extended by a 3–2 vote. Based on newspaper reports, he alleged that one of three board members voted as he did because the superintendent was not Hispanic or Latino. The superintendent also alleged that the other two voted for termination of his contract because he was sixty-six years old. If the allegations were true, it is hard to imagine a clearer case of impermissibly motivated personnel decision making.

The California high court first noted that the common law, in the form of judicial precedent, long has provided government officials broad immunity from lawsuits so that they have maximum discretion to make policy decisions without fear of liability. Votes by members of the school board whether to renew the contract of a superintendent fall into this category. The court then turned to the question of whether FEHA overrides the grant of immunity in Section 820.2 of the Tort Claims Act. That section conveys immunity to employees for discretionary acts "except as otherwise provided by statute." Board members are entitled to the same immunity. Because FEHA is a statute that prohibits the very kinds of reasons allegedly used by the three school board members, the superintendent argued that he could sue each of the board members individually. The justices did not agree. For this to be the case, the legislature would have had to include language in FEHA specifying that its provisions revoke the immunity provided in Section 820.2 for discretionary acts. Because there is no such indication in FEHA, the immunity provision of the Tort Claims Act protects the three board members in their individual capacities from the lawsuit. However, the court observed that, although the board members are immune, the school district itself likely could be sued because FEHA specifically states that both private and public *employers* can be held accountable for violating its terms (*Caldwell v. Montoya*, 1995). However, the justices did not decide the question of district liability because the issue was not before them.

Caldwell, the superintendent, subsequently did pursue litigation against the school district under FEHA (*Caldwell v. Paramount Unified School District*, 1995). The jury concluded that the board members were motivated by legitimate job-related reasons for not renewing his contract. Caldwell appealed once again, but the appellate court sustained the jury verdict. Aside from clarification of how FEHA affects the liability of school board members, the extensive litigation evident in the *Caldwell* case is a good illustration of why employers should avoid any reliance on, or even mention of, impermissible reasons for negative employment decisions. The focus should always be on job-related deficiencies.

LIABILITY UNDER FEDERAL LAW

Earlier in this book, we briefly examined the extent of liability under various federal statutes. Chapter 1 contains a chart describing the major federal laws impacting public schools and the consequences for violating them (see Table 1.1). We discussed federal statutes pertaining to employment discrimination in Chapter 5, federal disability law in Chapter 8, and racial and sexual harassment in Chapter 11. Here we discuss liability of schools and school employees under a well-known civil rights law, 42 United States Code (U.S.C.) Section 1983.

Liability of Schools Under 42 U.S.C. Section 1983

Personal injury and property damage cases are routinely the province of state courts. Aside from actions regarding disputes between citizens from different states involving at least $75,000 in controversy, the jurisdiction of federal courts is limited to federal wrongs. These fall primarily into the categories of violations of the U.S. Constitution and federal statutes. In Chapter 1 and elsewhere, many federal statutes have provisions describing how violations are to be addressed and what remedies are available. However, such is not the case for provisions of the federal Constitution. To bring federal wrongs committed by states and their political subdivisions within the jurisdiction of the federal courts, Congress enacted a key civil rights act after the Civil War. This statute, 42 U.S.C. Section 1983, provides that

Every person who, under color of any statute, ordinance, regulation, custom, or usage, of any State or Territory ... subjects, or causes to be subjected, any citizen of the United States or other person within the jurisdiction thereof to the deprivation of any rights, privileges, or immunities secured by the Constitution and laws, shall be liable to the party injured in an action at law, suit in equity, or other proper proceeding for redress [in federal court] ...

Section 1983, as it is commonly called, enables those who believe they are the victims of federal wrongs committed by persons employed by the government to bypass state courts and bring their claims directly to federal court. It is the primary basis for lawsuits involving alleged violation of federal constitutional rights such as freedom of speech and right to due process.

In an early decision, the U.S. Supreme Court interpreted the term *person* as used in the first part of Section 1983 to encompass municipalities. Thus, in most states the meaning of a "person" encompasses a public school district, as well as the individuals it employs, such as administrators, teachers, custodians, and the like, who are functioning in their official capacities. Likewise, charter schools as newly created mini-school districts are considered "persons" and thus subject to suit, as are their employees. At the same time, states themselves are immune from liability under the Eleventh Amendment to the U.S. Constitution. That amendment prevents states from being sued in federal court by citizens from other states or their own citizens without state permission, unless Congress has abrogated the immunity. Congress has not done so in Section 1983.

Unlike school districts in other states, California school districts are not considered municipalities under Section 1983 and cannot be sued under this statute. The U.S. Court of Appeals for the Ninth Circuit ruled in 1992 that California school districts are an arm of the state and thus immune under the Eleventh Amendment from federal claims (*Belanger v. Madera Unified School District*). The *Belanger* case involved a school principal who was reassigned to classroom teaching. She filed a Section 1983 lawsuit against the district, claiming she was denied equal protection of the laws because of her gender and was the victim of retaliation for testifying against the district in another gender discrimination lawsuit. Because the state controls school district funding as a result of the *Serrano v. Priest* equalization litigation and Proposition 13, as discussed in some detail in Chapter 3, the court noted that any judgment against the school district would have to be paid out of what essentially is a state fund. Second, while public schooling is generally considered a municipal function, this is not true in California. The court cited provisions of the California Constitution and the Education Code giving the state great control over the operations of school districts. The court also noted a California Supreme Court decision, *Hall v. City of Taft,* recognizing public schools as "a matter of statewide rather than local or municipal concern."

For all these reasons, the judges concluded that California school districts are not political subdivisions for purposes of Section 1983 but rather agents of the state performing central governmental functions. Because Congress did not abrogate state Eleventh Amendment immunity in enacting Section 1983, the lawsuit was dismissed due to lack of federal jurisdiction. Whether California charter schools, which are less subject to state control, might be similarly immune remains unclear.

In 1999, the Ninth Circuit revisited the question, this time in a case involving a suit in federal court against the Oakland school district based on allegations of a denial of rights protected by the California Fair Employment and Housing Act (FEHA). Once again, the Ninth Circuit refused to let the lawsuit continue because the Eleventh Amendment barred the claim (*Freeman v. Oakland Unified School District*). There was no indication that either California or Congress had abrogated the state's immunity from a FEHA lawsuit filed in federal court. However, the Ninth Circuit did note that the plaintiff could refile his claim in state court. This assumes, of course, that the period of time during which such a lawsuit can be filed had not ended while the federal action was underway.

The Ninth Circuit has ruled that neither the Local Control Funding Formula (LCFF) nor the Local Control and Accountability Plan (LCAP) that changed the way public schools and county offices of education are funded (see the discussion above in the update for Chapter 3). Thus Eleventh Amendment immunity from lawsuits under 42 U.S.C. Section 1983 continues (*Sato v. Orange County Dept. of Education*, 2017).

While the Eleventh Amendment bars lawsuits for damages against California school districts under Section 1983, it does not preclude courts from issuing court orders defining rights and legal relationships (known as declaratory judgments) or requiring or halting actions (known as injunctions). Attorneys' fees associated with such lawsuits also are not barred by the Eleventh Amendment (*Williams v. Vidmar*, 2005). And it is important to note that Congress can abrogate state Eleventh Amendment immunity under the Fourteenth Amendment, which prohibits states from denying persons of life, liberty, or property without due process of law and of equal protection of the laws. Congress has done so in statutes such as Section 504 of the 1973 Rehabilitation Act, Title VI of the 1964 Civil Rights Act against racial discrimination, and Title IX of the 1972 Education Amendments against gender discrimination.

Liability of School Employees Under 42 U.S.C. Section 1983

If a school district cannot be sued in federal court for federal wrongs under Section 1983, what about individual employees? When a lawsuit is filed against the employee in the employee's official capacity, that amounts to suing the district directly. Employees act in their official capacity when they are carrying out school district policies and administrative procedures. And because school districts are immune under the Eleventh Amendment, so too are employees in this instance.

However, public employees can be sued in their individual, as contrasted with their official, capacity under Section 1983. And in this instance, immunity is less certain. Employees are sued in their individual capacities when they stray beyond district policy and administrative procedures. Consider this situation. A school administrator routinely uses force to maintain discipline. In one instance, he slaps a student across the mouth and grabs him by the neck after the student said what the administrator thought was "Heil Hitler." The student, who is hospitalized, reports the incident to the police. The administrator pleads guilty to assault and battery and is placed on probation. Later, the administrator punches a student who was making noise during a special program held at the half-time of a basketball game; he throws another student into the lockers when he spots the student wearing a hat. The three students file a Section 1983 lawsuit against the school administrator, seeking damages.

Though federal courts have discretion in deciding whether a recognized federal right is at stake before moving directly to grant immunity, quite often the first question centers on the nature of the right at issue. If there is no recognized federal right, then the case will go nowhere. In some instances, stating the right is easy. As we have seen, students have rights to freedom of speech, religious exercise, and due process, among others. In other instances, identifying the right may be more difficult. Is there a constitutional right to be free from being handled in a physical manner, as described above? In the case from which these facts were taken, the Ninth Circuit recognized that there is a Fourteenth Amendment liberty right to be free from injury inflicted by a school official. This right is clearly established, originating with the 1977 U.S. Supreme Court decision involving the use of corporal punishment (*Ingraham v. Wright*). The Court ruled in that case that "where school authorities, acting under color of state law, deliberately decide to punish a child for misconduct by restraining the child and inflicting appreciable physical pain, we hold that Fourteenth Amendment liberty interests are implicated" (p. 674). Citing that ruling, the Ninth Circuit recognized that the students' right to be free from physical attacks is well recognized.

The U.S. Supreme Court has ruled that a public official is entitled to immunity unless the official knew or should have known that his actions would violate a clearly recognized federal right (*Harlow v. Fitzgerald*, 1982). Applying this test, the Ninth Circuit concluded that the administrator knew or should have known that his excessive use of force violated the students' clearly recognized constitutional right to be free from harm. Therefore, he was not entitled to qualified immunity (*P.B. v. Koch*, 1996).

A few years later, the Ninth Circuit ruled that a vice principal's taping an elementary student's head to a tree for five minutes because the student would not stop misbehaving constituted a violation of the student's well-recognized Fourth Amendment right to be free from unreasonable seizures (*Doe v. Hawaii Department of Education*, 2003). This being the case, the school official was not entitled to qualified immunity under Section 1983. In 2007 the Ninth Circuit relied on its analysis in *P.B. v. Koch* to hold that a special education teacher who slaps a four-year-old disabled child repeatedly and slams the child into a chair violates the child's constitutional right to be free from excessive force (*Preschooler II v. Clark County School Board of Trustees*). Because a special education teacher should know that such actions contravene the heightened protections for these children, the teacher is not entitled to qualified immunity from a Section 1983 lawsuit. Nor are school officials who permitted such acts to occur.

However, parents likely cannot use Section 1983 to sue for money damages when allegations are made that IDEA provisions have been violated. The Ninth Circuit ruled as much in a 2007 case involving a parent who sought to link Section 1983 with IDEA so she could receive compensation for lost income and the emotional distress of advocating for IDEA benefits for her son (*Blanchard v. Morton School District*). The appellate judges held that Section 1983 cannot be used in combination with IDEA, because IDEA is a sufficiently comprehensive statute and provides its own remedies (e.g., compensatory education, reimbursement for private school expenses). In a later ruling, the Ninth Circuit ruled that even a Section 1983 claim of nominal damages—usually a dollar—also is precluded under IDEA for the same reason (*C.O. v. Portland Public Schools*, 2012). Nominal damages are used to establish a viable legal claim that rights have been violated though there has been no financial loss. Note, however, that if a Section 1983 claim is not anchored in IDEA, as is the case with the *Preschooler II* case already described, then monetary damages may be sought.

Though normally a matter of state law, occasionally litigation arises in federal court under Section 1983 against school districts and personnel over injuries inflicted on a student by other students or outsiders who come on to the campus.

The argument is that the victims have a liberty right under the due process clause of the Fourteenth Amendment to be free from harm inflicted by third parties. However, to avoid having personal injury cases flooding federal courts, judges have construed this claim very narrowly. The U.S. Supreme Court has ruled that when a state confines someone in a state facility on a twenty-four-hour basis, then the state does have a special relationship with the person and is required under the due process clause to protect the person from injury inflicted by third parties. This is known as the "special relationship" exception. However, courts have not applied the special relationship exception to public schools, given that they are not custodial institutions like mental health facilities and prisons that deprive persons of their liberty. The U.S. Court of Appeals for the Ninth Circuit refused to do so in a case involving sexual acts by two developmentally disabled students in a Washington State high school bathroom (*Patel v. Kent School District*, 2011). The mother of the female student, A.H., argued that one of her daughter's teachers had not followed a provision of the student's IEP requiring the student to be supervised at all times including while in bathrooms. The teacher believed that the student needed to transition to using a bathroom on her own and allowed her to do so in the bathroom next to the teacher's classroom. Later, the teacher discovered that the male student had left the classroom shortly after A.H. and found the pair in the bathroom. She escorted A.H. back to the classroom and informed school officials and A.H.'s mother.

The Ninth Circuit also rejected the mother's argument that the teacher had placed the student in danger and was deliberately indifferent to her safety. This is known as the "state-created danger" exception to the absence of a Fourteenth Amendment requirement to protect individuals from third parties. Here, the judges noted that the teacher had regularly sought to protect A.H. The teacher provided feedback to school officials and to A.H.'s mother, and she had spoken with both A.H. and the male student about hugging in the hallway. When she noticed that the male student had left the classroom shortly after A.H., she rushed to the bathroom. Thus, the teacher had not acted with deliberate indifference. At worst, she had committed a lapse of judgment when she allowed A.H. to use the next-door bathroom on her own. The matter was dismissed from federal court. The mother was free to file a tort claim in state court.

As we noted in Chapter 11, students have a recognized right to be free from both racial and sexual harassment under Title VI of the 1964 Civil Rights Act and Title IX of the 1972 Education Amendments, respectively. Lawsuits under these statutes are filed against school entities. Section 1983 opens up lawsuits against school employees, including those working in charter schools. A 2003 ruling from the Ninth

Circuit conveys good insight into the application of Section 1983 in this context (*Flores v. Morgan Hill Unified School District*, 2003). The case involved same-sex student-on-student sexual harassment. Students who either were or were perceived to be lesbian, gay, or bisexual sued school officials in the Morgan Hill Unified School District for responding ineffectively to repeated harassment over a number of years. They alleged that teachers and administrators failed to stop name-calling and antigay remarks and that administrators responded to physical abuse with inadequate disciplinary action. The judges ruled that the Fourteenth Amendment's equal protection clause has been construed in the Ninth Circuit as early as 1990 to protect persons from harassment based on their sexual orientation.

Accordingly, school district antiharassment policies had to be enforced against peer harassment of homosexual and bisexual students in the same manner as against peer harassment of heterosexual students. The court found that not only had the named school officials taken ineffective action to stop the harassment, they also lacked an effective training program on how to deal with sexual orientation discrimination. The court ruled that there was sufficient evidence for a jury to conclude that the school officials intentionally discriminated against the students in violation of the equal protection clause, and therefore the officials were not entitled to qualified immunity.

Can a supervisor be liable for a subordinate's violation of federal rights in a Section 1983 lawsuit? The answer is yes, if the supervisor knew or should have known about the acts and failed to stop them. This is the teaching of a 1998 Ninth Circuit ruling involving a sixth grader whose student teacher allegedly fondled, kissed, straddled, and otherwise inappropriately touched her and other girls in the class (*Oona R.S. by Kate S. v. McCaffrey*, 1995). Boys in the class also were alleged to have engaged in harassment. The parents sought to have the student teacher removed from the class, but they maintained the principal declined to do so. The parents claimed the classroom teacher did not stop the harassment but did retaliate against the student by lowering her grade and depriving her of awards she had won. The teacher, principal, and director of elementary education sought dismissal of the claims against them. The Ninth Circuit first observed that a public school student has a clearly recognized right under federal law to be free from sexual abuse and harassment. Accordingly, "a supervisor may be found liable under [Section] 1983 if the supervisor is 'aware of a specific risk of harm to the plaintiff.'" Here, the teacher, principal, and director of elementary education were all in a supervisory capacity over the student teacher. They all had a duty to take action to protect students from the student teacher's sexual harassment and discrimination. Thus, they were not entitled to qualified immunity.

The lesson of these cases is quite clear. Because school personnel can be held liable in their individual capacities when federal rights are violated, it is wise to learn what these rights are and to act expeditiously to protect them.

SUMMARY

The California Tort Claims Act conveys broad immunity to school districts and their employees but does not apply to private schools and their employees. How the Act applies to charter schools has not yet been definitively determined. As a general rule, neither the school district nor the employee is liable when the employee is using appropriate discretion in carrying out his or her duties. However, if the employee is not exercising appropriate discretion while acting within the scope of employment when an injury occurs, the district bears the liability. This is particularly true where the law imposes a duty on school employees to ensure student safety. For this reason, districts carry insurance. An exception is when the employee is not acting within the scope of employment. In these instances, the employee alone will face liability. Clearly, the implication for employees is to carry out their responsibilities conscientiously. The implication for school districts is to make sure that school employees know what their job requirements are and that they follow school district policies and regulations in carrying them out. This is particularly true when there is a mandatory duty under the law because the district bears liability if the duty is not performed. The best example of a clearly established mandatory duty is the duty to supervise and protect students. However, that duty is mitigated somewhat in the context of athletic events because courts have ruled that students themselves must assume the risk of participating.

The school district's duty under the Tort Claims Act to protect innocent third parties from the actions of students arises only when the district has assumed the responsibility or when district officials have reason to believe that students could pose a harm to others. In either event, it must be established that the district's action constituted the proximate cause of the nonstudent's injury for there to be liability. Concern about injury to nonstudents is most apt to arise when counselors receive sensitive information from students and when students are attending school-sponsored activities off campus. The California Education Code requires disclosure of information from students that could harm others. Care must be taken in arranging school-sponsored activities so that student safety is assured and innocent third parties are protected.

A school district also bears liability under the Tort Claims Act for injuries caused by a dangerous condition of its property that it knew about but did not fix or that resulted from the negligence of its employees. Consequently, school personnel should make certain that school grounds and equipment are safe. At the same time, the Tort Claims Act provides considerable protection to school districts and their employees from liability for injuries sustained by nonstudents participating in hazardous recreational activities on school premises. Often, districts and district personnel try to ward off the threat of liability through the use of waivers. However, unless very carefully worded, waivers are not foolproof. While districts routinely provide insurance for school personnel, employees may choose to add personal coverage as well, because it may be needed in the case of injuries caused by their negligent use of an automobile or when they are determined to have acted outside the scope of employment.

Though judicial rulings have indicated that racial or sexual harassment committed by a school employee may not be actionable under the Tort Claims Act because it is not encompassed within the scope of employment, liability may be imposed on both the school district and the employee under other state laws. In particular, as we have seen in earlier chapters, California's Unruh Civil Rights Act and Fair Employment and Housing Act provide remedies for a wide range of discriminatory actions. Discrimination based on sexual preference and identity is encompassed within the terms of both. Further, the school district may be liable under the Tort Claims Act for its negligence in not having a well-designed hiring process that would screen out employees who pose a danger to students. This also carries implications for the writing of employment recommendations, because nondisclosure of facts when there is a foreseeable danger of harm may result in liability for both the writers and the schools that employ them.

Federal law provides an avenue of redress for wrongs involving federal constitutional and statutory rights. However, school districts are immune from many of these lawsuits, given the interpretation of a major federal civil rights statute by the U.S. Court of Appeals for the Ninth Circuit. How this applies to charter schools awaits a future ruling. Public school employees, including those in charter schools who are sued as individuals acting on their own, are not entitled to the same immunity if it is established that they knew or should have known that their actions would violate clearly recognized federal rights. Among these are freedom of speech, free exercise of religion, due process, and the right to be free from sexual abuse.

School districts are not immune from liability for racial and sexual harassment. As we noted in Chapter 11, Title VI of the 1964 Civil Rights Act and Title IX of the 1972 Education Amendments provide that the district's federal funding can be curtailed and that the victims of harassment and abuse can sue the district for damages. In addition, 42 U.S.C. Section 1983 permits lawsuits against individuals who committed the acts and even against their supervisors. Given the sanctions under both state and federal law for racial and sexual harassment, it is essential that both school districts and employees make every effort to avoid such situations.

In the end, the key to avoiding liability is to practice effective preventive action. This means knowing and following the law, complying with recognized ethical standards, and using common sense. Because one cannot be assured that a lawsuit or even a valid claim will never arise, it is also important to have adequate insurance protection.

APPENDIX A

GLOSSARY OF LEGAL TERMINOLOGY

The words and definitions in this glossary are intended to help the lay reader better understand some of the terminology used in this book, in judicial decisions, in legal memoranda, and in other materials on school law. We have included the legal terms the reader is most likely to encounter. For a more extensive list, consult Bryan A. Garner, ed., *Black's Law Dictionary. Abridged*, 8th ed. (see Appendix C).

actual damages The amount awarded to the prevailing plaintiff for out-of-pocket losses such as hospital expenses (compare *compensatory damages* and *punitive damages*).

agency fee A service fee that employees must pay to the union once a collective bargaining agent has been recognized as the exclusive representative of the employees in a bargaining unit, if the employees do not wish to become dues-paying members of the union.

amicus curiae "Friend of the court"; a person or organization allowed to appear in a lawsuit, usually to file arguments in the form of a brief supporting one side or the other, even though not a party to the dispute.

appellant The party appealing a court's decision (compare *plaintiff*).

appellee The party opposing an appeal of a court's decision (see *defendant*).

attorneys' fees Refers to the practice of according the winning party's costs to the losing party in a civil case. The 1976 Civil Rights Attorneys' Fees Awards Act gives courts this power in civil rights suits.

back pay Lost wages that must be paid to employees who have been illegally discharged or laid off.

cause of action A legal claim.

certiorari A writ issued by a court asking the lower court to submit the record in a case, thus indicating the willingness of the higher court to entertain the appeal; "cert." for short.

civil case Every lawsuit other than a criminal proceeding. Most civil cases involve a lawsuit brought by one person against another and usually concern money damages.

civil liberties Fundamental individual freedoms that are constitutionally protected. Provisions listed in the Bill of Rights of the U.S. Constitution, such as freedom of speech and religious exercise, are considered civil liberties.

civil rights Rights that provide access to the legal system and equitable treatment before the law. Civil rights can be provided by a constitution or action of a legislative body. Thus, one is entitled to freedom from discrimination based on race, color, religion, sex, or national origin in public and private employment by provisions of Title VII of the 1964 Civil Rights Act.

class action A lawsuit brought by one person on behalf of him- or herself and all other persons in the same situation.

code A collection of laws. The California Education Code is a grouping of state statutes affecting education.

collective bargaining The negotiating process for reaching an agreement pertaining to wages, hours, and other terms and conditions of employment between management and labor. In California, collective bargaining for public school employees is conducted in accord with the provisions of the Educational Employment Relations Act.

common law Law that develops by custom and is given expression through court rulings. Many student and teacher rights have developed this way, as has the tort of personal privacy invasion. Many common-law principles have been incorporated into legislative enactments (statutes).

compensatory damages An amount awarded to the plaintiff to compensate for pain and suffering.

complaint The first main paper filed in a civil lawsuit. It includes, among other things, a statement of the wrong or harm supposedly done to the plaintiff by the defendant and a request for specific help from the court. The defendant responds to the complaint by filing an "answer."

contract An agreement that affects the legal relationship between two or more persons. To be a contract, an agreement must involve persons legally capable of making binding agreements, at least one promise, consideration (that is, something of value promised or given), and a reasonable amount of agreement between the persons as to what the contract means.

criminal case A case involving crimes against the laws of the state; unlike civil cases, in criminal cases the state is the prosecuting party.

de facto "In fact, actual"; a situation that exists in fact, whether or not it is lawful. De facto segregation is that which exists regardless of the law or the actions of civil authorities (compare *de jure*).

defamation Impugning a person's character or injuring a person's reputation by false or malicious statements. This includes both *libel* and *slander* (see these terms).

defendant The person against whom a legal action is brought. This legal action may be civil or criminal. At the appeal stage, the party against whom an appeal is taken is known as the "appellee." has won the decision

de jure "Of right"; legitimate; lawful, whether or not in actual fact. De jure segregation is that which is sanctioned by law (compare *de facto*).

de minimis Trivial, small, unimportant, as in, "The matter is sufficiently de minimis that it should not be the subject of a formal lawsuit."

dictum See *obiter dictum*.

disclaimer The refusal to accept certain types of responsibility. For example, a summer school course listing may disclaim any responsibility for guaranteeing that the courses contained therein will actually be offered because courses, programs, and instructors are likely to change without notice.

due process Both the U.S. and California constitutions require that before a governmental entity can deprive a person of life, liberty, or property, due process of law must be provided. *Procedural due process* refers to a set of steps that are designed to elicit truth. They generally consist of notice of wrongdoing, a hearing for the presentation of evidence and of a defense, and a right to appeal to higher authorities. If one's life is at stake, each of these components is quite elaborate. Important liberty and property rights also require formal due process. For example, before a public school employee's contract can be terminated, the governing board must follow a set of formal due process procedures. *Substantive due process* requires that the decision itself must be fair and reasonable. For the due process clauses of the Fifth and Fourteenth Amendments to the U.S. Constitution to come into play, it first must be established that life, liberty, or property rights are implicated. However, the California Constitution due process clauses found in Article I, Section 7 (a) and Section 15 require only a showing that some statutory benefit or entitlement is at stake. The greater the benefit or entitlement, the more formal the due process requirements are.

eminent domain The authority of a governmental entity to claim private property for public use. The government typically has to provide the owner the fair market value of the property. Usually refers to land that the government needs for building roads, erecting schools, and the like.

en banc The hearing of a case by an appellate court in which the full complement of judges assigned to the court, rather than a small panel, presides.

expunge Blot out. For example, a court order requesting that a student's record be expunged of any references to disciplinary action during a particular time period means that the references are to be "wiped off the books" (see also *redact*).

fiduciary A relationship between persons in which one person acts for another in a position of trust. Some courts hold private schools to a fiduciary relationship with students and may intervene if the school has not acted fairly, as, for example, in expelling a student.

forum A place for communication. In the context of the First Amendment to the U.S. Constitution, a *public forum* means a place where First Amendment rights are almost unlimited in their scope, a *limited public forum* allows government some restriction over speakers and content of expression, and a *closed forum* refers to government property traditionally not open to public communication.

grievance An employee complaint concerning wages, hours, or conditions of work; that is, literally anything connected with employment. A grievance system consists of steps by which an individual employee or a group of employees seeks a solution to a complaint. First, the grievance is brought to the attention of the employee's immediate superior. If no satisfactory adjustment is made, the employee may continue to appeal to higher levels. While virtually all collective bargaining agreements contain a grievance system, such systems are also increasingly part of organizational life whether or not a union is present since they afford the means to channel and resolve disputes.

hearing An oral proceeding before a court or quasi-judicial tribunal.

holding The rule of law set forth in a case to answer the issues presented to the court.

informed consent A person's agreement to allow something to happen (such as surgery) that is based on a full disclosure of facts needed to make the decision intelligently. Certain types of student searches are best carried out with informed consent of the student being searched or his or her parents.

infra Later in the article or book. For example, *infra*, p. 235, means to turn to that page, which is further on. Opposite of *supra*.

injunction A court order requiring someone to do something or to refrain from taking some action.

in loco parentis "In place of a parent"; acting as a parent with respect to the care, supervision, and discipline of a child. The development of student rights law has somewhat curtailed, especially at the secondary school level, the traditional view that public school officials stand in loco parentis to students.

ipso facto "By the fact itself"; by the mere fact that.

jurisdiction Right of a court to hear a case; also the geographic area within which a court has the right and power to operate. *Original jurisdiction* means that the court will be the first to hear the case; *appellate jurisdiction* means that the court reviews cases on appeal from lower court rulings.

jurisprudence Philosophy of the law; the rationale for one's legal position.

justiciable Proper for a court to decide. For example, a justiciable controversy is a real dispute that a court may handle.

law Basic rules of order. Constitutional law reflects the basic principles by which government operates. Statutory law consists of laws passed by legislatures and recorded in public documents. Administrative laws are the decisions of administrative agencies, for example, a State Board of Education rule. Judicial law consists of the pronouncements of courts.

libel Written defamation; false and malicious written statements communicated to another, such as by publication, that injure a person's reputation.

litigation A lawsuit or series of lawsuits.

mandamus A court order commanding some official duty to be performed.

mediation The involvement of a neutral third party to facilitate agreement between the parties to a dispute.

moot For the sake of argument; not a case involving a current dispute.

negligence A tort or civil wrong that involves failure to live up to a standard of care, such as reasonableness, when one has a duty to do so, and as a result, someone or something is harmed. Different degrees of negligence trigger different legal penalties.

obiter dictum A digression from the central points of a court's decision; an incidental discussion that does not establish precedent; often shortened to *dictum*, or in the plural, *dicta*.

parens patriae The historical right of all governments to take care of persons under their jurisdiction, particularly minors and incapacitated persons. Thus, states have acted *parens patriae* in establishing public schooling systems for the benefit of all people within their borders.

per curiam An unsigned decision and opinion of a court, as distinguished from one signed by a judge.

petitioner The one bringing an action; similar to *plaintiff*. Opposite of *respondent*.

plaintiff The person who brings a lawsuit against another person. At the appeal stage, the person bringing the appeal is called the "appellant." and is usually the one losing in the lower court action or who disagrees with part of the decision.

plenary Complete or full in all respects; total.

police power The traditional power of governments to establish laws protecting the health, safety, and welfare of its citizens and to enforce them.

precedent A court decision on a question of law that gives authority or direction on how to decide a similar question of law in a later case with similar facts. Ruling by precedent is usually conveyed through the term *stare decisis*.

prima facie "Clear on the face of it"; presumably, a fact that will be considered to be true unless disproved by contrary evidence. For example, a prima facie case is one that will win unless the other side comes forward with different evidence to dispute it.

punitive damages An amount awarded to a person by a court that is over and above the damages actually sustained. Punitive damages are designed to punish the defendant and serve as a deterrent to similar acts in the future. Also termed *exemplary damages* (compare *actual damages* and *compensatory damages*).

quasi-judicial Refers to the case-deciding function of an administrative agency. Thus, a school board is a quasi-judicial body when it holds a formal hearing on a student expulsion case.

redact To delete or blot out. For example, in releasing documents to the public, it may be necessary to redact certain information that would violate student privacy rights (see also *expunge*).

remand To send back; for example, a higher court may send a case back to the lower court, asking that certain action be taken.

res judicata "A thing decided." Thus, if a court decides the case on its merits, the matter is settled and no new lawsuit can be brought on the same subject by the same parties.

respondent The party responding to an action; similar to *defendant*. The opposite of *petitioner*.

right to work Also known as the "open shop," the term is used to apply to laws that ban union-security agreements, such as the union shop, by rendering it illegal to make employment conditional on membership or nonmembership in a labor organization. Unions are particularly opposed to these state laws because they allow what are commonly referred to as "free riders"—those who share in the collective benefit but pay nothing for it.

sectarian Of or relating to religion or a religious sect.

secular Of or relating to worldly concerns; opposite of *sectarian*.

slander Oral defamation; the speaking of false and malicious words to a third party that injure another person's reputation, business, or property rights.

sovereign immunity The government's freedom from being sued for money damages without its consent. California school districts do not enjoy sovereign immunity in that they can be sued in state court under the terms of the California Tort Claims Act. However, they do enjoy immunity from most federal claims because they are considered part of the state, and the state enjoys immunity from suit in federal court under the Eleventh Amendment to the U.S. Constitution.

standing A person's right to bring a lawsuit because he or she is directly affected by the issues raised.

stare decisis "Let the decision stand"; a legal rule that, when a court has decided a case by applying a legal principle to a set of facts, the court should stick by that principle and apply it to all later cases with clearly similar facts unless there is a good, strong reason not to do so. This rule helps promote fairness and reliability in judicial decision making and is inherent in the American legal system (see also *precedent*).

state action Action by the government or an entity closely intertwined with the government. For the Fourteenth Amendment of the U.S. Constitution to apply to a given situation, there must be some involvement by a state or one of its political subdivisions. A public school falls into the latter category. Wholly private action is not covered by the Fourteenth Amendment. Thus, private schools and colleges, like corporate organizations and private clubs, are not subject to its strictures.

statute A law enacted by a legislative body.

summary judgment A decision for one side in a lawsuit rendered before the trial begins. Summary judgment occurs when there is no genuine issue of material fact, and the court can decide the issue as a matter of law.

supra Earlier in an article or book. For example, *supra*, p. 11, means to turn to that page, which appeared earlier. Opposite of *infra*.

tort A civil wrong done by one person to another for which a court may award damages to the person injured. Examples of torts are negligence, battery, and defamation. Lawsuits of this type against California school districts and their employees generally are governed by the terms of the California Tort Claims Act.

trial A process occurring in a court whereby opposing parties present evidence, subject to cross-examination and rebuttal, pertaining to the matter in dispute.

trial de novo A completely new trial ordered by a judge or appeals court; also applied to situations where a higher-level court looks at the case anew rather than relying on findings of the lower court.

ultra vires Going beyond the specifically delegated authority to act; for example, a school board that is by law restricted from punishing students for behavior occurring wholly off campus acts *ultra vires* in punishing a student for behavior observed at a private weekend party.

waiver The means by which a person voluntarily gives up a right or benefit. To be valid, waivers have to be worded very carefully. Thus, in a case where a parent is asked to sign a waiver absolving the school or teacher from liability in the event of an accident to his or her child, waivers must make clear what the parent is giving up, for example, the right to sue *even if* the school or teacher is negligent. Even if parents sign such a knowing waiver, the child may recover damages in his or her own right. The services of an attorney are best secured in drawing up waivers.

APPENDIX B
FINDING AND READING STATUTES AND JUDICIAL DECISIONS

In this book, we describe the law and provide references to key legislative enactments, called statutes, and to court decisions. Some readers may be interested in consulting the statutes and judicial decisions directly. In this appendix, we describe how to do this efficiently and effectively.

STATUTES

Statutes enacted by Congress and the California Legislature can be found in two ways. The first is to consult websites that list them, and the second is to consult printed volumes. The former is preferable because websites are easy to access and updated frequently. A list of several websites for obtaining legal information is contained in Appendix C.

Both federal and California statutes are grouped into codes. The United States Code contains all the laws enacted by Congress. In California, there are a number of codes of relevance to education, including the Penal Code, the Government Code, and, of course, the Education Code. The first task is to locate the relevant code. Once this is done, the statute can be found by section number. For example, an important federal statute that enables persons to bring lawsuits in federal court alleging federal wrongs is known as 42 U.S.C. Section 1983. The number to the left of the abbreviation is the volume number, and the number to the right of it is the section number. The abbreviation stands for "United States Code." Most large public libraries have one or more sets of volumes containing the United States Code. It is thus a simple task to find the correct volume number and then locate the desired section. Volumes entitled "United States Code Annotated" include brief summaries of judicial decisions involving the section as well, along with other important information, such as the administrative regulations that have been developed by federal agencies to implement the provisions.

Finding all the codes containing the statutes enacted by the California Legislature is easy. Simply access the California Education Department's website at www.cde.ca.gov and click on "Laws and Regulations." Follow the links to all twenty-nine California codes, including the Education Code. This website also contains the regulations (often called rules) issued by state agencies and approved by the Office of Administrative Law. Included among them are the regulations issued by the State Board of Education and the California Department of Education.

Hardback volumes containing the California statutes and administrative regulations can also be found in law school libraries and larger public libraries. It is important to consult the pocket part at the back of each volume, along with recently issued paperback supplements, to obtain current law. Volumes containing state statutes include references to administrative law provisions and brief summaries of interpretive judicial law relating to each statute. They also include historical information about the enactment of the statute and later amendments. For ease of reference, many administrators have a copy of the paperback *Desktop Edition: California Education Code*, published by West and updated annually. This large volume is useful for accessing statutory provisions quickly, but it does not include references to judicial decisions. Users of the desktop edition must remember to use the most recent edition because statute law is always changing.

JUDICIAL DECISIONS

Judicial decisions can be accessed online, in published volumes, and often by CD. Lawyers and legal commentators subscribe either to Westlaw or LexisNexis, comprehensive online databases for access to legal information. Both databases require training to use them effectively. Given user cost and sophistication, these systems are not well suited to the needs of laypersons. However, less sophisticated online systems for accessing court decisions and other information are available to the general public. We have included several of these in Appendix C. Printed volumes containing both federal and California judicial decisions are available in law libraries and in most public libraries.

Regardless of whether they are found on the Web or in a library, judicial decisions are reported in a specific format. We can use as an illustration the seminal decision of the U.S. Supreme Court declaring that government-maintained racial segregation in public schools is unconstitutional. The official citation for the case is *Brown v. Board of Education of Topeka, Kansas*, 347 U.S. 483, 74 S. Ct. 686, 98 L. Ed. 873 (1954). The name to the left of the "*v.*" is known as the plaintiff at the trial court level and as the appellant (or petitioner) in the event of an appeal. Because this case had been appealed to the U.S. Supreme Court, Brown is the appellant. The name to the right of the "*v.*" is the defendant at the trial court level and the appellee (or respondent) at the appellate level. Here the appellee is the Board of Education of Topeka, Kansas. Sometimes the names will reverse order. This occurs if the plaintiff wins at the trial court level and the defendant initiates an appeal, thus becoming the appellant. In the *Brown* case, the names did not change on appeal because the plaintiffs did not prevail in the lower court. The original defendants remain the appellees. The "*v.*" between the names stands for *versus* and indicates the adversary nature of litigation.

The numbers and letters following the case name identify where the case can be found. As with statutes, the number to the left of the abbreviation refers to printed volumes, and the number to the right refers to the first page of the decision. Thus, 347 to the left of the first abbreviation refers to the volume number, and 483 to the right of it refers to the page number. "U.S." is the abbreviation for *United States Reports*, the official volumes issued by the Government Printing Office. So, once we locate the *United States Reports* in a library, we will retrieve volume 347 and turn to page 483 to find the first page of the Supreme Court's complete *Brown* decision. The other abbreviations operate similarly and refer to commercially published reporters that contain additional information, such as headnotes and summaries useful to attorneys and legal researchers. "S. Ct." is the *Supreme Court Reporter*, and "L. Ed." is the *United States Supreme Court Reports*, Lawyer's Edition.

The published decisions of the U.S. Court of Appeals for the Ninth Circuit are found together with the decisions of the other federal circuits in the *Federal Reporter* series. Recent decisions are reported in the third edition of this series, abbreviated as "F.3d." Published decisions of federal district courts in California are found in the *Federal Supplement* series. Recent decisions are reported in the second edition of this series, abbreviated as "F. Supp. 2d." California state appellate court decisions can be found in the editions of the *California Reporter* and the *California Appellate Report*. Earlier decisions can be found in the *Pacific Reporter*. Very recent decisions, along with information about the California court system, also can be found on the California Courts website, www.courtinfo.ca.gov. Many law firms and libraries now have case law on CD, thus doing away with large collections of printed volumes.

Once a case is located, the reader usually will first find a brief syllabus of the ruling. Following the summary will be a list of headnotes, setting forth key points in the decision and directing the reader to where these points are discussed in the text of the opinion. The headnotes also provide links to other sources dealing with the same legal point. Following the headnotes will be a list of the attorneys who argued the case and the judge or judges who decided it. Next is the opinion of the court, along with the name of the judge who authored it. Federal district court decisions bear the name of the trial judge (the decisions of California trial court judges are not published). Federal and state appellate court decisions bear the name of one of the judges assigned to the case (normally, cases at both the federal and state appellate levels are heard by a panel of three judges). Numbers in brackets will be found throughout the opinion. These refer to the headnotes at the start of the opinion. If the opinion has been downloaded from a website, numbers will appear periodically in bold type. These refer to the pages in the printed volumes. If the case is reported in more than one printed volume, asterisks will appear before the numbers to distinguish one volume from another.

The reader may encounter one or more concurring opinions at the end of the court opinion. A concurring opinion indicates that the authoring judge agrees with the outcome of the case but for different reasons. Any dissenting opinions will follow the concurring opinions. A dissenting opinion indicates that the writer disagrees with the outcome for reasons stated in the dissenting opinion. Depending on the number of judges hearing the case, others may join in supporting concurring or dissenting opinions. And, in complex cases, it is not unusual to find judges issuing opinions that concur on some points but dissent on others. Neither the concurring nor the dissenting opinions will affect the actual decision of the court. However, it is often said that today's concurring or dissenting opinion may become tomorrow's majority opinion.

Unlike statutory and administrative law, which changes frequently, judicial law is built on the concept of *stare decisis*, meaning that a decision stands unless there is a good reason not to follow it. This adds consistency and reliability to the law over time. Accordingly, in crafting opinions, judges and their law clerks frequently refer to earlier decisions, often including excerpts to support particular points of law. They also will cite statutes and legal commentary. This extensive referencing sometimes makes opinions hard to read. And it may force the reader to review earlier decisions to understand fully the point of law under discussion.

Depending on the position of the court in the judiciary hierarchy, the decision may be appealed to a higher court. If affirmed, the lower court's decision becomes judicial precedent on the point or points of law involved. If overruled, the lower-court decision ceases to have value as legal precedent. Sometimes, a decision that has not been overruled is viewed as an anomaly by other courts and is not followed in later decisions. Or it may be that a statute that the court relied on in reaching a decision may later be changed by the legislature. Lawyers and legal researchers know this and employ the tools of legal research to track a decision over time to make sure that it is still good law. Fortunately, computerized legal retrieval systems have made this task a lot easier than in the days when only printed volumes were available.

Our advice to educators is to realize that sometimes it requires skill to find and understand the law. It is always wise to ask for assistance from legal librarians and others who can offer help when the need arises.

APPENDIX C

REFERENCES

The vast majority of the legal authority in the book can be found on the internet. There is also print material with the laws, regulations, and judicial decisions noted in the book. In this appendix we summarize these resources and note some additional resources relevant to researching the law.

The law is in constant flux. Cases are appealed and reversed. Statutes are amended and repealed. Courts sometimes invalidate regulations. While the following resources contain generally accurate information, additional legal research and/or consultation of a competent legal professional may be appropriate, depending on the intended use of the information.

LAWS AND REGULATIONS

- United States Code (https://uscode.house.gov/download/download.shtml). Search the entire United States Code by title and section. For example, the citation "20 U.S.C. § 1400" is Title 20, Section 1400 of the United States Code.
- Code of Federal Regulations (www.access.gpo.gov/nara/cfr/cfr-table-search.html). The Code of Federal Regulations contains the implementing regulations for the United States Code. The Code of Federal Regulations is arranged by title, part, and section. For example, the citation "34 C.F.R. § 300.503" is Title 34, Part 300, Section 503.
- California Code (www.leginfo.ca.gov). Contains the complete California Code. Search by code and section (e.g., Education Code Section 44942).

- *California Education Code: Desktop Edition.* This softbound desktop edition of the California Education Code is published annually. Order from Thomson West (https://store.legal.thomsonreuters.com/).
- California Code of Regulations (https://oal.ca.gov/publications/ccr/). Like its federal counterpart in the Code of Federal Regulations, the California Code of Regulations provides additional guidance and detail on the implementation of the California Code. Title Five of the California Code of Regulations is Education.

JUDICIAL DECISIONS

- FindLaw for Legal Professionals (www.findlaw.com). Contains links to state and federal judicial decisions. Decisions available on the internet, however, may be limited in some instances to those issued in the last eight to ten years.
- Appendix B, "Finding and Reading Statutes and Judicial Decisions," addresses the hardbound collections that contain federal and state judicial decisions.

GOVERNMENT AGENCIES

- U.S. Copyright Office (www.copyright.gov). Includes information about copyright laws and publications pertaining to the reproduction of copyrighted works by educators. Also includes information on copyright and digital distance education (www.copyright.gov/disted).
- U.S. Department of Education (www.ed.gov). Contains information regarding No Child Left Behind (NCLB), Family Education Rights and Privacy Act (FERPA), charter schools, school choice, and numerous education-related links of interest for students, parents, teachers, and administrators. This site contains a link to the Office for Civil Rights (OCR) and Office of Special Education and Rehabilitative Services (OSERS). OCR's site contains information regarding the laws OCR enforces (for example, Title IX of the Education Amendments of 1972, Section 504 of the Rehabilitation Act of 1973, and the Americans with Disabilities Act). OSERS's site contains information regarding the Individuals with Disabilities Education Act (IDEA), memoranda with interpretive guidance on IDEA, and links to special education research and statistics.

- U.S. Department of Labor (www.dol.gov). Contains information regarding employee leave rights under the Family and Medical Leave Act (FMLA).
- U.S. Equal Employment Opportunity Commission (www.eeoc.gov). Contains comprehensive information regarding federal employment discrimination laws, the filing of a discrimination complaint, and publications to assist employers with compliance.
- U.S. Patent and Trademark Office (www.uspto.gov). Contains information regarding copyrighted works including an overview of the TEACH Act (www.uspto.gov/web/offices/dcom/olia/teachreport.pdf).
- California Department of Education (www.cde.ca.gov). Contains information regarding state curriculum, testing, finance, and links to state special education sites like the Office of Administrative Hearings (OAH) (https://www.cde.ca.gov/sp/se/ds/) (scroll down to California Administrative Hearings Database) and special education decisions (https://www.cde.ca.gov/sp/se/ds/) (scroll down to Office of Administrative Hearings, Special Education Unit).
- Department of Fair Employment and Housing. Contains information regarding state employment discrimination laws and employee leave rights under the California Family Rights Act (CFRA).
- Public Employment Relations Board (www.perb.ca.gov). Contains information regarding the Educational Employment Relations Act (EERA) and a database of decisions.
- California Attorney General (https://oag.ca.gov/). Includes a searchable database of recent attorney general opinions, including a number of opinions relevant to education.

OTHER RESOURCES

- Cohen, Morris L., and Kent Olson. *Cohen and Olson's Legal Research in a Nutshell*, 12th ed., 2016. Easy-to-use guide to legal research, including how to access and use online legal research.
- Garner, Bryan A., ed. *Black's Law Dictionary, Abridged*, 10th ed., 2015. Softbound law dictionary that is a useful resource for school personnel who work with attorneys and legal materials.
- Stanford University Library's Copyright and Fair Use web page provides information on judicial as well as other law relating to copyright use (www.fairuse.stanford.edu/primary_materials).

LIST OF CASES

The official citations of all the cases cited in this book are included in this list; page numbers for where we refer to these cases can be found in the topic index. The basic citation system format is discussed in Appendix B. Information about accessing cases is given in Appendix C. We have modified the official legal system of citing cases somewhat in this index for the benefit of lay readers.

Modifications include identification of the districts of the California courts of appeal so that the readers can tell which of the six made the decision. This is apparent in the very first citation in the index. To indicate which decisions come from the California Supreme Court, we have included the simple designation "Cal." along with the date of the decision within the parentheses following the citation. While there are several reporters where the decisions of California courts can be found, we have opted to follow common practice and cite to official reporters as much as possible. We cite to the *California Reporter* series (abbreviated "Cal. Rptr.") for ease of reference for all but a few older court decisions. For the same reason, we also have opted to cite to the official *United States Reports* (abbreviated as "U.S.") for U.S. Supreme Court decisions for all but the most recent decisions. For very recent decisions that may not yet be included in the official reports, we use the *Supreme Court Reporter* (abbreviated as "S. Ct."). The italic words "*cert. denied*" that occasionally appear after a case citation mean that the U.S. Supreme Court refused to hear the case on appeal. This does not mean that the high court agreed with the lower court's ruling. It merely means that for whatever reason, the Supreme Court refused to take up the case. Except for the U.S. Supreme Court, we do not include the citation history of a case except where important to the continued validity of the decision being cited.

The abbreviation PERC stands for Public Employee Reporter for California, where the decisions of the Public Employment Relations Board (PERB) and its staff on collective bargaining matters can be found. The abbreviation IDELR refers to the *Individuals with Disabilities Education Law Report*, which contains decisions pertaining to children with disabilities.

Aaris v. Las Virgenes Unified School District, 75 Cal. Rptr. 2d 801 (Cal. App. 2 Dist. 1998)
Abood v. Detroit Board of Education, 431 U.S. 209 (1977)
Achene v. Pierce Joint Unified School District, 97 Cal. Rptr. 3d 899 (Cal. App. 4 Dist. 2009)
Acosta v. Los Angeles Unified School District, 37 Cal. Rptr. 2d 171 (Cal. App. 2 Dist. 1995)
Adair v. Stockton Unified School District, 77 Cal. Rptr. 3d 62 (Cal. App. 3 Dist. 2008)
Adams v. Oregon, 195 F.3d 1141 (9th Cir. 1999)
Adcock v. San Diego Unified School District, 109 Cal. Rptr. 676 (Cal. 1973)
Adelt v. Richmond School District, 58 Cal. Rptr. 151 (Cal. App. 1 Dist. 1967)
A.G. v. Paradise Valley Unified School District No. 69, 815 F.3d 1195 (9th Cir. 2016)
Aguirre v. Los Angeles Unified School District, 461 F.3d 1114 (9th Cir. 2006)
Agostini v. Felton, 521 U.S. 203 (1997)
Alexander v. Sandoval, 532 U.S. 275 (2001)
Alex G. ex rel. Stephen G. v. Board of Trustees of Davis Joint Unified School District, 332 F. Supp. 2d 1315 (E.D. Cal. 2004)
Allison C. v. Advanced Education Services, 28 Cal. Rptr. 3d 605 (Cal. App. 4 Dist. 2005)
Alma W. v. Oakland Unified School District, 176 Cal. Rptr. 287 (Cal. App. 1 Dist. 1981)
Ambach v. Norwick, 441 U.S. 68 (1979)
American Academy of Pediatrics v. Lungren, 66 Cal. Rptr. 2d 210 (Cal. 1997)
American Civil Rights Foundation v. Berkeley Unified School District, 90 Cal. Rptr. 3d 789 (Cal. App. 1 Dist. 2009).
American Civil Rights Foundation v. Los Angeles Unified School District, 86 Cal. Rptr. 3d 754 (Cal. App. 2 Dist. 2008)
American Library Association v. United States, 539 U.S. 194 (2003)
Anderson Union High School District v. Shasta Secondary Home School, 4 Cal. App.5th 262 (2016)
Arcadia Unified School District v. State Department of Education, 5 Cal. Rptr. 2d 545 (Cal. 1992)
Arizona Christian School Tuition Organization v. Winn, 131 S. Ct. 1436 (2011)

Arlington Central School District Board of Education v. Murphy, 126 S. Ct. 2455 (2006)

Association of Mexican-American Educators v. State of California, 231 F.3d 572 (9th Cir. 2000)

Atwater Elementary School District v. California Department of General Services, 59 Cal. Rptr. 3d 233 (Cal. 2007)

Avila v. Spokane School District 81, 852 F.3d 936 (9th Cir. 2017)

Baca v. Moreno Valley Unified School District, 936 F. Supp. 719 (C.D. Cal. 1996)

Bacus v. Palo Verde Unified School District, 52 Fed. Appx. 355 (9th Cir. 2002) (unpublished)

Bain et al. v. California Teachers Association et al., 156 F.Supp.3d 1142 (C.D. Cal. 2015)

Bakersfield City School District v. Superior Court, 13 Cal. Rptr. 3d 517 (Cal. App. 5 Dist. 2004)

Bakersfield Elementary Teachers Association v. Bakersfield City School District, 52 Cal. Rptr. 2d 486 (Cal. App. 5 Dist. 2006)

Banning Teachers Association v. Public Employment Relations Board, 244 Cal. Rptr. 671 (Cal. 1988)

Bassett v. Lakeside Inc., 44 Cal. Rptr. 3d 827 (Cal. App. 3 Dist. 2006)

Bartell v. Palos Verdes Peninsula School District, 147 Cal. Rptr. 898 (Cal. App. 2 Dist. 1978)

B.C. v. Plumas Unified School District, 192 F.3d 1260 (9th Cir. 1999)

Bekiaris v. Board of Education of City of Modesto, 100 Cal. Rptr. 16 (Cal. 1972)

Belanger v. Madera Unified School District, 963 F.2d 248 (9th Cir. 1992)

Bell v. Vista Unified School District, 98 Cal. Rptr. 2d 263 (Cal. App. 4 Dist. 2000)

Benjamin G. v. Special Education Hearing Office, 32 Cal. Rptr. 3d 366 (Cal. App. 1 Dist. 2005)

Bercovitch v. Baldwin School, 133 F.3d 141 (1st Cir. 1998)

Berkelman v. San Francisco Unified School District, 501 F.2d 1264 (9th Cir. 1974)

Bernstein v. Lopez, 321 F.3d 903 (9th Cir. 2003)

Berry v. Department of Social Services, 447 F.3d 642 (9th Cir. 2006)

Bethel School District No. 403 v. Fraser, 478 U.S. 675 (1986)

Beussink v. Woodland R-IV School District, 30 F. Supp. 2d 1175 (E.D. Mo. 1998)

Biscotti v. Yuba City Unified School District, 69 Cal. Rptr. 3d 825 (Cal. App. 3 Dist. 2007)

Blackwell v. Issaquena County Board of Education, 363 F.2d 749 (5th Cir. 1966)

Blair v. Bethel School District, 608 F.3d 540 (9th Cir. 2010)

Blanchard v. Morton School District, 509 F.3d 934 (9th Cir. 2007), *cert. denied*, 552 U.S. 1231(2008)

Board of Education v. Allen, 392 U.S. 236 (1968)

Board of Education v. Earls, 536 U.S. 822 (2002)

Board of Education of Hendrick Hudson School District v. Rowley, 458 U.S. 176 (1982)
Board of Education of Island Trees v. Pico, 457 U.S. 853 (1982)
Board of Education of Long Beach Unified School District v. Jack M., 139 Cal. Rptr. 700 (Cal. 1977)
Board of Education of Oklahoma City Public Schools v. Dowell, 498 U.S. 237 (1991)
Board of Education of Rogers, Arkansas v. McCluskey, 458 U.S. 966 (1982)
Board of Education of the Round Valley Unified School District v. Round Valley Teachers Association, 52 Cal. Rptr. 2d 115 (Cal. 1996)
Board of Education v. Sacramento County Board of Education, 102 Cal. Rptr. 2d 872 (Cal. App. 3 Dist. 2001)
Board of Education of Westside Community Schools v. Mergens, 496 U.S. 226 (1990)
Board of Regents v. Roth, 408 U.S. 564 (1972)
Bob Jones University v. United States, 461 U.S. 574 (1983)
Bolin v. San Bernadino City Unified School District, 202 Cal. Rptr. 416 (Cal. App. 4 Dist. 1984)
Bostock v. Clayton County, Georgia, 590 US 664 (2020)
Bowker v. Baker, 73 Cal. App.2d 653 (Cal. App. 4 Dist. 1946)
Bown v. Gwinnett County School District, 112 F.3d 1464 (11th Cir. 1997)
Boyd v. Eastin, 2002 WL 31854990 (Cal. App. 3 Dist. 2002) (unpublished)
Bravo ex rel. Ramirez v. Hsu, 404 F. Supp. 2d 1195 (C.D. Cal. 2005)
Brown v. Board of Education of Topeka, Kansas, 347 U.S. 483 (1954)
Brown v. Gilmore, 533 U.S. 1301 (2001)
Brown v. Woodland Joint Unified School District, 27 F.3d 1373 (9th Cir. 1994)
BRV, Inc. v. Superior Court, 49 Cal. Rptr. 3d 519 (Cal .App. 3 Dist. 2006)
Bullis Charter School v. Los Altos School District, 134 Cal. Rptr. 3d 133 (Cal. App. 6 Dist. 2011)
Butt v. State of California, 15 Cal. Rptr. 2d 480 (Cal. 1992)
C.A. v. William S. Hart Union High School District, 138 Cal. Rptr. 3d 1 (Cal. 2012)
Caldwell v. Montoya, 42 Cal. Rptr. 2d 842 (Cal. 1995)
Caldwell v. Paramount Unified School District, 48 Cal. Rptr. 2d 448 (Cal. App. 2 Dist. 1995)
California Association for Safety Education v. Brown, 36 Cal. Rptr. 2d 404 (Cal. App. 6 Dist. 1994)
California Charter Schools Association v. Los Angeles Unified School District, 151 Cal. Rptr. 3d 585 (Cal. App. 2 Dist. 2012)
California Parents for the Equalization of Educational Materials v. Torlakson, 267 F.Supp.3d 1218 (F.Supp.3d N.D. Cal., 2017)
California Parents for Equalization of Educational Materials v. Torlakson, 973 F.3d 1010 (9th Cir. 2020)

California School Boards Association v. State Board of Education, 113 Cal. Rptr. 3d 550 (Cal. App. 1 Dist. 2010)
California School Boards Association v. State of California, 121 Cal. Rptr. 3d 696 (Cal. App. 4 Dist. 2011)
California School Employees Association v. Bonita Unified School District, 77 Cal. Rptr. 3d 486 (Cal. App. 2d Dist. 2008)
California School Employees Association v. Livingston Union School District, 56 Cal. Rptr. 3d 923 (Cal. App. 5 Dist. 2007)
California Teachers Association v. Governing Board of the Hilmar Unified School District, 115 Cal. Rptr. 2d 323 (Cal. App. 5 Dist. 2002)
California Teachers Association v. Governing Board of San Diego Unified School District, 53 Cal. Rptr. 2d 474 (Cal. App. 4 Dist. 1996)
California Teachers Association v. Hayes, 7 Cal. Rptr. 2d 699 (Cal. App. 3 Dist. 1992)
California Teachers Association v. Huff, 7 Cal. Rptr. 2d 699 (Cal. App. 3 Dist. 1992)
California Teachers Association v. Public Employee Relations Board, 87 Cal. Rptr. 3d 530 (Cal. App. 4 Dist. 2009)
California Teachers Association v. Riles, 176 Cal. Rptr. 300 (Cal. 1981)
California Teachers Association v. State Board of Education, 271 F.3d 1141 (9th Cir. 2001)
California Teachers Association v. Vallejo City Unified School District, 56 Cal. Rptr. 3d 712 (Cal. App. 1 Dist. 2007)
Campaign for Quality Education et al. v. State of California/Robles-Wong v. State of California, 209 Cal.Rptr.3d 888 (Cal. App. 1 Dist. 2016)
Carey v. Population Services, International, 431 U.S. 678 (1977)
Casterson v. Superior Court, 123 Cal. Rptr. 2d 637 (Cal. App. 6 Dist. 2002)
Caviness v. Horizon Community Learning Center, 590 F.3d 806 (9th Cir. 2010)
C.B. ex rel. Baquerizo v. Garden Grove Unified School District, 635 F.3d 1155 (9th Cir.), *cert. denied*, 132 S. Ct. 500 (2011).
Cedar Rapids Community School District v. Garrett F., 526 U.S. 66 (1999)
Ceniceros v. Board of Trustees of the San Diego Unified School District, 106 F.3d 878 (9th Cir. 1997)
C.F. ex rel. Farnan v. Capistrano Unified School District, 654 F.3d 975 (9th Cir. 2011), *cert. denied sub nom. C. F. v. Corbett*, 132 S. Ct. 1566 (2012)
Chalifoux v. New Caney Independent School District, 976 F. Supp. 659 (S.D. Tex. 1997)
Chandler v. McMinnville School District, 978 F.2d 524 (9th Cir. 1992)
Chandler v. Siegelman, 230 F.3d 1313 (11th Cir. 2000), *cert. denied*, 533 U.S. 916 (2001)
Charles H. Allen et al., Petitioners-Appellants, and California School Employees Association and Pleasant Valley Elementary School District, Respondents, 8 PERC P 15051 (1984)

Chicago Teachers Union, Local No. 1 v. Hudson, 475 U.S. 292 (1986)
Christian Legal Society Chapter v. Martinez, 130 S. Ct. 2971 (2010)
City of Madison v. Wisconsin Employment Relations Commission, 429 U.S. 167 (1976)
City of San Jose v. Superior Court of Santa Clara, 2 Cal.App.5th 508 (2017)
Clark v. Arizona Interscholastic Association, 695 F.2d 1126 (9th Cir. 1982)
Clark v. Arizona Interscholastic Association, 886 F.2d 1191 (9th Cir. 1989)
Clausing v. San Francisco Unified School District, 271 Cal. Rptr. 72 (Cal. App. 1 Dist. 1990)
C.O. v. Portland Public Schools, 679 F.3d 1162 (9th Cir. 2012)
Coalition for Economic Equity v. Wilson, 122 F.3d 718 (9th Cir. 1997)
Cole v. Oroville Union School District, 228 F.3d 1092 (9th Cir. 2000), cert. denied sub nom., *Niemeyer v. Oroville Union School District*, 532 U.S. 905 (2001)
Colin ex rel. Colin v. Orange Unified School District, 83 F. Supp. 2d 1135 (C.D. Cal. 2000)
Collins v. Chandler Unified School District, 644 F.2d 759 (9th Cir.), cert. denied, 454 U.S. 863 (1981)
Compton Unified School District v. Compton Education Association, 11 PERC P 18067 (1987)
Conn v. Western Placer Unified School District, 113 Cal. Rptr. 3d 116 (Cal. App. 3 Dist. 2010)
Connick v. Myers, 461 U.S. 138 (1983)
Constantinescu v. Conejo Valley Unified School District, 20 Cal. Rptr. 2d 734 (Cal. App. 2 Dist. 1993)
Coomes v. Edmonds School District No. 15, 816 F.3d 1255 (9th Cir. 2016)
Copley Press, Inc. v. Superior Court, 74 Cal. Rptr. 2d 69 (Cal. App. 4 Dist. 1998)
Corales v. Bennett, 567 F.3d 554 (9th Cir. 2009)
County Sanitation District No. 2 v. Los Angeles County Employees Association, Local 600, 214 Cal. Rptr. 424 (Cal. 1985)
Cousins v. Weaverville Elementary School District, 30 Cal. Rptr. 2d 310 (Cal. App. 3 Dist. 1994)
Crawford v. Board of Education of the City of Los Angeles, 130 Cal. Rptr. 724 (Cal. 1976)
Crawford v. Board of Education of the City of Los Angeles, 458 U.S. 527 (1982)
Crawford v. Huntington Beach Union High School District, 121 Cal. Rptr. 2d 96 (Cal. App. 4 Dist. 2002)
Crowl v. Commission on Professional Competence of the Governing Board of San Juan Unified School District, 275 Cal. Rptr. 86 (Cal. App. 3 Dist. 1990)
Cuff v. Grossmont Union High School District, 164 Cal. Rptr. 3d 487 (Cal. App. 4 Dist. 2013)
Culbertson v. Oakridge School District No. 76, 258 F.3d 1061 (9th Cir. 2001)

Cumero v. Public Employment Relations Board, 262 Cal. Rptr. 46 (Cal. 1989)
C.W. v. Capistrano Unified School District, 784 F.3d 1237 (9th Cir. 2015)
Daugherty v. Vanguard Charter School Academy, 116 F. Supp. 2d 897 (W.D. Mich. 2000)
Davenport v. Washington Education Association, 551 U.S. 177 (2007)
Davis v. Monroe County Board of Education, 526 U.S. 629 (1999)
Davison v. Santa Barbara High School District, 48 F. Supp. 2d 1225 (C.D. Cal. 1998)
Dawson v. East Side Union High School, 34 Cal. Rptr. 2d 108 (Cal. App. 6 Dist. 1994)
DeNooyer v. Merinelli, 12 F.3d 211 (6th Cir. 1993) (unpublished disposition), *cert. denied sub nom. DeNooyer by DeNooyer v. Livonia Public Schools*, 511 U.S. 1031 (1994)
DiLoreto v. Board of Education, 87 Cal. Rptr. 2d 791 (Cal. App. 2 Dist. 1999)
DiLoreto v. Downey Unified School District Board of Education, 196 F.3d 958 (9th Cir. 1999), *cert. denied*, 529 U.S. 1067 (2000)
D.O. v. Escondido Union School District, 59 F.4th 394 (9th Cir. 2023)
Dobbs v. Jackson Women's Health Organization, 597 U.S. 215 (2022)
Doe v. Albany Unified School District, 118 Cal. Rptr. 3d 507 (Cal. App. 3 Dist. 2010)
Doe v. California Lutheran High School, 88 Cal. Rptr. 3d 475 (Cal. App. 4 Dist. 2009)
Doe v. Hawaii Department of Education, 334 F.3d 906 (9th Cir. 2003)
Donovan v. Poway Unified School District, 84 Cal. Rptr. 3d 285 (Cal. App. 4th Dist. 2008)
Downs v. Los Angeles Unified School District, 228 F.3d 1003 (9th Cir. 2000), *cert. denied*, 532 U.S. 994 (2001)
Durant v. Los Angeles Unified School District, 2003 WL 21949586 (Cal. App. 2 Dist. 2003) (unpublished)
Duval v. Board of Trustees, 113 Cal. Rptr. 2d 517 (Cal. App. 5 Dist. 2001)
Edwards v. Aguillard, 482 U.S. 578 (1987)
Edwards v. Lake Elsinore USD, 228 Cal. Rptr.3d 383 (Cal. App. 4 Dist. 2014)
Eisenstadt v. Baird, 405 U.S. 438 (1972)
Eklund v. Byron Unified School District, 154 Fed. Appx. 648 (9th Cir. 2005) (unpublished), *cert. denied*, 549 U.S. 942 (2006)
Elk Grove Unified School District v. Newdow, 542 U.S. 1 (2004)
Endrew F. v. Douglas County School District RE-1, 579 U.S. 969 (2017)
Engle v. Vitale, 370 U.S. 421 (1962)
Environmental Charter High School v. Centinela Valley Union High School District, 18 Cal. Rptr. 3d (Cal. App. 2 Dist. 2004)
Epperson v. Arkansas, 393 U.S. 97 (1968)
Eric M. v. Cajon Valley Union School District, 95 Cal. Rptr. 3d 428 (Cal. App. 4 Dist. 2009)
Espinoza v. Montana Department of Revenue, 591 U.S. 464 (2020)

Evens v. Superior Court, 91 Cal. Rptr. 2d 497 (Cal. App. 2 Dist. 1999)
Everson v. Board of Education, 330 U.S. 1 (1947)
Farrington v. Tokushige, 273 U.S. 284 (1927)
Fashion Valley Mall v. National Labor Relations Board, 69 Cal. Rptr. 3d 288 (Cal. 2007), *cert. denied*, 555 U.S. 819 (2008)
Fellowship of Christian Athletes v. San Jose Unified School District, 82 F.4th 664 (9th Cir. 2023)
Fields v. Palmdale School District, 427 F.3d 1197 (9th Cir. 2005), *opinion amended per curiam on denial of rehearing*, 447 F.3d 1187 (9th Cir.), *cert. denied*, 549 U.S. 1089 (2006)
Fischer v. Los Angeles Unified School District, 82 Cal. Rptr. 2d 452 (Cal. App. 2 Dist. 1999)
Fisher v. University of Texas at Austin, 2013 WL 315220 (2013)
Fleice v. Chualar Elementary School District, 254 Cal. Rptr. 54 (Cal. App. 6 Dist. 1988)
Florence County School District Four v. Carter, 510 U.S. 7 (1993)
Flores v. Morgan Hill Unified School District, 324 F.3d 1130 (9th Cir. 2003)
Florey v. Sioux Falls School District, 619 F.2d 1311 (8th Cir.), *cert. denied*, 449 U.S. 987 (1980)
Ford v. Long Beach Unified School District, 291 F.3d 1086 (2002)
Forest Grove School District v. T. A., 557 U.S. 230 (9th Cir. 2009)
Foster v. Mahdesian, 268 F.3d 689 (9th Cir. 2001), *cert. denied sub nom. Foster v. Garcy*, 535 U.S. 1112 (2002)
Franklin v. Gwinnett County Public Schools, 503 U.S. 60 (1992)
Frazer v. Dixon Unified School District, 22 Cal. Rptr. 2d 641 (Cal. App. 1 Dist. 1993)
Freedom from Religion Foundation, Inc. v. Chino Valley Unified School District Board of Education, 896 F.3d 1132 (9th Cir. 2018)
Freeman v. Oakland Unified School District, 179 F.3d 846 (9th Cir. 1999)
Freeman v. Pitts, 503 U.S. 467 (1992)
Fremont Unified School District v. Fremont Unified District Teachers Association, 14 PERC P 21107 (1990)
Fremont Union High School District v. Santa Clara County Board of Education, 286 Cal. Rptr. 915 (1991)
Friedrichs v. California Teachers Association, 136 S.Ct. 1083 (2016)
Friery v. Los Angeles Unified School District, 300 F.3d 1120 (2002), *opinion after certification question declined*, 448 F.3d 1146 (9th Cir. 2006)
Frontiero v. Richardson, 411 U.S. 677 (1973)
Fry v. Napoleon Community Schools, 580 U.S. 154 (2017)
Garcetti v. Ceballos, 547 U.S. 410 (2006)
Garrett v. Los Angeles City Unified School District, 172 Cal. Rptr. 170 (Cal. App. 2 Dist. 1981)

Gebser v. Lago Vista Independent School District, 524 U.S. 274 (1998)
Gellerman v. Calaveras Unified School District, 43 Fed. Appx. 28, 37 IDELR 125 (9th Cir. 2002) (unpublished)
Ghafu v. Bernstein, 32 Cal. Rptr. 3d 626 (Cal. App. 1 Dist. 2005)
Givhan v. Western Line Consolidated School District, 349 U.S. 410 (1979)
Goleta Union Elementary School District v. Ordway, 166 F. Supp. 2d 1287 (2001), supplemented, 248 F. Supp. 2d 936 (C.D. Cal. 2002)
Gong Lum v. Rice, 275 U.S. 78 (1927)
Gonzaga University v. Doe, 536 U.S. 273 (2002)
Good News Club v. Milford Central School, 533 U.S. 98 (2001)
Gordon v. Board of Education of the City of Los Angeles, 78 Cal. Rptr. 464 (Cal. App. 2 Dist. 1947)
Gordon J. v. Santa Ana Unified School District, 208 Cal. Rptr. 657 (Cal. App. 4 Dist. 1984)
Goss v. Lopez, 419 U.S. 565 (1975)
Governing Board of ABC Unified School District v. Haar, 33 Cal. Rptr. 2d 744 (Cal. App. 2 Dist. 1994)
Granowitz v. Redlands Unified School District, 129 Cal. Rptr. 2d 410 (2003)
Green v. Garriott, 212 P.3d 96 (Ariz. App. Div. 1 2009)
Gregory K. v. Longview School District, 811 F.2d 1307 (9th Cir. 1987)
Grimsley v. Board of Trustees, 235 Cal. Rptr. 85 (Cal. App. 5 Dist. 1987)
Griswold v. Connecticut, 381 U.S. 479 (1965)
Groff v. DeJoy, 600 U.S. 447 (2023)
Grove v. Mead School District No. 354, 753 F.2d 1528 (9th Cir.), cert. denied, 474 U.S. 826 (1985)
Grutter v. Bollinger, 539 U.S. 306 (2003)
Harik v. California Teachers Association, 326 F.3d 1042 (9th Cir.), cert. denied sub nom. *Sheffield v. Aceves*, 540 U.S. 965 (2003)
Harlow v. Fitzgerald, 457 U.S. 800 (1982)
Hartzell v. Connell, 201 Cal. Rptr. 601 (Cal. 1984)
Hazelwood School District v. Kuhlmeier, 484 U.S. 260 (1988)
Healy v. James, 408 U.S. 169 (1972)
Hector F. v. El Centro Elementary School District, 173 Cal. Rptr.3d 413 (Cal. App. 4 Dist. 2014)
Hedges v. Wauconda Community Unit School District No. 118, 9 F.3d 1295 (7th Cir. 1993)
Hemady v. Long Beach Unified School District, 49 Cal. Rptr. 3d 464 (Cal. App. 2 Dist. 2006)
Henderson v. Los Angeles City Board of Education, 144 Cal. Rptr. 568 (Cal. App. 2 Dist. 1978)

Hills v. Scottsdale Unified School District No. 48, 329 F.3d 1044 (9th Cir. 2003), cert. denied, 540 U.S. 1149 (2004)
Hoff v. Vacaville Unified School District, 80 Cal. Rptr. 2d 811 (Cal. 1998)
Hohe v. San Diego Unified School District, 274 Cal. Rptr. 647 (Cal. App. 4 Dist. 1990)
Honig v. Doe, 484 U.S. 305 (1988)
Hooks v. Clark County School District, 228 F.3d 1036 (9th Cir. 2000), cert. denied, 532 U.S. 971 (2001)
Horace Mann Insurance Company v. Analisa N., 263 Cal. Rptr. 61 (Cal. App. 4 Dist. 1989)
Horton v. Whipple, 58 Cal. App. 189 (Cal. App. 3 Dist. 1922)
Hosanna-Tabor Evangelical Lutheran Church v. Equal Employment Opportunity Commission, 132 S. Ct. 694 (2012)
Hoschler v. Sacramento City Unified School District, 57 Cal. Rptr. 3d 115 (Cal. App. 3 Dist. 2007)
Hoyem v. Manhattan Beach City School District, 150 Cal. Rptr. 1 (Cal. 1978)
Hudgens v. National Labor Relations Board, 424 U.S. 507 (1976)
Hunter ex rel. Brandt v. Regents of University of California, 190 F.3d 1061 (9th Cir.), cert. denied, 531 U.S. 877 (1999)
Hunter v. Regents of the University of California, 2001 WL 1555240 (Cal. App. 2 Dist. 2001) (unpublished)
In re Alexander B., 270 Cal. Rptr. 342 (Cal. App. 2 Dist. 1990)
In re Corey L., 250 Cal. Rptr. 359 (Cal. App. 1 Dist. 1988)
In re Humberto O., 95 Cal. Rptr. 2d 248 (Cal. App. 2 Dist. 2000)
In re J.D., 170 Cal. Rptr. 3d 464 (Cal. App. 1 Dist. 2014)
In re Joseph F., 102 Cal. Rptr. 2d 641 (Cal. App. 1 Dist. 2000)
In re Joseph G., 38 Cal. Rptr. 2d 902 (Cal. App. 4 Dist. 1995)
In re K.S., 108 Cal. Rptr. 3d 32 (Cal. App. 1 Dist. 2010)
In re Latasha W., 70 Cal. Rptr. 2d 886 (Cal. App. 2 Dist. 1998)
In re Lisa G., 23 Cal. Rptr. 3d 163 (Cal. App. 4 Dist. 2004), as modified (Jan. 10, 2005)
In re M.S., 42 Cal. Rptr. 2d 355 (Cal. 1995)
In re Michael M., 104 Cal. Rptr. 2d 10 (Cal. App. 5 Dist. 2001)
In re Miguel H., 103 Cal. Rptr. 3d 884 (Cal. App. 2 Dist. 2010)
In re Rafael C., 200 Cal. Rptr. 3d 305 (Cal. App. 1 Dist. 2016)
In re Randy G., 110 Cal. Rptr. 2d 516 (Cal. 2001)
In re William G., 221 Cal. Rptr. 118 (Cal. 1985)
In re William V., 4 Cal. Rptr. 3d 695 (Cal. App. 1 Dist. 2003)
Ingraham v. Wright, 430 U.S. 651 (1977)
Ingram v. Flippo, 89 Cal. Rptr. 2d 60 (Cal. App. 6 Dist. 1999)
Irvine Unified School District v. Irvine Teachers Association, CTA/NEA, 11 PERC P 18128 (1987)

Irving Independent School District v. Tatro, 468 U.S. 883 (1984)
Iverson v. Muroc Unified School District, 38 Cal. Rptr. 2d 35 (Cal. App. 5 Dist. 1995)
Jackson v. Birmingham Board of Education, 544 U.S. 167 (2005)
Jackson v. Pasadena City School District, 31 Cal. Rptr. 606 (Cal. 1963)
Jacobs v. Clark County School District, 526 F.3d 419 (9th Cir. 2008)
Janus v. American Federation of State, County and Municipal Employees, 585 U.S. 924 (2018)
J.C. ex rel. R. C. v. Beverly Hills Unified School District, 711 F. Supp. 2d 1094 (C.D. Cal. 2010)
J.H. v. Los Angeles Unified School District, 107 Cal. Rptr. 3d 182 (Cal. App. 2 Dist. 2010)
J.L. v. Mercer Island School District, 592 F.3d 938 (9th Cir. 2010)
John A. v. San Bernardino City Unified School District, 187 Cal. Rptr. 472 (1982)
John R. v. Oakland Unified School District, 256 Cal. Rptr. 766 (Cal. 1989)
Johnson v. Huntington Beach Union High School District, 137 Cal. Rptr. 43 (Cal. App. 4 Dist.), *cert. denied*, 434 U.S. 877 (1977)
Johnson v. Poway Unified School District, 658 F.3d 954 (9th Cir. 2011), *cert. denied*, 132 S. Ct. 1807 (2012)
Jonathan L. v. Superior Court, 81 Cal. Rptr. 3d 571 (Cal. App. 2 Dist. 2008)
Joyce v. Simi Valley Unified School District, 1 Cal. Rptr. 3d 712 (Cal. App. 2 Dist. 2003)
Juran v. Independence Oregon Central School District 13J, 898 F. Supp. 728 (D. Or. 1995)
Kahn v. East Side Union High School District, 4 Cal. Rptr. 3d 103 (Cal. 2003)
Katz v. Los Gatos-Saratoga Joint Union High School District, 11 Cal. Rptr. 3d 546 (Cal. App. 6 Dist. 2004)
Kavanaugh v. West Sonoma County Union High School District, 129 Cal. Rptr. 2d 811 (Cal. 2003)
Kennedy v. Bremerton School District, 597 U.S. 507 (2022)
Keyes v. School District No. 1, 413 U.S. 189 (1973)
Keyser v. Sacramento City Unified School District, 265 F.3d 741 (9th Cir. 2001)
Kimberly M. v. Los Angeles Unified School District, 263 Cal. Rptr. 612 (Cal. App. 2 Dist. 1989)
King v. Saddleback Junior College District, 445 F.2d 932 (9th Cir.), *cert. denied*, 404 U.S. 979 (1971)
Kirchmann v. Lake Elsinore Unified School District, 67 Cal. Rptr. 2d 268 (Cal. App. 4 Dist. 1997), *supplemented*, 100 Cal. Rptr. 2d 289 (Cal. App. 4 Dist. 2000) (Eleventh Amendment immunity protects school district from suit under 42 U.S.C. § 1983), *cert. denied*, 533 U.S. 902 (2001)
Klump v. Nazareth Area School District, 425 F. Supp. 2d 622 (E.D. Pa. 2006)

K.M. ex rel. Bright v. Tustin Unified School District, 725 F.3d 1088 (9th Cir. 2013)
Knapp v. Palisades Charter High School, 53 Cal. Rptr. 3d 182 (Cal. App. 2 Dist.), cert. denied, 128 S. Ct. 255 (2007)
Knight v. Jewett, 11 Cal. Rptr. 2d 2 (Cal. 1992)
Knox v. Service Employees International Union, Local 1000, 132 S. Ct. 2277 (2012)
Kotterman v. Killian, 972 P.2d 606 (Ariz.), cert. denied, 528 U.S. 921 (1999)
Lackner v. North, 37 Cal. Rptr. 3d 863 (Cal. App. 3 Dist. 2006)
Lamb's Chapel v. Center Moriches Union Free School District, 508 U.S. 384 (1993)
Lane v. Franks, 134 S.Ct. 2369 (2014)
Larry P. v. Riles, 793 F.2d 969 (9th Cir. 1984), as amended on denial of rehearing (1986) (en banc)
Lassonde v. Pleasanton Unified School District, 320 F.3d 979 (9th Cir. 2003), cert. denied, 540 U.S. 817 (2003)
Las Virgenes Educators Association v. Las Virgenes Unified School District, 102 Cal. Rptr. 2d 901 (Cal. App. 2 Dist. 2001)
Lau v. Nichols, 414 U.S. 563 (1974)
LaVine v. Blain School District, 257 F.3d 981 (9th Cir. 2001), cert. denied, 536 U.S. 959 (2002)
Lawrence v. Texas, 539 U.S. 558 (2003)
Lawson v. PPG Architectural Finishes, 12 Cal.5th 703 (2022)
League of United Latin American Citizens v. Wilson, 908 F. Supp. 755 (C.D. Cal. 1995), supplemented, 997 F. Supp. 1244 (C.D. Cal. 1997)
Lee v. Weisman, 505 U.S. 577 (1992)
Leeb v. Delong, 243 Cal. Rptr. 494 (Cal. App. 4 Dist. 1988)
Leger v. Stockton Unified School District, 249 Cal. Rptr. 688 (Cal. App. 3 Dist. 1988)
Leventhal v. Vista Unified School District, 973 F. Supp. 951 (S.D. Cal. 1997)
Lilley v. Elk Grove Unified School District, 80 Cal. Rptr. 2d 638 (Cal. App. 3 Dist. 1998)
Lindke v. Freed, 114 S.Ct. 756 (2024)
Lindros v. Governing Board of Torrance Unified School District, 108 Cal. Rptr. 185 (Cal.), cert. denied, 414 U.S. 1112 (1973)
L.J. v. Pittsburg Unified School District, 850 F.3d 996 (9th Cir. 2017)
Locke v. Davey, 540 U.S. 712 (2004)
Long Beach Unified School District v. State of California, 275 Cal. Rptr. 449 (Cal. App. 2 Dist. 1990)
Lopez v. Tulare Joint Union High School District, 40 Cal. Rptr. 2d 762 (Cal. App. 5 Dist. 1995)
Los Angeles Teachers Association v. Los Angeles City Board of Education, 78 Cal. Rptr. 723 (Cal. 1969)
Los Angeles Unified School District v. Superior Court, 60 Cal. Rptr. 3d 445 (Cal App. 2nd Dist. 2007)

Lovell v. Poway Unified School District, 90 F.3d 367 (9th Cir.), *cert. denied*, 518 U.S. 1048 (1996)
Lucas v. Fresno Unified School District, 18 Cal. Rptr. 2d 79 (Cal. App. 5 Dist. 1993)
Madsen v. Associated Chino Teachers, 317 F. Supp. 2d 1175 (C.D. Cal. 2004)
Mahmoud et al. v. Taylor et al., 606 U.S. ___ (2025)
Malcolm W. v. Novato Unified School District, 2002 WL 31770392 (Cal. App. 1 Dist. 2002) (unpublished)
Manguso v. Oceanside Unified School District, 200 Cal. Rptr. 535 (Cal. App. 4 Dist. 1984)
Mark H. v. Lemahieu, 513 F.3d 922 (9th Cir. 2008)
Mark H. v. Hamamoto, 620 F.3d 1090 (9th Cir. 2010)
Marken v. Santa Monica-Malibu Unified Sch. Dist., 136 Cal. Rptr. 3d 395 (Cal. App. 4. 2012)
Marsh v. Chambers, 463 U.S. 783 (1983)
Massey v. Banning Unified School District, 256 F. Supp. 2d 1090 (C. D. Cal. 2003)
May v. Evansville-Vanderburgh School Corporation, 787 F.2d 1105 (7th Cir. 1986)
M.C. v. Antelope Valley Union High School District, 858 F.3d 1189 (9th Cir. 2017)
McCarthy v. Fletcher, 254 Cal. Rptr. 714 (Cal. App. 5 Dist. 1989)
McCollum v. Board of Education, 333 U.S. 203 (1948)
McIntyre v. Sonoma Valley Unified School District, 141 Cal. Rptr. 3d 540 (Cal. App. 4 Dist. 2012)
McKinney v. Oxnard Union High School District Board of Trustees, 181 Cal. Rptr. 549 (Cal. 1982)
McMahon v. Albany Unified School District, 129 Cal. Rptr. 2d 184 (Cal. App. 1 Dist. 2002), *cert. denied*, 540 U.S. 824 (2003)
Mendoza v. State of California, 57 Cal. R.ptr. 3d 505 (Cal. App. 2 Dist. 2007)
Miller v. California, 413 U.S. 15 (1973)
Miller v. Chico Unified School District Board of Education, 157 Cal. Rptr. 72 (Cal. 1979)
Milliken v. Bradley, 418 U.S. 717 (1974)
Mills v. Board of Education of the District of Columbia, 348 F. Supp. 866 (1972)
Miranda v. Arizona, 384 U.S. 436 (1966)
Mississippi University for Women v. Hogan, 458 U.S. 718 (1982)
Mitchell v. Helms, 530 U.S. 793 (2000)
Modesto City Schools v. Education Audits Appeal Panel, 20 Cal. Rptr. 3d 831 (Cal. App. 3 Dist. 2004)
Montalvo v. Madera Unified School District Board of Education, 98 Cal. Rptr. 593 (Cal. App. 5 Dist. 1971)
Monteiro v. Tempe Union High School District, 158 F.3d 1022 (9th Cir. 1998)
Mooney v. Garcia, 143 Cal. Rptr. 3d 195 (Cal. App. 6 Dist. 2012)

Moran v. State of Washington, 147 F.3d 839 (9th Cir. 1998)
Moreno Valley Unified School District v. Public Employment Relations Board, 191 Cal. Rptr. 60 (Cal. App. 4 Dist. 1983)
Morgan v. Swanson, 659 F.3d 359 (5th Cir. 2011)
Morrison v. State Board of Education, 82 Cal. Rptr. 175 (Cal. 1969)
Morrow v. Los Angeles Unified School District, 57 Cal. Rptr. 3d 885 (Cal. App. 2 Dist. 2007)
Morse v. Frederick, 551 U.S. 393 (2007)
Mrs. B. v. Milford Board of Education, 103 F.3d 1114 (2nd Cir. 1997)
Mt. Healthy City School District Board of Education v. Doyle, 429 U.S. 274 (1977)
M.W. v. Panama Buena Vista Union School District, 1 Cal. Rptr. 3d 673 (Cal. App. 5 Dist. 2003)
Nathan G. v. Clovis Unified School District, 165 Cal. Rptr. 3d 588 (Cal. App. 5 Dist. 2014)
National Labor Relations Board v. Catholic Bishops of Chicago, 440 U.S. 490 (1979)
National Labor Relations Board v. Natural Gas Utility District of Hawkins County, Tennessee, 402 U.S. 600 (1971)
N.D. et al. v. State of Hawaii Department of Education, 600 F.3d 1104 (9th Cir. 2010)
Newdow v. Rio Linda Union School District, 597 F.3d 1007 (9th Cir. 2010)
Newport-Mesa Unified School District v. State of California Department of Education, 371 F. Supp. 2d 1170 (C.D. Cal. 2005)
New Jersey v. T.L.O., 469 U.S. 325 (1985)
New York v. Ferber, 458 U.S. 747 (1982)
New York Times v. Sullivan, 376 U.S. 254 (1964)
Nguon v. Wolf, 517 F. Supp. 2d 1177 (C.D. Cal. 2007)
Nicole M. v. Martinez Unified School District, 964 F. Supp.1369 (N.D. Cal. 1997)
Nordlinger v. Hahn, 505 U.S. 1 (1992)
North County Parents Organization v. Department of Education, 28 Cal. Rptr. 2d 359 (Cal. App. 4 Dist. 1994)
Nurre v. Whitehead, 580 F.3d 1087 (9th Cir. 2009), *cert. denied*, 130 S. Ct. 1937 (2010)
O'Connor-Ratcliff v. Garnier, 604 U.S. 205 (2024)
Ollier v. Sweetwater Union High School District, 858 F. Supp. 2d 1093 (S.D. Cal. 2012)
Oona R. S. By Kate S. v. McCaffrey, 143 F.3d 473 (9th Cir. 1998), *cert. denied*, 526 U.S. 1154 (1999)
Options for Youth-Victor Valley, Inc. v. Victor Valley Options for Youth Teachers Association, 27 PERC P 104 (2003)
Osborne v. Ohio, 495 U.S. 103 (1990)
Owasso Independent School District v. Falvo, 534 U.S. 426 (2002)
P. B. v. Koch, 96 F.3d 1298 (9th Cir. 1996)

Parents Involved in Community Schools v. Seattle School District No. 1, 551 U.S. 701 (2007)
Parents of Student W. v. Puyallup School District, 31 F.3d 1489 (9th Cir. 1994)
Patel v. Kent School District, 648 F.3d 965 (9th Cir. 2011)
Patten v. Grant Joint Union High School District, 37 Cal. Rptr. 3d 113 (Cal. App. 3 Dist. 2005)
Pasadena City Board of Education v. Spangler, 427 U.S. 424 (1976)
Payne v. Peninsula School District, 653 F.3d 863 (9th Cir. 2011)
Peloza v. Capistrano Unified School District, 37 F.3d 517 (9th Cir. 1994), *cert. denied*, 515 U.S. 1173 (1995)
Pennsylvania Association for Retarded Children v. Commonwealth of Pennsylvania, 343 F. Supp. 279 (E.D. Penn. 1972)
People v. Jose Y., 46 Cal. Rptr. 3d 268 (Cal. App. 2 Dist. 2006)
People v. Luera, 103 Cal. Rptr. 2d 438 (Cal. App. 2 Dist. 2001)
People v. Ramirez, 158 Cal. Rptr. 316 (Cal. 1979)
Perry Education Association v. Perry Local Educators' Association, 460 U.S. 37 (1983)
Peterson v. Minidoka County School District No. 331, 118 F.3d 1351 (9th Cir.), *amended*, 132 F.3d 1258 (9th Cir. 1997)
Peter W. v. San Francisco Unified School District, 131 Cal. Rptr. 854 (Cal. App. 1 Dist. 1976)
Petersil v. Santa Monica-Malibu Unified School District, 161 Cal. Rptr.3d 851 (Cal. App. 2 Dist. 2013)
Pickering v. Board of Education, 391 U.S. 563 (1968)
Pierce v. Society of Sisters, 268 U.S. 510 (1925)
Pinard v. Clatskanie School District 6J, 467 F.3d 755 (9th Cir. 2006)
Pinellas County School District, 20 IDELR 561 (OCR 1993)
Planned Parenthood of Central Missouri v. Danforth, 428 U.S. 52 (1976)
Plessy v. Ferguson, 163 U.S. 537 (1896), *overruled by Brown v. Board of Education of Topeka, Kansas*, 347 U.S. 483 (1954)
Plyler v. Doe, 457 U.S. 202 (1982)
Posey v. Lake Pend Oreille School District No. 84, 546 F.3d 1121 (9th Cir. 2008)
Poway Federation of Teachers v. Poway Unified School District, 12 PERC P 19102 (1988)
Poway Unified School District v. Superior Court, 73 Cal. Rptr. 2d 777 (Cal. App. 4 Dist. 1998)
Preschooler II v. Clark County School Board of Trustees, 479 F.3d 1175 (9th Cir. 2007)
Prince v. Jacoby, 303 F.3d 1074 (9th Cir. 2002), *cert. denied*, 540 U.S. 813 (2003)
Public Employment Relations Board v. Modesto City Schools District, 186 Cal. Rptr. 634 (Cal. App. 5 Dist. 1982)

Ramirez v. Long Beach Unified School District, 129 Cal. Rptr. 2d 128 (Cal. App. 2 Dist. 2002)
Randi W. v. Muroc Joint Unified School District, 60 Cal. Rptr. 2d 263 (Cal. 1997)
Ravenswood Teacher Association v. Ravenswood City School District, 26 PERC P 33118 (2002)
Ray v. Antioch Unified School District, 107 F. Supp. 2d 1165 (N.D. Cal. 2000)
Reed v. Reed, 404 U.S. 71 (1971)
Reed v. United Teachers Los Angeles, 145 Cal. Rptr. 3d 454 (Cal. App. 2 Dist. 2012)
Reeves v. Rocklin Unified School District, 135 Cal. Rptr. 2d 213 (Cal. App. 3 Dist. 2003)
Regents of the University of California v. Bakke, 438 U.S. 265 (1978)
Regino v. Staley, 133 F.4th 951 (9th Cir. 2025)
Reynolds v. United States, 98 U.S. 145 (1878)
Ridgecrest Charter Sch. v. Sierra Sands Unified Sch. Dist., 30 Rptr.3d 648 (Cal. App. 4th 2005)
Rim of the World Unified School District v. Superior Court, 129 Cal. Rptr. 2d 11 (Cal. App. 4 Dist. 2002)
Rizo v. Vovino, 854 F.3d 1161 (9th Cir. 2017)
Robb v. Bethel School District #403, 308 F.3d 1047 (9th Cir. 2002)
Robert L. Mueller Charter School, 27 PERC P 46 (2003)
Robins v. PruneYard Shopping Center, 153 Cal. Rptr. 854 (Cal. 1979), *aff'd*, 447 U.S. 74 (1980)
Roe v. Wade, 410 U.S. 113 (1973)
Ross v. Campbell Union School District, 138 Cal. Rptr. 557 (Cal. App. 1 Dist. 1977)
R.P. v. Prescott Unified School District, 631 F.3d 1117 (9th Cir. 2011)
Runyon v. McCrary, 427 U.S. 160 (1976)
Ryan v. California Interscholastic Federation—San Diego Section, 114 Cal. Rptr. 2d 798 (Cal. App. 4 Dist. 2001)
Sacramento City Unified School District v. Holland, 14 F.3d 1398 (9th Cir. 1994), *cert. denied*, 512 U.S. 1207 (1994)
San Antonio Independent School District v. Rodriguez, 411 U.S. 1 (1973)
Sanchez v. San Diego County Office of Education, 106 Cal. Rptr. 3d 750 (Cal. App. 4 Dist. 2010)
San Diego Teachers Association v. Superior Court, 154 Cal. Rptr. 893 (Cal. 1979)
San Diego Unified School District v. Commission on Professional Competence, 124 Cal. Rptr. 3d 320 (Cal. App. 4 Dist. 2011)
San Dieguito Union High School District v. Commission on Professional Competence, 220 Cal. Rptr. 351 (Cal. App. 4 Dist. 1985)
Sands v. Morongo Unified School District, 281 Cal. Rptr. 34 (Cal. 1991), *cert. denied*, 505 U.S. 1218 (1992)

Sanford Unified School District No. 1 v. Redding, 557 U.S. 1364 (2009)
San Francisco NAACP v. San Francisco Unified School District, 413 F. Supp. 2d 1051 (N.C. Cal. 2005)
San Francisco Unified School District v. Johnson, 92 Cal. Rptr. 309 (Cal. 1971)
San Leandro Teachers Association v. Governing Board of the San Leandro Unified School District, 95 Cal. Rptr. 3d 164 (Cal. 2009)
San Mateo City School District v. Public Employment Relations Board, 191 Cal. Rptr. 800 (Cal. 1983)
Santa Barbara School District v. Superior Court, 118 Cal. Rptr. 637 (Cal. 1975)
Santa Fe Independent School District v. Doe, 530 U.S. 290 (2000)
Sato v. Orange County Dept. of Education, 861 F.3d 923 (9th Cir. 2017)
Schaffer v. Weast, 546 U.S. 49 (2005)
School District of Abington Township v. Schempp, 374 U.S. 203 (1963)
Scott B. v. Board of Trustees of Orange County High School of the Arts, 158 Cal. Rptr. 3d 173 (Cal. App. 4 Dist. 2013)
Sequoia Union High School District v. Aurora Charter High School, 5 Cal. Rptr. 3d 86 (Cal. App. 1 Dist. 2003)
Serrano v. Priest, 96 Cal. Rptr. 601 (Cal. 1971) [*Serrano I*], 135 Cal. Rptr. 345 (Cal. 1976) [*Serrano II*], *cert. denied sub nom. Clowes v. Serrano*, 432 U.S. 907 (1977)
Serrano v. Priest, 226 Cal. Rptr. 584 (Cal. App. 2 Dist. 1986) [*Serrano III*], *cause dismissed* (Oct. 27, 1989)
Service Employees Industrial Union v. Los Angeles Unified School District, 7 PERC P 14069 (1983)
Settle v. Dickson County School Board, 53 F.3d 152 (6th Cir.), *cert. denied*, 516 U.S. 989 (1995)
Shanley v. Northeast Independent School District, 462 F.2d 960 (5th Cir. 1972)
Shelton v. Tucker, 364 U.S. 479 (1960)
Skelly v. State Personnel Board, 124 Cal. Rptr. 14 (Cal. 1975)
Skinner v. Vacaville Unified School District, 43 Cal. Rptr. 2d 384 (Cal. App. 1 Dist. 1995)
Smith v. Novato Unified School District, 59 Cal. Rptr. 3d 508 (Cal. App. 1 Dist. 2007), *cert. denied*, 552 U.S 1184 (2008)
South Bay Union School District v. Public Employment Relations Board, 279 Cal. Rptr. 135 (Cal. App. 4 Dist. 1991)
Spanierman v. Hughes, 576 F. Supp. 2d 292 (D. Conn. 2008)
St. Isidore of Seville Catholic Virtual School v. Drummond, 145 S. Ct. 1916 (2025) (mem.)
State Board of Education v. Honig, 16 Cal. Rptr. 2d 727 (Cal. App. 3 Dist. 1993)
Stockton Teachers Association CTA/NEA v. Stockton Unified School District, 139 Cal. Rptr. 3d 55 (Cal. App. 4 Dist. 2012)

Stone v. Graham, 449 U.S. 39 (1980) (per curiam)
Sullivan v. Centinela Valley Union High School District, 122 Ca. Rptr. 3d 871 (Cal. App. 4 Dist. 2011)
Summerfield v. Windsor Unified School District, 116 Cal. Rptr. 2d 233 (Cal. App. 1 Dist. 2002)
Swann v. Charlotte-Mecklenburg Board of Education, 402 U.S. 1 (1971)
Swanson v. Guthrie Independent School District I-L, 135 F.3d. 694 (10th Cir. 1998)
Tape v. Hurley, 66 Cal. 473 (Cal. 1885)
Tarasoff v. Regents of the University of California, 131 Cal. Rptr. 14 (Cal. 1976)
T.B. v. San Diego Unified School District, 806 F.3d 451 (9th Cir. 2015)
T.H. v. San Diego Unified School District, 19 Cal. Rptr. 3d 532 (Cal. App. 4 Dist. 2004)
Thompson v. Sacramento City Unified School District, 132 Cal. Rptr. 2d 748 (Cal. App. 3 Dist. 2003)
Timothy O. v. Paso Robles Unified School District, 822 F.3d 1105 (9th Cir. 2016)
Tinker v. Des Moines Independent Community School District, 393 U.S. 503 (1969)
Toney v. Young, 238 F.Supp.3d 1234 (E.D. Cal. 2017)
Torcaso v. Watkins, 367 U.S. 488 (1961)
Torsiello v. Oakland Unified School District, 242 Cal. Rptr. 752 (Cal. App. 1 Dist. 1987)
Town of Greece, N. Y. v. Galloway, 572 U.S. 565 (2014)
Troxel v. Granville, 530 U.S. 57 (2000)
Trinity Lutheran Church of Columbia, Inc. v. Comer, 582 U.S. 449 (2017)
Truth v. Kent School District, 542 F.3d 634 (9th Cir. 2008), *overruled on other grounds, Los Angeles County, CA v. Humphries*, 131 S. Ct. 447 (2010)
Tucker v. State of California Department of Education, 97 F.3d 1204 (9th Cir. 1996)
Union School District v. Smith, 15 F.3d 1519 (9th Cir. 1994), *cert. denied*, 513 U.S. 965 (1994)
United States v. Aguilera, 287 F. Supp. 2d 1204 (E.D. Cal. 2003)
United States v. Ballard, 322 U.S. 78 (1944)
United States v. Seeger, 380 U.S. 163 (1965)
United States v. Virginia, 518 U.S. 515 (1996)
United Teachers Los Angeles v. Los Angeles Unified School District, 142 Cal. Rptr. 3d 850 (Cal. 2012)
Valerie v. Davis, 307 F.3d 1036 (9th Cir. 2002)
Vallejo City Unified School District v. Vallejo Education Association, 17 PERC P 24166 (1993)
Van Duyn v. Baker School District, 502 F.3d 811 (9th Cir. 2007)
Van Orden v. Perry, 545 U.S. 677 (2005)

Vergara v. State of California, 209 Cal.Rptr.3d 532 (Cal. App. 2 Dist. 2016)
Vernonia School District v. Acton, 515 U.S. 646 (1995)
Virginia G. v. ABC Unified School District, 19 Cal. Rptr. 2d 671 (Cal. App. 2 Dist. 1993)
Vittal v. Long Beach Unified School District, 87 Cal. Rptr. 319 (Cal. App. 2 Dist. 1970)
Walczak v. Florida Union Free School District, 142 F.3d 119 (2nd Cir. 1998)
Wallace v. Jaffree, 472 U.S. 38 (1985)
Walnut Valley Unified School District v. Superior Court, 121 Cal. Rptr. 3d 383 (Cal. App. 2 Dist. 2011)
Ward v. Flood, 48 Cal. 36 (Cal. 1874)
Washington v. Davis, 426 U.S. 229 (1976)
Welch v. Oakland Unified School District, 111 Cal. Rptr. 2d 374 (Cal. App. 1 Dist. 2001)
Wells v. One2One Learning Foundation, 48 Cal. Rptr. 3d 108 (Cal. 2006)
West Virginia State Board of Education v. Barnette, 319 U.S. 624 (1943)
Westminster School District of Orange County v. Mendez, 161 F.2d 774 (9th Cir. 1947)
W.G. v. Board of Trustees of Target Range School District No. 23, 960 F.2d 1479 (9th Cir. 1992)
Widmar v. Vincent, 454 U.S. 263 (1981)
Wilson v. State Board of Education, 89 Cal. Rptr. 2d 745 (Cal. App. 1 Dist. 1999)
Winn v. Hibbs, 361 F. Supp. 2d 1117 (D. Ariz. 2005)
Wisniewski v. Board of Education of Weedsport Central School District, 494 F.3d 34 (2nd Cir. 2007), *cert. denied*, 552 U.S. 1296 (2008)
Wisconsin v. Yoder, 406 U.S. 205 (1972)
Woodbury v. Brown-Dempsey, 134 Cal. Rptr. 2d 124 (Cal. App. 4 Dist. 2003)
Woodland Joint Unified School District v. Commission on Professional Competence, 4 Cal. Rptr. 2d 227 (Cal. App. 3 Dist. 1992)
Worth County Schools, 27 IDELR 224 (OCR 1997)
Wysinger v. Crookshank, 82 Cal. 588 (Cal. 1890)
Yarber v. Oakland Unified School District, 6 Cal. Rptr. 2d 437 (Cal. App. 1 Dist. 1992)
Zalac v. Governing Board of the Ferndale Unified School District, 120 Cal. Rptr. 2d 615 (Cal. App. 1 Dist. 2002)
Zelman v. Simmons-Harris, 536 U.S. 639 (2002)
Zorach v. Clauson, 343 U.S. 306 (1952)

INDEX

Italic page numbers indicate material in tables or figures.

42 U.S.C. Section 1981, 41
42 U.S.C. Section 1983: 6, 8, 256–257, 370, 490, 491, 493, 496, 540, 549; liability of school employees, 534–538; liability of schools, 531–534; private school exemption, 41

Aaris v. Las Virgenes Unified School District, 513
Abood v. Detroit Board of Education, 177, 179
absences, 50, 54–55, 268, 270, 321
academic freedom, 250, 284–288, 290, 306
Acceptable Use Policies (AUPs), 88, 89, 92, 271
accountability,17; assessment and, 45, 102–105; of charter schools, 30, 35–36, 38, 184; distance learning and, 96; of employers, 492, 501, 531; instructional trends, 46; LCFF and, 78, 131; of school districts, 492, 501;of students, 517; voucher programs and, 44

accreditation of charter schools, 34–35
Achene v. Pierce Joint Unified School District, 209
ACLU. *See* American Civil Liberties Union
Acosta v. Los Angeles Unified School District, 515–516
acronyms, in special education, 335
Acton, Vernonia School District v., 450–451
ADA. *See* Americans with Disabilities Act (1990); average daily attendance (ADA)
Adair v. Stockton Unified School District, 161
Adams v. Oregon, 341
Adcock v. San Diego Unified School District, 245
Adelt v. Richmond School District, 204
adequate yearly progress, 27, 81, 103
ADHD (attention deficit hyperactivity disorder), 348–349, 372
administrative law, *3*, 9–12, 15, 550, 552, 545

administrative law judges (ALJs): layoffs or dismissals and, 207, 210, 218, 223, 228; MIRS process and, 207; OAH ALJs, 334, 337, 365; PERB ALJs, 155, 163, 169; special education law and, 334, 339, 346, 360, 364, 365, 366
administrative panels, 403, 404–405, 406, 410
Administrative Services Credential, 192
administrators, 3, 7, 10, 13; attendance and, 53, 56; charter schools and, 186; classroom instruction and, 78–79; collective bargaining and, 149, 153; contract law and, 12; copyright law and, 88; credentialing, 83; curriculum and, 71, 76, 181; discrimination and, 473, 474, 475, 479; educator expression rights and, 246, 247, 249, 250, 251, 252–253, 262; employee classification of, 190; employment rights of, 188–189, 229–230, 231; evaluations of, 205; IDEA and, 7, 333; harassment and, 491, 493, 495, 496; legal liability of, 506, 507, 508, 509, 510, 511, 516, 529, 532, 534–535, 537; off-campus speech and, 274; safe learning environments and, 46, 57, 63, 67, 68; schooling structure and, 21–24; special education law and, 357, 376; student discipline and, 380, 381, 384, 387, 389, 391, 392, 394, 395, 397, 400, 417; student search and, 450, 451, 456, 457, 458; student seizure and, 461; teacher academic freedom and, 285, 288; teacher dismissals and, 215; teacher staffing and, 222
Adventures of Huckleberry Finn, The (Twain), 77, 490
advertisements, 78, 213, 279, 318–319, 332, 344
advisory committees, 22, 80, 131, 144, 162, 424–425, 463, 491
affirmative action: for gender, 478; limits on, 474–478, 479, 497; prohibition against, 32; Supreme Court's decision to uphold, 466–467; for race, 466–467, 474–478, 479, 497
African American students. *See* Black students
Age Discrimination Act of 1975, 440, 485
Age Discrimination in Employment Act (1967), 7
agendas, public meeting, 420, 421–422, 424
age of majority, 360–361, 437
Agostini v. Felton, 294, 325
Aguilera, United States v., 453
Aguillard, Edwards v., 306
Aguirre v. Los Angeles Unified School District, 369
A.G. v. Paradise Valley Unified School District No. 69, 371, 415
AI. *See* artificial intelligence (AI)
AIDS prevention education, 24, 487
Alamo Heights Independent School District (Texas), 115
Albany Unified School District, Chen Through Chen v., 273
Albany Unified School District, McMahon v., 424
alcohol, advertising for, 93, 318
alcohol use, by teachers, 210, 216
alcohol use, by students, 378–379, 386, 389, 397, 408, 450, 460, 522
Alexander B., In re, 457
Alexander v. Sandoval, 490
all-comers policies, 32, 317

Allen, Board of Education v., 325
Allen, Charles H., et al., Petitioners-Appellants, and California School Employees Association and Pleasant Valley Elementary School District, Respondents, 176
Alma W. v. Oakland Unified School District, 509
Alum Rock school district, 42
Ambach v. Norwick, 284
American Academy of Pediatrics v. Lungren, 437
American Civil Liberties Union (ACLU), 289
American Civil Rights Foundation v. Berkeley Unified School District, 480
American Civil Rights Foundation v. Los Angeles Unified School District, 475
American Federation of State, County and Municipal Employees, Janus v., 179–180
American Federation of Teachers, 180, 185
American Library Association v. United States, 90
Americans with Disabilities Act (ADA, 1990), 237–240; charter schools, 191; FEHA compared with, 241; overview, 7; private schools, 41; Section 504 and, 237–240, 371–373, 374–374, 377
Amish, 24, 322
Analisa N., Horace Mann Insurance Company v., 509
Anderson Union High School District v. Shasta Secondary Home School, 31, 35–36
Antelope Valley Union School District, M. C. v., 353

Anti-Defamation League (ADL), 511
Anti-SLAPP Law (California), 511
Antioch High School, 455–456
Antioch Unified School District, Ray v., 493
API. *See* Academic Performance Index
appeals, expulsion, 19, 409–412
appellate courts, 13, 15, 544, 551, 552
appellate division, superior courts, 13
appellate jurisdiction, 545
arbitration, 3, 149, 152, 165, 170–174
Arcadia Unified School District v. State Department of Education, 133
Arizona, Miranda v., 456–457
Arizona Interscholastic Association, Clark v. (1982), 483
Arizona Interscholastic Association, Clark v. (1989), 483
Arkansas, Epperson v., 76, 284
Arkansas educator association rights, 260
Arlington Central Unified School District Board of Education v. Murphy, 369
armband protest. *See Tinker v. Des Moines Independent Community School District*
artificial intelligence (AI), 98–102, 259
Asian students, 80, 317, 468–470
assault, 283, 386, 388, 394, 443, 496, 504–505, 534. *See also* sexual assault or battery
Assembly Bill 8, 121
Assembly Bill 86, 358
Assembly Bill 112, 180
Assembly Bill 114, 359
Assembly Bill 119, 180
Assembly Bill 1955, 440–441, 488–489
Assembly Bill 2926, 135

assessment and accountability, 102–105. *See* accountability; student assessment
Associated Chino Teachers, Madsen v., 175
Association of Mexican-American Educators v. State of California, 83
association rights, 57, 260–261, 281–284, 291
athletes and athletics: California governance of, 17, 427; drug testing and use, 450–451, 458; due process and, 382–383; duty to supervise and, 511–516, 538; expulsion or suspension and, 397; FERPA and 8; gender discrimination and equity, 323, 483, 485–486, 487–488; injuries, 451, 511–516, 523, 538; insurance and, 528–529; mascot names, 65; recreational youth sports leagues, 58; safe and healthy environments, 65, 68; student records and, 443
attendance, 47–57; compulsory attendance laws, 22–23, 47–53, 112; distance learning and, 95; exemptions from, 53–55; homeschooling and, 24; interdistrict attendance appeals, 19; private schools and, 39; records, 53; truancy, 14, 55–57, 268. *See also* average daily attendance (ADA)
attendance zones and areas, 27, 32–33, 97, 140, 465, 467, 471, 475, 478, 480
attention deficit hyperactivity disorder (ADHD), 348–349, 372
attorneys: of foster children, 50; Miranda and, 456; parents as, 297, 389; public service employees, 190; school attorneys, 279, 300; special education and, 365, 366, 367, 369–370, 376, 377; student discipline and, 389, 402; student search and seizure, 456, 459; Title VII and, 237
attorneys' fees, 7, 10, 72, 218, 237, 369–370, 374, 375, 377, 429, 533, 541
Atwater Elementary School District v. Department of General Services, 217
at-will employment, 191
audio recorders in classroom, 87
Aurora Charter High School, Sequoia Union High School District v., 37
autism, 336, 339, 345–346, 349, 350, 356, 357
automatic external defibrillator, 67
average daily attendance (ADA), 49, 54, 55, 78; computing truancy and, 55; charter school funding and, 137, 139, 517; employment rights and, 189, 202, 208, 209, 219, 225; layoffs, non-reelection, and dismissals and, 208, 209, 219; LCFF and, 129, 130; quest for equity and, 116; revenue limit funding and, 125–126; synchronous online instruction and, 95
Avila v. Spokane School District 81, 364
AYP (adequate yearly progress), 27, 81, 103

Baca v. Moreno Valley Unified School District, 255, 256, 421
Bagley Act (1971) (California), 471–472
Bain et al. v. California Teachers Association et al., 179
Baird, Eisenstadt v., 437
Baird, Sedlock v., 308
Baker, Bowker v., 324

Baker School District, Van Duyn v., 341
Bakersfield Elementary Teachers Association v. Bakersfield City School District, 197
Balanced Treatment for Creation-Science and Evolution-Science in Public School Instruction Act, The (Louisiana), 306
Baldwin Park school district, 113
Baldwin School, Bercovitch v., 372
Ballard, United States v., 296
Banning Teachers Association v. Public Employment Relations Board, 155
Banning Unified School District, Massey v., 440
bargaining unit, 131, 149–151, 154–157, 160, 169, 174–176, 179, 181, 187, 541
Barnette, West Virginia State Board v., 2, 297
Bartell v. Palos Verdes Peninsula School District, 525
basic aid districts, 116, 118, 126, 130
battery, 60, 61, 385, 386. *See also* sexual assault or battery
Bassett v. Lakeside Inn, Inc., 519
bathrooms, 438, 447, 451, 452, 488, 504–505, 536
B.C. v. Plumas Unified School District, 458, 461
behavior intervention plan (BIP), 357–358, 376–377, 415
behavior plans, 343, 359, 384, 388
Bekiaris v. Board of Education of City of Modesto, 248
Belanger v. Madera Unified School District, 532
Bell v. Vista Unified School District, 428
Benjamin G. v. Special Education Hearing Office, 360

Bennett, Corales v., 268
Bercovitch v. Baldwin School, 372
Berkelman v. San Francisco Unified School District, 483
Bernstein, Ghafur v., 511
Bernstein v. Lopez, 229
Berry v. Department of Social Services, NEED pages
Bethel School District, Blair v., 247
Bethel School District v. Fraser, 268, 272, 274, 288
Beverly Hills school district, 113
Beverly Hills Unified School District, J.C. ex rel. R.C. v., 274
Bible: clubs, 313, 316, 317; college, 288; reading of, 298, 301, 306, 320; study of, 320; taught as history or literature, 305, 321
Biden, Joseph, 100
bilingual education, 22, 39, 72, 79, 424
Bill of Rights, 2, 450, 542. *See also specific amendments*
BIP. *See* behavior intervention plan.
Birmingham Board of Education, Jackson v., 485
Biscotti v. Yuba City Unified School District, 524
Black, Hugo, 265, 293
Blackmun, Harry, 437
Black's Law Dictionary, Abridged, 541
Black students: equal protection and, 112; intelligence tests and, 347; NAEP scores, 468; racial discrimination and, 467, 468, 469, 471, 491
Blackwell v. Issaquena County Board of Education, 264
Blain School District, LaVine v., 267
Blair v. Bethel School District, 247
Blanchard v. Morton School District, 535

B. L. Levy, Mahanoy Area School District v., 272
block grants, 34, 121, 127, 128, 130, 137
Board of Education, DiLoreto v., 319
Board of Education, Everson v., 293, 324
Board of Education, McCollum v., 293
Board of Education, Pickering v., 244–246, 247, 248, 250, 251–252, 264, 286
Board of Education of City of Modesto, Bekiaris v., 248
Board of Education of Hendrick Hudson School District v. Rowley, 333, 338–341, 356
Board of Education of Island Trees v. Pico, 91
Board of Education of Long Beach Unified School District v. Jack M., 438
Board of Education of Oklahoma City Public Schools v. Dowell, 466
Board of Education of Rogers, Arkansas v. McCluskey, 378
Board of Education of the City of Los Angeles, Crawford v., 472–474, 475, 476, 478, 479
Board of Education of the City of Los Angeles, Gordon v., 322
Board of Education of the District of Columbia, Mills v., 331, 332–333, 342, 363
Board of Education of the Round Valley Unified School District v. Round Valley Teachers Association, 154, 172, 173
Board of Education of Topeka, Kansas, Brown v., 2, 112, 114, 244, 465, 466, 470, 471, 497, 551
Board of Education of Weedsport Central School District, Wisniewski v., 271
Board of Education of Westside Community Schools v. Mergens, 282, 314, 316
Board of Education v. Allen, 325
Board of Education v. Earls, 451
Board of Education v. Sacramento County Board of Education, 405
Board of Regents v. Roth, 191
Board of Trustees, Duval v., 427
Board of Trustees, Grimsley v., 209
Board of Trustees of Target Range School District No. 23, W.G. v., 337
Board of Trustees of the San Diego Unified School District, Ceniceros v., 314
Bolin v. San Bernardino City Unified School District, 206
Boliou v. Stockton Unified School District, 218
bonding, for facilities funding, *124*, 135
Bonita Unified School District, California School Employees Association v., 173–174
Bonta, Rob, 324
Bostock v. Clayton County, Georgia, 236
Bowker v. Baker, 324
Bown v. Gwinnett County School District, 299
Bravo ex rel. Ramirez v. Hsu, 462
Bremerton School District, Kennedy v., 294, 303
Brown, Jerry, 51, 104
Brown Act (1953) (California), 420–429, 462–463; defining open meetings, 424–426; enforcement, 429; exceptions to open meetings, 426–428; key provisions, 421–424; school board meetings, 208, 255

Brown Act (1961) (California), 153, 186
Brown-Dempsey, Woodbury v., 402
Brown v. Board of Education of Topeka, Kansas, 2, 112, 114, 244, 465, 466, 470, 471, 497, 551
Brown v. Gilmore, NEED PAGE numbers
Brown v. Woodland Joint Unified School District, 307
BRV, Inc. v. Superior Court, 431
Bullis Charter School v. Los Altos School District, 36–37
bumping rights, in layoffs, 227
Burger, Warren, 268, 299
Burge v. Colton School District 53, 271
busing limits, 473–474
bus suspension, 413
Butt v. State of California, 220–221

CAHSEE (California High School Exit Exam), 11, 35, 104
Cajon Valley Union School District, Eric M. v., 518
Calaveras Unified School District, Gellerman v., 356
Caldwell v. Montoya, 531
Caldwell v. Paramount Unified School District, 531
California, Miller v., 89
California, Whitlow v., 51
California Alternate Performance Assessment (CAPA), 104
California Appellate Report, 551
California Association of Private School Organizations, 40
California Attorney General: on admission refusal, 52; on attendance record withholding, 53; on expulsion appeals, 412; on firearm possession, 392; on first grade admission, 52; on IEP team members, 352–353; on independent study funding, 54; on interdistrict transfers, 29; on legal liability, 500, 527; on news media on campus, 63, 352–353; on open meetings, 426, 428; on parental permission on absences, 55; role of, 18; on student discipline, 408; on student searches, 443, 459; on summer sessions, 325; on technology for meetings, 422
California Basic Education Skills Test (CBEST), 82, 83, 193
California Business and Professionals Code, 93–94
California Charter Academy, 35
California Charter Schools Association, 36
California Charter Schools Association v. Los Angeles Unified School District, 37
California Civil Rights Department, 237, 242
California Code, 392, 550
California Code of Civil Procedure, 64, 174
California Code of Regulations, 9, 11, 155, 192, 216, 334, 350, 503
California Commission on Teacher Credentialing (CCTC), 82, 82; certificated employees, 189; credentialing system, 192–193; disclosure exemptions, 432, internship credentials, 202; recommendations of school employees, 510; teacher evaluation and assessment, 82–83, 218

California Constitution, 3; on busing, 473; charter schools and, 38; on due process, 380, 382–383, 384, 543; educational mandate, 4–5, 165; on education funding, 111, 112, 113, 114, 118, 126, 128, 133, 325; on equal protection, 118, 221, 380, 472, 473–475, 476, 477, 478, *479*, 481, 484, 543; establishment clause, 307, 308; free speech protections, 174, 175, 246–247, 251, 266, 269; on individual rights, 5; movement toward adequacy and, 142, 143, 145; on religious freedom, 294–295; pornography and, 90; on public access, 419; on safe learning environments, 57, 378, 507; on school district operations, 532; on schooling structure, 15, 16, 17, 18, 20, 21, 44; on separation of church and state, 40, 296, 307, 311–312, 325, 328, 329; student search and seizure and, 440, 449, 450, 461

California Cradle-to-Career Data System, 94

California Department of Education (CDE), *3*; on artificial intelligence, 99, 101; on assessment and accountability, 102, 103, 104, 105; bullying and, 494; charter schools and, 30, 36, 140; comprehensive school safety plan guidance, 59; on curriculum censorship, 78; curriculum content standards, 72–73, 74; curriculum law and, 47; DASH Recognition Program and, 65–66; Eric Paredes Sudden Cardiac Arrest Prevention Act and, 512; on homeschooling, 24; LGBTQ students and, 488; nonpublic schools and, 359–360, 362, 381; on physical education, 67; private schools and, 12, 40; racial discrimination and, 471; on religion in schools, 301, 302; State Board of Education and, 9; structure for school governance, 16–18, *16*; teacher preparation and credentialing, 83; Title IX and, 485; Uniform Complaint Procedure, 11, 134; website, 8, 30, 47, 71, 101, 103, 550, 556

California Department of Fair Employment and Housing (now California Civil Rights Department), 11, 237, 556

California Department of Mental Health, 359

California Education Code: Desktop Edition, 550, 555

California Education for a Global Economy Initiative, 72

California English Language Development Test (CELDT), 80

California Family Rights Act (CFRA), 231

California Federation of Teachers (CFT), 148, 153

California High School Exit Exam (CAHSEE), 11, 35, 104

California Interscholastic Federation, 17, 29, 68, 383, 427–238, 512

California Interscholastic Federation-San Diego Section, Ryan v., 383

California Legislative Analyst's Office, 135

California Legislature, 3; administrative agencies and, 9–10; administrator training and, 22; artificial intelligence and, 101; attendance and, 57; California Partnership Academies and, 71; California schooling structure and, 15–18, 20, 21, 44; California Student Civil Liberties Act, 439; charter schools and, 30–31, 35–36, 38, 39, 163, 184; class size and, 78; collective bargaining and unions, 146, 148, 149, 152, 153, 159, 162, 176, 180, 183; curriculum content standards set by, 70, 71–73, 75; distance learning and, 94, 97; district unification and, 20; Expanded Learning Opportunities Program, 97; employee layoff rights and, 227; expulsion and, 394; extracurricular and athletic activities and, 383, 512; False Claims Act, 517; homeschooling and, 24; immunity and, 530; interdistrict school choice program and, 28; mental health services and, 359; Open Enrollment Act, 29; Parental Involvement Act, 25–26; Parent Empowerment Act, 27; privacy and, 441, 445, 488; private schools and, 39, 40; public records and, 429, 430, 432, 434, 435; racial discrimination and, 468–472, 478; religion and schools, 294, 295, 299, 305; Romero Act, 21; safe learning environment and, 57, 58, 59, 60, 64, 65, 67, 69; school funding and, 107, 108, 116–119, 121–122, 123–128, 133, 137, 139, 142, 144–145; special education and, 338–339, 359; statutory law, 5, 6, 8, 545, 547, 549–550; student assessment and, 104; teacher support and assessment, 83; Unruh Civil Rights Act, 495–497, 498, 508, 539; voucher programs and, 43. *See also individual Senate Bills*; Tort Claims Act

California Longitudinal Teacher Integrated Data Education System, 84

California Parents for the Equalization of Educational Materials v. Torlakson, 74, 307

California Office of Administrative Hearings (OAH), 217–218, 223, 334, 337–338, 340, 342, 350, 360, 363, 364, 365, 366, 368, 369, 370, 377, 415, 416, 418

California Office of Economic Opportunity, 42

California School Boards Association v. State Board of Education, 31

California School Boards Association v. State of California, 128

California School Employees Association (CSEA), 148, 153, 173–174

California School Employees Association v. Bonita Unified School District, 173–174

California School Employees Association v. Livingston Union School District, 226

California Standards for the Teaching Profession, 82, 205

California Standards Tests (CST), 102, 468

California Student Civil Liberties Act, 439

California Teachers Association (CTA), 124, 144, 148, 177, 181–183, 246, 285

California Teachers Association, Friedrichs v., 179
California Teachers Association, Harik v., 179
California Teachers Association et al., Bain et al. v., 179
California Teachers Association v. Governing Board of San Diego Unified School District, 247
California Teachers Association v. Governing Board of the Hilmar Unified School District, 161
California Teachers Association v. Hayes, 15, 107, 124
California Teachers Association v. Public Employee Relations Board, 183
California Teachers Association v. Riles, 325
California Teachers Association v. State Board of Education, 285
California Teachers Association v. Vallejo City Unified School District, 220
California v. Chino Valley Unified School District, 440
California Voting Rights Act, 20
California Youth Authority, 20
Camarillo High School, 474
Campaign for Quality Education et al. v. State of California, 145
Campbell Union School District, Ross v., 500
Capistrano Unified School District, C. F. ex rel. Farnan v., 286
Capistrano Unified School District, C. W. v., 370
Capistrano Unified School District, Peloza v., 261, 302, 307
caregiving affidavit, 48

Carey v. Population Services, International, 437
Carter, Florence County School District Four v., 368
Carter, Robert, 470
Casterson v. Superior Court, 520
Castro v. Clovis Unified School District, 270–271
catastrophic leave program, 232
categorical aid, 123, *124*, 126–127, 137–138
Catholic Bishops of Chicago, National Labor Relations Board v., 185
Caviness v. Horizon Community Learning Center, 185
C.A. v. William S. Hart Union High School District, 509
CBEST (California Basic Education Skills Test), 82, 83, 193
C. B. v. Garden Grove Unified School District, 368
CCTC. *See* California Commission on Teacher Credentialing (CCTC)
CDE. *See* California Department of Education (CDE)
Ceballos, Garcetti v., 249–250, 252, 253, 259
Cedar Rapids Community School District v. Garrett F., 357
cell phone searches, 455–456
Ceniceros v. Board of Trustees of the San Diego Unified School District, 314
censorship, 76–78, 91, 213, 257, 270, 274–279, 289, 291, 425
Center Moriches Union Free School District, Lamb's Chapel v., 294, 318

Centinela Valley Union High School District, Environmental Charter High School v., 38
Centinela Valley Union High School, Sullivan v. 208
Central High School (Columbus, Ohio), 382
certificated employees, 75, 188–191, 242; assignment of, 206; in charter schools, 139, 181; classifications of, 194–204; collective bargaining and, 148, 149, 154, 156, 157, *158*, 159, 160, 161, 172, 181; as counselors, 526; credentials, 192–193; definition of, 208; discipline of, 206–208; dismissal of permanent teachers, 210–217; dismissal hearing process, 217–219; distance learning and, 95; evaluation of, 83, 205; fringe benefits for, 428; layoff of, 172, 219–223; leave rights, 231–235; misclassification of, 222; non-re-election and dismissal of probationary teachers, 208–210; permanent, 202–204; probationary, 200–202; property rights of, 191–192; student discipline and, 381, 384 *386*, 391, 403; student supervision by, 503; substitute, 194–195; suspension and dismissal of, 207, 210–219; temporary, 195–199
C.F. ex rel. Farnan v. Capistrano Unified School District, 286
Chambers, Marsh v., 300
Chandler Unified School District, Collins v., 299
Chandler v. McMinnville School District, 281
Chandler v. Siegelman, 301

Channel One, 78
Charlotte-Mecklenburg Board of Education, Swann v., 465
Charter School Facility Grant Program, 36, 140
Charter School Revolving Loan Fund, 36
charter schools, 25, 30–39, 45; accountability and, 30, 35–36, 38, 184; accreditation of, 34–35; administrators in, 83; as alternative to low-performing public schools, 29; Americans with Disabilities Act and, 191; for at-risk students, 57; block grants and, 136–138; Brown Act and, 420–421; California Legislature and, 30–31, 35–36, 38, 39, 163, 184; class size and, 78; collective bargaining and, 148, 155, 162–164, 172–173, 181–187; constitutionality of, 38–39; county school board and, 21; curriculum content standards and, 72, 73, 75, 77; defamation lawsuits and, 511; dismissal from, 399–400; distance learning and, 517; Educational Code provisions and, 17; Eleventh Amendment and, 8, 532; enrollment, 1; facilities, 139–140; Fair Employment and Housing Act and, 240; Fourteenth Amendment and, 4; functioning as local education agencies, 31; funding, 27, 51, 128, 136–140, 146, 326–327, 517; gender balance and, 488; IDEA and, 335; independent study and, 54–55; laboratory schools and, 477–478; legal liability and, 500–501, 511, 512, 517, 520, 532, 533, 536, 538, 538;

minutes of instruction per grade level, 52; non-classroom-based, 98, 138–139; nonsuspect classifications used by, 478; number of, 20; online programs in, 98; operating, 33–38; *Pickering* decision, and 245; public employees and, 191; racial balance in, 477–478; religion and, 293, 305, 311, 316, 326–327; review and approval of, 9, 19; rights of expression and, 244, 245, 266, 281; safe learning environment and, 58, 59, 68, 69; special education and, 49, 55, 335; starting, 31–33; teacher qualification in, 81; Title IX and, 487; voucher programs and, 42
Charter Schools Act (1992, California), 30–31, 35, 38, 163, 184
Charter Schools Development Center, 36
Chatsworth High School, 449
Chen Through Chen v. Albany Unified School District, 273
Chicago Teachers Union, Local No. 1 v. Hudson, 177–178
Chico Unified School District, Miller v., 231
child abuse, 59, 68–69, 211, 218, 527–528
Child Abuse and Neglect Reporting Act, 68–69
Child Evangelism Fellowship, 320
child find and referral for initial assessment, 343–345
Children's Internet Protection Act (CIPA), 90–91, 92
child with a disability, defined, 238
Chinese American students, 80, 469–470

Chino Valley School District, 175, 324
Chino Valley Unified School District, California v., 440
Chino Valley Unified School District Board of Education, Freedom from Religion Foundation, Inc. v., 300
Choplick, Theodore, 447, 448
Christian Legal Society v. Martinez, 317
Chualar Elementary School District, Fleice v., 200, 203–204
CIPA. *See* Children's Internet Protection Act
City of San Jose v. the Superior Court of Santa Clara, 433–434
City of Madison v. Wisconsin Employment Relations Commission, 256
Civic Center Act (California), 58, 318, 320, 321, 328
Civil Rights Act (1964), 7, 465. *See also specific titles*
Civil Rights Project/*Proyecto Derechos Civiles*, 467
claim forms, 433
Clark, Tom, 296, 305
Clark County School Board of Trustees, Preschooler II v., 535
Clark County School District, Hooks v., 323
Clark County School District, Jacobs v., 280
Clark County School District, Planned Parenthood of Southern Nevada, Inc. v., 279
Clark v. Arizona Interscholastic Association (1982), 483
Clark v. Arizona Interscholastic Association (1989), 438

classified employees, 58, 189–190, 192, 223–228, 242; categories, 223–225; definition of 189; dismissal and layoff of, 160, 219, 226–228; evaluation and discipline of, 225–225, 229; leave rights of, 231–234; in merit system school districts, 228–229; non-reelection of, 188; property rights of, 191–192; termination of, 173

classroom-based instruction, defined, 138

classroom instruction, 47, 76, 78–84, 138, 285, 291, 328, 405

class size reduction, 78–79, 106, 108–109, 127

Clatskanie School District 6J, Pinard v., 266

Clausing v. San Francisco Unified School District, 506–507

Clauson, Zorach v., 293, 322

Clayton County, Georgia, Bostock v., 236

Cleveland: Pilot Project Scholarship Program, 326; voucher program, 43, 44

Clinical or Rehabilitative Services Credential, 192

closed forum, 61, 254, 275, 279, 282, 289, 313

Clovis Unified School District, Castro v., 270–271

Clovis Unified School District, Nathan G. v., 399

C.O. v. Portland Public Schools, 535

Coalition for Economic Equity v. Wilson, 475

Code of Federal Regulations, 334, 350, 554, 555

Cohen and Olson's Legal Research in a Nutshell (Cohen and Olson), 556

Coleman, James S., 108

Coleman Report, 108

Cole v. Oroville Union High School District, 312

Colin ex rel. Colin v. Orange Unified School District, 282

collective bargaining and unions, 148–187, 542; agency fees and, 541; bargaining units, 149–151; in charter schools, 35; contract administration, *150*, 152–153, 170–175, 176; contract law and, 13, 15; contract negotiation, *150*, 151–152, 163–170; curriculum and, 288; defining length of service, 227; EERA and, 8–9, 153–180; employee transfer and, 206; expression through school channels and, 254; future challenges of, 180–186; leave and, 231, 233; merit system districts and, 228–229; as official teacher representative, 255; organizational security arrangements, 175–180; Peer Assistance and Review and, 205; Public Employment Relations Board and, 154–155; scope of bargaining, 157–164; substitute teachers and, 224–225; teacher–student ratio and, 95; teacher layoff and, 227; teacher suspension and, 207, 225, 226; three stages of, 148–153; unionization stage of, 149–150; whistleblowers and, 263. *See also* Educational Employment Relations Act (1975) (California)

Collins v. Chandler Unified School District, 299

Colorado, Counterman v., 267
Colton School District 53, Burge v., 272
Columbus, Ohio, Public School System, 382
Commission on Professional Competence, 166–167, 188, 207, 212–215, 218, 242
Commission on Professional Competence, Crowl v., 214
Commission on Professional Competence, San Diego Unified High School District v., 211, 212–213, 214, 438
Commission on Professional Competence, San Dieguito Union High School District v., 217
Commission on Professional Competence, Woodland Joint Unified School District v., 188, 215
Commonwealth of Pennsylvania, Pennsylvania Association for Retarded Children (PARC) v., 331–333, 342, 363
community service, 55–56, 388, 390, 408–409, 417
community use policies, 318–321, 328
comparative religion classes, 305
compensatory education, 127, 367, 368, 369, 535
complaints about working conditions, 251–253
Compton Education Association, Compton Unified School District v., 168
Compton Unified School District v. Compton Education Association, 168
compulsory attendance laws, 22–23, 47–53, 112
concurring opinions, 14, 77, 284, 552

Conejo Valley Unified School District, Constantinescu v., 523–524
confidential employees, 155, 262
confidentiality, 69, 155, 389, 428, 445, 446, 452, 526–527
conflict of interest, 252
Connecticut, Griswold v., 436–437
Connell, Hartzell v., 133
Connick v. Myers, 251
Conn v. Western Placer Unified School District, 262
conscientious objector, 296
Constantinescu v. Conejo Valley Unified School District, 523–524
constitutional law, 2–5, 15, 42, 44, 78, 292–295, 313, 436, 463, 484, 545
contact sport, 29, 483, 486, 515–516, 523. *See also* athletes and athletics
continuation schools, 57, 76, 288, 390, 398–399
contract administration, *150*, 152–153, 170–175, 176
contract law, 12–13, 15
contract negotiation, *150*, 151–152, 163–170
controlled substances, 65, 211, 385, *385*, *386*, 389, 392–395, 415, 460
Coomes v. Edmonds School District No. 15, 253
Copley Press, Inc. v. Superior Court, 433
Copyright Act (1976), 84, 85, 87, 88
copyright law, 46–47, 84–88, 555
Corales v. Bennett, 268
Corey L., In re, 456–457
Corinne A. Seeds University Elementary School, 477
corporal punishment, 384, 500, 506–507, 534

counselors, and the duty to warn, 526–528
Counterman v. Colorado, 267
county boards of education, 18, 20, 28, 31, 33, 50, 53, 54, 57, 126, 155, 190, 202, 228, 403, 406, 409–412, 418, 428, 500, 518
county juvenile courts, 14
County Sanitation District No. 2 v. Los Angeles County Employees Association, Local 600, 168
county superintendents, 18–19, 21, 28–29, 34, 49, 56, 66, 155, 190, 202, 240, 262, 408, 428, 500, 518
court reporters, 13
courts of appeal, 3, 13, 14, 450, 557
Cousins v. Weaverville Elementary School District, 222
Coverdell Act, 499–500. *See also* No Child Left Behind Act (2001)
COVID-19 pandemic, 33, 95, 96–98, 101, 109, 132, 147
Crawford v. Board of Education of the City of Los Angeles (1976), 472–474, 476, 479
Crawford v. Huntington Beach Union High School District, 475, 478
creation-science, 306
credentials of certificated employees, 192–193. *See also* California Commission on Teacher Credentialing (CCTC)
C.R. ex rel. Rainville v. Eugene School District 4J, 273
Crookshank, *Wysinger v.*, 469
Crowl v. Commission on Professional Competence, 214
CSEA. *See* California School Employees Association

CTA. *See* California Teachers Association
Cuff v. Grossmont Union High School District, 527
Culbertson v. Oakridge School District No. 76, 320
Cumero v. Public Employment Relations Board, 176, 177
curriculum and instruction, 70–102; administrators and, 71, 76, 181; artificial intelligence and, 99–102; California schooling structure and, 17; charter schools and, 38, 72, 73, 75, 77; classroom free speech and, 275, 282, 283, 285, 287–288, 290; classroom instruction, 78–84; class size reduction and, 78–79; closed and open forums and, 425; collective bargaining and, 152, *158*, 161, 170, 181; copyright law and, 46–47, 84–88; curriculum censorship, 76–78; curriculum content standards, 70–76, 81, 83, 102, 104, 106, 205, 287, 290; curriculum support and training, 19; discrimination, and 484; distance learning and, 92–99; funding and, 109, 146; independent study, 25, 31, 35, 51, 54–55, 76, 139; Internet privacy and, 91–99; Internet use and, 88–99; kindergarten, 52; movement toward adequacy and, 141; No Child Left Behind and, 141; PPRA and, 446; physical education and, 514–515; religion and, 292, 295, 304–309, 318, 322; student assessment and, 103–105, 106; students with disabilities and, 340, 349, 352, 354

C.W. v. Capistrano Unified School District, 370
cyberbullying, 92, 98, 272, 274, 397

Danforth, Planned Parenthood of Central Missouri v., 437
dangerous condition of school property, 11, 26–27, 523–524, 538–539
Dariano v. Morgan Hill Unified School District, 270
Daugherty v. Vanguard Charter School Academy, 305–306
Davenport v. Washington Education Association, 178
Davis, Washington v., 490
Davison v. Santa Barbara High School District, 496
Davis v. Monroe County Board of Education, 493
Dawson v. East Side Union High School, 78
de facto segregation, 465–466, 472, 473, 478. *See also* racial discrimination
defamation, 277, 403, 510–511, 527, 543, 545, 546, 547
de jure segregation, 465–466, 471, 475, 497, 543. *See also* racial discrimination
Delong, Leeb v., 276, 277, 278
Department of Education, North County Parents Organization v., 430, 466
Department of General Services, Atwater Elementary School District v., 217
desegregation. *See* racial discrimination
Desktop Edition of the California Code, 1, 550, 555

Des Moines Independent Community School District, Tinker v. See Tinker v. Des Moines Independent Community School District
Detroit Board of Education, Abood v., 177, 179
developer fees, 123, *124*, 135–136
Dickson County School Board, Settle v., 310
differential pay, 232–233
DiLoreto v. Board of Education, 319
DiLoreto v. Downey Unified School District Board of Education, 319
Director of Education. *See* Superintendent of Public Instruction (SPI)
disability, defined, 238–240, 241–242, 348–350, 372, 374–375. *See also* Americans with Disabilities Act (1990); Individuals with Disabilities Education Act (IDEA); special education
discipline, employee, 188–189; classifications and, 194; of classified employees, 224; 225–226; collective bargaining and, 35, 156, 163, 173–174; for egregious misconduct, 211; evaluation and, 204; merit system school districts and, 228–229; personnel files and, 230, 231; of probationary and permanent employees, 206–208
discipline, student. *See* student discipline
discretion: abuse of, 37; in charter schools, 37; collective bargaining and, 156, 157, 161, 163, 169, 171, 172; in classification of employees, 227; compensatory education and, 368; counselor, 527, 528; in

discretion (*Cont.*)
  evaluating teachers, 190, 191, 204, 220; first-grade admission and, 52; funding and, 117, 127–128, 134, 142, 147; IEP teams and, 336, 346, 352–353, 376; library-book removal and, 91; legal liability and, 501, 502, 503, 508, 530, 538; physical education and, 53, 67; in private schools, 12, 41, 329; in providing transportation, 329; racial and ethnic balances, 27; religion and, 321; special education and, 336, 346, 352–353, 356, 365, 368; student discipline and, 379, 393–395, 400, 402, 406, 411, 412, 417–418; teacher academic freedom and, 284, 288
discretionary expulsion, 394–396
discrimination: administrators and, 473, 474, 475, 479; age discrimination, 7, 440, 485; Americans with Disabilities Act and, 237–240, 371–372, 374, 377; assessments and, 347; artificial intelligence and, 101; California Fair Employment and Housing Act and, 240–242, 439, 530, 539; charter schools and, 32, 191; civil rights and, 542; employment discrimination, 11, 237, 240, 385, 531, 556; Equal Access Act, 313–318; Equal Employment Opportunity Commission, 235, 236, 237, 240; federal statutes affecting California public schools, 7–8; gender discrimination, 8, 11, 323–324, 464, 480–489, 492–497, 532, 533, 537; limited open forum and, 89, 254, 256, 281–282; national origin discrimination, 6, 7, 27, 83, 142, 235, 236, 241, 243, 269, 421, 465, 475, 484, 489, 495, 542; private schools and, 41; Proposition 209 and, 27; racial discrimination under California law, 468–480; racial discrimination under federal law, 465–468; religion and, 7, 74, 296, 310, 314–316, 317, 318, 319, 321, 327; retaliation for union activity, 209; right of association and, 282–283; Safe Place to Learn Act and, 57; Section 504 and, 237–240, 371–374; sexual orientation and transgender discrimination, 323–324, 488, 494, 537; Title VI and, 77, 83, 142, 489–490; textbook selection and, 73; Title VII and, 6, 235–237, 465, 485; Title IX and, 484–487; Uniform Complaint Procedure and, 11; Unruh Civil Rights Act and, 539; viewpoint discrimination, 279, 314, 315, 319, 321, 421; wealth discrimination, 114, 115, 118

dismissal, 62, 188, 242; in *Bekiaris v. Board of Education of City of Modesto*, 248; of certificated employees, 194, 198, 201, 202, 206–219; at charter schools, 399–400; of classified employees, 223, 225, 226–228, 229; closed meetings and, 426–427, 428; collective bargaining and, 35, 160, 163, 166, 173; discipline and, 206; employee classification and, 194, 198; free speech and, 244, 248, 249–250, 253; hearing process, 217–219; of permanent teachers, 210–217; personnel files and, 230–231; in *Pickering v. Board of Education*, 245; of probationary teachers, 206–208; of substitute teachers, 194

dispute resolution, 32, 153, 399
dissenting opinions, 14, 109, 222, 281, 311, 314, 316, 460, 515, 552
distance learning, 87, 93, 95–98, 517
district power equalizing, 118–119, 146
Distinguished After School Health (DASH) Recognition Program, 65–66
Dixon Unified School District, Frazer v., 426
Dobbs v. Jackson Women's Health Organization, 437
Doe, Gonzaga University v., 10, 444
Doe, Honig v., 416
Doe, Plyler v., 4, 51
Doe, Santa Fe Independent School District v., 300
Doe v. Albany Unified School District, 53
Doe v. California Lutheran High School, 497
Doe v. Hawaii Department of Education, 462, 535
D.O. v. Escondido Union School District, 346
Donovan v. Poway Unified School District, 494
Douglas County School District, Endrew F., 339, 340, 341, 376
Dowell, Board of Education of Oklahoma City Public Schools v., 466
Downey Unified School District Board of Education, DiLoreto v., 318–319
Downs, Robert, 286–287
Downs v. Los Angeles Unified School District, 286–287
Doyle, Mt. Healthy City School District Board of Education v., 247–251, 263

drug abuse, by teachers, 210
drug paraphernalia, 93, *387*, 395, 448, 449
drug rehabilitation programs, for students, 408
drug testing, 450–451, 458
due process clause, 2, 74, 383, 437, 536, 543
due process hearings, 229, 335, 336, 339, 345, 350, 362, 363–370, 373, 377, 414, 416
Dunsmuir Joint Union High School District, 431
duty to supervise and protect, 511–516, 538
duty to warn, 526–528
Duval v. Board of Trustees, 427

Earls, Board of Education v., 451
East Side Union High School, Dawson v., 78
East Side Union High School District, Kahn v., 513
Eckhardt, Christopher, 264
Economic Impact Aid, 127
Edgewood Independent School District (Texas), 115
Edison Brentwood Academy, 162–163
Edison Schools, 163
Edmonds School District No. 15, Coomes v., 253
Educational Employment Relations Act (EERA) (1975) (California), 8–9, 148–149; arbitrator's role, 171–174; bargaining units, 149–150; collective bargaining under, 153–187; contract administration, 170–175; contract negotiation, 163–170; covered employees and schools, 155–156;

Educational Employment (*Cont.*) curriculum development and, 152; grievance and arbitration system, 170–171; National Labor Relations Act and, 148, 183–185, 186; organizational security arrangements, 175–180; protected acts under, 154, 182–183; Public Employment Relations Board and, 154–155; scope of bargaining, 157–163, *158*; unfair labor disputes, 174–175. *See also* collective bargaining

educational foundations, 134

educational management organizations (EMOs), 163, 183

Educational Revenue Augmentation Fund (ERAF), 123, 125

Education Audits Appeal Panel, Modesto City Schools v., 54

Education Code, 1, 8–9, 10, 12, 17–22, 542, 549, 550, 554, 555

Education Consolidation and Improvement Act (1981), 326

Education Empowerment Act (1998) (California), 446

Education for All Handicapped Children Act (EAHCA) (1975), 332, 335, 363. *See also* Individuals with Disabilities Education Act (IDEA)

educator association rights, 260–261

Edwards v. Aguillard, 306

Edwards v. Lake Elsinore Unified School District, 234–235

EEOC. *See* U.S. Equal Employment Opportunity Commission

EERA. *See* Educational Employment Relations Act (1975) (California)

EAHCA. *See* Education for All Handicapped Children Act

egregious misconduct, 217, 210, 211, 218

Eisenstadt v. Baird, 436–437

El Centro Elementary School District, Hector F. v., 495

Electronic Communications Privacy Act, 89

electronic devices, 271–272, 434, 439, 455

Elementary and Secondary Education Act (ESEA), 27, 46, 90, 102, 325. *See also* Title I funding

Eleventh Amendment, 8, 532, 533, 534, 547

Elk Grove Unified School District, Lilley v., 512, 513, 516

Elk Grove Unified School District v. Newdow, 297

El Modena High School, 282–283

email, 89, 253, 430, 434

emergency credentials, 192–193, 203–204

Emergency Substitute Permit, 193

employment, 188–243; administrators, 229–230; antidiscrimination laws, 235–242; employee classifications and categories, 189–191; employee leave rights, 231–235; personnel file, 230–231; property rights, 191–192. *See also* administrators; certificated employees; classified employees; teachers

Employment Division, Department of Human Resources v. Smith, 322

encroachment, 127

Endrew F. v. Douglas County School District, 339, 340, 341, 376

Engle v. Vitale, 298

English immersion, 72, 79, 285

English–Language Arts content standards, 70, 75
English Language Proficiency Assessment for California (ELPAC), 80
English learners, 47, 72, 75, 79–80, 97, 105, 122, 127, 129–130, 424
Environmental Charter High School v. Centinela Valley Union High School District, 38
Epperson v. Arkansas, 76, 284
Equal Access Act (1984), 282, 291, 313–314, 317, 328
Equal Employment Opportunity Commission, Hosanna-Tabor Evangelical Lutheran Church v., 41
Equality of Educational Opportunity study, 108
equal protection clause: employment law and, 221; gender discrimination and, 440, 481, 482, 483, 484, 537; racial discrimination and, 2, 74, 465, 466, 467, 469, 479, 489, 490; school funding and, 112–113, 116, 118, 120, 121, 145; special education and, 331; undocumented immigrants and, 4
Equal Rights Amendment (ERA), 480–481, 484
E-rate funds for Internet use, 90
Eric M. v. Cajon Valley Union School District, 518
Eric Paredes Sudden Cardiac Arrest Prevention Act, 512
Escondido Union School District, D.O. v., 346
ESEA. *See* Elementary and Secondary Education Act
Espinoza v. Montana Department of Revenue, 327
establishment clause, 293–294; aid to religious private schools, 326–327, 329; of California Constitution, 307, 308; campus access for religious groups, 314, 316, 318, 319, 320, 321; in elementary schools, 306; evolution and, 307; Fourteenth Amendment and, 293; free exercise clause and, 295, 295; free speech and, 314, 316; graduation prayer and religious speeches, 312; Jefferson, Thomas, and, 293; parent groups and, 306; Pledge of Allegiance and, 297; promotion of religion and, 286, 297; religion in the classroom and, 304, 306, 307–308, 314; right of association and, 282; school prayer, 298, 299, 300, 302–304; secularism and, 296; Ten Commandments and, 304, 317–319;
ESY. *See* extended school year
Eugene School District 4J, C.R. ex rel. Rainville v., 273
evaluation of employees: of administrators, 205; CCTC and, 82–83, 218; of certificated employees, 83, 204–206; of classified employees, 225–225, 229; curriculum and, 81–84
Evansville-Vanderburgh School Corporation, May v., 301–302
Evens v. Superior Court, 439
Everson v. Board of Education, 293, 324
Every Student Succeeds Act (ESSA), 45, 81, 103, 106, 141
excess tax districts, 126
exclusionary rule, 404, 450
exclusivity, in collective bargaining, 150, 176

excursions: fees for, 133; voluntary, 520
Executive Order N-12-13 (Newsom), 99–100
Executive Order on Safe, Secure, and Trustworthy Artificial Intelligence (Biden), 100–101
Expanded Learning Opportunities Program, 97
explosives, *385, 386*, 392
expression rights, educator, 30, 244–263, 260–261; complaints about working conditions, 251–253; expression through school channels, 254–259; *Mt. Healthy* test, 247–249; right of association, 260–261; speaking out on matters of public concern, 244–247; teacher academic freedom, 284–288; use of electronic communication devices, 259–260; whistleblowing, 261–263
expression rights, student, 30, 263–284; in the classroom, 288–289; through dress, grooming, and uniforms, 279–281; through electronic communication, 271–272; face-to-face communication, 264–269; as graduation speakers, 313; off-campus speech and, 272–274; political speech, 273; protected identities and, 269–271; religion and, 265–266, 280, 281–282; right of association, 281–284; through school channels, 274–279
expression rights in the classroom, 30; students, 288–289; teachers, 284–288
expression through school channels: educators, 254–259; students, 274–279

expulsion, 391–396; appeals, 19, 378; discretionary, 394–396; mandatory recommendation, 391–394; mandatory recommendation unless inappropriate, 394; pending, 50; special education and, 401, 412, 415, 417–418; temporary, 267; transfers and, 29
expulsion process, 400–412; appeal, 409–412; governing board final determination, 405–408; hearing, 401–405; postexpulsion educational programming, 408–409; recommendation for expulsion, 400–401; readmission following expulsion, 409; subpoenas for hearings, 402, 405, 407
expulsion records, 407, 444
extended school year (ESY), 336, 357, 376

FAA. *See* functional analysis assessment
face-to-face communication, 87, 254, 264–269, 287
facilities funding, 36, *124*, 135–136
fact-finding panels, 166–167
Fair Employment and Housing Act (FEHA, California), 191, 238, 240–242, 439, 530–531, 533, 539
fair share service fee, 175, 176
fair use doctrine, 84, 87, 88
False Claims Act (California), 517
Falvo, Owasso Independent School District v., 442
Family and Medical Leave Act (FMLA), 231, 556
Family Educational Rights and Privacy Act (FERPA, 1974), 555; claim

forms, 433; enforcement, 10; exceptions, 527; inspection of instructional materials and, 446; noncompliance penalties, 6; overview, 8; privacy and the Internet, 92. *See also* Protection of Pupil Rights Amendment
FAPE. *See* free appropriate public education
Farrington v. Tokushige, 39
Fashion Valley Mall v. National Labor Relations Board, 5
Faulkner, William, 77, 490
FBA. *See* functional behavioral assessment
federal courts, 6, 8, 10, 12, 14, 15
Federal Reporter series, 551
Federal Supplement series, 551
federal supremacy clause, 4
FEHA. *See* Fair Employment and Housing Act (California)
Fellowship of Christian Athletes v. San Jose Unified School District Board of Education, 283–284, 317, 320
Felton, Agostini v., 294, 325
Ferber, New York v., 90
Ferguson, Plessy v., 469, 470
Ferndale Unified School District, 198
FERPA. *See* Family Educational Rights and Privacy Act (1974)
Field Act (California), 35
Fields v. Palmdale School District, 23
field trips, voluntary, 520
fighting, 393–394, 462, 504, 506
filtering/blocking devices, internet, 90, 91–92
FindLaw for Legal Professionals, 555
firearms, 62, 64, 93, *385–387*, 391–392, 408, 453, 455, 456, 527

firearms, imitation, *387*, 392
First Amendment: aid to private schools and, 325, 329; campus access for outside groups and, 61, 314–317, 318; community use policies and, 318, 319; curriculum and, 74; electronic communication devices and, 259; exercise of religion and, 295, 303; expression through school channels and, 254, 256, 257, 275; face-to-face communication and, 266–269; free speech under, 5; graduation activities and, 312, 313; inappropriate materials and, 89–90; instructional materials and, 77; library book removal and, 91; open meetings and, 421, 423, 424; Pledge of Allegiance and, 297; public employee testimony and, 250; religion in the classroom and, 293, 294, 305, 306, 308–309; right of association and, 281–282, 284; speaking out on matters of public concern and, 244–245, 246–247; student discipline and, 379; student dress and grooming, 279; teacher academic freedom and, 285, 286; unions and, 177, 178, 179–180; working condition complaints and, 253. *See also* establishment clause; expression rights
first grade, admission to, 52, 53
Fischer v. Los Angeles Unified School District, 208, 427
Fitzgerald, Harlow v., 535
flag, saluting, 2, 297
Fleice v. Chualar Elementary School District, 203–204
Fletcher, McCarthy v., 76

Flippo, Ingram v., 429
Flood, Ward v., 469, 470
Florence County School District Four v. Carter, 368
Flores v. Morgan Hill Unified School District, 537
Florey v. Sioux Falls School District, 310–311
Florida voucher program, 43
Florida Union Free School District, Walczak v., 341
Ford, Gerald, 333
Ford v. Long Beach Unified School District, 347
Forest Grove School District v. T.A., 369
Fortas, Abe, 264, 265, 275, 284
Foster v. Mahdesian, 178
foster youth, 25, 47, 49–50, 79, 129–130, 233, 336
foundation funding, 110–112, 113, 115, 116–118, 121, 125
four-month positions, 197–198
Fourteenth Amendment: corporal punishment and, 534; civil rights law and, 6; curriculum content standards and, 74; distribution of school resources and, 111–112, 113, 115, 116, 145; due process, 2, 380, 381–382, 417, 437, 536, 543; Eleventh Amendment immunity and, 533; EMOs and, 185; gender and, 481–483; participation in interscholastic sports and, 383; private schools and, 4; property rights and, 191; protection of students and, 534, 536; religion and, 74, 293, 295; search and seizure and, 437, 440, 447; sexual orientation and, 537; speaking out on matters of public concern and, 245; student dress and grooming and, 279–280; student lifestyle rights and, 440; undocumented immigrant children and, 4. *See also* equal protection clause

Fourth Amendment: expulsion and, 404; student searches, 447–449, 450, 452, 455, 456, 458; student seizures, 461, 462

Franklin v. Gwinnett County Public Schools, 492

Franks, Lane v., 250

Fraser, Bethel School District v., 268, 272, 274, 288

Frazer v. Dixon Unified School District, 426

Frederick, Morse v., 269

free appropriate public education (FAPE), 7, 330, 333, 335, 337–343, 375–377; due process and, 336, 363, 364, 367–368; extended school year and, 357; IEP alterations and, 353; initial assessment and, 345–346; least restrictive environment and, 341–343; placement and, 359–360; private school students and, 362–363; procedural component, 337–338; Section 504 and, 373; stay-put and, 366; student discipline and, 413, 418; substantive component, 338–341

Freed, Lindke v., 256–258

Freedom from Religion Foundation, Inc. v. Chino Valley Unified School District Board of Education, 300

freedom of the press. *See* expression rights

free exercise clause, 74, 295–296, 303, 326

Freeman v. Oakland Unified School District, 533
Freeman v. Pitts, 466
free speech rights. *See* expression rights
Fremont Unified District Teachers Association, Fremont Unified School District v., 169–170
Fremont Unified School District v. Fremont Unified District Teachers Association, 169–170
Fremont Union High School District v. Santa Clara County Board of Education, 396–397
Fresno Unified School District, 511
Fresno Unified School District, Lucas v., 503
Friedrichs v. California Teachers Association, 179
Friery v. Los Angeles Unified School District, 476, 477
Frontiero v. Richardson, 481
Frudden v. Pilling, 281
Fry v. Napoleon Community Schools, 374
functional analysis assessment (FAA), 358, 376–377
functional behavioral assessment (FBA), 357–359, 376–377, 414–415

Galloway, Town of Greece v., 294, 300
gangs, 60, 280, 281, 457
Gann, Paul, 119
Gann Limit. *See* Proposition 4 (1979)
Garcetti v. Ceballos, 249–250, 252, 253, 259
Garcia, Mooney v., 420
Garcia Marquez, Gabriel, 76
Garden Grove Unified School District, C. B. v., 368

Gardner, John, 76
Garner, Bryan A., 541, 556
Garnier, O'Connor-Ratcliff v., 256–257
Garrett F., Cedar Rapids Community School District v., 357
Garrett v. Los Angeles City Unified School District, 438–439
Garriott, Green v., 327
GATE. *See* gifted and talented education
Gateway Academy, 511
Gebser v. Lago Vista Independent School District, 492–493
Gellerman v. Calaveras Unified School District, 356
gender discrimination, 8, 11, 464, 480–489, 492–495
general education classrooms, special education students in, 342–343, 349
general education teachers, on IEP teams, 352
general education teaching credentials, 82–83
general-purpose funds, 34, 125, 126, 137, 146
Ghafur v. Bernstein, 511
gifted and talented education, 26, 79
Givhan v. Western Line Consolidated District, 247, 251, 252
Golden West Middle School, 60
Gong Lum v. Rice, 470
Gonzaga University v. Doe, 10, 444
Good News Club v. Milford Central School, 319–320
Gordon J. v. Santa Ana Unified School District, 404, 450
Gordon v. Board of Education of the City of Los Angeles, 322
Gorsuch, Neil, 294, 303

Goss v. Lopez, 382–384, 417
Governing Board of ABC Unified School District v. Haar, 212
Governing Board of San Diego Unified School District, California Teachers Association v., 247
Governing Board of the Ferndale Unified School District, Zalac v., 198–199
Governing Board of the Hilmar Unified School District, California Teachers Association v., 161
Governing Board of San Leandro Unified School District, San Leandro Teachers Association v., 174–175
Governing Board of Torrance Unified School District, Lindros v., 285
governing boards: admission policies and, 51; appeals to, 11, 445; attendance law and, 48, 49, 51; California schooling structure and, 20, 21; charter school petitions and, 32–33; Civic Center Act and, 58, 318, 321; code of ethics, 216–217; contract negotiations and, 164–165; curriculum and instructional materials, 73, 76, 80; delegation of power of, 12; dismissal or suspension of teachers, 217–218, 226–227, 437–438; election of, 20; as employer, 65, 94, 155, 190–191, 195, 224–225; employee free speech and, 245–246, 247, 248, 249, 252, 255, 256; expulsion of students, 393, 394, 395, 396, 398, 399, 400–412, 417–418; Fair Employment and Housing Act and, 240; field trips and, 520; Internet access and, 91; layoffs and, 219–220, 223, 226–227; legal liability and, 499–500, 520; meetings of, 419, 420–421, 422–423, 426–429, 444, 462; in merit system school district, 228–229; open enrollment policy and, 26; probationary employees and, 200, 202, 203, 204; right of association and, 283; school hours and, 63; school publications and, 289; segregated schools and, 468, 470; student discipline and, 380, 381, *385–386*, 388, 390, 393, 394, 395, 396, 398, 399, 400–412, 415, 417–418; student dress and grooming, 280, 281; student privacy and, 441, 444; teacher discipline and, 207, 208, 209–210, 225–226; teacher evaluation and, 204–206, 225–226; teachers serving at pleasure of, 12, 242; transfers and, 29; transportation and, 133, 324; unfair labor charges and, 174–175, 176; whistleblowing and, 252

Government Code (California), 8–9, 128, 153–154, 157–158, 161, 166, 175–176, 210, 232, 252, 261, 421, 423, 425, 501, *502*, 549

governor, 13, 15–17, *16*, 44, 123, 144, 154

grades, 26, 32, 50, 273, 278, 287, 382, 537

graduation prayer and religious music and speeches, 311–313. *See also* school prayer

Graham, Stone v., 304, 317

Granowitz v. Redlands Unified School District, 389

Grant High School (Los Angeles Unified School District), 457

Granville, Troxel v., 23

Green v. Garriott, 327
Gregory K. v. Longview School District, 341
Grendel (Gardner), 76
grievances, 3, 13, 15, 149, *150*, 152, 156, *158*, 159, 165, 170–171, 230, 245, 251, 333, 544
Grimsley v. Board of Trustees, 209
Griswold v. Connecticut, 436–437
Grossmont Union High School District, Cuff v., 527
Groff v. DeJoy, NEED PAGE numbers
group searches, 457–461, 463
Grove v. Mead School District No. 354, 322
Gun-Free School Zone Act (California), 62, 392
Guthrie Independent School District, Swanson v., 323–324
Gwinnett County Public Schools, Franklin v., 492
Gwinnett County School District, Bown v., 299

Haar, Governing Board of ABC Unified School District v., 212
Hahn, Nordlinger v., 120–121
hair rules, 279–180
Hamamoto, Mark H. v., 373–374
Harik v. California Teachers Association, 179
Harlow v. Fitzgerald, 535
Harper v. Poway Unified School District, 270
Hartzell v. Connell, 133
hate crimes, 32, 235, 439, 472, 494
Hawaii, private foreign language schools in, 39
Hawaii Department of Education, Doe v., 462, 535
Hawaii Department of Education, N.D. et al. v., 366
Hawkins test, 184
Hayes, California Teachers Association v., 15, 107, 124
hazardous recreational activities, *502*, 515–516, 523, 539
Hazelwood School District v. Kuhlmeier, 91, 274, 276, 288, 309
hazing, 40, *387*, 433
Healdsburg Union School District, 159
Health Services Credential, 192
hearing officers, 173, 217, 222, 226, 229, 336, 342, 363–364, 366, 370, 403–406, 410, 415
hearings, expulsion, *385*, 389, 393–395, 399–406, 410–411, 417, 432
Hector F. v. El Centro Elementary School District, 495
Hedges v. Wauconda Community Unit School District No. 118, 321
Helms, Mitchell v., 326
Hemady v. Long Beach Unified School District, 515
Henderson v. Los Angeles City Board of Education, 425
Hills v. Scottsdale Unified School District No. 48, 320–321
HIV/AIDS prevention education, 24, 487
Hoff v. Vacaville Unified School District, 520–522
Hogan, Mississippi University for Women v., 482
Hohe v. San Diego Unified School District, 525–526

holiday observances, 55, 310–311, 321, 328
Holland, Sacramento City Unified School District v., 342
homeschooling, 1, 24–25, 40, 45, 53, 98, 302, 323
homosexuality, 91, 211, 261, 270, 282–283, 286, 493–495, 537
Honig, State Board of Education v., 118
Honig injunction, 415–416
Honig v. Doe, 416
Hooks v. Clark County School District, 323
Horace Mann Insurance Company v. Analisa N., 509
Horizon Community Learning Center, Caviness v., 185
Horton v. Whipple, 1
Hosanna-Tabor Evangelical Lutheran Church v. Equal Employment Opportunity Commission, 41
Hoschler v. Sacramento City Unified School District, 208
hostile environments, 77, 236, 387, 396, 490–491, 496
Hoyem v. Manhattan Beach City School District, 518
Hsu, Bravo ex rel. Ramirez v., 462
Hudgens v. National Labor Relations Board, 5
Hudson, Chicago Teachers Union, Local No. 1 v., 177–178
Hudson notice, 177–178
Hughes, Spanierman v., 259
Humberto O., In re, 56
Hunter ex rel. Brandt v. Regents of the University of California, 477
Hunter v. Regents of the University of California, 477
Huntington Beach Union High School District, Crawford v., 475
Huntington Beach Union High School District, Johnson v., 313
Hurley, Tape v., 469
hybrid claims, 322–323

IAES. *See* interim alternative educational settings
IDEA. *See* Individuals with Disabilities Education Act (IDEA)
IDEA 2004. *See* Individuals with Disabilities Education Improvement Act (2004)
IEE. *See* independent educational evaluation
IEP. *See* Individualized Education Program (IEP)
immunity of state against suit, 499–501, 503
impasse, in contract negotiation, 165–169, *166*, 338
Impressions, 307, 425, 426
Independence Oregon Central School District 12J, Juran v., 460
independent educational evaluation (IEE), 336, 348, 350–351, 360, 367
independent study, 25, 31, 35, 51, 54–55, 76, 139, 517
Indian students. *See* Native American students
Individualized Education Program (IEP), 330, 375–376; behavior-related assessments and plans, 357–359, 384; child fined, referral, assessment and eligibility, 343, 345–351; contents, 336, 353–355; defined, 336; disciplinary removals, 413; extended school year, 318–319; FAPE and,

337–341; initial assessment and, 345–348; mental health services, 359; parental rights, 444; placement, 359–360; process, 351–360; special education and related services, 355–357; student discipline and, 384, 412, 413, 414–415, 418; team meetings, 351–353; teams, 337; transition plans, 361–362
individual searches, 452–457
individual services plan (ISP), 344, 363
Individuals with Disabilities Education Act (IDEA), 333–336, 345–346, 347, 348, 375, 377; attorneys' fees, 369–370; assessments and, 340, 351; behavior-related assessments and plans, 357–359; charter schools and, 335; child find and referral for initial assessment, 343–345; due process and, 364–365, 366, 367–369; eligibility for special education and, 348–350; federal funding and, 132; free appropriate public education and, 337–338, 356, 373; IEP contents, 353, 355; implementation of, 9; least restrictive environment requirement, 341–343; mental health services, 359; overview, 3, 7; parental rights and, 323, 414, 444; private schools and, 41, 362–363; Section 504 versus, 373–374; student discipline and, 380, 412, 415, 416, 418; transition plans, 360–361, 362. *See also* special education; special needs students
Individuals with Disabilities Education Improvement Act (2004), 334, 344, 370
Ingraham v. Wright, 534

Ingram v. Flippo, 429
injury: athletic, 451, 511–516, 523, 538; dangerous conditions of school property, 523–525; employee leave rights and, 232; employee liability, 534–538; injurious objects, 459; insurance against, 539; negligence and, 67, 232; to nonstudents, 520–523; parental liability, 26; school liability, 58, 531–535; self-injury, 358; stay put exceptions and, 336, 366; student discipline and, *385, 386, 387,* 388–389, 393–394, 396, 415–416, 418; to students off campus, 517–520; to students on campus, 503–508; *Tarasoff* ruling, 526–527; waivers of liability, 525–526; workplace-violence prevention plan, 64; *See also* Tort Claims Act (California)
in loco parentis doctrine, 263, 272, 521, 544
instant messaging, 271
Institute for Research on Educational Policy and Practice, 144
instructional material selection and disposal, 73
insurance, 249, 350, 502–503, 509, 528–530
intelligence tests, 347
interdistrict transfers, 28, 29, 42, 45, 47, 478
interim alternative educational settings (IAES), 366, 415–416, 418
internet, 85, 88–102, 212–213, 260, 380, 392, 397, 438, 441, 442, 554
interns, 71, 200–202
interscholastic sports. *See* athletes and athletics

interstate commerce, 6, 184
intradistrict open enrollment, 26, 29
intradistrict transfers, 26, 29, 475
Invasion of Privacy Act (California), 439
invocations, 499–300, 311–312, 328
IQ tests, 347
Irvine Teachers Association, CTA/NEA, Irvine Unified School District v., 169
Irvine Unified School District v. Irvine Teachers Association, CTA/NEA, 169
Irving Independent School District v. Tatro, 356–357
I.R. v. Los Angeles Unified School District, 365
ISP. *See* individual services plan
Issaquena County Board of Education, Blackwell v., 265
Iverson v. Muroc Unified School District, 516

Jack M., Board of Education of Long Beach Unified School District v., 438
Jackson, Robert, 2, 297
Jackson v. Birmingham Board of Education, 485
Jackson v. Pasadena City School District, 114, 471–472, 473–474, 475, 476, 478, 479
Jackson Women's Health Organization, Dobbs v., 437
Jacobs v. Clark County School District, 280
Jacoby, Prince v., 314, 315–316
Jaffree, Wallace v., 299
Janus v. American Federation of State, County and Municipal Employees, 179–180

Japanese American students, 470
Jarvis, Howard, 119
J.C. ex rel. R.C. v. Beverly Hills Unified School District, 274
J. D., In re, 455
Jefferson, Thomas, 293
Jefferson County school system, 467
Jewett, Knight v., 514
J.H. v. Los Angeles Unified School District, 503
Jimenez v. Roseville City School District, 516
J.L. v. Mercer Island School District, 340
John A. v. San Bernardino City Unified School District, 403
John R. v. Oakland Unified School District, 508–509
Johnson, San Francisco Unified School District v., 471
Johnson v. Huntington Beach Union High School District, 313
Johnson v. Poway Unified School District, 285–286, 302
Jonathan L. v. Superior Court, 25
Joseph F., In re, 60
Joseph G., In re, 453
Jose Y., People v., 459–460
Joyce v. Simi Valley Unified School District, 524–525
judicial decisions, finding and reading, 550–553
judicial law, 1, 3, 13, 44, 302, 304, 334, 545, 550, 552
Juran v. Independence Oregon Central School District 12J, 460
Jurupa Valley High School (Riverside County), 323–324

juvenile courts, 14, 19, 25, 50, 56, 61, 387, 433, 447, 449, 456, 457, 459, 460, 461

K–12 Pupil Online Personal Information Protection Act, 94
Kahn v. East Side Union High School District, 513
Katz v. Los Gatos-Saratoga Joint Union High School District, 49
Kavanaugh v. West Sonoma County Union High School District, 195
Kennedy, Anthony, 269, 294, 467
Kennedy v. Bremerton School District, 294, 303
Kent School District, Patel v., 536
Kent School District, Truth v., 283, 316
Kern County superintendent, 19
Keyes v. School District No. 1, 466
Keyser v. Sacramento City Unified School District, 249
Kimberly M. v. Los Angeles Unified School District, 508
kindergarten, 51–52, 53, 70, 129, 320, 338, 387
King v. Saddleback Junior College District, 279
Kirchmann v. Lake Elsinore Unified School District, 251
K. J., In re, 454
Klump v. Nazareth Area School District, 455
K.M. ex rel. Bright v. Tustin Unified School District, 371
Knapp v. Palisades Charter High School, 501
Knight v. Jewett, 514
knives, 385, 386, 388, 392, 399–400, 408, 452, 457, 459–460, 461

Knox v. Service Employees International Union, Local 1000, 178
Koch, P.B. v., 535
Kozinski, Alex, 270
K.S., In re, 454
Kuhlmeier, Hazelwood School District v., 91, 274, 276, 288, 309

laboratory schools, 477–478
labor unions. *See* unions
Lackner v. North, 522
Lago Vista Independent School District, Gebser v., 492–493
Lake Elsinore Unified School District, Kirchmann v., 251
Lake Pend Oreille School District No. 84, Posey v., 253
Lakeside Inn, Inc., Bassett v., 519
Lake Tahoe Unified School District, 519
Lamb's Chapel v. Center Moriches Union Free School District, 294, 318
Lane v. Franks, 250
Larry P. v. Riles, 347
Lassonde v. Pleasanton Unified School District, 313
Las Virgenes Educators Association v. Las Virgenes Unified School District, 287
Las Virgenes Unified School District, Aaris v., 513
Las Virgenes Unified School District, Las Virgenes Educators Association v., 287
Latasha W., In re, 459–460
Latino students, 464, 467, 468, 470, 530
Lau v. Nichols, 80
LaVine v. Blain School District, 267

law of the district, defined, 10
Lawrence v. Texas, 437
laws and regulations websites, 47, 554–555
Lawson v. PPG Architectural Finishes, 263
layoffs, *158*, 159, 160, 172, 188–189, 190, 193, 198, 199, 204; of certificated employees, 172, 219–223; of classified employees, 160, 219, 226–228; of permanent teachers, 193; of probationary teachers, 158, 159, 193, 219, 220, 223; rights of permanent classified employees, 227
LEA. *See* local educational agency
League of United Latin American Citizens v. Wilson, 4. 51
Learning Tree, The (Parks), 322
least restrictive environment (LRE), 340, 341–343, 376
leave rights, employee, 189, 191, 231–235, 556
leaves of absence, student, 54
Leeb v. Delong, 276, 277, 278
Lee v. Weisman, 312
legal liability under California law, 499–531; counselors and duty to warn, 526–528; danger condition of school property, 523–525; Fair Employment and Housing Act, 530–531; injury to nonstudents, 520–523; injury to student athletes and cheerleaders, 511–516; injury to students off campus, 517–520; injury to students on campus, 503–508; insurance and, 528–530; of school employees when acting outside scope of employment, 508–511; when students don't learn, 516–517; Tort Claims Act, 500–530; waivers of liability, 525–526
legal liability under federal law, 531–538; of school employees, 534–538; of schools, 531–533
Leger v. Stockton Unified School District, 504
legislative body, definition of, 425
Legislature. *See* California Legislature
Lemahieu, Mark H. v., 373
Leroy Greene School Facilities Act (1998) (California), *124*, 136
Leventhal v. Vista Unified School District, 420–421, 426–427
liability, waivers of, 525–526, 548
libel, 275, 501, 501, 511, 543, 545
libraries, public, 19, 90, 549, 550
library book removal, 91
Lilley v. Elk Grove Unified School District, 512, 513, 516
limited open forum, 89, 254–256, 282–283, 314, 318–321, 420–421
Lindros v. Governing Board of Torrance Unified School District, 284
Lindke v. Freed, 256–258
Lisa G., In re, 452
Livingston Union School District, California School Employees Association v., 226
L.J. by and through Hudson v. Pittsburg Unified School District, 349, 350
lobbying by unions, 176–177, 183, 186
Local Control Funding Formula (LCFF), 78–79, 105, 128–131, 132, 136, 137, 141, 144, 146, 147, 198, 533
local educational agency (LEA), 31, 69, 104, 326, 329, 334, 335, 366, 415

loco parentis doctrine, 263, 272, 521, 544
Long Beach Unified School District, Ford v., 347
Long Beach Unified School District, Hemady v., 515
Long Beach Unified School District, Ramirez v., 519
Long Beach Unified School District, Vittal v., 204
Long Beach Unified School District v. State of California, 128
long-term removals, in special education, 413–415
Longview School District, Gregory K. v., 341
Loper Bright Enterprises v. Raimondo, 10
Lopez, Bernstein v., 229
Lopez, Goss v., 382–384, 417
Lopez v. Tulare Joint Union High School District, 288, 289
Lorenz, Reno, 449
Los Altos School District, Bullis Charter School v., 36–37
Los Angeles City Board of Education, Henderson v., 425
Los Angeles City Board of Education, Los Angeles Teachers Association v., 246
Los Angeles City Unified School District, Garrett v., 438–439
Los Angeles County Employees Association, Local 600, County Sanitation District No. 2 v., 168
Los Angeles County superintendent, 18–19
Los Angeles Teachers Association v. Los Angeles City Board of Education, 246

Los Angeles Unified School District, 21, 37, 97, 170, 221, 286–287, 438, 457, 472, 475–477
Los Angeles Unified School District, Acosta v., 515
Los Angeles Unified School District, Aguirre v., 369
Los Angeles Unified School District, American Civil Rights Foundation v., 475
Los Angeles Unified School District, Downs v., 286–287
Los Angeles Unified School District, Fischer v., 208, 427
Los Angeles Unified School District, Friery v., 476, 477
Los Angeles Unified School District, I. R. v., 365
Los Angeles Unified School District, J.H. v., 503
Los Angeles Unified School District, Kimberly M. v., 508
Los Angeles Unified School District, Morrow v., 426
Los Angeles Unified School District, Service Employees Industrial Union v., 162
Los Angeles Unified School District v. California Charter Schools Association, 37
Los Angeles Unified School District v. Superior Court, 429
Los Gatos-Saratoga Joint Union High School District, Katz v., 49
lottery, state, 123, *124*, 134
Louisiana creation-science statute, 306
Lovell v. Poway Unified School District, 266–267

Lowell High School (San Francisco Unified School District), 482–483
low-income students, 42–44, 66, 79, 97, 103, 109, 122, 125, 127, 129, 130, 132, 141, 143, 146, 220–222, 464, 468, 519
LRE. *See* least restrictive environment
Lucas v. Fresno Unified School District, 503
Luera, People v., 90
Lungren, American Academy of Pediatrics v., 437

Madera Unified School District, Belanger v., 532
Madera Unified School District Board of Education, Montalvo v., 279
Madsen v. Associated Chino Teachers, 175
Mahdesian, Foster v., 178
Mahanoy Area School District v. B. L. Levy, 272
majority, age of, 360–361, 437
Malcolm W. v. Novato Unified School District, 491
management employees, defined, 155
management prerogative, 152, *158*
mandatory consulting, *158*
mandatory recommendation for expulsion, *385*, 391–394, 417
mandatory recommendation for expulsion unless inappropriate, 394
mandatory subjects of bargaining, 150, 151, 152, 154, 157, 159, 205
Manguso v. Oceanside Unified School District, 510
Manhattan Beach City School District, Hoyem v., 518

manifestation determination, 50, 414–415, 418
Mark H. v. Hamamoto, 373–374
Mark H. v. Lemahieu, 373
Marken v. Santa Monica-Malibu Unified School District, 431–432
Marshall, Thurgood, 109, 245, 470
Marsh v. Chambers, 300
Martinez, Christian Legal Society v., 317
Martinez Unified School District, Nicole M. v., 496, 508
Massey v. Banning Unified School District, 440
May v. Evansville-Vanderburgh School Corporation, 301–302
McCaffrey, Oona R.S. by Kate S. v., 537
McCarthy v. Fletcher, 76
McCluskey, Board of Education of Rogers, Arkansas v., 378
McCollum v. Board of Education, 293
McCrary, Runyon v., 41
McGuffey's Reader, 292
McIntyre v. Sonoma Valley Unified School District, 196
McKinney-Vento Homeless Assistance Act, 445
McKinney v. Oxnard Union High School District, 474, 479
McMahon v. Albany Unified School District, 424
McMinnville School District, Chandler v., 281
McNeil v. Sherwood School District 88J, 272–274
McReynolds, James, 23
M.C. v. Antelope Valley Union School District, 353

INDEX | 609

Mead School District No. 354, Grove v., 322
media: multi-, 85, *86*, 87; news, 63, 274, 422–423, 429, 433; school, 315; services, 19; social, 94, 256–258, 260, 270–271, 324, 398, 441
mediation: for IDEA disputes, 365, 366; for labor disputes and contract negotiation, 153, 154, 159, 160, 165–167, *166*; truancy, 56
medical care authorization, 48
medical services, in special education, 356
meet and confer rights, *150*, 157, 186
Mello-Roos Community Facilities District Act (1982) (California), *124*, 136
Mendez, Westminster School District of Orange County v., 470
Mendoza v. State of California, 21
mental health services, for students with disabilities, 330, 359
mental illness, in employees, 207–208
Mercer Island School District, J.L. v., 340
Mergens, Board of Education of Westside Community Schools v., 282, 314
merit system school districts, 224, 228–229
metal detectors, 459, 460, 461, 463
Mexican American students, 109, 115, 470
Mexico, students living in, 49
Meyers-Milias-Brown Act (1968) (California), 153
Michael M., In re, 269–270
Miguel H., In re, 62
Milford Board of Education, Mrs. B. v., 341

Milford Central School, Good News Club v., 319–320
Miller, Hal, 231
Miller v. California, 89
Miller v. Chico Unified School District, 231
Mills v. Board of Education of the District of Columbia, 331, 332–333, 342, 363
Milwaukee voucher program, 43, 44
Minidoka County School District No. 331, Peterson v., 302
Minimum Foundation School Program (Texas), 115
Mirabelli v. Olson, 440
Miranda rights, 454, 456–457
Miranda v. Arizona, 456–457
Mississippi University for Women v. Hogan, 482
Mitchell v. Helms, 326
Modesto City Schools District, Public Employment Relations Board v., 167
Modesto City Schools v. Education Audits Appeal Panel, 54
Moment of Quiet Reflection in Schools Act (1997) (Georgia), 299
Monroe County Board of Education, Davis v., 493
Montalvo v. Madera Unified School District Board of Education, 279
Montana Department of Revenue, Espinoza v., 327
Monteiro v. Tempe Union High School District, 77, 491
Montoya, Caldwell v., 531
Mooney v. Garcia, 420
Moran v. State of Washington, 249
Moreno Valley Unified School District, Baca v., 255, 256, 421

Moreno Valley Unified School District v. Public Employment Relations Board, 167
Morgan Hill Unified School District, Dariano v., 270
Morgan Hill Unified School District, Flores v., 537
Morgan v. Swanson, 265
Morongo Unified School District, Sands v., 311
Morrison, Toni, 77
Morrison factors, 211–212, 213, 216, 261
Morrison v. State Board of Education, 211–213, 216, 261, 438
Morrow v. Los Angeles Unified School District, 426
Morse v. Frederick, 268–269
Morton School District, Blanchard v., 341
Mount Pleasant Valley Elementary School District, 176
Mrs. B. v. Milford Board of Education, 341
M.S., In re, 270
Mt. Healthy City School District Board of Education v. Doyle, 247–251, 263
Mt. Healthy test, 247–251
multimedia copyright law, 86, 87
Multiple Subject Teaching Credential, 192, 201
municipal courts, 56
Muroc Joint Unified School District, Randi W. v., 510
Muroc Unified School District, Iverson v., 516
Murphy, Arlington Central Unified School District Board of Education v., 369

music copyright law, 85, 86, 87
M.W. v. Panama Buena Vista Union School District, 505
Myers, Connick v., 251

NAACP. *See* National Association for the Advancement of Colored People
NAEP. *See* National Assessment of Educational Progress
Napoleon Community Schools, Fry v., 374
Nathan G. v. Clovis Unified School District, 399
Nation at Risk, A, 102
National Assessment of Educational Progress (NAEP), 102, 103, 468
National Association for the Advancement of Colored People (NAACP), 470, 496
National Average School Funding Guarantee and Parental Right to Choose Quality Education Amendment (1988) (California), 43
National Board for Professional Teaching Standards, 205
National Education Association (NEA), 148, 177, 180, 185. *See also* California Teachers Association (CTA)
National Heritage Academies, 305
National Labor Relations Act (NLRA), 148, 183–185
National Labor Relations Board, Fashion Valley Mall v., 5
National Labor Relations Board, Hudgens v., 5
National Labor Relations Board v. Catholic Bishops of Chicago, 185
National Labor Relations Board v. Natural Gas Utility District of Hawkins County, Tennessee, 184

national origin discrimination, 6, 7, 27, 83, 142, 235, 236, 241, 243, 269, 421, 465, 475, 484, 489, 495, 542
Native American students, 468, 469
Native American studies, 73
Natural Gas Utility District of Hawkins County, Tennessee, National Labor Relations Board v., 184
Nazareth Area School District, Klump v., 455
NCLB. *See* No Child Left Behind Act (2001)
N.D. et al. v. Hawaii Department of Education, 366
negligence, defined, 501
Neighborhood Children's Internet Protection Act, 90
Newdow, Elk Grove Unified School District v., 297
Newdow v. Rio Linda Union School District, 297
Newport-Mesa Unified School District v. State of California Department of Education, 347
New Jersey v. T.L.O., 447–449, 450, 453–454, 458, 460
Newsom, Gavin, 99, 100, 440
New York v. Ferber, 90
New York Times v. Sullivan, 511
Nguon v. Wolf, 440
Nichols, Lau v., 80
Nicole M. v. Martinez Unified School District, 496, 508
Nineteenth Amendment, 480
No Child Left Behind Act (NCLB, 2001), 10, 27, 45, 46, 81, 102–103, 106, 141, 310, 499, 555
non-classroom-based charter schools, 98, 138–139

non-curriculum-related student groups, 282, 291
nonmandatory bargaining items, 165
nonnegotiable topics, *158*
nonpublic agency (NPA), 64, 360
nonpublic school (NPS), 359–360, 362–363, 381. *See also* private schools
Nordlinger v. Hahn, 120–121
North County Parents Organization v. Department of Education, 430, 466
North, Lackner v., 522
Northeast Independent School District, Shanley v., 397
Northwest Ordinance (1787), 292
Norwick, Ambach v., 284
Novato Unified School District, Malcolm W. v., 491
Novato Unified School District, Smith v., 277
NPA. *See* nonpublic agency
NPS. *See* nonpublic school
Nurre v. Whitehead, 311
nutritional foods and beverages, 65

OAH. *See* Office of Administrative Hearings
Oakland Unified School District, Alma W. v., 509
Oakland Unified School District, Freeman v., 533
Oakland Unified School District, John R. v., 508–509
Oakland Unified School District, Torsiello v., 519
Oakland Unified School District, Welch v., 200–201
Oakland Unified School District, Yarber v., 523

Oakridge School District No. 76, Culbertson v., 320
obscenity, 89
Oceanside Unified School District, Manguso v., 510
O'Connor, Sandra Day, 314, 326, 482
O'Connor-Ratcliff v. Garnier, 256–257
off-campus injury, 517–520
off-campus student behavior, 396–398
Office of Administrative Hearings (OAH), 217–218, 223; due process hearings, 363, 364, 377; expulsion hearings and, 415; special education and, 334, 336, 338, 340, 342, 350, 360, 368, 369, 370, 415–416; stay put and, 365, 366; website, 556
Ohio, Osborne v., 90
Old Order Amish, 24, 322
Ollier v. Sweetwater Union High School District, 486
Olson, Kent, 556
Olson, Mirabelli v., 440
One Hundred Years of Solitude (Garcia Marquez), 76
One2One Learning Foundation, Wells v., 517
online courses, 95, 96. See also distance learning
Oona R.S. by Kate S. v. McCaffrey, 537
open forum, defined, 89. See also limited open forum
open meetings, 420–429: charter schools and, 30; defining, 424–426; enforcement of, 429; exceptions to, 426–428. See also Brown Act (1953) (California)
Options for Youth-Victor Valley, Inc. v. Victor Valley Options for Youth Teachers Association, 184–185

Orange Unified School District, Colin ex rel. Colin v., 283
Oregon, Adams v., 341
Oregon public school attendance law, 22–23
Orange County Dept. of Education, Sato v., 533
organizational security arrangements, *158, 159,* 175–180
Oroville Union High School District, Cole v., 312–313
Osborne v. Ohio, 90
outsiders: on campus, 57–58, 60–61, *62*; expression through school channels, 78, 279
overcrowding grants, 136
Owasso Independent School District v. Falvo, 442
Oxnard Union High School District, McKinney v., 474, 479

Pacific Reporter, 551
Palisades Charter High School, Knapp v., 501
Palmdale School District, Fields v., 23
Palos Verdes Peninsula School District, Bartell v., 525
Panama Buena Vista Union School District, M.W. v., 505
Paradise Valley Unified School District No. 69, A.G. v., 371, 415
Paramount Unified School District, Caldwell v., 531
parcel taxes, *124,* 134
Parental Choice in Education initiative (1993), 43
parental consent, 50, 55, 346, 347, 348, 359, 390, 443, 445, 446, 471

INDEX | 613

Parental Empowerment Act (1998) (California), 45
Parental Involvement Act (1998) (California), 25–26
parental notice, 343, 391
Parent Empowerment Act (2010) (California), 27
parent groups, 134, 306
parents: advisory committees, 131, 424; assessment and, 80, 81; attendance and, 47–48, 49, 50, 51–53, 54; bilingual education and, 72; charter schools and, 30, 182; choice, 26–29, 326–327, 329; class size and, 78; community announcements and, 320–321; curriculum and, 74, 76, 77; discipline and, 390–391, 397–399, 401, 402, 405–410, 413–414, 416–418; due process and, 368–370; expulsion and, 401–402, 405–407; FERPA and, 8, 10; freedom of expression and, 263, 264, 267, 268, 269, 271–274, 277, 281; funding and, 133, 134; homeschooling, 1, 24–25, 40, 45, 53, 98, 302, 323; IEP team meetings and, 352–353; Internet and, 89, 92, 93, 94, 96, 98; involuntary transfers and, 398–399; kindergarten enrollment and, 51–52, 53; LCAPs and, 131; parent–teacher associations, 58, 134; postexpulsion educational programming and, 408; privacy and 420–421, 425, 431–432, 437–438, 440–447; private schools and, 22–24, 41–44; in public schools, 25–26; reimbursement for educational expense, 368–369; religion and, 295, 298, 302, 305–308, 309, 312, 319–325; rights and responsibilities, 22–29; safe school environment and, 63, 64, 66, 68; special education and, 332, 334–339, 341, 342, 343–348, 350–354, 355, 356–357, 359–370, 376–377; stay-put and, 365–366; student records and, 441–446; student searches and seizures, 450, 452–453, 455, 459–460; teenage parenting, 288; transportation and, 471; truancy and, 55–56. *See also* Family Educational Rights and Privacy Act (1974); hybrid claims
Parents Involved in Community Schools v. Seattle School District No. 1, 466–467
Parents of Student W. v. Puyallup School District, 368, 369
Parks, Gordon, 322
PAR. *See* Peer Assistance and Review
particular kinds of services (PKS) layoffs, 219
Pasadena City Board of Education v. Spangler, 466
Pasadena City School District, Jackson v., 114, 471–472, 473–474, 475, 476, 478, 479
Paso Robles Unified School District, Timothy O. v., 345
Patel v. Kent School District, 536
Paul D. Coverdell Teacher Protection Act (2001), 499–500. *See also* No Child Left Behind Act (2001)
Payne v. Peninsula School District, 374, 375
P.B. v. Koch, 535
Peer Assistance and Review (PAR), 205
peer harassment, 8, 57, 396, 493, 495, 537

Peloza v. Capistrano Unified School District, 261, 302, 307
Peninsula School District, Payne v., 374, 375
Pennsylvania Association for Retarded Children (PARC) v. Commonwealth of Pennsylvania, 331–333, 342, 363
People v. Jose Y., 459–460
People v. Luera, 90
People v. Ramirez, 383
PERB. *See* Public Employment Relations Board (PERB)
permanent certificated employees, 203, 207, 219, 234–235
permanent classified employees, 226–227, 228, 242
permanent teachers, 188, 189–190, 202–204: in charter schools, 30, 183; as default classification, 194; discipline of, 206–208; dismissal of, 210–219; evaluation of, 204–206; layoffs, 193; on leave, 195; non-re-election of, 208–210; probationary classification and, 200, 202; provisional credentials and, 203, 220; reemployment list, 223; temporary classification and, 195, 197, 198, 199
permissive subjects of bargaining, 151
Perry, Van Orden v., 304, 318
Perry Education Association v. Perry Local Educators' Association, 61, 89, 254–256
personal necessity leave, 231–232
personnel commission, 228–229
personnel director, 228
personnel exception to Brown Act, 421, 426–427
personnel file, 189, 205, 206, 230–231, 431

Petersil v. Santa Monica-Malibu Unified School District, 196
Peterson v. Minidoka County School District No. 331, 302
Peter W. v. San Francisco Unified School District, 517
Pickering v. Board of Education, 244–246, 247, 248, 250, 251–252, 264, 286
Pico, Board of Education of Island Trees v., 91
Pierce Joint Unified School District, Achene v., 209
Pierce v. Society of Sisters, 22–24, 39, 41–42, 324
Pilling, Frudden v., 281
Pilot Project Scholarship Program (Cleveland), 326
Pinard v. Clatskanie School District 6J, 266
Pinellas County School District (Office for Civil Rights case), 372
Pitts, Freeman v., 466
Pittsburg Unified School District, L.J. by and through Hudson v., 349, 350
PKS layoffs. *See* particular kinds of services layoffs
placement, in special education, 359–360, 362–363, 365–369, 377
Planned Parenthood of Central Missouri v. Danforth, 437
Planned Parenthood of Southern Nevada, Inc. v. Clark County School District, 279
Pleasanton Unified School District, Lassonde v., 313
Pledge of Allegiance, 297
Plessy v. Ferguson, 469, 470

Plumas Unified School District, B.C. v., 458, 461
Plyler v. Doe, 4, 51
police officers, 56, 59, 60, 214, 444, 454, 457–458, 459
political activity and speech, 70, 175, 246, 247, 270
Population Services, International, Carey v., 437
pornography, 90
Portland Public Schools, C.O. v., 535
Posey v. Lake Pend Oreille School District No. 84, 253
poverty, as suspect classification, 115
Poway Federation of Teachers v. Poway Unified School District, 162
Poway Unified School District, Donovan v., 494
Poway Unified School District, Harper v., 270
Poway Unified School District, Johnson v., 285–286, 302
Poway Unified School District, Lovell v., 266–267
Poway Unified School District, Poway Federation of Teachers v., 162
Poway Unified School District v. Superior Court, 433
Powell, Lewis F., 116, 281–282, 284
PPG Architectural Finishes, Lawson v., 263
prayer, 286, 294, 295, 298–304, 305–306, 310, 311–313, 314
preinterns, 200
preschool teacher, 192, 193
Preschooler II v. Clark County School Board of Trustees, 485
Prescott Unified School District, R.P. v., 370

Priest, Serrano v. (1971), 107, 111, 112–114, 115, 116, 145, 146
Priest, Serrano v. (1976), 5, 107, 111, 116–119, 145, 146, 484
Priest, Serrano v. (1986), 107, 111, 121–122, 146
Prince v. Jacoby, 314, 315–316
principals: California schooling system and, 21–22; credentials, 21–22, 192; expression rights and, 247, 268, 270, 274–275, 276–279, 286–287; expulsion and, 400, 401, 404; legal liability and, 503, 504, 505, 525, 527; playground supervision and, 503; safe school environment and, 58, 60, 61, 62, 63, 67; student discipline and, 381, 384, 386, 388–389, 393, 394, 395, 397, 399; student lifestyle rights and, 440; substitute, 22; teacher preparation and evaluation, 81; Title VII and, 236–237; Uniform Complaint Procedure and, 11; unions and collective bargaining and, 156, 163
print items copyright law, 85, *86*
prior review of school-sponsored publications, 276–278, 289
privacy: California versus U.S. Constitution, 5; artificial intelligence and, 100–101; Brown Act and, 421; corporal punishment and, 507; counselors and, 527–528; electronic devices and, 271; FERPA, 6, 8, 10, 92, 433, 446, 527, 555; Internet, 88–90, 92–98; lifestyle, 260–261; marital, 279; personal, 436–447; personnel files and, 431; public records, and, 429, 430–436; right of association and, 261; student

privacy (*Cont.*)
   dress and grooming, 279; obscene material and, 90; social media and, 260; student record and, 441–446; student searches and, 447–461; student seizures and, 461–461; student surveys and, 446–447; transgender status and, 323
private funding, 146
private schools, 39–41: attendance and, 39, 53; California schooling system and, *16*, 17; choice and, 181; charter schools and, 30; contract law and, 12; direct aid to, 325–326; discrimination and, 485, 487, 489, 494, 495, 496–497; disability and, 237, 374; enrollment numbers, 1; exemption to Section 1983, 41; Fair Employment and Housing Act and, 240; foster children and, 49, 50; Fourteenth Amendment and, 4; IDEA and, 41, 362–363; indirect aid to, 326–328; instructional materials, 75; legal liability and, 501, 504, 512, 527, 531, 535, 538; parent rights and responsibilities, 22–24, 26; religion and, 40–41; safe school environment in, 57, 59, *62*, 67, 68, 69; special education and, 41, 344, 359–360, 362–363, 368–369, 317; statutory law and, 6, *7*, 8; student assessment and, 40; student lifestyle rights in, 440; student records, 445; student transfer and, 29; teacher credentialing in, 83; Title VI and, 489–490; Title IX, 485, 487, 489; unions and, 148, 163, 185; vouchers and, 41–44, 185. *See also* nonpublic school (NPS); religious private schools

privatization, 187, 329
probationary certificated employees, *158*, 159, 195, 203, 209, 223
probationary classified employees, 227
probationary teachers, 194, 195, 200–202; becoming a permanent employee, 202–204; classified employees, 223–224, 226, 227, 228; evaluation, 206; layoffs, *158*, 159, 193, 219, 220, 223; leave rights, 234–235; nonextension, 154, 172; non-reelection and dismissal, 154, 172, 188, 189–190, 195–196, 200, 203–204, 208–210, 227, 228; reemployment list, 234; temporary classification and, 195–198, 199
procedural due process, 382–383, 543. *See also* due process
profanity, 76, 274, 285, 288, 289, 291, *387*, 391, 456
professional clear credential, 82
program improvement schools, 29
prohibited subjects of bargaining, 151
property rights in employment, 191–192, 194, 204, 206, 208, 209
property tax, 47, 48, 49, 107, 110, 111, 113, 115–121, 123, *124*, 125–126, 130, 135, 141, 145–146. *See also* Proposition 13 (1978)
Proposition 1 (1979), 474, *479*
Proposition 4 (1979), 119, 128. *See also* Proposition 13 (1978)
Proposition 7 (1974), 118
Proposition 13 (1978), 107, 110, 119–122, 128, 134, 135, 141, 146, 532. *See also* property taxes; Proposition 4 (1979)
Proposition 21 (1972), 472, 473, *479*
Proposition 38 (1988), 43

Proposition 39 (2000), 36, 135, 139
Proposition 46 (1986), 135
Proposition 47 (2002), 135, 140
Proposition 55 (2004), 135, 140
Proposition 98 (1988), 123, 124, *125*, 130, 142, 144, 146
Proposition 174 (1993), 43
Proposition 187 (1994), 4, 51
Proposition 209 (1996), 27, 474, 477, 479, 480, 484
Proposition 227 (1998), 47, 72, 79, 285
Protection of Pupil Rights Amendment (PPRA), 446. *See also* Family Educational Rights and Privacy Act (1974)
provisional credential, 203, 220
PruneYard Shopping Center v. Robins, 5
Public Charter School Grant Program, 36
Public Employment Relations Board (PERB): charter schools and, 181–183, 184–185; contract administration and, 171, 174–175; contract negotiation and, 165–170; elections, 157; role of, 154–155; stages of bargaining and, 149, 151; subjects and scope of bargaining, 156, 159, 161, 161–163; unfair labor disputes and, 174–175; website, 556
Public Employment Relations Board, Banning Teachers Association v., 155
Public Employee Relations Board, California Teachers Association v., 183
Public Employment Relations Board, Cumero v., 176, 177
Public Employment Relations Board v. Modesto City Schools District, 167
Public Employment Relations Board, Moreno Valley Unified School District v., 167
Public Employment Relations Board, San Mateo City School District v., 159–160
Public Employment Relations Board, South Bay Union School District v., 165
public forum, 5, 61, 174, 254, 256–257, 275, 281, 284, 289, 301, 311, 319, 544. *See also* limited open forum
Public Records Act (California) (PRA), 59, 424, 429–436, 463
public school employee, defined, 155
public school employer, defined, 155
Pupil Personnel Services Credential, 192
Puyallup School District, Parents of Student W. v., 368, 369

Quality Education Investment Act (QEIA), 144, 181
Quincy High School (Plumas Unified School District), 458

race, and socioeconomic status, 467, 468, 480
racial balancing, 32, 467, 474–478
racial discrimination, 465–480; California law, 11, 27, 468–480, 479; employment and, 235–237, 241–243; federal law, 6, 7, 77, 83, 142, 465–468; fostering diversity, 478–480; funding systems and, 142; historical perspectives on, 468–470; intelligence tests and, 347; limits on affirmative action and racial balancing, 474–478; limits on busing, 473–474; private schools and, 41; remedying, 470–473
racial harassment, 57, 77, 489–491, 496

Rafael C., In re, 456
Raimondo, Loper Bright Enterprises v., 10
Ralph M. Brown Act. *See* Brown Act (1953) (California)
Ramirez, People v., 383
Ramirez v. Long Beach Unified School District, 519
Randi W. v. Muroc Joint Unified School District, 510
Randy G., In re, 461–462
Ravenswood Teachers Association v. Ravenswood City School District, 162–163
Ray v. Antioch Unified School District, 493
Reading Instruction Competency Assessment, 82
reasonable accommodations, 7, 239–240, 242
reasonable modifications, 374
reassignment of employees, *158*, 159, 190, 204–206, 220, 229–231, 248–249, 252, 302
recommendations, employment, 216, 539
Redding, Sanford Unified School District No. 1 v., 455
Redlands Unified School District, Granowitz v., 389
Redwood City Elementary School District, 37
Reed v. Reed, 481
Reed v. United Teachers of Los Angeles, 221
Reeves v. Rocklin Unified School District, 61
references, employment, 510
Regents of the University of California, Hunter ex rel. Brandt v., 477

Regents of the University of California, Hunter v., 477
Regents of the University of California, Tarasoff v., 526–527
Regino v. Staley, 324, 440
regulations and laws websites, 554–555
Rehabilitation Act (1973). *See* Section 504 of the Rehabilitation Act of 1973
Rehnquist, William, 327
reimbursement for educational expenses, 323, 325, 363, 367, 368–369, 410, 535
related services, 333, 335, 355, 336, 360, 375, 376
religion: aid to religious private schools, 324–328; association rights and, 261, 281–282; campus access for religious groups, 313–321; charter schools and, 30; in the classroom, 304–310; community use policies and, 318–321; constitutional law and, 292–295; discrimination and, 7, 74, 296, 310, 314–316, 317, 318, 319, 321, 327; free exercise of, 295–296; government support of, 298–301; graduation prayer and religious speeches, 311–313; hate crime and, 325, 439; holiday observances, 310–311; Pledge of Allegiance and, 297; religious exercise, 55, 298, 301–304, 320; in private schools, 40–41; at a public university, 282; religiously based exemptions, 321–323; religious music, 310–311; school prayer, 298–304; student religious papers and presentations, 309–310; teacher academic freedom and, 306; teaching about, 305–309; transgender

students and, 323–324. *See also* establishment clause
religious private schools, 7, 41, 43, 292, 294, 295, 305, 324–328, 329, 362, 496–497. *See also* private schools
religion in the classroom, 304–310
religious retreats, absences for, 55, 321
religious symbols, 304, 305, 310, 317
Reporting by School Employees of Improper Governmental Activities Act (California), 261–262
reputation as protected liberty, 383
resource specialist program (RSP), 355, 359
respondeat superior doctrine, defined, 501–502
restrooms, 438, 447, 451, 452, 488, 504–505, 536
revenue limit funding, 117–118, 119, 121, *124*, 125–126, 128–129, 136–137, 219
Reynolds v. United States, 293
Rice, Gong Lum v., 470
Richardson, Frontiero v., 481
Richmond School District, Adelt v., 204
right of association, 57, 260–261, 281–284, 291
right of expression. *See* expression rights
Riles, California Teachers Association v., 325
Riles, Larry P. v., 347
Rim of the World Unified School District v. Superior Court, 407, 444
Rio Linda Union School District, Newdow v., 297
Rizo v. Vovino, 241
Robert L. Mueller Charter School (Public Employment Relations Board decision), 181

Roberts, John, 10, 269, 326, 327
Robles-Wong v. State of California, 145
Robins, PruneYard Shopping Center v., 5
Rocklin High School, 61
Rocklin Unified School District, Reeves v., 61
Rodda Act. *See* Educational Employment Relations Act (EERA) (1975) (California)
Rodriguez, San Antonio Independent School District v., 115–119, 145
Rose for Emily, A (Faulkner), 77, 490
Roseville City School District, Jimenez v., 516
Ross v. Campbell Union School District, 500
Roth, Board of Regents v., 191
Round Valley Teachers Association, Board of Education of the Round Valley Unified School District v., 154, 172–173
Rowley, Board of Education of the Hendrick Hudson School District v., 300–302, 333, 338–341, 356
R.P. v. Prescott Unified School District, 370
RSP. *See* resource specialist program
Rules of Conduct for Professional Educators, 216
Runyon v. McCrary, 41
Ryan v. California Interscholastic Federation-San Diego Section, 383

Sacramento City Unified School District, Hoschler v., 208
Sacramento City Unified School District, Keyser v., 249
Sacramento City Unified School District, Thompson v., 504–505

Sacramento City Unified School District v. Holland, 342
Sacramento County Board of Education, Board of Education v., 405–406
Saddleback Junior College District, King v., 279
safe learning environment, 57–69
Safe Place to Learn Act (California), 57–58, 494
salaries, 115; charter schools and, 139; closed-session meetings and, 428; collective bargaining and, 160–161, 165, 170, 176, 186; FEHA and, 241; general-purpose funds and, 125; leave rights and, 232–233; salary schedules, 160–161, 229, 428
San Antonio Independent School District v. Rodriguez, 109, 114–115, 145
San Bernardino City Unified School District, Bolin v., 206
San Bernardino City Unified School District, John A. v., 403
Sanchez v. San Diego County Office of Education, 520
San Diego Teachers Association v. Superior Court, 168
San Diego Unified School District, 167, 246–247, 525
San Diego Unified School District, Adcock v., 245
San Diego Unified School District, Hohe v., 525–526
San Diego Unified School District, T.B. v., 370
San Diego Unified School District, T.H. v., 393–394
San Dieguito Union High School District v. Commission on Professional Competence, 217, 438

San Jose Unified School District Board of Education, Fellowship of Christian Athletes v., 283–284, 317, 320
Sandoval, Alexander v., 490
Sands v. Morongo Unified School District, 311
Sanford Unified School District No. 1 v. Redding, 455
San Francisco, racial discrimination in, 468–469, 470
San Francisco County superintendent, 19
San Francisco Unified School District, 79–80
San Francisco Unified School District, Berkelman v., 483
San Francisco Unified School District, Clausing v., 506–507
San Francisco Unified School District v. Johnson, 471
San Francisco Unified School District, Peter W. v., 517
San Leandro Teachers Association v. Governing Board of San Leandro Unified School District, 174–175
San Marin High School, 491
San Mateo City School District v. Public Employment Relations Board, 159–160
Santa Ana Unified School District, Gordon J. v., 404, 450
Santa Barbara High School District, Davison v., 496
Santa Barbara School District v. Superior Court, 472, 479
Santa Clara County Board of Education, Fremont Union High School District v., 396–397

Santa Fe Independent School District v. Doe, 300
Santa Monica-Malibu Unified School District, Marken v., 431–432
Santa Monica-Malibu Unified School District, Petersil v., 196
satellite charter schools, 35
Sato v. Orange County Dept. of Education, 533
SBE. *See* State Board of Education (SBE)
Scalia, Antonin, 294, 312, 451
Schaffer v. Weast, 367
Schempp, School District of Abington Township v., 295, 298, 305
school boards. *See* governing boards
school choice, 22, 26–29, 36, 41–45, 181, 185, 328–329, 466–467
school day length, 52
school district internships, 200–202
School District No. 1, Keyes v., 466
School District of Abington Township v. Schempp, 295, 298, 305
school districts, unified, 20, 21
school finance, 107–109, 145–147; categorical aid, 123, *124*, 126–127, 137–138; centralized, 107; charter school funding, 136–140; components, *124*; current system and changes to, 123–136; district power equalizing, 118, 119, 146; facilities funding, 135–136; federal funds, 132; foundation funding, 110–112; Fourteenth Amendment and, 145; litigation, 112–119; Local Control Accountability Plans, 131–132; Local Control Funding Formula, 78–79, 105, 128–131, 132, 136, 137, 141, 144, 146, 147, 198, 533; movement toward adequacy, 140–145; other sources of revenue, 134; Proposition 13, 119–122; Proposition 98, *125*; Quality Education Investment Act and, 144, 181; revenue limit funding, 117–118, 119, 121, *124*, 125–126, 128–129, 136–137, 219; state-centered funding, 122; student fees, 132–134; unequal treatment based on wealth, 112, 113–114, 117–119, 121, 126
school hours, 56, 60, 63
schooling structure, California, 15–22, *16*
school law components, 1–15, *3*; administrative law, 9–12; constitutional law, 2–5; contract law, 12–13; judicial law, 13–15; statutory law, 6–9, *7–8*
school prayer, 294, 295, 298–304, 305, 328; Equal Access Act and, 314; private prayer and religious exercise, 301–304; school-sponsored or endorsed public prayer, 299–301. *See also* graduation prayer and religious speeches; religion in the classroom
school psychologists, 192, 219, 331, 347, 348, 350, 526
school site councils, 22, 58, 424, 459, 463
school superintendents, California schooling structure and, 18–19, 21–22; charter schools and, 32, 34; classification and certification of, 190, 192; collective bargaining and, 155, 164, 184; contract law and, 12; expression rights and, 247, 248–249, 251, 255, 262, 276, 277–278; Fair Employment and Housing Act

school superintendents (*Cont.*) and, 240, 530; legal liability and, 500, 510–511, 518, 519, 530; roles and duties of, 229–230; safe school environment and, 59, 63, 66; search and seizure and, 420–421, 424, 425, 426, 427, 428, 431, 445, 451; student discipline and, 381, 388, 392, 394, 395, 398, 400, 400–401, 402, 405, 408; student transfers and, 28–29; teacher employment and discipline, 202, 203, 205, 206; truancy and, 55, 56–57

school visitors, 60–61, *62*

school visits by parents, 26, 391

Schwarzenegger, Arnold, 144

Scott B. v. Board of Trustees of Orange County High School of the Arts, NEED PAGE numbers

Scottsdale Unified School District No. 48, Hills v., 320–321

Seattle School District No. 1, Parents Involved in Community Schools v., 466–467

Section 504 of the Rehabilitation Act of 1973, *7*, 41, 237–239, 330, 370, 371–375, 377, 485, 533

Section 1983. *See* 42 U.S.C. Section 1983

secularism, 42, 293, 294, 295–296, 298, 299, 304, 305, 306–307, 310–311, 317–318, 325–236, 328

Sedlock v. Baird, 308

Seeger, United States v., 296

segregation. *See* racial discrimination

Senate Bill 90, 116

Senate Bill 112, 180

Senate Bill 285, 180

Senate Bill 484, 104, 105

Senate Bill 553, 64

Senate Bill 740, 140

Senate Bill 866, 180

senior management, 190, 224–225, 230

separation of church and state. *See* establishment clause; religion

Sequoia National Forest summer camp, 519

Sequoia Union High School District v. Aurora Charter High School, 37

Serrano v. Priest (1971), 107, 111, 112–114, 115, 116, 145, 146

Serrano v. Priest (1976), 5, 107, 111, 116–119, 145, 146, 484

Serrano v. Priest (1986), 107, 111, 121–122, 146

service credentials, 192–193

Service Employees Industrial Union v. Los Angeles Unified School District, 162

Service Employees International Union, Local 1000, Knox v., 178

Seth's Law. *See* Safe Place to Learn Act (California)

Settle v. Dickson County School Board, 310

sex education, 24, 283, 328, 487

sexual assault or battery, *385*–386, 392–393, 395, 401, 404, 492, 493, 505

sexual harassment and abuse: California Education Code, 494–495; legal liability, 508–509, 537–538; student discipline, 273, *387*, 389, 393, 395, 396, 508; of students by school personnel, 212, 537; Title VI, 465; Title VII, 236; Title IX, Civil Rights Act, *8*, 492–493; Unruh Civil Rights Act and, 495–497

sexual orientation, 235; AB 1955 and, 441; California Education Code

and, 494; California Fair Employment and Housing Act and, 241, 439; charter schools and, 32; Fourteenth Amendment and, 537; rights of association and, 283; rights of expression and, 269, 270; Safe Place to Learn Act and, 57; Sex Equity in Education Act and, 488, 489; student organizations and, 317; Title VII and, 236; Unruh Civil Rights Act and, 495, 497
Shanley v. Northeast Independent School District, 397
Shasta Secondary Home School, Anderson Union High School District v., 31, 35–36
sheltered English immersion classrooms, 285
Shelton v. Tucker, 260
Shepard, Matthew, 283
Sherwood School District 88J, McNeil v., 273–274
short-term employees, 224–225, 242
short-term removals, in special education, 413–414
Siegelman, Chandler v., 301
silent meditation, 299
Simi Valley Unified School District, Joyce v., 524–525
Simmons-Harris, Zelman v., 326
Single Gender Academies Pilot Program, 484
Single Subject Teaching Credential, 192
Sioux Falls School District, Florey v., 310–311
Skelly conference, 208, 217, 226
Skelly v. State Personnel Board, 208
Skinner v. Vacaville Unified School District, 506

skipping, in layoffs, 220–221
Smith, Employment Division, Department of Human Resources v., 322–323
Smith, Union School District v., 360
Smith v. Novato Unified School District, 277
sniffer dogs, 458, 461
social media, 94, 256–258, 260, 270–271, 324, 398, 441
Society of Sisters, Pierce v., 22–24, 39, 41–42, 324
socioeconomic status, and race, 467, 468, 480
software copyright law, 85, *86*
Soma, *387*
"some educational benefit," in special education, 340–341, 343, 375–376
Sonoma Valley Unified School District, McIntyre v., 196
South Bay Union School District v. Public Employment Relations Board, 165
Spanaway Lake High School (Washington), 315
Spangler, Pasadena City Board of Education v., 466
Spanierman v. Hughes, 259
speaking out on matters of public concern, 244–247
special education: ADA, 374–375; behavior-related assessment and plans, 357–359; categorical aid, 126–127; charter schools and, 55; child find and referral, 343–348; criteria for, 350; discipline and, 412–417; due process, 363–370; eligibility for, 348–350; exiting from, 361–362; extended school year, 336, 357; FAPE, 337–343; funding, 125,

special education (*Cont.*)
126, 127; history of law, 330–334; IEE, 350–351; IEP process, 351–360; initial assessment, 345–348; liability, 505, 506, 516, 353; local plan area, 49; LRE, 341–343; mental health services, 359; placement, 359–360; preschool teachers, 193; private schools and, 362–363; regulations concerning, 9; related services, 355–357; Section 504, 371–375; sources of law, 334–335; student records concerning, 53; terms and acronyms, 335–336; transitions plans and age of majority, 360–362. *See also* special needs students

Special Education Hearing Office, Benjamin G. v., 360

special education teachers, 193, 253, 352, 376, 535

special needs students: categorical funding, 121; assessment for, 104, 105; child find, referral, assessment, and eligibility, 343–351; collective bargaining and, 161; COVID-19 pandemic and, 97; discrimination and, 469, 495; English learners, 72; expulsion, 401, 412, 415, 417–418; liability, 505, 524; school safety and, 59; transportation of, 50. *See also* Individuals with Disabilities Education Act (IDEA); special education

specific learning disability (SLD) eligibility category, 336, 349, 350

spending and funding, per-pupil, 107, 109, 113, 115, 117, 121–122, 125–127, 134, 137, 145, 146, 484

SPI. *See* Superintendent of Public Instruction (SPI)

Spokane School District 81, Avila v., 364

sports. *See* athletes and athletics; contact sports

squeeze formula. *See* revenue limit funding

Staley, Regino v., 324, 440

Standardized Testing and Reporting (STAR), 103–104

State Board of Education (SBE), 3; appointment or election of, 16; assessment and, 104–105; authority of, 9–10; charter schools and, 30, 31, 33, 34, 138, 139, 184; curriculum content standards, 70, 71, 73, 74–75; employee and student lifestyle, 438; granting waivers, 20, 52; racial discrimination, 471; regulations, 550; role, 16, 17, 18–19, 20; special education law, 334, 335; student fees, 134; teacher dismissal or reassignment, 210, 211, 217, 223, 228, 230

State Board of Education, California School Boards Association v., 31

State Board of Education, California Teachers Association v., 285

State Board of Education v. Honig, 18

State of California, Mendoza v., 21

State Board of Education, Morrison v., 211–213, 216, 261, 438

State Board of Education, Wilson v., 9, 38, 184

State Department of Education, Arcadia Unified School District v., 133

State of California, Association of Mexican-American Educators v., 83

State of California, Butt v., 220–221

State of California, Campaign for Quality Education et al. v., 145

INDEX | 625

State of California, Long Beach Unified School District v., 128
State of California, Robles-Wong v., 145
State of California, Vergara v., 222
State of California, Williams v., 11, 142
State of California Department of Education, Newport-Mesa Unified School District v., 347
State of California Department of Education, Tucker v., 302
State of Washington, Moran v., 249
State Personnel Board, Skelly v., 208
statutes: defined, 6; finding and reading, 549–550. *See also specific statutes*
statutory law, 3, 6–9
stay-put placement and provision, 365–366, 377, 414
Stevens, John Paul, 299
Stewart, Potter, 260, 284, 298
St. Isidore of Seville Catholic Virtual School v. Drummond (2025), 327
Stockton Teachers Association CTA/NEA v. Stockton Unified School District, 199
Stockton Unified School District, Adair v., 161
Stockton Unified School District, Boliou v., 218
Stockton Unified School District, Leger v., 504
stolen property, 387, 395, 502
Stone v. Graham, 304, 317
strikes, teacher, 149, 165, 167–170
student assessment, 17, 102–105; alternative, 104, 354; in charter schools, 35, 75; collective bargaining and, 170, 181; curriculum content standards, 70–76; educating targeted groups and, 79–81; FAA, 336, 358, 376–377; FBA, 357–359, 414–415, Every Student Succeeds Act and, 141; mandated, 109, 146;NCLB, 27, 46, 81, 102–102, 106; parental right to inspect materials, 25; private schools and, 40; racial discrimination and, 347; of sex education and HIV/AIDS prevention education, 24; special education and, 340, 343–348, 350–352, 355, 357–359, 361
student discipline, 378–; acts and consequences, 385–387; California's legal framework for, 380–384; discipline short of suspension, 384; discretionary discipline, 394–396; dismissal from charter schools, 399–400; due process and, 381–384; expulsion, 391–396; expulsion appeal, 409–412; expulsion hearing and final determination, 410–408; expulsion process, 400–412; importance of rules for, 378–380; involuntary transfer, 398–399; mandatory recommendation for expulsion, 391–394; mandatory recommendation for expulsion unless inappropriate, 394–395; postexpulsion educational programming, 408–409; readmission following expulsion, 409; recommendation for expulsion, 400–401; special education and, 412–417; suspension, 384–391; types of, 384–; who can discipline, 381
student dress and grooming, 50, 133, 279–281, 291

student lifestyle rights, 439–441
student newspapers, 274–279, 280, 290, 291, 397
Student Online Personal Information Protection Act, 94–95
Student Test Taker Privacy Protection Act, 94
student records, 8, 9, 25–26, 60, 53, 94, 267, 287, 323, 407, 432, 441–447, 5–6, 526, 544
student religious groups, 282, 313–321
student religious papers and presentations, 309–313
student searches, 447–463; constitutional law and, 2, 404, 419, 447–451;; group, 457–461; individual, 452–457; standards, 447–451; truant students and, 56. *See also* student seizures
student seizures, 461–463
student surveys and profiling, 446–447
Stull Act (California), 204, 209, 230
subpoenas for expulsion hearings, 402, 405, 407
substitute employees, 8, 22, 169, 191, 193, 194–195, 200, 206, 217, 223–225, 232–233–235, 242
Sullivan v. Centinela Valley Union High School, 208
Sullivan, New York Times v., 511
Summerfield v. Windsor Unified School District, 200, 203–204
Superintendent of Public Instruction (SPI), 3; attendance strategies and, 57; authority of, 9, 11; California schooling structure and, 16–18, *16*, 21; lawsuits files by, 144, 511; private school affidavits, 40; role of, *16*, 17; safe school environments and, 69;

school accountability and, 71, 105; school funding and, 137, 144; selection of, 17; student assessment and, 105; student transfers and, 28; teacher evaluation and assessment, 83
superintendents. *See* school superintendent
Superior Court, BRV, Inc. v., 431
Superior Court, Casterson v., 520
Superior Court, Copley Press, Inc. v., 433
Superior Court, Evens v., 439
Superior Court, Jonathan L. v., 25
Superior Court, Los Angeles Unified School District v., 429
Superior Court, Poway Unified School District v., 433
Superior Court, Rim of the World Unified School District v., 407, 444
Superior Court, San Diego Teachers Association v., 168
Superior Court, Santa Barbara School District v., 472, *479*
Superior Court of Santa Clara, City of San Jose v., 433–434
superior courts, 3, 13
supervised suspension classroom, 391
supervisory employees, defined, 156
supplementary aids and services, in special education, 341, 343, 373, 375, 377
supremacy clause, 4
Supreme Court Reporter, 551, 557
suspension: of employee pay, 160; of employees, 207, 210–219; of order to expel, 407–408, 418; of students, 56–57, *62*, 264, 267, 268, 271, 274, 279, 379, 381–382, 384–391, 393, 400–401, 440, 450

Swann v. Charlotte-Mecklenburg Board of Education, 465
Swanson, Moran v., 265
Swanson v. Guthrie Independent School District, 322–323
Sweetwater Union High School District, Ollier v., 486

Tamalpais High School, 491
Tape v. Hurley, 469
Tarasoff v. Regents of the University of California, 526–527
Tatro, Irving Independent School District v., 356–357
T.A., Forest Grove School District v., 369
tax credits, 181, 185, 327
T.B. v. San Diego Unified School District, 370
teachers: 4-8-1–*See* academic freedom; certificated employees; employment; expression rights, educator; permanent teachers; probationary teachers; special education teachers; strikes, teacher
teachers' aides, 68, 343, 356, 445
Tempe Union High School District, Monteiro v., 77, 491
temporary certificated employees, 195, 196, 198, 201
Ten Commandments, 304, 317–319
Tenth Amendment, 2, 4
terroristic threats, 387, 395
Texas, Lawrence v., 437
Texas school funding, 109, 115
T.H. v. San Diego Unified School District, 393–394
Thirteenth Amendment, 7, 41, 469
Thompson v. Sacramento City Unified School District, 504–505
threats of violence, 62, 63, 64, 262, 266–267, 269–272, 273–274, 289, 385, 386–399, 396
three-month positions, 197–198
tie-breaking criteria, in layoffs, 220
time, place, and manner rules, 246, 266, 278, 288, 291, 301
Timothy O. v. Paso Robles Unified School District, 345
Tinker v. Des Moines Independent Community School District, 263–266; censorship, 76; expression targeting protected identities, 270; face-to-face communication, 264–265, 266, 268; free speech off campus, 273, 274; free speech on campus, 272; interstudent communication, 265–266, 275, 280; religion and, 301; student classroom expression, 288, 289; student discipline, 379; wearing political symbols, 264, 267, 280, 291, 379
Title I funding: charter schools and, 27; disadvantaged children and, 46, 127, 132; discrimination and, 374; fluctuations of, 199; private schools and, 325; reasonable accommodations, 375; school accountability, 102, 103. *See also* Elementary and Secondary Education Act
Title III, 127
Title VI, Civil Rights Act (1964), 7, 77, 80, 83, 142, 465, 485, 489–492, 533, 536, 539
Title VII, Civil Rights Act (1964), 235–237; California Basic Education Skills Test, 83; discrimination and, 465, 485; employment, 240–242; FEHA and, 241–242; harassment

Title VII, (Cont.)
and, 489; influence, 6; overview, 7; private schools, 41; religion and, 294, 304
Title IX, Civil Rights Act (1964), 11, 483
Title IX, Education Amendments (1972), 8, 9, 41, 483, 484–487, 492–493, 495, 496, 498, 533
T.L.O., New Jersey v., 447–449, 450, 453–454, 458, 460
Tokushige, Farrington v., 39
Toney v. Young, 253
Torcaso v. Watkins, 296
Torlakson, California Parents for the Equalization of Educational Materials v., 74, 307
Torsiello v. Oakland Unified School District, 519
Tort Claims Act (California), 500–530, 502, 538–539; claim forms, 433; counselors and duty to warn, 526–528; dangerous condition of school property, 523–525; employees acting outside the scope of their employment, 496, 508–511; Fair Employment and Housing Act and, 530; injury to nonstudents, 520–523; injury to student athletes and cheerleaders, 511–516; injury to students off campus, 517–520; injury to students on campus, 503–508; insurance, 528–530; liability when students don't learn, 516–517; waivers of liability, 525–526
torts, defined, 501
Town of Greece v. Galloway, 294, 300
tracking, of students, 83–84
transcripts, 2, 32, 410, 444–445

transgender persons, 73, 323–324, 448, 493, 494
transition plans, 330, 360–361
Trinity Lutheran Church of Columbia, Inc. v. Comer, 326
Troxel v. Granville, 23
truancy, 14, 55–57, 268
Truth v. Kent School District, 283, 316
Tucker, Shelton v., 260
Tucker v. State of California Department of Education, 302
Tulare Joint Union High School District, Lopez v., 288, 289
Tustin Unified School District, K.M. ex rel. Bright v., 371
Twain, Mark, 77, 490

undocumented persons, 4, 51
unified school districts, 20, 21
Uniform Complaint Procedure, 11, 134
uniforms, 12, 65, 132, 280–281
unionization stage (collective bargaining), 149–150, *150*
unions. See California Teachers Association (CTA); collective bargaining and unions; Educational Employment Relations Act (1975) (California)
unitary status, 466
United States, American Library Association v., 90
United States, Reynolds v., 293
United States Code, 392, 531, 549–550, 554
United States Code Annotated, 550
United States Reports, 551, 557
United States Supreme Court Reports, Lawyer's Edition, 551

United States v. Aguilera, 453
United States v. Ballard, 296
United States v. Seeger, 296
United States v. Virginia, 482
United Teachers of Los Angeles, Reed v., 221
university internships, 200, 202
University of California, 52, 72, 74, 100
University of California at Berkeley, 100, 526
University of California at Los Angeles Graduate School of Education, 477
University of Missouri, 281
Unruh Civil Rights Act (1959) (California), 495–497, 498, 508, 539
U.S. Congress, 2, 3, 6, 7, 9, 14. *See also specific federal laws*
U.S. Constitution: charter schools and, 38, 185; copyright law and, 84; constitutional law, 2–5, 15, 42, 44, 78, 292–295, 313, 436, 463, 484, 545; due process clause, 2, 74, 383, 437, 536, 543; education as a right and, 114, 115–116; employment and, 191; obscene materials and, 90; religion and, 292–295, 296, 297, 299, 312, 313, 329; teacher credentials and, 82. *See also* equal protection clause; establishment clause; *specific amendments and Supreme Court cases*
U.S. Department of Education (USDOE): accrediting bodies, 34; applicable programs, 446; authority, 9; Every Student Succeeds Act (ESSA), 45, 81, 103, 106, 141; Family Educational Rights and Privacy Act and, 6, 10, 92, 433, 444, 446, 527, 555; Family Policy Compliance Office, 10, 442; on graduation speakers, 313; IDEA interpretation, 334; *A Nation at Risk*, 102; National Assessment of Educational Progress, 102, 103, 468; No Child Left Behind, 10, 27, 45, 46, 81, 102–103, 106, 141, 310, 499, 555; Office for Civil Rights, 9, 372–373, 375, 485, 487, 489, 555; Office of Special Education and Rehabilitative Services, 9, 334, 555; on parental rights to see disciplinary records, 442; Protection of Pupils Rights Amendment, 446; racial harassment and, 489–490; religion and, 301; Title VI and IX guidance, 489, 490; website, 555

U.S. Department of Education Office for Civil Rights: disabilities, 7; Section 504 and, 372; Title IX and, 9, 485; website, 487

U.S. Department of Labor, website, 556
U.S. Equal Employment Opportunity Commission (EEOC), 235–237, 240

Vacaville Unified School District, Hoff v., 520–522
Vacaville Unified School District, Skinner v., 506
Vallejo City Unified School District, California Teachers Association v., 220
Vallejo City Unified School District v. Vallejo Education Association, 169
Vallejo Education Association, Vallejo City Unified School District v., 169
Valley High School (Tulare Joint Union High School District), 288–289

Vanguard Charter School Academy, Daugherty v., 305
Van Duyn v. Baker School District, 341
Van Nuys High School, 475–476
Van Orden v. Perry, 304, 318
Vergara v. State of California, 222
Vernonia School District v. Acton, 450
vicarious liability, defined, 501, 503
Victor Valley Options for Youth Teachers Association, Options for Youth-Victor Valley, Inc. v., 184–185
Victor Valley Union High School District, 184
video recording copyright law, 86, 87
video teleconferencing, 96, 422
Vidmar, Williams v., 533
viewpoint discrimination, 279, 314, 315, 319, 321, 421
Vincent, Widmar v., 281–282
violence, threats of, 62, 63, 64, 262, 266–267, 269–272, 273–274, 289, 385, 386–399, 396
Virginia, United States v., 482
Virginia Military Institute, 482
Vista Unified School District, Bell v., 428
Vista Unified School District, Leventhal v., 420–421, 426–427
Vitale, Engle v., 298
Vittal v. Long Beach Unified School District, 204
voucher programs, 1, 39, 41–44, 45, 118, 181, 185, 326–327, 329
Vovino, Rizo v., 241

waivers of liability, 525–526, 548
Walczak v. Florida Union Free School District, 341
Wallace v. Jaffree, 299
Ward v. Flood, 469, 470

warn, duty to, 526–528
Wasco Union High School District, 76–77
Washington v. Davis, 490
Washington Education Association, Davenport v., 178
Watkins, Torcaso v., 296
Watson Initiative (1972) (California), 119
Wauconda Community Unit School District No. 118, Hedges v., 321
wealth, as suspect classification, 113–114
Weast, Schaffer v., 367
Weaverville Elementary School District, Cousins v., 222
Web-based learning, 88, 97–98
Weisman, Lee v., 312
Welch v. Oakland Unified School District, 200–201
Wells v. One2One Learning Foundation, 517
Western Association of Schools and Colleges (WASC), 34, 40
Western Line Consolidated District, Givhan v., 247, 251, 252
Western Placer Unified School District, Conn v., 262
Westminster School District of Orange County v. Mendez, 470
West Sonoma County Union High School District, Kavanaugh v., 195
West Virginia State Board of Education v. Barnette, 2, 297
W.G. v. Board of Trustees of Target Range School District No. 23, 337
Whipple, Horton v., 1
Whistleblower Protection Act (California), 251, 261

whistleblowing, 262–263
White, Byron, 275, 448
Whitehead, Nurre v., 311
white students, 270, 467, 468, 471, 475, 476, 480, 490
Whitlow v. California, 51
Wicca belief system, 295, 307
Widmar v. Vincent, 281–282
William G., In re, 448–449, 450, 452
William S. Hart Union High School District, C.A. v., 509
Williams v. State of California, 11, 142, 143, 144
William V., In re, 450, 458
Wilson, Coalition for Economic Equity v., 475
Wilson, League of United Latin American Citizens v., 4, 51
Wilson, Pete, 123
Wilson v. State Board of Education, 9, 38, 184
Windsor Unified School District, Summerfield v., 200, 203–204
Winton Act (1965) (California), 153, 157, 161, 186
wireless electronic devices, 271, 272
Wisconsin Employment Relations Commission, City of Madison v., 256
Wisconsin v. Yoder, 24, 322
Wisniewski v. Board of Education of Weedsport Central School District, 271

Wolf, Nguon v., 440
Woodbury v. Brown-Dempsey, 402
Woodland Joint Unified School District, Brown v., 307
Woodland Joint Unified School District v. Commission on Professional Competence, 188, 215
workplace-violence prevention plan (Senate Bill 553), 64
workplace-violence restraining orders (WVRO), 63–64
work-to-rule job action, 169
World Changers, 315–316
Worth County Schools (Office for Civil Rights case), 372
Wright, Ingraham v., 534
Wysinger v. Crookshank, 469

Yarber v. Oakland Unified School District, 523
Yoder, Wisconsin v., 24, 322
Young, Toney v., 253
Yuba City Unified School District, Biscotti v., 524

Zalac v. Governing Board of the Ferndale Unified School District, 198–199
Zelman v. Simmons-Harris, 326
zero-tolerance policy, 393
Zorach v. Clauson, 293, 322